THE

TRIBES AND CASTES OF BENGAL

By H.H. RISLEY,

INDIAN CIVIL SERVICE, OFFICER D'ACADEMIE FRANCAISE

ETHNOGRAPHIC CLOSSARY

Vol. II

τίς πόθεν εἰς ἀνδρῶν ; πόθι τοι πόλις ἠδὲ τοκῆες ;

ODYSSEY i, 170.

Selling Agents :

FIRMA KLM PRIVATE LIMITED

KOLKATA

Published by :-
Firma KLM Private Limited
257B, B. B. Ganguly Street
Kolkata-700 012
e-mail : firmaklm@yahoo.com
Website : www.firmaklm.net
Phone No. : 033-2237-4391/2221-7294

1st Edition : Calcutta 1891 (Bengal Secretariat Press)
Reprint : Calcutta 1998
Reprint : Kolkata, 2014

ISBN 81-7102-071-2

Price : ₹ 2500.00 (Set of 2 volumes)

Printed by :-
Unik Colour Printing Works
20A, Patuatola Lane
Kolkata-700009

TO THE MEMORY OF

Dr. James Wise,

SOME TIME CIVIL SURGEON OF DACCA,

THIS VOLUME,

EMBODYING IN PART THE RESULTS OF HIS RESEARCHES DURING THIRTEEN YEARS' RESIDENCE IN EASTERN BENGAL,

IS DEDICATED.

ETHNOGRAPHIC GLOSSARY.

VOL. II.

L

Láb, a title of Baniyás, of the Khandiwár sub-caste of Bais Baniyás and of the Oswal Baniyás in Behar.

Lábar, a *gáin* of the Sándilya *gotra* of the Uttar-Bárendra Brahmans in Bengal.

Labnagar Kumet, a section of the Majraut sub-caste of Goálás in Behar.

Lachh, a section of Rautiás in Chota Nagpur.

Ladilá, a section of Bábhans in Behar.

Ladu, a sub-section of the Kautsasa section of Utkal Brahmans in Orissa.

Láek, a section of Utkal or Orissa Brahmans.

Lagdingpá, a *rui* or sept of the Bedtshan-gye sub-tribe of Dejong Lhoris or Bhotias of the south.

Lagmetá, a *mul* or section of the Naomuliá or Majraut sub-caste of Goálás in Behar.

Lagori, a sept of Hos in Singbhum.

Láhá, a title of the Desá sub-caste of Gandhabaniks; of Mayarás, Kaibarttas, and of Subarnabaniks in Bengal.

Láhágot, a *mul* or section of the Naomuliá or Goriá sub-caste of Goálás in Behar.

Lahakpá, a *thar* or sept of Mangars in Darjiling.

Lahaniá, a section of Goálás in the North-Western Provinces and Behar.

Lahati, a section of Nowars in Darjiling.

Laher, a sub-sept of the Hemrom and Márndi septs of Santáls.

Laherá, a synonym for Láheri.

Láheri, a group of the Bárendra Goálás in Bengal.

Láheri, a *gáin* of the Sándilya *gotra* and a title of Bárendra Brahmans in Bengal.

Laheri, *Laherá*, a Behar caste engaged in the manufacture and sale of lac bangles (*láh ká churi*). The group is probably a functional one, consisting of members of several different castes who happened to adopt that particular profession. In Behar it is divided into two sub-castes—Dakhinhá and Tirhutiá—residing respectively north and south of the Ganges. There are two sections,—Kási and Mahuriá. Prohibited degrees are reckoned by the standard formula calculated to seven generations in the descending line.

Origin and internal structure.

Laheris admit both infant and adult-marriage, but regard the former practice as the more respectable. The ceremony is of the standard type, but no *tilak* is paid to the parents of the bridegroom. Polygamy is resorted to only in the event of the first wife proving barren. Widows are allowed to marry again by the *sagai* form. In such cases it is deemed right and proper for a woman to marry her late husband's younger brother if one has survived him, but she is under no positive obligation to do so. A faithless wife can be divorced by establishing her guilt before a panchayat. If, however, the offence

Marriage.

has been committed with a member of the caste, it is usually condoned on payment of a fine in the form of a feast given to the heads of the caste. Adultery with an outsider involves instant expulsion from the community.

Inheritance. In deciding questions of inheritance and succession the caste profess to be guided by the Mitákshará, which is the personal law of most Hindus in Behar. Disputes, however, rarely go beyond the pancháyat, a highly primitive tribunal, which cannot be credited with very precise knowledge of the written law. To this circumstance, no doubt, we owe the preservation among their scanty customs of the usage known in the Panjáb as *chundávand*, by which the sons, however few, of one wife take a share equal to that of the sons, however many, of another. In applying this rule no distinction is drawn between the status of the wives, and the sons of a wife married by the *sagai* form get the same share as the sons of a woman who was married as a virgin by the regular ceremony.

Religion. Laheris consider themselves to be orthodox Hindus, and regard Bhagavati as the deity whom they are more especially bound to worship. Tirhutiá Brahmans serve them as priests, and do not suffer in social esteem by so doing. Their functions, however, extend only to attendance at marriages and watching over the observances due to the greater gods of the Hindu Pantheon. The minor deities, Bandi and Goraiyá, are worshipped by the heads of families themselves without the assistance of Brahmans. Goats, wheaten cakes, milk, and sweetmeats form the usual offerings, which are afterwards eaten by the members of the household.

Social status and occupation. In point of social standing the Laheris rank with Koiris and Kurmis, and Brahmans will take water from their hands. Besides their original occupation of making lac bracelets, many of them are engaged in cultivation as occupancy raiyats. As a rule, however, they will not guide the plough with their own hands, and none of them are found in the lower grades of the agricultural system.

The following statement shows the number and distribution of the Laheri caste in 1872 and 1881:—

DISTRICT.	1872.	1881.	DISTRICT.	1872.	1881.
Bardwan	333	168	Tirhut { Mozufferpur ...	6,643	2,212
Bankura	28	8	Tirhut { Darbhanga ...		2,673
Birbhum	98	149	Saran	617	324
Midnapur	206	15	Champaran	1,273	995
Hughli	246	24	Monghyr	1,995	2,209
24-Parganas	282	......	Bhagalpur	1,306	1,016
Nadiya	30	205	Purniah	601	708
Khulna	......	103	Maldah	163	......
Murshedabad	274	81	Santál Parganas ...	11	393
Dinajpur	98	74	Cuttack	4,656	3
Pabna	5	......	Puri	1,879	......
Dacca	2	79	Balasore	1,018	39
Faridpur	353	153	Tributary States ...	914	......
Tipperah	6	326	Hazaribagh	......	684
Noakhali	18	8	Lohardagá	......	1,430
Patna	1,424	1,081	Singbhum	......	9
Gya	2,051	714	Manbhum	......	99
Shahabad	243	24	Tributary States ...	......	65

Lah-ogpá, dwelling below *la* or mountain-top or pass; a *rui* or sept of the Ruichhung sub-tribe of Dejong Lhoris or Bhotias of the south.

Lahoni, a *thar* or section of Nepáli Brahmans.

Lahtaur, a sept of Rájputs in Behar.

Láhuliá, a sept of Rájputs in Behar.

Láik, a title of Telis and Mayarás in Bengal.

Laiyál, a *thar* or section of Nepáli Brahmans.

Lakándri, a *thar* or sept of Mangars in Darjiling.

Lakargarhá, a sub-caste of Sunris in Manbhum.

Lákat, a sept of Rájputs in Behar.

Lakhansariá, a section of Madhesiá Halwáis in Behar.

Lakhauriá, a division of Brahmans in Behar.

Lakhauriár, a section of Káyasths in Behar.

Lakhiputra, a synonym for Doai.

Lakhnauá, a section of the Banodhiá and Jaiswár Kalwárs in Behar.

Lakhotia, a section of Mahesris in Behar.

Lakhsariá, a section of Bháts.

Lakrihár, a section of Bansphor Doms in Western Behar.

Laksha, a *gáin* of the Bátsya *gotra* of Bárendra Brahmans in Bengal.

Laksham Seriá, a section of the Biyáhut and Kharidáhá Kalwárs in Behar.

Lakshan or *Saranbanda*, a class of Sannyásis or Fakirs.

Lakshanpuriá, a *mul* or section of the Naomuliá or Majraut sub-caste of Goálás in Behar.

Laktomáháng, a sept of Limbus in Darjiling.

Lakwár, a section of the Maghayá sub-caste of Barhis in Behar.

Lál, Lála, a title of Káyasths, Khatris, of the Banodhiá sub-caste of Kalwárs and Sunris in Behar.

Lálá, a synonym for Káyasth in Behar.

Lálbegi, a class of Mahomedan sweepers supposed to have come from Upper India, some with sepoy regiments, others as wanderers in search of work. Though styled Mahomedans, they neither practise circumcision nor abstain from pork. The Lalbegi are employed as sweepers in European households, and are always addressed as jama'dár by the other servants.

They eat the leavings of Europeans, and drink any sort of wine or spirits. They will not, however, eat with the Raut, who in their turn pride themselves on abstaining from food that has come from a European table. Nor will they touch a dead body.

The religious rites of the Lalbegi are partly Hindu, partly Muhammadan. As with Mussulmáns generally, marriages are arranged by an old woman who acts as match-maker. No *kabin* or marriage settlement is drawn up, but an *ikrár* or bond is executed, in which both promise to love one another, and the bridegroom undertakes not to bring a second wife into his house. Previous to the wedding day the Khandúri ceremony is observed, as well as other Muhammadan customs, but the services of the Kohárji Brahman are not required. Should the marriage be celebrated in the bridegroom's house, a fee of twenty annas is paid to the pancháyat; if in the bride's, only five annas.

A few of the Lalbegi keep the fast of Ramazán, although they dare not enter a public mosque.

Their funeral ceremonies are peculiar. The dead may not be buried in a Mussulmán cemetery, but are consigned to the ground in some waste and jungly spot. The corpse is wrapped in five shrouds, a handkerchief is placed under each arm and in each hand, a *kasáwá* or napkin is bound round the head, and a *khirqá* or blouse is put on the body. After the grave has been filled in, a cloth cover (*phúl ka chadar*) is laid over it, while four pieces of "Agar" wood are inserted at the corners and set fire to. The rest of the funeral ceremonies are strictly Mahomedan. For four days after a death a fire is not allowed to be lighted in the dwelling-house of the deceased, the family in the meantime receiving food from their neighbours; but on the fifth day a tray laden with betel-nuts and adorned with flowers is placed in front of the hut, and a feast is given to the whole tribe.

The Lalbegis follow many Hindu customs, observing the Díwálí and the Holí as the greatest festivals of the year. On these occasions a mud image of a mosque with five domes is made, supposed to be a model of one still existing at Ghazní, in Kábul, which belonged to Lál Beg, the eponymous ancestor of the tribe. In front of the image a cock is sacrificed, and offerings of *pilao*, *sherbet*, and sweetmeats are made in his name. Lál Beg is identified by Sir H. Elliot[1] with Lál Guru, the same as the Rákshasa Aronákarat; but in Benares[2] he is confounded with Pír Zahr, perhaps the famous Chishtíya saint Sayyíd Sháh Zuhúr. In the Panjáb, again, Mihtars adore Lál Pír, or Bábá Faqír, as the dyers do Pír 'Alí Rangrez, and the blacksmiths Hazrat Dáúd. It seems not improbable, therefore, that the Lalbegí, like many other tribes converted to Mahomedanism, have adopted a Mahomedan saint as their common ancestor.

Lál-Chátái, a sub-group of Hele Kaibarttas in Central Bengal.

Lál-Gámia, a group of the Mihtar sub-caste of Telis in Behar.

Lál-Goálá, a hypergamous group of Goálás in Eastern Bengal.

Lalihar, a bird, a totemistic sept of Lohárs in Chota Nagpur.

Láma, a *thar* or sept of Gurungs in Darjiling.

Lámá Khor, a section of Murmis in Darjiling.

Lamamaka, a sept of Hos in Singbhum.

Lámbá, a section of Goálás in the North-Western Provinces and Behar.

Lambacha, a sept of the Tungjainya sub-tribe of Chakmás in the Hill Tracts of Chittagong.

Lámgáde, Lamgadeh, a section of Kámis and a *thar* or sept of Mangars in Darjiling.

Lamgoriá, a section of Bábhans in Behar.

[1] *Supplemental Glossary*, i. 82.
[2] Sherring, *Hindu Tribes of Benares*, p. 397.

Lámi Chhanya, a *thar* or sept of Gurungs and Mangars in Darjiling.

Lamjál, a *thar* or sept of Mangars in Darjiling.

Lampochhá, a sept of the Rautár sub-tribe of Thárus in Behar.

Lamsani Tongi, a *thar* or sept of the Das-Gurung sub-tribe of Gurungs in Darjiling. It was separated from its parent *thar*, the Lehbo Lamsani.

Lang, a kind of bird, a totemistic sept of Mundas in Chota Nagpur.

Láng Chenre, a section of the Mahili-Munda sub-caste of Mahilis in Chota Nagpur.

Langjharájhari, a *mul* or section of Kesarwáni Baniyás in Behar.

Langsál or **Lamsál**, a *thar* of the Bachh *gotra* of Nepáli Brahmans.

Laoti, he who was obeyed, a sept of the Pánthar sub-tribe of Limbus in Darjiling.

Láphaunchhá, a *thar* or sept of Khambus in Darjiling.

Lápung, a small bird, a totemistic sept of Mundas in Chota Nagpur.

Larapá, monkey-eater, a sept of Mundas in Chota Nagpur.

Larauni, a *mul* or section of the Chhamuliá Madhesiá sub-caste of Halwáis in Behar.

Larhora or *Purbál Mehter*, a sub-caste of Doms in Behar who reverence Supat Bhagat, a devotee whom they believe to be the *purka* or founder of their sub-caste. They make baskets and remove filth.

Lari, a sub-caste of Goálás in Chota Nagpur.

Larka, the fighters, a title of the Ho tribe in Singbhum.

Larkor, a title of Jaunpuri Chamárs in Behar whose women act as midwives.

Larma, a sept of Chakmás in the Hill Tracts of Chittagong.

Larsunar, a sept of Mundas in Chota Nagpur.

Lartangar, a *mul* or section of the Kanaujiá sub-caste of Sonárs in Behar.

Láruli, a *gáin* of the Bharadwája *gotra* of Bárendra Brahmans in Bengal.

Larwár, a *dih* or exogamous section of the Gharbait sub-caste of Amáts in Behar.

Larwariá, a section of Bábhans in Behar.

Laskar, a title of Pods in Bengal.

Lát, a sub-sept of the Kisku, Saren, and Tudu septs of Santáls, whose ancestor baked meat in a leaf platter.

Latá-baidya, a synonym for Bárui.

Latá Punra, a section of Pundarik or Pundas, so called from their selling vegetables grown from *latá* or creeper.

Láter, a sub-tribe of Dhimáls in the Darjiling Terai.

Lathaur, a sub-caste of Telis in Behar, a section of Rajwárs and Rautiás in Chota Nagpur.

Latihar, a variant for Láheri or Churihár, who manufacture lac bracelets or *churis*.

Lau, a sub-section of the Hárita section of Utkal Brahmans in Orissa.

Laugi, a title of Nágars in Behar.

Lauki, a title of Hindu Joláhas in Behar.

Laungijarhuá, a *mul* or section of the Sátmuliá or Kishnaut sub-caste of Goálás in Behar.

Lauriá, a section of Goálás in Behar.

Lautni, a sept of Rájputs in Behar.

Láwápur, a section of Majraut Goálás in Behar.

Láyá, a synonym for Maulik.

Leba, a sept of Chakmás in the Hill Tracts of Chittagong.

Lechenche, the dissolute one, a sept of the Yangorup sub-tribe of Limbus in Darjiling.

Legbahang, a sept of the Tambrkhola sub-tribe of Limbus in Darjiling.

Legma, the worker in mud, a sept of the Chhothar sub-tribe of Limbus in Darjiling.

Leh Láma, a *thar* or sept of Gurungs in Darjiling the members of which are called in to officiate at the obsequies of the dead by throwing earth on the grave, and to read the funeral prayers.

Lekhogma, he of the swollen testes, a sept of the Yangorup sub-tribe of Limbus in Darjiling.

Lenda, earthworm, a totemistic sept of Mundas in Chota Nagpur.

Leng, a totemistic sept of the Bhumij tribe in Manbhum, the members of which will not touch or eat a mushroom.

Lenká, a title of Chásás in Orissa.

Lepcha, *Rong*, *Khamba*, *Mon*, a Mongolian tribe of Sikkim, Western Bhutan, Eastern Nepal, and Darjiling. They are divided into two branches—**Rong** and **Khamba**. The former claim to be the original inhabitants of Sikkim, while the Khamba are believed to have immigrated some 250 years ago from the Kham province of China, whither a deputation of Lamas had been sent to choose a ruler for Sikkim. The Raja selected by them brought with him a number of his own tribe, who retained the name of their original home as associating them with the ruling family. The distinction, however, has not operated as a bar to intermarriage, and the two branches are now thoroughly amalgamated. Both, in fact, probably come of the same original stock, and represent two successive migrations of Mongols into Sikkim.

Origin.

"In person," says Dr. Campbell,[1] "the Lepchas are short, averaging about five feet in height: five feet six inches is tall, and four feet eight inches is a common stature among the men. The women are shorter in the usual proportion. The men are bulky for their height, but rather fleshy than sinewy. The muscular development of their limbs is inferior to that of the Mágars, Gurungs, Murmis, and other

Physical type.

[1] *Journal of Ethnological Society of London*, vol. I, No. 2.

Parbattiahs. They are very fair of skin, and boys and girls in health have generally a ruddy tinge of complexion. This is lost, however, in adolescence, although the fairness continues. The features are markedly Mongolian, but there is a fulness and roundness of feature accompanied by a cheerful expression and laughing eye which renders the face a most pleasing one. The total absence of beard and the fashion of parting the hair along the crown of the head adds to a somewhat womanly expression of countenance in the men, and the loose bedgown sort of jacket, with wide sleeves, which they wear, contributes still more to render it rather difficult for strangers to distinguish the sexes, especially in middle age. The men very often look like women, and the women sometimes like men. The hair is worn long by both sexes; the younger men allowing it to hang loose over the shoulders, the elders plaiting it into a tail, which sometimes reaches to the knees. The women of rank wear their hair in two, and sometimes in three tails, tying it with braids and silken cords and tassels. The Lepchas, both male and female, are dirty in person, rarely having recourse to ablution. In the cold and dry season this renders them unpleasant inmates of a close dwelling, but in the rains, when they move about and are frequently wet, they are clean and sweet. The temperament of the Lepcha is eminently cheerful, and his disposition really amiable. In ordinary intercourse they are a very fascinating people, and possess an amount of intelligence and rational curiosity not to be met with among their Bhotia, Limbu, Murmi, or Gurung neighbours, and indeed rarely, if ever, to be seen among people so completely secluded from foreign intercourse as they always have been. The marked contrast in these respects between the Lepchas and the listless, uninquiring natives of the plains renders association with them a source of much pleasure to Europeans. They are wonderfully honest, theft being scarcely known among them; they rarely quarrel among themselves. I have never known them to draw their knives on one another, although they always wear them. For ordinary social purposes of talking, eating, and drinking, they have great unanimity, but for any more important purposes of resistance to oppression, the pursuit of industry or trade, their confidence in one another is at a low pitch; they fly bad government rather than resist it, and used to prefer digging for yams in the jungle and eating wretchedly innutritious vegetables to enduring any injustice or harsh treatment. They are singularly forgiving of injuries, when time is given them, after hasty loss of temper. Although they were ready enough to lodge complaints before the Magistrate against one another in cases of assault and other offences, they rarely prosecuted to a decision, generally preferring to submit to arbitration or making mutual amends and concessions."

Internal structure.

The internal structure of the tribe, so far as I have been able to ascertain it, is shown in Appendix I. The subject is most obscure, and Lepchas themselves seem unable to throw much light upon it. Besides the main divisions of Rong and Khamba, which, as has been stated above, have no special bearing on marriage, the Lepchas recognize ten groups, which they call *thars*. These appear to have been at one time exogamous, and the Adinpuso *thar* is said to be so still. The rest, however, have lost their exogamous character, and their members may marry women of their own or of other groups. Two *thars*, Barphungpuso and Adinpuso, rank higher than the other eight, and do not permit intermarriage with them. The distinction is said to arise from the fact that the officials of the Sikkim State are invariably chosen from these two *thars*, and they probably are the descendants of the Khamba clansmen who followed the chief from Tibet. Village headmen (*mandals*) are drawn from among the eight lower *thars*, and these groups represent the main body of cultivators in Sikkim. Members of these *thars* again may intermarry with Limbus, which is forbidden for Barphungpuso and Adinpuso.

The primitive rule of exogamy having thus fallen into disuse, the Lepchas supply its place by a table of prohibited degrees which does not differ materially from that expressed by the common formula *mamera*, *chachera*, etc., already often referred to. Intermarriage is barred only for three generations in the descending line, except when a *mith* or adoptive relationship has been entered into, in which case the prohibition is said to extend to nine generations. The ceremony observed in *mith* is of the same general character as among the Murmis, but Lamas, not Brahmans, officiate as priests, and Tibetan scarves are exchanged as pledges of amity instead of the rupees used by the Murmis. The wives of the two friends take part in the ceremony, and are not troubled by the strict etiquette which among the Nepalese regulates the conduct of a wife towards her husband's *dost*.

Marriage.

Lepcha girls usually marry between the ages of sixteen and eighteen. Men marry later owing to the difficulty of getting together the bride-price, which ranges from Rs. 40 to Rs. 100 according to the rank of the parties. The freest courtship is permitted, and sexual license before marriage is tolerated. If a girl becomes pregnant, the man is expected either to marry her or to pay some compensation to her parents for the reduction in value which she has undergone. Formal proposals of marriage are usually made to the bride's parents by *pibus* or go-betweens acting on behalf of the lover. If the proposal is accepted, the *pibus* go to the bride's house with Rs. 5 as earnest-money, and ten seers of *maruá* beer and a Tibetan scarf. An auspicious day for the marriage is then fixed by the Lamas. The ceremony, performed first at the bride's and then at the bridegroom's house, is of a very simple character. Bride and bridegroom sit side by side on a carpet, and the Lama ties a silk scarf round the neck of each and then changes the scarves, so that the bride wears the bridegroom's and *vice versâ*. Rice is sprinkled over their heads, they eat together, and drink *maruá* beer out of the same cup. The proceedings end with a feast. The married couple spend three days in the husband's house, and then usually go on a month's visit to the bride's parents.

When a man is too poor to pay the bride-price, he is often allowed to marry, as it were, on credit; but the bride does not leave her father's house, and the husband goes to live with her and work for his father-in-law until the full amount has been made up.

Polyandry, though comparatively rare, is not entirely unknown among the Lepchas. As might be expec[illegible] the Tibetan form of the custom is followed, and the younger brothers share the favours of the eldest brother's wife. Polygamy is permitted, but is not practised on a large scale.

A widow may marry again, and is subject to no express restrictions in her choice of a second husband. It is considered, however, proper for her to marry her late husband's younger brother, and if she marries an outsider, this brother-in-law usually keeps the children, and in any case may claim repayment of the bride-price. The full ceremony may be employed at the marriage of a widow, but the parties usually content themselves with the mere announcement by a Lama that they have become man and wife.

If a married couple cannot agree, arbitrators (*pibus*) are appointed to attempt to adjust their differences. If they fail after two or three attempts, a formal divorce is effected with the concurrence of the Lama who married the pair. The wife returns to her father's house, and her husband pays some compensation to her parents. When a woman is taken in adultery, a pancháyat considers the case and determines the amount of fine (*gysh*) to be paid to her husband by the paramour. The amount of the fine is not fixed by custom, nor does it bear any stated proportion to the bride-price. Where adultery is proved, the husband has a right to divorce his wife without paying compensation to her parents, and to take away her ornaments. Physical chastisement is never inflicted, nor is the right of divorce invariably exercised. Divorced wives may marry again by the same ceremony as is in use at the marriage of a virgin.

Inheritance.

In matters of inheritance and succession the Lepchas follow a tribal custom of their own, which is administered by the pancháyats of the tribe, and rarely comes before the regular courts. At a man's death his property is supposed to be divided equally among his sons, but the rule of equal division is liable in practice to be modified by other considerations. Thus the widow and daughters of the deceased usually live with the eldest son, and where this is the case he gets an extra share of the property. In Sikkim, again, it is held that the rule of equal division only applies where the sons render equal service to the Raja of the country, so that if one son does service and the others do not, that one gets an extra share of the property. A similar principle is recognized by the Lepchas of Darjiling. In dividing an inheritance account is taken by the pancháyat of the extent to which the different heirs have contributed to the improvement of the property, and their shares are adjusted accordingly. Brothers have no claim by right of descent, but shares may be awarded to them by the pancháyat in proportion to the work they have done during the lifetime of the deceased. Wills are unknown; but a father may make a verbal declaration in favour of a particular son, and the pancháyat will give effect to this declaration of his wishes. If sons survive, the unmarried daughters are maintained by them, and neither they nor married daughters take any share in the property. If, however, there are no sons, a married daughter may succeed, provided that she and her husband have lived in her father's house. The whole system, however, is extremely fluid and indefinite, and the rules stated above are in practice constantly modified by the pancháyat with the object of doing substantial justice to the various claimants.

Religion.

Most Lepchas at the present day profess to be Buddhists, and follow in a more or less intelligent fashion the observances of the northern sect of that religion. It is clear, however, that at no very distant time their sole belief was a form of Shamanistic Animism of the same general character as that described in the article on the Limbus. Conspicuous traces of this faith still survive among them, imperfectly hidden by the thin veil of Buddhistic usage. In the belief of the average Lepcha, mountain and forest, rock and stream represent ill-defined but formidable powers who threaten mankind with a variety of physical ills, and require to be constantly appeased through the agency of Bijuás or exorcists. Not all of these powers are evil, and some are even credited with taking a kindly interest in human affairs. But savage theology, expressing doubtless the experience of primitive man as to the distribution of good and evil in the world, teaches that the good gods abide in their own place and take no heed of mankind, while the malevolent deities are in a constant state of jealous and mischievous activity. The former therefore gradually drop out of notice and fade from the memories of men, while the latter, strong in the fears they inspire, may even outlive an entire change of religion on the part of their votaries. The snow-clad giant Kinchinjanga, chief among the elemental deities of the Lepchas, who vexes men with storm and hail and sends down avalanches and torrents to wreck their fields and sweep away their homes, has been translated to the milder system of Buddhism, where he figures as the tutor of Sakya Muni himself. Eshegenpu, Palden Lhamo, Lapen-Rimbuchi, Genpu-Maling-Nagpu, and Wasungma are less easy to identify; but the fact that they receive offerings of meat and *maruá* beer in addition to the flowers, fruit, rice, and incense sanctioned by Buddhist usage, lends some weight to the conjecture that they belong to an earlier and more barbarous system. Chirenzi or Lachen-Om-Chhup-Chhimu is said by the Lepchas to be the same as Mahadeva. His wife is Umadevá. Both are believed to have been worshipped by the Lepchas before the introduction of Buddhism.

Tibetan Lamas serve the tribe as priests, and preside at all Buddhist ceremonies. Lepchas themselves rarely become Lamas, but many of them are exorcists (Bijuás or Ojhas), and exercise considerable influence by their power of averting the ill-will of the gods and appeasing the spirits of the dead.

Disposal of the dead.

The dead are usually buried, fully clothed and in a sitting position, facing towards the east. Before burial the corpse is kept sitting in the house for two or three days with food before it. The grave is lined with stones and a round cairn built on the top surmounted by a flag. Among the Rong Lepchas an Ojha is called in about a month after death to perform a simple propitiatory rite, at which a cow or a goat is killed and much *maruá* beer is drunk. This is sometimes repeated on the first anniversary of the death. The object is to put the dead man's spirit to rest, and to prevent him from plaguing the living with bad dreams. At harvest time offerings of rice, *maruá* beer, and various kinds of food are presented by the head of the household for the benefit of ancestors in general.

The higher classes of Khamba Lepchas burn their dead, pound the fragments of the bones which remain, and throw them into a river, not into a *jhorá* or hill stream. The subsequent propitiatory ceremony is sometimes very elaborate, as in the case of the obsequies of the sister of the Sikkim Raja, described by Mr. J. Ware Edgar, C.S.I., in the following passage[1]:—

"Before the figure [meant to represent the dead person, in this case the Sikkim Rajah's sister, who was a nun] was a table on which were different kinds of food; on another table at the side were various things which had belonged to the woman when alive; while on a third, 108 little brass lamps were arranged in rows. Long lines of monks in dark red robes and with very tall caps of bright crimson on their heads sat on carpets placed in the middle of the chapel and chanted litanies throughout each day of my stay at Toomlong.

"It chanced that I saw the conclusion, and learned the meaning of this ceremony at Pomiongchi, where the lay-figure of the nun was taken some days after I left Toomlong. There for three days the figure was seated before the altar, and the monks chanted the litanies for the departure of the soul of the dead nun * * * On the third day the relations, friends, and dependents of the deceased brought or sent gifts of food or clothing or money, which were all laid before the figure of the dead woman; while the head Lama, standing in front of his chair and turning towards the figure, stated the nature of each gift and the name of the donor. Towards evening the tea-cup of the nun was freshly filled with tea and her murwa jug with murwa, and all the monks solemnly drank tea with her. Then many people who had known and loved the nun when alive went up, and, prostrating themselves before the figure, kissed the hem of the robe as a last farewell, while the monks chanted the litanies more zealously than ever, and the head Lama, who had left his chair and gone to one of the tables, went through some elaborate ceremonies the meaning of which I could not make out. At about nine o'clock the chanting ceased, and the Lama again standing in front of his chair made a long speech to the soul of the nun, in which he told her that all that could be done to make her journey to another world easy had been done, and that now she would have to go forth alone and unassisted to appear before the king and judge of the dead * * * * * * *
When the Lama had finished his address, some of the monks took

---

[1] *Report of a Visit to Sikkim*, pp. 57-58.

down the lay-figure and undressed it; while others formed a procession and conducted the soul of the nun into the darkness outside the monastery, with a discordant noise of conch-shells, thigh-bone trumpets, Tibetan flutes, gongs, cymbals, tambourines, drums, and other most disagreeable but nameless instruments."

Food.

"The Lepchas," says Dr. Campbell,[1] "have no caste distinctions. Those who live under the Nepal Government are obliged to conform to the Hindu laws of that State, which prohibit the killing of the cow. This they do, however, with a very bad grace, and rarely forego an opportunity of visiting Darjiling to indulge their beef-eating propensities. They are gross feeders, eating all kinds of animal food, including the elephant, rhinoceros, and monkey, and all grains and vegetables known to us, with the addition of many roots and plants altogether excluded from our culinary list. Pork is their most favourite flesh; next to that beef, goat, and mutton. The yak is considered the best beef, the next to that the flesh of the Sikkim cow, a fine animal, and last the Bengali and common cow. All birds are included in their list of eatable game. Of the carrion of wild animals, that of the elephant is most prized. The favourite vegetable food is rice; next to it wheat, barley, maize, millet. murwa, and a fine species of yam called "bookh," which grows all over these mountains, at elevations of from 1,500 to 3,000 feet. During the rains, when grain is scarce, they contentedly put up with ferns, bamboo roots, several sorts of fungi, and innumerable succulent plants found wild on the mountains. A large-rooted arum is much used at this season, after being soaked in water for six days to remove its acrid juice; still it often produces colic, and is poisonous. Fond of fermented and spirituous liquors, the Lepchas are nevertheless not given to drunkenness; their common beverage is a kind of beer made from the fermented infusion of Indian corn and murwa, which is weak, but agreeably acid and very refreshing. They drink this at all times when procurable, and when making a journey it is carried in a large bamboo "chunga," and diligently applied to throughout the day. They have no distilled liquor of their own, but they greatly admire and prize all our strong waters—our port and sherry, cherry brandy, and maraschino. Tea is a favourite beverage, the black sort brought from China in large cakes being that preferred. It is prepared by boiling, after which the decoction is churned up in a "chunga," with butter and salt. Milk is never taken with tea. Their cooking is careless, coarse, and not cleanly. Rice is generally boiled when travelling in pieces of the large bamboo; at home, in coarse iron pots. Vegetables are always boiled in oil, when the latter is procurable, and spiced with capsicum and ginger, of which these hills possess very fine kinds. Salt is not a commonly used condiment, the chief source of its supply till lately being Tibet, whence rock-salt is brought on men's backs: the easier communication with the plains of Bengal by the new Darjiling road admits of the importation of this article at a cheaper rate, and sea-salt is rapidly taking the place of the other.

[1] *Journal of the Ethnological Society of London*, vol. 1, No. 2, pp. 147-49.

"The Lepcha dress is simple and graceful. It consists of a robe of striped red and white cotton cloth crossed over the breast and shoulders, and descending to the calf of the legs, leaving the arms bare; a loose jacket of red cotton cloth is worn over the robe by those who can afford it, and both are bound round the waist by a red gridle; some strings of coloured beads round the neck, silver and coral earrings, a bamboo bow and quiver of iron-pointed arrows, and a long knife complete the dress of the men. The knife, called "ban" by the Lepchas, and "chipsa" by the Bhotias, is constantly worn by the males of all ages and ranks; it hangs on the right side, suspended from the left shoulder, and is used for all purposes. With the "ban" the Lepcha clears a space in the forest for his house and cultivation; it is the only tool used by him in building; with it he skins the animals that fall a prey to his snares and arrows; it is his sword in battle, his table knife, his hoe, spade, and nail-parer. Without the "ban" he is helpless to move in the jungle; with it he is a man of all work: the expertness with which it is used by the boys of a few years old even is the astonishment of strangers. The women are less neatly dressed than the men: a piece of plain unbleached cotton cloth, or the cloth of the castor oil insect—the indi—rolled round to form a sort of petticoat, with a loose red gown of the same, and a profusion of mock coral and coloured bead necklaces, form their entire wardrobe. They are the domestic and farm drudges of the men, performing all out and in-door work along with their husbands, and much besides. It is not unusual to meet a stout and active man, bow in hand, sauntering along the road followed by his wife and sisters heavily loaded with grain or merchandise. It is the delight of a Lepcha to be idle; he abhors the labour of practising any craft, but he expects that while he is amused and unemployed the female part of the household shall be busily engaged in the field, or in looking after the pigs and poultry. In recent times they have taken to work in tea plantations and as chair-bearers: and the necessity for money, since we introduced it into their country, has made them more steady workers."

Dress.

[2] "The Lepchas are poor agriculturists, their labours in this art being confined to the careless growing of rice, Indian corn, murwa (*Sessasum Orientalis*), and a few vegetables, of which the brinjal, cucumber, and capsicum are the chief. Their habits are incurably erratic: they do not form permanent villages, and rarely remain longer than three years in one place, at the expiration of which they move into a new part of the forest, sometimes near, often distant, and there go through the labour of clearing a space for a house, building a new one, and preparing the ground for a crop. The latter operations consist in cutting down the smaller trees, lopping off the branches of the large ones, which are burnt, and scratching the soil with the "ban," after

Occupation.

---

[1] The "ban" is a straight sword with a wooden scabbard open along one side.

[2] *Journal of the Ethnological Society of London*, vol. [illegible]. No. 2, p. 151.

which, on the falling of a shower of rain, the seed is thrown into the ground. Their houses are built entirely of bamboo, raised about five feet from the ground, and thatched with the same material, but a smaller species, split up."

The Lepchas numbered 3,952 in 1872 and 202 in 1881 in the district of Darjiling.

Lepuriet, a *mul* or section of the Naomuliá or Majraut sub-caste of Goálás in Behar.

Let, a sub-caste of Bágdis found in Murshedabad and Birbhum.

Lethrani, the designation of the women of the Limbu caste in Darjiling.

Levátiá, a section of Majraut Goálás in Behar.

Lhasung, a sub-sept of the Pon-po sept of Dejong Lhoris or Bhotias of the south, the members of which officiate as priests of all the septs.

Lha-yo, a *thar* or sept of Mangars in Darjiling.

Lhebo Lamsani, a *thar* or sept of the Das-Gurung sub-tribe of Gurungs. There is a tradition that in ancient times two Gurungs —father and son—quarrelled and separated from each other. The father's party remained at Lehbo and the son's party emigrated to a distant place. The latter were called Lamsani Tangi (*tangi* in Gurung means 'separated').

Lhopa, a native of Bhotan.

Lhopa Bhotia, a synonym for Dejong Lhori.

Lhoringten, the chief of Morang, a sept of the Chaibisa sub-tribe of Limbus. This *thar* was formerly under the Morang Raja.

Lhorong, a sub-tribe of Yakhas in Darjiling.

Libang, the archer, a sept of the Miákhola sub-tribe of Limbus in Darjiling.

Lihimba, dove, a totemistic sept of Juángs in Orissa.

Lila, fish, a totemistic sept of Oraons in Chota Nagpur.

Lilla, wild cow, a totemistic sept of Mundas in Chota Nagpur.

Liluai, a sept of Birhors in Chota Nagpur.

Limbu, a large tribe, probably of Mongolian descent, ranking next to the Khambu and above the Yakha among the three upper divisions of the Kiránti group. The precedence given to the Khambus is supposed to be due to their having a larger proportion of Khas and Newar blood, while the Limbus have interbred freely with the Lepchas. The Yakha are a minor tribe, concerning which little is known. Unlike the other two, they have no generally recognized honorific title, though they claim to be addressed as *dewan* and call themselves Yak Thomba or yakherds, with reference to the tradition that this was their characteristic occupation before the tribe crossed the Himalaya into Eastern Nepal. The name Limbu, or Das Limbu, from the ten sub-tribes (really thirteen) into which they are supposed to be divided, is used only by outsiders. Tibetans have no special name

Traditions of origin.

for the Limbus; they call all the tribes of the Indian side of the Himalaya by the general name Moupa or dwellers in the ravines. The Lepchas and Bhotias or Tibetans settled in Bhotan, Sikkim, and Nepal speak of the Limbus as Tsong, because the five *thums* or sub-tribes included in the class known as Lhása-gotra emigrated to Eastern Nepal from the district of Tsang in Tibet. Lepchas call them Chang, which may be a corruption of Tsong. By other members of the Kiránti group they are addressed by the honorific title of Subah or Suffah, a chief.

The Limbus, according to Dr. Campbell, "form a large portion of the inhabitants in the mountainous country lying between the Dud-Kosi and the Kanki rivers in Nepal, and are found in smaller numbers eastwards to the Mechi river, which forms the boundary of Nepal and Sikkim. In still fewer numbers they exist within the Sikkim territory, as far east as the Tista river, beyond which they rarely settle. In Bhutan they are unknown except as strangers." Hodgson locates them between the Arun Kosi and the Mechi, the Singilela ridge being their boundary on the east. The Limbus themselves claim to have held from time immemorial the Támba Khola valley on the upper waters of the Támba Kosi river; and the fact that one of their sub-tribes bears the name Támbakhola suggests that this valley may have been one of their early settlements. They have also a tradition that five out of their thirteen sub-tribes came from Lhása, while five others came from Benares. The former group is called the Lhása-gotra, and the latter the Kási-gotra; but the term *gotra* has in this case no bearing on marriage. All that can safely be said is that the Limbus are the oldest recorded population of the country between the Támra Kosi and the Mechi, and their flat features, slightly oblique eyes, yellow complexion, and beardlessness may perhaps afford grounds for believing them to be the descendants of early Tibetan settlers in Nepal. They appear to have mixed little with the Hindus, but much with the Lepchas, who of late years have migrated in large numbers from Sikkim to the west. Dr. Campbell compares the two tribes in the following words:—"The Limbu is a very little taller in stature than the Lepcha, somewhat less fleshy, and more wiry in the limbs, as fair in complexion, and as completely beardless. He is scarcely ever as ruddy as the Lepchas sometimes are; his eyes are, if anything, smaller, and placed more to the front than the Lepcha's, and his nose, although somewhat smaller, is rather higher in the bridge than that of the Lepcha. He wears his hair long, but does not plait it into a tail; has no fancy for bead necklaces; wears a *kukri* instead of the *bán*,[1] and wide trousers and a jacket or *chapkan* in preference to the robe and long jacket of the Lepchas."

At the time of the Gurkha conquest of Nepal the country east of the Arun Kosi was held by petty Limbu chiefs on quasi-feudal terms from the Hindu Rajas of Bijapur and Makwánpur, at whose courts representative Limbus discharged the duties of *Chauntra* or prime minister. Taking refuge in the hill forts with which each

---

[1] The long, straight knife used by the Lepchas.

chiefship was provided, the Limbus offered a gallant resistance to the invading Gurkhas, and the latter underwent many repulses before their supremacy was fully established. Although used to bearing arms, and deeming themselves a military race, they do not rank among the regular fighting tribes of Nepal, and they are not admitted into the Gorkháli regiments of the Nepalese army. Their principal occupations at the present day are agriculture, grazing, and petty trade. They serve in the Kiranti regiments raised about 30 years ago by Jang Bahadur, and some of them have enlisted in our own Gurkha battalions. Some authorities believe them, with the rest of the Kiranti, to be inferior in soldierly qualities to the Khas, Mangar, and Gurung tribes, from whom our best recruits are drawn, but this opinion seems to be giving away, among the present generation of Gurkha officers, to a more favourable estimate of their military capacity, and their behaviour in the Sikkim compaign of 1888 is understood to have borne out the latter view.

Internal structure.

The internal structure of the tribe is extremely complicated, and can best be studied in the Appendix, where it is shown in a tabular form. The Limbus are divided into thirteen endogamous sub-tribes, each of which is again broken up into a number of exogamous septs. The names of the septs are extremely curious. Two or three at the most are totemistic, a few are local or territorial, and one only is eponymous. By far the greater number of them refer to some personal adventure or peculiarity of the original founder of the sept, and they suggest the existence of a considerable body of rather grotesque folklore. The rule of exogamy goes by the male side, and is supplemented by forbidding intermarriage between persons descended in a direct line from the same parents as long as any relationship can be traced. Intermarriage between cousins is barred for three generations, or, as some say, for seven. In practice, however, while the rule forbidding marriage within the *thar* is most strictly observed, there seems to be much uncertainty about prohibited degrees, and I believe near alliances with the mother's kindred are by no means uncommon. A further complication is introduced by the restrictions on intermarriage arising from *mith* (Limbu *saiba*) friendship or on fictitious brotherhood among most of the hill races. Two men contract friendship by a special ritual at which a Brahman, or, when the parties are Buddhists, a Lama, officiates, and reads *mantras* or mystic formulæ, while the two friends thrice exchange rupees, handkerchiefs, or scarves, and daub each other between the eyebrows with the paste made of rice and curds which is used in the marriage ceremony. The effect of the union is that the friends are reckoned as brothers, and intermarriage between the two families is prohibited for several (some say eighteen) generations. Any breach of the rule is punished in British territory by exclusion from caste. In Nepal, I am informed, more severe punishments, such as death or slavery, are inflicted.

Members of the Murmi, Lepcha, and Bhotia tribes may be admitted into the Limbu tribe after being approved by the tribal council, called by the Limbus *thum-thum*, and giving a feast to the local community. In some cases the new member is required to file a written statement to the effect that he has entered the tribe and will abide by its rules. Khambus and Yakhas, being Kirantis themselves, may be admitted into the tribe by the simpler and more direct process of adoption. In any case the children of a Limbu man by a Bhotia, Lepcha, Gurung, Sunawar, Mangar, or Murmi woman, or of a Limbu woman by a man of any of these groups, are admitted without question into the Limbu community.

Religion.

The phlegmatic and utilitarian habit of mind which a German ethnologist has noticed as characteristic of the Mongolian races comes out conspicuously in the nonchalant attitude of the Limbus towards religion. Where their surroundings are Hindu, they describe themselves as Saivas, and profess to worship, though with sparing and infrequent observance, Mahádeva and his consort Gauri, the deities most favoured by the lax Hinduism of Nepal. In a Buddhist neighbourhood the yoke of conformity is still more easy to bear: the Limbu has only to mutter the pious formula, *om mani padme om*, and to pay respect and moderate tribute to the Lamas, in order to be accepted as an average Buddhist. Beneath this veneer of conformity with whatever faith happens to have gained local acceptation, the vague shapes of their original Pantheon have survived in the form of household or forest gods, much in the same way as Dionysus and other of the Greek gods may be traced in the names and attributes of the saints who preside over the vintage, the harvest and rural festivals of various kinds in remote parts of Greece at the present day. Under such disguises, which serve to mask departures from the popular creeds, the Limbus worship a host of spiritual beings whose attributes are ill-defined, and whose very names are not easy to ascertain. Yuma, Kapoba, and Thebá rank as household gods, and are propitiated once in five years, or whenever disease or loss of property threaten the family, by the slaughter, outside the house, of buffaloes, pigs or fowls. The votaries eat the sacrifice, and thus, as they express it, "dedicate the life-breath to the gods, the flesh to ourselves." No special days are set apart for the ceremony; but it cannot be performed on Sunday, as that day is sacred to Himariya. Those who wholly neglect the duty are supposed to suffer in person or property, and the common hill disease of goitre is believed to be one of the special modes by which the gods manifest their displeasure. Temples and idols are alike unknown, nor, so far as I can ascertain, does the imagination of the Limbus trouble itself to clothe its vague spiritual conceptions with any bodily form.

Himariya, the god of the forest, is propitiated on Sundays by offerings of sheep, goats, fowls, pigeons and Indian-corn A stone under a tree by the roadside is smeared with vermilion and bound with thread, and this place of sacrifice is marked by consecrated rags tied to a bamboo pole.

In addition to these more or less beneficent, or at least neutral, divinities, the Limbus are compassed about by a multitude of nameless evil spirits, "who require peculiar management in warding off their caprices." To appease and propitiate these is the special function of the Bijuás, a class of wandering mendicants peculiar to Sikkim and the eastern parts of Nepal. Bijuás are wholly illiterate, and travel about the country muttering prayers and incantations, dancing, singing, prescribing for the sick and casting out devils. They wear a purple robe and broad-brimmed hat, and are regarded with great awe by the people, into whom they have instilled the convenient belief that their curses and blessings will surely be fulfilled, and that ill-luck will attend any one who allows a Bijuá to leave his door dissatisfied.

While the Bijuá acts as exorcist and devil-worshipper for all the Himalayan races, the equally illiterate Phedangma is the tribal priest of the Limbus for the higher grades of spirits, and officiates at sacrifices, marriages, and funerals. He is also called in at births to foretell the destiny of the infant, and to invoke the blessings of the gods. The office frequently descends from father to son, but any one may become a Phedangbo who has a turn for propitiating the gods, and for this reason the occupation shows no signs of hardening into a caste.

Animism.

It will be apparent from the facts stated above that the leading principle of the Limbu religion is *animism*, "the belief in the existence of souls or spirits of which only the powerful—those on which man feels himself dependent, and before which he stands in awe—acquire the rank of divine beings and become objects of worship."[1] Among the Limbus, as among the aborigines of Chota Nagpur, who appear to have reached a very similar stage of development. this belief has given birth to a number of primitive miscellaneous divinities whose functions are very vaguely defined, and who do not owe allegiance to any centralised authority. This multiplicity of deities would of itself seem to favour the growth of Shamanism, a phenomenon which Sir John Lubbock regards as a widely distributed phase of thought forming a necessary stage in the progress of religious development. Others have gone so far as to use Shamanism as a sort of general name for all those animistic religions which make prominent use of the agency of the Shaman. Without disputing the convenience, or indeed the necessity, of introducing a class-name of some kind, I would urge that Shamanism is a term singularly ill-suited to serve as the designation of a large group of religions. For in the first place the practice which it denotes is common to religions of all varieties of culture, and is by no means confined to the religions specially called Shamanistic; and secondly, the word, while calling attention to the superficial, fails to connote the essential characteristics of the class of religions in question. It may, indeed, possibly be the case, as has been hinted above, that the complicated departmentalism of certain animistic religions, where the supreme power is cut up into fractions and distributed among an army of gods, ghosts and demons, has led to the development of Shamanism by leaving it uncertain to whom a man should apply for the alleviation of any particular evil. The Shaman, like the touts who

[1] Tiele, *Outlines of the History of the Ancient Religions*, p. 9.

hang about our public offices, professes to help people out of this difficulty, and to show them not only to what god their petitions should be addressed, but in what form they should be couched, and by what ceremonies introduced. But even on this showing the practice is the consequence, not the cause, of certain primitive ideas; and it is these ideas, not any of their more or less variable consequences, which a definition should aim at expressing. Taken by itself, then, the word Shamanism seems to fall short of completeness as a description of the Limbu religion. For all religious of that type the term animism should be retained as denoting the *entourage* of vague spiritual influences which is of their essence. In dealing with these surroundings different agencies are resorted to: sometimes the fetish predominates; sometimes the medicine man. According as one or the other of these predominates, the particular form of animism may conveniently be styled fetishistic or Shamanistic. Following this principle, the Limbu religion may be defined as a rather elementary form of Shamanistic animism, in which the Bijuá and Phedangma play the part of Shaman, the former operating on the demons, and the latter having for his department the gods. Finally, we may perhaps hazard the conjecture that the original religion of the Limbus is closely akin to the Pon or ancient religion of Tibet. In both we find the forces of nature and the spirits of departed men exalted into objects of worship. In both systems temples and images are unknown, while propitiatory offerings occupy a prominent place. To complete the parallel, neither recognize a definite priestly order, while both encourage resort to Shamans or medicine men to ward off the malign influences which surround the human race.

Disposal of the dead.

Both cremation and burial are in vogue among the Limbus, the latter being the more common, and probably the older, practice. The corpse is placed lying on its back with the head to the east. The grave is lined with stones, and a cairn, consisting of four tiers for a man and three for a woman, erected on the top. The Phedangma attends at the funeral and delivers a brief address to the departed spirit on the general lot of mankind and the doom of birth and death, concluding with the command to go whither his fathers have gone and not to come back to trouble the living with dreams. Neither food nor clothes are placed in the grave, but sometimes a brass plate with a rupee in it is laid under the head of the corpse. For nine days after the funeral the sons of the deceased live on plain rice without any salt; and for a month or two the relatives wear flowers in their hair and avoid merry-makings. The special and characteristic sign of mourning is a piece of white rag tied round the head. There is no periodical ceremony for the propitiation of ancestors.

Inheritance.

At a man's death his sons, natural or adopted, divide his property; but an adopted son or a natural son by a wife informally married (*kachchi sádi*) takes only one-half of a legitimate son's share. The division of the property is usually made by the tribal council (*thum-thum*), who set apart an extra share for the eldest son. The youngest son is allowed to choose his share first, and the other shares are then allotted by the *thum-thum*. Failing sons, the sons-in-law actually living in or willing to live in the family homestead are entitled to divide the property. Brothers are the next heirs, and married sisters, if they attend the funeral, usually get a small share in the inheritance, although it is said that they have no positive right to claim this concession. An exception to these rules of devolution occurs in the case of *daijo* or property given to a sister or daughter or acquired from a maternal uncle or father-in-law. This is equally distributed among the sons of the woman to whom or on whose behalf it was given, and in the event of her dying without children it reverts to her own family. This simple customary law is administered by the headmen of the tribe and hardly any instances are known of Limbus having resorted to our courts for the settlement of disputes regarding property.

Social status.

The Limbus stand wholly outside of the Hindu caste system, and their social position can only be defined with reference to the other Himalayan races. They belong to the upper division of the Kiránti group, which inhabits the middle hills of the Himalayas, and rarely descends below an elevation of 2,000 feet. Within this division the Limbu take rank below the Khambu and above the Yákha, but this distinction is probably unknown beyond the limits of the Kiránti group, and in the eyes of society at large the three tribes occupy practically an equal position. They consider themselves, and are regarded by others, as superior to the Danuár, Hayu, and Thámi, who make up the lower division of the Kiránti. Their relations to the people of Nepal are less easy to define. They are certainly deemed inferior to the Khas, and probably also to the Mangars and Gurungs, both of whom are classed as military tribes. Newars hold a place second only to the Khas; Gurungs are inferior to the Newars. Mangar and Sunwar have their place next to the Gurungs; Limbus, Khambus, and Yakhas are inferior to the Mangar and Sunwar.

In the matter of food, they have very few prejudices. They eat beef, pork, and the flesh of all clean-feeding animals, and drink wine. In fact, the only restrictions on their diet appear to be those imposed on certain *thars* by the obligation not to eat the totem or beast-eponym of the group. They will eat with all the castes of the hills except the Kami, Damai, Sarki, and Gain.

The Census Report of 1881 returned 2,429 Limbus in the district of Darjiling.

Linda, eel, a totemistic sept of Oraons in Chota Nagpur.

Lin-dseh-bo, a *rui* or sept of the Bedtshan-gye sub-tribe of Dejong Lhoris or Bhotias of the south.

Lingdam, a sept of the Char-khola sub-tribe of Limbus, said to be admitted from the Lepchas.

Lingden, a sept of the Yangorup sub-tribe of Limbus, said to be admitted from the Lepchas.

Lingdenbeh, a sept of Limbus in Darjiling.

Lingkhim, a sept of the Tambrkola sub-tribe of Limbus in Darjiling.

Linglámphen, a sept of Limbus in Darjiling.

Ling-tamba, a *rui* or sept of Dejong Lhoris, whose ancestor had emigrated from Bhotan.

Liokichá, a *thar* or sept of Sunuwárs in Darjiling.

Lipo, a tree, a totemistic sept of Mundas in Chota Nagpur.

Litiya, a bird, a totemistic sept of Mundas in Chota Nagpur.

Lo, a section of Murmis in Darjiling.

Loáyat, a synonym for Kuri or Mayará in Tipperah.

Lodah, a sub-tribe of Bhumijs in Chota Nagpur.

Lodarwa, a *mul* or section of the Kanaujia sub-caste of Sonárs in Behar.

Lodh, a title of Dakshin-Rárhi and Bangaja Káyasths in Bengal.

Lodhiyá, a sub-caste of Binds in Behar.

Logáin, a *mul* or section of the Kanaujia sub-caste of Sonárs in Behar.

Logna Kotra, small deer, a totemistic sept of Mundas in Chota Nagpur.

Logo, a sept of Mundas in Chota Nagpur believed to be totemistic.

Lohá, iron, a totemistic sept of Tántis, Oraons, and Gonds in Chota Nagpur.

Lohágun, a section of Kámis; a *thar* or sept of Mangars in Darjiling.

Lohait-Kuri, a small caste found along the banks of the Meghna, who represent themselves as the descendants of a Kaibartta fisherboy, bought during a season of famine by a Kuri, or parcher of grains, who took this means of securing a husband for his daughter. The caste has separated into two subdivisions, those following the father's profession of fisherman having repudiated connection with the maternal branch, who parch grain.

The Loháit-Kuri at present associates neither with the Kaibarttas nor with the Kuri or Mayará. The majority are fishermen, who will not cast a net or fish from the shore, but angle with a rod from boats drifting with the stream. The name Lohait-Kuri is said to come from their using large rectangular iron hooks, with a shank nearly two inches long. Iron sinkers are preferred to leaden ones, and the only bait used is a small fish.

A Patit Brahman ministers to them, and the *sráddha* is kept at the expiry of a lunar month. Like other fishermen, they observe the Jál-pálani for seven days. A heavy fee is paid for a wife, as the caste is a small one, and one hundred rupees is not an unusual bride-price, while a widower may have to pay as much as two hundred. The Loháit-Kuris carry on a considerable trade with their own boats, but will not accept service with any other caste.

Lohar, a sub-caste of Barhis in Behar who work only in iron. They are, however, distinct from, and do not intermarry with, the Lohár caste. The latter are probably of Dravidian descent, while the former appear to be an occupational group

Lohár, a synonym for Kámár in Behar; a *mul* or section of the Naomuliá or Majraut sub-caste of Goálás in Behar; a section of Kámis in Darjiling.

Lohár, the blacksmith caste of Behar, Chota Nagpur, and Western Bengal. The Lohárs are a large and heterogeneous aggregate, comprising members of several different tribes and castes, who in different parts of the country took up the profession of working in iron. Of the various sub-castes shown in Appendix I, the **Kanaujiá** claim to be the highest in rank, and they alone have a well-marked set of exogamous sections. They regard Viswámitra as their legendary ancestor, and worship him as the tutelary deity of their craft. The **Kokás** Lohárs seem to be a branch of the Barhis, who have taken to working in iron and separated from the parent group for that reason. The **Maghaiya** seems to be the indigenous Lohárs of Behar, or opposed to the Kanaujiá and **Mathuriyá**, who profess to have come in from the North-West Provinces. **Kamár-Kalla** Lohárs may perhaps be a degraded offshoot from the Sonar caste. The **Mahur** or **Mahulia** say they came from the North-Western Provinces, and the fact that all Hindus can take water from their hands renders it likely that they may have broken off from some comparatively respectable caste. Their traditions, however, are not definite enough to enable this conjecture to be verified. The **Kamiá** Lohárs found in Champáran have immigrated from Nepal, and are regarded as ceremonially unclean. Many of them have become Mahomedans. In the Santál Parganás, a sort of ethnic border land between Bengal and Behar, we find three sub-castes of Lohárs,—**Birbhumiá**, from the neighbouring district of Birbhum; **Govindpuriá**, from the subdivision of Govindpur, in Northern Manbhum; and **Shergarhiá**, from the *parganá* of that name in Bardwan. The names give no clue to the tribal affinities of these three groups, but the fact that they have the totemistic section **Sal-máchh** shows them to be of non-Aryan descent, probably Bauris or Bágdis, who took to iron-working and called themselves Lohárs. Of the four sub-castes into which the Lohárs of Bankura are divided, two bear the names **Gobrá** and **Jhetiá**, which occur among the sub-castes of the Bauris. Two others—**Angariá** and **Pánsili**—I am unable to trace. The Manbhum Lohárs acknowledge three sub-castes,—**Lohár-Mánjhi**, **Danda-Mánjhi**, and **Bágdi-Lohár**, names which suggest a connexion with the Bágdi caste. Lastly, in Lohardagá we have the **Sad-Lohárs**, claiming to be immigrant Hindus; the **Manjhal-Turiyás**, who may well be a branch of the Turi caste; and the **Mundá-Lohárs**, who are certainly Mundás. The great number of the sub-castes, coupled with the fact that in some cases we can determine with approximate certainty the tribes of which they once formed part, seem to point to the conclusion, not merely that the aggregate termed the Lohar caste is made up of drafts locally levied from whatever groups were available for employment in a comparatively menial occupation, but that all castes whose functions

Tradition of origin.

Internal structure.

are concerned with the primary needs of social life are the result of a similar process.

Marriage.

Further indications of the different elements from which the caste has been formed may be traced in its social customs. The Lohárs of Chota Nagpur and Western Bengal practise adult as well as infant-marriage, a price is paid for the bride, and the marriage ceremony is substantially identical with that in use among the Bágdis. Polygamy they allow without imposing any limit on the number of wives a man may have, and they recognize the extreme license of divorce characteristic of the aboriginal races. In Behar, on the other hand, infant-marriage is the rule and adult-marriage the rare exception. The ceremony is modelled on the orthodox type. A bridegroom-price is paid, and polygamy is lawful only on failure of issue by the first wife. As to divorce, some diversity of practice seems to prevail. Kanaujiás profess to prohibit it altogether, while other sub-castes admit it only with the permission of the pancháyat, and regard the remarriage of divorced wives with disfavour. Widow-marriage is recognized both in Behar and elsewhere; but this is by no means a distinctively Dravidian usage, but rather a survival of early Aryan custom, which has fallen into disuse among the higher castes under the influence of Brahmanical prejudice.

Religion.

Equally characteristic differences may be observed in the religious usages of the main branches of the caste. Kanaujiá Lohárs and all the Behar sub-castes, except the Nepalese Kamiás, pose as orthodox Hindus, employ Maithil Brahmans, and worship the standard gods. In Chota Nagpur and Western Bengal, though some profession of Hinduism is made, this is little more than a superficial veneer laid on at a very recent date, and the real worship of the caste is addressed to Manasá, Rám Thákur, Baranda Thákur, Phulai Gosáin, Dalli Gorai, Bhádu, and Mohan Giri. In the latter we may perhaps recognize the mountain god (Marang Buru) of the Mundas and Santáls. To him goats are sacrificed on Mondays or Tuesdays in the months of Mágh, Ashár, and Agraháyan, the flesh being afterwards eaten by the worshippers. The Lohárs of Bankura and the Santál Parganás have taken to employing low Brahmans, but in Lohardagá the aboriginal priest (*páhan*) and the local sorcerer (*mati*, *ojhá*, or *sokhá*) minister to their spiritual wants. The Sad-Lohárs alone show an advance in the direction of orthodoxy, in that they employ the village barber to act as priest in the marriage ceremony.

Occupation.

In Behar the caste work as blacksmiths and carpenters, while many have taken to cultivation. They buy their material in the form of pigs or bars of iron. Iron-smelting is confined to the Lohárs of Chota Nagpur, and is supposed to be a much less respectable form of industry than working up iron which other people have smelted. In the Santál Parganás Lohárs often cultivate themselves, while the women of the household labour at the forge. None of the Western Bengal Lohárs combine carpentry with working in iron.

Social status.

In Behar Lohárs rank with Koiris and Kurmis, and Brahmans take water from their hands. The status of the caste in Western Bengal is far lower, and they are associated in matters of food and drink with Bauris, Bagdis, and Máls.

The following statement shows the number and distribution of Lohárs in 1872 and 1881 :—

District.	1872.	1881.
Bardwan	The figures are included in the table on Kámárs.	202
Bankura		5,507
Birbhum		1,007
Midnapur		312
Hughli		87
24-Parganas		57
Nadiya		1
Jessore		238
Dinajpur		101
Rajshahye		10
Bogra		19
Pabna		10
Darjiling*		577
Kuch Behar		3
Faridpur		2
Maimansinh		6
Chittagong		19
Patna	7,304	8,054

District.	1872.	1881.
Gya	17,216	16,659
Shahabad	27,959	30,268
Tirhut { Mozufferpur ...	57,341	38,245
Tirhut { Darbhanga ...		11,831
Saran	38,449	42,025
Champaran	26,953	24,015
Monghyr	7,179	4,232
Bhagalpur	23,405	9,789
Purniah	16,083	7,953
Maldah	......	307
Santál Parganás	14,870	2,913
Cuttack	The figures are included in the table on Kámárs.	300
Balasore		33
Tributary States		1,387
Hazaribagh		8,422
Lohardagá		34,108
Singhbhum		1,826
Manbhum		1,531
Tributary States		10,302

Lohará, a sept of Mundas in Chota Nagpur.

Lohar-Agariá, a sub-tribe of Agariás in Chota Nagpur.

Loharatengi, a section of Rajwars in Western Bengal.

Loharbans, iron, a totemistic sept of Chiks; a section of Ghásis in Chota Nagpur.

Lohár-Kámár, a sub-caste of Kámárs in Midnapur.

Lohárkoriyá, a section of Bháts.

Lohár Mánjhi, a sub-caste of Lohárs in Manbhum.

Lohatiá, a section of Sonárs in Behar.

Lohchab, a section of Goálás in the North-Western Provinces and Behar.

Lohrá, a synonym for Asura and Lohár.

Lohra Asur, a sub-tribe of Asuras in Chota Nagpur.

Lohrakhukhri, a kind of wild mushroom, a totemistic sept of Mundas in Chota Nagpur.

Lohriá, an iron-smelter.

Lohsá, a sub-caste of Kámárs in Manbhum.

Lohtamiá, a sept of Rájputs in Behar.

Lohutiá, a *mul* or section of the Ghosin sub-caste of Goálás in Behar.

Loityal, a *thar* or section of Nepáli Brahmans.

Lokándri, a section of Kámis in Darjiling.

Lokárk, a *pur* or section of Sákadwipi Brahmans in Behar.

Lokmahung, a sept of the Phedáb sub-tribe of Limbus in Darjiling.

Loksohm, a sept of the Yongorup sub-tribe of Limbus, said to be admitted from the Lepchas.

Lolutra, a *mul* or section of the Chhamuliá Madhesiá sub-caste of Halwáis in Behar.

Lomasá, a Brahmanical section of Khatris in Bengal.

Longa, a bird with long tail, a totemistic sept of Mundas in Chota Nagpur.

Lopáte, a *thar* or sept of Gurungs in Darjiling.

Lopchan, a section of Murmis in Darjiling.

Lori, a *dugu* or section of the Kochh-Mándái in Dacca.

Loskra, a sept of Chakmás in the Hill Tracts of Chittagong.

Lotháng, a *thar* or sept of Gurungs in Darjiling.

Lowa, a sept of Páns in Chota Nagpur.

Loyá, a section of Mahesris in Behar.

Loyna, a sept of Chiks in Chota Nagpur.

Lu, a title of Tántis in Bengal.

Ludhi, a sub-caste of Baniyás who deal in *lodh* or catechu.

Ludhna, a sub-caste of Bhuiyas in Singbhum.

Lugniár, hare, a totemistic sept of Mundas in Chota Nagpur.

Lugum, a tree, a totemistic sept of Mundas in Chota Nagpur.

Lugumah, a sept of Limbus in Darjiling.

Lugunki, a sept of Mundas in Chota Nagpur.

Luhá, a sept of the Pánthar sub-tribe of Limbus in Darjiling.

Lukhasan, a section of Goálás in Behar.

Luksom, a sept of Lepchas in Darjiling.

Lukum, a sept of Rájputs in Behar.

Lulang, a sept of the Tungjainya sub-tribe of Chakmás in the Hill Tracts of Chittagong.

Lumphongma, those who shared the land, a sept of the Phedáb sub-tribe of Limbus in Darjiling.

Lumria, fox, a totemistic sept of Lohárs in Chota Nagpur.

Lungyeli, a *thar* or sept of Mangars in Darjiling.

Luniá, a synonym for Nuniá.

Luniwál, a section of Goálás in the North-Western Provinces and Behar.

Lupu, paddy husks, a totemistic sept of Mundas in Chota Nagpur.

Lutí, small black fly, a totemistic sept of Mundas in Chota Nagpur.

M

Machhilhá, a section of Sonárs in Behar.

Machhuá, a sub-caste of Bagdis and Kewats; a synonym for Gonrhi, Kewat, and Tiyar; a title of Máls and of low class Mahomedans who sell fish retail. The latter do not catch fish themselves, but obtain their supplies on a system of advances from the regular fishing castes. Hindus who follow the same avocation are called Nikári, *q.v.*

Machi, a section of Sonárs in Behar.

Machiwár, fish, a totemistic sept of Páns in Chota Nagpur.

Machli, fish, a totemistic sept of Mundas; a section of Sáráks in Chota Nagpur.

Madak, a synonym for Madhunápit and Mayará.

Mádalwár, a section of Turis in Chota Nagpur.

Madán, a *thar* or sept of Gurungs in Darjiling.

Madári, a sub-caste of Máls, who are often employed as snake-charmers.

Maden, the son of his mother, a sept of the Chhothar and Phedáb sub-tribes of Limbus in Darjiling. The name may possibly have reference to a system of female kinship which has now fallen into disuse.

Maderwár, a sept of Kharwars in Chota Nagpur.

Mádhab, a family of the Kulin group of Jugis in Bengal.

Mádhabáchárjya, a sect of Vaishnavs in Bengal.

Madha Gaurá, a sub-caste of Gaura Brahmans in Behar.

Mádhái, a *mel* or hypergamous sub-group of Rárhi Brahmans in Bengal.

Madhepuriet, a *mul* or section of the Naomuliá or Majraut sub-caste of Goálás in Behar.

Madhesia, a sub-caste of Goálás, Halwáis, and Kándus in Behar.

Madhubaniá, a *pur* or section of Sákadwipi Brahmans in Behar.

Madhu Goálá, a sub-caste of Goálás in Bengal.

Madhugrámi, a *gáin* of the Bátsya *gotra* of Uttar-Bárendra Brahmans in Bengal.

Madhukari, a sub-caste of Tántis in Bengal.

Madhukuliya, Madhukulya, an exogamous section of Baidyas; of Baruis and Nápits in Bengal, a section of Sánkháris, Tántis, Telis, and Subarnabaniks in Bengal; of Kaibarttas in Central Bengal; of Sutradhars and Bauris in Western Bengal; of Khyáns in Northern Bengal.

Madhu-Madak, a sub-caste of Madhunápits in Bengal.

Madhunapit, *Madak*, a confectioner caste of Bengal Proper who regard themselves as distinct from the Mayará. In explanation of their origin the story is told that the religious reformer Chaitanya being one day in

Origin.

a hurry ordered two of his servants to shave him. They carried out the command, but pointed out to their master that expulsion from caste privileges was the penalty which their obedience had brought upon them. Chaitanya accordingly bade them become confectioners and make sweetmeats for him. Since that time their descendants have followed the same trade, and their purity, according to Hindu ideas, is such that even goddesses partake of the dainties they prepare. Another more romantic version is that a barber named Madhu, who was called in to shave the head of Chaitanya on the occasion of his becoming a Sannyási, was so impressed with the importance of the function he had performed that he asked to be released from his hereditary profession; for, he said, having touched the head of Chaitanya, how could he cut the toe-nails of ordinary men? As Chaitanya flourished about the beginning of the sixteenth century, this legend would make the Madhunápit caste a comparatively recent offshoot from the Nápit. Such an origin, however, is not in great favour among the members of the caste, who prefer to assume a special act of creation.

Marriage.

The sub-castes and sections of the Madhunápit are shown in Appendix I. Neither series throws any light upon the origin of the caste. A man may not marry a woman belonging to his own section, nor one who stands towards him in the religious relation of *sapinda* or *samánodaka*. Madhunápits marry their daughters as infants, forbid widows to remarry, and do not recognize divorce. Although not mentioned by name in the various couplets defining the Nava-Sákha, the Madhunápit are generally admitted to belong to that group, and Brahmans will take water from their hands. Considering that the Napit and Madak are unquestionably members of the Nava-Śákha group, and the Madhunápit certainly derive their origin from one or other of these castes, their title to be Nava-Sákha seems to be beyond dispute. Most of them are Vaishnavas by creed.

Occupation.

The Madhunápit, says Dr. Wise, is the most respected confectioner in Eastern Bengal, for the caste Mayará or Madak is rarely met with, and the Halwai is usually a Ghulám Káyasth, a Khontta Brahman, or a Kándu. They assume great airs, neither intermarrying with other castes—not even with barbers—nor shaving themselves. In former days they would not fry sweetmeats in ghi or butter, but now they are less fastidious. The common sweetmeats prepared by the Madhunápit are *jalebi*, *amriti*, *khájá*, *chhená perá*, *laddu*, *gajá*, and *sar-bhájá*. The delicacies offered to idols are *perá*, *barfi*, *iláchi dáná*, *batásá*, and *sandes*.

The Madhunápit do not cultivate the soil, but are found employed as writers, goldsmiths, grocers, cloth merchants, and policemen.

Madhurá, a sub-caste of Bábhans in Behar.

Madhuras, a totemistic sept of Mundas in Chota Nagpur who cannot eat honey.

Madhurasiárk, a *púr* or section of Sákadwipi Brahmans in Behar.

Madhurishi, a section of Mayarás in Bengal.

Madhust, a section of Maghaiyá Kumhárs in Behar.

Madhwál, a sept of Rájputs in Behar.

Madhyabhág, a *samáj* or local group of the Sándilya *gotra* of the Páschátya Baidik Brahmans in Bengal.

Madhya-bhág or **Madhyamkul**, a sub-caste of Háris in Bengal.

Madhyagrámi, a *gáin* of the Kásyapa *gotra* of Bárendra Brahmans in Bengal.

Madhyakul, a group of the Aswini Tántis in Bengal.

Madhyalá, a hypergamous group of Jugis in Bengal.

Madhyalya, a hypergamous group of the Bangaja Káyasths.

Madhyam Kurmi, a sub-caste of Kurmis in Manbhum.

Madhya-sreni, a sub-caste of Brahmans and Káyasths in Western Bengal.

Madhyasreni Káyastha, a sub-caste of Káyasthas in Midnapur.

Mádowán, a *mul* or section of the Ghosin sub-caste of Goálás in Behar.

Madrishi, honey-bee, a totemistic section of Sunris in the Santál Parganás and Manbhum.

Madrisi or **Madhukulya**, a section of Goálás in Bengal.

Mádura, *Mádar*, a contraction of Mahádanda, a sub-caste of Kewats in Behar who sell *sál* leaves and wood.

Mag, a synonym for Magh.

Mágadha, a territorial division of Brahmans in Behar.

Magadha Goárá, a sub-caste of Goálás in Orissa.

Magahgoriah, a variant for Maghaya Goálá or Maghaya Gonrh.

Magahiyá, a sub-caste of Doms in North Behar, who are cultivators and thieves, in Gya basket-makers, and in Bengal musicians and basket-makers; a sub-caste of Dhánuks, Dosádhs, Hajjáms in Behar, and of Kámárs in Manbhum; of Kándus, Támbulis, Kahárs, and Chamárs in Behar; and of Máls in the Santál Parganás.

Magai or *Mágadhi*, a sub-caste of Goálás in Bengal.

Magar, a synonym for Mangar.

Maggah, a section of the Tirhutiya sub-caste of Doms in Behar.

Magh, *Mag*, the popular designation of a group of Indo-Chinese tribes, who describe themselves by the various titles of **Maramagri**, **Bhuiyá Magh**, **Baruá Magh**, **Rájbansi Magh**, **Marmá** or **Myam-ma**, **Roáng Magh**, **Thongtha** or **Jumiá Magh**. Concerning the use and derivation of the name Magh there has been much discussion, and the question cannot be considered as having been finally settled.

Origin.

Wilson,[1] followed by Ritter,[2] Fr. Muller,[3] and Colonel Yule,[4] defines it as "a name commonly applied to the natives of Arakan, particularly those bordering on Bengal or residing near the sea,—the people of Chittagong." Sir Arthur Phayre, quoted by Colonel Yule, derives the name from "*Maga*, the name of the ruling race for many centuries in *Magadha* (modern Behar). The kings of Arakan were no doubt originally of this race; for though this is not distinctly expressed in the histories of Arakan, there are several legends of kings from Benares reigning in that country, and one, regarding a Brahman, who marries a native princess and whose descendants reign for a long period." Dalton[5] appears to take much the same view regarding the Arakanese as an outlying branch of the Burmese, and adding that the name Magh is exclusively a foreign epithet, unknown to the Arakanese themselves. Mantegazza[6] follows Dalton on the whole, but seems to look upon the term Magh as rather a tribal name than the general designation of the people who inhabit a particular tract of country.

Internal structure.

In its actual use at the present day the term Magh includes three endogamous groups:[7] the Thongtha, Thongcha, or Jumiá Magh;[8] the Marma, Myamma, Roáng or Rakhaing Magh;[9] and the Máramagri, otherwise known as Rájbansi, Baruá, or Bhuiyá Magh. The first and second have been described by Lewin under the name Khyoungtha or 'children of the river,' a designation based upon locality and not corresponding to any real tribal distinction. Both the Jumiá and the Roang Maghs probably belong to the same original stock, but the former have so long been settled in the Chittagong country that they regard themselves as the aborigines of the Hill Tracts, while the latter belong to a more recent stream of immigrants from Arakan.[9] The physical characteristics of both tribes are unmistakeably Mongolian. Their stature is low, the face broad and flat, cheekbones high and wide, nose flat and bridgeless,

---

[1] *Glossary*, *s.v.* Magh.
[2] *Erd-Kunde*, v, 324.
[3] *Allgemeine Ethnographie*, 405.
[4] *Anglo-Indian Glossary*, *s.v.* Mugg.
[5] *Ethnology of Bengal*, 112.
[6] *Studii sull'Etnologia dell'India*, p. 331.
[7] *Hill Tracts of Chittagong*, p. 36.
[8] Some remarks on the defects of Captain Lewin's classification of the hill tribes into Khyoungtha and Toungtha will be found in the article on Chakma above. To those objections it should be added that the classes Khyoungtha and Toungtha do not appear to be mutually exclusive. Captain Lewin himself states (p. 37) that "Khyoungtha means those who inhabit the banks of mountain streams and support themselves by hill cultivation;" and if this definition be accepted, it is difficult to see how the line between the two classes should be drawn.
[9] Roáng seems to be a corruption of Rakhaing, the indigenous name for the Arakan country or its inhabitants. Arakan, again, is the European form of Rakhaing or Rakhang. Colonel Yule (*Anglo-Indian Glossary*, art. Arakan) thinks that we may have got Arakan through the Malay. but the early connexion of the Arabs with Chittagong seems to justify the conjecture that the word may be simply Al-Rakhang.

and eyes small with eyelids obliquely set;[1] while according to Lewin the men have neither beard nor moustache. The Maramagri or Rájbansi Magh are of an entirely different type. They are supposed by Colonel Phayre to be "the offspring of Bengali women by Burmans when the latter possessed Chittagong;" and this theory of their origin is borne out by the fact that their exogamous septs are similar to those of the Thongtha and Marmá. All external indications of their Mongolian descent have, however, been obliterated by generations of intermarriage with the non-Aryan Bengalis of Chittagong and Noakhali; and the Rájbansi Maghs, who are largely employed as cooks in Calcutta, have the glossy black complexion, wavy hair, and abundant beard and moustache which characterise the lower castes of Eastern Bengal. It may be added that their somewhat insolent bearing and excitable manner of speech complete the contrast with the stolid, but amiable Mongolians, from whom they are remotely descended.

The septs of the three sub-tribes are shown in Appendix I. Most of them, as Lewin has pointed out, appear to be the names of the rivers on which the original settlements of the sept were situated. They observe the simple rule that a man may not marry a woman of his own sept, supplemented by a table of prohibited degrees, which does not differ materially from that arrived at by the standard formula already often referred to. In applying these prohibitions, however, there seems to be some laxity where descent is traced through females, for I am informed that a man may marry the daughters of his father's sister and of his mother's brother—a connexion which would not ordinarily be allowed.

Marriage.

The Maramagri marry their daughters either as infants or as adults, and there is some tendency among them to regard the former usage as more respectable from the social point of view. Marmás and Thongchas adhere to the more primitive custom of adult-marriage, and more or less expressly tolerate sexual intercourse as one of the necessary incidents of pre-matrimonial courtship. Their marriage ceremony, says Lewin,[2] "is distinctive and uncommon. On a young man attaining a marriageable age, that is, about 17 to 18, his parents look about for some young girl who would be a good wife to him, unless, as is more often the case, he has fixed upon a partner for himself. Having determined upon a suitable match, a male relative of the family is sent off to the girl's parents to arrange matters. On arriving at their village he proceeds to the house, and before going up the house ladder he gives the usual salutation, with both hands joined and raised to the forehead. '*Ogatsa*,' he says, 'a boat has come to your landing place; will you bind it or loose it?' A favourable response is given, and he then goes up into the house. On seating himself he asks, 'Are the supports of the house firm?' If the

---

[1] The apparent obliquity of the Mongolian eye is due to a peculiar conformation of the eyelids, and does not extend to the orbit itself. See Topinard, *Eléments d'Anthropologie Générale*, p. 998.

[2] *Hill Tracts of Chittagong*, p. 49.

answer is, 'They are firm,' it is favourable, and matters may then be more fully entered into. The affair is taken into consideration, and he returns to his own village to report good progress to the bridegroom's parents, and to request them to fix a day for taking the omens. On the appointed day the parents meet, the young people being supposed to know nothing of all this. A fowl is killed by the fathers, its tongue taken out, and, according to certain marks thereon, the matter is pronounced good or bad. The bridegroom's parents sleep for the night at the house of the intended bride, and all parties look anxiously for dreams by which to foretell the happiness or the reverse of the union. On going away, should everything be propitious, their intended daughter kneels at their feet for a blessing, and they present her with a new petticoat and a silver ring. Learned persons are then called in, who, by consulting the stars and casting the nativity of the parties, determine a favourable day and hour when the ceremony shall be undertaken. Meantime the parents on both sides prepare pigs and spirits, rice and spices, unlimited, for the marriage feast. They also send round to all their kith and kin a fowl and a letter giving notice of the intended marriage; in some places a pice or copper coin is substituted for the fowl. On the auspicious day, and at the hour appointed, the bridegroom and all his relatives set out for the bride's house, dressed in the gayest colours, both men and women, with drums beating before them. On arriving at the entrance of the village the female relatives of the bride bar the approach with a bamboo. Across this barrier the bridegroom has to drink a loving cup of fraternity, generally spirits. Should the females on the bride's side muster strong, the road will probably be barred five or six times before the entry into the village is fairly made. The bridegroom, however, does not drink all that is given him, but after taking the liquor in his mouth he is allowed to eject it again upon the ground.

"In the village, on some open turfy spot, a number of bamboo booths have been erected, adorned with flowers and green boughs, and filled with materials for feasting. Here also sit an opposition party of drummers, and mighty is the row as the bridegroom's party defiles on to this spot. A separate and specially beautified booth has been erected for the young lover and his parents, and here they sit in state and receive visits from all the village. The bride in like manner, surrounded by her near relatives, sits in her father's house. The boys of the village, irrepressible as is the wont of that species, make raids upon both parties, for the purpose of chaffing and getting alternate feasts of comestibles. They also organize an amateur band of music, and serenade the bride towards evening with fiddles and flutes. Of course, all the girls of the village are congregated at the bride's father's house, and, as license and riot are the order of the day, the fun here grows fast and furious. Towards nightfall the bridegroom ascends to his bride's house amid a tempest of cheers and a hailstorm of drums. After this outburst a temporary lull ensues, to permit of the ceremony being performed. The bride is brought forth from an inner chamber in the arms of the women. On the floor of the house are placed water in jars, rice, and mango leaves. Round these a new-spun cotton-thread is wound and carried again round the two contracting parties as they stand opposite to each other. The 'poongyee,' or priest, now comes forward; he recites some prayers in a language that is not understood even by himself (probably Pali), and then taking cooked rice, a handful in each hand, he crosses and recrosses his arms, giving seven alternate mouthfuls to the bride and bridegroom; after this he takes their hands and crooks the little finger of the bridegroom's right hand into the little finger of the bride's left. The ceremony is then concluded by more unintelligible mutterings. The bridegroom now takes the bride by the hand, and together they make the circuit of the room, saluting lowly the elder relatives of both families. They then sit down—the bride to the left of her husband, and their clothes are tied together. The wedding guests then come forward and place at their feet, each according to his or her means, some presents of clothes or household furniture. After this a saturnalia ensues, of dancing, drinking, fighting, and love-making. The bride and bridegroom are expected to sit up all night. I should add that the happy man does not consummate his marriage until he and his wife (sleeping apart) have for seven days eaten together seven times a day."

The bride-price among Thongchas and Marmas is said to be about Rs. 30. With the Maramagris, who as a class are wealthier, the average amount paid for a wife is Rs. 60, which may rise to Rs. 80 if the bridegroom is of inferior status, as, for example, in the event of a Bhuiyá Magh marrying the daughter of a Rájbansi Magh. The ceremony in use among the Máramagris is of the same general character as that described above, the essential portion being the crooking together of the little fingers of the bridegroom's left hand and the bride's right, while the priest pours water over the hands thus joined. This is followed by *sindurdán* or smearing vermilion on the bride's forehead—a form which appears to have been borrowed from the Hindus. The Marmá ritual is still more like that of the Thongchas, and does not include *sindurdán*. In the course of the wedding the bride and bridegroom eat some curry and rice from the same dish, and what they leave is kept in a covered earthen vessel for seven days, during which time the married couple may not leave the village or cross running water. On the eighth the vessel is opened, and if maggots are found in the food it is deemed an excellent omen, showing that the marriage will be a fruitful one.

Polygamy is recognized: a man may have as many wives as he can afford to maintain. The first wife, however, is regarded as the highest in rank, and takes precedence of all subsequent wives, who are expected to treat her with special consideration.

In all the sub-tribes widows are allowed to marry again, and are fettered by no restrictions in their choice of a second husband. No special ritual is ordained for this purpose, and as a rule the parties simply go and live together as man and wife. Divorce is permitted with the sanction of the tribal pancháyat, on the ground of adultery or inability to live happily together. A written agreement is usually drawn up, and sometimes, when the authority of the pancháyat is deemed insufficient, this "writing of divorcement" is laid before the Magistrate of the district. Among the Thongchas the parties give one another flowers, and after bathing go off in different directions, exchanging all kinds of abusive epithets. Divorced wives may marry again by the ritual in use for the remarriage of widows.

Religion.

All Maghs are Buddhists of the Southern school, and regard the northern Buddhists of Tibet as wholly unorthodox. The wilder sections of the Thongchas, however, retain some vestiges of an earlier animistic faith, which bids them sacrifice cattle, goats, and swine, and make offerings of rice, fruits, and flowers to the spirits of hill and river. Among the Maramagris, on the other hand, the tendency is to follow after modern Hinduism, particularly in its Tantric developments, and to add the gross worship of Siva and Durga to the simple observances prescribed by their own communion. It thus comes to pass that while the Buddhist *Phungyis* or *Ráolis* are the recognized priests of all the tribes, considerable respect is shown to Brahmans, who are frequently employed to determine auspicious days for particular actions, and to assist in the worship of the Hindu gods. Among the Thongchas old women often devote themselves to the service of religion, and although not charged with special ceremonial functions, are regarded as in some sense priestesses, and are called by the distinctive name *lerdama*.

Disposal of the dead.

The funeral ceremonies of the Maghs are thus described by Lewin:—"When a person has died, his relatives assemble. Some one of them sits down and commences to beat the funeral roll on the drum; the women weep and cry, and the men busy themselves, some in performing the last offices to the corpse, of washing, dressing, etc., while others go off to the woods and bring wood for the funeral pile, and bamboos with which to construct the bier. About 24 hours generally elapse from the time of death to that of cremation. In bearing the corpse from the house to the burning ground, if the deceased were a man of wealth or influence, the body may be borne on a wheeled car; all women also have this privilege; the plebs, however, are simply carried to the funeral pile on the shoulders of their relatives. The procession is after this fashion:—First come the priests, if there are any in the vicinity to attend; they march gravely at the head of the party, bearing on their shoulders their curved palm-leaf fans, clad in their ordinary saffron-coloured robes, and attended by their disciples. Next come relatives of the deceased, two and two, bearing food, clothes, etc., which have been offered as alms to the priests on behalf of the departed. Next is borne the bier, carried on bamboos by six men, and accompanied by as many drums as can be procured. Behind the coffin come the male relatives; and lastly, the procession is closed by the women of the village, clad in their best. The funeral pile is composed of four layers of wood for a woman, three for a man. The body is placed on the pile; the leading priest takes an end of the dead man's turban, and, holding it, repeats some passages of the law, four of the deceased's male relatives standing meanwhile at the four corners of the pile and sprinkling a few drops of water thereon. The nearest blood relative, male or female, of the dead man then fires the pile. When the fire is extinguished the ashes are scrupulously collected together and buried over the spot; a small conical mound of earth is heaped up, and a very long bamboo pole, with an equally lengthy flag, is erected over the grave. On returning from the place all parties bathe themselves. If it is the master of the house who has died, the ladder leading up to the house is thrown down, and they must effect an entrance by cutting a hole in the back wall and so creeping up. The relatives eat and drink, and each contributes according to his means to defray the expenses incurred. After seven days the priests reassemble at the house to read prayers for the dead."

In the case of priests and persons of high social position the corpse is dried or embalmed and kept for a year in a special coffin, while arrangements are being made for an elaborate funeral, which usually takes place on the 1st of Baisakh. A temporary pagoda is built of bamboo decorated with coloured paper and flags, and is set up in some open place faced by a row of bamboo cannon mounted on wheels, crammed to the muzzle with tightly-rammed powder and fitted with a long fuse. These cannon are presented by persons desirous of doing honour to the deceased, and it is deemed an act of great merit to send a cannon to the funeral of a Phungyi. On the arrival of the coffin a mimic conflict—a 'tug of war'—takes place over it, the women pulling it one way and the men the other. According to another account the contest is not between the men and the women, but between the unmarried and married persons of either sex. The coffin is then placed in the pagoda, and the bamboo cannon are discharged in order of the precedence of those who presented them. Last of all the pagoda and coffin are burned, and a long bamboo, carrying a triangular flag forty-five feet long, is set up on the place. A funeral offering (*kongmu*) of various kinds of food is placed on the ground on the eighth day, and this ceremony is repeated every year.

Social status.

The social status of the Maghs does not admit of very precise definition, as the entire community is outside of the regular caste system, and orthodox Hindus will take neither food nor water from their hands. In the matter of diet they are highly promiscuous, eating beef, pork, fowls, fish of all kinds, snakes, field-rats, lizards, and certain kinds of worms. Both sexes indulge freely in spirituous liquors. For all this they are not wholly free from prejudice as to the caste of the persons with whom they will take food; and no Maghs, except those who are fishermen themselves, will eat, drink, or smoke in the same hookah with members of the fishing castes, such as Kaibarttas and Málos, or with the Jugi caste of weavers. Tántis and Nápits, on the other hand, are considered ceremonially pure, and Maghs will take water from their hands.

Occupation.

The Thongcha sub-tribe live almost entirely by the peculiar method of cultivation known in Chittagong, Assam, and Northern Bengal by the name *jhúm;* in Burmah and Arakan as *tungyá;* and in Chota Nagpur and the Central Provinces called *dáhá* or *paráo.* Captain Lewin describes the system as follows:—

Jhum cultivation.

"In the month of April a convenient piece of forest land is fixed upon, generally on a hillside, the luxuriant under-growth of shrubs and creepers has to be cleared away, and the smaller trees felled: the trees of larger growth are usually denuded of their lower branches, and left standing. If possible, however, the jhumiá fixes upon a slope thickly covered with a bamboo jungle of the species called 'dolloo.' This compared with a dense tree jungle is easy to cut, and its ashes, after burning, are of greater fertilising power. Although the clearing of a patch of dense jungle is no doubt very severe labour, yet the surroundings of the labourer render his work pleasurable in comparison with the toilsome and dirty task of the cultivators of the plains. * * * * *

By his comparatively pleasurable toil the hill-man can gain two rupees for one which the wretched ryot of the plains can painfully earn, and it is not to be wondered at that the hill people have a passion for their mode of life, and regard with absolute contempt any proposal to settle down to the tame and monotonous cultivation of the dwellers in the low-lands.

"The jhum land once cleared, the fallen jungle is left to dry in the sun, and in the month of May it is fired: this completes the clearing. The firing of the jhums is sometimes a source of danger, as at that season of the year the whole of the surrounding jungle is as dry as tinder and easily catches fire. In this way sometimes whole villages are destroyed, and people have lost their lives. I have myself seen a whole mountain-side on fire for four days and four nights, having been ignited by jhum-firing. It was a magnificent sight, but such a fire must cause incalculable injury to the forest: young trees especially would be utterly destroyed. Generally, however, by choosing a calm day, and keeping down the fire at the edges of the jhum, by beating with boughs, the hill people manage to keep the firing within certain prescribed limits. A general conflagration, such as I have mentioned, is of quite exceptional occurrence. If the felled jungle has been thoroughly dried, and no rain has fallen since the jhum was cut, this firing will reduce all, save the larger forest trees, to ashes, and burn the soil to the depth of an inch or two. The charred trees and logs previously cut down remain lying about the ground: these have to be dragged off the jhum and piled up all round, and with the addition of some brushwood form a species of fence to keep out wild animals.

"Work is now at a standstill, till the gathering of the heavy clouds and the grumbling of thunder denote the approach of the rains. These signs at once bring a village into a state of activity; men and women, boys and girls, each bind on the left hip a small basket filled with the mixed seeds of cotton, rice, melons, pumpkins, yams, and a little Indian corn; each takes a 'daô'[1] in hand, and in a short time every hillside will echo to the 'hoiya,' or hillcall (a cry like the Swiss jodel), as party answers party from the paths winding up each hillside to their respective patches of cultivation. Arrived at the jhum, the family will form a line, and steadily work their way across the field. A dig with the blunt square end of the daô makes a narrow hole about three inches deep: into this is put a small handful of the mixed seeds, and the sowing is completed. If shortly afterwards the rain falls, they are fortunate and have judged the time well; or (unparalleled luck) if they get wet through with the rain as they are sowing, great will be the jollification on the return home, this being an omen that a bumper season may be expected.

"The village now is abandoned by every one, and the men set to work to build a house, each in his own jhum, for the crop must be carefully watched to preserve it from the wild pig and deer, which would otherwise play havoc among the young shoots of the rice. The jhums of the whole village are generally situated in propinquity: a solitary jhum is very rare. During the rains mutual help and assistance in weeding the crop is given; each one takes his turn to help in his neighbour's jhum; no hoeing is done; the crop has merely to be kept clear from weeds by hand labour, and an ample return is obtained. If the rain be excessive, however, the cotton crop is liable to be spoilt, as the young plants die from too much water.

"The first thing to ripen is Indian corn; this is about the end of July. Next come the melons, of which there are two or three sorts grown in the jhums: afterwards vegetables of all sorts become fit for gathering; and finally, in September, the rice and other grain ripens. At this time the monkeys and jungle fowl are the chief enemies of the crop. In the month of October the cotton crop is gathered last of all, and this concludes the harvest. The rice having been cut, is beaten from the ear in the jhum: it is afterwards rolled up in rough, straw-covered bales and carried to the granary in the village.

* * * * *

---

[1] "The 'daô' is the hill knife, used universally throughout the country. It is a blade about 18 inches long, narrow at the haft, and square and broad at the tip; pointless, and sharpened on one side only. The blade is set in a handle of wood; a bamboo root is considered the best. The fighting 'daô' is differently shaped. This is a long pointless sword, set in a wooden or ebony handle; it is very heavy, and a blow of almost incredible power can be given by one of these weapons. With both the fighting and the ordinary daô one can make but two cuts; one from the right shoulder downwards to the left, one from the left foot upwards to the right. The reason of this is that in sharpening the blade one side only gives the edge, slanting to the other straight face of the blade. Any attempt to cut in a way contrary to those mentioned causes the daô to turn in the hand on the striker, and I have seen some bad wounds inflicted in this manner. The weapon is identical with the "parang latok" of the Malays. The ordinary hill daô is generally stuck naked into the waist-band on the right hip, but the fighting daô is provided with a scabbard and worn at the waist. The daô to a hillman is a possession of great price. It is literally the bread-winner. With this he cuts his jhum and builds his houses; without its aid the most ordinary operations of hill life could not be performed. It is with the daô that he fashions the women's weaving tools; with the daô he fines off his boat; with the daô he notches a stair in the steep hillside leading to his jhum; and to the daô he frequently owes his life, in defending himself from the attacks of wild animals."

Besides grain and cotton, the hill tribes grow tobacco. This is planted principally in small valleys on the banks of the hill streams." In order to scare birds, deer, and wild pigs from the growing crop, a cleft bamboo is planted in the middle and connected by a long cane with the hut built for watching the crop in such a manner that by pulling the cane the two halves of the bamboo can be clashed together and a harsh rattling noise produced.

The Marmás and Maramagris have for the most part adopted a settled mode of life and taken to plough cultivation. They also catch and sell fish, hew wood, dug-out canoes, and weave baskets and mats. The Rájbansi Maghs are accomplished cooks, and are largely employed by Europeans in that capacity. As a rule they take a keen interest in their profession, and it may be that their skill is in some measure due to their freedom from the social and religious prejudices which debar other classes of native cooks from tasting the dishes which they prepare.

Maghá Chewár, a *mul* or section of the Sâtmuliá or Kishnaut sub-caste of Goálás in Behar.

Maghad Khandi, a sub-caste of Telis in Bengal.

Maghaiá, a sept of Lohárs in Chota Nagpur.

Maghaiyá, a sub-caste of Kumhárs and Telis in Behar and Chota Nagpur.

Maghayá, a native of Mag-há (Magadha) or South Behar; a designation of numerous sub-castes, such as Barai, Beldar, barber, Dhanuk, Dhobi, Gangotá, Goálá, Kándu, Nunia, Sunri, and Teli castes in Behar; a sub-caste of Barhis in Behar who work in both wood and iron and do the rougher woodwork required for houses, as distinguished from the Kanaujiás, who are joiners and cabinet-makers. Representatives of this sub-caste are found both in the town of Bhágalpur and in the north of the district, but intermarriage between the two groups is believed to be rare. The headman of the former is styled *Sátun*, while the headman of the latter bears the usual title of *Manjhan*; a sub-caste of Bhars in Manbhum, comprising the five sections of Mayur, Bel, Báerisi, Kásyab, and Bráhmarshi, of which the first four are totemistic and the last appears to have been borrowed from the Brahmans; a sub-caste of Doms in Behar who play the *dhol* and *turi*; a sub-caste of Halwáis or confectioners in Behar, who have to some extent abandoned their distinctive occupation and find employment as servants and petty shopkeepers dealing in miscellaneous articles. Many of them fry rice, *chura*, etc., and are called *bhuja bhura*; a sub-caste of Koiris in Behar, which, though endogamous as regards the rest of the caste, intermarries with the Chirme or Chirmáit sub-caste; a sub-caste of Kumhárs in Behar and Western Bengal, which used formerly to be endogamous, but now intermarries with the Tirhutiá sub-caste; a sub-caste of Thatherá or brass-chaser in Behar.

Maghayá Bráhman, a synonym for Bábhan.

Maghi, a sept of Chiks in Chota Nagpur.

Maghniá, a sept of Lohárs in Chota Nagpur.

Magi, a sub-caste of Kumhárs in Dacca and Tántis in Bengal; a sub-caste of Báitis in Faridpur.

Magrathi, a *thar* or sept of Mangars in Darjiling.

Maguri, a title of Bangaja Káyasths in Bengal.

Mahabara, a totemistic sept of Chiks in Chota Nagpur who never kill or chase the wild boar.

Mahabhát, a section of the Kamár sub-caste of Dosádhs in Behar.

Mahábrahman, Mahápátra or **Kantáha**, a division of Brahmans in Behar who officiate as priests on cremation.

Mahádanda, a sub-caste of Kewats in Behar.

Mahádanta, a title of Brahmans.

Mahájan, money-lender, a title of the Ariár sub-caste of Bais Baniyás.

Máhakariá, a section of Goálás in the North-Western Provinces and Behar.

Mahalá, a section of Goálás in the North-Western Provinces and Behar.

Mahaldár, a title of men who measure grain for Mahajáns, also called Kayáls; a title of Jaunpuri Chamárs and Muchis in Behar whose women act as midwives; a title of certain Musalmans, also called Pajrá, who sell fish and are boatmen.

Mahali, a synonym for Mahili; a sept of Lohárs in Chota Nagpur.

Mahali-Munda, a sub-tribe of Mundas in Chota Nagpur; a sept of Lohárs in Chota Nagpur.

Mahallá-navis, an honorary title of Káyasths in Bengal.

Mahámandá, a section of the Mahmudábáz sub-caste of Nápits in Central Bengal.

Mahánadi, a river, a sept of Bediyas and Chiks in Chota Nagpur.

Mahánadiá, a sept of Gonds in Chota Nagpur.

Mahánáik or *Sreshta-Khandáit*, a sub-caste of Khandáits in Balasore and Cuttack.

Mahánandiá, a sept of Páns in Chota Nagpur.

Maháni, a title of Támbulis, Telis, and other trading castes.

Mahant, S.; the head of a religious establishment of the mendicant orders of the Hindus.

Mahanta, a priest of the Jugi caste in Tipperah; a spiritual guide in the Vaishnava sect; a title of Kurmis in Western Bengal.

Mahanti, *Máhinti*, a titular section of Utkal or Orissa Brahmans; a title of Chásás and Karans in Orissa.

Mahápátra, a hypergamous group of the Bangaja sub-caste of Káyasths in Bengal; a title of Brahmans and Karans in Orissa; a title of Khandáits in Chota Nagpur.

Mahar, a section of Goálás in Behar.

Mahará, a title of the Dhusiá sub-caste of Chamars; a title of Kahars in Behar who carry palanquins and work as boatmen.

Mahárái, a title of Kurmis in Behar.

Mahárāj, a title affected by certain mendicants and Brahmans; a title of respect applied to Behar Brahmans who are employed as cooks.

Mahárāná, a title of Nágars in Behar.

Mahárāno, a *mul* or section of the Naomuliá or Majraut sub-caste of Goálás in Behar.

Mahárāshtra, a *thar* or section of Nepáli Brahmans.

Mahárāshtriya, a territorial division of the Pancha Drávira Brahmans who live in the south of the Vindyá range, a country of the Marathi language.

Mahárath or *Mahárathi*, great charioteer, a title of Khandáits in Orissa.

Maháraus, a sept of the Suryabansi sub-tribe of Rájputs in Behar.

Maharná, a section of Kewats in Behar.

Maháset, a group of Maghaiyá Telis and Sunris in Behar.

Mahásib, literally 'an accountant,' a section of the Maghayá sub-caste of Telis; a title of Sunris in Behar.

Mahasthán, Mastán or **Háliá**, a sub-caste of Utkal Brahmans in Orissa.

Mahat, a sub-caste of Goálás in Chota Nagpur; a title of up-country Brahmans and of some trading castes; a title of the Kochh tribe in Northern Bengal.

Máhátá, a title of Khatris in Bengal.

Maháthá, a section of Maghaiyá Kumhárs in Behar.

Mahathwár, a section of the Chamár and Bhuiyá castes.

Mahátmá, a *mul* or section of the Ghosin sub-caste of Goálás; a section of the Chaubhán sub-caste of Nuniás and a section of the Banodhiá and Jaiswár Kalwárs in Behar.

Mahátman, a section of the Maghayá sub-caste of Kumhárs in Behar.

Mahato, a title of Goálás, Kurmis, Koiris, Kahárs, Kumhárs, Rajwárs, Dhánuks, Mundas, Chiks or Páns and Pásis; a sept of Oraons in Chota Nagpur.

Mahatoar, a sept of Páns and Agariás in Chota Nagpur.

Mahauliá, a section of Kaserás in Behar.

Mahaut, a sept of Thárus in Behar.

Máhbariá, a *kul* or section of Bábhans in Behar.

Mahbho, a sept of the Yangorup sub-tribe of Limbus in Darjiling; branch of the same sept may not intermarry.

Mahbu, the physician, literally a shaker—one who, being ridden by ghosts or devils, shakes himself free: hence a physician; a sept of the Charkola sub-tribe of Limbus in Darjiling.

Mahdauriár, a *pur* or section of Sákadwipi Brahmans in Behar.

Mahendra Khyáni, a group of the Bárendra Sunris in Eastern Bengal.

Máhepurá, a *mul* or section of the Chhamulia Madhesiá sub-caste of Halwáis in Behar.

M[illegible]er, a section of Kumhárs in Singbhum.

Mahesbaráit, a section of the Kamár sub-caste of Dosádhs in Behar.

Maheeri, a trading caste of Northern India and Marwar, closely allied to the Agarwáls and Oswáls with whom they eat and drink. Like the Agarwáls, they have a sub-caste called Dasá, said to be illegitimate and perhaps coming of slave mothers. The Mahesri are almost invariably Hindus, while the Agarwál and Oswál castes contain a large proportion of Jains. They have 72 exogamous subdivisions (*gots*), a few of which are shown in Appendix I. Like the Agarwáls, they observe a complex rule of exogamy. A man may not marry into (*a*) his own section, (*b*) his mother's, (*c*) his maternal grandmother's, (*d*) his father's maternal grandmother's, (*e*) his mother's maternal grandmother's.

Maheswar, a *pur* or section of Sákadwipi Brahmans, and of Maghaiyá Kumhárs in Behar.

Mahili, *Mahali*, a Dravidian caste of labourers, palanquin-bearers, and workers in bamboo found in Chota Nagpur and Western Bengal. They are divided into five sub-castes—**Bansphor-Mahili**, who make baskets and do all kinds of bamboo work; **Pátar-Mahili**, basket-makers and cultivators; **Sulunkhi-Mahili**, who are cultivators and labourers; **Tánti-Mahili**, who carry palanquins; and **Mahili-Munda**, a small outlying sub-caste confined to Lohardagá. A comparison of the totemistic sections of the Mahilis shown in Appendix I with those of the Santáls seems to warrant the conjecture that the main body of the caste, that is to say the group comprising the Bansphor, Sulunkhi, and Tanti Mahilis, is merely a branch of the Santáls, separated at a comparatively recent date from the parent tribe. The exact causes of the separation are, of course, lost in the obscurity which enshrouds the early history of all tribal movements. But the fact that the Mahilis make baskets and carry palanquins, occupations which every Santál would deem degrading, suggests that the adoption of these pursuits may have given the first impulse to the formation of the new group. The Mahili-Munda possibly parted from the Mundá tribe for similar reasons. Besides the sections shown in the Appendix the entire sub-caste regard the pig as their totem, and consider it wrong to eat pork. It is rumoured, indeed, that appetite often gets the better of tradition, but that in such cases the carcase alone is eaten, and the consequences of breaking the taboo averted by throwing away the head. The Pátar-Mahili are a Hinduised sub-caste of South-East Manbhum, who employ Brahmans as priests and abstain from eating beef.

Origin and internal structure.

A man may not marry a woman of his own section or of the section to which his mother belonged before her marriage. Beyond these limits marriage is regulated with reference to the standard formula for prohibited degrees.

Marriage.

Mahilis marry their daughters both as infants and as adults, but the former practice is deemed the more respectable, and there can, I think, be little doubt that in this, as in other castes on the borders of Hinduism, the tendency at the present day is towards the entire abolition of adult-marriage. The customary bride-price paid for a Mahili girl is supposed to be Rs. 5, but the amount is liable to vary according to the means of the bridegroom's parents. On the wedding morning, before the usual procession starts to escort the bridegroom to the bride's house, he is formally married to a mango tree, while the bride goes through the same ceremony with a *mahuá*. At the entrance to the bride's house the bridegroom, riding on the shoulders of some male relation and bearing on his head a vessel of water, is received by the bride's brother, equipped in similar fashion, and the two cavaliers sprinkle one another with water. The bride and bridegroom are then seated side by side on a plank under a canopy of *sál* leaves erected in the courtyard of the house, and the bridegroom touches the bride's forehead five times with vermilion, and presents her with an iron armlet. This is the binding portion of the ritual.

So far as positive rules are concerned, the Mahilis appear to impose no limit on the number of wives a man may have. It is unusual to find a man with more than two; and practically, I understand, polygamy is rarely resorted to unless the first wife should happen to be barren. Widows may remarry, and are under no restrictions in their choice of a second husband, though it is deemed right and proper for a widow to marry her deceased husband's younger brother if such a relative exists. Divorce is permitted on the ground of adultery or inability to agree. When a husband divorces his wife he gives her a rupee and takes away the iron armlet (*lohár kháru*) which was given her at her wedding. He must also entertain his caste brethren at a feast by way of obtaining their sanction to the proceedings. Divorced wives may marry again.

Like the Bauris and Bágdis, the Mahilis admit into their caste men of any caste ranking higher than their own. The conditions of membership are simple. The person seeking admission into the Mahili community has merely to pay a small sum to the headman (*parganáit*) of the caste and to give a feast to the Mahilis of the neighbourhood. This feast he must attend himself, and signify his entrance into the brotherhood by tasting a portion of the food left by each of the guests on the leaf which on these occasions serves as a plate.

Inheritance.

In matters of inheritance and succession the Mahilis profess to follow whatever law applies to the Hindus of the locality—the Dáyabhága in Manbhum and the Mitákshará in Lohardagá. Statements of this kind, however, import little more than a vague assumption of conformity with what is supposed to be the custom of all respectable men; and there is no reason to believe that the headman (*parganáit*) and caste-council (*pancháyat*), who settle the civil disputes of the caste, have any knowledge of, or pay the smallest regard to, the rules of the regular Hindu law. The questions which come before this primitive tribunal are usually very simple. Its decisions are accepted without question, and I know of no instance where an attempt has been made to correct them by appealing to the regular courts. It does not follow, however, that Mahilis and castes of similar standing have escaped the influence of the Codes and have preserved a distinct customary law of their own. On the contrary, the written law certainly filters down to these lower grades of society, not through the regular channels of text-books and courts, but in virtue of their tendency to imitate the usages of the groups immediately above themselves. If men of these lower castes are asked what law they follow, a common answer is that they have the same law as their landlords; and the landlords, to whatever caste they may belong, almost invariably get their law from the text-books and the courts. To this influence it is probably due that the practice of giving an extra share (*jeth-angs*) to the eldest son in dividing an inheritance is gradually dying out among the Mahilis, and the tendency is towards an equal division of property.

Religion.

The religion of the Mahilis is at present a mixture of half-forgotten animism and Hinduism imperfectly understood. They affect indeed to worship all the Hindu gods, but they have not yet risen to the distinction of employing Brahmans, and their working deities seem to be Bar-pahárí and Manasá. The former is merely another name for the well-known mountain god of the Mundas and Santáls, while the latter is the snake goddess, probably also of non-Aryan origin, whose cult has been described in the article on the Bágdis. To these are offered goats, fowls, rice, and ghi, the offerings being afterwards eaten by the worshippers themselves.

Disposal of the dead.

The Mahilis of Northern Manbhum bury their dead face downwards; but this practice is not universal, for the Pátar Mahilis and the Mahilis of the Santál Parganas burn their dead and bury the ashes near at hand. On the eleventh day after death offerings of milk, ghi, and rice are made at the place of burial. Similar offerings are presented in the months of Kártik and Chait for the propitiation of departed ancestors in general. The anniversary of the death of an individual ancestor is not observed.

Social status and occupation.

Mahilis rank socially with Bauris and Dosadhs. They eat beef, pork, and fowls, and are very partial to strong drink. Field-rats, which are reckoned a special delicacy by the Oraons, they will not touch. They will eat cooked food with the Kurmi, the Bhumij, and the Deswali Santáls. They believe their original occupation to be basket-making and bamboo work generally. Many of them are now engaged in agriculture as non-occupancy raiyats and landless day-labourers.

The following statement shows the number and distribution of Mahilis in 1872 and 1881 :—

DISTRICT.	1872.	1881.	DISTRICT.	1872.	1881.
Bardwan	64	57	Maldah	1,365	218
Bankura	......	77	Santál Parganás	9,581	1,232
Birbhum	......	35	Cuttack	......	53
Midnapur	3,497	986	Balasore	......	7
Nadiya	18	31	Tributary States	......	694
Khulna	......	10	Hazaribagh	1,979	2,296
Dinajpur	3	302	Lohardagá	8,989	7,510
Rajshahye	28	196	Singbhum	1,301	1,196
Pabna	60	......	Manbhum	7,896	4,772
Monghyr	375	......	Tributary States	111	13
Bhagalpur	548	......			

Mahili-Mundá, a sub-caste of Mahilis in Western Bengal.

Mahintá, a *gáin* of the Bátsya *gotra* of Rárhi Brahmans in Bengal.

Mahisirupján, a *mul* or section of the Naomulia or Majraut sub-caste of Goálás in Behar.

Máhkur, Mákur, a sub-caste of Goálás in Chota Nagpur.

Mahlaingtsa, a sept of Maghs in the Hill Tracts of Chittagong.

Mahli, a sept of Birhors in Chota Nagpur.

Mahmudábáz, a sub-caste of Nápits in Eastern Bengal.

Máhmudpuriá, a sub-caste of Kámárs in Western Bengal.

Mahrá, a *mul* or section of the Biahut sub-caste of Kalwárs in Behar.

Máhrá, a title of Chamárs and men employed to herd cattle.

Mahrághási, a sub-caste of Ghásis in Chota Nagpur who serve as bearers.

Mahrajiá, a section of Bháts.

Mahrána, a *pangat* or section of Bánsphor Doms, and of Dosadhs in Behar.

Mahrano, a title of Hindu Joláhás in Behar.

Mahrasiá, a *pur* or section of Sákadwipi Brahmans in Behar.

Mahrat, a *mul* or section of the Ayodhiá sub-caste of Hajjáms in Behar.

Mahraul, a *mul* or section of the Goria sub-caste of Goálás in Behar.

Mahraur, a sept of the Chandrabansi Rájputs in Behar. They cannot intermarry with persons of the Besáin and Chaubhán septs, being supposed to have had their common origin in the same saint.

Mahtá, a section of Goálás in the North-Western Provinces and Behar.

Mahtha, a section of the Amashta sub-caste of Káyasths in Behar.

Máhto, (i) a village headman; (ii) a title applied in Behar to Kurmis who by age or by personal influence have attained a leading position in their villages. In some parts of the country the title is used as almost synonymous with Kurmi; and a Kurmi, when asked to what caste he belongs, will reply "Máhto;" (iii) a title of the following castes:—Dhánuks, Dosádhs, Goria Goálás, Koiris, Sunris; the Bhojpuriá and Ayodhiá sub-castes of Nuniás in Behar; also Thárus; the Bediyas, Mahilis, Nágeswars, and Kharwars in Chota Nagpur; Cheros and the Malwe Rájputs in Chota Nagpur; Tántis, Kewats, Binds and Dhobis in Behar.

Mahtoar, a totemistic sept of Chiks in Chota Nagpur.

Mahtwar, a section of Goálás in Behar.

Mahuá, a tree, a totemistic sept of Páns, Doms, Bedyas, and Chamárs in Chota Nagpur.

Mahuár, a sept of Rájputs in Behar.

Mahuári, a section of Bábhans and of the Biyáhut and Kharidáhá Kalwárs in Behar.

Mahukal, a bird, a totemistic sept of Mundas, Bediyas, and Kharwars; a section of Mahilis in Chota Nagpur.

Mahuli, a section of the Sátmuliá Maghayá sub-caste of Kándus in Behar.

Mahur or *Mahuliyá*, a sub-caste of Lohárs in Behar.

Máhuri, a sub-caste of Baniyás in Behar, who occupy nearly as high a rank as the Agarwáls in social estimation. Like the Sikhs, the Máhuris strictly prohibit the use of tobacco, and a man detected smoking would be expelled from the community. Another peculiar usage is that marriages are always celebrated at the bridegroom's house, and not at the bride's. Trade and money-lending are the proper occupations of the Máhuri. Some of them have acquired substantial tenures and set up as landholders and zamindars.

Mahuriá, a section of Láheris in Behar.

Mahwá, a section of the Tirhutia sub-caste of Doms in Behar.

Maiduchhá, a *thar* or sept of Khambus in Darjiling.

Maikam, a *thar* or sept of Khambus in Darjiling.

Mai ketári beguná bágh, "harrow, sugarcane, egg-plant, garden," a formula or shibboleth distinguishing a section of the Maghayá sub-caste of Koiris in Behar.

Maikhola, a sub-tribe of Limbus in Darjiling.

Máil, a *mul* or section of the Chhamuliá Madhesiá sub-caste of Halwáis in Behar.

Máilidhurlak, a *mul* or section of the Naomuliá or Majraut sub-caste of Goálás in Behar.

Mailwár, a section of Cheros, Khariás, Kharwars, and Lohárs in Chota Nagpur.

Máilwar, a *mul* or section of the Naomuliá or Majraut sub-caste of Goálás in Behar.

Mainá, a bird, a totemistic sept of Goálás, Parhaiyas, Mundas, and Bediyas in Chota Nagpur.

Mainkiswar, a section of the Kamár sub-caste of Dosádhs in Behar.

Mainpuri, a class of Baniyás in Behar.

Máir, a sub-caste of Sonárs in Behar who do not permit the remarriage of their widows.

Mairiá, a section of Bábhans in Behar.

Maisásari, a sub-caste of Kurmis in Orissa.

Máitál, a title of Kánsáris or braziers in Western Bengal.

Maitbukru, a place where he buries his bones, being his ancestral birthplace, a section of Mahilis in Chota Nagpur.

Maithil or **Tirhutiá**, a territorial division of the Pancha Gaura Brahmans in Behar, deriving its name from Mithilá or Tirhut.

Máiti, *Máti*, a title of Utkal Brahmans and of Kaibarttas in Orissa and Bengal.

Maitra, a *gáin* of the Kásyapa *gotra* of Bárendra Brahmans in Bengal.

Majar or **Minjur**, peacock, a totemistic sept of Mundas and Páns in Chota Nagpur.

Májháliár, a *mul* or section of the Sátmuliá or Kishnaut sub-caste of Goálás in Behar.

Majhal-Turiyá, a sub-caste of Rajwárs in Lohardagá.

Májhasthán, a sub-caste of Kumhárs in Pabna.

Májhaurá, a section of the Biyáhut and Kharidáhá Kalwárs in Behar.

Majhiaur, a sept of the Rautár sub tribe of Thárus in Behar.

Majhiya, a section of Rajwárs in Western Bengal.

Majhrot, a title of Maithil Brahmans in Behar.

Majhwat, a sub-caste of Goálás in Chota Nagpur.

Máji, a title of Kandhs in Orissa.

Majilpur, a *samáj* or local group of the Dákshinátya Baidik Brahmans in the 24-Parganás.

Majlishi, a sub-caste of Sunris in Eastern Bengal.

Majlisi (Maudgalya), a section of Kaibarttas in Murshedabad.

Majraut or **Naomuliá**, a sub-caste of Goálás in Behar.

Majumdár, an honorary title of Brahmans, Káyasths, Báruis, Jugis, and Sunris in Bengal; a hypergamous group of Kaibarttas in Bakarganj.

Majurrishi, a section of Mayarás in Bengal.

Makadá, a section of Goálás in the North-Western Provinces and Behar.

Makhaiwár, a *pur* or section of Sákadwipi Brahmans in Behar.

Mákhpawár, a *pur* or section of Sákadwipi Brahmans in Behar.

Maki, *Muki*, a synonym for Ghási.

Mákunda, a sub-group of the Háliyá or Hele Kaibarttas in Central Bengal.

Makundpuri, a section of Sonárs in Behar.

Mál, a Dravidian cultivating caste of Western and Central Bengal, many of whom are employed as *chaukidárs* or village watchmen and have gained an evil reputation for their thieving propensities. Beyond the vague statements current among the Máls of Eastern Bengal, that they were wrestlers (*Malla*, *Mála*) at the court of the Dacca Nawábs and gained their name from this profession, the caste appear to have no

Traditions of origin.

traditions, and their origin has formed the subject of much discussion, the general drift of which is stated by Mr. Beverley[1] as follows :-

"In his late work on the Ancient Geography of India, General Cunningham quotes a passage from Pliny, in which the *Malli* are mentioned as this :—'*Gentes : Calingæ proximi mari, et supra Mandei Malli, quorum mons Mallus finisque ejus tractus est Ganges.*' In another passage we have, '*Ab iis (Palibothris) in interiore situ Monedes et Suari, quorum mons Mallus*' ; and putting the two passages together, General Cunningham 'thinks it highly probable that both names may be intended for the celebrated Mount Mandar, to the south of Bhagalpur, which is fabled to have been used by the gods and demons at the churning of the ocean.' The *Mandei* General Cunningham identifies 'with the inhabitants of the Mahanadi river, which is the *Manada* of Ptolemy.' 'The *Malli* or *Malei* would therefore be the same people as Ptolemy's *Mandalæ*, who occupied the right bank of the Ganges to the south of Palibothra,' the *Mandalæ* or *Mandali* having been already identified with the *Monedes* and the modern Munda Kols. 'Or,' adds General Cunningham, 'they may be the people of the Rajmahal hills who are called Maler, which would appear to be derived from the Canarese *Male* and the Tamil *Malei*, a 'hill.' It would therefore be equivalent to the Hindu *pahári* or *párbatiya*, a 'hillman." Putting this last suggestion aside for the present, it seems to me that there is some little confusion in the attempt to identify both the *Monedes* and the *Malli* with the Mundas. If the *Mandei* and the *Malli* are distinct nations—and it will be observed that both are mentioned in the same passage—the former rather than the latter would seem to correspond with the *Monedes* or Mundas. The *Malli* would then correspond rather to the *Suari, quorum mons Mallus*—the hills bounded by the Ganges at Rajmahal. They may therefore be the same as the Mals. In other words, the Mals—the words Maler and Malhar seem to be merely a plural form—may possibly be a branch of the great Sauriyan family to which the Rajmahal Pahárias, the Oraons, and the Sabars all belong, and which Colonel Dalton would describe as Dravidian. Fifteen hundred or two thousand years ago this people may have occupied the whole of Western Bengal. Pressed by other tribes, they have long since been driven into corners, but not without, as it were, leaving traces of their individuality behind. In Mal-bhumi (Manbhum) instead of 'the Country of the Wrestlers,' as Dr. Hunter puts it, we seem to have the land of '*Mons Mallus*' and the Mals. The Maldah district may also possibly owe its name to their having been settled there. As to the name, indeed it is quite possible that it means nothing more than highlanders; the word *Mallus* being simply the Indian vernacular for the Latin *mons*. If a native were asked the name of a hill in the present day, he would reply, as Pliny's informant probably replied years ago, that it was a 'hill;' and if asked the name of the people who lived there, he would probably say they were 'hillmen.'

"These Mals appear to have been driven eastwards and to have spread over the whole of Bengal, where they have become merged

---

[1] *Report of the Census of Bengal*, 1872, by H. Beverley, p. 184.

in the mass of low-caste Hindus. This will account to some extent for what Colonel Dalton calls the Dravidian element in the composition of the Bengali race. Under the Hindu system the Mals, like other aboriginal tribes who came within the pale of Hinduising influences, appear to have formed one of the forty-five tribes of Chandals, the lowest or sweeper class among Hindus. Chandals are found in every district of Bengal, their aggregate number in the present day being over a million and a half. In Mymensingh, where we find 20,000 Mals, we have 123,000 Chandals. In the south-eastern districts they seem to have lost their name in the generic term of Chandals, but in the eastern districts they still retain it. In Birbhum and Bankura, in each of which districts there are about 9,000 Mals, there are not as many hundred Chandals. In Murshedabad there are 29,000 Mals against 22,000 who described themselves as Chandals. Most officers say the Mals are identically the same as the Chandals. Some say they are wrestlers, others attribute to them the same occupation as that of the Madaris or Sampheriyas, viz., that of snake-charmers. Others, again, say they are Musalmans, and identify them with Bediyas or Babajiyas; but in this explanation there seems to be some confusion, the two last tribes not being generally considered identical. The Babajiyas, though an itinerant tribe like the Bediyas, are employed, like the stationary Pasaris, in selling drugs. The returns, however, show that some of the Mals are Musalmans."

Internal structure.

The most primitive specimens of the caste are met with in Bankura, where they have distinctly totemistic sections, and are divided into the following sub-castes:—Dhaliá, Gobrá or Gurá, Khera, Rájbansi, and Sánágánthá. In Midnapur and Manbhum we find Dhunakátá, Rájbansi, Sápuryá or Bedya Mál, and Tungá; in Birbhum Khaturía, Mallik, and Rájbansi; in the Santál Parganás Deswar, Magahiyá, Rajbansi or Rájá Mál, Rárhi Mál, and Sindurá; while in Murshedabad the sub-castes are the same as in Bankuar, except that Dhaliá is not known. The origin of these groups is extremely obscure, and I doubt whether any amount of inquiry would throw much light on the subject. Rájbansi, for example, is the name adopted by a very large proportion of the Kochh tribe; but there is no reason to suppose that the Máls are Kochh, and they might easily have acquired the name Rájbansi in the same manner as the Kochh have done by identifying themselves with the lineage of a local Rájá, who may or may not have belonged to the same race. The simplest solution of the difficulty, appears to be to assume that Mál is nothing more than a variant of Málé, 'man,' the name by which the Málé Pahāriás describe themselves. It is possible, again, that the Rájbansi Máls may be the same as Rája Máls whom Buchanan noticed among the Mál Pahāriás at the beginning of the century. The monkey-catching Gobras bear the same name as one of the sub-castes of Bágdis; and Khera is not far removed from Khairá, whom some regard as a branch of the Doms. The Sánágánthá take their name from making *sánás*, the uprights through which weavers pass their thread. The **Dhunákátá Máls** collect resin (*dhuna*) by tapping *sál* trees; the **Tungá** sub-caste are cultivators; while the **Sapuriá** or **Bedya Máls** live by charming snakes, catching monkeys, hunting or conjuring, and roam about the country carrying with them small tents of coarse gunny-cloth. Although they catch snakes, Sápuriá Máls hold the animal in the highest reverence, and will not kill it, or even pronounce its name, for which they use the synonym *latá*, 'a creeper.'

Kinship with the Bediyás.

The names of the last-mentioned group raise the probably insoluble question of the connexion of the Máls with the Bediyás. Dr. Wise treats both Mál and Samperiá or Sápuriá as subdivisions of the Bediyá tribe; but it is equally possible that the Mál may be the parent group, and that the Bediyás may have separated from it by reason of their adhering to a wandering mode of life when the rest of the tribe had taken to comparatively settled pursuits. There certainly seem to be reasons for suspecting some tolerably close affinity between the two groups. The Máls of Dacca, for instance, are called **Ponkwah**, from their dexterity in extracting worms from the teeth, a characteristic accomplishment of the Bediyás. They repudiate the suggestion of kinship with the latter tribe, but it is said that many can recollect the time when relationship was readily admitted. At present, however, in spite of some survival of roving habits, peculiar physiognomy, and distinctive figures, Máls are with difficulty recognized. Many of them are small bankers (*mahájans*), never dealing in pedlar's wares, but advancing small sums, rarely exceeding eight rupees, on good security. The rate of interest charged is usually about fifty per cent. per annum; but this demand, however exorbitant, is less than that exacted by many money-lenders in the towns. The Dacca Máls never keep snakes, and know nothing about the treatment of their bites. The women, however, pretend to a secret knowledge of simples and of wild plants. They are also employed for cupping, for relieving obscure abdominal pains by friction, and for treating uterine diseases, but never for tattooing. The Máls of Eastern Bengal do not intermarry with Bediyás, and even within the limits of their own group a sharp distinction used to be observed between settled Máls and gipsy Máls; so that if one of the former sought to marry a girl of the latter class, he was required to leave his home, give up his cultivation, and adopt a wandering life. This custom has gradually given way to a keener sense of the advantages of settled life, but its general disuse is said to be still resented by the elders of the caste.

Plausible as the conjecture may be which would trace some bond of kinship between the Bediyás and the Máls, the evidence bearing on the point is not precise enough to enable us to identify the Sápuriá Máls of Midnapur with the Sámperiya Bediyás of Eastern Bengal.* Snake-charming is an occupation likely enough to be adopted by any caste of gipsy-like propensities, and there is no reason why both Máls and Bediyás should not have taken to it independently. Further particulars will be found in the article Bediyá.

Exogamy.

The Máls of Western and Central Bengal seem on the whole to be the most typical representatives of the original Mál tribe. Among them the primitive rule of exogamy is in full force, and a man may not marry a woman who belongs to the same totem group as himself. Prohibited degrees are reckoned by the standard formula calculated in the descending line to five generations on the father's and three on the mother's side. Outsiders belonging to higher castes may be admitted into the Mál community by giving a feast to the Máls of the neighbourhood and drinking water in which the headman of the village (*mánjhi*) has dipped his toes. No instance of any one undergoing this disagreeable ordeal has been quoted to me, and such cases must be very rare.

Marriage.

Girls may be married either as infants or after they have attained puberty, the tendency being towards the adoption of the former custom. The ceremony takes place just before daybreak in a sort of arbour made of *mahuá* and *sidhá* branches in the courtyard of the bride's house. After the bride has been carried seven times round the bridegroom the couple are made to sit side by side facing the east, and a vessel of water which has been blessed by a Brahman is poured over their heads after the manner of the Mundas and Oraons.[1] Garlands of flowers are then exchanged, the clothes of the pair are knotted together, and if adult they retire into a separate room in order to consummate their union. On their reappearance they are greeted by the company as husband and wife. Polygamy is permitted, but most Máls are too poor to maintain more than one wife. A widow may marry again,[2] but no special ritual is in use, except among the Rájá Máls of Birbhum, who exchange necklaces of beads or seeds of the tulsi (*Ocymum sanctum*); and such marriages, which are called *sanga*, are effected by paying a small fee to the headman (*khámid* or *mánjhi*) and to the father of the widow. Divorce may be effected, with the sanction of the panchâyat, on the ground of adultery by the wife, and divorced women may marry again in the same manner as widows.

Religion.

Máls profess to have completely adopted Hinduism, and no vestiges of any more primitive religion can now be traced among them. They seem to belong to whatever Hindu sect is popular in the locality where they are settled; and in different districts they describe themselves as Vaishnavas, Saivas, or Sáktas, as the case may be. The snake goddess Manasá is believed to be their special patroness, and is worshipped by them in much the same fashion as by the Bágdis. Sacrifices of rice, sweetmeats, and dried rice are also offered by the heads of families to the tutelary goddess of each village, who bears the name of the village itself with the termination *sini*

[1] According to some accounts Jalmá, the goddess of water, must first be worshipped with gifts of flowers at a neighbouring tank, and water drawn from this tank must be used in the marriage in addition to water blessed by a Brahman.

[2] This is the general rule, but the Rájbansi Máls of Midnapur have recently abandoned widow-marriage.

added; so that the goddess of the village Páthará would be called Pátharásini. In most districts they have not yet attained to the dignity of employing Brahmans, but elders of the caste or headmen of villages serve them as priests (*khámud*). In the Santál Parganás, however, the Brahmans of the Let sub-caste of Bágdis officiate also for the Rájá Máls. The dead are burned, usually at the side of a stream, into which the ashes are thrown. A meagre imitation of the orthodox *sráddh* ceremony is performed on the eleventh day after death in ordinary cases, and on the third day for those who have died a violent death. On the night of the Káli Pujá in Kártik (October–November) dried jute stems are lighted in honour of departed ancestors, and some even say that this is done to show their spirits the road to heaven. Libations of water are offered on the last day of Chait. Female children are buried mouth downwards, and the bodies of very poor persons are often buried with the head to the north in the bed of a river.

Disposal of the dead.

Occupation and social status.

Agriculture is supposed to be the original profession of the caste, and most Máls, except those of distinctly gipsy habits, are now engaged in cultivation as occupancy or non-occupancy raiyats and landless day-labourers. None appear to have risen to the higher rank of zamindar or tenure-holder, except in Bankura, where one *sardár ghatwál*, one *sadiál*, 56 *tábidárs*, and 35 *chákarán chaukidárs* are Máls. In Manbhum, on the other hand, which some believe to be the original home of the caste, no Máls are found in possession of these ancient tenures, though some are employed as ordinary village *chaukidárs*. The women of the caste and some of the men often make a livelihood by fishing—a fact which accounts for their bearing the title of Machhuá. Their social status is very low, and is clearly defined by the fact that Bágdis and Koras will not take water from their hands, while they will take water and sweetmeats not only from those castes, but also from Bauris. Máls pride themselves on abstaining from beef and pork, but eat fowls, all kinds of fish, field-rats, and the flesh of the *gosámp* (*Lacerta godica*). The Rájá Máls, however, do not touch fowls.

The following statement shows the number and distribution of Máls in 1872 and 1881:—

DISTRICT.	1872.	1881.	DISTRICT.	1872.	1881.
Bardwan	3,078	734	Jalpigori	16	......
Bankura	8,436	12,348	Dacca	4,663	7,835
Birbhum	9,346	21,630	Faridpur	957	2,272
Midnapur	5,726	4,042	Bakarganj	2,945	877
Hughli	1,058	807	Maimansinh	20,166	14,782
Howrah		16	Tipperah	3,970	4,755
24-Parganás	955	329	Chittagong	1	9
Nadiya	4,467	4,696	Noakhali	3	21
Khulna	......	70	Shahabad	907	7 016
Jessore	5,577	2,398	Bhagalpur	71	607
Murshedabad	29,281	8,368	Maldah	2,062	885
Dinajpur	1,446	1,026	Santál Parganás	8,820	489
Rajshahye	1,064	267	Tributary States, Orissa ...	1,092	......
Rangpur	386	313	Lohardaga	960	......
Bogra	818	743	Singbhum	1,367	31
Pabna	1,682	1,310	Manbhum	4,031	1,675
Darjiling	. 2	......	Tributary States	1,042	......

Mál, a sub-caste of Bhuiyas in Singbhum; a title of Kaibarttas; a section of the Maghayá sub-caste of Koiris and a section of Turis; a sub-sept of the Saren sept of Santáls.

Mál or **Már**, a sub-caste of Mauliks in Chota Nagpur.

Málá, a title of Kapális and Kawális in Eastern Bengal.

Málabhumiá, a sub-caste of Muchis in Bengal.

Máládhárkháni, a *mel* or hypergamous sub-group of Bárhi Brahmans in Bengal.

Malár, a synonym for Kathak in Singbhum.

Malar, a sept of Mundas and Ghásis in Chota Nagpur.

Malauriár, a *pur* or section of Sákadwipi Brahmans in Behar.

Máldhiá, a section of the Sátmuliá Maghayá sub-caste of Kándus in Behar.

Málé, *Mál, Sámariá Malé, Savar Paháriá, Sauriá, Sámil Paháriá, Asal Paháriá, Sangi*, a Dravidian tribe of the Rajmahál hills, closely akin to the Oraons, and probably an isolated branch of the large and widely diffused Savar tribe. The actual name of the tribe appears to be Mál, which is combined with the pronouns *en*, *em*, and *é* in order to form the present of the verb substantive. Thus Málen is the first person singular, I am a Mál; Málé, the third person singular; Malem, the first person plural; and Máler (used in the spelling Malair by Lieutenant Shaw as the name of the tribe), the third person plural. The selection of Málé as the tribal name for the purpose of this work is therefore both arbitrary and incorrect, and can only be justified by the necessity of having some distinctive designation to mark off these Máls from the Mál Paháriás of the southern hills and from the Mál caste of Bengal. In respect of physical characteristics the Málé represent the extreme type of the Dravidian race as we find it in Bengal. The nasal index measured on 100 men of the tribe yields an average of 94·5, which closely approaches the proportions ascertained for the Negro. The average stature is low, the complexion dark, and the figure short and sturdy.

Origin.

Early history of the tribe.

Owing to the rocky and forest-bound character of their country, and their incessant internal struggles, the Málés of the Rájmahál hills maintained a virtual independence during the period of Musalmán ascendancy in Bengal. It appears that, although they never completely recognized the imperial authority, they had a rude indigenous system of government, which was worked in moderate accord with the *zamindárs* of the low country bordering on the hills. The hills included in each *tappá* or subordinate fiscal division were subject to one or more divisional headmen, called *sardárs*, to whom the village headmen (*mánjhis*) were in their turn subordinate. The *sardárs*, who were possibly more civilized than the rest of the tribe, received from the *zamindárs* allotments of land in the plains on *jágir* or service tenures, in consideration of which they made themselves responsible for the prevention and detection of crime among the hill people. Besides this, the passes leading from the hills into the plain country were guarded by outposts of Málés, whose duty it was to stop any bodies of men from making raids upon the plains, and to give warning of an impending inroad. For further security, the *zamindárs* themselves maintained at the foot of the hills a chain of *chaukis* or police outposts, which were independent of the Málé guardians of the passes within the hills. Once every year, at the Dasahará festival, the divisional headman (*sardár*) of each *tappá* came down to the plains with his subordinate *mánjhis*, and there partook of a feast and received a turban at the *zamindár's* expense, at the same time formally renewing his engagements to keep the peace within his jurisdiction. For a long time this system kept crime within bounds, and promoted good feeling between the Málés and the people of the low country; but about the middle of last century a show of independence on the part of the hill people was treacherously resented by the *zamindárs*, who took the opportunity of the annual public feast to murder several of the village headmen. On this the Málés within the hills gave up the guardianship of the passes, and commenced a series of depredations, which were held in some check up to 1770 by the line of *zamindári* police posts without the hills. In that year, however, the famine which desolated the neighbouring districts pressed with peculiar severity upon the alluvial strip of country lying between the Rájmahál hills and the Ganges; the police outposts were abandoned, and the plains thus lay at the mercy of the Málés, who, owing to their aboriginal practice of living upon jungle foods, had escaped the extremity of distress. It was therefore in the years following the famine of 1770 that the raids of the hillmen upon the low country became most frequent and most systematic. Plunder no doubt was their main object, and the desire to revenge the treacherous murder of their headmen; but many of their inroads were in the first instance instigated by the landholders, who were in the habit of offering the Málés a free passage through their own lands on condition that they ravaged those of the neighbouring *zamindárs*. At any rate, the terror they occasioned was so widespread that the alluvial country was deserted by its cultivators; no boat dare moor after dusk on the southern bank of the Ganges; and even the Government mail-runners, who in those days passed along the skirts of the hills, by way of Rájmahál and the Teliá Garhí Pass, were frequently robbed and murdered at the foot of the hills. Up to 1778 the British Government, like the Muhammadans before them, made various attempts to suppress the Málés by military force. In 1772 a corps of light infantry, armed expressly for jungle fighting, was raised and placed under command of Captain Brooke. But the Málés never gave the troops a chance in the open country; while in the tangled undergrowth of the hills firearms had no decided advantage over the strong bamboo bows and heavy poisoned arrows of the hillmen. Besides this, the absence of roads, the difficulty of keeping up supplies, and the fatally malarious climate of the Rájmahál jungles, made the permanent subjection of the Málés a hopeless undertaking for native troops. In 1778 Captain Brown, then commanding the corps of light infantry, submitted to

Government a scheme for the pacification of the hillmen, the essential elements of which were the following:—*First,* the *sardárs* or divisional headmen of the Málés were to be restored to their original position as chiefs of the tribe, receiving formal *sanads* of appointment from Government, and in their turn entering into engagements, renewable annually, to perform certain specified duties. Similar engagements were to be taken from the *mánjhis* or village headmen, binding them to obey the *sardárs* in all matters laid down in the *sanads.* *Second,* those *sardárs* whose *tappás* bordered upon the public road were to receive a fixed pecuniary allowance, nominally for the purpose of maintaining police to protect the mail-runners, but in fact as a bribe to deter them from committing robberies themselves. *Third,* all transactions with the hill people were to be carried on through their *sardárs* and *mánjhis,* but intercourse with the inhabitants of the plains was to be encouraged by establishing markets on the outskirts of the hills. *Fourth,* the old *chauki bandi* or chain of police outposts, which had been abandoned in 1770, was to be completely re-established and maintained by Government until the service lands attached to them had been brought under cultivation. But the control of these outposts was to be taken from the *zamindárs* and made over to *thánádárs* or police officers appointed by Government, who were again to be subordinate to *sazáwals* or divisional superintendents. This police force was further to be strengthened by conferring grants of lands below the hills on invalid sepoys, on the condition that they settled on their allotments and gave assistance in the event of a Málé inroad. The total annual expense of the scheme was estimated at £100. Early in 1778 Captain Brown's scheme was approved by Government; and both the chain of police posts below the hills and the system of allowances to the *sardárs* on the public road were partially established before the end of the year. But in 1779 the hill country of Rájmahál was transferred from Captain Brown's jurisdiction, and it thus fell to Mr. Augustus Cleveland, who had been appointed Collector of Bhágalpur, to carry out the foregoing scheme. In the following year (1780) Mr. Cleveland reported that forty-seven hill chiefs had of their own will submitted to Government authority. With the view of retaining these men as loyal subjects he subsequently proposed that a corps of hill archers, four hundred strong, should be enrolled from among the Málés and officered by eight *sardárs* or divisional headmen, under the command of the Collector of Bhágalpur. The officers were to be paid Rs. 5, and the common soldiers Rs. 3, per mensem. Every village headman, he suggested, should be called upon to furnish recruits to the corps, and should receive for this service an allowance of Rs. 2 a month. The yearly expense of this arrangement, including the cost of the purple jackets and turbans which were to form the uniform of the corps, was estimated by Mr. Cleveland at £3,200. Warren Hastings, who was then Governor-General, at first objected to the enrolment of the corps of archers on the ground of this heavy expense, and sanctioned a scheme which Mr. Cleveland had proposed in the meantime, for granting pensions of Rs. 10 a month to all divisional headmen (*sardárs*) and of Rs. 5 a month to their *náibs* or deputies; *mánjhis* or village headmen were to receive no allowance at all. But towards the end of 1780 the enrolment of a corps of archers was sanctioned, mainly in consequence of the Commander-in-Chief having expressed his approval of the scheme when passing through Bhágalpur on his way to the Upper Provinces. At the same time the fiscal divisions of Ambár and Sultánábad were transferred to Mr. Cleveland's jurisdiction, it having been found that the chiefs of the southern portion of the Rájmahál hills would not give in their allegiance as long as they were exposed to continual inroads from the inhabitants of those *parganás*. Shortly afterwards, at the special request of the *sardárs* and *mánjhis* of Belpattá, that fiscal division was also placed under Mr. Cleveland, pensions being granted to the chiefs and recruits furnished for the hill archers.

Not long after the enrolment of the hill archers an outbreak that occurred in the hills was quelled by them so effectively that a proposal by Mr. Cleveland that the corps should be drilled and armed like regular sepoys was readily sanctioned, and Lieutenant Shaw was appointed adjutant; the name of the corps being at the same time changed to "The Bhágalpur Hill Rangers," by which name they were known until disbanded on the reorganization of the Native army after the Mutiny in 1857.

From the first enrolment of the hill archers petty offences committed by the members of the corps were punished by a rude court-martial of the officers. In 1782, however, one of the archers murdered a Málé woman, and in order to punish this, the first serious crime that had occurred, Mr. Cleveland proposed the formation of a distinct tribunal, the jurisdiction of which should be limited to members of the corps. This, which was at first styled court-martial, and afterwards hill assembly, was to consist of three or more officers of the corps, the power of appointing and dissolving the court resting with Mr. Cleveland. Mr. Cleveland was also to approve of all sentences passed by the court, except when capital punishment was awarded. In that case an assembly of five or more hill chiefs (*sardárs*) was to be convened, and a final decision to be passed in accordance with the opinion of the majority. Mr. Cleveland further proposed that offences committed by the inhabitants of the hills generally, with the exception of those who were enrolled in the corps of archers, should be withdrawn from the jurisdiction of the ordinary courts and placed under a tribunal of chiefs (*sardárs*) presided over by himself. The entire scheme, both as regards the court-martial for the archers and the assembly of *sardárs* for the hillmen generally, was approved by Government in April 1782. Shortly afterwards Mr. Cleveland reported that he had arranged for assemblies to be held twice a year, and gave the following account of the proceedings of the first trial:—"I have settled with the chiefs that they are regularly to assemble here twice a year for the purpose of trying all prisoners who may be brought before them; and as particular cases occur which may require immediate inquiry, they have agreed to attend whenever I find it necessary to summon them. One assembly has been already held, at which 1 principal chief (*sardár*), 74 *mánjhis*, and 120 common hill people were tried for plundering the *parganá* of Kharakpur of near nine hundred head of cattle. The trial lasted three days, and was conducted with as much ceremony and formality as the nature and disposition of the people would admit of. I have the pleasure to observe, however, that the chiefs appeared to conduct themselves throughout the trial with the greatest attention and impartiality, and the result of their proceedings, which I have confirmed, is as follows:—One principal chief, Bidji of Titoriá, and one common hill man, Chandra of Pupat, to be hanged immediately; and the sentence was accordingly carried into execution this morning, in the presence of the corps of hill archers and all the principal hill chiefs and *mánjhis*. One *mánjhi*, Jaruá of Tátakpárá, to be hanged twenty days hence, unless the whole cattle plundered are delivered up in that time, in which case he is to be pardoned. Seven *mánjhis* to be confined for their lives, unless the whole of the cattle plundered are delivered up in twenty days, in which case they are to be pardoned. Sixty-five *mánjhis* and 120 common hill people acquitted."

The rules of Mr. Cleveland's Hill Assembly were subsequently incorporated in Regulation I of 1796, which "provided that the Magistrate should commit all important cases to be tried before an assembly of hill chiefs. He was to attend the trial as superintending officer, and confirm or modify the sentence, if not exceeding fourteen years' imprisonment. Higher sentenecs were referred to the Nizámat Adalat, as the Supreme Criminal Court was then called. This unusual procedure was followed till 1827, when the law was repealed by Regulation I of that year; the mountaineers were then declared amenable to the ordinary courts, but some of the hill *mánjhis* were to sit with the Magistrate as assessors when he tried cases in which the hill men were concerned; and the *mánjhis* were also authorized to adjudicate summarily in disputes about land, succession, and claims to money when the value of the claim did not exceed one hundred rupees." It appears that the Hill Assembly, when no longer kept together by the personal influence of Mr. Cleveland, became almost unmanageable. Considerable difficulty was experienced in getting the chiefs to meet at all; and when present they would not attend to the proceedings of the court, while their sentences were hasty and capricious in the extreme. It was found, too, that even when the assemblies could be induced to do their work, the power they had been entrusted with was too uncontrolled, and that the total personal exemption of the Málés from the jurisdiction of the ordinary courts was a measure of doubtful policy, the more so as it seems to have been held that under Regulation I of 1796 the Magistrate had no power to try and punish Málés for petty offences on his own motion. Regulation I of 1827 has now been repealed by Act XXIX of 1871.

In 1783, the year before his death, Mr. Cleveland proposed that the Málés should be given extensive grants of waste land at the foot of the hills on the following terms:—(1) Every *sardár* was to have a rent-free *jágir* or service tenure, in perpetuity, of from 100 to 300 *bighás* of land. (2) Any Málé of lower rank than a chief might be allowed any quantity of land rent-free for ten years, it being liable to subsequent assessment at equitable rates. (3) In order to secure that the foregoing provisions should really come into operation, Mr. Cleveland suggested that all *sardárs* and *mánjhis* holding pensions from Government should forfeit their pensions unless they settled in the plains within twelve months. It was hoped that by thus forcing the hill men to settle in the plains they would become civilized by intercourse with the lowlanders; while as they learned more productive methods of agriculture it would be possible to make them contribute to the cost of administration. But the scheme was never carried out, and the immigration of Santáls from the west has now almost completely cut off the Málés from close intercourse with the plains. In any case, it may be doubted whether they would have left their hills; while from all that is known of the Oraons and other Dravidian races, Mr. Cleveland's expectation that the Málés would take to manufactures appears to have been utterly unfounded.

Traditions.

The traditions of the Málé are meagre. In Lieutenant Shaw's well-known monograph on the tribe[1] published in 1795, a story is told of seven brothers who were deputed by the gods to people the earth. A feast was made, and it was arranged that each brother was to take of such food as he liked and go to the land which he had chosen to dwell in. One took one thing and one another, and their choice determined the caste of their descendants. From the brother who took goat's flesh sprang the Hindus; another who took flesh of all kinds, but refused pork, became the father of the Mahomedans; another chose pork, and from him are the Kiratis; another is the ancestor of the 'Kawdir' (Kádar), and so on. Only the eldest brother, who was sick, got all sorts of food in an old dish. He was left in the hills as an outcast, and from him the Málé are descended. This myth is clearly only an echo of the similar story told by the Mundas and Hos. Both versions agree in their general tenor and in some of their details; both must have arisen after the tribes had been for some time in contact with Hindus, and both, it may be added, find it necessary to provide a place for the English in their account of the making of mankind.

Internal structure.

All my correspondents agree in assuring me that the Málés have no endogamous or exogamous subdivisions, and that their marriages are regulated solely by the standard formula for reckoning prohibited degrees which is explained in the introduction. If this is correct, a point upon which I am not yet fully convinced, the fact is remarkable. The Málés have been less exposed to Hindu influences than their kinsmen, the Oraons, yet the latter retain a long list of exogamous totems, while the former have no exogamous groups at all, and in this respect are more modern than most Hindu castes. The question seems to me to call for further inquiry. One would wish to know whether the Málé ever observed the characteristic Dravidian system of exogamy; and if so, how it came to fall into disuse.

---

[1] *Asiatic Researches*, vol. IV.

Free courtship is allowed, and girls are married, when of full age, to men of their own choice. Sexual intercourse before marriage is not recognized in theory, but if an unmarried girl becomes pregnant a sacrifice is offered to atone for the indiscretion, and arrangements are made to get her married without delay.

Marriage

Marriage brokers (*sithu*) are employed to conduct the preliminary negotiations, and to settle the difficult question of the bride-price. When this has been satisfactorily arranged, an auspicious day is fixed, when the bridegroom goes with his friends to the bride's house, taking with him a goat to furnish forth the wedding feast, and the bride-price, a portion of which is sometimes paid beforehand through the *sithu*. The parties are made to sit opposite each other, the bridegroom facing east and the bride west, while her girl friends comb and oil her hair. Then the father takes the bride by the hand and gives her to the bridegroom, pointing out that she is not halt, maimed or blind, and enjoining him to treat her kindly. This done, the *sithu* takes the bridegroom's right hand, dips the little finger in *sindur*, and makes five dots with it on the girl's forehead, afterwards using her finger to perform the same office for the bridegroom. Guns are fired to mark the completion of this essential rite, and the married couple then eat together out of the same dish in symbol of their union. The proceedings are concluded by a feast.

Divorce is permitted with the sanction of the leading men of the village. If the husband demands a divorce on the ground that his wife is barren, that she has committed adultery, or that she is incurably lazy, he is entitled to claim a refund of the bride-price which he paid for her in the first instance. He forfeits this right if the reasons which he gives are deemed to be frivolous and insufficient. If the wife claims a divorce on whatever grounds, her family must refund the bride-price. The ritual observed consists in tearing a *sál* leaf or breaking a small branch or a piece of string in token of separation, and pouring a vessel of water over the woman's head. Divorced women may marry again.

Divorce.

The religion of the Málés is animism of the type common among Dravidian tribes. At the head of their system stands the Sun called Dharmer Gosain, and represented by a roughly-hewn post set up in front of each house. He is worshipped with offerings of fowls, goats, sindur, and oil at the commencement of the harvest season, and at other times when any misfortune befalls the family. When people are gathered together for this purpose, the village headman, who acts as priest, goes round the congregation with an egg in his hand, and recites the names of certain spirits. He then throws away the egg, apparently as a propitiatory offering, and enjoins the spirits to hold aloof and abstain from troubling the sacrifice. Among the minor gods mentioned by Lieutenant Shaw, Raksi now appears as the tutelar deity of strong drink, who is worshipped by the headman of the village before beginning to distil liquor from the fresh *mahua* crop.

Religion.

According to Lieutenant Shaw, Raksi is sought out when a man-eating tiger infests a village or a bad epidemic breaks out, and is worshipped in the form of a black stone set up under a tree and hedged round with *Euphorbia* plants. Chal or Chalnad is a god presiding over a group of ten villages, and represented by a black stone set up under a *mukmum* tree. Goats and pigs are the animals usually offered to him, and the sacrifice of a cow, said by Lieutenant Shaw to be performed every three years, seems to have fallen into disuse. Pau-Gosain, the god of highways, lives under a *bel*, *kurare*, or *mukmum* tree. He is invoked by persons going on a journey. When Lieutenant Shaw wrote the offering was a cock. Now it is a white goat, and the sacrifice is said to be a very expensive one, by reason of the large amount of rice-beer—ten or twelve maunds—that must be offered to the god and drunk by his assembled votaries. The tutelary deity of the village, spoken of by Lieutenant Shaw under the name of Dwára Gosain, is now called Bára-Dwári, because he is supposed to live in a temple with twelve doors. The whole village worship him in the month of Mágh. Colonel Dalton suggests that this god may perhaps be the same as the Oraon Dárá. Kul Gosain, 'the Geres of the mountaineers,' and Autga, the god of hunting, appear not to be known at the present day. Gumo Gosain, or the god of the pillar, is represented in every household by the wooden post (*gumo*) which supports the main rafters of the roof. On this the blood of a slain goat is sprinkled to propitiate the spirits of ancestors. The fact that this god is common to the Málés and Mál Pahāriás (see page 70 below), and is worshipped by both in the same way, seems to tell strongly in favour of the common origin of the two tribes. As in Lieutenant Shaw's time, Chamda Gosain still ranks high among the tribe, and demands offerings on a larger scale than any other god. A sacrifice consisting of twelve pigs and twelve goats, with rice, oil and *sindur* in proportion, must put a severe strain on the resources of a Málé villager. In order to commemorate the event, three bamboos decorated with streamers of bark painted black and red at the ends, the natural colour being left in the centre, are set up to represent Chamda Gosain in front of the house of the person who organizes the sacrifice. One bamboo has ninety streamers, another sixty, and the third twenty, and the poles are also decorated with peacock's feathers. The night is spent in dancing, and in the morning sacrifices are offered in the house and in the fields for a blessing on the family and on the crops. The bamboos are then taken inside and suspended from the roof of the house to show that the owner has performed the full sacrifice.

The question whether the Málés have any functionaries who can properly be called priests is in some respects an obscure one. According to Buchanan, they formerly had priests called Naiyas or Laiyas, a designation common enough in Western Bengal, but these, it is said, have now disappeared, and their functions have devolved upon the Demános, who were originally only diviners selected for their supposed intimacy with the spirits, their capacity for going into trances, and so forth, these powers being in some mysterious way bound up with their long hair, which may on no account be cut. More recent observers, however, assure me that the Demáno merely directs religious and ceremonial observances, but does not himself officiate as priest. The duties of priest are discharged by the village headman or the chief member of the household, or by any influential person chosen for the occasion, and the Demáno is merely a spiritual director endowed with certain supernatural powers, such as that of discerning the causes of all diseases, so that when a man falls ill he can say which of the gods has afflicted him and what sort of sacrifice should be offered to bring about his recovery. On the occasions when Chamda Gosain and Gumu Gosain are worshipped, the Demáno is decorated with a necklace of cowrie shells. No Demáno may eat turmeric. Besides the Demáno there is another class of divines called Cherin, whose duty is to select persons to officiate as priests. This he does by balancing a bow on his two hands and watching its oscillations, while he calls out one by one the names of the persons present, the idea being that the god thus signifies from whose hands he wishes to receive the offering. The flesh of the animals offered in sacrifice is eaten by the male worshippers : women may not partake of it.

Disposal of the dead.

As a rule the Málé bury their dead, the corpse being laid on a layer of *bhelak* leaves with the head pointing towards the north. The bodies of those who died of snake-bite or have come to a violent end are exposed in the jungle. According to Colonel Dalton, the bodies of Demános are dealt with in this fashion, on the ground that if they are buried in the village, their ghosts walk and cause annoyance to the living. On the fifth day after death a feast is given, to which all members of the family are invited. Six months or a year later a special ceremony is held for the purpose of appeasing the spirit of the dead man. The chief part is played by the Demáno, who represents the deceased, and is dressed so as to personate him as closely as possible. In this character he demands clothes, ornaments, food and whatever the dead man was fond of in this life, the belief being that if they are given to the Demáno, the spirit will in some unexplained fashion have the use of them in the world of the dead. When the Demáno has got all that he asked for, he goes into a fit and remains insensible for some minutes, during which time he is supposed to be in communication with the spirit of the deceased. On his revival the company partake of a feast.

The property left by the dead man cannot be divided until this second feast has taken place. According to Colonel Dalton, the eldest son takes half, and the remainder is equally divided among the agnates. Some say, however, that division among the sons takes place on a sort of diminishing scale according to order of birth, the eldest getting the largest share, the second less, and so on.

Mode of living.

The Málé villages are usually built on the summits of the range of hills occupied by the tribe. Their houses are constructed of wattled bamboo, the interstices of which are filled with grass, no mud being used. They cultivate by burning the underwood and sowing seed in the ashes, a system usually known as *jhum* or *poráo*, but by them called *kale mandote*, or 'jungle-burning.' Although addicted to this destructive method of agriculture, the Málé are great lovers of trees, which they plant freely on their village sites. In matters of diet they acknowledge none of the restrictions recognized by Hindus. They eat beef, pork, domestic fowls, all kinds of fish, and the leavings of people of other castes, and indulge freely in strong drink.

Male Kumchhá, a *thar* or sept of Khambus in Darjiling.

Malhá, a title of Kaibarttas in Orissa.

Malhán, a section of the Baranwar sub-caste of Baniyás in Behar.

Málhátiá, a *mul* or section of Kesarwáni Baniyás in Behar.

Máli, *Málákár*, a caste employed in making garlands and providing flowers for the service of Hindu temples. In Bengal the caste is included among the Nava-Sákha, and its members profess to trace their descent from the garland maker attached to the household of Rája Kansa of Mathurá, who, when met by Krishna, was asked for a chaplet of flowers and at once gave it. On being told to fasten it with a string, he, for want of any other, took off his sacred thread and tied it, on which Krishna most ungenerously rebuked him for his simplicity in parting with his *paitá*, and announced that for the future his caste would be ranked among the Súdras. Like others of the higher castes, the Málákárs claim to have originally come from Mathurá in the reign of Jahangír. They are few in number, but in every Hindu village there is at least one representative, who provides daily offerings of flowers for the temples and marriage tiaras for the village maidens.

Tradition of origin.

They are divided into two main groups—the **Phulkátá-Máli**, who make ornaments, toys, etc., from the pith of the solá, and the **Dokáne-Máli**, who keep shops. The former group is again broken up into **Rárhi**, **Bárendra**, and **Athghariá**, the last of whom are supposed to be descended from eight families outcasted for some cause now forgotten. Their sections, which are shown in Appendix I, belong to the ordinary Brahmanical series, and are supplemented by the regular rules regarding prohibited degrees. In Dacca, according to Dr. Wise, the caste has only one *gotra*, Alamyán, and two *dals*, or unions, between which there is no real difference. If, however, a member of one union marries into a family belonging to the other, the marriage feast will be more expensive than if he took a bride from his own, as he must invite the members of both *dals* to the ceremony. The bridal dresses must be made of red silk brought from Murshedabad, as cotton cloth is prohibited. The bride is always carried in a pálkí or palanquin, while the bridegroom rides on a pony or in a Sedan chair. Mális marry their daughters as infants, forbid widows to marry again, and do not recognize divorce. If a wife is proved to be unfaithful, she is turned out of the caste, and her husband performs a sort of penance to purify himself from the slur of having associated with her.

Internal structure.

Religion.

The Málákárs are all Vaishnavas by creed, and it is said that none of them worship Siva. A Gosáin is their guru, while their Brahman is common to them and to the Nava-Sákha.

Occupation.

"A Máli will not cultivate with his own hands, and never works as a kitchen-gardener, the gardeners of Bengal being generally Chandáls and Uriyas. Many Mális, however, hold land as occupancy raiyats, which they cultivate by means of hired labourers. In Dacca members of the caste keep shops for piece-goods, practise medicine, act as vaccinators, and take service in temples. Their principal occupations, however, are making wreaths, fabricating artifical chaplets and toys from the pith of the solá (*Hedysarum lagenarium*). The garlands placed every morning before idols are collected and arranged by Málákárs, who nevertheless refuse to paint figures, this being the profession of the Ganak and Rangrez. All the tinsel decorations put on the images and their carriages are designed by Málákárs. At marriages their services are indispensable, for they prepare the crowns (*Mukuta*) worn by the bridal pair. Morover, no bride would consider the attire complete unless her hair was adorned with a Khopajúrá, or ornament for the hair-knot, made with leaves of the jack-tree mixed with white Bela blossoms, while at one side of it they place a rose or some other bright flower. For the bouquet delivered on the bridal morning the Málákár expects to be paid a rupee.

"The profession of a Málákár requires a considerable knowledge of flowers, for some are forbidden to be used in religious services and others can only be exhibited before the shrines of the deities to whom they belong. Thus the 'Dhatúrá' is sacred to Siva; the 'Aparájitá' (*Clitoria ternatea*) to Káli; the 'Bákas' (*Justicia adhatoda*) to Saraswati; and the 'Asoka' (*Jonesia asoca*) to Sashthi. The 'Javá' (*Hibiscus rosa Sinensis*) or China rose is of most unlucky omen, and can only be presented to Káli, but not to other idols, nor employed at weddings.

"Strong scented blossoms are selected for religious offerings, and these in Bengal are the 'Champá' (*Michelia Champaca*), 'Chamelí' (*Jasminum grandiflorum*), 'Juí' (*Jasminum auriculatum*), 'Bela' (*Jasminum Zambac*), 'Gandhráj' (*Gardenia florida*), and the 'Hársingár' (*Nyctanthes arbor tristis*).

"Chaplets offered to idols must be tied with the dried fibres of the plantain stem, not with string, and if picked and arranged by one not a Málákár they are unclean. From sixteen to twenty-four annas a month are received by the garland-maker for providing a daily supply of flowers to a temple; but, as with everything else, the price of bouquets has greatly risen, and a rupee only procures about half the quantity it formerly did.,

"One of the chief occupations of this caste is inoculating for small-pox and treating individuals attacked by any eruptive fever. Hindus believe that Sítalá, the goddess of small-pox, is one of seven sisters, who are designated Motiya, Matariyá, Pakauriya, Masúriká, Chamariya, Khudwá, and Pansá. The first four are varieties of small-pox, the names referring to the form, size, and colour of the pustules; the fifth is *Variola maligna*; the sixth is measles; and the seventh is water-pox. Every Málákár keeps images of one or more of these goddesses, and on the first of Chait (March 15th) a festival is held, and the Málákárs superintend the details. It is popularly called 'Málibágh,' from the garden where the service is performed, and thither Hindus and Muhammadans repair with offerings of clotted milk, cocoanuts, and plantains in the hope of propitiating the dreaded sisters.

"When small-pox rages, the Málákárs are busiest. As soon as the nature of the disease is determined, the Kabíráj retires and a Málákár is summoned. His first act is to forbid the introduction of meat, fish, and all food requiring oil or spices for its preparation. He then ties a lock of hair, a cowrie-shell, a piece of turmeric, and an article of gold on the right wrist of the patient. The sick person is then laid on the 'Májh-pattá,' the young and unexpanded leaf of the plantain tree, and milk is prescribed as the sole article of food. He is fanned with a branch of the sacred *nim*, and any one entering the chamber is sprinkled with water. Should the fever become aggravated and delirium ensue, or if a child cries much and sleeps little, the Máli performs the Máta pujá. This consists in bathing the image of the goddess causing the disease and giving a draught of the water to drink. To relieve the irritation of the skin, pease-meal, turmeric, flour, or shell-sawdust is sprinkled over the body.

"If the eruption be copious, a piece of new cloth in the figure of eight is wrapped round the chest and shoulders. On the night between the seventh and eighth days of the eruption the Máli has much to do. He places a waterpot in the sick room, and puts on it alwá rice, a cocoanut, sugar, plantains, a yellow rag, flowers, and a few *nim* leaves. Having mumbled several *mantras*, he recites the *kissa*, or tale, of the particular goddess, which often occupies six hours.

"When the pustules are mature, the Máli dips a thorn of the karaundá (*Carissa*) in til oil, and punctures each one. The body is then anointed with oil, and cooling fruits given. When the scabs (dewli) have peeled off, another ceremonial, called 'Godám,' is gone through. All the offerings on the waterpot are rolled in a cloth and fastened round the waist of the patient. These offerings are the perquisite of the Máli, who also receives a fee.

"These minute, and to our ideas absurd, proceedings are practised by the Hindus and Muhammadans, including the bigoted Farazi, whenever small-pox or other eruptive fever attacks their families. Government vaccinators earn a considerable sum yearly by executing the Sítalá worship, and when a child is vaccinated a portion of the service is performed."

Social status.

The Mális of Behar hold a respectable position among the castes of that province. They rank with Kumhárs, Koiris, and Kahars, and Brahmans will take water from their hands. The main difference between them and the Bengal Mális is that they practice widow-marriage, and do not take an extreme view of the necessity of getting their daughters married as infants. With this exception, the account given above of the Bengal Mális applies for the most part to the Behar members of the caste.

The following statement shows the number and distribution of Mális in 1872 and 1881 :—

DISTRICT.	1872.	1881.	DISTRICT.	1872.	1881.
Bardwan	3,376	2,171	Chittagong	856	106
Bankura	535	1,634	Noakhali	339	37
Birbhum	886	2,225	Patna	4,996	5,611
Midnapur	6,186	7,942	Gya	8,877	7,671
Hughli	2,652	2,469	Shahabad	3,432	5,109
Howrah		1,163	Tirhut { Mozufferpur ...	16,223	11,543
24-Parganás	2,586	2,390	Tirhut { Darbhanga ...		10,004
Nadiya	2,980	6,345	Saran	4,691	6,909
Khulna	......	2,176	Champaran	4,974	7,367
Jessore	1,811	4,323	Monghyr	5,360	5,249
Murshedabad...	2,483	3,613	Bhagalpur	2,877	4,428
Dinajpur	2,184	3,133	Purniah	4,663	25
Rajshahye	458	890	Maldah	567	883
Rangpur	2,068	1,456	Santál Parganás	1,962	3,728
Bogra	1,075	864	Cuttack	3,346	4,493
Pabna	2,966	1,731	Puri	11,669	11,186
Darjiling	143	220	Balasore	1,306	1,690
Jalpigori	500	980	Tributary States	10,606	9,777
Kuch Behar	......	2,156	Hazaribagh	1,556	2,765
Dacca	2,757	2,769	Lohardagá	5,205	2,750
Faridpur	1,347	2,310	Singbhum	34	2,369
Bakarganj	2,204	1,401	Manbhum	4,105	3,601
Maimansinh	11,836	2,379	Tributary States	224	452
Tipperah	5,244	2,480			

Máli, a synonym for Bhuinmáli; a sept of the Malwe Rájputs in Chota Nagpur.

Malik, a title of Rájputs, Telis and Doms in Behar.

Málik, a title of Kandhs in Orissa.

Malikauliá, a section of Bábhans in Behar.

Malitwár, a section of Bábhans in Behar.

Maljáda, a bastard or son of a harlot.

Málkarnauti, a *mul* or section of the Sátmuliá or Kishnaut subcaste of Goálás in Behar.

Málkas, a section of Oswáls.

Malkhájania, from *malkhájaná*, a payer of land revenue, a zemindar.

Málkiá, a *mul* or section of the Sátmuliá or Kishnaut subcaste of Goálás in Behar.

Malla, wrestler, a title of Khandáits in Orissa and of the Aguri or Ugrakshatri caste in Western Bengal.

Mallabhumia, a sub-caste of Bauris in Western Bengal.

Malláh, *Ar.*, a sailor, a boatman, a generic term current in Behar and Bengal as the popular designation of various boating and fishing castes. Mr. Sherring notices this general use of the word, but adds that there is a special tribe of Mallahs divided into the following sub-castes:—(1) **Mallah**, (2) **Muria** or **Muriári**, (3) **Panduki**, (4) **Bathawa** or **Badhariyá**, (5) **Chaini**, **Chain** or **Chai**, (6) **Suráyá**, (7) **Guriyá**, (8) **Tiar**, (9) **Kulwant** or **Kulwat**, (10) **Kewat**,

He also mentions the tradition that all these "are descended from a common father, by name Nikhád, but that the Kewats alone were born in lawful wedlock." Nikhád is merely a variant for Nishád or Nishada, a Dravidian tribe mentioned in the Rig-Veda, from which several of the fishing castes may possibly derive their origin. It is clear, however, that while the ten groups enumerated by Mr. Sherring may at one time have belonged to a single tribe, that tribe must have broken up some time before the Arabic word *Malláh* can have been current in India long enough to stand any chance of being adopted as a tribal name. If, then, Mr. Sherring's statement is correct, a point on which there is room for some difference of opinion, it merely shows that a certain number of distinct fishing castes believe themselves once to have formed part of a larger group, to which they give the modern name Malláh, a foreign word denoting an occupation, not a caste, and throwing no light on the affinities of the people who use it.

The castes to which the term Malláh is ordinarily applied in Bengal are the following:—Gonrhi, Chain, Bind, Kewat, Tiyar, Muriári, Surahiya, Málo, and Jáliyá Kaibartta.

Mallametiá, *Mátiá*, or *Mátiál*, a sub-caste of Bágdis in Bengal, by profession fishermen and earth-workers.

Mallik, a sub-caste of Máls in Birbhum; an honorary title of Brahmans, Doms, Káyasths, Kaibarttas, and Subarnabaniks in Bengal; a section of the Biyáhut and Kharidáhá Kalwárs and of Mális and Sonárs in Behar.

Malo, a sub-section of the Kautsasa section of Utkal Brahmans.

Málo, a title of the class of Rájputs to which the Raja of Bishenpur claims to belong. It is a plausible conjecture that this name, unheard of among admitted Rájputs, may have arisen from the connexion of the Raja with the Mál tribe, who are numerous in Bankura.

Málo, *Málo-Pátni*, a Dravidian boating and fishing caste, supposed by Buchanan to have come from Western India. This opinion, however, is unsupported by any evidence beyond a resemblance of names, which may be either wholly accidental or may have arisen from the tribal name Málo being confounded with the Arabic word Malláh, 'a boatman.' Dr. Wise considers the three fisher castes—the Kaibartta, Málo, and Tiyar—to be "undoubtedly representatives of the pre-historic dwellers in the Gangetic delta. As a rule they are short and squat, of a dark-brown colour, often verging upon black. Although Hindus by creed, they are fond of showy garments, of earrings, and of long hair, which is either allowed to hang down in glossy curls on their shoulders or fastened in a knot at the back of the head. The whiskers and moustaches are thin and scrubby, the lips often thick and prominent, the nose short with the nostrils expanded. The physiognomy indicates good temper, sensuality, and melancholy rather than intelligence and shrewdness." The sections of the Málos, shown in Appendix I, seem on the whole to bear out the view that

Internal structure.

they are the remnant of a distinct aboriginal tribe, and not merely an occupational group. These sections are peculiar to the Málos, and do not appear to have been borrowed from any other caste. I am unable to analyse them completely, but I venture the conjecture that some of them are totemistic, the totems being the rivers, which the Málos regularly worship. There are no sub-castes. The Rájbansi, which some authorities are disposed to regard as a sub-caste of the Málo, are clearly Kochh, who have taken to fishing, while the Kátar or Bepári Málo, who deal in, but do not catch, fish, and derive their name from their practice of cutting up their wares and selling them by weight, are Muhammadans in no way connected with the Málo caste.

Marriage.

The rule of exogamy is in full force among the Málo. A man may not marry a woman of his own section or of the section to which his mother belongs. For the rest, marriage is regulated by counting degrees down to seven generations in the descending line. Females are married as infants. A price is paid for the bride, which of late years has risen to the large sum of Rs. 100. The ceremony is of the orthodox type, the giving of the bride and the bridegroom's formal acceptance of the gift being the essential and binding portion of the rite. Polygamy is permitted in theory, and a man may marry two sisters, provided that he takes the eldest first. In practice, however, I understand it is unusual to marry a second wife unless the first proves barren. Widows may not marry again, nor is divorce permitted. A woman taken in adultery is abandoned by her husband and turned out of the caste.

Religion.

Málos as a rule belong to the Vaishnava sect. Their *purohit* is a Patit Brahman, and their *guru* a Gosain. Special reverence is paid by them to the great rivers on which they live, and these, together with their boats and nets, have their regular seasons of worship. Khala-Kumári is worshipped in Srávan (July–August), offerings are made to Bura-Buri in fulfilment of vows, and lights are launched on the water in honour of Khwája Khizr.

Disposal of the dead.

The dead are usually burned on the bank of a river, and the ashes cast into the water. *Sráddh* is performed on the thirty-first day after death, then once a month for a year, and again on the first anniversary of the death. Usually, however, the monthly *sráddhs* are lumped together towards the close of the year. In the case of persons who die a violent death, the first *sráddh* is performed on the fourth day, and a final *sráddh* on the thirty-first day.

Social status.

Although the social rank of the Málos is low, and Brahmans will not take water from their hands, the Nápit and Dhobá usually work for them. They are on good terms with the Tiyar and Kaibartta, and members of the three castes will even smoke together. The Málo, however, says Dr. Wise, "is the lowest in rank, while the Kaibartta and Tiyar still dispute about their relative positions. The Kaibartta, again, is more thoroughly Hinduised than either of the other two. A ridiculous distinction is always cited in proof of the inferior rank of the Málo. The Kaibartta and Tiyar in netting always pass the netting needle from above downwards, working from left to right; while the Málo passes it from below upwards, forming his meshes from right to left. It is remarkable that the same difference is adduced by the Behár fisherman as a proof of the degraded rank of the Banpar." The only titles met with among Málos are Mánjhi, Pátra, and Bepári, while among other fisher castes no honorary distinctions exist. Under the Muhamadan Government they served as boatmen, chaprásís, mace-bearers (asabardár), and staff-bearers (sonte-bardár) in processions. They were also employed in conveying treasure from Dacca to Murshedabad, while a tradition still survives that early in this century two of their number became great favourites with Nawáb Nasrat Jang, who presented them with golden spinning wheels for their wives' use. The Málos therefore extol the golden age that has passed, and inveigh against the equality and degeneracy of the present.

Occupation.

Málos generally use a shorter Jalká boat than the Tiyars, but when they fish with the long Uthár net they fasten two boats stem to stern. Like the Kaibartta, the Málo is often a cultivator, and in Bhowál he has been obliged by changes in the course and depth of the rivers to relinquish his caste trade. Málos manufacture twine, but not rope, and traffic in grain, while those who have saved a little money keep grocer's shops or become fishmongers. Málo women sell fish in the bazars, but in some places this practice is considered derogatory to their gentility and is prohibited.

The following statement shows the number and distribution of Málos in 1872 and 1881:—

District.	1872.	1881.	District.	1872.	1881.
Bardwan	9,338	454	Bakarganj	1,751	989
Bankura	6,983	32,079	Maimansinh	13,909	11,454
Birbhum	586	3,158	Tipperah	2,600	1,720
Midnapur	39,804	40,236	Chittagong	525	31
Hughli	} 1,820	{ 2,097	Noakhali	110	......
Howrah		657	Patna	17,559	19,099
24-Parganás	2,338	1,548	Gya	11,518	11,906
Nadiya	13,311	10,672	Shahabad	15,267	14,913
Khulna	......	3,390	Tirhut { Mozufferpur ...	} 159 730	{ 89,273
Jessor	12,600	10,765	Tirhut { Darbhanga ...		115,217
Murshidabad	7,388	7,598	Saran	21,849	22,599
Dinajpur	1,203	1,222	Champaran	15,331	55,222
Rajshahye	1,768	1,484	Monghyr	15,836	21,850
Rangpur	1,392	1,148	Bhagalpur	11,754	18,891
Bogra	3,637	1,120	Purniah	21,016	27,570
Pabna	16,490	6,846	Maldah	1,646	4,281
Darjiling	26	1,175	Santál Parganas	1,865	2,889
Jalpaiguri	251	3	Hazaribagh	1,466	3,475
Kuch Behar	......	133	Lohardaga	7,250	10,924
Dacca	6,437	1,949	Singbhum	...	443
Faridpur	6,033	2,389	Manbhum	1 671	1,918

Málo-Pátni, a synonym for Málo.

Mál Pahária, a Dravidian tribe inhabiting the Rámgarh Hills in the Santál Parganás, who until recently lived by hunting and *jhúm* or *karáo* cultivation. Their tribal affinities are extremely obscure, and have formed

Origin.

the subject of some discussion. Buchanan[1] gives the following account of them:—"The northern tribe[2] consider their southern neighbours as brethren, and call them Maler,[3] the name which they give themselves; but the southern tribe, shocked at the impurity of the others, deny this consanguinity, and most usually call the northern tribe Chet, while they assume to themselves the denomination of Mál or Már, which, however, is probably a word of the same derivation with Maler. The Mál, however, divide themselves into three tribes—Kumárpali, Dángrpali, and Márpali; and they often call the northern mountaineers Sumarpali, thus, as it were, acknowledging a common origin, which I have little doubt is the fact. The manners and language of the three southern Pali are the same, and they speak a very impure dialect of the Bengalese. The three Pali were originally local distinctions, but now all live intermixed, have exactly the same customs and language, and intermarry but there are five real hereditary distinctions, which descend in the male line. The highest rank consists of the Rajas or chiefs and their descendants, all of whom are called Singhas or lions. Next to these are certain families that were at one time rich, and are called Grihi. They assisted their poorer brethren with loans, and seem to have been a kind of bankers, like the Vaisyas of the Hindus. They never seem to have held any office in the State. The third in rank were the Manjhis or chiefs of villages, and none but persons of this rank were ever permitted to hold this office. The persons of the Ahriti or fourth class were by birth hunters, and at first in all probability were the lower and labouring class, like the Sudras of the Hindus; for what is now considered as the lowest and fifth class is composed of the Naiyas, who are allowed to have originally been the priests, but have been totally discarded from that office." Against Dr. Buchanan's description of the Mál Paháriás as a Hinduised branch of the Maler, we have to set Colonel Dalton's opinions[4] that the former tribe "appear to be altogether unconnected with the Rájmahál hillmen," and Mr. Ball's statement,[5] based upon personal observation, that the Mál Paháriás "are altogether distinct in appearance, customs, and language from the Asal Paháriás, who occupy the Rájmahál hills proper." It should be observed, however, that even in Dr. Buchanan's time (1807–1814) a wide breach had been established between the two groups, and the southern Paháriás at least strenuously disowned all kinship with the northern. Sixty years later the breach must have been greatly widened by the Mál Paháriás continually adopting Hindu customs, while the Malés seem to have stubbornly resisted all impulses in that direction, and this movement may possibly account for the impression formed by Mr. Ball. On the question of language the evidence seems to be inconclusive. Colonel Dalton gives a very meagre list of words obtained by Dr. Coates from a Mál Pahária prisoner in the Hazáribágh Central Jail. On this he observes:—"I cannot say I have

[1] *Eastern India*, ii, 126.
[2] The Malés of Rajmahal.
[3] Malér is the plural of Malé.
[4] *Ethnology of Bengal*, p. 274.
[5] *Jungle Life in India*, p. 229.

found in it analogues sufficient to justify its association with the Dravidian dialects, but it is equally unlike Kol."[1] A comparison of the list with Mr. Droese's Malto Vocabulary shows, however, that some slight correspondence may be traced between the language of the Malé and the mongrel dialect spoken by the Mál Pahárias. Thus, *chapta*, 'the foot'; Malto, sole of the foot: *ekore*, 'to go'; Malto, *eke*: *tindiáná*, 'to eat,' seems to be a causal formed in Hindi fashion from the Malto *tinde*, 'to feed:' *maler*, 'a man,' is the nominative plural of *male*: *bátker*, 'a woman,' and *batker*, 'a daughter,' are curiously like the Malto *baty*, 'virginal,' and *bátgni*, 'a maiden': *chichu* is the Malto word for fire: *amma* is not far removed from *amu*, the Malto for water: *chiore*, 'to give,' appears to be from the same root as *chiye*: *malaga*, 'no,' merely adds a syllable to the Malto *mala*: and *kúkrá*, 'a cock,' may perhaps be connected with the Malto *kúkre*, 'to cry out.' These slight resemblances of course fall far short of establishing the identity of the two tribes, but they tend on the whole to show that Buchanan's opinion is not so clearly untenable as has been sometimes supposed to be the case. Mr. Droese, with whom I discussed the subject some years ago, considered the two tribes to be of common origin. This view is borne out by the fact that they understand one another's language readily, though they assert that the dialects are different; as well as by the identity of their ancestral worship, a point in which all races display a remarkably conservative spirit. As for the antagonism which at present prevails between the north and south Pahárias, it is only another instance of what has been commonly observed in Chota Nagpur, that two sections of the same tribe which in any way happen to become separated are often far more strongly opposed to one another than if they had been originally distinct tribes.

Internal structure.

The Mál Pahárias are divided into two sub-tribes—Mál Pahária proper and Kumár or Komar-Bhág. The latter group, which corresponds with Buchanan's Kumárpali, is the more Hinduised of the two. The septs are given in Appendix I. They appear to be identical with Buchanan's "hereditary distinctions." He would doubtless have discovered the fact that they are exogamous had the subject of exogamy attracted any attention at the time when he wrote. Their names are apparently titular, and throw no light upon the affinities of the tribe. The Mál Pahárias also observe a table of prohibited degrees, which differs little from that defined by the standard formula referred to in the article on Bais. They have no traditions worth mentioning, except a vague legend that their first parents were born from a cow. The same story is told of the ancestor of the Pachete family in Manbhum, whose estate borders on the country where the Mál Pahárias are now found. It is possible, indeed, that the Pachete Ráj may in early times have extended further to the east, and that the head of that house may have been the Raja of whom Buchanan speaks as having formerly appointed from among the Mál

[1] *Ethnology of Bengal*, p. 274.

Pahárias a dewan, a faujdár to command in predatory expeditions, and the mánjhis or headmen of villages. This, however, is the purest conjecture. The tendency to borrow a myth current in a landholding family may be frequently observed in Chota Nagpur.

Marriage.

Marriage is either infant or adult. Girls are rarely married before the age of ten or eleven, and usually not until they are fully grown up. In the latter case sexual intercourse before marriage is tacitly recognized, it being understood that if an unmarried girl becomes pregnant her lover will come forward and marry her. A professional match-maker (*sithu*) is usually employed by the bride groom's people to search for a suitable wife. When his selection has been made, a visit of inspection is paid by the parents; and if the proposed bride is approved of, the price to be paid for her is settled by personal discussion. Custom ordains that the amount shall be an *odd* number of rupees, not less than five, nor more than twenty-five. It must be paid either in a lump sum or by instalments before the marriage can be celebrated. On the occasion of the final payment the bridegroom's parents send by the *sithu* some *bájrá* beer and a *sári* for the bride, which is made over to her maternal uncle to be kept till the day of the wedding. Particular inquiries were made regarding the reason for thus selecting the maternal uncle as a sort of trustee for the bride's *peculium*, but no definite result was arrived at; and this usage, undoubtedly one of great antiquity, seems only to be explicable as a survival of female kinship, a system of which no other traces are met with in the tribe. Shortly after the bride-price has been paid, the *sithu* is again sent to the bride's house, this time bearing an arrow wound round with yellow thread tied in as many knots as there are days to the date proposed for the wedding. The bride's people make their preparations accordingly, undoing a knot as each day passes. On the day before the bridegroom arrives and is lodged near the bride's house. Early next morning a big feast is given, after which the bridegroom takes his seat facing the east in a sort of arbour of *sál* branches built for the purpose. Here he is joined by the bride, dressed, like him, in a new cotton wrapper dyed yellow with turmeric, who sits besides him while the maidens of his company comb out her hair. A *sál* leaf cup is offered to the bridegroom, containing red lead, which he daubs on the bride's forehead and the parting of her hair. The girls who combed the bride's hair take her hand, dip a finger into the red lead, and make seven spots on the bridegroom's forehead. This final and binding rite is received with a shout of applause, which is the signal for the Dom musicians in attendance to beat the drums for a dance. Towards evening the wedded pair go off to the bridegroom's house, where the whole party spend the night in dancing and drinking. Polygamy is permitted, and, in theory at least, there are no restrictions on the number of wives a man may have. Practically, however, the poverty of the tribe and their hand-to-mouth fashion of living set strict limits to the exercise of this right, and few Pahárias indulge themselves with the luxury of a second wife, except when the first happens to be barren. A man may marry two sisters, but he must follow the order of age, and if already married to a younger sister, may not take an elder sister to wife.

A widow may marry again. She is expected to marry her late husband's younger brother if there is one; but if he does not wish to marry her, any member of the caste not barred by the prohibited degrees may have her on paying a bride-price of Rs. 2 to her late husband's relatives. No ceremony is required, nor is *sindur* used. The husband merely gives the woman a new cloth and takes her to his house. A wife may be divorced with the sanction of the caste council or pancháyat for adultery or persistent and incurable ill-temper. As a rule arrangements of this sort are effected by mutual consent, the parties tearing a *sál* leaf in two before the pancháyat as a symbol of separation. The seducer of a married woman is required to repay to her husband the sum which she cost him as a virgin. Divorced wives may marry again in the same manner as widows, and for the same bride-price, which is paid to their own, not to their late husband's relations.

Religion.

At the head of the Pahariá religion stands the sun, to whom reverential obeisance is made morning and evening. On occasional Sundays a special worship is performed by the head of the family, who must prepare himself for the rite by eating no salt on the previous Friday and fasting all Saturday, with the exception of a light meal of molasses and milk, taken at sunset after bathing. Before sunrise on Sunday morning a new earthen vessel, a new basket, some rice, oil, areca nuts, and vermilion, and a brass *lota* of water with a mango branch stuck in it, are laid out on a clean space of ground in front of the house. The worshipper shows these offerings to the rising sun and prays, addressing the luminary as 'Gosain,' that he and his family may be saved from any specific danger or trouble that is supposed to threaten them. The rice is then given to a goat, which is decapitated while eating by a single blow from behind. The body of the animal is then cooked and served up at a feast, of which the neighbours partake; the head alone, which is deemed *prasád*, or sacred, being carefully reserved for the members of the family. Next in honour to the sun are Dharti Mái, mother earth; her servant, or as some say sister, Garámi; and Singhbáhini, who bears rule over tigers, snakes, scorpions, and all manner of noxious beasts. To the earth goats, pigs, fowls, etc., are offered in Ashar and Magh, and buffaloes or goats are sacrificed about the time of the Hindu Durga Pujá to the goddess Singhbáhini, who is represented for sacrificial purposes by a lump of clay daubed with vermilion and oil and set up in front of the worshipper's house. The village Mánjhi officiates as priest. The Mágh worship of Dharti Mái is clearly the festival described by Colonel Dalton under the name Bhuindeb, the earth god.[1]

"The Máls plant in their dancing place two branches of the *sál* tree, and for three days they dance round these branches, after which they are removed and thrown into a river, which reminds one of

[1] *Ethnology of Bengal*. p. 274.

the Karma festivals as solemnised by the Oraons and Kols in Chota Nagpur. On this occasion the men and women dance *vis-à-vis* to each other, the musicians keeping between. The men dance holding each other above their elbows, the left hand of one holding the right elbow of the other, whose right hand again holds the left elbow of the arm that has seized him. The fore-arms touching are held stiffly out and swayed up and down. They move sideways, advance, and retire, sometimes bending low, sometimes erect. The women hold each other by the palms, interlacing the fingers, left palm upon right palm, and left and right fore-arms touching. They move like the men."

Two curious points may be added. The man at whose instance or for whose benefit the ceremony is performed must sleep the night before on a bed of straw; and the dancing party, who are greatly excited with drink, shout continually *búr*, *búr* (*pudendum muliebre*), a mode of invocation believed to be especially acceptable to the goddess. In this somewhat indelicate cry we may perhaps see a barbarous and undraped reference to the *vis genetrix naturæ* so prominent in many early forms of belief.

Besides these greater elemental deities, the Mál Pahárias recognize and propitiate a number of vaguely-defined animistic powers, chief among whom is Chordánu, a malevolent spirit, needing to be appeased at certain intervals with sacrifices and the first fruits of whatever crop is on the ground. To the same class belongs Mahádáná, for whom eggs are the appropriate offering. Among the standard Hindu deities Kali and Lakhi Mai (Lakshmi) are honoured with sparing and infrequent worship, the offerings in this case being the perquisite of the village headmen.

Ancestor worship is in full force, and the *sacra privata* of a Mál Pahária household correspond precisely with those observed by the Málé tribe. The Lares are known to both by the familiar term Gumo Gosain or Deota, the gods of the wooden pillar (*Gumo*),[1] which supports the main rafters of the house. Around this centre are grouped a number of balls of hardened clay, representing the ancestors of the family, to whom the first fruits of the earth are offered, and the blood of goats or fowls poured forth at the foot of the pillar that the souls may not hunger in the world of the dead. As every household is guarded by its ancestral gods, so every village has a tutelary deity of its own—*Larem agri custodem*, who lives in a *sál* tree within the village. This tree is daubed with red lead and worshipped on certain occasions, and may on no account be cut down. The tribe have no priests, and the head of the household or village, as the case may be, performs all religious and ceremonial observances. Brahmans, however, are to some extent held in honour, and presents are given to them on festal occasions.

Disposal of the dead.

The dead are usually burned, and a piece of bone is saved from the flames to be thrown into a river or a deep tank the waters of which do not run dry. The relatives are deemed impure, and may not eat salt for five days. At

---

[1] The word is Malto.

the end of that time they are shaved, and partake of a feast provided by the eldest son. The funeral expenses are a first charge on the estate, and after these have been paid the balance is equally divided among the sons, daughters getting no share. Very poor persons, who cannot afford to give a feast, bury their dead in a recumbent position with the head towards the south, and give nothing but a little salt and meal (*sattu*) to the friends who attend the funeral. In Buchanan's time it was the universal custom to bury the dead on the day of death. No *sráddh* is performed by the Mál Pahāriás proper, but some of the wealthier members of the Kumár Bhág sub-tribe are beginning to adopt a meagre form of this ceremony in imitation of their Hindu neighbours.

Occupation.

The tribe believe *jhúm* tillage and hunting to be their original occupations, and a large proportion of the tribe still adhere to these primitive modes of livelihood. Their system of *jhúm* cultivation is thus described by Buchanan :—"On the hills the *bári* is neither ploughed nor hoed. The men cut the trees and burn them, and the women sow the seed. In the first year they scatter over the surface seed of the kinds of millet called *kheri* and *kangni*, and with a stick pointed with iron (*khantá*) form small holes, in which they drop seed of maize, *janirá*, and a pulse called *borá* or *kalai*. In the second year they plant only maize and *janirá*." By the third year the land is worked out, and the cultivator must seek a fresh patch of jungle for his operations. A large tract of hill land is therefore required to keep a Pahāriá village going. Buchanan observed that although their progress in agriculture was greater than that of their northern neighbours, their huts were much more wretched and dirty, their clothing more scanty, and their women less cleanly and worse provided with ornaments. In bad seasons they supplement their scanty food-supply with jungle roots and herbs, of which, like the Sikkim Lepchas, they have a minute empirical knowledge. Of late years many have taken to plough cultivation at the foot of the hills, where they hold land as occupancy raiyats at the rents fixed in the current settlement. Standing as they do wholly outside the regular caste system, they can hardly be said to have any social status in the ordinary sense of that phrase. From the Hindu point of view their diet is certainly unclean, for pork, fowls, and all kinds of fish are deemed lawful food; but the fact of their abstaining from beef, snakes, lizards, and field-rats would probably lead the average Hindu to regard them as a shade purer than the Málés and their congeners the Oraons.

Mál Pahāriá proper, a sub-tribe of Mál Pahāriás in the Santál Parganás.

Málpánj, a section of Mahesris in Behar.

Malta, a sept of Chiks in Chota Nagpur.

Maluá, *Máluá*, a sub-caste of Bauris in Western Bengal whose original residence is said to have been Manbhum; a section of Chiks or Páns in Chota Nagpur; a sub-tribe of Kandhs in Orissa.

Máluá or **Manuá**, a sub-caste of Karangás in Western Bengal.

Malwar, a class of braziers who make *kháru* and other brass ornaments for the hand.

Malwe or **Már-Rájput,** a sub-tribe of Rájputs in Chota Nagpur.

Mán, a title of Bangaja Káyasths in Bengal.

Mana, a title of Dakshin-Rárhi and Bangaja Káyasths.

Mananmanáras, a *mul* or section of the Chhamuliá Madhesiá sub-caste of Halwáis in Behar.

Manár, a title of Cheros in Chota Nagpur.

Manariá, a section of Bábhans in Behar.

Manchhihá, Manchiá, a *kul* or section of Bábhans in Behar.

Mándái, a synonym for Kochh.

Mandal, (i) a headman of a village; (ii) a title of Kaibarttas, Chandals, Goálás, Sunris, Sadgops, Telis, Tantis, and Báuris; of Nápits, Kurmis, Kapális, Pods, Santáls, and Subarnabaniks; (iii) a sub-caste of Dhánuks in Purniah. Some Brahmans in Bankura bear the title; of Rájputs in Behar; a title of Khambus in Darjiling.

Mandap, a section of Kumhárs in Singbhum.

Mandar, probably a variant of Mandal, a title of cultivating Dhánuks; a *pangat* or section of Dosadhs and Kadars; a title of the Cháb and Kurin sub-castes of Gonrhis; a title of the Maghayá sub-caste of Koiris and Telis; a section of the Chaubhán sub-caste of Nuniyás and of Sunris and Khatwes in Behar; a section of the Kanaujiá sub-caste of Goálás and a title of Kishnaut Goálás in Behar; a title of Gangotás and Kewats and of Kharwárs in Lohardagá.

Mandaráná, a sub-caste of Sutradhars in Western Bengal.

Mandárane, a sub-caste of Sunris in Western Bengal.

Mandari, a title of Hindu Joláhas in Behar.

Mándároná, a group of the Áswini Tántis and of Dwádas Telis in Bengal; a sub-caste of Doms in Bengal.

Mándhayá, a section of Goálás in the North-Western Provinces and Behar.

Mándiár, a sept of Rájputs in Behar.

Mandilwar, a section of the Amashta sub-caste of Káyasths in Behar.

Manding, *man,* medicine, a practiser of medicine, a sub-sept of the Nah-pá sept of Sherpa Bhotias.

Mandrá, a section of Bábhans in Behar.

Mandri, a section of the Kádar caste in Behar.

Mandriár, a section of Mahilis in Chota Nagpur.

Mandus, a title of Ganjwár Sunris in Behar.

Manem-ma, a sept of the Phágu sub-tribe of Yakhas in Darjiling.

Maner, a section of the Sátmuliá Maghayá sub-caste of Kándus in Behar.

Manerar, a section of Awadhiá Hajjáms in Behar.

Maneriá, a section of the Biyáhut and Kharidáhá Kalwárs in Behar.

Mángaf, a section of the Biyáhut and Kharidáhá Kalwárs in Behar.

Mangal, a section of the Agarwála caste in Behar.

Mangar, crocodile. a totemistic section of Kurmis in Chota Nagpur and Orissa; a section of Binjhiás in Chota Nagpur.

Mangar, *Magar*, *Thomi*, one of the fighting tribes of Nepal, belonging, with the Gurung Khas and Sunuwar, to the Mukhya group, and highly esteemed for their military qualities. The Mangars believe their original *habitat* to have been the valley of Dhoreh on the banks of the Karnali-Bheri river in Western Nepal: thence they spread to Likhukhola, and thus gradually made their way into Eastern Nepal. The internal structure of the tribe, so far as I have been able to ascertain it, is shown in tabular form in Appendix I. The subject, however, is an extremely obscure one, and I am not yet in a position to throw much light upon it. There are four sub-tribes—**Athárah Panth**, **Burathoki**, **Gharti**, and **Sakhali**. The Gharti are probably descended from emancipated slaves (see article **Gharti**); the origin of the rest is uncertain. The exogamous septs are very numerous, and the list given in Appendix I contains many names of the territorial type common in India along with others which seem to be nicknames of the founders of septs, such as are found among the Tibetans and Limbus. Judged by their physical characteristics, the Mangars must be classed as Mongoloid, their naso-malar index being slightly lower than that of the Tibetans, while their complexion, eyelids, stature and the general cut of their features stamp them as a cross in which the Mongolian element on the whole predominates. The septs are exogamous, the rule being that a man may not marry a woman of his own sept. There seem to be no rules excluding more than one sept in marriage. Prohibited degrees are reckoned by the standard formula for three generations in the descending line.

Origin and internal structure.

Girls are married after they attain maturity, and sexual license before marriage is tolerated on the understanding that if a girl becomes pregnant, the father of her child shall at once be called upon to marry her. The marriage ceremony is of the Hindu type, *sindurdán*, or the smearing of vermilion on the bride's forehead, being its binding portion. Brahmans usually officiate, but this is not essential. A man may marry two or three wives, the only limit in practice being his ability to maintain them. A widow may not marry again by the standard ritual (*byáh*) appointed for the wedding of a spinster, but a man may take her to live with him, and she is counted as his wife. Her children by her second husband are considered legitimate; they rank as Mangars (instead of belonging to a special category like the offspring of Brahman widows in Nepal), and they share

Marriage.

in their father's property on equal terms with the children of a wife married in the regular form. Moreover, if any one runs away with a widow, he has to pay damages to the man she is living with just as if she were his regular wife. In Nepal husbands are entitled to wreak summary vengeance on the seducers of their wives. An adulterer taken in the act is killed offhand, and the faithless wife has her nose cut off. In such cases the question of divorce clearly does not arise. But in British territory, and I believe frequently in Nepal itself, disagreements of this sort are settled without resort to bloodshed. The wife goes off with her paramour, and the husband claims from the latter as damages the amount of the bride-price which he paid for the woman in the first instance. The pancháyat enforces his claim, and justice is held to have been satisfied.

Religion.

The religion of the Mangars may best be described as lax Hinduism tempered by survivals of an earlier animistic cult. Satya Narain is one of their favourite deities. Sansári and Aitâbáreh are also worshipped with offerings of goats, fowls and pigeons. Upadhya Brahmins assist at the cult of Satya Narain and of the recognized Hindu gods; but Sansari and Aitábáreh are worshipped by the heads of households without the assistance of priests. Brahmans are not held to be degraded by serving as priests in Mangar families.

Disposal of the dead.

The funeral ceremonies of the Mangars, which are the same as those of the Gurung and Sunuwars, are curious and interesting. Immediately after death the corpse is tied with three pieces of rope to a stout pole and carried to the grave. There it is stripped, dressed in new clothes, and laid on its back in the grave with the head pointing to the north. The forehead is smeared with sandal wood paste. One of the maternal relatives of the deceased, usually the maternal uncle, is then chosen to act as priest for the occasion, and to conduct the ritual appointed for the propitiation of the dead. First of all he puts in the mouth of the corpse some silver coins and some coral, which is greatly prized by the Himalayan races. Then he lights a wick soaked in clarified butter, touches the lips with fire, scatters some parched rice about the mouth, and lastly covers the face with a cloth called *pujunri*. Two bits of wood, about three feet long, are set up on either side of the grave. In the one are cut nine steps or notches forming a ladder for the spirit of the dead to ascend to heaven ; on the other every one present at the funeral cuts a notch to show that he has been there. As the maternal uncle steps out of the grave, he bids a solemn farewell to the dead and calls upon him to ascend to heaven by the ladder that stands ready for him. When the earth has been filled in, the stick notched by the funeral party is taken away to a distance and broken in two pieces, lest by its means the dead man should do the survivors a mischief. The pole used to carry the corpse is also broken up, and the spades and ropes are left in the grave.

When the mourners return home, one of their party goes ahead and makes a barricade of thorn bushes across the road midway between the grave and the house of the deceased. On the top of the thorns he puts a big stone on which he takes his stand, holding a pot of burning incense in his left hand and some woollen thread in his right. One by one the mourners step on the stone and pass through the smoke of the incense to the other side of the thorny barrier. As they pass, each takes a piece of thread from the man who holds the incense and ties it round his neck. The object of this curious ceremony is to prevent the spirit of the dead from coming home with the mourners and establishing itself in its old haunts. Conceived of as a miniature man, it is believed to be unable to make its way on foot through the thorns, while the smell of the incense, to which all spirits are highly sensitive, prevents it from surmounting this obstacle on the shoulders of one of the mourners.

Occupation and social status.

Agriculture, trade and soldiering are the chief occupations of the Mangars, but no means of earning a livelihood comes amiss to them, provided that it does not involve doing things which are recognized as the proper business of the lower castes. They abstain from beef, but eat pork and domestic fowls, and indulge freely in strong drink. Before marriage a Mangar will eat any sort of food with a Gurung or Khas, but after he has been married, he can only take chupatties from these castes, and may not take rice or dál. Mangars smoke in the same hookah with Gurungs, Khas and Brahmans.

Mangaráj, a title of Khandáits in Orissa.

Mán-Gauránga, a sub-caste of Sutradhars in Murshedabad.

Mang-beh-pá, a *rui* or sept of Dejong Lhori Bhotias, the members of which are of a low mixed origin.

Manglagpa, a sept of the Pánthar sub-tribe of Limbus in Darjiling, whose ancestor was ridden by a god and danced.

Mangmu, a sept of the Yangorup sub-tribe of Limbus in Darjiling.

Mangoyak, a sept of Limbus in Darjiling.

Mangráti, a section of Kámis in Darjiling.

Mangrauni, a section of Bábhans in Behar.

Mangthong, a sept of the Phágu sub-tribe of Yakhas in Darjiling.

Mang-tshang-wa, a *rui* or sept of the Ruichhung sub-tribe of Dejong Lhoris or Bhotias of the south.

Mangyong, a sept of Limbus in Darjiling.

Manháriá, shopkeepers who deal in miscellaneous goods, chiefly fancy articles.

Mani, a sub-caste of Sunris in Maldah.

Manihári, a functional group of Jugis in Bengal.

Manikchakdudhpurá, a *mul* or section of the Naomuliá or Majraut sub-caste of Goálás in Behar.

Mánikmahanta, *Mánikmanta*, a title of Kurmis.

Manikshariá, a section of Bábhans in Behar.

Manimanáras, a section of Madhesiá Halwáis in Behar.

Manjar, cat, a totemistic section of Rautiás and a sept of Kharwars in Chota Nagpur.

Manjari, a section of Kámárs in Singbhum and the Santál Parganás.

Manjhal-Turiyá, a sub-caste of Lohárs in Chota Nagpur.

Manjhan, the title of the headman of the Tior and Dom castes in Behar who has under him a messenger bearing the title of *Chharidár*. The Maghaya Barhis and the Aráiyá Telis of North Bhágalpur also have headmen bearing this title. In the case of the latter the jurisdiction of each *manjhan* is said to extend to 22 villages.

Mánjhi, (i) the steersman of a boat, a ferryman: hence, a boatman generally. (ii) A village headman among the Santáls, and a title by which Santáls frequently describe themselves in answer to inquiries as to their caste. (iii) A title used by the Kaibartta, Kahár, Kumhár, Teor, Patni, Kochh, Bágdi, Málá, Jeliá, Goálá, the Máls of the Rájmahál hills, the Khetauris in the Santál Parganás: a section of Sunris in Behar; a title and a sept of Bauris and Kharwars; a title of Asuras, and Korwas in Chota Nagpur; a sept of Nágesars in Chota Nagpur; a title of Binjhiá, Rautiá, Oraon, Turi; a title of Kapális and Kawális in Eastern Bengal; a section of Kádars; a title of Málos in Eastern Bengal; of Parhaiyas and Khandáits in Chota Nagpur; a section of Doms and Dosádhs in Behar; a title of Cheros and Mahilis; a title and a sept of Mál Paháriás; a title of Tántis in Behar.

Manjhiá, a sub-tribe of Kharwárs in Southern Lohardagá.

Mánjhi-Khil, a sub-sept of the Hansda, Marndi, and Tudu septs of Santáls.

Mánki, *Mánki Sáhib,* an honorific title bestowed in Bankura on the eldest son of a well-to-do cultivator of the Bhumij tribe. In Chotá Nagpur Proper the term denotes the headman of a group or circle of villages. It is also the designation of a sept and a sub-tribe of Mundas. See **Murá**.

Mánná, a title of Kaibarttas, Mayarás, and Nápits in Bengal.

Manoharshahi, a group of the Fatehsing Telis in Murshedabad; a sub-caste of Kotáls in Western Bengal.

Manrayạ, a *kul* or section of Bábhans in Behar.

Mantiáni, a title of the Bárui caste in Bengal.

Mantrawár, a section of Kurmis in Chota Nagpur and Orissa.

Már, *Málwé Rajput*, a small cultivating caste of Chota Nagpur, who say that they came from Malwa and were formerly Kshatriyas, but dropped the sacred thread and took to the plough. Colonel Dalton thought them 'more Aryan than anything else, with a dash of aboriginal blood.' But if this view be correct, it seems difficult to account for their abandoning the characteristic Rájput sept names and adopting the totems peculiar to Dravidian tribes 'They have Brahmans for priests, worship the host of Hindu gods, and, like the Kandhs, especially adore those among their ancestresses who became Sátis, though in their present degraded state they allow of widow-marriage, and a man always takes to wife, by the custom called *sagai*, his elder brother's widow.'

Már, rice broth, a totemistic sept of Mundas in Chota Nagpur.

Marai, a wild animal, a totemistic sept of Páns and Gonds in Chota Nagpur.

Maraiá, a section of the Kádar caste in Behar.

Maraiya, a title of Barhis in Behar.

Maralbai, a sept of Rájputs in Behar.

Máramagri, *Rájbansi*, *Baruá* or *Bhuiyá Magh*, a sub-tribe of Maghs in the Hill Tracts of Chittagong.

Marandi, a sept of Santáls.

Marar, a title of Kumhárs and Tántis in Behar; a title of Surahiyás, Tiyars, Kewats, and of Gareris; a section of the Bánsphor sub-caste of Doms in Behar.

Marár, a title of Amáts in Behar, indicating some degree of social importance and deemed superior to either Ráut or Khawas; a title of Sunris, Jolhas; a title of the headmen of the Dom caste in Behar who have under them servants called Chharidárs to execute or communicate their orders; a title of the Dhusiá sub-caste of Chamárs; a title of the Majraut sub-caste of Goálás; a section of the Játhot division of the Párbatti-Kurin sub-caste of Gonrhis; a title applied in Behar to Kurmis who by age or personal influence have attained a leading position in their villages; a title of Beldárs and Nuniás.

Marare-Sihaul, a *mul* of the Kásyap section of Maithil Brahmans in Behar.

Marare-Jagaul, a *mul* of the Kásyap section of Maithil Brahmans in Behar.

Marare-Ukki, a *mul* of the Kásyap section of Maithil Brahmans in Behar.

Marare-Barhampur, a *mul* of the Kásyap section of Maithil Brahmans in Behar.

Marare-Adauri, a *mul* of the Kásyap section of Maithil Brahmans in Behar.

Marare-Misrauli, a *mul* of the Kásyap section of Maithil Brahmans in Behar.

Marare-Rajaurá, a *mul* of the Kásyap section of Maithil Brahmans in Behar.

Marare-Jagatpur, a *mul* of the Kásyap section of Maithil Brahmans in Behar.

Mardahá, a *pangat* or section of Dosádhs in Behar.

Mardaniá, barbers, a sept of the Rautár sub-tribe of Thárus in Behar.

Márh, a title of Kaibarttas in Bengal.

Márhwár, a sept of Rájputs in Behar.

Maria, a sept of Chiks in Chota Nagpur.

Mariáli, a sub-caste of Tántis in Bengal.

Mariár, a sept of Rájputs in Behar.

Marich-bhuswal, a section of Sonárs in Behar.

Marichigrám, a *samáj* or local group of the Sábarna *gotra* of

Páschátya Baidik Brahmans in Bengal.

Marichwár, a sub-tribe of Thárus in Behar.

Marik, a title of Tántis and a section of the Bánsphor sub-caste of Doms in Behar.

Márik, a title of Báruis in Bengal; a section of the Kádar caste in Behar which intermarries with the Bárik, Kápari, Mánjhi, Mandar, and Naiyá sections, but not with the rest; a title of Hindu Jolhas, Doms, Dosádhs, Goálás, Koiris, Kumhárs, and other castes in Behar.

Marj-bhuswal, a section of Sonárs in Behar.

Markam, a sept of Goálás in Chota Nagpur.

Márkanda, Márkandárk, a *pur* or section of Sákadwipi Brahmans in Behar.

Márkande, a small cultivating caste found in Bhágalpur and the Santál Parganás. They have neither sub-castes nor sections, and I can find no evidence tending to affiliate them with any existing caste or tribe. Their own tradition is that they are descended from Márkandeya Muni, a sage who was outcasted for eating the leavings of certain Brahmans who had invited him to a feast.

Origin.

The Márkande practise infant-marriage and allow polygamy without setting any definite limit on the number of wives a man may have. Widows may marry again, and enjoy full freedom of choice in selecting a second husband. Divorce is not recognized. A faithless wife is simply turned out of the caste.

Marriage.

In matters of religious and ceremonial observances the Márkande exhibit little divergence from the standard of orthodox Hinduism. In the worship of the greater gods they employ Brahman *purohits*, who are not held to be degraded by serving the caste in this capacity. The minor god Karmani is worshipped by the members of the household without the assistance of priests.

Religion.

In point of social standing Márkandes rank with Goalas, Kurmis, and Koiris. Brahmans will take water and certain kinds of sweetmeats from their hands. Their sole occupation is agriculture. The bulk of the caste are occupancy raiyats, but some have risen to the position of tenure-holders.

Social status.

The following statement shows the number and distribution of the Márkande caste in 1872 and 1881:—

District.	1872.	1881.
Shahabad	6	......
Darbhanga	......	5
Monghyr	5,780	1,983
Bhagalpur	3,587	3,384
Purniah	6,561	3,598
Santál Parganás	3,044	4,390

Márkandeya, a *gotra* or section of the Baidya caste in Bengal.

Marli, a sept of Hos and Santáls.

Marmá, *Myammá* or *Roáng Magh*, a sub-tribe of Maghs in the Hill Tracts of Chittagong.

Marmu, a sept of Mundas in Chota Nagpur.

Márndi, grass, a totemistic sept of Santáls.

Marotsa, a sept of Maghs in the Hill Tracts of Chittagong.

Márre, a section of Bábhans in Behar.

Marri, a section of Máhilis in Manbhum, the members of which do not allow their daughters to enter their houses after marriage.

Marrik, a section of Rajwárs in Western Bengal.

Marsyángdi, a *thar* or sept of Mangars in Darjiling.

Marturiá, a section of Lohárs in Behar.

Maruá, a *mul* or section of the Chhamuliá Madhesiá sub-caste of Halwáis in Behar.

Maruá, *Maruábádi* (*maruá* = Indian corn (*Eleusine corocana*) and *ábádi* = cultivator), a contemptuous epithet applied to Hindustanis and especially to up-country boatmen who ply on the Bengal rivers on account of their stupidity in comparison with Bengalis.

Maruáhá, a *mul* or section of the Tinmuliá Madhesiá sub-caste of Halwáis in Behar.

Maruiporá, a sub-caste of Brahmans in Bengal, who have degraded themselves by officiating as priests at the funerals of Sudras.

Marwahe, a section of the Bahánnajáti sub-caste of Khatris in Bengal.

Márwári, literally a native of Málwa or Márwár. Most of the Márwáris found in Bengal are bankers and traders, usually Jains. The name gives no definite indication of caste, but it will be found as a rule that a Márwári belongs to the Agarwal, Oswal, Maheswari, or Srimal castes. In fact all traders from Rajputana and the neighbouring districts are commonly called Márwáris.

Máryá, a small iron-working caste, possibly of Dravidian descent, found in the Santál Parganas. The information at my disposal does not warrant any conjecture regarding their origin. So far as I can ascertain, they have neither sub-castes nor sections, and their marriages are regulated by a very rough enumeration of prohibited degrees, which admits of intermarriage between persons descended from the same parents after the expiry of three generations on the father's side and one on the mother's. Daughters are married either as infants or as adults, and polygamy is allowed without any theoretical limitation on the number of wives a man may take. Widows may marry again, but are under no restriction in their choice of a second husband. Divorce is permitted for adultery or for inability to agree, and divorced women may marry again.

Marriage.

Máryás profess to be Hindus, but they do not employ Brahmans for religious and ceremonial purposes, and the functions of the priest are discharged by selected members of the caste The dead are burned and the ashes

Religion.

buried, but no regular *sráddh* is performed, and the only funeral observance consists of a feast given to the caste brethren by a man's heir ten days after his death.

Social status. The caste ranks with Lohárs, Chamárs, and the lowest grades of Dravidian Hindus. They eat fowls and indulge freely in spirituous and fermented liquors. Iron-working is believed to be their original occupation, and most of them are blacksmiths at the present day. Some, however, have taken to cultivation, and a few are said to have risen to the comparatively high position of tenure-holders.

The Census Report of 1881 returned 857 Máryás in the Santál Parganás.

Masálchi, a title of Bágdis, probably arising from their employment as palanquin-bearers, one of the duties of a bearer being to carry a torch. It is also possible that the term may denote an office held by the Bagdi caste under one of the Rajas of Western Bengal.

Masanta, a title of Tilis in Bengal.

Masáre keraut, a section of the Biyáhut and Kharidáhá Kalwárs in Behar.

Másaur, a section of the Sátmulia Maghayá sub-caste of Kándus in Behar.

Masawár, a sub-caste of Kumhárs in Chota Nagpur and Behar.

Máschatak, a *gáin* of the Sándilya *gotra* of Rárhi Brahmans in Bengal.

Máski, a *thar* or sept of Mangars in Darjiling.

Másle, a sub-caste of Telis in Bengal.

Masnath, a sub-caste of Telis in Behar.

Maurakhiyá, a section of the Bánsphor sub-caste of Doms in Behar.

Mastán, Mahasthán or **Háliá**, a sub-caste of Utkal Brahmans.

Másya, a functional group of Jugis in Bengal.

Matasyási, a *gáin* of the Sándilya *gotra* of Bárendra Brahmans in Bengal.

Matha Ság, a vegetable, a totemistic sept of Mundas in Chota Nagpur.

Mathgrámi, a *gáin* of the Kásyapa *gotra* of Bárendra Brahmans in Bengal.

Mathia, brass bracelet, a totemistic sept of Mundas in Chota Nagpur.

Mathrwár, a section of Kurmis in Chota Nagpur and Orissa.

Máthur, a division of Brahmans and a sub-caste of Káyasths in Behar.

Mathurábási, a section of Goálás in Behar.

Mathurá or **Mathurábási**, a sub-caste of Goálás in Orissa.

Mathuriá, a sub-caste of Telis, Barhis and Lohars in Behar and Chota Nagpur.

Mátiá, a sub-caste of Bágdi in Bengal who are cultivators and earth-workers.

Mátial, a sub-caste of Kewats in Orissa.

Mátiál, a sub-caste of Bágdis in Bengal who sell fish and vegetables.

Mátiál, *Metel*, *Metiá*, "terræ filius," a title of Kaibarttas in Orissa and also of Bágdis, Bauris, Koras, and other earth-working castes in Bengal. As a rule the term is used only by outsiders.

Matibans-Tánti, a sub-caste of Tántis in Orissa.

Matkum, a title of the Bhumij tribe in Manbhum.

Matsendra, king of fish, a section of Jugis.

Mattariá, a sub-caste of Halwáis in Behar.

Matti, a title of Goálás in Behar.

Matwárá, a section of Rajwárs in Western Bengal.

Maudgalya, a *gotra* section of Brahmans, Baidyas, Káyasths, Subarnabaniks and Telis in Bengal; a section of Sudras in Eastern Bengal; of the Paschim Kuliyá Sadgops; an eponymous section of Kámárs, Mális, Madhunápits, and Nápits in Bengal; a section of Bárendra Sunris in Eastern Bengal.

Maudgalya or **Madhukulya**, a section of Pods in Central Bengal.

Maugh, fish, a totemistic sept of Mundas in Chota Nagpur.

Maughá, a group of the Bárendra Sunris in Eastern Bengal.

Mauhariá, a sub-caste of Rástogis in Behar.

Maulavi, a title of Bauris in Western Bengal.

Maulik, a synonym for Dhimál.

Maulik, a hypergamous group of Káyasths, of the Dákshinátya Baidik Brahmans, Baidyas, Sadgops, Chásádbohás, and Subarnabaniks in Bengal. The name appears to be connected with *mul*, root, stock, or origin.

Maulik, *Láyá*, *Náyá*, a Dravidian caste of Manbhum and Western Bengal, who claim affinity with the Mal Pahariás of Rájmahál, and who may possibly be an offshoot from that tribe, to whom, as being the earliest settlers in the country, the duty of propitiating the forest gods may easily have come to be assigned.

Internal structure.

The Maulik of Northern Manbhum and the Santál Parganás are divided into six sub-castes—**Chandana**, **Hariyán** or **Jehariyá**, **Mál** or **Már**, **Sauriyá**, **Rájbansi**, and **Deobansi**. The last two groups call themselves Hindus, and allege that their ancestors were at one time in possession of the Pándra estate in Manbhum. The sections of all the sub-castes are totemistic. A man may not marry a woman belonging to his own section, nor one who falls within the usual formula for reckoning prohibited degrees.

Marriage.

Adult-marriage was formerly in vogue among the Mauliks, as it is still among the Mundas and Oraons. Of late years the example of the Hindus around them has led to the adoption of infant-marriage; and this practice, involving, as is ordinarily believed, an advance in social respectability, tends to become constantly more popular. The earlier custom, however, still survives, and sexual indiscretions before marriage are said to be not uncommon, and as a rule are leniently dealt with. After the bride has been selected and a small bride-price paid, the bridegroom is married to a mango-tree and the bride to a mahuá. This is followed by the ordinary ceremony performed under an open canopy made of sál leaves. The two Hinduised sub-castes employ a Brahman to recite *mantras* on this occasion; for the others a man of their own caste serves as priest. The binding portion is the marking of the bride's forehead with vermilion, which is done by the bridegroom with the *jánti* or cutter used for slicing areca nut.

Polygamy is not formally recognized, but a man is allowed to take a second wife if his first wife is barren. A widow may marry again by the *sangá* form, and is subject to no restrictions in her choice of a second husband. Great license of divorce is allowed, the tearing of a *sál* leaf in symbol of separation being the only form required to complete the act. Divorced wives may marry again.

Religion.

Although, as has been stated above, the Deobansi and Rajbansi sub-castes call in Brahmans of low rank, known locally as Pánres, to assist in their marriage ceremony, even they have not yet taken to worshipping Hindu deities or employing Brahmans as their family priests, and the caste as a whole still adheres to the rude animism characteristic of the aboriginal races of Western Bengal. Their offices as priests of the various spiritual powers who haunt the forests, rocks, and fields and bring disease upon man and beast are in great request. A Bhumij or a Kurmi who wishes to propitiate these dimly-conceived but potent influences will send for a Maulik to offer the necessary sacrifices in preference to a Láyá or priest of his own caste—a fact which speaks strongly for the antiquity of the settlement of the former in the country. Besides serving as priests, they also collect lac, catechu, and other jungle produce, and work as cultivators and day-labourers. Their social rank, according to orthodox ideas, is exceedingly low, and no Hindu will take water from their hands. Mauliks themselves will eat boiled rice with Bhuiyas, and sweetmeats, etc., with Santáls and Mundas. The more advanced Deobansi and Rájbansi sub-castes abstain from beef, and believe themselves to be thereby raised in ceremonial purity and social estimation above their fellows. It is curious to observe that while the non-Hinduised Mauliks will eat no one's leavings, the more orthodox sub-castes have no prejudices on this point so far as the members of the higher Hindu castes are concerned, and will eat the leavings of Brahmans, Rájputs, and Káyasths.

The following statement shows the number and distribution of Mauliks in 1872 and 1881:—

DISTRICT.	1872.	1881.	DISTRICT.	1872.	1881.
Monghyr	5,402	608	Lohardagá	371	......
Bhagalpur	......	95	Singhhum	578	......
Santál Parganás	9,179	3,524	Manbhum	687	5,446
Hazaribagh	688	18	Tributary States	......	179

Maulo, a title of Muchis in Western Bengal.

Maulwár, a sept of the Suraj-bansi division of Rájputs in Behar.

Maunachh, a sept of Rájputs in Behar.

Maunas, a section of Brahmans; a sept of Rájputs in Behar.

Maura, a *mul* or section of the Kanaujiá sub-caste of Hajjáms in Behar.

Maureswari, a sub-caste of Telis in Bengal.

Maurhiá, a section of the Banodhiá and Jaiswár Kalwárs in Behar.

Mauriyár, a *pur* or section of Sákadwipi Brahmans in Behar.

Mautkaha, a *gotra* or section of Nepáli Brahmans.

Mawáli, a title of Chandáls in Eastern Bengal.

Mawar, peacock, a totemistic sept of Chiks in Chota Nagpur.

Mawár, a title of Bábhans in Behar.

Mayáháng, a *thar* or sept of Khambus in Darjiling.

Mayará, *Modak, Mairá, Kuri,* the confectioner caste of Bengal Proper, a heterogeneous functional group, to be distinguished from the Madhunápit, on whom popular usage sometimes confers the titles Modak and Kuri. Some, indeed, regard the Madhunápit as merely a sub-caste of Mayará, but it will be seen from the article on Madhunápit that there are grounds for believing that group to be a distinct homogeneous caste owing its origin to a schism among the Nápits. In Central Bengal the Mayará caste is divided into four sub-castes—**Rárh-ásram, Máyur-ásram, Aja-ásram,** and **Dharm-ásram** or **Dharm-sut.** In Dacca, where there are comparatively few Mayarás and the occupation of sweetmeat-making is almost wholly in the hands of the Madhunápit, the former group has only two sub-castes—**Ekpátiá** and **Dopátiá.** The distinction between these is curious: the former in their marriage ceremony simply carry the bride seven times round the bridegroom, while the latter carry both round in concentric circles, the bridegroom following the inner and smaller circle of the two.

Origin and internal structure.

The sections of the Mayará caste which are given in the Appendix show a singular mixture of elements derived from the Brahmanical *gotras* and survivals from the earlier totemistic sections which we find among the non-Aryan castes. It is impossible now to determine what tribes may have contributed to form the Mayará caste as we now find it, but the fact that distinct traces of totemism may be discerned will perhaps be held to justify the conjecture that the group is not wholly of Aryan extraction. As a rule marriage within the section is strictly prohibited, but in some parts of the country the law of exogamy is disregarded, and marriage is regulated solely by calculation of prohibited degrees. Mayarás have not yet developed a full-blown system of hypergamy, but they appear to be on the road towards doing so, for the families who bear the titles **Ásh, Barát, Dás,** and **Nandi** are called

Kulins. At present, however, the distinction is meaningless so far as marriage is concerned. Men belonging to Maulik families may marry Kulin women, and the only privilege attached to Kulinism is the right to receive presents of cloth, etc., at marriages and other domestic festivals.

Marriage.

Mayarás profess to marry their daughters as infants, but they are not so particular in this matter as the higher castes, and instances of girls marrying after puberty, though rare, are said to occur occasionally without entailing any serious loss of reputation for the family concerned. The marriage ceremony is performed in accordance with orthodox usage; *sampradán*, or the giving and receiving of the bride, being the essential portion of the rite. A price, varying according to the social status of the parties, is paid for the bride. Polygamy is permitted, no limit being placed, in theory at least, on the number of wives a man may have. Widows may not marry again, and divorce is not recognized. A woman taken in adultery is turned out of the caste.

Religion.

The caste profess to be orthodox Hindus, belonging for the most part to the Vaishnava sect. They regard Ganes as their special deity, and make images in his honour. The special season for his worship is towards the end of the cold weather, before the sugarcane crop has been cut, and freshly-prepared molasses cannot be used in the manufacture of sweetmeats until the god has been duly propitiated. Brahmans officiate as their priests, and are not looked down upon by other members of the sacred order. In Manbhum, Mohan Giri, Sahib Miá, Sashthi, and Bhádu are among their minor gods, whom the members of each household worship with sacrifices of goats and offerings of rice, fruit, and sweetmeats. In this domestic worship Brahmans take no part. The dead are burned and the ashes thrown into the Ganges or any river that may be conveniently situated for the purpose. *Sráddh* is performed on the thirty-first day after death.

Occupation.

Mayarás believe the making of sweetmeats to be their original occupation, but many of them at the present day have entered Government service or taken to trade, while a few are engaged in agriculture as tenure-holders and occupancy raiyats. They will, however, on no account cultivate sugarcane themselves or take any part in the preparation of molasses. In a country where sweetmeats form a staple article of diet, and are often the only food that an orthodox Hindu can partake of on a journey, when he has no time to go through the elaborate process of preparing his own food, it is essential that there should be no doubt about the social status and ceremonial purity of the caste which supplies the community with sweetmeats. Mayarás therefore rank among the Navasákha, and Brahmans will take water from their hands. Their own rules regarding diet are those of most respectable Hindus. They will eat cooked food only with Brahmans, and will take water or sweetmeats from members of the Navasakha group.

The following statement shows the number and distribution of Mayarás in 1872 and 1881, the figures for Halwáis being included in the former year for the districts of Bengal Proper :—

District.	1872.	1881.	District.	1872.	1881.
Bardwan	17,040	12,240	Darjiling	90	65
Bankura	3,719	7,579	Jalpigori	270	1,104
Birbhum	10,066	8,165	Kuch Behar	......	336
Midnapur	6,010	7,068	Dacca	2,112	1,297
Hughli	8,278	6,382	Faridpur	897	831
Howrah		2,769	Bakarganj	1,450	270
24-Parganás	6.864	2,190	Maimansinh	5,017	4,780
Nadiya	9,337	17,076	Tipperah	5,901	666
Khulna	......	737	Chittagong	231	238
Jessore	1,942	3,322	Noakhali	616	428
Murshedabad	3,062	5,359	Maldah	279	1,219
Dinajpur	546	494	Santál Parganás	The figures are included in the table on Halwás.	9,045
Rajshahye	909	898	Lohardagá		26
Rangpur	5,798	18,150	Singbhum		572
Bogra	200	1,080	Manbhum		11,363
Pabna	1,522	1,894	Tributary States		71

Mayur, a totemistic section of the Bhar caste in Manbhum, the members of which will not touch or kill the peacock.

Mayur-ásram, a sub-caste of Mayarás in Central Bengal.

Mazumdár, a title of Nápits in Bengal.

Mech, *Mechi*, a Mongoloid tribe found in the Goalpárá district of Assam and in the Himalayan Terai from the Bhutan Duárs westward to the Konki river. In Northern Bengal they have given their name to the Mechi river, and in Goalpárá to the large tract of country called Mechpárá, the proprietor of which, however, calls himself a Rájbansi and repudiates all connexion with the Mech tribe.[1] Ritter[2] identifies them with the Dhimál, and remarks that in point of agricultural skill they are about on a level with the Gáros. Fr. Müller[3] classes them among the Lohitic races, and says they are of the same stock as the Káchári or Bodo. A good observer[4] writes thus of the Mech :—"They are probably the original inhabitants of the Darjiling Terai, and are a distinctly Mongolian race, with fair skins and large bones and limbs. Their physical appearance and characteristics are quite distinct from the Tháru of the Western Terai. They are disappearing, absolutely dying out, faster than any race of which I have known or read. The reason is, no doubt, that their distinctive cultivation is by *jhum*, which is barred by Government forest conservancy, and the spread of settled plough cultivation from the South." In another place Mr. Oldham speaks of the Dhimál and Rájbansi as "dark-skinned Dravidians, and lays stress on the contrast between them and the fair-complexioned Mech. The compiler of the *Assam Census Report*, on the other hand, includes the Mech and the Kochh under the generic term Bodo, and appears to regard both as belonging substantially to the same race.

Origin.

[1] Dalton, *Ethnology of Bengal*, p. 88.
[2] *Erdkunde*, iv, 109.
[3] *Allgemeine Ethnographie*, p. 406.
[4] Mr. W. B. Oldham, late Deputy Commissioner of Darjiling.

A singular reference to both Mech and Dhimál is met with in the Limbu legend that when the three brothers, their ancestors, were first dropped by the gods from Heaven they fell in Benares, whence they wandered northward, seeking the place appointed for them to dwell in. So they came to the *Khachar*, or *mule-country*, as the Nepalese call the tract at the foot of the hills between the Brahmaputra and Kosi rivers. There the youngest brother determined to settle, and became the father of the Kochh, Dhimál, and Mech; while the two others went further into the hills, and their descendants are the Limbus and Khambus of Nepal. A third story makes Assam the proper home of the Mech, and seeks to connect them with the Gáros. Others, again, say that the Mech and Dhimál are descended from Nepalese who, being driven out of Nepal for breaches of caste rules, settled in Khachar and married women of the locality. Without attaching any historical value to these traditions, we may perhaps infer from them that considerable intermixture of blood has taken place between the inhabitants of the hills and the plains, and that types originally distinct may in this way have been greatly modified and to some extent amalgamated. The process of fusion has, however, not yet gone so far as to render it impossible to discern in the Mech traces of a primary Mongolian stock, while the Dhimál tribe appears to be connected by features and complexion with the black races, who may be conveniently designated aboriginal.

Internal structure.

The Mech of the Darjiling and Jalpigori district are divided into two sub-tribes[1]—Agniá-Mech and Játi-Mech, which are practically endogamous, seeing that a member of the former group cannot marry into the latter without thereby forfeiting his position in his own group. The Agniá sub-tribe have twelve exogamous septs, which are shown in Appendix I, while the Játi-Mech regulate marriage by the standard formula calculated to three generations in the descending line. The same rule is observed on the mother's side by the Agniá-Mech, who, however, extend the prohibition in the male line to seven generations.

The Agniá-Mech admit only Rájbansis into their own group; while the Játi-Mech receive also Dhimáls, Dhekrás, and Agniá-Mech. In all cases the new member has to give a feast as a sort of entrance-fee and by way of proclaiming his membership. Such admissions are usually brought about by men of the higher groups taking mistresses from the women of the lower, and thus forfeiting their place in their own society.

Marriage.

Among the Agniá-Mech the usual age for marriage is twelve years for females and sixteen for males, though here, as elsewhere, the influence of Hinduism shows itself in the desire on the part of well-to-do people to get their daughters married at a still earlier age. For the most part, however, the earlier usage of free courtship still holds its ground, and the

---

[1] Further east, I understand, that four sub-tribes are known—Agniá-Mech, Assam-Mech, Káchrá-Mech, and Thampái-Mech. Káchrá-Mech are probably the same as the Kachári.

consent of the parents is sought only after the young people have arranged matters between themselves. Even then, if objections are raised, the girl often solves the difficulty by going off with her lover and thus compelling her parents to take steps to get her married. The same system prevails among the Játi-Mech, but with them the age for marriage ranges from sixteen to twenty for both males and females, and it is not uncommon to find a woman married to a man younger than herself. The bride-price, called *mothom thcká* by Agniá and *chumná* or *sodhá* by the Játi-Mech, is supposed to be fixed with reference to the beauty and accomplishments, and may rise in the Agniá sub-tribe as high as Rs. 120 or even more. Among the Játi-Mech it is supposed to be fixed at Rs. 63, but this amount may be, and usually is, reduced by haggling.

In both sub-tribes the marriage ceremony is exceedingly simple. Among the Agniá-Mech the essential and binding portion of the rite is the formal washing of the bride's feet in the presence of the friends and relatives of both parties with water poured from a bamboo water-vessel (*chungá*). This being done, she enters a room where the bridegroom is awaiting her, and consummation is supposed to take place at once. When she comes out a cock and a hen are sacrificed and two betel leaves and areca nuts offered to Siva, the latter articles being afterwards eaten by the wedded pair. Feasting then commences by the bride serving first the bridegroom, and after him the other guests, with meat and boiled rice. The Játi-Mech do not wash the bride's feet, but make the pair exchange betel leaves and areca nuts. This is held to be the essential rite, and is followed by the sacrifice of a cock and hen to Siva.[1]

A widow may marry again, but if she has children it is deemed more respectable for her to live as a widow with her late husband's relatives, to whom in any case her children belong. If, however, she determines to contract a second marriage, she may not marry any relative, whether elder or younger, of her deceased husband, but must return to her parents' house and get married from there by an informal ceremony called *nika*, in which the bridegroom makes with his little finger a single spot of vermilion on the bride's forehead. Fowls are sacrificed as in the regular form, but the bride's feet are not washed, nor does she exchange betel leaves and areca nuts with the bridegroom. The bride-price for a woman marrying a second time is reduced to one-half of the original amount, and if she marries a third time to one-fourth. In the presumably rare case of a woman marrying for the fourth time, no bride-price at all is paid. A remarried widow is deemed to be socially the inferior of a woman

---

[1] Some of my correspondents distinguish three modes or forms of marriage: thus—(1) the ordinary marriage, in which the parents' consent is obtained before the girl goes to her husband; (2) the *dakuá* marriage, in which the bride elopes or is carried off, and may be reclaimed by her parents if the bride-price is not paid; (3) the *ghar sundi* marriage, when a girl takes a fancy to a man, goes to his house of her own accord, and sits as a suppliant by the symbol of the *ghar-devi*, which stands in the corner of the chief room. In such cases, after refusing the girl as a matter of form, the man is bound ultimately to yield to her importunity. Clearly, however, these are not so much forms of marriage as modes of proposing marriage.

married as a virgin, and is not entitled to serve boiled rice to the guests assembled on any public or ceremonial occasion. Divorce may be effected, with the sanction of the pancháyat, at the wish of the parties or on the ground of the wife's adultery. In the latter case the seducer is liable to repay the bride-price to the injured husband, and cannot marry the woman until he has done so. Divorced wives can only be remarried by the curtailed ceremony in use at the remarriage of a widow, and they hold the same social status as the latter. Their children also belong to the father. It would seem at first sight that the unrestricted courtship permitted by the Mech can hardly promote a high standard of female chastity, and in fact sexual intercourse before marriage, though not expressly recognized, is virtually tolerated, it being understood that if a girl becomes pregnant her lover will at once come forward and marry her. Regarding married women, however, a different order of ideas prevails, and as soon as a girl has finally pitched upon a husband, she is required to be strictly faithful to him. A curious usage, to which parallels may be found in European folklore, deserves notice in this connexion. In the courtyard of every Mech house a sij plant (*Euphorbia Indica*) is carefully tended as the abode of the god Siva and as the emblem of conjugal fidelity. Should the leaves of the plant wither, this is supposed to show that something is wrong with one of the women of the household. Rice is deposited under the tree, and on the next day a pancháyat is called, before which all the women are summoned and a handful of rice is given to each to chew. She who fails to masticate her portion is held guilty of unchastity, and if married is at once turned out of the house. If it is an unmarried girl who breaks down in the chewing ordeal, she is called upon to disclose the name of her paramour, so that arrangements may be made to get her married at once.

Religion.

The religion of the Mech, like that of the Dhimál, is still in an early stage of transition from animism to Hinduism. They describe themselves as Hindus of the Saiva sect, and worship Siva under the name of Batho, and his consort Káli as Bali Khungri. To the former the Agniá-Mech sacrifice buffaloes, goats, and pigeons; while his wife has to put up with the less respectable offerings of pigs, fowls, and goats, which the Játi-Mech offer indifferently to either. The Játi-Mech also reverence as a household goddess (*ghar-deoi*), a nameless personage, supposed to be the mother of Siva, who is represented by a lump of sun-dried clay set in the corner of the chief room. Pigs, fowls, plantains and parched rice are offered to her on any day in the week except Sunday, Tuesday, or Wednesday. Among their other deities may be mentioned Tsimising, Tista Burhi (Buchanan's 'old lady of the Tista'), Mahesh Thákur, Sonnisi and Mahákál. They have no Brahmans, and priests (*dhámi* or *ojhá*) chosen from among the tribe to serve them for religious and ceremonial purposes.

Disposal of the dead.

Those who can afford a funeral pyre prefer to burn the dead, while the poorer members of the tribe bury, placing the corpse face upwards with the head pointing towards the south. In the latter case a small fire is kindled upon the grave, in which food and drink are burned for the benefit of the deceased. The Agniá-Mech perform a meagre propitiatory rite on the eighth day, and the Játi-Mech on the fourth day, after death. With both the important part of the proceedings is the feast which is given to the friends and relatives of the deceased. Some repeat the ceremony every year after the manner of the Hindus, but this is unusual.

Social status.

Judged by the Hindu standard, the social status of the Mech is extremely low. Both Rájbansis and Dhimáls look down upon them; and they themselves, while claiming higher rank than Garos, Lepchas, and Tibetans, admit the social superiority of the Rájbansis. Dhimáls they appear to look upon as standing on much the same level as themselves, though the former profess to be stricter in matters of food and drink, and strenuously disclaim kinship and social intercourse with the Mech. They eat pork, fowls, all kinds of fish, lizards, and the *imphu* silk-worm, but abstain from beef, the flesh of the long-tailed sheep, snakes, field-rats, and the leavings of other people. Buffalo flesh now ranks as beef, at any rate with the Agniá-Mech; but this seems to be a comparatively modern reform, for some Mech are said to eat buffalo flesh, and those who do not seem to pride themselves on their asceticism. Spirituous liquors are indulged in without stint.

A curious story is told in the Terai to account for the fact that the Nepalese will take water from the hands of the Mech. It is said that some twenty years ago Jang Bahadur, then Prime Minister of Nepal, while shooting in the Terai, fell in love with a Mech girl, the daughter of Ujir Singh Jamadar, of Dhulábári, and took her with him to Nepál as his mistress. As the price of her person, and in accordance with the wishes of the tribe, he issued an edict that in future no subject of Nepal should refuse to take water from a Mech, or, as my informant adds, from a Dhimál also. I am unable to say what amount of truth there may be in this tale, but if such an edict were ever actually published, it can hardly have done more than recognize and confirm a practice already existing. Even Jang Bahadur's despotic power must have yielded to popular prejudice if the Nepalese had really deemed the Mech unclean. The fact, however, seems to be that there is a considerable strain of Nepalese blood among the Mech, and other facts may be mentioned which go to confirm this view. Like the Nepalese, for example, the Mech have much greater liberty in matters of food before marriage than after, so that an unmarried man may take rice from people who are not deemed pure enough to give food to a married man. Both observe the Tihar festival; both call the bride-price *sodhá* or *theká*. These coincidences may of course be due merely to that transfusion of custom which is everywhere observable; but taking all the circumstances into consideration, I think it more likely that they have arisen from intermixture of the two races.

Occupation.

Husbandry by the *jhúm* method is regarded by the Mech as their original occupation, but of late years many have taken to settled cultivation as raiyats of *jots* in the Terai. The rearing of the *imphu* silkworm, which spins the silk used in the chequered cloths worn by the Mech, was at one time a regular industry, but has fallen off notably within the last generation.

The following statement shows the number and distribution of the Mech tribe in 1872 and 1881:—

DISTRICT.	1872.	1881.
Bogra	... .	31
Rangpur	... .	6,835
Darjiling	... 893	1,063
Jalpigori	... 40	8,760
Kuch Behar	... .	224

Mecharí, a sept of Tántis in Chota Nagpur.

Mechi, a synonym for Mech.

Mecho, a hypergamous group of Kaibarttas in Jessore.

Medari, a *gáin* of the Sábarna *gotra* of Bárendra Brahmans in Bengal.

Meghalbariárpur, a *mul* or section of the Naomuliá or Majraut sub-caste of Goálás in Behar.

Meghi, a *thar* or sept of Gurungs in Darjiling.

Mehalo, a title of Doms in Behar.

Meháus, a section of the Sátmuliá Maghayá sub-caste of Kándus in Behar.

Mehdipur Mohdia, a *mul* or section of the Naomuliá or Majraut sub-caste of Goálás in Behar.

Meheden, a section of the Bárajáti sub-caste of Khatris in Bengal.

Meherá, a section of the Chárjáti sub-caste of Khatris in Bengal.

Mehmánpur, a *mul* or section of the Naomuliá or Majraut sub-caste of Goálás in Behar.

Mehos, a *mul* or section of the Maghayá sub-caste of Kándus in Behar.

Mehrá, a sept of Rájputs in Behar.

Mehran, a section of Sunris in Behar.

Mehrána, a title of the Tirhutiá sub-caste of Kumhárs in Behar.

Mehri, a sept of Rájputs in Behar.

Mehtar, *Mihtar*, a sub-caste of Háris who remove night-soil.

Mehtar, a section of Maghayá Kumhárs; a title of Nuniás, of the Dhusia and Dohar sub-castes of Chamárs; a section of the Kulsunri sub-caste of Sunris and of the Dharkár sub-caste of Doms in Behar.

Mehtaria, a section of Maghayá Dhobis in Behar; also a title of Chamárs.

Mekchan, a section of Murmis in Darjiling.

Mekhun, a *dugu* or section of the Kochh-Mandai in Dacca. The name indicates the original habitat of the group, probably a hill or village in Assam, and at the present day has no bearing upon marriage.

Memophagpa, a sept of the Chaibisa sub-tribe of Limbus in Darjiling.

Mendru, a sept of Rájputs in Behar.

Meng, a *thar* or sept of Mangars in Darjiling.

Mengi, a *thar* or sept of Gurungs in Darjiling.

Menwạ́r, a section of Bháts in Behar.

Menyangbo, the unsuccessful one, a sept of the Yangorup sub-tribe of Limbus in Darjiling.

Meongba, a sub-sept of the Thekim sept of Limbus in Darjiling.

Mephagpa, the butcher, literally pig-roaster, a sept of the Pánthar sub-tribe of Limbus in Darjiling.

Mert, a sept of Bhuiyás in Chota Nagpur.

Mesha, sheep, a title of Tántis in Bengal.

Mesh-rási, a section of Málos in Eastern Bengal.

Mete, a title of Kaibarttas in Bengal.

Methi, a section of Oswáls in Behar.

Methuá, a synonym for Dhángar in Chota Nagpur.

Mewakhola or **Terothar**, a sub-tribe of Limbus in Darjiling.

Mihtar, a sub-caste of Telis in Behar.

Millak, a section of Mahesris in Behar.

Millong, a sept of the Tungjainya sub-tribe of Chakmás in the Hill Tracts of Chittagong.

Min, *sál* fish, a totemistic section of the Kumhár caste in Manbhum; a section of Jugis in Bengal.

Minag-pá, a *rui* or sept of Sherpa Bhotias of Nepal.

Mind, a sept of Mundas in Chota Nagpur.

Minj, a snake, the totem of a section of Oraon-Dhángars settled for several generations in Behar.

Minji, eel, a totemistic sept of Oraons in Chota Nagpur.

Mir or *Mair*, a sub-caste of Sonárs in Behar.

Mirchaiá, a section of the Baranwar sub-caste of Baniyás in Behar.

Mirchwán, a section of Sonárs in Behar.

Mirdáha, a section of the Kádar caste in Behar which intermarries with the Darbe, Mánjhi, Kampti, and Báre sections, but not with the rest; a section and a title of Maghaya Doms; a title of men of the Turi and Dosadh castes who follow the profession of hawkers or falconers; a title of Binjhiás and Khandáits in Chota Nagpur.

Miriásin, a class of Mahomedan musicians in Behar who also deal in and apply leeches.

Mirich bhusait, a *mul* or section of the Ayodhiabási sub-caste of Sonárs in Behar.

Mirshikár, a chief huntsman; a low class of Mahomedans who live by snaring birds.

Mising, a sept of Tipperahs in the Hill Tracts of Chittagong.

Misir, a section of the Sribástab sub-caste of Káyasths in Behar.

Misr or **Misra**, a title of Gaura, Maithil, Kanaujiá, and Sáraswat

Brahmans and of Bábhans in Behar.

Misra, a title of the Dákshinátya Baidik Brahmans in Bengal; a *thar* of the Atri *gotra* of Nepáli Brahmans; a section of Gaura Brahmans in Behar; a section of Utkal or Orissa Brahmans.

Mistri, a synonym for Barai, Karangá, and Dhobi in Behar.

Mistri, a carpenter or mason. *Occ.* A title of Barhis, Kanaujiá Lohárs, and of Kámárs in Behar; a title of Sutradhars, Chásádhobás, Dhobás, and Pods in Bengal.

Mithan, a section of Agarwáls in Behar.

Mithoriá, a section of Majraut Goálás in Behar.

Mitra, a title of Káyasths and Báruis in Bengal.

Mitraseni Behará, a sub-caste of Bhuinmális in Bengal.

Mittal, a *gotra* or section of Agarwáls in Behar.

Moáli, a *gáin* of the Kásyapa *gotra* of Bárendra Brahmans in Bengal.

Mobrishya, a section of Sánkháris in Bengal.

Mochháre, a sept of the Agniá sub-tribe of Meches in the Darjiling Terai.

Mochi, a title of Jaunpuri Chamárs who make shoes; also a title of Dhusiá Chamars in Behar.

Mochián, a *mul* or section of the Kanaujiá sub-caste of Sonárs in Behar.

Modak, a synonym for Mayará.

Modási, a group of the Rájbansi sub-caste of Kochhs in Northern Bengal.

Modgalya, a section of Gandhabaniks in Bengal.

Modhágrámi, a *gáin* of the Kásyapa *gotra* of Bárendra Brahmans in Bengal.

Modi, a title of Baniyás, Halwáis, Kalwars, Koras, and Sunris in Behar.

Mogalkáchá, a *mul* or section of the Naomuliá or Majraut sub-caste of Goálás in Behar.

Mogha, a title of men who dress as females and earn their living by dancing and singing.

Moghaliá, a section of the Dhusiá sub-caste of Chamárs.

Mohali, a sub-caste of Doms in Behar. The similarity of name suggests a connection with the mat and basket-making caste of Mahili in Western Bengal.

Mohani, a title of Gonrhis in Behar.

Mohár, a *mul* or section of the Chhamuliá Madhesiá sub-caste of Halwáis in Behar.

Mohara, a *thar* or sept of Dámis in Darjiling whose chief profession is sewing.

Mohbaita, a section of the Pachainya sub-caste of Doms in Behar.

Mohdiar, a section of Ghásis in Chota Nagpur.

Moirá, a synonym for Mayará.

Moktán, a section of Murmis in Darjiling.

Molá, a sub-caste of Báuris in Western Bengal.

Molá, a section of Doms in Western Bengal.

Molán, a section of Goálás in the North-Western Provinces and Behar.

Moldhiá, a section of Goálás in the North-Western Provinces and Behar.

Moldiar, a section of Bábhans in Behar.

Molima, Molima-Sege, a sept of Chakmás in the Hill Tracts of Chittagong.

Molo, a sub-caste of Korás in Western Bengal.

Momin, 'faithful'; a synonym for Musalmán; a designation of Mahomedan Jolahas which distinguishes them from the Hindu Jolahas.

Mon, a synonym for Lepcha.

Mongar, a section of Goálás in Behar.

Mongbai, a sept of Tipperahs in the Hill Tracts of Chittagong.

Monghyr, a *dih* or local section of the Maghayá sub-caste of Telis in Behar. The system of exogamy among this sub-caste of Telis seems, however, either to be dying out or to be of recent introduction, for some of the Maghayás say they have no *dihs*, but merely prohibit marriage within nine *pi.his* or degrees of relationship.

Monglá, a sept of the Tungjainya sub-tribe of Chakmás in the Hill Tracts of Chittagong.

Mongri, thorny fish, a totemistic sept of Páns in Chota Nagpur.

Mongtupo, a sept of the Yangorup sub-tribe of Limbus in Darjiling.

Monmatar, *Motia*, *Motari* (from *mot*, *B.*, 'a burthen') a porter, a carrier of burthens, and generally a day-labourer employed otherwise than in agriculture.

Mor, peacock, a totemistic section of Khandáits in Orissa and Chota Nagpur.

Mormu, deer, a totemistic sept of Lohárs in Chota Nagpur.

Morpachi, a sept of Goálás in in Chota Nagpur.

Moti, a sept of Gonds in Chota Nagpur.

Motiomán, a sept of Kaurs in Chota Nagpur.

Motliá, a section of Goálás in the North-Western Provinces and Behar.

Motrihá, a section of the Banodhiá and Jaiswár Kalwárs in Behar.

Mo-u, a sept of the Tungjainya sub-tribe of Chakmás in the Hill Tracts of Chittagong.

Mowar, a section of Bábhans in Behar.

Mowl, a sept of Mundas in Chota Nagpur.

Mradha, a title of Háris in Bengal.

Mridha, the head of the menial servants in a zamindár's establishment.

M·ung, a synonym for Tipperah.

Muchi, *Rishi*,[1] the leather-dressing and cobbler caste of Bengal, by origin doubtless a branch of the Chamárs, though its members now repudiate that name and claim to be a distinct caste of somewhat higher social position. Mr. Nesfield observes that "the industry of tanning is preparatory to, and lower than that of, cobblery: and hence * * * * the caste of Chamár ranks decidedly below that of Muchi. The ordinary Hindu does not consider the touch of a Muchi so impure as that of a Chamár, and there is a Hindu proverb to the effect that 'dried or prepared hide is the same thing as cloth,' whereas the touch of the raw hide before it has been tanned by the Chamár is considered a pollution. The Muchi does not eat carrion like the Chamár, nor does he eat swine's flesh; nor does his wife ever practise the much-loathed art of midwifery. He makes the shoes, leather aprons, leath[illegible] buckets, harness, portmanteaux, etc., used by the [illegible] people of India. As a rule he is much better off than the Chamár, and this circumstance has helped amongst others to raise him in the social scale." It may be gathered from this description that in the North-West Provinces the Muchi never dresses freshly-skinned hides, but confines himself to working up leather already tanned by the Chamár. This distinction does not appear to be so sharply drawn in Bengal, where Muchis tan hides like the Chamárs, but will only cure those of the cow, goat, buffalo, and deer.

Traditions of origin.

The origin of the Muchi caste is given in the following legend, related to Dr. Wise by one of their Brahmans, and afterwards reported to me substantially in the same form from an independent source:—One of the Prajá-pati, or mind-born sons of Brahmá, was in the habit of providing the flesh of cows and clarified butter as a burnt offering (Áhuti) to the gods. It was then the custom to eat a portion of the sacrifice, restore the victim to life, and drive it into the forest. On one occasion the Prajá-pati failed to resuscitate the sacrificial animal, owing to his wife, who was pregnant at the time, having clandestinely made away with a portion. Alarmed at this he summoned all the other Prajá-patis, and they sought by divination to discover the cause of the failure. At last they ascertained what had occurred, and as a punishment the wife was cursed and expelled from their society. The child which she bore was the first Muchí, or tanner, and from that time forth mankind being deprived of the power of reanimating cattle slaughtered for food, the pious abandoned the practice of killing kine altogether. Another story is that Muchirám, the ancestor of the caste, was born from the sweat of Brahmá while dancing. He chanced to offend the irritable sage Durvása, who sent a pretty

[1] Buchanan met with a tribe of fishermen in Puraniya called Rishi, and considered them to be an aboriginal tribe of Mithilá. Rishi, however, is often used as a pseudonym to hide the real paternity of a caste: thus the Músahar often calls himself "Rishi-bálaka," or son of a Rishi, and the Bengali Chamár tries to pass incognito as a Rishi. In the case of the Músahar it is possible that Rishi may be Rikhi or Rikh-Mun, the bear, one of the original totems of the Bhuiyá or Músahar tribe, and the same may hold go[illegible] for the Chandál. This explanation, however, is mainly conjectural.

Brahman widow to allure him into a breach of chastity. Muchirám accosted the widow as mother, and refused to have anything to do with her; but Durvása used the miraculous powers he had acquired by penance to render the widow pregnant, so that the innocent Muchirám was made an outcaste on suspicion. From the widow's twin sons Bara Rám and Chhota Rám descended the Bará-bhágiyá and Chhota-bhágiyá sub-castes, which are the two main divisions of Muchis at the present day. The Chhota-Bhágiyá deal in hides, act as musicians, and do various kinds of leather work; while the Bará-bhagiyá profess to be only cultivators. The latter are again divided into Uttar-Rárhi and Dakin-Rárhhi, who do not intermarry or eat together. The other sub-castes, Chásá-Kurur or Chásá-Kolai, are agriculturists; the Betuá make cane baskets and also cultivate; the Jugi-Muchi or Korá weave coarse cloth of cotton, often mixed with silk; the Tikákar Konai, who make the *tiká* or charcoal balls used for lighting pipes; and the Baitál, Kurur, Mála bhumiá, Sabarkárá, and Sánki, are shoemakers, cobblers, and curriers. Muchis have only two sections, Kásyapa and Sándilya, which have been borrowed from the Brahmanical system, and has no bearing upon the prevention of intermarriage between near relatives.

Marriage.

They follow the ordinary rules as to prohibited degrees, and permit the marriage of two sisters to the same man, provided that the younger is not married first. Both infant and adult-marriage are recognized for girls, but the former practice is deemed the more respectable, and is resorted to in the large majority of cases. In the Dacca district a father generally receives from fifty to sixty rupees for his daughter, from which it may be inferred that the custom of polygamy has tended on the whole towards the preponderance of males in the caste. In other districts, however, the bride price is not so high, and in Pabna it is said to vary from Rs. 5 to Rs. 25-4, according to the means of the bridegroom. The marriage ceremony is a simplified form of that in use among the higher Hindu castes; *sindurdán*, or according to some the burning of *khai* or parched paddy before the bride and bridegroom. being the binding portion. The bride is dressed in red garments. In former years, says Dr. Wise, the marriage ceremonies of the Rishi were scenes of debauchery and intemperance, but of late intoxicating liquors have been prohibited until all the regular forms have been observed. Even Hindus, who rarely have anything favourable to say of the Rishi, confess that now-a-days, owing to some unknown cause, both the Chamárs and Rishis have become more temperate and more attentive to their religious duties than formerly. Polygamy is permitted with no restriction on the number of wives, except the man's ability to maintain them and their children. Divorce is permitted on the ground of adultery. Usually the pancháyat of the caste are called together by their president (*parámánik* or *moidli*) to give their sanction to the proceedings; and if this is not done at the instance of the husband, the wife has a right to appeal to the pancháyat. With the permission of that body divorced wives may marry again by the *sanga* or *nika* form. Widows also may marry a second time by this ritual, the binding portion of which consists of exchanging garlands made of the flowers of the *tulsi* (*Ocymum sanctum*). Here also the sanction of the pancháyat is required, and a feast is given to the members. A small sum, varying from Re. 1 to Rs. 5, is paid as *pan*. Indications are not wanting that the opinion of the caste tends to condemn widow-marriage, and that the custom may be expected to die out within a generation or two unless some special influence is brought to bear in its favour. Already some Muchis hold that only virgin widows can properly marry again, and that the remarriage of a full-grown woman who has already lived with her husband is little better than concubinage. The children of *sanga* marriages are deemed to be in some sense degraded, and, if males, have to pay a heavy fine before they can obtain wives. Like Bauris and Bágdis, the Muchis admit into their community members of any caste higher than their own. The new member is required to give a feast to the caste pancháyat, and to eat with them in token of fellowship. Instances of men of other castes thus becoming Muchis are rare, and occur only when a man has been turned out of his own caste for having intercourse with a Muchi woman and taking food from her hands.

Religion.

The majority of the caste are believed to belong to the Saiva sect, but a large proportion of the Betuá sub-caste are Vaishnavas. They imitate the Sudras in most of their religious ceremonies, while others peculiar to themselves resemble those of the Chamárs. Though regarded as utterly vile, they are permitted to make offerings at the shrines of Káli, which a Jugi is not allowed to do. They keep many Hindu festivals, the chief being that in honour of Viswakarmá on the last day of Bhádra. When small-pox prevails they offer a pig to Sitalá, first of all smearing the animal's snout with red lead and repeating certain incantations, after which it is set free, and any one can seize it. Like the Chamár, Dhobá, Dosadh, and other low castes, the Muchis worship Jalka Devi whenever cholera or other epidemic disease breaks out. The Muchi women, however, only collect contributions in their own quarter, and wear the wreath of plantain, date-palm, or *bená* (*Andropogon muricatus*) for two and a half days instead of for six, as is the custom of the Chamárs. Muchirám Dás, the reputed ancestor of the caste, and Rui Dás, are also popular objects of worship.

Priests.

A Brahman was bestowed on the Bará-bhágiyá Muchis by Ballál Sen, and the story goes that in the palace of that monarch a certain Brahman having made himself especially troublesome by insisting upon being appointed as priest to one of the newly-formed castes, had it intimated to him by the Raja that he would belong to the caste which should first appear to him in the morning. There was also a Muchi, a celebrated player on the *naqúrah*, or kettledrum, whose duty it was to sound the *reveille*. It was easily arranged that the Brahman should first cast his eyes on him when he awoke, and his descendants have ever since ministered to this despised race. They rank among the lowest of the Barna-Brahmans, and neither members of the sacred order nor men belonging to the *A'charani* castes will take water from their hands. The Chhota-bhágiyá have priests of their own. Muchis burn their dead and perform *sráddh* on the thirtieth day after death. In the case of men who have died a violent death there is no *sráddh*, but a *práyaschitta*, or expiatory ceremony, is performed.

The Chhota-bhágiyá and Betuá sub-castes, like the Chandáls, observe ten days of impurity and celebrate the *sráddh* on the eleventh.

Social status.

The social position of Muchis is, as has been intimated above, perhaps a shade higher than that of Chamárs, but this is not saying much, and both castes may properly be placed in one class at the bottom of the scale of precedence recognized by the average Hindu. None of the regular village servants will defile himself by working for a Muchi, and thus the caste has been compelled to provide itself with barbers and washermen from among its own members. Illegitimate children are usually brought up to these professions, and wherever the community is a large one no inconvenience is felt. Their rules regarding diet are in keeping with their standing in society. The Chhota-bhágiyá sub-caste eat beef, as the Chamárs do; are very partial to chickens, and regard pork as a delicacy. The Bara-bhágiyá, Betuá, and Chásá-kolai abstain from beef and pork, but not from fowls; and they are far less particular than the higher castes as to the kinds of fish which they eat. Like the Chamárs, all Muchis are great spirit-drinkers, and notorious for their indulgence in the more dangerous vice of gánja-smoking. No other caste will eat food prepared by a Muchi, but Doms will take water from their hands and will smoke from the same hookah.

Occupation.

Muchis work as tanners, shoe-makers, saddlers, musicians, and basket-makers. Their mode of preparing skins is as follows:—The raw hide is rubbed, and then soaked for fifteen to twenty days in a strong solution of lime. It is then deprived of its hair and of any fat that remains, and steeped for six days in acid tamarind juice. Finally, it is put in a vat containing a solution of lac and pounded babúl (*Acacia*), garan (*Ceriops Roxburghianus*), and sundarí (*Heritiera minor*) barks, the hide being after this immersion regarded as properly cured.

The town Muchis buy hides from their brethren resident in those parts of the country where cattle abound. The village Muchis of the Chhota-bhágiyá sub-caste, while they pride themselves on not skinning the carcasses of their own cattle, row up and down the rivers in their neighbourhood in search of carcasses, and when epidemic diseases attack the herds they find so much to do that the villagers attribute the spread of the disease to them. It is doubtless often the case that they puncture a healthy cow with an Acacia thorn impregnated with virus, but they are rarely, if ever, detected at this villainous trade. The people, however, firmly believe that they increase their profits in this way. In Western Bengal and Chota Nagpur, where the *sál* jungles form the chief pasturing grounds, Muchis destroy cattle with arsenic rolled up in a bundle of *mahuá* petals. These are a favourite food for cows, and can be strewn on the ground without rousing any suspicion.

The Muchi will not touch a corpse, but will skin the carcass of a dead animal. The skin of the buffalo sacrificed at the Durgá Púja is their perquisite, and the skinning of the animal often gives rise to bitter quarrels between rival families.

Most Muchis make shoes, but of inferior quality to those manufactured by the Chamárs. The Betuá sub-caste are famous for making baskets with rattan (*Calamus rotang*), which natives assert are so closely woven that they will hold water. They also collect the roots of the dub grass (*Panicum*), and manufacture the brush (*manjan*) used by weavers for starching the warp. In some parts the Muchi castrates bull calves, but this they stoutly deny. Others, again, work as sweepers and remove night-soil, but those who do so are excluded from intermarriage with the rest of the caste, and appear to be on the way to form a sub-caste of their own.

The tablá-wála, or drum-maker, is always a Muchi. Goats' skins are used for the covering, while cows' hides supply the strings for tightening the parchment. On every native drum, at one or both ends, black circles (*khiran*) are painted to improve the pitch. The Muchi prepares a paste of iron filings and rice, with which he stains the parchment. At all Hindu weddings they are employed as musicians, and engaged in bands, as among Muhamadans. Their favourite instruments are drums of various shapes and sizes, the violin, and the pipe.

The female Muchi differs from the Chamáín in never acting as a midwife, in wearing shell bracelets instead of huge ones of bell-metal, and in never appearing as a professional singer.

The following statement shows the number and distribution of Muchis in 1881, the figures for 1872 having been included with those of Chamárs:—

District.	1881.	District.	1881.
Bardwan	48,684	Darjiling	71
Bankura	9,094	Dacca	411
Birbhum	25.716	Faridpur	3,336
Midnapur	11,854	Bakarganj	1,547
Hughli	10,909	Maimansinh	6.902
Howrah	3,517	Tipperah	2,613
24-Parganás	24.814	Chittagong	584
Nadiya	34.068	Noakhali	221
Khulna	41,147	Maldah	2.883
Jessore	22,347	Santál Parganás ...	5,651
Murshedabad	10,076	Cuttack	862
Dinajpur	3.305	Puri	56
Rajshahye	2,795	Balasore	249
Rangpur	2,831	Tributary States ...	571
Bogra	1,908	Singhbhum	577
Pabna	4,890	Manbhum	7,307

Muchirám Dás, a title of Muchis in Bengal.

Muddapuriá, a section of the Komár sub-caste of Dosádhs in Behar.

Mudgal, a section of Karans in Orissa.

Mudgul, a section of the Srotriya sub-caste of Utkal Brahmans.

Mudi, petty shop-keepers selling rice, *dál*, sugar, etc.; a title of Binds and Bágdis; a synonym for Korá, professional diggers and excavators; a title of bullock-drivers engaged in trade; a section of Oraons whose chief profession is earthwork. They also carry palanquins and cultivate land.

Mudir, frog, a totemistic section of Jagannáthi Kumhárs in Orissa.

Mudu, a sept of Tántis in Chota Nagpur.

Muduk, a sept of Mundas in Chota Nagpur.

Muduli, a title of Chásás in Orissa.

Mugrish, a section of Khyáns in Northern Bengal.

Muharrir, Mohari, a vernacular writer, a clerk who either does not know English or is employed in a post which requires no knowledge of English.

Muhkim, supervisor, a title of Tántis in Bengal.

Mujaimiya, a *kul* or section of Bábhans in Behar.

Mujaniar, a sept of Korwas in Chota Nagpur.

Mujganji-Parámánik, a sub-caste of Nápits in the 24-Parganás.

Mujgarni, a group of the Dhapárá sub-caste of Kumhárs in Pabna.

Mujni, a section of Koiris in Behar.

Mujniá, a section of the Biyáhut and Kharidábá Kalwárs in Behar.

Mukáranchhá, a *thar* or sept of Khambus in Darjiling.

Mukariá, a section of the Dhaprá sub-caste of Doms in Behar.

Mukeri, a person employed in grinding wheat-flour.

Mukh, a section of Maghaiyá Kumhárs in Behar.

Mukhaiti, a *gáin* of the Bharadwája *gotra* of Rárhi Brahmans in Bengal.

Mukhi, a section of Ghásis in Chota Nagpur: hence *Mukhiáin*, an opprobrious term applied to women of the Ghási and other low castes from their quarrelsome habits.

Mukhiá, a *mul* or section of the Ghosin sub-caste of Goálás in Behar; a section of Kewats; a title of Binds and Kurmis in Behar; a title of Khambus in Darjiling.

Mukhiár, a title of Tiors and of the Cháb sub-caste of Gonrhis in Behar.

Mukhiyá, a section of the Játhot division of the Párbatti-Kurin sub-caste of Gonrhis in Behar.

Mukhya-Kulin, a hypergamous group of Rárhi Brahmans in Bengal.

Mukmed, a section of the Maghayá sub-caste of Barhis in Behar.

Mukruár, spider, a sept of Asuras in Chota Nagpur.

Muktáng, a section of Murmis in Darjiling.

Mukta-sil, a title of barbers in Eastern Bengal.

Mukund, a section of Barhis in Behar.

Mul, a *gáin* of the Kásyapa *gotra* of Rárhi Brahmans in Bengal; a sept of Tántis in Chota Nagpur.

Mula, a group of the Bárendra Goálás in Bengal.

Mulhatiá, a section of the Kasarwáni sub-caste of Baniyás in Behar.

Mulki, a sub-tribe of Rájputs in Western Bengal.

Mulmaháli, a section of the Biyáhut and Kharidáhá Kalwárs in Behar.

Mulukjuri, a *gáin* or sub-section of Saptasati Brahmans in Bengal.

Mulukuas, a *thar* or sept of Khambus in Darjiling.

Munda, *Mura*, *Horo-hon*, a large Dravidian tribe of Chota Nagpur classed on linguistic grounds as Kolarian, and closely akin to the Hos and Santáls, and probably also to the Kandhs. The name Munda is of Sanskrit origin. It means headman of a village, and is a titular or functional designation used by the members of the tribe, as well as by outsiders, as a distinctive name much in the same way as the Santáls call themselves Mánjhi, the Bhumij Sardár, and the Khambu of the Darjiling hills Jimdár. The general name Kol, which is applied to both Mundas and Oraons, is interpreted by Herr Jellinghaus to mean pig-killer, but the better opinion seems to be that it is a variant of *horo*, the Mundári for man. The change of *r* to *l* is familiar and needs no illustration, while in explanation of the conversion of *h* into *k*, we may cite *hon*, the Mundári for 'child,' which in Korwa becomes *kon* and *koro*, the Muási form of *horo*, 'a man.' It may be added that the Kharias of Chota Nagpur call the Mundas Kora, a name closely approaching Kol.

Origin.

The Munda myth of the making of mankind tells how the self-existent primeval deities Ote Borám and Sing Bonga created a boy and a girl and put them together in a cave to people the world. At first they were too innocent to understand what was expected of them, but the gods showed them how to make rice-beer, which inflames the passions, and in course of time their family reached the respectable number of twelve of either sex. As is usual in myths of this class, the children were divided into pairs; and Sing Bonga set before them various kinds of food for them to choose from before starting in the world. The fate of their descendants depended on their choice. Thus "the first and second pair took bullocks' and buffaloes' flesh, and they originated the Kols (Hos) and the Bhumij (Matkum); the next took of the vegetables only, and are the progenitors of the Brahmans and Chhatries; others took goats and fish, and from them are the Sudras. One pair took shell-fish and became Bhuiyás; two pairs took pigs and became Santáls. One pair got nothing, seeing which the first pairs gave them of their superfluity, and from the pair thus

Tradition.

provided spring the Ghasis, who toil not, but live by preying on others."[1]

Internal structure.

The Mundas are divided into thirteen sub-tribes, several of which, such as Kharia-Munda, Mahili-Munda, Oraon-Munda, appear to be the result of crosses with neighbouring tribes, while others again, like Bhuinhár-Munda and Mánki-Munda, have reference to the land and communal system of the tribe. The Mahili-Munda sub-tribe has the pig for its totem, and for them pork is tabooed. But appetite has proved stronger than tradition, and the taboo is satisfied by throwing away the head of the animal, the rest of the carcase being deemed lawful food. The septs or *kilis*, which are very numerous, are mainly totemistic, and the totem is taboo to the members of the sept which bears its name. A list of the septs is given in Appendix I. If it were possible to identify them all, and to ascertain precisely to what extent and in what manner the taboo of the totem is observed by each, the information would probably throw much light upon the growth of early tribal societies.

Marriage.

A Munda may not marry a woman of his own sept. The sept-name goes by the father's side, and inter-marriage with persons nearly related through the mother is guarded against by reckoning prohibited degrees in the manner common in Behar. Adult marriage is still in fashion, and sexual intercourse before marriage is tacitly recognized, but in all respectable families matches are made by the parents, and the parties themselves have very little to say in the matter. The bride-price varies from Rs. 4 to Rs. 20. *Sindurdán*, or the smearing of vermilion on the bride's forehead by the bridegroom and on the bridegroom's forehead by the bride, is the essential and binding portion. The practice described by Colonel Dalton of marrying the bride to a *mahuá* tree and the bridegroom to a mango seems now to have been abandoned. Traces still survive among the Mundas of a form of marriage, resembling the Santáli *nir bolok*. It is called *dhuko era*, meaning a bride who has entered the household of her own accord. The children of a woman thus married seem to have an inferior status in respect of their rights to inherit the landed property of their father. The late Babu Rákhál Dás Háldár, Manager of the estate of the Maharájá of Chota Nágpur, gave me an illustration of this fact. Some years ago the *mundá* or headman of one of the villages of the Government estate of Barkagarh died, leaving an only son by a *dhuko era* wife, and a question was raised as to the latter's right to succeed. Under Colonel Dalton's orders, a number of headmen of villages were called together, and their opinions were taken. No decided results, however, could be arrived at. Some thought the son should get the whole property. Others proposed to exclude him altogether, and a third party considered him entitled to maintenance. Eventually the question was compromised by admitting the son's right to one-fourth of the land and the whole of the personal property. The case is a curious comment on the

---

[1] Dalton, *Ethnology*, p. 185.

uncertainty of tribal custom. Widows may marry again by the ritual known as *sagai*, in which *sindurdán* is performed with the left hand. Divorce is allowed at the instance of either party, and divorced women are permitted to marry again. In cases of adultery the seducer is required to pay to the husband the full amount of the bride-price.

Religion.

At the head of the Munda religion stands Sing-Bonga, the sun, a beneficent but somewhat inactive deity, who concerns himself but little with human affairs, and leaves the details of the executive government of the world to the gods in charge of particular branches or departments of nature. Nevertheless, although Sing-Bonga himself does not send sickness or calamity to men, he may be invoked to avert such disasters, and in this view sacrifices of white goats or white cocks are offered to him by way of appeal from the unjust punishments believed to have been inflicted by his subordinates. Next in rank to Sing-Bonga comes Buru-Bonga or Marang-Buru, also known as Pát-Sarná, a mountain god, whose visible habitation is usually supposed to be the highest or most remarkable hill or rock in the neighbourhood. "In Chota Nágpur," says Colonel Dalton,[1] "a remarkable bluff, near the village of Lodhma, is the Marang-Buru or Maha-Buru for a wide expanse of country. Here people of all castes assemble and sacrifice—Hindus, even Mahomedans, as well as Kols. There is no visible object of worship; the sacrifices are offered on the top of the hill, a bare semi-globular mass of rock. If animals are killed, the heads are left there, and afterwards appropriated by the páhan or village priest." Marang-Buru is regarded as the god who presides over the rainfall, and is appealed to in times of drought, as well as when any epidemic sickness is abroad. The appropriate offering to him is a buffalo. Ikir Bonga rules over tanks, wells and large sheets of water; Garhá-era is the goddess of rivers, streams and the small springs which occur on many hill sides in Chota Nágpur; while Náge or Nága-era is a general name applied to the minor deities or spirits who haunt the swampy lower levels of the terraced rice-fields. All of these are believed to have a hand in spreading disease among men, and require constant propitiation to keep them out of mischief. White goats and black or brown cocks are offered to Ikir Bonga, and eggs and turmeric to the Náge. Deswáli or Kárá-Sarná is the god of the village who lives with his wife Jáhir Burhi or Sarhul-Sarná in the Sarná or sacred grove, a patch of the forest primeval left intact, to afford a refuge for the forest gods. Every village has its own Deswáli, who is held responsible for the crops, and receives periodical worship at the agricultural festivals. His appropriate offering is a *kárá* or he-buffalo; to his wife fowls are sacrificed. Gumi is another of the Sarná deities whose precise functions I have been unable to ascertain. Bullocks and pigs are sacrificed to him at irregular intervals. Chandor appears to be same as Chando Omol or Chanala, the moon worshipped by women, as the wife of

---

[1] *Ethnology of Bengal*, 188.

Sing Bonga and the mother of the stars. Colonel Dalton mentions the legend that she was faithless to her husband, and he cut her in two, 'but repenting of his anger he allows her at times to shine forth in full beauty.' Goats are offered to her in the Sarná. Háprom is properly the homestead, but it is used in a wider sense to denote the group of dead ancestors who are worshipped in the homestead by setting apart for them a small portion of every meal and with periodical offerings of fowls. They are supposed to be ever on the watch for chances of doing good or evil to their descendants, and the Munda fully realise the necessity for appeasing and keeping them in good humour.

Festivals.

The festivals of the tribe are the following:—(1) Sarhul or Sarjum-Bábá, the spring festival corresponding to the Baha or Bah-Bonga of the Santáls and Hos in Chait (March-April) when the *sál* tree is in bloom. Each household sacrifices a cock and makes offerings of *sál* flowers to the founders of the village in whose honour the festival is held. (2) Kadletá or Batauli in Asarh at the commencement of the rainy season. "Each cultivator," says Colonel Dalton, "sacrifices a fowl, and after some mysterious rites a wing is stripped off and inserted in the cleft of a bamboo and stuck up in the rice-field and dung-heap. If this is omitted, it is supposed that the rice will not come to maturity." (3) Naná or Jom-Naná, the festival of new rice in Asin when the highland rice is harvested. A white cock is sacrificed to Sing-Bonga, and the first fruits of the harvest are laid before him. Until this has been done, it would be an act of impiety to eat the new rice. (4) Khariá puja or Kolom Singh, called by the Hos Deswáli Bonga or Mágh Parab celebrating the harvesting of the winter rice, the main crop of the year. Five fowls and various vegetables are offered to Deswáli, the god of the village at the *khalihan* or threshing floor. Among the Hos of Singbhum the festival is kept as a sort of *saturnale*, during which the people give themselves up to drunkenness and all kinds of debauchery. This is less conspicuously the case with the Mundas of the plateau who live scattered among Hindu and Christian neighbours, and do not form a compact tribal community like the Hos of the Kolhan. The festival, moreover, is kept by the Mundas on one day only, and is not spread over a month or six weeks, during which time the people of different villages vie with each other in dissipation, as they do in the Kolhán.

The funeral ceremonies of Mundas do not differ materially from those of the Hos, of which Colonel Dalton's description has been quoted in the first volume of this Glossary.

Succession.

Succession among the Mundas is governed by their own customs, which appear to have been little affected by the influence of Hindu law. Property is equally divided among the sons, but no division is made until the youngest son is of age. With them, as with the Santáls, daughters get no share in the inheritance; they are allotted among the sons just like the live-stock. "Thus if a man dies, leaving three sons and three daughters and thirty head of cattle, on a division each son would get ten head of cattle and one sister; but should there be only one sister, they wait till she marries and divide the *pan*," or bride-price, which usually consists of about six head of cattle. Among the Hos of Singbhum the bride-price is higher than with the Mundas, and the question of its amount has there been found to affect seriously the number of marriages.

Village communes and officials.

According to ancient and universal tradition, the central table land of Chota Nagpur Proper was originally divided into *parhás* or rural communes, comprising from ten to twenty-five villages, and presided over by a divisional chief, called the *rájá* or *múnda* of the *parhá*. In 1839, titular *rájás* of the *parhá* were still existing in the Fiscal Division of Khukrá near Ránchí, who retained considerable authority in tribal disputes, and at times of festival and hunting. But this element in the Munda village system has now fallen into decay, and survives only in the *jhandás* or flags of the *parhá* villages, and in the peculiar titles bestowed on the cultivators themselves. The exclusive right to fly a particular flag at the great dancing festivals is jealously guarded by every Munda village, and serious fights not unfrequently result from the violation of this privilege. Besides this, individual villages in a *parhá* bear specific titles, such as *rájá*, *diwán*, *kunwár*, *thákur*, *chhotá lal*, etc., similar to those which prevail in the household of the reigning family, which obviously refer to some organization which no longer exists. I am informed that these officials still make the arrangements for the large hunting parties which take place at certain seasons of the year.

A Kol village community consists, when perfect, of the following officers:—*Múnda*, *máhato*, *páhn*, *bhandári*, *goráit*, *goálá*, and *lohár*. Washermen, barbers, and potters have been added since 1839, and even now are only found near much frequented halting places, and in villages where the larger Hindu tenure-holders live. The Kols invariably shave themselves, and their women wash the clothes.

(1) Munda.—The *múnda* is the chief of the *bhuinhárs*, or descendants of the original clearers of the village. He is a person of great consequence in the village; and all demands from the *bhuinhárs*, whether of money or labour, must be notified by the owner of the village through the *múnda*. He is remunerated for his trouble by the *bhuinhári* land, which he holds at a low rate of rent, and receives no other salary. In parganá Lodhmá, and in the south-eastern portion of Lohardagá he sometimes performs the *máhato's* duties as well as his own, and he then gets a small *jágir* of half a *páwá* of land rent-free.

(2) Mahato.—The functions of a *máhato* have been compared to those of a *patwári* or village accountant, but he may be more aptly described as a rural settlement officer. He allots the land of the village among the cultivators, giving to each man a *goti* or clod of earth as a symbol of possession; he collects the rent, pays it to the owner, and settles any disputes as to the amount due from the *raiyats*; and, in short, manages all pecuniary matters connected with the land. He is appointed by the owner of the village, and receives one *páwá*

of *rájhas* land rent-free, as a *jágir* or service-tenure. But the office is neither hereditary nor permanent, and the *máhato* is liable to be dismissed at the landlord's discretion. Dismissal, however, is unusual, and the *máhato* is often succeeded by his son. Where the *máhato* collects the rents, he almost universally receives a fee, called *báttá*, of half an *ánná* from each cultivator, or of one *ánná* for every house in the village. In one village *báttá* amounts to four *ánnás* and a half on every *páwá* of land. Occasionally, where there is no *bhandári* or agent for the owner's rent-paying land, the *máhato* gets three bundles (*karais*) of grain in the straw, containing from ten to twenty *sers* apiece, at every harvest. Thus during the year he would receive three bundles of *gondli* from the cold weather crop, and the same amount from the *gorá* or early rice, and the *don* or late rice. In *khálsá* villages, which are under the direct management of the Mahárájá, the *máhato* often holds, in addition to his official *jágir*, a single *páwá* of land, called *kharcha* or *rozina khet*, from the proceeds of which he is expected to defray the occasional expenses incurred in calling upon cultivators to pay their rent, etc.

The functions of the *máhato* are shown in greater detail in the following extract from Dr. Davidson's Report of 1839 :—" On a day appointed, the *thikádár* or farmer proceeds to the *akhrá* or place of assembly of the village, where he is met by the *máhato*, *páhn*, *bhandári*, and as many of the *rayats* as choose to attend. He proceeds, agreeably to the dictation of the *máhato*, to write down the account of the cultivation of the different *rayats*, stating the number of *páwás* held and the rent paid by each. Having furnished this account, any new *rayats* who may wish to have lands in the village, after having the quantity and rent settled, have a *goti* given to them. If any of the old *rayats* require any new land, a *goti* is taken for that, but not for the old cultivation. The *máhato* collects the rent as the instalments become due, according to the above-mentioned account given to the farmer; and all differences as to the amount of rent payable by a *rayat*, if any ever arise, which very seldom happens, are settled by the opinion of the *máhato*. So well does this mode answer in practice, that in point of fact a dispute as to the amount of rent owed by a *rayat* is of rare occurrence. When a farmer wishes to cheat a *rayat*, he accuses him of having cultivated more land than he is entitled to, or of owing him *manwár* or grain-rent for land held in excess; and if such a thing as a dispute as to the amount of rent owed ever does arise, the *máhato's* evidence is generally considered conclusive by both parties."

(3) PAHN.—The importance of the *páhn*, or priest of the village gods, may be inferred from the current phrase in which his duties are contrasted with those of the *máhato*. The *páhn*, it is said, "makes the village" (*gáon banátá*), while the *máhato* only "manages it" (*gáon chalátá*). He must be a *bhuinhár*, as no one but a descendant of the earliest settlers in the village could know how to propitiate the local gods. He is always chosen from one family; but the actual *páhn* is changed at intervals of from three to five years by the ceremony of the *súp* or winnowing-fan, which is used as a divining rod, and taken from house to house by the boys of the

village. The *bhuinhár* at whose house the *súp* stops is elected *páhn*. On the death of a *páhn*, he is frequently, but not invariably, succeeded by his son. Rent-free lands are attached to the office of *páhn* under the following names:—(1) *Páhni*, the personal *jágir* or service-tenure of the priest, generally containing one *páwá* of land. (2) *Dálikatári*, for which the *páhn* has to make offerings to Jáhir Búrhí, the goddess of the village. It is called *dálikatári*, as it is supposed to defray the expenses of the *Karm* festival, when a branch (*dáli*) of the *karma* tree is cut down and planted in the fields. (3) *Desauli*, a sort of *bhutkheta* or devil's acre, the produce of which is devoted to a great triennial festival in honour of Desauli, the divinity of the grove. This land is either cultivated by the *páhn* himself, or by *raiyats* who pay him rent. (4) *Pánbhárá* and *táhálu* are probably the same. Lands held under these names are cultivated by the *páhn* himself or his near relations; and whoever has them, is bound to supply water at the various festivals.

(4) Bhandárí.—The *bhandári* or bailiff is the landlord's agent in respect of the management of the village. He is usually a Hindu, and represents the landlord's point of view in village questions, just as the *páhn* is the spokesman of the *bhuinhárs* or original settlers. He generally holds one *páwá* of land rent free from the owner, receiving also from every *raiyat* three *karais* or sheaves of each crop as it is cut—one of *gondli*, one of early rice, and one of wet rice. Instead of the land, he sometimes gets Rs. 3 or Rs. 4 in cash, with 12 *káts* or 4½ cwt. of paddy.

(5) Gorait.—The *goráit* is, in fact, the *chaukidár* or village watchman. He communicates the owner's orders to the *raiyats*, brings them to the *máhato* to pay their rents, and selects coolies when required for public purposes. As a rule he holds no service land, but receives the three usual *karais* or sheaves from every cultivator.

(6) Ahir or Goala.—The *áhir's* duty is to look after the cattle of the village, and to account for any that are stolen. He is remunerated by a payment of one *kát* of paddy for each pair of plough-bullocks owned by the cultivators whose cattle are under his charge. He also gets the three *karais* or sheaves at harvest time, besides an occasional *súp* or winnowing fan full of paddy. If cows are under the *áhir's* charge, the milk of every alternate day is his perquisite. In the month of *Ághan* (December) he takes five *sers* of milk round to the cultivators, receiving in return *pakhirá* or 20 *sers* of paddy as a free gift. He always pays the *ábwáb* known as *dádani ghi*, and in some villages has to give the *baitháwán ghi* as well. In a very few cases the *áhir* holds half a *páwá* of land rent-free.

(7) Lohar.—The *lohár* or blacksmith gets one *kát* of paddy and the three *karais* for every plough in the village, and is also paid two or three *ánnás* for every new *phár* or ploughshare. In a very few villages he holds half a *páwá* of land rent-free.

The *kotwál* or constable and the *chaukidár* or watchman do not belong to the genuine Muṅda village system, and need not be mentioned here.

In the Fiscal Division of Torí the bulk of the inhabitants belong to the Kharwár sub-tribe of Bhogtás, and the village system differs from that which prevails on the central plateau. Here the *páhn* is the only official who holds service land, and he gets half a *pátti*, or not quite two standard *bighás*. He performs the village *pujás*, and often does the work of a *máhato*, when the owner of the village is an absentee. But even then the landlord sometimes employs a bailiff, called *bárhil*, to collect the rents.

In the tract known as the Five Parganás, including Támár, Bundu, Sillí, Ráhe, and Barandá, as well as in the *Mánkipatti*, or that part of Sónpur *parganá* which borders on Singbhum district, we meet with *mánkis* and *múndas* who are undoubtedly the descendants of the original chiefs, and still hold the villages which their ancestors founded. Here the *parhá* divisions exist in their entirety, as groups of from twelve to twenty-four villages, each of which has its own *múnda* or village head; while the whole commune is subject to a divisional headman called *mánki*, who collects the fixed rents payable by the *múndas*. The chief village officer is the *páhn*, who holds from one to five *káts* of land rent-free as *dálikatári*. A *kát* in this sense is a measure of land analogous to, if not identical with, the *khandi* of the Kolhán in Singbhum, and denotes the quantity of land which can be sown with one *kát* of seed. In this part of the country the *múnda* sometimes has a deputy called *diwán* who assists him to collect his rents, and *bhandáris* are occasionally met with.

Mundabárik, a class of barbers in Chota Nagpur who only shave Mundas.

Munda-Khariá, a sub-caste of Khariás in Chota Nagpur.

Munda-Lohár, a sub-caste of Lohárs in Lohardagá.

Mundá-Mahili, a sub-caste of Mahilis in Chota Nagpur.

Munda-Mánjhi, a sub-tribe of Mundas in Chota Nagpur.

Munda-Oraon, a sub-tribe of Oraons in Chota Nagpur.

Mundiba, *mahuá* tree, a totemistic sept of Juángs in Orissa.

Mundoraj, a tree, a totemistic sept of Mundas in Chota Nagpur.

Mundra, a section of Mahesris in Behar.

Mundri, quail, a totemistic sept of Mundas in Chota Nagpur.

Mundu or Badar, a dense jungle, a sub-sept of the Saren sept of Santáls.

Munduáb, small mushroom, a totemistic sept of Juángs in Orissa.

Munduia, a sept of Hos in Singbhum.

Mundus, a section of the Kulsunri sub-caste of Sunris in Behar.

Munga, coral, a totemistic sept of Kharwars in Chota Nagpur; a section of the Karan sub-caste of Káyasths in Behar.

Munga Ság, a vegetable, a totemistic sept of Mundas in Chota Nagpur.

Muniar-Ganjhu, a sub-caste of Kharwárs in Hazaribagh.

Muṇiṣ, an agricultural labourer.

Munjaniar, a fruit from which oil is made, a totemistic sept of Chiks in Chota Nagpur.

Munjniar, a wild creeper, a totemistic sept of Oraons in Chota Nagpur.

Munri, fried rice, a totemistic sept of Mundas in Chota Nagpur.

Munshi, an honorary title of Brahmans.

Munsif, an honorary title of Káyasths in Bengal.

Muntri, a section of Goálás in Behar.

Mura, a synonym for Munda, an honorific title bestowed in Bankura on the eldest son of a well-to-do cultivator of the Bhumij tribe. See **Mánki**.

Murão, a synonym for Koiri.

Murári, *Muráli*, a corruption of Mundári, sometimes used outside of Chota Nagpur as a synonym for Munda.

Murba, a section of the Dhaprá and Pachainyá sub-caste of Doms in Behar.

Murchulia, a sept of Páns in Chota Nagpur.

Murdáfarash, a sub-caste of Doms in Bengal who attend to the cremation and disposal of dead bodies, or undertakers, each in charge of a burning *ghát*. They do the same work as Gangáputras, but the latter rank higher.

Murga, cock, a totemistic sept of Oraons in Chota Nagpur.

Murgear, a section of Khariás in Chota Nagpur.

Murgi, hen, a totemistic sept of Binjhiás and Kharwars in Chota Nagpur.

Murhia or **Sebaka**, a group of the Paudá sub-caste of Utkal Brahmans in Orissa.

Muri, a totemistic sept of Korwas in Chota Nagpur whose ancestors made a *chutá* of four sculls and cooked their dinner; a sept of Mundas whose totem is wild fowl.

Muria or **Muriári**, a sub-caste of Malláhs in Behar.

Muriari, *Mariyári*, a boating, fishing, and cultivating caste of Behar. The origin of the Muriari is uncertain. Buchanan,[1] who calls them Mariyári Málas, was of opinion that they belonged to an aboriginal race from the upper valley of the Ganges. Other authorities, however, connect them with the Kewat. Their only tradition is the somewhat vague one that their progenitor was a certain Kál Dás, who came from 'the south country.'

Origin.

The Muriyári marry their daughters as infants or as adults according to their means, the former practice being of course the more fashionable of the two. Polygamy is sanctioned in theory, but is found too expensive in actual life for many to indulge in it. A widow may marry again by *sagai*. She is expected to marry her husband's younger brother if he leaves one, but otherwise her choice is free. Divorce is not allowed.

Marriage.

Their religion, marriage ceremony, funeral observances, and so forth, are of the orthodox type. Maithil Brahmans act as their priests, and are said to

Religion.

[1] Martin's *Eastern India*, i. 172.

incur no social degradation by doing so. Bandi, Parameshwari, and the Panch Pir are their favourite minor gods, to whom they offer flowers, betel leaves, sweetmeats, etc., in a part of their own houses which is plastered with cow-dung for the occasion and called *gosainghar*.

Social status.

The social position of the Muriyári is much the same as that of Gangotás, Kurmis, and Koiris, and Brahmans will take water and certain kinds of sweetmeats from their hands. Their diet is that of most orthodox Hindus, except that, like most of the boating and fishing castes, they indulge freely in spirits. In Bhágalpur Muriyáris who have taken to cultivation call themselves **Maghaya´**, and profess to look down upon the boating and fishing members of the caste, whom they represent as having come from the North-Western Provinces. It is not clear that this divergence of occupation has as yet led to the formation of two distinct sub-castes. The cultivating section of the caste, indeed, appears not to be a very strong one, and few of its members have risen above the status of a non-occupancy raiyat, while many are landless day-labourers paid in cash or kind. In this connexion it deserves notice that in Arrah, where the Mariyári are very numerous, they are employed as ferrymen, boatmen, and fishermen, but refuse to carry palanquins or to settle down as cultivators. Many large boats manned by them arrive at the Váruni fair in November, laden with pulse and other vegetable products.

The following statement shows the number and distribution of the Muriári caste in 1881 :—

Monghyr	385
Bhágalpur	272
Purniah	1,764
Maldah	1,051
Santál Parganás	255

Murkia, a section of Mahesris in Behar.

Internal structure.

Murmi, *Tamang Bhotia*, *Isháng*, *Sain*, a Mongolian or semi-Mongolian caste, who claim to be among the earliest settlers in Nepal. About their origin little is known, nor do their own traditions throw much light upon the question ; but their physical characteristics, and the fact that their exogamous divisions (*thars*) bear Tibetan names, seem to lend support to the opinion that they are descended from a Tibetan stock, modified more or less by intermixture with Nepalese races. Like most Himalayan castes, the Murmis have a large number of *thars*, which are shown in Appendix I. The form of exogamy observed is the simple one that a man may not marry a woman of his own *thar*. For the rest marriage is regulated by the standard formula *mamera*, *chachera*, etc., calculated to seven generations in the descending line. In the case of descents through females these prohibitions are not so strictly observed, and public opinion does not disapprove of marriages with tolerably near relatives, provided that the primary rule of marrying outside the *thar* is not departed from. The question of prohibited degrees among the Murmis is greatly complicated by the rules regarding adoptive brotherhood (*mith*, *dosti*, *kanyaketi*)—a very obscure subject which I have been unable to work out thoroughly. When a man desires to adopt another man as his brother, he sends a message intimating his feelings, and if the reply is favourable presents are exchanged. A day is then fixed for the performance of the regular ceremony, at which a Brahman officiates as priest. The two friends stand facing one another, each with a rupee at his feet. The rupees are solemnly interchanged, and the pair bedaub one another between the eyebrows with the mixture of rice and curds used in the marriage ceremony. A fee of Re. 1 is paid to the Brahman, and the proceedings end with a feast.

Marriage.

The fictitious relationship thus established is regarded as equivalent to actual kinship. The adopted brothers may not address or speak of one another by name, nor may they talk to each other's wives, even though these may have taken part in the ceremony. Their descendants, again, are supposed not to intermarry till seven generations have passed. Some, indeed, say that this prohibition extends to the entire *thar*, and enumerate several *thars* which may not intermarry by reason of their founders having contracted *mith*. Others, again, say that *mith* can only be entered into by members of the same *thar*, whose descendants in the first generation would in any case be forbidden to intermarry. Great importance is attached to the observance of the rules connected with *mith*. In British territory a man who infringes them by marrying a woman within the forbidden degrees is punished by exclusion from the caste, and no Murmi will eat, drink, or smoke with him. In Nepal the penalties are said to be far more severe: the offender is denounced as *hár-phurá*, and is liable to be sold as a slave, or, according to some accounts, to be punished capitally. Murmis may contract *mith* with Bhotias, Lepchas, Limbus, Khambus, Yakhas, Mangars, Gurungs, and Sunwars; and members of the last six castes may even be admitted into the Murmi community.

With the Murmis, as with most of the Himalayan castes, adult-marriage prevails, and sexual intercourse before marriage is tolerated, it being understood that if a girl becomes pregnant she will disclose the name of her lover, and he will come forward to marry her. A bride-price (*sot*) of Rs. 50 to Rs. 60 in ornaments and cash is paid to the bride's parents. The marriage takes place at night in the house of the bride. A Lama officiates as priest and besmears the foreheads of the couple with a mixture of curds and rice. The bridegroom then puts vermilion on the bride's forehead and the parting of her hair and changes places with her, after which the Lama brings their heads together so that their foreheads touch (*lagan*). This is deemed the binding portion of the ceremony. Polygamy is permitted, but is not much resorted to in practice, and it is unusual to find a Murmi with more than one wife. Widows are not allowed to marry again by the regular ritual; but they may be kept as mistresses, and the children of women so kept are said to be considered not inferior to those born in regular wedlock. Divorce is permitted on the ground of adultery or unsuitability of temper. Divorced wives may not marry again, but become concubines on the same terms as widows.

In the matter of inheritance the Murmis follow a tribal custom of their own. Sons inherit in equal shares; failing sons, the father succeeds; then the daughters take equal shares. Failing daughters, the widow inherits, and in any case she must be maintained by the persons who succeed to the property.

Religion.

The religion of the caste is not easy to define. We may discern in it a substratum of primitive animism overlaid by elements borrowed from Hinduism, and, less freely, from Buddhism. Everything tends towards gradual adoption of the Nepalese form of Hinduism, and Buddhist usages are believed to be on the decline, though the Lama still serves as priest at a Murmi wedding, and flags stamped with the sacred *om* may be seen flying in Murmi villages. Notwithstanding this general tendency towards the triumph of Hinduism, some of the popular deities of the caste seem to belong to an earlier type. The stone fetish called Thangbaljho is honoured by winding cloth round it and sprinkling rice on its top; and every September goats and fowls are sacrificed and their blood poured forth on the stone. Similar offerings are made to Purbujá devatá, a forest god who lives in a tree and visits with fever and rheumatism those who neglect his worship. Bhim Singh, one of the Pándava brothers, is worshipped at the Durga Puja with sacrifices of buffaloes, goats, fowls, and ducks. Sherkijho is a fetish of ill-defined attributes; while Gyong and Changreshi appear to be deified Lamas. Behind these again are the village and household gods, a shifting and shadowy multitude, which no man can number or describe, clamouring, like the ghosts who crowded round Odysseus, for their share of sacrifice and libation.

Brahmans have not yet been called in to organize this chaotic Pantheon. Their functions are confined to presiding over the ceremony of *mith*, and occasionally assisting at the worship of some of the standard Hindu gods. The daily religion of the caste is looked after by Lamas or by any Murmi who has a turn for ceremonial ministration.

Disposal of the dead.

The rich burn their dead and preserve a piece of bone to be deposited in a private *gumpa*. The ordinary practice is to bury, the body being laid in the grave with the head to the north and fire applied to the mouth. A small enclosure roofed in with a big stone is built round the grave, a cairn is piled on the stone, and a flag is planted hard by. For seven days after death the relatives of the deceased observe formal mourning and do not eat salt with their food. On the eighth day a propitiatory offering of meat, rice, eggs, plantains, and sweetmeats is presented at the grave, and a feast is given by the chief mourner. For the next six months small daily offerings are made in the house to a piece of cloth torn from the shroud of the deceased: at the end of that time a Lama is called in and the final ceremony is performed.

Occupation and status.

The bulk of the Murmi caste are cultivators, and regard agriculture as their original and fitting occupation. Many of them serve in the police, and Lama Murmis are enlisted as recruits by the 1st Gurkhas. In Nepal they are not reckoned among the regular fighting castes, but they are admitted into the Kiránti regiments raised by Jang Bahadur some thirty years ago. A considerable number are employed as labourers on the tea gardens near Darjiling. In the matter of diet they have few scruples: they eat beef, pork, fowls, and frogs, and indulge freely in spirituous liquors. Notwithstanding this, their social status in the Himalayan region is respectable, and Nepalese Brahmans and Chattris will take water and sweetmeats from their hands. They themselves eat with Limbus, Khambus, Lepchas, and Bhotias.

In 1872 the Murmis numbered 6,557 in Darjiling and 23 in Jalpigori, while in 1881 they numbered 5,324 only in Darjiling.

Murmu, nilgao, a totemistic section of Kurmis in Chota Nagpur and Orissa; a sept of Hos and Santáls.

Murmuár, a totemistic section of Máhilis in Manbhum, the members of which will not touch, kill, or eat the murmu or nilgái.

Murmurwar, a sept of Kharwars in Chota Nagpur.

Muro, a sub-sept of the Murmu sept of Santáls.

Muromah, a sept of Mundas in Chota Nagpur.

Murtel, a *thar* of the Gargya *gotra* of Nepáli Brahmans.

Murti, a section of the Sátmuliá Maghayá sub-caste of Kándus in Behar.

Murum, stag, a totemistic sept of Mundas in Chota Nagpur.

Murwá, a section of the Tirhutiyá sub-caste of Doms in Behar.

Mus, rat, a totemistic sept of Goálás, Chamárs, and Kharwars in Chota Nagpur; a section of Kurmis in Chota Nagpur and Orissa; a totemistic sept of Chiks and Doms.

Musa or **Musu**, mouse, a totemistic sept of Mundas and Páns in Chota Nagpur.

Musahar, *Bhuiyá*, *Sádá Banráj*, *Banmánush*, a Dravidian cultivating and servile caste of Behar, who appear to be an offshoot from the Bhuiyá tribe of Chota Nagpur. The grounds for this opinion are stated at length in the article **Bhuiyá** and need not be repeated here. The question of the origin of the caste has been examined by Mr. J. C. Nesfield in an elaborate monograph on *The Musheras of Central and Upper India,* published in the *Calcutta Review* for January 1888.

Origin according to Mr. Nesfield.

Mr. Nesfield's inquiries into the traditions of the Musahars (as I prefer to spell the name) tend to connect them with the Cherus and Savars, who play a prominent part in the legendary history of the Ganges valley. From this it would follow, if the standard classification be accepted, that the Musahars belong to the Kolarian group of tribes, while my hypothesis would class them among the Dravidians. The distinction, however, between Kolarian and Dravidian appears to me, and, I believe, also to Mr. Nesfield, to rest solely upon peculiarities of language, which in this case at any rate do not correspond to real differences of race. If the test of language is rejected, and we look only to physical characteristics, the so-called Dravidians and Kolarians can only be regarded as local varieties of one and the same stock. This being so, there is really no material difference between Mr. Nesfield's view and my own. He connects the Musahars of the North-Western Provinces with the Dravidian Savars and Cherus; I trace the Musahars of Behar to the equally Dravidian Bhuiyás of Southern Chota Nagpur. Both hypotheses may conceivably be correct. We both agree in thinking the Musahars a fragment of some Dravidian tribe recently and imperfectly absorbed into the Hindu caste system; and if this main point be conceded, it is not very important to determine from which of the known Dravidian tribes the fragment was broken off.

The meaning and derivation of the name Musahar have often been discussed, and Mr. Nesfield has the following remarks on the subject:—

"The name given to the tribe in this essay has been spelt throughout as Mushéra, which is a slight departure from the spelling or spellings hitherto adopted in English books. The name has been supposed to be made up of two Hindi words signifying 'rat-taker.' Hence in Buchanan's *Eastern India* they are described as a people 'who have derived their name from eating rats.' But rat-catching or rat-eating is by no means the peculiar, or even a prominent, characteristic of the tribe; and the name in Upper India at least is pronounced by the natives of the country as Mŭshera, and not as Mūsahar (rat-taker) or Mūsarhá (rat-killer). In an old folk-tale which has recently come to my knowledge, the name is made to signify flesh-seeker or hunter, being derived from *măsŭ*, 'flesh,' and *héra*, 'seeker,' and a legend is told as to the event which led to the tribe being driven to maintain itself by hunting wild animals. This is a more comprehensive title than rat-catcher, besides resting on better authority. Probably, however, both derivations are fanciful,—Hindi versions of a name which is not of Hindi origin. It is certain that the more isolated members of the tribe, who still speak a language of their own unconnected with Hindi, call themselves by a name which sounds like Mŭshéra; and it is not likely that men who have preserved their original speech continuously for so many centuries would have designated themselves by a name borrowed from a foreign language.

"There are one or two other names by which the tribe is known besides Mushéra. In all the districts of Oudh in which the tribe is found, they are commonly, and in some places exclusively, known by the title of Banmánush, or man of the forest. The name Banmánush is of purely Hindi origin; and though intended to be a term of reproach applied by Hindus to a people from whom they stand aloof as impure and savage, it has been accepted by Mushéras themselves, many of whom scarcely know themselves by any other title, and all of whom are entirely ignorant of its origin and meaning. Other names, less commonly known or used, are Deosiyá, derived from their great ancestor Deosi; Banráj, or king of the forest, a less contemptuous, or perhaps an ironical, form of the name Banmánush; and Maskhán, or eater of flesh, another form of the name Maséhra or Mushéra. Sometimes, if a Mushéra is asked to which of the great Indian castes he belongs, he will tell you that he is an Ahir, or rather a subdivision of Ahir, the caste of cowherd; and he appears to be rather anxious to have his title to this honour recognized. But in point of fact he has no claim to any such lineage. Mushéras are the hereditary enemies of Ahirs, as all their legends testify, and many are the petty raids that they have made against them for the possession of cattle and forest."

I am myself inclined to believe that the popular etymology "rat-catcher" or rat-eater is the true one, and that the word is an opprobrious epithet bestowed by the Hindus on the caste with reference to their fondness for eating field-rats. From Vedic times down to the present day we find the promiscuous habits of the non-Aryans in respect of food exciting the special aversion of the Aryan colonists and forming the basis of depreciatory names which tend to supplant the original tribal designation. It can hardly be expected that the givers of contemptuous names should be guided by a nice sense of scientific precision, and would stop to consider whether the practice of eating rats was really the peculiar or prominent characteristic of a particular tribe. The nickname would be bestowed at random, and it is conceivable that even in the same part of the country it might be conferred upon several different tribes.

Internal structure.

The internal structure of the caste is shown in Appendix I. So far as I can ascertain, the only sub-castes are Tirhutiá and Maghaiyá, and it is doubtful whether the distinction between these amounts to true endogamy or represents anything more than the fact that marriage between families living on opposite sides of the Ganges is comparatively uncommon. The divisions Rikhmun and Balakmun appear now to be purely titular groups, which bear no definite relation to marriage. It is a plausible conjecture that they were at one time exogamous sections, which broke up into smaller groups and thus lost their exogamous character. On the north of the Ganges the system of exogamy followed by the Tirhutiá Musahars is very elaborate, and a man may not marry a woman belonging to his own section, or the sections of which his mother and his paternal and maternal grand mothers were members. If, again, the excluded ascendants of a particular couple happened to be of the same section, the marriage is forbidden, although the boy and girl themselves belong to different sections. Among the more primitive Musahars further south the simpler rule prevails that a man may not marry a woman of his own section. This is the case also among the Bhuiyás; and there seem to be grounds for inspecting that the minute regulations which the Tirhutiá Musahars affect to observe have been borrowed by them from some of their Hindu neighbours.

On the north of the Ganges, Tirhutiá Musahars are said to practise infant-marriage; while in Shahabad girls are usually not married until they have passed the age of puberty, and sexual intercourse before marriage is said to be tolerated. A bride-price of Rs. 2 is paid for a virgin, but the tender is reduced to half if there are reasons to doubt her integrity. The marriage ceremony is based on the Hindu model, and does not differ materially from that in vogue among other low castes in Behar. The well-known formula—

Marriage.

Gangá ká páni samundar ki sank
Bar Kanyá jag jag anand

(May Ganges water and sea-shell betide
Enduring bliss to bridegroom and to bride)

is recited by one of the elders present, and water and rice are sprinkled on the bridegroom's head. The bride is then lifted by her mother, and the bridegroom marks her forehead five times with vermilion. Consummation follows at once, and the married couple usually leave for the bridegroom's house next day.

Polygamy is said to be unknown. The remarriage of widows by the *sagai* form is permitted, and is not fettered by the common condition requiring the widow to marry her late husband's younger brother. Divorce is allowed, with the sanction of the caste panchâyat, for infidelity on the part of the wife. The husband breaks in two a piece of dried grass (*khár*) in the presence of the pancháyat, and formally renounces his wife by saying that in future he will look upon her as his mother. Divorced women may marry again by the ritual appointed in the case of widows.

The religion of the Musahars illustrates with remarkable clearness the gradual transformation of the fetichistic animism characteristic of the more primitive Dravidian tribes into the debased Hinduism practised in the lower ranks of the caste system. Among the standard gods of the Hindu Pantheon, Káli alone is admitted to the honour of regular worship. To her the men of the caste sacrifice a castrated goat, and the women offer five wheaten cakes with prayers that her favour may be shown to them in the pains of childbirth. In parts of Gya and Hazaribagh an earlier stage of her worship may be observed. Her shrine stands at the outskirts of the village, and she is regarded as a sort of local goddess, to be appeased on occasion, like the Thakuráni Mai of the Hill Bhuiyas, by the sacrifice of a hog. It is curious to observe that the definite acceptance of Káli as a member of the Hindu system seems rather to have detracted from the respect in which she was held before she assumed this comparatively orthodox position. Her transformation into a Hindu goddess seems to have rendered her less malignant. Her worship, though ostensibly put forward as the leading feature of the Musahar religion, seems to be looked upon more as a tribute to social respectability than as a matter vitally affecting a man's personal welfare Káli, or Debi Mai, as she is commonly called, may be appeased by an occasional

Religion.

sacrifice, but the Birs require to be kept constantly in good humour, or they may do serious mischief. The six Birs or heroes known as Tulsi Bir, Rikmun, Ram Bir, Bhawár Bir, Asan Bir, and Charakh Bir are believed to be the spirits of departed Musahars who exercise a highly malignant activity from the world of the dead. Rikmun is often spoken of as the *purka* or ancestor of the caste, and when a separate sacrifice is offered to him the worshipper recites the names of his own immediate forefathers. On ordinary occasions the Birs are satisfied with offerings of sweetmeats prepared in ghi, but once in every two or three years they demand a collective sacrifice of a more costly and elaborate character. A pig is provided, and country liquor, with a mixture of rice, molasses, and milk is offered at each of a number of balls of clay which are supposed to represent the Birs.[1] Then a number of Bhakats or devotees are chosen, one for each Bir, with the advice and assistance of a Brahman, who curiously enough is supposed to know the mind of each Bir as to the fitness of his minister. The shaft of a plough and a stout stake being fixed in the ground, crossed swords are attached to them, and the Bhakats having worked themselves up into a sort of hypnotic condition, go through a variety of acrobatic exercises on the upturned sword-blades. If they pass through this uninjured, it is understood that the Birs accept the sacrifice. The pig is then speared to death with a sharp bamboo stake, and its blood collected in a pot and mixed with country liquor. Some of this compound is poured forth on the ground and on the balls of clay, while the rest is drunk by the Bhakats. The ceremony concludes with a feast in which the worshippers partake of the offerings.

Priesthood.

The Musahars have not yet attained to the dignity of keeping Brahmans of their own, though they call in Brahmans as experts to fix auspicious days for marriages and important religious ceremonies, to assist in naming children, and even to interpret the will of characteristic Musahar deities like the Birs. In the matter of funeral ceremonies the tendency is to imitate Hindu usage. A meagre version of the standard *sráddh* is performed about ten days after death, and once a year, usually in the month of October, regular oblations are made for the benefit of deceased ancestors. It deserves notice that with Musahars, as with Doms, the sister's son of the deceased officiates as priest at the *sráddh*.

Social status.

The social status of the caste is pretty closely defined by the fact that they will eat any kind of food with all Hindu castes except Chamars, Dosadhs, Dhobi, Dom, and Mihtar, but Doms alone will take food from them. In matters of diet they have few scruples, eating pork, fowls, frogs, tortoises, alligators, jackals, cats, wild and tame snakes, snails, and various sorts of lizards, particularly the gosámp or iguana, while field-rats are esteemed a special delicacy. Beef and the flesh of

---

[1] Some speak of the balls as the "houses" of the Birs, but this seems to be a modern refinement on the primitive idea, which recognizes no distinction between the god himself and the fetish which represents him.

horses and donkeys they hold to be forbidden. In the North-West Provinces, according to Mr. Nesfield, the Dolkárha or palanquin-bearing Musahars eat horse flesh and keep fowls, while the Pahári and Dehâti sub-tribes abstain from both, and regard the horse as a tabooed animal, whom it is sin for a Musahar to touch. The Paháris, however, eat beef when they can get it, and are only deterred from extensive cattle-lifting by their fear of the pugnacious grazier castes. Musahars are skilled, too, above other men in the knowledge of forest products, and use for food a number of roots, leaves, and fruits of which the ordinary Hindu knows nothing. They will not, however, cut or injure the *karhar* tree, which is also held sacred by the Chamárs.

Occupation.

In Behar the bulk of the caste are field-labourers and palanquin-bearers, and only a few have attained to the dignity of cultivating on their own account, or have become possessed of occupancy rights. Further west the hill Musahars, described by Mr. Nesfield, "do not even know the use of the plough." but burn patches of forest and raise small crops in the ashes. Wherever the caste is found they strive to eke out the scanty yield of their agricultural labours by a variety of semi-savage pursuits, their heritage from more primitive modes of life. The rearing of *tasar* silkworms, collecting stick-lac, resin and gum, making catechu, supplying Baidyas and Pansaris with indigenous drugs, stitching leaf plates and cutting wood for sale—all these may be reckoned among the characteristic occupations of the Musahar. We may add the watching of fields and crops by night, which Mr. Nesfield shrewdly connects with the notion that the Banmánush, or "man of the forest" (a common designation of Musahars), is best able to propitiate the primeval deities whose ancient domain has been invaded by the plough. An interesting parallel may be found in Colonel Dalton's statement that in Keonjhar, Bonai, and other Tributary States to the south the Bhuiyás, whom I hold to be the parent tribe from which the Musahars have sprung. "retain in their own hands the priestly duties of certain old shrines to the exclusion of Brahmans." The whole subject of the occupations of the Musahars is discussed with the utmost thoroughness in Mr. Nesfield's admirable monograph.

The following statement shows the number and distribution of Musahars in 1872 and 1881 :—

District.	1872.	1881.	District.	1872.	1881.
Bardwan	......	3	Gya	60,895	16,247
24-Parganás	......	5	Shahabad	10,117	13,313
Murshedabad...	......	1,091	Tirhut { Mozufferpur ...	83,068	38,555
Dinajpur	......	45	Tirhut { Darbhanga ...		66,828
Rangpur	......	17	Saran	5,317	6,465
Bogra	......	18	Champaran	26,844	38,053
Darjiling	......	383	Monghyr	112,565	123,337
Faridpur	......	1	Bhagalpur	69,907	79,584
Maimansinh	......	159	Purniah	20,214	31,225
Chittagong	......	6	Santál Parganás	14,353	18,548
Maldah	......	159	Hazaribagh	4,217	8,753
Patna	27,308	36,864	Lohardaga	64	......

Musalmániá or *Turk-Naua*, a sub-caste of Hajjáms in Behar who are Mahomedans.

Musamiá, a section of Kamár-kalla Sonárs in Behar.

Musawir, a painter.

Mushahar, a subdivision of Bhuiyas—low Bhuiyas as distinguished from the higher Ghatwal Bhuiyas. The former take service, while the latter do not.

Mushrif, an honorary title of Káyasths in Bengal.

Musipur, a group of Maghaiyá Telis in Bengal.

Mustaufi, an honorary title of Káyasths in Bengal.

Musuhang, the lowland chief, a sept of the Phedáb sub-tribe of Limbus in Darjiling.

Mutabar, a title of Kapális, signifying a headman of the panchâyat of the caste.

Mutai, a *thar* or sept of Dámis in Darjiling whose chief profession is sewing.

Muthá, a section of Koránch Kándus; a title of headman among the Kandh tribe in Orissa.

Muthbári, a *thar* or section of Nepáli Brahmans.

Mutri, a sept of Mundas in Chota Nagpur.

Mutriar, a sept of Lohárs in Chota Nagpur.

N

Nábik, a title of Kaibarttas.

Nád, a title of Bangaja Káyasths.

Nadhiá, a section of Goálás in the North-Western Provinces and Behar.

Nadi Samp, river snake, a totemistic sept of Mundas in Chota Nagpur.

Nág, "snake," a totemistic section of the Kumhár, Koiri, and Rajwár castes in Chota Nagpur, the members of which will not touch or kill a snake; a title of Káyasths; of the Kut sub-caste of Gandhabaniks; a totemistic section of Nuniás; a family title of Kashta Baidyas; a section of Binjhiás, Barais, Báruis, Rautiás; a totemistic sept of Ahirs, Bairágis, Bedias, Birhors, Chamárs, Bhuiyás, Kharwárs, and Nágesars in Chota Nagpur; a section of Goálás and a sept of Rájputs in Behar; a sept of Asuras, Gonds; a section of Kahárs, Khariás; a section of Chiks or Páns in Chota Nagpur; of Telis in Bengal; a totemistic section of Khandaits; of Kámárs in Singbhum and the Santál Parganás; of Dhanuks and Doms; a sub-sept of the Kisku sept of Santáls; a title of Sánkháris; a section of Máls in Bankura; a sept of Bhumij, Mundas, Santáls, Lohars, Parhaiyas, Pators; a title of Mayarás in Bengal.

Nágá, *Náger*, *Nágabás*, *Nágamahanta*, (i) corruption of *Nanga*, 'naked;' a small sect of religious mendicants, many or most of whom have now taken to cultivation, call themselves a caste, and are regarded by other people as low-caste Brahmans; they take alms at *sráddhs*: (ii) a title of Maháráshtriya Brahmans.

Nagar, a section of Goálás in Behar.

Nágar, a small cultivating caste of Bhágalpur and the Santál Parganás. The affinities of the Nágars are obscure. They have lost their original sections, and the whole caste now professes to belong to the *Kásyapa gotra*, a section-name borrowed from the Brahmanical system and inoperative for the purpose of controlling intermarriage. They are divided into five sub-castes—**Jethaut, Pulauns, Nágbansi, Káthautiá, Bhátnágar.** Of these all are endogamous except the first two, which have begun to intermarry within the last fifteen years. In all the sub-castes the degrees prohibited for marriage are defined by the formula *chacherá*, *mamerá*, etc., calculated to seven generations in the descending line.

Origin and internal structure.

Both infant and adult-marriage are in vogue, and polygamy is recognized in the event of the first wife being barren. The marriage ceremony is of the standard low-caste type, *sindurdán* being its essential portion.

Marriage.

Widows may marry again by the *sagai* form, and are subject to no restrictions in their choice of a husband. Divorce is not permitted.

Religion.

In their religious and ceremonial observances Nágars do not appear to depart materially from the standard ordinances of popular Hinduism. They employ Brahmans as their priests, who are received on terms of equality by other members of the sacred order.

Social status.

Their social status is low, and they rank just above the Dosádhs, with whom they will smoke, using the same hookah. Neither Brahmans nor members of the castes from whom Brahmans can take water will accept water from the hands of a Nágar. Some few have risen to the position of tenure-holders, but the large majority of the caste are occupancy or non-occupancy raiyats and landless day-labourers.

The following statement shows the number and distribution of Nágars in 1872 and 1881:—

District.	1872.	1881.	District.	1872.	1881.
Murshedabad	......	2,403	Monghyr	7,876	9,786
Dinajpur	......	4	Bhágalpur	3,998	3,264
Jalpigori	......	94	Purniah	2,853	1,030
Shahabad	2	......	Maldah	......	12,319
Darbhanga	696	473	Santál Parganás	211	267
Champaran	1,254	171			

Nágar, a hypergamous group of Maithil Brahmans; in Behar a synonym for Nat, *q.v.*

Nágarchi, a synonym for Dámi in Darjiling.

Nagare-Chhutár, a sub-caste of Sutradhars in the Santál Parganás.

Nagariá, a section of the Banodhiá and Jaiswár Kalwárs in Behar.

Nágasá, an eponymous section of Karans and Khandáits in Orissa.

Nágásan, a *mul* or section of the Naomuliá or Goriá sub-caste of Goálás in Behar.

Nágasya, a section of Telis in Chota Nagpur.

Nágbans, cobra, a totemistic sept of Oraons in Chota Nagpur.

Nágbansi, (i) in Behar a section of Bábhans and also of Dosádhs and Nágars; a sept of Rájputs; a title of Támbulis; (ii) in Chota Nagpur a sub-tribe of pseudo-Rájputs, probably of Dravidian descent, to which the Maharája of Chota Nagpur belongs; a title of Mundas in Chota Nagpur.

Nágbansi Munda, a sub-tribe of Mundas in Chota Nagpur.

Nágbasriár, a section of Kurmis in Chota Nagpur and Orissa.

Nag-Chhang Shakzang, a synonym for Sherpa Bhotia of Nepal.

Nágduar, a water insect, a totemistic sept of Mundas in Chota Nagpur.

Nagen, a sept of Limbus in Darjiling.

Nager, a maker of stones for rings, an occupation followed by Mahomedans.

Nágesar, *Nágasia, Kisan*, a small Dravidian tribe of Chota Nagpur, described by Colonel Dalton as of dark complexion, short stature, and very ugly features. They have two sub-tribes, one of which uses vermilion (*sindur*) in their marriage ceremony, while the other substitutes oil. The names **Sendará** and **Teliá** have reference to this practice. Their sections bear totemistic names which occur among the Mundas and among many other Dravidian tribes. According to Colonel Dalton adult-marriage is in vogue, but matches are arranged by the parents. The standard bride-price is two baskets of rice and one rupee in cash.

In Sargujá the Nágesar worship the sun with offerings of white cocks, and sacrifice goats to Shikária deota, but their chief god is said to be the tiger. In Jashpur they swear by the tiger, but do not worship him, and their chief god is Moihidhúnia, to whom fowls are offered every year and a buffalo once in three years. They also recognize Darha, the village god of the Mundas, and keep the Sarhed festival like them.

Nágeswar, a *mul* or section of the Chhamuliá Madhesiá sub-caste of Halwáis in Behar.

Nágh, a *mul* or section of the Ghosin sub-caste of Goálás in Behar.

Nágneswar, a *mul* or section of the Chhamuliá Madhesiá sub-caste of Halwáis in Behar.

Nagpuriá, a sept of Birhors in Chota Nagpur.

Nágrá, a *mul* or section of the Sátmuliá or Kishnaut sub-caste of Goálás in Behar.

Nágraj, a *mul* or section of the Goriá sub-caste of Goálás in Behar.

Nágrishi, snake, a totemistic section of the Paripál sub-caste of Sunris in Manbhum; a section of Mayarás and Subarnabaniks in Bengal.

Nagrua, a kind of mud, a totemistic sept of Mundas in Chota Nagpur.

Naguriá, a sept of Hos and Santáls.

Náha, Náhá, a title of Báruis in Western Bengal; a title of Bangaja Káyasths in Bengal.

Nahadiá, a section of Goálás in the North-Western Provinces and Behar.

Nah-dik, a sub-sept of the Pon-po sept of Dejong Lhoris or Bhotias of the south.

Nah-pá, a *rui* or sept of Sherpa Bhotias of Nepal.

Naheri, a title of Hajjáms in Behar.

Nahlibo, he who chased his wife, a sept of the Miákhola sub-tribe of Limbus in Darjiling. The story is that the wife of the founder of the *thar* ran away from him, but he caught her and brought her back and afterwards had a large family by her.

Nahmah-pá, a *rui* or sept of the Ruichhug sub-tribe of Dejong Lhoris or Bhotias of the south.

Nái, a synonym for Nápit in Bengal and for Hajjám in Behar.

Naia, the village priest in the communal organization of a village (*Sans.* Náyaka), vulgarly called *laya*.

Náiár, a section of the Bahánnajáti sub-caste of Khatris in Bengal.

Naigrámi, a *gáin* of the Sábarna *gotra* of Bárendra Brahmans in Bengal.

Náik (*Sans.* Náyaka), leader, a title of Acharji or astrological Brahmans in Orissa; of Khandáits in Chota Nagpur and Orissa; of the Dhusiá sub-caste of Chamárs in Behar; of Kaibarttas in Bengal; of Chásás and Kewats in Orissa; of Mál Pahárias, Rájputs, and Telis in Behar; of Khariás, Binjhiás, Ghásis, Chiks, Paturias, and Telis in Chota Nagpur; also a section of Sunris in Behar.

Náiki-Khil, a sub-sept of the Hansda, Hemrom, Marndi, and Tudu septs of Santáls.

Naimba, a coolie class in Nepal.

Naini, a woman who performs the duties of a Naiá or village priest.

Naitam, a sept of Gonds in Chota Nagpur.

Naithung, a sept of Tipperahs in the Hill Tracts of Chittagong.

Naiyá, a small Dravidian caste found only in Bhágalpur. The sections of the Naiyás appear to be totemistic, and this fact, coupled with their bearing the title **Pujáhá**, leads me to regard them as a caste formed by the fortuitous aggregation of a number of Naiyás or Lájás, priests of the aboriginal forest deities, into an endogamous group. For an instance of this process having taken place under very similar conditions, see the article on **Maulik**. A subcaste of the Kádar bears the same name, and it is perhaps owing to this that the Naiyás were not separately enumerated in the Census of 1881.

Naiyá, a sub-caste of Kádars; a section of the Kádar caste in Behar which intermarries with all the other sections except the Marik, Hazári, Naiyá, Kampti, and Báre.

Nakat, a section of Oswáls.

Nákhudá, a commander of a vessel, a title of Gonrhis in Behar.

Naknesá, a section of Madhesiá Halwáis in Behar.

Nakutwár, a *mul* of the Kausika section of Maithil Brahmans in Behar.

Nalakhiá, a section of the Biyáhut and Kharidáhá Kalwárs in Behar.

Nálsi, a *gáin* or sub-section of Saptasati Brahmans in Bengal.

Nal Tiyar, a sub-caste of Tiyars in Bengal.

Nalu, a title of Bangaja Káyasths in Bengal.

Nama, a synonym for Chandál.

Namadháni, a title of Chandáls in Eastern Bengal who live on agriculture.

Namah, short for Nama Sudra, a title of Chandáls in Bengal.

Namahatá, a title of Brahmans and Kayasths in Bengal.

Namang-po, a *rui* or sept of Dejong Lhoris, the members of which are of a low mixed origin.

Nama Sudra, a synonym for Chandál.

Námátá, a synonym for Lohárs in Manbhum who serve as servants to local zamindars.

Námbochhá, a *thar* or sept of Khambus in Darjiling.

Nambon, a sub-sept of the Pon-po sept of Dejong Lhoris or Bhotias of the south.

Námdung, a *thar* or sept of Khambus in Darjiling.

Namjali, a *thar* or sept of Mangars in Darjiling.

Nam-tsang-koba, a *rui* or sept of the Bedtshan-gye sub-tribe of Dejong Lhoris or Bhotias of the south.

Námzingmung, a sept of Lepchas in Darjiling.

Nánaksái, a *gáin* or sub-section of Saptasati Brahmans in Bengal.

Nánakshálhi, a worshipper of Guru Nának, a synonym for Sikh.

Nanda, a group of the Srotriya sub-caste of Utkal Brahmans.

Nandan, a title of Bangaja Káyasths.

Nandanábási, a *gáin* of the Sándilya *gotra* of Bárendra Brahmans in Bengal.

Nandark, a *pur* or section of Sákadwipi Brahmans in Behar.

Nandbansi, a sub-caste of Goálás in the North-Western Provinces and Behar.

Nandi, a *gáin* of the Sábarna *gotra* of Rárhi Brahmans in Bengal; a family title of Kashta Baidyas, Báruis, Káyasths, Mayarás, Nápits, Sánkháris, Subarnabaniks, Tántis, and Tilis in Bengal.

Nándi, a section of the Bahánnajáti sub-caste of Khatris in Bengal.

Nandigrámi, a *gáin* of the Bharadwája *gotra* of Bárendra Brahmans in Bengal.

Nandkiriár, a section of Káyasths in Behar.

Nangeswari, a class of mendicants who go about naked.

Nángtoyár, a section of Kurmis in Chota Nagpur and Orissa who give children their first rice naked.

Nániá, a section of Goálás in the North-Western Provinces and Behar.

Naniár, a section of Khariás in Chota Nagpur.

Nanjorá, a section of Bábhans in Behar.

Nánkár, a section of the Dhengar sub-caste of Gareris in Behar.

Naomuliá or **Majraut,** a sub-caste of Goálás in Behar.

Naorakhiá, a section of Bhojpuriá Halwáis in Behar.

Náphák, a *dugu* or section of the Kochh-Mandai in Dacca. The name indicates the original habitat of the group, probably a hill or village in Assam, and now-a-days has no bearing upon marriage.

Nápit, the barber caste of Bengal, descended, according to one opinion, from a Kshatriya father and Sudra mother, and according to Parásara from a Kuveri father and a Pattikár mother. Some, again, ascribe the origin of the caste to an act of special creation on the part of Siva, undertaken to provide for the cutting of his wife's nails. Several different versions of this myth are current, all of which are too childish to be worth quoting here. The caste is clearly a functional group, formed in all probability from the members of respectable castes who in different parts of the country adopted the profession of barbers.

Origin.

Nápits are divided into the following sixteen sub-castes:—**Anarpuriá, Bámanbane, Bárendra, Uttar-rárhi, Dakshin-rárhi, Paschim-rárhi, Mahmudábáz, Saptagrám, Sátghariá, Khottá.** There are two sub-castes

Internal structure.

in Noakháli—**Bhuluá-Nápit** and **Sundipá-Nápit**, while in the 24-Parganás there are four—**Háldár-Parámánik**, **Koliá-Parámánik**, **Hansadahá-Parámánik**, and **Mujganji-Parámánk**. No trustworthy tradition seems[1] to be extant regarding the origin of these groups, but their names appear to indicate that they are based upon territorial distinctions, and refer to the early settlements of certain main divisions of the caste. The Uttar-rárhi claim to be of higher rank than the Dakshin and Paschim-rárhi, and support their claim by the foolish tale that one of their ancestors was so skilful an operator that he used to shave the Raja of Nadiya without waking him. In recognition of his services he received a large grant of land, with the injunction that neither he nor his descendants should touch the feet of a woman or of a man of low caste. The three Rárhi sub-castes have Kulins and Mauliks among them; but these divisions are not strictly hypergamous, and a Maulik man may marry a Kulin woman, an arrangement wholly impossible among the castes which regularly practise Kulinism. Knarpuriá Nápits do not practise the profession of the caste, but make their living by trade, medicine, and all kinds of clerical work. Many of them are employed as *náibs* and *muharrirs* in the management of landed property. The sections, which are shown in Appendix I, have for the most part been borrowed from the Brahmans; and the exceptions to this rule observed among Mahmudábáz Nápits throw no light upon the origin of the caste as a whole. The theory is that a man may not marry a woman of his own *gotra*; but this prohibition appears not to be very strictly observed, and marriage is regulated for the most part by counting prohibited degrees.

Marriage.

Girls are married as infants between the ages of from six to ten years. A professional matchmaker (*ghatak*) belonging to the Nápit caste, or one of the friends of the bridegroom's family, finds out a suitable match and carries on the preliminary negotiations. A formal visit is then paid by the bridegroom's people for the purpose of seeing the bride and settling the important question of bride-price (*pan*), the amount of which is supposed never to be less than Rs. 100, while it may rise as high as Rs. 200 or Rs. 250. The guardians of the bride also visit and inspect the bridegroom. On these occasions small presents of betel-leaves, areca nuts, fresh fish, milk, etc., are exchanged. The amount of *pan* having been agreed to, the guardians of the bridegroom bestow their blessing (*ásirbad*) on the bride and present her with some article of jewellery. Her people do the same for the bridegroom and give him a few rupees. The date of the wedding is then fixed, and an instalment of the *pan* is paid.

Two days before the bridegroom himself, and the bride through her guardians, perform *nándimukh sráddh* for the propitiation of their ancestors. This is followed on the next day by *aahibás*, when the bridegroom, copiously anointed with turmeric and mustard oil, wearing new clothes, and having his right wrist bound round with cotton and blades of grass, sits on a wooden seat, while a basket containing

[1] Some authorities regard the Madhunápit as a sub-caste of barbers. This opinion, however, rests merely on an obscure tradition, and I have preferred to treat them as a separate caste.

five saucers (*pradip*) for burning oil, five lumps of coloured earth, a looking-glass, a small wooden box (*kotuá*), some vermilion, turmeric, paddy, and grass is carried seven times round him by a married woman whose husband is alive. The basket, with the things in it, is carefully kept that it may be taken next day to the bride's house.

On the wedding day the bridegroom is seven times rubbed with mustard oil and turmeric, and after bathing is dressed in a red silk wrapper. Towards evening he is taken in a palanquin with much discordant music to the bride's house, where the women of the family receive him and carry the basket already referred to round him seven times, touching him with it on the forehead at each turn, and crying *ulu ulu* for good luck.

The bride and bridegroom, both dressed in red silk, are then conducted to the *chháyá-mandap* or ceremonial canopy, which is set up in the courtyard. A sketch plan of this, showing approximately the relative positions of the chief parties to the ceremony, is given below:—

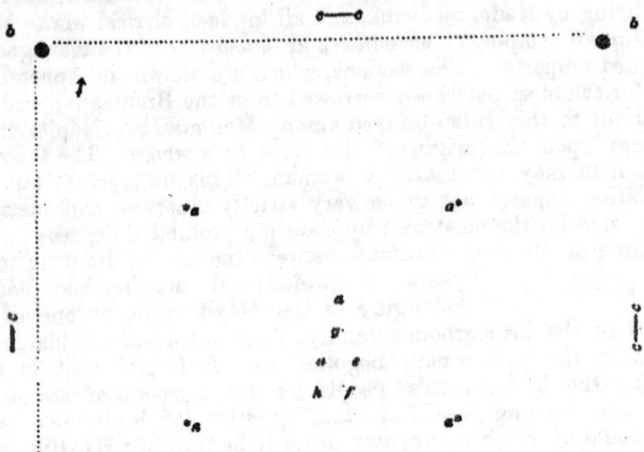

a. Vessels of water covered with mango boughs.
b. Tall shoots of bamboo drawn together at the top, so as to meet over the central water vessel.
c—c. Lines of cotton thread joining the bamboos at about five feet from the ground.
* Plantain stems fixed in the ground.
d. The bridegroom, facing east.
e. The bride, facing west.
f. The bride's father, facing north.
g. The priest.
h. The barber, facing the bride and pronouncing the Gaur-vachana discourse.

The leading persons being placed as shown above, the priest dictates certain *mantras* or sacred texts, which are repeated by the bridegroom, the bride, and her father in turn, while the bride places her hands, palm downward, on the palms of the bridegroom, where a silver coin or some small fruit has been previously placed. This joining of the hands completes the ceremony, and it remains only for the barber to repeat to the wedded pair *Gaur-vachana*, an admonitory discourse about the marriage of Siva and Párvati, having for its moral the duty of submitting to one another and of bearing with each other's infirmities of temper. The bride and bridegroom are then taken to the *básarghar*,[1] a room in the house where they spend the night in the company of a number of young married women, friends of the family, who enjoy the privilege of tormenting the bridegroom with all manner of small witticisms and practical jokes. Early next morning the bride is taken in procession to the bridegroom's house, where she stays for a week and consummation usually takes place. At the end of that time she returns to her father's house and stays there until finally fetched by the bridegroom a year or so afterwards.

Polygamy is permitted, and there seems to be no theoretical limit to the number of wives a man may have. In practice, however, most people content themselves with one. Divorce is allowed on the ground of unchastity with the sanction of the pancháyat, a powerful and well-organized body, who summon both husband and wife before them and inquire into the facts. If the pancháyat decline to grant a divorce their orders are enforced, and the husband compelled to take his wife back by the penalty of excommunication.

Religion.

Most Nápits are Vaishnavas, and comparatively few Sáktas or Saivas are found among the caste. They employ Brahmans as priests, who are received on equal terms by other members of the sacred order. The dead are burned, and *sráddh* performed in the orthodox fashion on the thirty-first day after death.

Social status.

The social standing of the caste is high. They are included in the standard couplet of Parásara defining the Nabasákh group, and Brahmans will take water from their hands. Their own rules regarding diet are the same as are followed by most respectable Hindus. Vaishnava Nápits do not eat flesh, but as a rule allow themselves fish, except the *nánen*, *ghárua pángurá*, *bághár*, and *gajár*. Some, however, affect special purity by abstaining from all kinds of animal food. Sáktas, on the other hand, may take mutton and the flesh of goats which have been sacrificed. Indulgence in spirituous or fermented liquors is supposed to be prohibited, but in practice this question seems to depend more upon individual tastes than upon any general rule.

Occupation.

In Bengal, as elsewhere in India, the barber is an indispensable member of the village community, and the office often descends from father to son, carrying with it in some cases a small allotment of service land, held rent-free

---

[1] For a description of a typical scene in the Básarghar, see pp. 95 ff of *Bengal Peasant Life* by the Rev. Lál Behári Day.

or at a low quit-rent. In large towns they work independently, and there is no regulation against their following their occupation wherever they like. As a rule, the working classes only shave every eight days, but the higher ranks do so every four, sometimes every second day. For shaving every four days, eight annas a month is usually charged, and for a single shave one *paisá*, which also includes the charge for ear-cleaning, nailparing, shampooing, and cracking each joint of the body. In the houses of the rich the barbership is often a hereditary post, as is that of the purohit, dhobá, and dáí, while he, like them, has free access to all parts of the house during the day. The barber pares the nails of Hindu females as well as males, and his presence is required at all domestic occurrences. The day a child is born he pares the mother's nails, and returns on the ninth and thirtieth days to repeat the operation. At the houses of Muhamadans he is only present on the sixth day, the *chhathi*. For these services he is given pulse, rice, oil, salt, turmeric, and two *paisá*, the rich generally adding a piece of cloth and a rupee. At marriages, as has been mentioned above, his presence is essential, and for some castes he performs the functions of a priest. His wife, unlike the Hajjámin of Behar and Upper India, has usually no occupation in Bengal, but the women of the Saptagrámi sub-caste are employed as female barbers.

In addition to all these vocations, the barber, like his European namesake of the seventeenth century, practises surgery, opening boils and abscesses, inoculating for small-pox, and prescribing in all forms of venereal disease. Often he is also an exorciser of devils, and is called in to cure convulsions in newly-born children by *jharna-phunkná*, or muttering spells and making passes with a *nim* branch. When a member of the Nápit caste wishes to study medicine, he is associated with a Kabíráj, who is then called Adhyápaka, or tutor. The pupil is not bound as an apprentice, but he must obey his master as implicitly as the disciple his guru. He compounds salves and simples, and daily receives instruction from his teacher. The Nápits who practise inoculation for small-pox are generally most reckless, spreading the disease without the slightest consideration for the unprotected. They possess a text-book, Vasanta-ṭiká, but few study it.

Nápits have the reputation of being thrifty and very acute, and many plying their trade in one of the large towns hold land in the country, which is sublet to others. Those who practise medicine often amass considerable wealth and attain great influence in rural society. Others, again, make a living by trade; some few have found their way in Government service and the legal profession; while many devote themselves to agriculture as tenure-holders or occupancy raiyats, rising in rare cases to the position of zamindars. A Nápit, however, will on no account till the soil with his own hands or earn his living by fishing, nor will he, like the Hajjám of Behar, accept domestic service in the houses of low-caste men. In Eastern Bengal he poses as a clean Súdra, condescending to shave Europeans and Muhamadans, but refusing to have anything to do with the Chandál, Bhúinmálí, and castes of similar standing. He will shave a Sunri, but will not pare his nails, and will not attend at the wedding of any but the clean Súdras.

Although the Bengal Nápits, unlike the barber-surgeon of the Middle Ages in Europe, does his work more or less in the open air, and has no shop where idlers lounge and the plethoric are bled, he enjoys much the same reputation for loquacity and spreading scandal. Constant observation of his neighbours gives him remarkable insight into the character of all ranks in Hindu society. His experience takes a wider range than that of the average villager, and renders him by comparison a man of the world, full of anecdote and repartee, and often gifted with a talent for debate which enables him to take a prominent part in the affairs of the community. The secrets of many households are known to him, and, if rumour is to be believed, he plays the go-between in many an intrigue. Nápits are very clannish, and an insult received by one is resented by the whole body; while melancholy indeed is the fate of a Hindu who offends his barber. The whole *dal* or union of the village will refuse to shave him, and at last, driven to desperation, he is glad, by the payment of an exorbitant fee, to be restored to their good graces.

The following statement shows the number and distribution of Nápits in 1872 and 1881:—

District.	1872.	1881.	District.	1872.	1881.
Bardwan	26,092	17,897	Darjiling	435	820
Bankura	7,423	12,222	Jalpigori	2,505	4,834
Birbhum	7,746	8,194	Kuch Behar	......	3,048
Midnapur	42,249	45,989	Dacca	18,206	21,715
Hughli	22,287 (Hughli and Howrah)	13,987	Faridpur	12,685	18,897
Howrah		11,454	Bakarganj	40,044	33,486
24-Parganás	36,060	21,803	Maimansinh	19,875	32,768
Nadiya	21,657	19,449	Tipperah	21,643	32,206
Khulna	......	16,289	Chittagong	15,697	15,480
Jessore	29,660	25,002	Noakhali	10,528	12,671
Murshedabad	15,057	13,459	Hill Tracts	4	104
Dinajpur	11,653	12,206	Purniah	......	11
Rajshahye	7,949	8,455	Maldah	6,357	7,864
Rangpur	13,726	12,940	Santál Parganás	.....	14,673
Bogra	3,854	3,917	Singbhum	1,875	1,423
Pabna	10,623	11,698	Manbhum	13,504	15,174

Nápit, a synonym for Bhandári.

Nar, *Nat*, *Nartak*, *Nátak*, a dancing and musician caste of Eastern Bengal, whom Dr. Wise identifies with the Brahmanical Kathak of Hindustán, mainly on the strength of a tradition that they first came to Dacca in the days of the Nawabs. Another theory of their origin makes them out to be the same as the Nuri who manufacture lac bracelets. Ward mentions that in his day none of the caste were to be found in Bengal, and that the Brahmans trace their descent from a Málákár and a female Şúdra. The modern Naţas, not satisfied with this pedigree, claim to be the offspring of Bharadwája Muni and a dancing girl, and assert that the Gaṇak Brahmans are sprung from a son of the same holy man, so the Naṛs of Bikrampur affect to trace their origin to a dancer banished from Indra's heaven and condemned to follow his profession on earth. In

Hindustán the Kathaks still wear the Brahmanical cord and confer the Asír-bád, or benediction, on Ṣúdras; but in Bengal the Naṛs no longer do so, as the original settlers, being few in number, were obliged to take wives from mean castes, and became degraded. Although the Naṛ caste requires to support a Brahman of its own, the Ṣúdra Nápit and Dhobá work for it. The Naṛs have one *gotra*, the Bharadwája, and their patronymics are Nandí and Bhakta, by which latter title the caste is sometimes known, but whenever an individual excels in music, he is dignified by the title Ustád. Like other Ṣúdras, the Naṛs celebrate the *sráddha* on the thirtieth day, are generally Vaishnavas in creed, and have a Patit Bráhman to officiate to them. They decline to play in the houses of the Chaṇḍáls, Bhúinmális, and other low castes, and as their services are no longer required, have ceased to perform before Muhamadans. The Hindu Naṛ occupies a position corresponding to that of the Muhamadan Bájunia, but the former is more sought after, as no Hindu will have a Muhamadan musician in his house if he can possibly avoid it.

When young the Naṛ boys, then called Bhagtiyás, are taught dancing, but on reaching manhood they become musicians, or Sampardá, and attend on dancing girls (Bái), who are usually Muhamadans. If they have no ear for music, they become cultivators or shop-keepers. In former days no Hindu girls ever danced in public, although dancers among the Bází-gar and other vagrant tribes were common, but at present Baistabís and Hindu prostitutes are found among professional Nách girls. There has been a tendency within the last thirty years for the Naṛ caste to separate into two classes—one teaching boys to dance and playing to them, the other attending the Muhamadan Bái. The latter class are the better paid and more skilful musicians, and a band (Sampardái) accompanying a popular dancing girl often earn as much as twenty rupees a night, while the former consider they are well paid if they get five rupees for one night's amusement. The musical instruments generally used by the Naṛs are the Sárungí, Behla and Kásí varieties of fiddles, the Tablá or drum, and the Manjírá or cymbals. Naṛs treat their instruments with great veneration, and always, on first rising in the morning, make obeisance before them. On the Ṣrí Panchamí in Mágh, sacred to Saraswatí, a Naṛ will not play a note until the worship of the goddess is finished. Like the Ṛishí women, the Naṛ women will not play, sing, or dance in public, although at marriages of their own people they still do so.

It is currently believed that many Naṛs have of late years become Muhamadans, but this accusation is denied by the caste. It is nevertheless true that when a Sampardá falls in love with a dancing girl, his only chance of marrying her is by becoming a Muhamadan.

Naradwár, a section of Bábhans in Behar.

Narangbali, a section of the Karan sub-caste of Káyasths in Behar.

Nara-Sundar, a title of Nápits in Bengal.

Naraune-Teghrá, a *mul* of the Parásara section of Maithil Brahmans in Behar.

Naraune-Saktárápur, a *mul* of the Parásar section of Maithil Brahmans in Behar.

Narauni, (i) a *mul* or section of the Tinmuliá, Madhesiá, and Bhojpuriá sub-castes of Halwáis in Behar; (ii) a sept of Chandrabansi Rájputs.

Nárbá, a section of Murmis in Darjiling.

Nardauchhá, a *thar* or sept of Khambus in Darjiling.

Narhan, a *dih* or exogamous section of the Gharbáit sub-caste of Amáts in Behar.

Narhatiár, a section of Káyasths in Behar.

Nári, a low class of people who make lac bracelets. *Occ.*

Nárikátá, cutters of the navel-string, a sub-caste of Háris. The men cultivate and the women act as nurses (*dhái*).

Nári-tepá, pulse-feeler, a title of Baidyas used by outsiders.

Nariyá, a *mel* or hypergamous sub-group of Rárhi Brahmans in Bengal.

Narjenáre, a sept of the Agniá sub-tribe of Meches in the Darjiling Terai.

Nartoroá, a sub-caste of Korwás in Chota Nagpur.

Narwáre-Rámpur, a *mul* of the Kásyapa section of Maithil Brahmans in Behar.

Naskar, a title of Brahmans, Kayasths, and Kaibarttas in Bengal.

Naskarpurá, a section of Pátnis in Bengal.

Natabaidya, a nonym for Nat.

Natanya, a section of Kumhárs in Singbhum.

Náth, (i) a lord; master; a title, perhaps ironical of, and a synonym for, the Jugi caste in Bengal. (ii) A title of Dakshin-Rárhi and Bangaja Káyasths and Subarnabaniks in Bengal. Intermarriage is prohibited within the title. (iii) A section of the Orissa Brahmans. (iv) A title of Binjhiás.

Náthán, a sub-caste of Báruis in Bengal.

Náthji, a title of Jugis in Bengal.

Nathur, a title of Rájputs in Singbhum.

Nau, Nauá, a synonym for Nápit in Bengal and for Hajjám in Behar.

Nauá, a sub-tribe of Thárus in Nepal.

Nauákuri, a section of Kurmis in Chota Nagpur and Orissa.

Nauhatta, a sub-caste of Beldars in Behar.

Naukandri, a Nepal caste who work as carpenters.

Nau-lákh Khambu, a synonym for Khambu.

Nauli-Karan, a sub-caste of Karans in Orissa.

Nauniyár, a synonym or variant for Rauniár, which is a sub-caste of Baniyás in Behar.

Nauriyá, a section of the Bansphor sub-caste of Doms in Behar.

Nautana, a sub-caste of Kumhárs in Jessore.

Nauthni, a sept of Chandrabansi Rájputs in Behar.

Navadwip, a *samáj* or local group of the Bharadwája *gotra* of Páschátya Baidik Brahmans in Nadiya.

Nawalpuriá, a sept of the Rautár sub-tribe of Thárus in Behar.

Naya, priests (worshippers of the titular deity) of Santáls, Bhuiyas, Mauliks, Rajwars, etc.

Náyá, a synonym for Maulik.

Náyári, a *gáin* of the Sábarna *gotra* of Rárhi Brahmans in Bengal.

Necháhli, a *thar* or sept of Khambus in Darjiling.

Nedhuri, a *gáin* of the Sábarna *gotra* of Bárendra Brahmans in Bengal.

Nekári, *Nikári*, a synonym for Machhuá, *q.v.*

Neki, a section of Murmis in Darjiling.

Nekutwár-Barahi, a *mul* of the Kausik section of Maithil Brahmans in Behar.

Nembang, the swollen one, a sept of the Charkhola sub-tribe of Limbus in Darjiling.

Nembong, a sub-sept of the Phejom sept of Limbus in Darjiling.

Nenijor, a section of the Sátmulia Maghayá sub-caste of Kándus in Behar.

Neogi, an honorary title of Brahmans, Kayasths, Sadgops, etc., in Bengal.

Neopáni, Nivipánya, a *thar* of the Kaundin *gotra* of Nepáli Brahmans.

Nepáli, a sub-caste of Brahmans in Nepal.

Nepáliyá, a *thar* of the Dharta-Kausik *gotra* of Nepáli Brahmans.

Neprá, a section of the Sátmuliá Maghayá sub-caste of Kándus in Behar.

Nermáh, a sept of Limbus in Darjiling.

Nesur, a section of Murmis in Darjiling.

Netriá, a section of Kámárs in Singbhum and the Santál Parganás.

Neul, weasel, a totemistic section of Jagannathi Kumhárs in Orissa.

Neurádarvesh, *Náradarvesh*, *Neurājáti*, *Nárajati*, a title of a sect of Vaishnavas who shave their heads.

Newra, mongoose, a totemistic sept of Chiks in Chota Nagpur.

Niáli, a section of Kaibarttas in Orissa.

Nich Kurmi, a sub-caste of Kurmis in Chota Nagpur who marry their daughters as adults and permit sexual license before marriage.

Nichondia, a sub-caste of Baniyás in Behar.

Nidráli, a *gáin* of the Bátsya *gotra* of Bárendra Brahmans in Bengal.

Nigam, a sub-caste of Káyasths in Behar.

Nigániá, a section of Goálás in the North-Western Provinces and Behar.

Nigham, a *mul* or section of the Kanaujiá sub-caste of Sonárs in Behar.

Nij, a sub-sept of all the septs of Santáls.

Nikari, a *gáin* of the Sábarna *gotra* of Bárendra Brahmans in Bengal.

Nikári, *Nikiri*, Hindu fishmongers, who do not catch fish themselves, but obtain their supplies on a system of advances from the regular fishing castes. Mahomedans who follow the same avocation are called Mechuá, *q.v.*

Nikhar, a sub-caste of Gareris in Behar.

Nikharbans, a sept of Chiks in Chota Nagpur.

Nikhati, a *gáin* of the Bharadwája *gotra* of Bárendra Brahmans in Bengal.

Nikitia-Kandh, a sub-tribe of Kandhs in Orissa.

Niktawár, Nikutwár, a section of Bábhans in Behar.

Nikthá, a section of the Banodhiá and Jaiswár Kalwárs in Behar.

Nikum, a section of Goálás in the North-Western Provinces and Behar.

Nikumbh, a sept of the Surajbansi division of Rájputs in Behar.

Niluá, a sub-caste of Jugis in Northern Bengal whose special business it is to dye in blue.

Nimáchandpurá, a *mul* or section of the Naomuliá or Majraut sub-caste of Goálás in Behar.

Nimái, a family of the Kulin group of Jugis in Bengal.

Nimak, salt, a totemistic sept of Mundas in Chota Nagpur.

Nimámbaunchhá, a *thar* or sept of Khambus in Darjiling.

Nimandih, a section of Káyasths in Behar.

Nimavat, a sect of Vaishnavas.

Nimri, a sept of Rájputs in Behar.

Nimuani, a sept of Chiks in Chota Nagpur.

Nimundih, a sept of the Suryabansi Rájputs in Behar.

Ninauchhá, a *thar* or sept of Khambus in Darjiling.

Ninglehku, one who cuts poisonous plants, a sept of the Phedáb sub-tribe of Limbus in Darjiling.

Ninhiám, a *mul* or section of the Chhamuliá Madhesiá sub-caste of Halwáis in Behar.

Niparia, a *mul* or section of the Kanaujiá sub-caste of Hajjáms in Behar.

Nir, a sub-caste of Tántis in Bengal.

Nirábil, a *pathi* or hypergamous sub-group of Bárendra Brahmans in Bengal.

Nirbán, a section of Goálás in the North-Western Provinces and Behar.

Nirbhaya, a title of Sunris in Bengal.

Nirola, a *thar* or section of Nepáli Brahmans.

Nisán, a sept of the Chandrabansi division of Rájputs in Behar.

Nisank, a group of the Srotriya sub-caste of Utkal Brahmans.

Nishi, a synonym for Muchi.

Niskalanka, a section of Telis in Bengal.

Niti Siná, a sub-caste of Dhobás in Central Bengal.

Niyárishi, a section of Telis.

Niyáriyá, *Neyári*, *Niyariyá*, *Niyárdhoá*, a low caste who sift and wash the ashes and refuse of goldsmiths' shops for the scraps of precious metal which may be recovered by this process.

Nobáláre, a sept of the Agniá sub-tribe of Meches in the Darjiling Terai.

Nobonapuria, a section of the Kamár sub-caste of Dosádhs in Behar.

Nodá, a sub-caste of Bágdis found in the 24-Parganás and Hughli, said to have come from Bankura.

Nogo, a sept of Limbus in Darjiling.

Nohár, a variant of Lohár.

Noinjorá, a section of Sonárs in Behar.

Nois, a sept of Mundas in Chota Nagpur.

Nolka, a section of Oswáls in Behar.

Nomahang, a *thar* or sept of Khambus in Darjiling.

Nonaitwár, a *mul* of the Sándil section of Maithil Brahmans, and a *kul* or section of Bábhans in Behar.

Noniyán, a synonym for Nuniá.

Nonoár, a section of Goráits in Chota Nagpur.

Non-pá, a *rui* or sept of Sherpa Bhotias of Nepal.

Nowattiá, a sept of Tipperahs in the Hill Tracts of Chittagong.

Nrisingha, a section of Gandhabaniks in Bengal.

Nunáon, a section of the Biyáhut and Kharidáhá Kalwárs in Behar.

Nun-Bind, a sub-caste of Binds in Eastern Bengal.

Nuneswar, a section of the Biyáhut and Kharidáhá Kalwárs in Behar.

Nunetwár, a *mul* of the Sándil section of Maithil Brahmans in Behar.

Nungoliá, a synonym for Nuniá.

Nunhar, a section of the Biyáhut and Kharidáhá Kalwárs in Behar.

Nuniá, *Noniyán*, a Dravidian caste of Behar and Upper India engaged in cultivation, saltpetre-making, and various kinds of earthwork. The caste seem to have no traditions except of a silly story that the Awadhia are descended from an ascetic named Bidur Bhakat, who broke his fast on salt earth, and being thereby disqualified for the higher life of meditation, was condemned by Rám Chandra to betake himself to the manufacture of saltpetre. This throws small light on the origin of the Nuniás. It seems, however, to be generally believed that they are closely connected with the Binds and the Beldárs, and I venture the conjecture that the Binds may be the modern representatives of an aboriginal tribe from which the Nuniás have branched off as saltpetre-makers and the Beldárs as earth-workers. All three groups are now endogamous. The hunting and fishing proclivities of the Binds seem to suggest that they are the oldest of the three, while the totemistic sections of the Nuniás stamp them as Dravidian. The Beldars are probably a more recent offshoot, but the fact that the name Beldár (mattock-bearer) is assumed by members of any caste when employed on earthwork renders it difficult to determine their precise affinities.

Origin.

The Nuniás of Behar are divided into seven sub-castes:—Awadhiá or Ayodhiabási, Bhojpuriá, Kharáont, Maghayá, Orh, Pachainyá or Chauhán, and Semarwár. Their sections, which are given in Appendix I, appear to be for the most part totemistic. A man may not marry a woman belonging to his own section, but no other sections are barred to him; and the rule of simple exogamy is supplemented by the standard formula *mamerá*, *chacherá*, etc., already quoted. It deserves notice that intermarriage in the *chacherá* line is forbidden as long as any relationship can be traced, while in the other three lines the prohibition only extends to three or, as some say, to five generations. All Nuniás who can afford to do so marry their daughters as infants, adult-marriages being considered unfashionable, if not disreputable. Polygamy is permitted, but it is unusual to find a man with more than two wives; and I gather, although there is no distinct rule on the subject, that practice is held to be justified only by the necessity of procuring offspring. Widows are allowed to marry again by the *sagai* form, and are subject to no restrictions in their choice of a second husband except those arising from consanguinity. It is considered, however, right for a widow to marry her deceased husband's younger brother. Divorce is effected on grounds of adultery or incompatibility of temper by the order of the caste council (pancháyat). A divorced woman may marry again by the *sagai* form unless she has gone wrong with a man of another caste—an offence which entails summary expulsion.

Internal structure.

Tirhutiá Brahmans serve the Nuniás as priests, and officiate at their marriages. The marriage ceremony is of the standard type. The bridegroom-price (*tilak*) is fixed by custom at a sum varying from Re. 1 to Rs. 5

Marriage.

and a pair of *dhotis*. After the marriage the bride does not go with the *barát* to her husband's house, but stays with her parents until she attains puberty, when her husband goes to fetch her with a few of his friends and brings her home in procession (*dira gawau*). Consummation is not effected until after this ceremony. Awadhiya Nuniás have a curious custom called *ásmáui shádi*, which requires that the bride and bridegroom shall be held off the ground during the marriage ceremony.

Religion.

In matters of religion the Nuniás follow the ordinary forms of Hinduism current in Behar. Most of them are Sáktas, and there are said to be comparatively few Vaishnavas in the caste. Bhagavatiji is their favourite goddess. Bandi, Goraiyá, and Sitalá are worshipped on Tuesdays, Wednesdays, and Saturdays. There are no deities specially worshipped by women and children, but women take part in the worship of Sitalá. Sannyási fakirs are the gurus of the caste. The dead are burned, and *sráddh* performed on the thirteenth day after death. The ashes are thrown into any river that may be handy. The bodies of children dying under five years of age are buried—a point wherein Nunias depart from the usual custom, which is to bury after eighteen months.

Occupation.

The caste believe the extraction of salt and saltpetre from saline earth to be their original occupation, and it is possible, as has been suggested above, that they may have broken off from the Binds by reason of their adopting this profession. At the present day we find them also employed in road-making, tank-digging, well sinking, building and thatching houses, and all kinds of agricultural field labour. Many of them also hold lands of their own, and a few have gained a more secure position as occupancy raiyats. Nuniás who have no land often wander about during the dry season in search of work, and build small grass huts for temporary shelter. None of them are artisans. In Bengal, according to Dr. Wise, Nuniás readily obtain service with Goálás or other clean Sudras, but refuse to work as labourers or domestic servants with low-caste families. The social standing of Nuniás seems to vary in different parts, and does not admit of very precise definition. In Patna, Mozufferpur, and parts of Monghyr they rank with Kurmis, Koiris, Kumhárs, etc., and Brahmans will take water and certain kinds of sweetmeats from their hands. In Bhágalpur, Purniah, Champarun, Shahabad, and Gya they are placed on the same level as Tantis, and none of the higher castes will take water from them. In addition to the various kinds of food that are lawful for Hindus of the middle class, Nuniás eat field-rats and pork, and drink fermented and spirituous liquors. It is significant of the Nuniás' point of view in such matters that they think little of Bhakats, who practise small forms of asceticism by abstaining from certain kinds of food and drink; and I am informed that very few Bhakats are found among them.

Social status.

The following statement shows the number and distribution of Nuniás in 1872 and 1881:—

District.	1872.	1881.	District.	1872.	1881.
Bardwan	......	33	Patna	10,316	18,349
Bankura	......	1	Gya	14,916	16,908
Birbhum	......	25	Shahabad	13,183	18,686
Midnapur	......	4,667	Tirhut { Mozufferpur ...	} 69,242	{ 41,616
Hughli	......	39	Tirhut { Darbhanga ...		37,776
24-Parganás	......	451	Saran	65,854	68,368
Nadiya	......	25	Champaran	35,102	45,324
Murshedabad...	......	80	Monghyr	9,318	9,369
Dinajpur	......	1,336	Bhágalpur	3,436	7,377
Rajshahye	......	23	Purniah	971	1,984
Rangpur	......	1,365	Santál Parganás	347	1,662
Bogra	......	287	Cuttack	} *	{ 725
Pabna	......	28	Puri		......
Darjiling	......	362	Balasore		1
Jalpigori	......	275	Tributary States		1
Kuch Behar	......	702	Hazaribagh	278	2,316
Maimansinh	......	2,218	Lohardagá	2,635	4,116
Maldah	......	344	Singbhum	4	32
			Manbhum	228	533

* The figures are included with "other labouring castes."

Nuniár, a subdivision of Baniyas who deal in saltpetre.

Nuniyár, a section of Káyasths in Behar.

Nunkhariá, a section of the Biyáhut and Kharidáhá Kalwárs in Behar.

Nuri, a title of Joláhas in Behar who make lac bracelets, dye for the lips, etc.; the same as Churihár and Laheri. A Bengal caste of jewellers and lac-workers said to have been brought from Orissa by one of the Rajas of Krishnagar

O

Oari, a section of the Karan sub-caste of Káyasths in Behar.

Oaria, verandah, a totemistic sept of Mundas in Chota Nagpur.

Obarsári, a totemistic sept of the Bhumij tribe in Chota Nagpur.

Obung-gyakpa, the dweller above the fountain, a sept of the Phedáb sub-tribe of Limbus in Darjiling.

Odania, a territorial section of Binds in Behar.

Odhalaba, fox, a totemistic sept of Juángs in Orissa.

Oh-Ár, a sept of the Chandrabansi Rájputs in Behar.

Ohdár, a title of Khandáits and Kharwárs in Chota Nagpur.

Oinwár, a *mul* of the Kásyapa section of Maithil Brahmans in Behar.

Ojhá, a group of the Ádi-Gaura sub-caste of Gaura Brahmans; a title of Bábhans; a section of the Pargah caste in Behar.

Ojhá, Ujhá, or **Jhá**, a title of Maithil Brahmans in Behar.

Ojhaiyá, a sept of the Rautár sub-tribe of Thárus in Behar.

Okinwár, a *kul* or section of Bábhans in Behar.

Okrabo, a sept of the Phágu sub-tribe of Yakhas in Darjiling.

Olingthopa, a section of Mangars in Darjiling.

Om, a title of Dakshin-Rárhi Káyasths in Bengal.

On-chhombo, the horse-seller, a sept of the Tambrakhola sub-tribe of Limbus in Darjiling.

Ongdáhba, a *rui* or sept of Dejong Lhoris whose ancestor had emigrated from Bhotan.

Ongyo, a sept of the Tungjainya sub-tribe of Chakmás in the Hill Tracts of Chittagong.

Onwár, a section of Bábhans in Behar.

Ophia, a sept of Parhaiyas in Chota Nagpur.

Or, a sub-caste of Turis in Chota Nagpur.

Orá, a sept of Maghs in the Hill Tracts of Chittagong.

Oráon, *Uráon*, *Kunokh*, *Kunrukh*, a Dravidian cultivating tribe of Chota Nagpur, classed on linguistic grounds as Dravidian, and supposed to be closely akin to the Málés of the Rájmahál hills. Their traditions say that their

Tradition of origin.

original home was in the west of India, whence they came to the Kaimur hills and the plateau of Rohtás in Shahabad. Driven from Rohtás by the Muhamadans, the tribe split into two divisions. One of these, under the Chief, followed the course of the Ganges, and finally settled in the Rájmahál hills; while the other, led by his younger brother, went up the Son into Palamau, and turning eastward along the Koel took possession of the north-western portion of the Chota Nagpur plateau. Some say that they expelled the Mundas from this portion of the country, and forced them to retire to their present settlements in the south of Lohardagá; but this statement is not borne out by local tradition, nor can it be reconciled with the fact that the few Mundas found in the Oráon *parganás* on the plateau are acknowledged and looked up to as the descendants of the founders of the villages in which they live.

Physical characteristics.

The colour of most Oráons is the darkest brown, approaching to black; the hair being jet black, coarse, and rather inclined to be frizzy. Projecting jaws and teeth, thick lips, low narrow foreheads, broad flat noses, are the features which strike a careful observer as characteristic of the tribe. The eyes are often bright and full, and no obliquity is observable in the opening of the eyelids. No signs of Mongolian affinities can be detected in the relative positions of the nasal and malar bones, and the average naso-malar index for a hundred Oráons measured on the system recommended by Mr. Oldfield Thomas omes to 113·6.

Dress and ornaments.

"The dress of the men," says Colonel Dalton, "consists of a long narrow strip of cloth carefully adjusted as a middle garment, but in such a manner as to leave the wearer most perfect freedom of limb, and allow the full play of the muscles of the thigh and hip to be seen. They wear nothing in the form of a coat; the decorated neck and chest are undraped, displaying how the latter tapers to the waist, which the young dandies compress within the smallest compass. In addition to the cloth, there is always round the waist a girdle of cords made of *tasar* silk or of cane. This is now a superfluity, but it is no doubt the remnant of a more primitive costume, perhaps the support of the antique fig leaves. After the age of ornamentation is passed, nothing can be more untidy or unprepossessing than the appearance of the Oráon. The ornaments are nearly all discarded, hair utterly neglected, and for raiment any rags are used. This applies both to males and females of middle age. The ordinary dress of the women depends somewhat on the degree of civilization, and on the part of the country in which you make your observations. In the villages about Lohardagá, a cloth from the waist to a little below the knee is the common working dress; but where there is more association with other races, the persons of young females are decently clad in the coarse cotton cloth of the country, white with red border. Made-up garments are not worn except by the converts to Christianity. The one cloth, six yards long, is gracefully adjusted so as to form a shawl and a petticoat. The Oráons do not, as a rule, bring the upper end of the garment over the head, and so give it the functions also of a veil as it is worn by the Bengali women; they simply throw the end of the dress over the left shoulder, and it falls with its fringe and ornamented border prettily over the back of the figure. Vast quantities of red beads and a large heavy brass ornament, shaped like a torque, are worn round the neck. On the left hand are rings of copper, as many as can be indued on each finger up to the first joint; on the right hand a smaller quantity. Rings on the second toe only, of brass or bell-metal, and anklets and bracelets of the same material are also worn. The hair is, as a rule, coarse and rather inclined to be frizzy, but by dint of lubrication they can make it tolerably smooth and amenable; and false hair or some other substance is used to give size to the mass (the chignon) into which it is gathered, not immediately behind, but more or less on one side, so that it lies on the neck just behind, and touching the right ear; and flowers are arranged in a receptacle made for them between the roll of hair and the head. The ears are, as usual with such people, terribly mutilated for decorative purposes; spikes and rings are inserted into holes made in the upper cartilage, and the lobe is widely distended. When in full dancing costume, they add to their head-dress plumes of heron feathers, and a gay bordered scarf is tightly bound round the upper part of the body."

Bachelor's dormitory.

In matters of domestic economy the Oráons are a slovenly race, and their badly-built mud huts afford no sufficient accommodation for the unmarried members of the family. In the older Oráon villages this difficulty is provided for by a house called the dhúmkúria, in which all the bachelors must sleep under penalty of a fine. Where the girls sleep is, says Colonel Dalton, "somewhat of a mystery." In some villages a separate building, under the charge of an elderly woman, is maintained for their use; and more commonly they are distributed among the widows of the village. "But however billeted, it is well known that they often find their way to the bachelors' hall, and in some villages actually sleep there."

This curious institution is not peculiar to the Oráons. We meet with it among the Juángs, the Hill Bhuiyás of Keonjhur and Bonai, and the Jhumiá Maghs of the Chittagong Hill Tracts. The Oráon system, though already looked upon as an ancient custom, and apparently tending to disuse in newly-formed villages, is still very elaborate. "The Dhúmkúria fraternity are under the severest penalties bound down to secrecy in regard to all that takes place in their dormitory; and even girls are punished if they dare to tell tales. They are not allowed to join in the dances till the offence is condoned. They have a regular system of fagging in this curious institution. The small boys serve those of larger growth, shampoo their limbs, and comb their hair, etc., and they are sometimes subjected to severe discipline to *make men* of them." It is difficult not to see in this a survival of more primitive modes of life, possibly even of the initiatory ceremonies to which many tribes of savages attach so much importance.

Internal structure.

The internal structure of the Oráon tribe is shown in a tabular form in Appendix I. The exogamous septs are extremely numerous, and all that can be identified are totemistic, the totem being taboo to the members of the sept. The rule of exogamy in force is the simple one that a man may not marry a woman of his own sept. The sept name descends in the male line, and there is no objection to a man marrying a woman belonging to the same sept as his mother. In addition to this some system of prohibited degrees seems to exist among them, though no one can state it clearly, nor is it expressed in a definite formula. Still every Oráon will admit that he cannot marry his maternal aunt or his first cousin on the mother's side, though he will probably not be able to say how far these prohibitions go in the descending line. So also no one can marry his younger brother's widow or the elder sister of his deceased wife, though marriage with an elder brother's widow or a deceased wife's younger sister is deemed permissible.

Marriage.

Seventeen years ago, when Colonel Dalton published his account of the Oráons, infant-marriage is said to have been entirely unknown among the tribe. A few of the wealthier men, who affect to imitate Hindu customs, have now taken to this practice, and marry their daughters before they have attained puberty. Among the mass of the people, however, girls marry after they are grown up, and the freest courtship prevails at dances, festivals, and social gatherings of various kinds. Young men woo their sweethearts with offerings of flowers for the hair and presents of grilled field-mice, "which the Oráons declare to be the most delicate of food." Sexual intercourse before marriage is tacitly recognized, and is so generally practised that in the opinon of the best observers on Oráon girl is a virgin at the time of her marriage. To call this state of things immoral is to apply a modern conception to primitive habits of life. Within the tribe indeed the idea of sexual morality seems hardly to exist, and the unmarried Oráons are not far removed from the condition of modified promiscuity which prevails among many of the Australian tribes. Provided that the exogamous circle defined by the totem is respected, an unmarried woman may bestow her favours on whom she will. If, however, she becomes pregnant, arrangements are made to get her married without delay, and she is then expected to lead a virtuous life. Prostitution is unknown. Intrigues beyond the limits of the tribe are uncommon, and are punished by summary expulsion.

Colonel Dalton gives the following account of the Oráon marriage system :—

"When a young man makes up his mind to marry, his parents or guardians go through a form of selection for him; but it is always a girl that he has already selected for himself, and between whom and him there is a perfect understanding. The parents, however, have to arrange all preliminaries, including the price of the damsel, which is sometimes as low as Rs. 4 (8*s*.) In the visits that are interchanged by the negotiators, omens are carefully observed by the Oráons, as by the Mundas, and there are, consequently, similar difficulties to overcome; but when all is settled, the bridegroom proceeds with a large party of his friends, male and female, to the bride's house. Most of the males have warlike weapons, real or sham, and as they approach the village of the bride's family the young men from thence emerge, also armed, as if to repel the invasion, and a mimic fight ensues, which, like a dissolving view, blends pleasantly into a dance. In this the bride and bridegroom join, each riding on the hips of one of their friends. A bower is constructed in front of the residence of the bride's father, into which the bride and bridegroom are carried by women, and made to stand on a curry-stone, under which is placed a sheaf of corn, resting on a plough yoke. Here the mystery of the *sindúrdán* is performed; but the operation is carefully screened from view, first by cloths thrown over the young couple, secondly by a circle of their male friends, some of whom hold up a screen cloth, while others keep guard with weapons upraised and look very fierce, as if they had been told off to cut down intruders, and were quite prepared to do so. In Oráon marriages the bridegroom stands on the curry-stone behind the bride, but in order that this may not be deemed a concession to the female, his toes are so placed as to tread on her heels. The old women under the cloth are very particular about this, as if they were specially interested in providing that the heel of the woman should be properly bruised. Thus poised the man stretches over the girl's head and daubs her forehead and crown with the red powder *sindúr;* and if the girl is allowed to return the compliment (it is a controverted point whether she should do so or not), she performs the ceremony without turning her head, reaching back over her own shoulder and just touching his brow. When this is accomplished, a gun is fired; and then, by some arrangement, vessels full of water, placed over the bower, are capsized, and the young couple and those who stand near them receive a drenching shower-bath. They now retire into an apartment prepared for them, ostensibly to change their clothes, but they do not emerge for some time, and when they appear they are saluted as man and wife. Dancing is kept up during their retirement, one of the performers executing a *pas seul* with a basket on her head, which is said to contain the trousseau. The Oráons have no prescribed wedding garments. They do not follow the Hindu custom of using saffron-coloured robes on such occasions. The bride is attired in ordinary habiliments, and no special pains are taken to make her lovely for the occasion. The bridegroom is better dressed than usual. He wears a long coat and a turban. Nor have the Oráons any special days or seasons for marriages. The ceremony may take place in any month of the year, but, with all natives, the hot, dry months are generally selected if possible. There is then not much work on hand; granaries are full, and they prefer those months for marching and camping out."

Polygamy is permitted, and in theory at least there is no limit to the number of wives a man may have. This luxury, however, is but little sought after. Oráons are usually too poor to maintain many wives, and the majority content themselves with one. Widows may marry again, and are subject to no restrictions in selecting their second husbands. In such marriages the full ceremony is not performed: it is deemed sufficient for the female relatives of the bridegroom to smear vermilion on the bride's forehead and the parting of her hair. Sometimes even this meagre form is omitted, and a valid marriage is constituted by the mere fact of the parties living together. Notwithstanding this laxity of formal observance, the children of a widow are recognized as holding equal rank with those of a woman married by the full ritual used in a first marriage. Divorce is readily effected at the will of either husband or wife. The consent of the pancháyat is not required, nor is the intention to separate attested by any particular form. A husband turns away his wife, or a wife runs off from her husband, and the fact in either case is accepted as constituting a valid divorce. If a woman has children, her husband may be compelled to contribute to their maintenance if he divorces the mother on any other ground than adultery. Similarly, when a wife deserts her husband, not on account of ill-treatment, but merely because she takes a fancy to another man, her parents may be called upon to repay the bride-price which they received at her marriage. Divorced wives may marry again on the same terms and by the same form as widows.

Religion.

"The religion of the Oráons," says Colonel Dalton, "is of a composite order. They have, no doubt, retained some portion of the belief that they brought with them to Chota Nagpur; but, coalescing with the Mundas and joining in their festivals and acts of public worship, they have to a certain extent adopted their ideas on religion and blended them with their own. There is, however, a material distinction between the religious systems of the two people. The Mundas have no symbols and make no representations of their gods; the Oráons, and all the cognates whom I have met with, have always some visible object of worship, though it may be but a stone or a wooden post, or a lump of earth. Like the Mundas, they acknowledge a Supreme God, adored as Dharmi or Dharmesh, the Holy One, who is manifest in the sun; and they regard Dharmesh as a perfectly pure, beneficent being, who created us, and would in his goodness and mercy preserve us, but that his benevolent designs are thwarted by malignant spirits whom mortals must propitiate, as Dharmesh cannot or does not interfere if the spirit of evil once fastens upon us. It is therefore of no use to pray to Dharmesh or to offer sacrifices to him; so though acknowledged, recognized, and reverenced, he is neglected, whilst the malignant spirits are adored.

"I do not think that the Oráons have an idea that their sins are visited on them, either in this world or in a world to come. It is not because they are wicked that their children or their cattle die, or their crops fail, or they suffer in body; it is only because some malignant demon has a spite against them, or is desirous of harming them. Their ideas of sin are limited. Thou shalt not commit adultery, thou shalt not steal, thou shalt not bear false witness against thy neighbour, is about as much of the Decalogue as they would subscribe to. It is doubtful if they see any moral guilt in murder, though hundreds of them have suffered the extreme penalty of the law for this crime. They are ready to take life on very slight provocation, and in the gratification of their revenge an innocent child is as likely to suffer as the actual offender. There is one canon of the Mosaical law that they in former years rigorously enforced—'Thou shalt not suffer a witch to live.' I have dwelt on this subject in treating of the Mundas. If left to themselves, the life of elderly females would be very insecure. As it is, a suspected old woman (and sometimes a young one, especially if she be the daughter of a suspected old one) is occasionally condemned, well drubbed and turned out of the village; and she does not always survive the treatment she is subjected to. If we analyse the views of most of the Oráon converts to Christianity, we shall, I think, be able to discern the influence of their pagan doctrines and superstitions in the motives that first led them to become catechumens. The Supreme Being who does not protect them from the spite of malevolent spirits has, they are assured, the Christians under His special care. They consider that, in consequence of this guardianship, the witches and *bhúts* have no power over Christians; and it is, therefore, good for them to join that body. They are taught that for the salvation of Christians one great sacrifice has been made, and they see that those who are baptized do not in fact reduce their live-stock to propitiate the evil spirits. They grasp at this notion; and long afterwards, when they understand it better, the atonement, the mystical washing away of sin by the blood of Christ, is the doctrine on which their simple minds most dwell. I have not found amongst the pagan Oráons a trace of the high moral code that their cousins of the Rájmahál hills are said to have accepted, I consider that they have no belief whatever in a future state, whilst to the Rájmahális is attributed a profound system of metempsychosis. The Oráons carry that doctrine no further than to suppose that men who are killed by tigers becoms tigers, but for other people death means annihilation. As the sole object of their religious ceremonies is the propitiation of the demons, who are ever thwarting the benevolent intentions of Dharmesh, they have no notion of a service of thanksgiving; and so far we may regard the religion of the Mundas as of a higher order than theirs. When suffering or misfortune befall a man, he consults an augur, or *ojhá*, as to the cause of his affliction, and acts according to the advice given. The *ojhá* has it in his power to denounce a mortal or a particular devil. The method employed has been described in the account of the Mundas, and the result is the same. If a fellow-being is denounced, it is said that he has caused his familiar to possess and afflict the sufferer; and the person denounced is seized and tortured, or beaten, to force him to effect the expulsion of the evil spirit. But the family or village *bhút* may be accused. The *ojhá*, under inspiration, of course, decides what is to be sacrificed, and frequently ruins, if he does not cure, the patient consulting him. In the process of propitiation, the fetish nature of the Oráon belief is shown. The sorcerer produces a small image of mud, and on it sprinkles a few grains of rice. If fowls are to be the victims, they are placed in front of this image; and if they peck at the rice, it indicates that the particular devil is satisfied with the intention of his votaries, and the sacrifice proceeds. The flesh of the animals killed is appropriated by the sorcerer, so it is his interest to have a hecatomb if possible. In regard to the names and attributes of the devils, the Oráons who live with Mundas sacrifice to Marang Búrú and all the Munda Bongas. The Oráons on the western portion of the plateau, where there are few Mundas, ignore the Bongas and pay their devotion to Darhá, the Sarna Burhi (Lady of the Grove), and the village *bhúts*, who have various names. Chanda or Chandi is the god or goddess of the chase, and is always invoked preparatory to starting on great hunting expeditions. Any bit of rock, or stone, or excrescence on a rock, serves to represent this deity. The hill near Lodhma, known to the Mundas as Marang Búrú, is held in great reverence by the Oráons. To the spirit of the hill, whom they call Baranda, they give bullocks and buffaloes, especially propitiating him as the *bhút*, who, when malignantly inclined, frustrates God's designs of sending rain in due season to fertilise the earth. In some parts of the country Darhá is almost the only spirit they propitiate. If fowls are offered to him, they must be of divers colours, but once in three years he should have a sheep from his votaries; and once in the same period a buffalo, of which the *ojhá* or *páhn* gets a quarter. The Oráon must always have something material to worship, renewed every three years. Besides this superstitious dread of the spirits above named, the Oráon's imagination tremblingly wanders in a world of ghosts. Every rock, road, river, and grove is haunted. He believes that women who die in childbirth become ghosts, called *chorail;* and such ghosts are frequently met hovering about the tombstones, always clad in robes of white, their faces fair and lovely, but with backs black as charcoal, and inverted feet, that is, they walk with their heels in front. They lay hold of passers-by and wrestle with them, and tickle them; and he is lucky, indeed, who, thus caught, escapes without permanent injuries." Women who die within fifteen days of their confinement are believed to be likely to become *chorails*; but this danger may be averted by offering sacrifices for the repose of their spirits.

The Oráons do not employ Brahmans, and their religious and ceremonial observances are supervised by priests of their own tribe known as Naiyas.

Festivals.

"The Oráons and Mundas keep the same festivals; but, according to Mr. Luther, the *Karm* is, with the former, the most important. It is celebrated at the season for planting out the rice grown in seed-beds, and is observed by Hindus as well as by Kols and other tribes. On the first day of the feast the villagers must not break their fast till certain ceremonies have been performed. In the evening a party of young people of both sexes proceed to the forest, and cut a young *karma* tree (*Nauclea parvifolia*), or the branch of one, bearing which they return in triumph,—dancing, and singing, and beating drums,—and plant it in the middle of the *ákhra*. After the performance of a sacrifice to the Karma Deota by the *páhn*, the

k

villagers feast, and the night is passed in dancing and revelry. Next morning all may be seen at an early hour in holiday array; the elders in groups, under the fine old tamarind trees that surround the *ákhra*, and the youth of both sexes, arm-linked in a huge circle, dancing round the *karma* tree, which, festooned with garlands, decorated with strips of coloured cloth, sham bracelets and necklets of plaited straw, and with the bright faces and merry laughter of the young people encircling it, reminds one of the gift-bearing tree so often introduced at our own Christmas festival, and suggests the probability of some remote connection between the two. Preparatory to the festival, the daughters of the headmen of the village cultivate blades of barley in a peculiar manner. The seed is sown in moist, sandy soil, mixed with a quantity of turmeric, and the blades sprout and unfold of a pale yellow or primrose colour. On the *karma* day, these blades are taken up by the roots, as if for transplanting, and carried in baskets by the fair cultivators to the *ákhra*. They approach the *karma* tree, and, prostrating themselves reverentially, place before it some of the plants. They then go round the company, and, like bridesmaids distributing wedding favours, present to each person a few of the yellow barley blades, and all soon appear, wearing, generally in their hair, this distinctive decoration of the festival. Then all join merrily in the *karma* dances, and malignant indeed must be the *bhút* who is not propitiated by so attractive a gathering. The morning revel closes with the removal of the *karma*. It is taken away by the merry throng and thrown into a stream or tank; but after another feast dancing and drinking are resumed. On the following morning the effects of the two nights' dissipation are often, I fear, very palpable." Colonel Dalton notices that the *karma* festival is celebrated by Hindus as well as by the aboriginal tribes, and quotes a passage from the Bhavishya Purána, the object of which appears to be to explain how a festival of an aboriginal people came to be adopted by the Hindus. He also points out that the necessity of the females of the family joining in the ceremony is an argument against its Hindu origin.

"The Oráons have some observances during the Sarhúl festival that differ a little from those of the Mundas. Their idea is that at this season the marriage of Dharti, the earth, is celebrated; and this cannot be done till the *sál* trees give the flowers for the ceremony. It takes place, then, towards the end of March or beginning of April; but any day whilst the *sál* trees are in blossom will answer. On the day fixed the villagers accompany their *páhn* to the *sarna*, the sacred grove, a remnant of the old *sál* forest, in which the Oráons locate a popular deity, called the Sarna Búrhi, or woman of the grove, corresponding with the Jáhir Era and Desauli of the Mundas. To this dryad, who is supposed to have great influence on the rain (a superstition not unlikely to have been founded on the importance of trees as cloud-compellers), the *páhn*, arriving with his party at the grove, offers five fowls. These are afterwards cooked with rice, and a small quantity of the food is given to each person present. They then collect a quantity of *sál* flowers and return laden with them to the village. Next day the *pákn*, with some of the males of the village, pays a visit to every house, carrying the flowers in a wide, open basket. The females of each house take out water to wash his feet as he approaches, and, kneeling before him, make a most respectful obeisance. He then dances with them, and places over the door of the house, and in the hair of the women, some of the *sál* flowers. The moment that this is accomplished, they throw the contents of their water-vessels over his venerable person, heartily dousing the man whom a moment before they were treating with such profound respect. But to prevent his catching cold they ply him with as much of the home-brew as he can drink, consequently his reverence is generally gloriously drunk before he completes his round. The feasting and beer-drinking now become general; and after the meal the youth of both sexes, decked with *sál* flowers (they make an exceedingly becoming head-dress), flock to the *ákhra*, and dance all night and best part of next day."

Disposal of the dead.

"Where a death occurs in an Oráon family, it is made known by the lamentations of the women, who loosen their hair (a demonstration of grief which appears to prevail in all countries) and cry vigorously. They lay out the body on the common cot, called *chárpái*; and, after washing it carefully, convey it to the appointed burning-place, covered with a new cloth, and escorted by all the villagers, male and female, who are able to attend. In some families the funeral procession proceeds with music, but others dislike this custom, and nothing is heard but the cries of the women. When they have arrived at the place where the funeral pile has been prepared, the body is again washed, and the nearest relations of the deceased make offerings of rice, and put rice into the mouth of the corpse, while others put pice or other coin. The body is then placed on the pile and anointed; further offerings of rice are made, and the pile is ignited by a father or mother, a wife or husband. When the body has been consumed, notice is given in the village, and there is another collection of friends and relatives to collect the charred bones which remain. These are placed in a new earthen vessel, and ceremoniously taken to the village; and as the procession returns, parched rice is dropped on the road to mark the route selected. The cinerary urn is suspended to a post erected in front of the residence of the deceased; the guests are feasted, and the party then breaks up. In the month of December or January next ensuing, the friends and relations are all again collected to witness the disposal of the bones, in the place that, from the first establishment of the community, has been appropriated to the purpose. This is a point on which the Oráons are exceedingly tenacious; and even when one of them dies far from his home, his relations will, if possible, sooner or later, recover the fragments of his bones, and bear them back to the village, to be deposited with the ashes of his ancestors. The burial ground is always near a river, stream, or tank. As the procession proceeds with music to this place, offerings of rice are continually thrown over the cinerary urn till it is deposited in the grave prepared for it, and a large flat stone placed above. Then all must bathe, and after paying the musicians the party returns to the village. The money that was placed in the mouth of the corpse and afterwards saved from the ashes is the fee of the musicians. The person who carried the bones to the grave has to undergo purification by incense and the sprinkling of water. It is to be observed that this ceremony occurs in each village but once in the year; and on the appointed day the ashes of all who have died during the year are simultaneously relegated to their final resting place. No marriage can take place in a village whilst the bones of the dead are retained there. The most ardent lovers must patiently await the day of *hadbári* or sepulture. The marriage season commences shortly afterwards."

Social status.

In the eyes of the average Hindu the Oráons have no social status at all, and are deemed to be entirely outside the regular caste system. In the important matter of diet the main body of the tribe have as yet made no concessions to Hindu prejudice. Beef, pork, fowls, all kinds of fish, alligators, lizards, field-rats, the larvæ of bees and wasps, and even the flesh of animals which have died a natural death, are reckoned lawful food. Oráons, in fact, will eat almost anything, and are looked down upon as promiscuous feeders by the Bagdis, Bauris, and other dwellers upon the outskirts of Hinduism. A common charge is that they eat snakes and jackals, but this is only partially true, for the flesh of these animals is used solely for certain obscure medicinal purposes, and is not recognized as a regular article of diet. It is a singular fact that the Oráons hold the ass to be sacred, and will not kill it or eat its flesh, thus assigning to the animal much the same position and dignity as the Hindus give to the cow. No reason can be given by the members of the tribe for delighting to honour an animal which is in no way characteristic of heir present habitat; nor do I find any evidence to support the obvious conjecture that the ass may have been a tribal totem. The question of such totems and its bearing upon the problem of the origin of exogamy has been discussed at length in the Introduction to the first volume.

Occupation.

The Oraons claim to have introduced plough cultivation into Chota Nagpur, and thus to have displaced the barbarous *dáhá* method of tillage which is carried on by burning the jungle and sowing a crop of pulse or Indian-corn in the ashes. They were certainly among the earliest settlers on the plateau of Chota Nagpur, and many of them even now hold *bhuinhári* tenures in right of being the first clearers of the soil. These rights, however, are now fast passing out of their hands, and the modern competition for land tends rather to reduce them to the position of tenants-at-will or landless agricultural labourers. "Their lot," says Colonel Dalton, "is not a happy one. Not one of their own people now occupies a position which would give him the power to protect, or the influence to elevate, them from the state of degradation into which a majority of the tribe have long fallen. They submit to be told that they were especially created as a labouring class. They have had this so often dinned into their ears, that they believe and admit it; and I have known instances of their abstaining from claiming, as authorised by law, commutation for the forced labour exacted by their landlords, because they considered that they were born to it. There are indeed some amongst them, stern yeomen, who cling with tenacity to the freeholds they have inherited, and will spend all they possess in defending them, but the bulk of the people seldom rise, in their own country, above the position of cottiers and labourers. There the value of labour has not risen in proportion to the advance that has taken place in other parts of India; and Oráons are easily induced to migrate for a time to other climes, even to regions beyond the great 'black water,' where their work is better remunerated. But those who return with wealth thus accumulated regard it not. They spend in a month what would have made them comfortable for life, and relapse into their lot of labour and penury, as if they had never had experience of independence and plenty. I believe they relish work, if the task-master be not over-exacting. Oráons sentenced to imprisonment without labour, as sometimes happens, for offences against the excise laws, insist on joining the labouring gangs, and wherever employed, if kindly treated, they labour as if they felt an interest in the work. In cold weather or hot, rain or sun, they go cheerfully about it; and after some nine or ten hours of toil, they return blithely home, in flower-decked groups, holding each other by the hand or round the waist, and singing.

"The constitution of the Oráon village is the same as that of the Mundárí. In each the hereditary *múnda* or headman and the hereditary *páhn* or priest have their lands on privileged terms, as the descendants of the founders of the village. The hereditary estates of the two families are called *khúnts*, and there is sometimes a third *khúnt*, called the *máhato;* on all of these a very low rent is fixed, but there are conditions of service attached. These may now be commuted to cash payments at the instance of either party. There is also, under charge of the *páhn*, the land dedicated to the service of the village gods. The priestly office does not always descend from father to son. The latter may be ignorant and disqualified, or he may be a Christian; therefore, when vacated, it is filled by divination. The magic *súp*, or winnowing-sieve, properly spelled like a divining-rod, conducts the person holding it to the door of the man most fitted to hold the office. A priest there must be; an Oráon community cannot get on without one. The fate of the village is in his hands; in their own phraseology, it is said that 'he makes its affairs.' He is also master of the revels which are for the most part connected with religious rites. The doctrine of the Oráons is that man best pleases the gods when he makes merry himself; so that acts of worship and propitiatory sacrifices are always associated with feasting, drinking, dancing, and love-making. The *múnda* or *máhato* is the functionary to whom the proprietor of the village looks for its secular administration. In contradistinction to the *páhn* who makes (*banátá*) the affairs, the *máhato* administers (*chalátá*) them; and he may be removed if he fail to give satisfaction."

The following statement shows the number and distribution of Oráons in 1872 and 1881 :—

District.	1872.	1881.	District.	1872.	1881.
Bardwan	981	2,413	Chittagong	1	43
Bankura	105	76	Noakhali	......	25
Birbhum	5,159	5,567	Patna	6	97
Midnapur	528	83	Gya	35	11
Hughli	} 626	{ 240	Shahabad	712	106
Howrah		19	Darbhanga	880	1,224
24-Parganás	3,362	1,439	Saran	37	108
Nadiya	265	633	Champaran	2,288	1,493
Khulna	......	14	Monghyr	8	43
Jessore	2	133	Bhagalpur	5,612	3,182
Murshedabad...	6,131	2,499	Purniah	8,066	7,864
Dinajpur	2,735	2,187	Maldah	3,165	2,622
Rajshahye	6,019	2,825	Santál Parganás	3,081	1,964
Rangpur	248	79	Cuttack	......	20
Bogra	167	422	Balasore	......	67
Pabna	200	185	Tributary States	......	50
Darjiling	1,648	605	Hazaribagh	1,775	1,493
Jalpiguri	453	210	Lohardagá	151,810	60,924
Kuch Behar	......	3	Singbhum	1,937	1,503
Dacca	2	......	Manbhum	19	670
Faridpur	11	......	Tributary States	53,342	48,975
Maimansinh	5	60			

Oráon, a section of Ghásis; a sept of Mundas in Chota Nagpur.

Oráon-Khariá, a sub-caste of Khariás in Chota Nagpur.

Oraon-Munda, a sub-tribe of Mundas in Chota Nagpur.

Orea, basket-maker, a sept of Mundas in Chota Nagpur.

Orgonra, hawk, a totemistic sept of Oraons in Chota Nagpur.

Orh, a sub-caste of Nuniás in Behar and of Kaibarttas in Orissa. It deserves notice that Od or Odh is a well-known vagrant caste of earth-workers in the Panjáb, Rájputána, and Western Hindustan. See Mr. Ibbetson's Report on the Census of the Panjáb, p. 308.

Orha, *Ourha*, synonyms for Uriya, a native of Orissa.

Orhchásá or *Mundi-chásá*, a sub-caste of Chásás in Orissa.

Orh-Pán or **Uriya-Pán**, a sub-caste of Páns in Orissa.

Oriá, a sub-caste of Sonárs in Behar.

Or-Máhali, a sub-caste of Máhilis who are basket-makers, the same as Doms.

Osái, a section of the Biyáhut and Kharidáhá Kalwárs in Behar.

Osiár, a *pur* or section of Sákadwipi Brahmans in Behar.

Ostá, **Ostad**, a title of Hajjáms in Behar.

Osti, a *thar* or section of Nepáli Brahmans.

Osui, a sept of Tipperahs in the Hill Tracts of Chittagong.

Oswál, a wealthy and respectable trading caste of Behar and Upper India, who say that their name is derived from Osiá or Osnagar, a town in Márwár. Colonel Tod places them among the mercantile clans of Rájputs, and they themselves, like many other trading castes, claim

Origin.

to be pure Vaisyas. However this may be, no one can fail to observe in them a refined type of features and a comparatively fair complexion—characteristics which can only be accounted for by supposing them to be of tolerably pure Aryan descent. A few of the sections of the caste are shown in Appendix I. They differ entirely from those of the Agarwáls. The Oswáls observe a complex rule of exogamy. A man may not marry into (*a*) his own section, (*b*) his mother's, (*c*) his maternal grandmother's, (*d*) his paternal grandmother's, (*e*) his paternal great-grandmother's. This, though reaching much further than the common rule which bars only a man's own section, does not enable the caste to dispense entirely with the usual system of counting prohibited degrees. There is only one sub-caste, the **Dasá**, which is debarred from intermarriage with Oswáls proper. According to Mr. Ibbetson[1] the word "means 'hybrid,' and is used for members of other castes who have departed from the custom of the caste or whose descent is not pure."

Marriage.

Oswáls marry their daughters as infants, prohibit widow-marriage, and do not recognize divorce. Like the Agarwáls, they also forbid polygamy. Many of the caste are Swetambari Jains, but in spite of this difference of religion they intermarry freely with Hindu Oswáls, most of whom belong to the Vaishnava sect, and thus do not offend Jain prejudice by partaking of animal food. Gaur Brahmans serve the Oswáls as priests, and do not forfeit their high position by doing so. The social rank of Oswáls is about the same as that of Agarwáls, and Brahmans will take water and certain kinds of sweetmeats from their hands.

The Oswáls were not returned separately in the Census Report of 1872. The following statement, however, will show the distribution of the caste in 1881:—

DISTRICT.	1881.	DISTRICT.	1881.
Bardwan	2	Maimansinh	11
Rangpur	106	Patna	2
Pabna	3	Shahabad	41
Bogra	4	Monghyr	23
Darjiling	164	Santál Parganás	3
Jalpigori	3	Lohardagá	7
Kuch Behar	20		

Otoniá, a section of the Biyáhut and Kharidáhá Kalwárs in Behar.

[1] *Panjáb Census Report*, para. 533.

P

Páb, a synonym for Pán.

Pábai ke kisán, a section of the Biyáhut and Kharidáhá Kalwárs in Behar.

Paban, a family name of the Grihasth group of Jugis in Bengal.

Pacháin, a *thar* or sept of Mangars in Darjiling.

Pacháinya, a sub-caste of Doms in Behar.

Pachainyá or *Chauhán*, a sub-caste of Nuniás in Behar.

Páchak, a maker of digestive pills and preserves; also a title applied to a Brahman cook.

Páchál, a title of Kaibarttas.

Pachás-ghariá, a group of the Bar-gohri sub-caste of Khandáits in Chota Nagpur.

Pachautá, a section of Madhesiá Halwáis in Behar.

Pachbhajuá, a section of Bábhans in Behar.

Pacheriá, a section of Goálás in the North-Western Provinces and Behar.

Pachgauti, a section of Rájputs in Behar.

Pachgotya, a section of Bábhans in Behar.

Pachhainya, a sub-caste of Agarwáls.

Pachhainyá Madesiá, a sub-caste of Halwáis in Behar.

Pachhaniá, a sept of Rájputs in Behar.

Pachhián, a sub-caste of Chamárs in Behar.

Pachhimá Bráhman, a synonym for Bábhan.

Pachhwár, a *pur* or section of Sákadwipi Brahmans in Behar.

Pachia, a sept of Gonds in Chota Nagpur.

Pachimá or *Kanaujiá*, a sub-caste of Kumhárs in Manbhum.

Pachi Pargana, a *mul* or section of the Naomuliá or Majraut sub-caste of Goálás in Behar.

Pach Kásyapa, a section of Sonárs in Behar, apparently adopted from the Brahmanical system.

Pachlor, a *mul* or section of the Kanaujiá sub-caste of Sonárs in Behar.

Pachmait, a section of Maghayá Kumhárs in Behar.

Páchnariá, a section of the Biyáhut and Kharidáhá Kalwárs in Behar.

Páchottar, a *mul* or section of the Tinmuliá and Chhamuliá Madhesiá and Bhojpuriá sub-castes of Halwáis in Behar.

Pachpákar, a section of Sonárs in Behar.

Pachpaniá, a sub-caste of Gulguliás in Hazaribagh and Gya.

Pachtar, a section of Madhesiá Kándus in Behar.

Pachtariá, a sept of Rájputs in Behar.

Padahári, a group of the Paudá sub-caste of Utkal Brahmans.

Paderáchhá, a *thar* or sept of Khambus in Darjiling.

Padhán, corruption of Pradhán, a title of Chásás in Orissa.

Padhániá, a section of Goálás in the North-Western Provinces and Behar.

Padmaráj, *Padaráj*, lotus-king; a title of Pods and Jaliyas in Bengal.

Padma-rási, a section of Málos in Eastern Bengal.

Padowar, a sept of Páns in Chota Nagpur.

Págmal, a family name of the Kulin group of Jugis in Bengal.

Págulwár-Barhiám, a *mul* of the Sándil section of Maithil Brahmans in Behar.

Pagulwár-Tarálohi, a *mul* of the Sándil section of Maithil Brahmans in Behar.

Pagulwár-Dhen, a *mul* of the Sándil section of Maithil Brahmans in Behar.

Páhari, a sub-caste of Ghásis in Chota Nagpur; a section of Saraogis in Behar.

Paháriá-Agariá, a sub-tribe of Agariás in Chota Nagpur.

Paháriá-Asur, a sub-tribe of Asuras in Chota Nagpur.

Paháriá-Binjhiá, a sub-tribe of Binjhiás in Chota Nagpur, so called from living in the hills.

Paharia-Korwa, a sub-tribe of Korwas in Chota Nagpur.

Pahasrait, a section of the Pachainyá sub-caste of Doms in Behar.

Pahlampuri, a section of Kanaujiá Lohárs in Behar.

Pai, a title of Bangaja Káyasths.

Paiharwáre, a section of Madhesiá Halwáis in Behar.

Páik, a foot soldier, a title of Goálás, Khandáits, Chásádhobás, Pods, and Dhobis. In Midnapur and Cuttack the *Páiks* hold small landed tenures and serve as rural police and village watchmen. Ahir Paiks prepare *churá*.

Paikár, a dealer, a wholesale purchaser, a broker. In the silk industry of Bengal the term is applied to the agents who buy silk cocoons from the cultivators and deliver them to the factory.

Paikará, a sub-tribe of Kaurs in Chota Nagpur.

Pailáhá, a section of the Biyáhut and Kharidáhá Kalwárs in Behar.

Pailá-Sudhá, a sub-caste of Sudhás in Orissa.

Pailwár, a sub-caste of Dosádhs; a sept of Rájputs in Behar.

Paindi, a *thar* or sept of Gurungs in Darjiling.

Painju, a *thar* or sept of the Das-Gurung sub-tribe of Gurungs, so named after a place in the frontiers of Nepal and Tibet near the head waters of the Káligangá.

Paitál, a title of Tántis or weavers, who manufacture silk cloth and also hats.

Paithán, a section of Awadhiá Hajjáms in Behar.

Paiti, a title of Támbulis in Behar.

Pákar, a fruit, a totemistic sept of Konrs in Chota Nagpur.

Pakarye-Maheshi, a *mul* of the Kásyap section of Maithil Brahmans in Behar.

Pákari, a *gáin* of the Sábarna *gotra* of Bárendra Brahmans in Bengal.

Pákbasanta, bird, a totemistic section of Bágdis in Bengal.

Pákháli, a synonym for Dhobá.

Pakharpailo, a sub-section of the Bharadwája section of Utkal Brahmans.

Pakhichátá, a section of Telis in Chota Nagpur.

Pákhimárá, 'bird-killer,' a title of Bediyás.

Pakhora, a sept of Mundas in Chota Nagpur.

Pakhrin, a section of Murmis in Darjiling.

Pakhuá, a sept of Korwas in Chota Nagpur.

Pakli, a section of Karan Káyasths in Behar.

Pakonyal, a *thar* or section of Nepáli Brahmans.

Pakra, a section of Goriá or Dahiár Goálás in Behar.

Pákrási, a *gáin* of the Kásyapa *gotra* of Rárhi Brahmans in Bengal.

Pákuri, a title of Goálás in Behar.

Pál, a title of Dakshin-Rárhi and Bangaja Kayasths, Telis, Sadgops, Kumhars, Támbulis, Tántis, Subarnabaniks, and Sutradhars in Bengal. Intermarriage is usually prohibited within the title.

Páladhi, a *gáin* of the Kásyapa *gotra* of Rárhi Brahmans in Bengal.

Palainggritsa, a sept of Maghs in the Hill Tracts of Chittagong.

Palaingtsa, a sept of Maghs in the Hill Tracts of Chittagong.

Palak Pánre, a *mul* or section of the Biáhut sub-caste of Kalwárs in Behar.

Palámi, a *thar* or sept of Gurungs in Darjiling.

Palankhái, a title of Bágdis in Western Bengal.

Palása, a sept of Maghs in the Hill Tracts of Chittagong.

Palásram, a group of the Sundi sub-caste of Suuris in Bengal.

Palaur, a section of Maheris in Behar.

Páli, a *mul* or section of the Sátmuliá or Kishnaut sub-caste of Goálás, and a section of the Sátmuliá Maghayá sub-caste of Kandus in Behar.

Pálit, a title of Káyasths in Bengal.

Páliwár-Mangrauni, a *mul* of the Bátsya section of Maithil Brahmans in Behar.

Paliwár-Mahesi, a *mul* of the Bátsa section of Maithil Brahmans in Behar.

Paliwár-Dibrá, a *mul* of the Bátsa section of Maithil Brahmans in Behar.

Paliwár-Sakuri, a *mul* of the Bátsa section of Maithil Brahmans in Behar.

Paliwár-Haripur, a *mul* of the Bátsa section of Maithil Brahmans in Behar.

Paliwár-Samaul, a *mul* of the Bátsa section of Maithil Brahmans in Behar.

Paliwár-Kachhrá, a *mul* of the Bátsa section of Maithil Brahmans in Behar.

Paliwár-Phuldáha, a *mul* of the Bátsa section of Maithil Brahmans in Behar.

Paliwár-Mahendra, a *mul* of the Bátsa section of Maithil Brahmans in Behar.

Paliwár-Jarhatyá, a *mul* of the Bátsa section of Maithil Brahmans in Behar.

Paliya, *Poliya*, *Pola*, a Dravidian cultivating caste of Northern Bengal, originally Kochh.

Paliyár-Parghá, a sub-caste of Parghás.

Pálki, a sept of Rájputs in Behar.

Pallab or Ballabh, a sub-caste of Goálás in Bengal.

Pallal, a group of Bárendra Goálás in Bengal.

Palli, a sub-tribe of Savars in Orissa.

Palmohá, a sub-caste of Koiris in Behar.

Palsái, a *gáin* of the Kásyapa *gotra* of Rárhi Brahmans in Bengal.

Pálu, a sept of Limbus in Darjiling.

Palwár, an up-country caste, by profession dealers in *ghi*, boatmen, cultivators, makers of brick-dust; some are also engaged as moharirs in the firms of tradesmen. Suryabansi is their title.

Pamár, a sept of the Suryabansi division of Rájputs in Behar.

Pamia, a tree, a totemistic sept of Mundas in Chota Nagpur.

Pán, *Pánwa*, *Pánr*, *Páb*, *Pánika*, *Chik*, *Chik-Baráik*, *Baráik*, *Ganda*, *Mahato*, *Sáwasi*, *Tánti*, a low weaving, basket-making, and servile caste scattered under various names throughout the north of Orissa and the southern and western parts of Chota Nagpur. "In feature," says Colonel Dalton, "these people are Aryan or Hindu rather "than Kolarian or Dravidian. Their habits are all much alike, "repudiating the Hindu restrictions upon food, but worshipping "Hindu gods and goddesses, and having no peculiar customs which "stamp them as of the other races.[1]" In Singbhum they are said by the same authority to be "domesticated as essential constituents of every Ho village community," and "now almost undistinguishable from the Hos.[2]" In another place they are described as "in all probability remnants of the Aryan colonies that the Hos subjugated.[3]"

Origin.

From these somewhat contradictory utterances it is not quite easy to gather what was Colonel Dalton's final opinion as to the origin of the Páns. In one place he credits them with features of an Aryan or Hindu type, in another he speaks of them as almost undistinguishable from the Hos—the most markedly Negrito-like

[1] Dalton, *Ethnology of Bengal*, p. 325.
[2] Dalton, *op. cit.*, 196, 325.
[3] Dalton, *op. cit.*, p. 185.

representatives of the Dravidian race. The distinction between Kolarian and Dravidian mentioned by him is of course purely linguistic, as has been explained in the introduction to these volumes.

The suggestion that the Páns may be the remnants of Aryan colonies subjugated by the Hos takes us back into prehistoric times, and raises the probably insoluble question: Were there ever Aryan colonies in the region where we find the Páns; and if so, is there anything to show that the Hos subjugated them? To the best of my knowledge the only evidence for the existence of such colonies consists of certain scanty architectural remains buried here and there in the jungles of Chota Nagpur, and of the shadowy tradition that the Singbhum copper mines were worked by the Jains. This seems a slender foundation for the conjecture that the Páns of the present day are the descendants of prehistoric Aryan colonists who were subdued by the Dravidian races of Chota Nagpur and settled down as helots in communities of alien blood, retaining their religion, but parting with that purism in matters of food which has always distinguished the Aryan in comparison with the Dasyu.

Traditions.

Fortunately there is no necessity to enter upon this speculative line of inquiry. Not only do their own traditions claiming descent from the snake throw doubt on the Aryan pedigree which has been made out for them, but the most cursory examination of the exogamous divisions of the Páns affords convincing evidence of their Dravidian origin. The caste has a very numerous set of totems, comprising the tiger,[1] the buffalo, the monkey, the tortoise, the cobra, the mongoose, the owl, the king-crow, the peacock, the centipede, various kinds of deer, the wild fig, the wild plum, and a host of others which I am unable to identify. They have in fact substantially the same set of totems as the other Dravidian tribes of that part of the country, and make use of these totems for regulating marriage in precisely the same way. The totem follows the line of male descent. A man may not marry a woman who has the same totem as himself, but the totems of the bride's ancestors are not taken into account, as is the case in the more advanced forms of exogamy. In addition to the prohibition of marrying among totem kin, we find a beginning of the supplementary system of reckoning prohibited degrees. The formula, however, is curiously incomplete. Instead of mentioning both sets of uncles and aunts and barring seven generations, as is usual, the Páns mention only the paternal uncle and exclude only one generation. They are therefore only a stage removed from the primitive state of things when matrimonial relations are regulated by the simple rule of exogamy, and kinship by both parents has not yet come to be recognized.

Like most castes which are spread over a large area of country, the Páns appear under several different names, the origin of

[1] It is a singular fact that the tiger gives its name to two separate groups. One of these is called *Kulhai*, a word which must have denoted tiger in the original language of the Pans (compare the Santali Kulh); while the other, *Bághail*, is obviously of Hindi origin.

which it is now difficult to trace. Thus in Manbhum they call themselves **Baráik**, 'the great ones,' a title used by the Jadubansi Rájputs, the Binjhias, Rautiás, and Khandáits; in Western Lohardagá and Sargujá we meet them under the name of **Chik** or **Chik Baráik**; in Singbhum they are **Sawási** or **Tánti**, and in the Western Tributary States they are called **Ganda**, a name which suggests the possibility of descent from the Gonds, a tribe which in former times appears to have extended further to the east, and to have occupied a more dominant position than is the case at the present day.

Internal structure.

In Orissa five sub-castes are known:—(1) **Orh-Pán** or **Uriya-Pán**, a semi-Hinduised group supposed to have sprung from a *liaison* between a Pán woman and a member of one of the lower Uriya castes, but now claiming a higher social status than the Páns of the original stock; (2) **Buna-Pán**, including those Páns who weave cloth only; (3) **Betra-Pán** or **Ráj-Pán**, basket-makers and workers in cane, also employed as musicians, syces, and chaukidárs. (4) **Pán-Baistab**, composed of Páns who have become Vaishnavas and who officiate as priests for their own caste. As a general rule it may be laid down that religious differences within the pale of Hinduism do not lead to the formation of endogamous groups. Among Agarwals and Oswals Jains and Hindus intermarry. It is only in Orissa that the Vaishnava members of several castes seem to cut themselves off from their own caste and from the general body of Vaishnavas, and form a new subcaste under a double name denoting the origin of the groups. (5) **Patradiá**, consisting of those Páns who live in the villages of the Kandh tribe, work as weavers and perform for the Kandhs a variety of servile functions. The group seems also to include the descendants of Páns, who sold themselves as slaves, or were sold as Merias or victims to the Kandhs. The precise history of the Patradiá sub-caste is of course obscure, but I see no reason to doubt the possibility of an endogamous group being formed in the manner alleged. There is no question whatever as to the Páns occupying a separate quarter,—a kind of Ghetto,—in the Kandh villages, where they weave the cloth that the tribe requires, and also work as farm-labourers, cultivating land belonging to the Kandhs, and making over to their landlords half the produce as rent. These Páns naturally come to be looked down upon by other Páns who serve Hindus or live in villages of their own and then come to be ranked as a separate sub-caste as regards the slave class alleged to be included in the group. We know that an extensive traffic in children destined for human sacrifice used to go on in the Kandh country, and that the Páns were the agents who "sometimes purchased, but more frequently kidnapped, the children, whom they sold to the Kandhs, and were so debased that they occasionally sold their own offspring, though they knew of course the fate that awaited them." Moreover, apart from the demand for sacrificial purposes, the practice of selling men as agricultural labourers was until a few years ago by no means uncommon in the wilder parts of the Chota Nagpur Division, where labour is scarce and cash payments are almost unknown. Numbers of formal bonds have come before me whereby men sold not only themselves, but their children for a lump sum to enable them to marry, and on several occasions attempts have been made to enforce such contracts in the courts, and to prevent the *Kamiá*, as a slave of this class is called, from emigrating to the tea districts of Assam, or from otherwise evading the obligations he had taken upon himself. There is nothing therefore antecedently improbable in the existence of a slave sub-caste among the Páns.

Marriage.

Pán girls are usually married after they are fully grown up, and the Hindu practice of infant-marriage is confined to a few well-to-do members of the Orh-Pán sub-caste, who have borrowed it from their orthodox neighbours as a token of social respectability. The standard bride-price is said to be Rs. 2 in cash, a maund and a half of husked rice, a goat and two *sáris*—one for the bride and one for her mother-in-law. In Orissa the simple marriage ceremony in vogue is performed by a member of the Pán-Vaishnava sub-caste, who, as has been mentioned above, serve the Páns as priests, and are often spoken of inaccurately as their "Brahmans." In Chota Nagpur, where the organization of the caste is less elaborate than in Orissa, men of the Nágeswar caste not unfrequently serve the Páns as priests; or again any member of the caste with a turn for ceremonial functions may officiate, and the post is usually filled by a Bhakat or devotee. The most essential portions of the ritual are believed to be *sindurdán*, the smearing of vermilion on the bride's forehead, and the parting of her hair and tying together the hands of the bride and bridegroom.

The widows may marry a second time, and it is deemed the proper thing for her to marry her deceased husband's younger brother. She may in no case marry the elder brother. Divorce is permitted, for almost any reason, with the sanction of the caste pancháyat. In Orissa the headman of the caste, styled Dalai or Behera, presides on such occasions, and a *chháda-patra* or bill of divorcement is drawn up. The husband is also required to provide her with food and clothing for six months. Divorced wives are allowed to marry again.

Religion.

The professed religion of the Páns is a sort of bastard Hinduism, varying with the locality in which they happen to be settled. In Orissa and Singbhum they incline to Vaishnavism, and tell a silly story about their descent from Duti, the handmaiden of Rádhá, while in Lohardagá the worship of Mahádeva and Devi Mái is more popular. This veneer of Hinduism, however, has only recently been laid on, and we may discern underneath it plentiful traces of the primitive animism common to all the Dravidian tribes. Man is surrounded by unseen powers—to call them spirits is to define too closely—which need constant service and propitiation, and visit a negligent votary with various kinds of diseases. The Páns seem now to be shuffling off this uncomfortable creed and deserting their ancient gods, while as yet they have not taken vigorously to Hinduism, and they are described by one observer as having very little religion of any kind. Among the minor gods in vogue among them mention may be made of Pauri Pahári or Bar-Pahár, a divinity of unquestionably Dravidian origin, who inhabits the highest hill in the neighbourhood and demands the sacrifice of a he-goat in the month of Phálgun, and occasional offerings of ghi all the year round. The snake is also worshipped as the ancestor of the caste. An attempt was made recently by the Páns of Moharbhanj to induce Brahmans to officiate for them as priests at marriages and funeral ceremonies. but no Brahmans could be persuaded to undertake these offices.

Disposal of the dead.

The southern Páns usually bury their dead in Orissa with the head pointing to the east, while in Singbhum it is turned towards the north. In Lohardagá both cremation and burial are in vogue. Rape seed and water are offered to the deceased and to his ancestors on the eleventh day after death.

Social status and occupation.

The social status of the caste according to Hindu ideas is exceedingly low. They eat beef, pork, and fowls, drink wine, and regard themselves as better than the Hári in virtue of their abstaining from horse flesh. In Lohardagá they eat *kachi*, drink and smoke with Mundas and Oraons. Their original occupation is admitted to be weaving, but many of them have now taken to cultivation. The Buná Páns of Orissa are noted thieves.

The following statement shows the number and distribution of Páns in 1872 and 1881 :—

District.	1872.	1881.	District.	1872.	1881.
Birbhum	......	36	Chittagong	2	......
Midnapur	9,709	......	Tipperah	......	5
24-Parganás	11	......	Cuttack	64,765	78,967
Khulna	......	2	Puri	5,243	6,124
Rangpur	......	57	Balasore	36,546	48,192
Bogra	......	15	Tributary States	112,628	106,567
Dacca	52	......	Lohardagá	12,387	217
Bakarganj	41	41	Mánbhum	..	536
Maimansinh	94	......	Tributary States	30,463	719

Pán, a sect of Dasnámi Sannyásis; a title of Telis and Aguris in Western Bengal.

Panarha, a title of Chamárs in Behar.

Panchabati, a *gáin* of the Sábarna *gotra* of Bárendra Brahmans in Bengal.

Pancha Drávira, one of the two main divisions of Brahmans dwelling in the south of the peninsula.

Pancha Gauriya, one of the two main divisions of Brahmans dwelling in the valleys of the Ganges and Jumna.

Panchakoti, a sub-caste of Brahmans, Baidyas, and Bauris in Western Bengal.

Panchapándava, "the five Pándus," a title of Kshatriyas.

Panchaparibár, a man with five families: a *pangat* or sect of Bairágis in Bengal.

Panchásiá, a sub-caste of Sunris in Tipperah.

Panchaubhe-Khajuli, a *mul* of the Sábarna section of Maithil Brahmans in Behar.

Panchaubhe-Jhauá, a *mul* of the Sábarna section of Maithil Brahmans in Behar.

Panchaubhe-Birpur, a *mul* of the Sábarna section of Maithil Brahmans in Behar.

Panchaubhe-Barhmaul, a *mul* of the Sábarna section of Maithil Brahmans in Behar.

Panchaubhe-Bhithi, a *mul* of the Sábarna section of Maithil Brahmans in Behar.

Panchaubhe-Dadri, a *mul* of the Sábarna section of Maithil Brahmans in Behar.

Panchaubhe-Kariaun, a *mul* of the Sábarna section of Maithil Brahmans in Behar.

Panchbatiár, a *pur* or section of Sákadwipi Brahmans in Behar.

Panchbhaiá, a functional section of Bábhans and Turis in Behar.

Panchbiha, a section of Tántis and Páns in Chota Nagpur.

Panchhai, a *pur* or section of Sákadwipi Brahmans in Behar.

Panchhiá, a sept of Páns in Chota Nagpur.

Panchjáti, a sub-caste of Khatris in Bengal.

Panchkanthi, a *pur* or section of Sákadwipi Brahmans in Behar.

Panchkuti, a *thar* or sept of Dámis in Darjiling whose chief profession is sewing.

Panchnámá mandar, a title of Nágars in Behar.

Panchobe, a *kul* or section of Bábhans in Behar.

Panchsamáj, a group of the Bárendra Sunris in Eastern Bengal.

Pánchsata Baháttarghar, a sub-caste of Kaibarttas in Central Bengal.

Pánchsau-ghariá, a group of the Bar-gohri sub-caste of Khandáits in Gángpur.

Pánchuriá, an endogamous division of Bárendra Brahmans in Bengal. They are held in the same estimation among Bárendras as Pirális among Rárhis.

Pandá, a sub-caste of Utkal Brahmans in Orissa, who serve in temples resorted to by pilgrims. The term is especially applied to temple priests in Orissa.

Pandar, a tree, a totemistic sept of Mundas in Chota Nagpur.

Pánde, a title of Bábhans; a section of the Sribástab sub-caste of Káyasths in Behar; also a designation of clerks of the Káyasth caste in Chota Nagpur.

Pánde or Panre, a title of Gaura, Kanaujiá, and Sáraswat Brahmans in Behar.

Pándiám, a section of Telis in Chota Nagpur.

Pandiár, a *pur* or section of Sákadwipi Brahmans in Behar.

Pandit, (i) a learned man hence, ironically, a title of Bágdis, Doms, Jugis, and other low castes, who do not employ Brahmans. (ii) A section of the Banpár sub-caste of Gonrhis in Behar. (iii) A title of Kumhárs. (iv) A title of Sáraswat Brahmans in Behar; a *thar* or section of Nepáli Brahmans. (v) A title of priests of Barnasankar castes in Tipperah.

Panditratni, including Kesabi, Gurbhabáni, Máládhári, and Brahmachári, a *mel* or hypergamous sub-group of Rárhi Brahmans in Bengal.

Pandki, a section of Ghásis in Chota Nagpur.

Pándrá, a section of Saraogis in Behar.

Pandrasau-ghariá, a group of the Bar-gohri sub-caste of Khandáits in Gangpur and Bonai.

Pandubi, a sub-caste of Malláhs in Behar.

Panduchone, a sept of Mundas in Chota Nagpur.

Panduki or *Pandki*, dove, a totemistic sept of Mundas and Telis in Chota Nagpur.

Paner, *Paneri*, *Panhári*, a seller of *pán* or betel leaf, a title of Barais and Támbulis in Behar.

Paneru, a *thar* or section of Nepáli Brahmans.

Pang-Karmo, *pang*, 'pasture,' and *karmo*, 'white'—a dweller in high pastures, a sub-sept of the Nah-pá sept of Sherpa Bhotias.

Páni, a section of Utkal or Orissa Brahmans.

Pániá, a dealer in pán or betel-leaf, a title of Barais and Támbulis in Behar.

Pánihá chaur, a section of the Biyáhut and Kharidáhá Kalwárs in Behar.

Pánika, a synonym for Pán.

Paniyár, a section of the Maghayá sub-caste of Kumhárs in Behar.

Pánjá, heap of bricks, a title of Bárendra Brahmans and Kaibarttas in Bengal.

Panjiár, **Panjiárá**, a caste official who keeps up genealogies and registers of marriages in Behar; a section of Maghayá Kumhárs and a *pangat* or section of Dosádhs ; a title of Nágars ; a section of the Banapár sub-caste of Koiris and Sunris ; a title of Goálás and Telis in Behar; a title of Kharwárs in Lohardagá.

Pánjibaddh, a hypergamous group of Maithil Brahmans in Behar.

Pánkharayá, a section of the Biyáhut and Kharidáhá Kalwárs in Behar.

Pankhi, a bird, a totemistic sept of Mundas in Chota Nagpur.

Pánkunda, a *samáj* or local group of the Sándilya *gotra* of Páschátya Baidik Brahmans in Bengal.

Pánpátra, a group of the Daspárá sub-caste of Kumhárs in Pabna.

Panr, a sept of Mundas in Chota Nagpur.

Pánr, a synonym for Pán.

Pánre, a section of Kanaujiá Lohárs and of the Banpár sub-caste of Gonrhis in Behar.

Pánre ke pánre, a section of the Biyáhut and Kharidáhá Kalwárs in Behar.

Pánru, snake, a totemistic sept of Lohárs in Chota Nagpur.

Pansain, a section of the Amashta Káyasths in Behar.

Pánsha, a sub-caste of Támbulis in Behar who deal in betel-leaves.

Pansili, a sub-caste of Lohárs in Chota Nagpur.

Pán-Tanti, a class of Tántis or weavers in Chota Nagpur who allow widows to marry, eat fowls, drink wine, etc., while the other class, Aswini Tántis, do no such things.

Panthar, a sub-tribe of Limbus in Darjiling.

Pánthi, a *thar* or sept of Mangars in Darjiling. See **Pánti**.

Panthpákar, a section of the Biyáhut and Kharidáhá Kalwárs; a *mul* or section of the Tinmuliá Madhesiá sub-caste of Halwáis and of the Ayodhiábási sub-caste of Sonárs in Behar.

Pánti, *Pánthi*, a title of Telis and Támbulis in Bengal who sell *pán* (piper betel).

Pánwa, a synonym for Pán.

Panwár, a sept of the Surajbansi division of Rájputs in Behar.

Pápriwál, a section of Saraogis in Behar.

Papson, the adopted one, a sept of the Chaibisa sub-tribe of Limbus in Darjiling.

Parabwár, a *dih* or exogamous section of the Gharbáil subcaste of Amáts in Behar.

Párájuli, a *thar* of the Kaundin *gotra* of Nepáli Brahmans.

Parak, a *dagu* or section of the Kochh-Mandai in Dacca. The name indicates the original habitat of the group, probably a hill or village in Assam, and now-a-days has no bearing upon marriage

Paramánanda Misra, a *mel* or hypergamous sub-group of Rárhi Brahmans in Bengal.

Parámánik, a title of Tántis, Telis, Nápits, Bágdis, Doms, Bauris, and of Goálás in Bengal; of Kurmis in Behar; a section of Pátnis and of the Chapotá subcaste of Hindu Joláhas in Behar; a hypergamous division of Telis and Tiyars in Bengal.

Paramánna, a title of Kaibarttas in Bengal.

Parásara, a *gotra* or section of Brahmans; of Tántis in Bengal; an eponymous sept of Rájputs in Behar; a section of Bábhans in Behar, borrowed from the Brahmanical system and superadded to the original exogamous groups (*kuls*) characteristic of the caste; a *gotra* or section of Joláhas in Behar. This designation has been borrowed from the Brahmans in comparatively recent times, and, being used indiscriminately by all Joláhas, does not operate as a bar to intermarriage. In fact, the Behar Joláhas have no working exogamous sections, and reckon prohibited degrees by the formula *mamera*, *chachera*, etc., explained in the article on Bais. A section of Karans in Orissa; of Káyasths, Madhunápits, Támbulis, Sánkháris, and Subarnabaniks in Bengal; an eponymous section of Bhuinmális in Eastern Bengal.

Parásar Dás, a synonym for, and sub-caste of, Kaibarttas.

Páráswar, a *thar* of the Basishth *gotra* of Nepáli Brahmans.

Parayá, a sept of Hos in Singbhum.

Parbate, a section of Kámis in Darjiling

Parbateh, a *thar* or sept of Mangars in Darjiling.

Parbatti-Kurin, a sub-caste of Gonrhis in Behar, which, though endogamous as regards the other sub-castes of Gonrhis, allows of intermarriage with the Kol sub-caste.

Parbatya, a *thar* or section of Nepáli Brahmans.

Párbbat, a sect of Dasnámi Sannyásis.

Parbe, a *pangat* or section of Dosádhs in Behar.

Pardhán (Pradhán), a title of Khandait Páiks, Khariás, and Kharwars in Chota Nagpur; a section of Sunris in Behar.

Pardhiel Kokaw, a totemistic sept of Mundas in Chota Nagpur.

Parel, a title of Kaibarttas in Bengal.

Parel, Pondyál, a *thar* of the Atrái *gotra* of Nepáli Brahmans.

Parewá, pigeon, a totemistic sept of Bediás in Chota Nágpur.

Párgáchá, a *thar* or sept of Sunuwárs in Darjiling.

Parganábhusári, a *dih* or local section of the Maghayá sub-caste of Koiris in Behar.

Parghá, *Parighá*, a small cultivating and labouring caste, probably of Dravidian descent, found in Monghyr, Bhágalpur, and the Santál Parganás.

Origin.

The origin of the Parghá is obscure, and their traditions throw no light upon their tribal affinities. One legend of the common miraculous type says that the first Parghá was created from the sweat of one of the Hindu gods in order to be a warrior. Another describes them as Paliyá or 'fugitive' Rájputs, who fled from the north-west before the avenging Parasu Rám, and on the way tore off their Brahmanical threads and threw them into the river Son. The Paliyás of Dinájpur, themselves originally Kochh, have a similar tradition, and so have other Dravidian castes whom fortune has placed in a position to pass themselves off as Rájputs. There would indeed be nothing *primá facie* improbable in the hypothesis that the Parghá may be nothing more than an outlying branch of the Paliyá; but arguments based on similarity of names are apt to prove fallacious, and I know of no definite evidence either for or against such a conjecture. Mr. C. F. Magrath, in his memorandum on the castes of Behar included in the Report of the Census of Bengal for 1872, was disposed to infer from their location that they must be a Hinduised offshoot of the Bhuiyás; but this suggestion again seems to be unsupported by any tangible evidence.

Internal structure.

The Parghás of Bhágalpur are divided into two sub-castes—Supa-Parghá and Paliyár-Parghá, and into several sections, which are shown in Appendix I. The section-names are of no special interest. Most of them are terms, such as Marar, Raut, and the like, used by many other castes as titles. I am informed, however, on good authority that among the Parghá these groups are exogamous. Prohibited degrees are reckoned by the usual formula calculated to seven generations in the descending line.

Girls of the Parghá caste may be married either as infants or as adults, but the former practice is deemed the more respectable, and no father who could afford to get his daughter married as a child would allow h · to reach the age of puberty unmarried. The standard low-caste ritual is followed, in which the smearing of vermilion on the bride's forehead is believed to constitute the valid and binding portion. Polygamy is permitted in the sense that a man may take a second wife if the first is barren. Widows may marry again, and are bound by no restrictions, except those arising from the prohibited degrees, in their choice of a second husband. Divorce is not formally recognized; and when a woman goes wrong, she is simply cast off by her husband. She is not, however, turned out of the caste, and she may marry again.

Marriage.

The religion of the Parghás offers no points of special interest, and appears to differ little from that of other Hindus of about the same social standing. Maithil Brahmans serve them as priests, but their rank is low among those of the sacred order. The funeral ceremonies of the caste are for the most part framed on the orthodox model, and are performed on the thirteenth day after death; but in the case of persons who die by a violent death, some Parghás construct a small round heap of dried mud, which is called after the dead and worshipped with offerings of goats and sweetmeats as a minor god.

Religion.

The bulk of the caste are occupancy or non-occupancy raiyats and landless day-labourers; some are tenure-holders, and a few exceptionally fortunate individuals have risen to the status of zemindars holding petty estates. In point of social standing Parghás rank a little lower than Dhánuks. They observe the standard scruples regarding food, and profess to abstain from spirituous liquors.

Occupation and social status.

The following statement shows the number and distribution of the Parghá caste during 1872 and 1881:—

DISTRICT.	1872.	1881.
Champaran	4	...
Monghyr	979	444
Bhágalpur	6,466	6,145
Santál Parganás...	1,850	1,161

Parhaiyá, *Parhiá*, a small Dravidian tribe of Palamau, described briefly by Colonel Dalton and at greater length by Mr. L. R. Forbes in his report on the settlement of Palamau. Their sections are totemistic. Colonel Dalton speaks of them as 'the mere remnant of a tribe who, according to their own traditions in this district and the traditions of other races (Lohardagá), once the population.' They worship Dharti Mai, the earth goddess, and Gohet.

Parhápe, a section of Bábhans in Behar.

Parhar, a section of Goálás in the North-Western Provinces and Behar.

Parhatiá, a sub-section of the Bharadwája section of Utkal

Páriál, a *gáin* of the Sábarna *gotra* of Rárhi Brahmans in Bengal.

Parián, a section of Sonárs in Behar.

Pariár, a *pur* or section of Sákadwipi Brahmans in Behar.

Párich, a *mul* of the Kásyapa section of Maithil Brahmans in Behar.

Párichsardár, a head of the *párichs* or exogamous sections into which some castes are divided.

Paridá, a title of Chásás in Orissa.

Parighá, a synonym for Parghá.

Párihál, a *gáin* of the Sándilya *gotra* and a *mel* or hypergamous sub-group of Rárhi Brahmans in Bengal.

Parihar, a section of Kumhárs in Lohardagá.

Parihár, a sept of the Chandrabansi and Suryabansi sub-tribes of Rájputs; a section of the Banpár sub-caste of Gonrhis and of Sunris in Behar.

Pariharbári, a section of the Biyáhut and Kharidáhá Kalwárs in Behar.

Parihasta, a title of Maithil Brahmans in Behar.

Parijai Kavala, a *thar* or section of Nepáli Brahmans.

Paripál, a sub-caste of Sunris in the Santál Parganás and Manbhum.

Parirá, a sub-tribe of Savars in Orissa.

Pariá, a title of Agariás, Asuras, Binjhiás, Oraons, and Khariás in Chota Nagpur.

Párkhari, a sept of Limbus in Darjiling.

Parkhiá, a virtuoso, an examiner of jewels.

Párnágrahi, a group of the Srotriya sub-caste of Utkal Brahmans.

Párni, a title of several fishermen castes—Chandál, Málo, Kochh, etc., who act as ferrymen.

Parrarit, a section of Maghaiyá Kumhárs in Behar.

Parsaiá, a *mul* or section of the Ayodhiabási sub-caste of Sonárs in Behar.

Parsariá, a *kul* or section of Bábhans in Behar.

Parsautiá, a section of the Sútmuliá Maghayá sub-caste of Kándus in Behar.

Parselá, a *mul* or section of the Ghosin sub-caste of Goálás in Behar.

Parsi, Parsu, a bush, a totemistic sept of Mundas in Chota Nagpur.

Parubo, a *rui* or sept of Dejong Lhoris whose ancestor had emigrated from Bhotan.

Parue-Mahendra, a *mul* of the Kásyap section of Maithil Brahmans in Behar.

Párui, a sub-caste of Chandáls in Eastern Bengal; a title of Kaibarttas in Bengal.

Parurá, a section of Awadhiá Hajjáms in Behar.

Parus, a section of the Maghayá sub-caste of Barhis in Behar.

Parwariá, a section of the Dhaprá sub-caste of Doms in Behar.

Paryá, *Parkyá*, "a low Brahman who takes from Hindus alms, such as oil, old black blankets, etc.; all black things on every Saturday, which is accounted a black day." *Fallon, s.v.*

Pásbán, "watchman," a title of Dosádhs in Behar, where members of that caste are largely employed as *chaukidárs* or village watchmen.

Páschátya Baidik, a sub-caste of Baidik Brahmans in Bengal.

Paschimá, a sub-caste of Kámárs in Eastern Bengal.

Paschim-Kabát, west gate, a title of Khandáits in Orissa.

Paschim-Kuliyá, a sub-caste of Sadgops in Bengal.

Paschim-rárhi, a sub-caste of Nápits in Bengal.

Paserea, a class of people who hawk about goods for sale; pedlars.

Pási, a Dravidian caste of Behar, whose original occupation is believed to have been the tapping of the palmyra, date, and other palm trees for their sap. The name Pási is usually derived from *pása*, a noose or cord, which Mr. Nesfield interprets as disclosing that they have only recently emerged from the hunting state. It seems, however, more probable that the name refers, not to the snaring of wild animals, but to the sling or noose used by Pásis in climbing palm trees.

Origin.

Pásis are divided into four sub-castes—**Báydhá**, **Gaiduha**, **Kamáni**, and **Tirsuliá**. There are also Mahomedan Pásis, distinguished by the designation **Turk**. The Byádhá sub-caste say that their original occupation was to collect the water-chestnut or singhárá (*Trapa bispinosa*, Roxb.), but now they tap date trees like the other sub-castes. There is only one section, **Kásyapa**, which has been borrowed from the Brahmanical system in comparatively recent times, and has no bearing on the regulation of marriages. Prohibited degrees are reckoned by the standard formula *mamerá*, *chacherá*, etc., calculated to seven generations in the descending line.

Internal structure.

Pásis marry their daughters as infants or as adults according to their means, the former practice being deemed the more respectable. The marriage ceremony is of the ordinary low-caste type. It is preceded by *lagan*, when a Brahman stirs up in water two grains of rice, representing the bride and bridegroom, and sprinkles vermilion over them as soon as the grains float into contact with each other. This favourable omen having been observed and a trifling sum paid as bride-price, a date for the marriage is fixed. The binding portion of the ceremony is the smearing of vermilion on the bride's forehead with the bridegroom's left hand. Opinions differ as to the practice of the caste in the matter of polygamy. Some say that a man may have as many wives as he can afford to maintain; others that he can only take a second wife with the consent of his first wife, and for the purpose of obtaining offspring. A widow may marry again by the *sagai* form, but is expected to marry her deceased husband's younger brother if there is one. Failing him, she may marry any one not within the prohibited degrees Divorce is effected, by the consent

Marriage.

of the panchâyat, when a woman is convicted of adultery with another member of the caste. Women divorced on these grounds may marry again on paying a fine, which usually takes the form of a feast to the caste panchâyat. Adultery with an outsider admits of no such atonement, and a woman detected in this offence is turned out of the caste, and usually becomes a regular prostitute.

Succession.

In matters of inheritance the caste professes to be guided by the principles of the Mitakshará law, which are enforced in cases of dispute by the caste-council (pancháyat). Daughters, however, and daughters' sons, do not inherit so long as any *deádi* relative survives.

Religion.

Most Pásis belong to the Sákta sect of Hindus, and regard Bhagavati as the goddess whom they are chiefly bound to worship. In their religious and ceremonial observances the Kamáni sub-caste alone employ Tirhutiá Brahmans, who are said to incur no social degradation by serving them. The other sub-castes call in degraded (*patit*) Brahmans for marriges only. Such Brahmans rank very low in social reputation, and their employment by the Pásis seems to be a reform introduced at a very recent date, for in all funeral ceremonies and at sacrifices offered to the greater gods whenever the services of a Brahman are not available the worshipper's sister's son (*bhánjá*) performs the functions of the priest. Among the Pásis of Monghyr this ancient custom, which admits of being plausibly interpreted as a survival of female kinship, still prevails in such force that the caste has not yet been convinced of the necessity of engaging Brahmans at all. The guru of the Pásis is usually a Nának-Shahi ascetic.

The minor-gods of the Pásis are very numerous. Bandi, Goraiyá, Sokhá, Sambhunáth, Mahámáyá, Rám Thakur, Mián Kabutrá, Naiká Gosáin, Masán, Ostád, and Kartar are the names mentioned in different parts of Behar. Goats, pigeons, cakes, milk, etc., are offered to them six times in the year, the offerings being afterwards eaten by the worshippers. In the month of Jeth the sickle (*hansuli*) used for cutting the palm tree is set up and solemnly worshipped with offerings of flowers and grain.

Social status and occupation.

Pásis rank socially below Tatwás, and on much the same level as Binds and Cháins, except that, unlike these, they nowhere attain to such consideration that Brahmans will take water from their hands. Most of them eat fowls and field-rats, and indulge freely in spirituous and fermented liquors. Many of them have taken to cultivation instead of, or in addition to, their traditional avocation, and hold land as occupancy or non-occupancy raiyats. Others are employed as day-labourers, porters, coolies, or servants to low-caste shop-keepers. In Bengal there is comparatively little demand for their services as palm-tappers, for the owners of toddy and date palms either extract the juice themselves or employ Bhuinmális to do so, and shops for the sale of spirituous liquors are usually owned by Sunris or outcaste Sudras. According to Dr. Wise, the extraction of the juice of the *tál*, or palmyra palm, as well as that of the *khajúr*, or date palm, is a most important operation in

Eastern Bengal, although it has not given rise to the formation of a special caste. The *tál* trees are tapped from March to May; the date palms in the cold season. The juice of the former, or toddy (*tári*), is used in the manufacture of bread, and as an intoxicating liquor by adding sugar and grains of rice. Hindustání drunkards often add *dhatúrá* to increase its intoxicating properties. In Dacca a *tál* grove is usually rented, and on an average twelve annas a tree are obtained. The quantity of juice extracted varies from an average of five to ten pounds. When fresh this sells for two annas a seer, but if a day old for only one anna. Date palm *tárí* is rarely drunk, being popularly believed to cause rheumatism, but is extensively used in preparing sugar. A date palm is generally leased for seven annas a year.

The following statement shows the number and distribution of Pásis in 1872 and 1881:—

DISTRICT.	1872.	1881.	DISTRICT.	1872.	1881.
Bardwan	318	254	Tipperah	21	......
Bankura	4	6	Patna	33,299	37,135
Birbhum	6	45	Gya	34,060	39,309
Midnapur	643	213	Shahabad	9,541	11,973
Hughli	813	75	Mozufferpur...	19,339	11,711
Howrah		446	Darbhanga		12,810
24-Parganás	1,226	648	Saran	4,767	5,562
Nadiya	1	1	Champaran	1,658	2,535
Khulna	......	1	Monghyr	12,362	13,998
Murshedabad	265	56	Bhagalpur	5,258	6,690
Dinajpur	90	47	Purniah	620	2,030
Rajshahye	1	924	Maldah	312	567
Rangpur	194	1	Santál Parganás	1,716	2,205
Bogra	......	2	Cuttack	1,062	631
Pabna	12	2	Puri	1,246	3,074
Darjiling	......	13	Balasore	1,266	63
Jalpigori	4	63	Tributary States	206	164
Kuch Behar	......	3	Hazaribagh	2,404	3,882
Dacca	19	43	Lohardagá	1,103	2,400
Faridpur	25	9	Singbhum	27	36
Bakarganj	68	......	Manbhum	97	57
Maimansinh	25	......	Tributary States	41	172

Pasupatiyá, a worshipper of Siva under the name of Pasupati, 'Lord of Animals.'

Pataiwár, a *dih* or exogamous section of the Gharbáit subcaste of Amáts in Behar.

Patálang, a sept of Limbus in Darjiling.

Pátalkat, a class of stonecutters in Gyá whose ancestors are said to have been brought from Jaipur to build the Vishnupad temple. They make stone cups, idols, and toys.

Pátar (*Sans.* Pátra), a title of Kaibarttas and various other castes; a section of tho Pargha caste in Behar.

Pátár, a section of Bhojpuriá Halwáis in Behar.

Patá-Ratnauli, a sub-group of Maghaiya Telis in Behar.

Pátári, a *gáin* or sub-section of Saptasati Brahmans in Bengal.

Patariár, a section of Mahilis in Chota Nagpur.

Pátar Máhili, a sub-caste of Máhilis in the south of Manbhum

Pata Sayá, a sept of Hos in Singbhum.

Patatri, a Sanskrit word for 'bird,' a title of the low class mountebanks called *Harbolás*, who imitate the tunes of birds and make their livelihood thereby.

Pátbandh, a sub-tribe of Kharwárs in Palámau.

Pate, a group of the Srotrya sub-caste of Utkal Brahmans.

Páthá, goat, a title of Bárendra Brahmans in Bengal.

Pathaiár, a *pur* or section of Sákadwipi Brahmans in Behar.

Páthak, a title of Kanaujiá and Sáraswat Brahmans in Behar; of Dákshinátya Baidik Brahmans in Bengal; a section of Utkal or Orissa Brahmans; a title of Bábhans in Behar.

Pathal, a section of Khariás in Chota Nagpur.

Páthar, a headman among tank-diggers in Tipperah; a hypergamous group of Kaibarttas in Bakarganj.

Pather, *Pattar*, *Patra*, a title of Bhuiyas in Western Bengal.

Patheri, a title borne by persons employed in stringing beads and trinkets with silk.

Páthu, a title of Maithil Brahmans in Behar.

Pathuri, a title of Kaibarttas.

Páthuri, dealers in articles of stone.

Pathuriá, a *mul* or section of the Ayodhiabási sub-caste of Sonárs in Behar. A prostitute.

Pati, a section of Utkal or Orissa Brahmans.

Pátia Dás, a synonym for Doai.

Pátial, a mat-making caste of Eastern Bengal who deny that they ever cultivate the soil with their own hands. Some say that they are a branch of the Káyasths, but no tangible evidence in support of this view seems to be available. The mats made by them, coarse, dark-coloured, and thick, are called Motápátí, to distinguish them from the finer kinds made at Silhet, known as Sítalpátí. The only plant cultivated for mat-making is the Mathara (*Maranta dichotoma*), which grows luxuriantly in low, marshy country. It flowers in June and July, and is cut, while still green, about the middle of September, the stems being divided into slips and hung from the rafters, and when required for use steeped in water.

Among the Silhet Pátials women make the mats; consequently the money value of a girl who is a skilful workman is considerable, and a father receives from three to five hundred rupees when his daughter marries. In Dacca, on the other hand, men are the sole workers. Although chiefly found in Dacca, the Pátials are scattered throughout Eastern Bengal, wherever the nature of the soil admits of the cultivation of the Maranta. The caste is exclusively Vaishnava. The headman has the title Pradhán, or Mu'tabar.

Pátikar, *Patuá*, *Sálubi*, an endogamous class of low Mahomedans, who paint pictures illustrating Hindu mythology and hawk them from door to door with songs. Although Pátikars are supposed to be Mahomedans, they, like the Nasyas of Rangpur, are very lax in their religious practices. They worship the rose as a *pir*, and have a great respect for the black kite, which they believe to be a bird of good omen.

Patita-Kshatri, a synonym for Koch.

Patiyár, a *pur* or section of Sákadwipi Brahmans in Behar.

Pátkumiá, a sub-tribe of Bhumij in Manbhum.

Patmurmurara, a sept of Kharwars in Chota Nagpur.

Patnáik, a title of Kaibarttas in Bengal.

Pátni, *Pátuni*, *Pátauni*, *Dom-Pátni*, a low boating, fishing, basket-making, trading, and cultivating caste of Eastern Bengal, whose dark complexion, short and muscular frame, snub nose, and expanded nostrils stamp them as of Dravidian descent. They are, says Dr. Wise, very reserved and uncommunicative, but there can be little doubt they were originally Doms. In Rangpur, and throughout the valley of the Brahmaputra, they are still designated Dom-Pátni, and in Bengal this is applied to them as a term of abuse. Their other titles are Gangáputra, Ghát-mánjhí, or simply Mánjhí.

Origin.

According to some authorities they are descended from a Rajaka, or washerman, and a woman of the Vaisya caste. Pátnis, however, claim to be the offspring of Mádhava, who ferried Ráma across a river on his way from Ayodhyá to Mithila, and relate how Mádhava, having witnessed the resuscitation of Ahalyá, was afraid to transport the god to the other bank until he had extracted the promise that Ráma would sit on the gunwale with his feet in the water. The simplicity of this ferryman was remarkable. When Ráma landed, Mádhava complained that the colour of the boat had been changed to a hideous yellow, and that he was ruined. The reply was that the ferry-boat had been converted into pure gold, and as a punishment for the Pátni's stupidity Ráma announced that his descendants would always be ferrymen, and that he himself would after death become the ferryman of the Vaitarani, or Hindu Styx.

Another fiction in the history of the Pátnis pertains to the reign of Ballál Sen. The monarch became enamoured of a ferryman's daughter named Padmá-vatí, and married her. At the feast *Pákasparsa*, when the bride cooks and the bridegroom for the first time eats from her hands, the Pátnis, with inborn obtuseness, and to the great grief of the queen, presented themselves at the end of the festival. For this misconduct they were degraded and enrolled among the *Nicha* or low castes.

Internal structure.

The Pátnis are divided into five sub-castes—**Ját-Pátni**, who are agriculturists and small traders, usually keeping shop as *mudis* or grocers; **Ghát-Pátni**, **Balami** or **Ghátwál**, who work as boatmen and take charge of ferries; **Dom-Pátni**, **Machhwá**, or **Nagárchi**, who fish, keep pigs, and get casual employment as musicians at weddings and festivals of various kinds; **Bansphor** and **Dágará**, who hunt, manufacture sieves and baskets of cane, and tie the framework of *kánchá* houses. The last two, from the nature of their pursuits, are more or less nomadic, making only temporary settlements in neat round huts of *sirki*, which they build on the outskirts of villages near rivers. All the sub-castes are endogamous. The Dom-Pátnis are said to admit outsiders into their sub-caste on condition of undergoing a degrading ceremony, one feature of which is that the proselyte must drink water in which the others have washed their feet.

The exogamous sections of the Pátnis shown in Appendix I appear to be for the most part of the territorial type, and do throw no light upon the tribal affinities of the caste. It deserves notice that one of the sections bears the name Tentuliá, which also denotes one of the Bágdi sub-castes. The prohibited degrees are much the same as with other low-caste Hindus.

Marriage.

Pátnis marry their daughters as infants by the standard ceremony. A bride-price (*pan*) is paid by the parents of the bridegroom to those of the bride. Polygamy is recognized in theory, but rarely resorted to in practice. Widows are not allowed to marry again, and divorce is not permitted. Traces of widow-marriage still survive among the Pátnis of Noakhali, but even there the custom is looked upon as disreputable, and seems likely soon to die out.

Religion.

In religious and ceremonial observances Pátnis conform on the whole to the practice of orthodox low-caste Hindus. They employ Patita or Varna Brahmans, who generally assume pompous titles, such as Chakravartti and the like, by way of covering the degradation incurred by serving the Pátni as priests. The Gosains, on the other hand, who act as the gurus of the caste, are received on equal terms by other Brahmans. Most Pátnis belong to the Saiva sect, whose tenets involve little interference with their flesh-eating and spirit-drinking propensities. Only a few Vaishnavas are to be found among them, except in Noakhali, where Vaishnavism is the prevalent faith, and the Pátnis give to it a nominal adherence, which does not, however, prevent them from indulging their tastes in matters of food and drink.

Disposal of the dead.

The dead are burned, and *sráddh* is performed on the thirty-first day after death. Like most Hindu boatmen, they invoke the Pánch Pir on embarking or when overtaken by a storm. The chief religious festival is the Gangá Pujá, and Pátnis never enter upon the work of a ferry without first sacrificing a white kid to the river goddess. They also propitiate Pavan, the Hindu ruler of the winds, with offerings of salt, sugar, milk, and *gánjá*.

Social status.

In point of social status Pátnis rank with Jeliyás, Málos, and the fishing Kaibarttas. Brahmans will not take water from their hands, and they have barbers and washermen of their own caste, as the regular Nápit and Dhobá will not work for them. They consider, however, that they have raised themselves in the social scale by prohibiting the remarriage of widows, and in various small matters they ape the prejudices of the higher castes. For example, they will caulk a boat, but deem it derogatory to paint it, and though they indulge freely in intoxicating drinks, they will never own to doing so.

The following statement shows the number and distribution of the Pátnis in 1872 and 1881 :—

District.	1872.	1881.	District.	1872.	1881.
Bardwan	125	14	Bogra	1,407	1,134
Bankura	......	51	Pabna	3,551	4,782
Birbhum	104	33	Jalpigori	35	60
Midnapur	195	842	Kuch Behar...	......	93
Hughli	393	174	Dacca	4,695	4,147
Howrah		115	Faridpur	1,389	3,363
24-Parganás	1,374	592	Bakarganj	4,518	3,836
Nadiya	3,564	3,696	Maimansinh	21,726	26,952
Khulna	......	3,670	Tipperah	6,305	6,814
Jessore	4,369	232	Chittagong	150	51
Murshedabad	2,529	2,066	Noakhali	2,419	2,104
Dinajpur	1,806	1,296	Purniah	......	6
Rajshahye	2,052	1,167	Maldah	1,126	1,066
Rangpur	2,178	1,770	Santal Parganás	......	8
			Manbhum	......	17

Pátni, a section of Saraogis in Behar.

Pátodi, a section of Saraogis in Behar.

Pátoli, a title of Jaliyás, fishermen.

Pátori, a section of Majraut Goálás in Behar.

Páthpariya, synonym for *páthak*, a Brahman who reads epic poems, Puranas, etc., in public.

Patra, *Pathara*, a title of Tántis, cocoon-weavers.

Pátra, *Pátor*, a synonym for Mahápátra, *q.v.*; a title of Kaibarttas, Pods, and Tántis in Bengal; a title of Málos in Eastern Bengal; a sept of Mál Paháriás; a title of Mahilis, Khandáits, and Telis in Chota Nagpur.

Patradás, a title of the Kurar or Kural sub-caste of Muchis, who work as cobblers and beat drums at festivals.

Patraḍiá, a sub-caste of Pāns in Orissa.

Pátrishi (the bean), a totemistic section of Bágdis; a section of Máls in Midnapur and Manbhum.

Pattadár, an honorary title of Káyasths in Bengal.

Páttar, a sub-caste of Tántis in Bengal; a class of fishermen in Eastern Bengal who enclose portions of newly-formed *char* lands at high tide by small weirs made of reed grass (*sirki*), and catch the fish when the water recedes. They do not use nets. Páttars also sell fish purchased from Jeliyás and other fishing castes.

Páttár, a class of Mahomedans who string silver and gold ornaments.

Pátuá, a group of the Karalái sub-caste of Kaibarttas in Noakháli.

Pátua, *Patu*, *Potá*, *Pole*, *Potuá*, *Patudár*, a class of people, both Hindu and Mahomedan, whose profession is painting Hindu deities.

Pátuli, a title of Kaibarttas.

Pátuni, a synonym for Dom in Northern Bengal.

Páturá-Chhutár, a sub-caste of Sutradhars in the Santál Parganás.

Paturiá, a Mahomedan dancing girl.

Páturiá, a sub-caste of Bauris in Western Bengal.

Patwa, *Pathera*, *Patheri*, a maker of fancy silk strings and fringes. Patwas also prepare and hawk about *tasar* silk. They are divided into three endogamous groups—Gauria, Rewar, and Tánti.

Patwár, a generic term in Central Bengal for persons employed in *zamindári* business, possibly a survival from times when there were *patwáris* in Bengal.

Patwári, a sept of Thárus in Behar.

Patwe, a *pangat* or section of Dosádhs in Behar.

Pátyakar, a synonym for Patiál, mat-makers and labourers.

Paulastya, a section of Brahmans.

Paundrakáli, a *gáin* of the Bátsya *gotra* of Bárendra Brahmans in Bengal.

Paunia, certain castes in Behar entitled to receive gifts from the village community, viz. Nauá, Dhobi, Lohár, Kumhár, Churihár, Teli, Chamár, Máli, Barhi, Laheri, Ghási, and Koiri.

Pauriá, a sub-caste of Koiris in Chota Nagpur.

Pauriá or Pauliá, a sept of Santáls.

Pauriár, a section of Awadhiá Hajjáms in Behar.

Pawaiyár, a *pur* or section of Sákadwipi Brahmans in Behar.

Páwariá, *Pawriá*, a class of Mahomedan women who dance and sing in male costume at the births of children in the houses of well-to-do people.

Pechá, a bird, a totemistic sept of Bediyas in Chota Nagpur.

Pechgotra, a section of the Ayodhiá sub-caste of Nuniás in Behar.

Pekhá, a sept of Limbus in Darjiling.

Pengi, a *thar* or sept of Gurungs in Darjiling.

Penkál-Máchh, a section of Máls in Midnapur and Manbhum.

Peo, a bird, a totemistic sept of Mundas in Chota Nagpur.

Peroan, pigeon, a totemistic sept of Mundas in Chota Nagpur.

Peshákar, *Peshákária*, a prostitute.

Petehimba, a sub-sept of the Thekim sept of Limbus in Darjiling.

Pethokote, a sept of Mangars in Darjiling.

Petungbah, a sept of Limbus in Darjiling.

Phádám, a sept of the Agniá sub-tribe of Meches in the Darjiling Terai.

Phágu, a sub-tribe of Yakhas in Darjiling.

Phaguahi, a sept of Gonds in Chota Nagpur.

Phaksa, a sept of Chakmás in the Hill Tracts of Chittagong.

Phalechhuah, a sept of Limbus in Darjiling.

Phansia, a section of Ghásis in Chota Nagpur.

Pharia, a synonym for Kunjrá —vegetable-sellers.

Pharkiet, a section of the Maghayá sub-caste of Kumhárs in Behar.

Pharphar, a *gáin* or sub-section of Saptasati Brahmans in Bengal.

Pharsádhenti, a sept of Kaurs in Chota Nagpur.

Phawahong, the name of a village, a sept of the Yangorup sub-tribe of Limbus in Darjiling.

Phedáb or Bhuiphuta, a sub-tribe of Limbus in Darjiling.

Phe-dang-sirri, a sept of Chakmás in the Hill Tracts of Chittagong.

Phedungsa, a sept of Chakmás in the Hill Tracts of Chittagong.

Phehim, the singer, a sept. of the Phedáb sub-tribe of Limbus in Darjiling.

Phejom, the *kukri*-bearer, including (*a*) Nembong, (*b*) Sardakpeapi, a sept of the Pánthar sub-tribe of Limbus in Darjiling.

Phekuram, a special ancestral deity of the Bahiot sub-caste of Amáts in Behar.

Phema, a sept of Chakmás in the Hill Tracts of Chittagong.

Phenduá, the hammerer of iron, a sept of the Tambrkhola sub-tribe of Limbus in Darjiling. This *thar* were formerly the blacksmiths of the tribe.

Phensa-pá, a *rui* or sept of Dejong Lhoris who are descendents of emigrants from Bhotan and Nepal.

Pheodan, the water-carrier, a sept of the Pánthar sub-tribe of Limbus in Darjiling.

Pherká, a title of Bágdis in Western Bengal.

Phetiá, a sept of Rájputs in Behar.

Pheyak, a sept of Limbus in Darjiling.

Phirti, a group of the Karalái sub-caste of Kaibarttas in Noakháli.

Phlumáchhá, a *thar* or sept of Khambus in Darjiling.

Pho-omphu, the hangman, a sept of the Phedáb sub-tribe of Limbus in Darjiling.

Photádár, a title of the Ariár sub-caste of Bais Baniyás and a *pangat* or section of Dosádhs in Behar.

Photro, a sept of the Charkhola sub-tribe of Limbus in Darjiling.

Phrangroatsa, a sept of Maghs in the Hill Tracts of Chittagong.

Phul, a group of the Bárendra sub-caste of Sunris in Eastern Bengal; flower, a sept of Chiks in Chota Nagpur.

Phulaus, a sub-caste of Nágars in Behar.

Phulehli, a *thar* or sept of Khambus in Darjiling.

Phulgot, a totemistic section of Nuniás in Behar.

Phulhári, a title of Háris in Eastern Bengal who are not sweepers, but are engaged as chaukidárs and gardeners.

Phuli, a *mul* or section of the Chhamuliá Madhesiá sub-caste of Halwáis in Behar.

Phuliá, a *mel* or hypergamous sub-group of Rárhi Brahmans in Bengal.

Phulkátá-Máli, a sub-caste of Mális in Bengal.

Phulmáli, a synonym for Máli.

Phulnápit, a sub-caste of Nápits in Western Bengal who have given up their profession of shaving and taken to cultivation.

Phulwar, a sept of Goálás in Chota Nagpur.

Phungthag, he who stole to order; a sept of the Phedáb sub-tribe of Limbus in Darjiling.

Phungun, a sept of Chiks in Chota Nagpur.

Phunknali, a sub-section of the Bharadwája section of Utkal Brahmans.

Phunvál, a *thar* or section of Nepáli Brahmans.

Phuowali, a mendicant caste of the Darjiling Terai regarding which little is known.

Phurkeli, a *thar* or sept of Khambus in Darjiling.

Phurti, a sept of Mundas in Chota Nagpur.

Phuti, rainbow, a totemistic sept of Mundas in Chota Nagpur.

Phutka, vegetable, a totemistic sept of Lohárs in Chota Nagpur.

Phyagpa, the knife-grinder, a sept of the Pánthar sub-tribe of Limbus in Darjiling.

Phyuyáli, a *thar* or sept of Mangars in Darjiling.

Pichagma, the son of the monkey, a sept of the Chaibisa sub-tribe of Limbus in Darjiling. This *thar* is said to have formerly worshipped the monkey.

Pikord, a bird, a totemistic sept of Mundas in Chota Nagpur.

Pil, a title of Dakshin Rárhi and Bangaja Káyasths.

Pilá, a totemistic sept of the Bhumij tribe in Chota Nagpur.

Pilchwár, a section of Bábhans in Behar.

Pilich, a section of the Sátmuliá Maghayá sub-caste of Kándus in Behar.

Piliksawár, a section of Bábhans in Behar.

Pilkhait, a section of Bábhans in Behar.

Pilua, a section of Mahilis in Chota Nagpur.

Pindwál, a section of Koránch Halwáis in Behar.

Pinguá, a sept of Hos in Singbhum.

Pipar, a fruit, a sept of Telis in Chota Nagpur.

Pipariá, a *mul* or section of the Kanaujiá sub-caste of Sonárs in Behar.

Pipi, a title of Bangaja Káyasths.

Pippalái, a *gáin* of the Bátsya *gotra* of Rárhi Brahmans in Bengal.

Pippali, a *gáin* of the Bharadwája *gotra* of Bárendra Brahmans in Bengal.

Pipret, a *mul* or section of the Naomuliá or Majraut sub-caste of Goálás in Behar.

Pipriáti, a section of Barhis in Behar.

Pirabhanga, a sept of Chakmás in the Hill Tracts of Chittagong.

Piráli, an endogamous division of the Rárhi Brahmans in Bengal. The popular story of the origin of this group is that their ancestor was degraded for having accidentally smelled food which had been prepared in the house of a Mahomedan. They are held in the same estimation among Rárhis as Pánchuriás among Bárendras.

Piruwal, a sub-caste of Khatris in Bengal.

Pishle, a sub-caste of Telis in Bengal.

Pitamundi, a *gáin* of the Kásyapa *gotra* of Rárhi Brahmans in Bengal.

Pithákoteh, a *thar* or sept of Mangars in Darjiling.

Pithári, a *gáin* or sub-section of Saptasati Brahmans in Bengal.

Pithoár, a section of Goráits in Chota Nagpur.

Pitraihá, a *mul* or section of the Banodhiá sub-caste of Kalwárs in Behar.

Pitule-Kámár, a sub-caste of Kámárs in Midnapur.

Plembochhá, a *thar* or sept of Khambus in Darjiling.

Poa, a sept of Chakmás in the Hill Tracts of Chittagong.

Pod, *Padmaráj*, *Chási*, a fishing, cultivating, landholding, and trading caste of Lower Bengal, found in large numbers in the 24-Parganás. Their origin is uncertain. Babu Bankim Chandra Chatterji, quoted at page 188 of the Census Report of 1872, notices their "marked approach to the Turanian and aboriginal type" of features, and seeks to identify them with the Pundra mentioned in the Mahábhárata as one of the five chief races of Eastern India between Magadha and the sea. The educated members of the caste claim for it a mixed descent from a Káyasth father and a Nápit mother. Others tell a highly indelicate story regarding the miraculous birth of the first Pod from Revati, the wife of Balarám.

Origin.

The Pods are divided into four sub-castes—**Bágande, Banglá, Khottá**, or **Mauná** and **Uraiyá**. The first two are found chiefly in the 24-Parganás and Jessore, the third in Murshedabad and Maldah, and the fourth in Midnapur and Balasore. All these groups are endogamous. Each is subdivided into *gotras* or sections borrowed from the Brahmanical system. The prohibited degrees are the same as among the higher castes.

Internal structure.

Pods marry their daughters between the ages of five and nine years, forbid widow-marriage, and do not recognize divorce. The morality of Pod widows, however, is alleged to be singularly lax, and the caste is tolerant

Marriage.

towards sexual indiscretions, so that the illegitimate children of widows and of divorced women are received into the community. Their marriage is of the orthodox type, the ceremony of *Kusandika* alone being omitted. *Sampradán*, or the offering of the bride to the bridegroom and his acceptance of the gift, forms the binding portion of the ritual.

Religion.

In addition to the well-known sects of Saiva, Sákta, and Vaishnava, we find among the Pods a large number of Sauras and Gánapatyas, sects very sparingly represented among the higher classes of Hindus in Bengal. The caste employ as their priests Rárhi Brahmans, who are held to be so far degraded by serving them that high class Brahmans will not take food or water from their hands. The gurus of the Pods are Rárhi Gosáins, but these, I understand, have in no way forfeited their position among Brahmans, though in some cases they eat and drink in Pods' houses. An instance of this was brought to my notice recently as evidence of the growth of the spirit of religious toleration among the educated Hindus of Calcutta and its suburbs.

Social status.

The social status of Pods is decidedly low. They will eat sweetmeats, drink and smoke with the fishing sub-castes of Bágdis: and these are ordinarily deemed to be nearly their equals in rank. Brahmans and members of the Nava Sákha group will not take water from them; and the Sutradhar and Kapáli, while they will eat sweetmeats, drink and smoke in company with a Pod, will not use the same pipe or drink from the same *lotá*. In matters of diet their practice is orthodox on all points except the indulgence in strong drink. They will eat the leavings of Brahmans. Vaishnava Pods abstain from all kinds of flesh.

Occupation.

The great majority of the caste are engaged in agriculture, as tenure-holders, and occupancy or non-occupancy raiyats. A few have risen to be zamindárs, and some at the other end of the scale work as nomadic cultivators on freshly-cleared land in the Sundarbans, changing their location every two or three years according to the fortune of their crops. Many Pods have taken to trade, and gold-smiths, blacksmiths, tinsmiths, carpenters, thatchers, etc., are found among them.

The following statement shows the number and distribution of Pods in Bengal in 1872 and 1881:—

District.	1872.	1881.	District.	1872.	1881.
Bardwan	226	42	Dinajpur	24	71
Bankura	3	196	Rajshahye	12	41
Birbhum	68	90	Rangpur	1	57
Midnapur	4	10,530	Bogra	4	80
Hughli	} 16,727	{ 1,958	Pabna	......	9
Howrah		14,138	Dacca	101	......
24-Parganás	240,076	217,236	Faridpur	73	
Nadiya	4,250	2,220	Bakarganj	314	......
Khulna	...	66,780	Maimansinh	63	13
Jessore	21,562	7,017	Tipperah	35	33
Murshedabad	86	8,137	Maldah	66	8,216

Poddár, a title of the Ariár sub-caste of Bais Baniyás and of Sonárs in Behar; of Sunris and of Subarnabaniks in Bengal who are money-lenders and dealers in gold and silver ornaments.

Podoro, a sept of Hos in Singbhum.

Podret, a section of Maghayá Kumhárs in Behar.

Pohobait, a section of the Pachainyá sub-caste of Doms in Behar.

Poiá, a sept of Gonds in Chota Nagpur.

Poiti, a sept of Gonds in Chota Nagpur.

Pokharmiá, a section of Lohárs in Behar.

Pokhrel, a section of Kámis in Darjiling.

Poma, a sept of Chakmás in the Hill Tracts of Chittagong.

Pomo, the large family, a sept of the Ahtharai sub-tribe of Limbus in Darjiling.

Pondha, the wanderer, a sept of the Yangorup sub-tribe of Limbus in Darjiling.

Pongwar, a *thar* or sept of Mangars in Darjiling.

Pongyangu, he who carries his goods on his back, a sept of the Phedáb sub-tribe of Limbus in Darjiling.

Ponkrishi (jungle cock), a totemistic section of Bágdis in Western Bengal

Pon-po, a *rui* or sept of the Bodtshan-gye sub-tribe of Dejong Lhoris or Bhotias of the south. This sept is composed of the five following sub-septs:—Chhungpá, Lhasung, Nah-dik, Nambon, and Yo-chang.

Ponthák, a sept of Limbus in Darjiling.

Porári, a *gáin* of the Kásyapa *gotra* of Rárhi Brahmans in Bengal.

Poriál, a title of Telis.

Porri, a sept of Gonds in Chota Nagpur.

Portel, a section of Kámis in Darjiling.

Porti, crocodile, a totemistic sept of Mundas in Chota Nagpur.

Potá, a section of Kámárs in Singbhum and the Santál Parganás.

Potadár, *Poddar* (properly Fotadár, from Persian *fotáh*, a bag or purse), a cash-keeper, a money-changer; an officer in Government treasuries who examines and weighs coins.

Prachanda, furious, a title of Bárendra Brahmans in Bengal.

Práchir, a section of Pátnis in Eastern Bengal.

Pradhán, (i) a title of Kaibarttas, Suklis, Sunris, and others in Bengal; a title of Kotáls and Binjhiás; of Khandáits in Chota Nagpur; Pátnis, Chamárs, and Santáls; (ii) a village headman in Singbhum; (iii) a section of Sunris in Behar; (iv) a hypergamous division of Tiyars.

Praharáj, a title of Khandáits in Orissa.

Prajápati, a synonym for Kumhár.

Prámánik, a group of the Daspárá sub-caste of Kumhárs in Pabna. See **Parámánik**.

Pramodni, a *mel* or hypergamous sub-group of Rárhi Brahmans in Bengal.

Prási, a section of the Biyáhut and Kharidáhá Kalwárs in Behar.

Prasidha, an eponymous sept of Rájputs in Behar.

Pratihár, including Bangrám and Gográm, a hypergamous group of the Paschim Kuliyá Sadgops in Western Bengal.

Pratilomaj, see **Anulomaj**.

Prayágwál, a priestly class of Brahmans in Prayág or Allahabad.

Prohá-kerauta, a section of Sonárs in Behar.

Puár, a sept of Rájputs in Behar.

Pubiá, Jaiá, a sub-caste of Utkal Brahmans in Orissa.

Puhániá, a section of Goálás in the North-Western Provinces and Behar.

Puhár, a title of Chásás in Orissa.

Puhoá, a sub-caste of Goálás in Behar.

Puilá, a title of Bágdis in Western Bengal.

Puin, a title of Bangaja Káyasths.

Pujáha, a title of the Naiyá caste in Behar, which appears to have reference to their original functions as priests of the aboriginal or forest deities.

Pujhor, priests, a sept of Mál Pahárias in the Santál Parganás.

Puktebu, a sept of the Yangorup sub-tribe of Limbus in Darjiling.

Pulámi, a *thar* or sept of Mangars in Darjiling.

Pulauns, a sub-caste of Nágars in Behar.

Pumá, a sept of the Tungjainya sub-tribe of Chakmás in the Hill Tracts of Chittagong.

Pun, a *thar* or sept of Mangars in Darjiling.

Pundárika, the white lotus (*Nelumbium speciosum*), a title of Pods, Kaibarttas, and occasionally of Jáliyas.

Pundarikáksha, *Pundari*, *Punra*, lotus-eyed; a name of Vishnu; a title of Pods who rear cocoons and cultivate chillies, ginger, etc.

Pundárk, a *pur* or section of Sákadwipi Brahmans in Behar.

Pundul, a sept of Rájputs in Behar.

Pung, a *thar* or sept of Mangars in Darjiling.

Pungi, a *thar* or sept of the Das-Gurung sub-tribe of Gurungs in Darjiling, so called after the name of a place in Nepal.

Pungsika, a *gáin* of the Sábarna *gotra* of Rárhi Brahmans in Bengal.

Punrakhiá, a *pur* or section of Şákadwipi Brahmans in Behar.

Punrapaita, a title of Punras who rear silk-worms only.

Punriár, a section of Kurmis in Chota Nagpur and Orissa.

Pur, a section of Goálás in Behar.

Pura, a title of Maithil Brahmans in Behar.

Purá, a hypergamous group of Karans in Orissa.

Purabi, an endogamous division of Nepáli Brahmans.

Puráin, a section of Awadhiá Hajjáms in Behar.

Puraliá, a section of Kámárs in Singbhum and the Santál Parganás.

Puran, a section of Bháts who read out verses in *sabhás* or caste assemblies; a sept of Tipperahs in the Hill Tracts of Chittagong; a synonym for Bhuiyá in Moharbhanj.

Purandari, a sub-caste of Tántis in Bengal.

Purandwár, a sub-caste of Háris in Bengal.

Purásaini, a *thar* or section of Nepáli Brahmans.

Purbba, a *gáin* of the Bátsya *gotra* of Rárhi Brahmans in Bengal.

Purbba Banga, a *samáj* or endogamous group of the Páschátya Baidik Brahmans in Eastern Bengal.

Purbbakul, a sub-caste of Tántis in Bengal.

Purbba Kuliyá, a sub-caste of Sadgops in Bengal.

Purbbasthâli, a *samáj* or endogamous group of the Páschátya Baidik Brahmans in Nuddia.

Purbe, a section of Sunris and of the Chapotá sub-caste of Hindu Joláhas in Behar.

Purbiá, a sub-caste of Sunris in Behar.

Purbiya, Purbiyá, a sub-caste of Agarwáls, a sub-tribe of Thárus in Nepal.

Purbiyá Khatri, the distinctive designation of the Bengal branch of the Khatri caste.

Purbiyá Madesiá, a sub-caste of Halwáis in Behar.

Puri, a sect of Dasnami Sannyásis.

Purthi, a sept of Hos in Singbhum.

Purti, a section of Khariás; a sept of Lohárs and Páns in Chota Nagpur.

Purubansi, a sept of Rájputs in Behar.

Purukhiru Naráin, a section of the Kamár sub-caste of Dosádhs in Behar.

Pusá, a section of the Pachainyá sub-caste of Doms in Behar.

Pusadih, a section of the Tirhutiya sub-caste of Doms in Behar.

Pusáitá, a section of the Dhaprá sub-caste of Doms in Behar.

Pusál, a *thar* or sept of Mangars in Darjiling.

Pusetá, a section of the Pachainyá sub-caste of Doms in Behar.

Pushali, Pushilál, a *gáin* of the Kásyapa *gotra* of Rárhi Brahmans in Bengal.

Pushána, a *gáin* of the Sándilya *gotra* of Bárendra Brahmans in Bengal.

Pusra, fruit of kusum tree, a totemistic sept of Oraons in Chota Nagpur.

Pusway, a section of Binjhiás in Chota Nagpur.

Putam, dove, a totemistic sept of Mundas in Chota Nagpur.

Puti, a *gáin* of the Bharadwája *gotra* of Bárendra Brahmans in Bengal.

Putitunda, a *gáin* of the Bátsya *gotra* of Rárhi Brahmans in Bengal.

Putri, a tree, a totemistic sept of Oraons in Chota Nagpur.

Pu-tsho-bo, a *rui* or sept of the Bedtshan-gye sub-tribe of Dejong Lhoris or Bhotias of the south, whose ancestor was a mixed progeny of Lepcha mother and Tibetan father.

Pu-tsibo, a *rui* or sept of Dejong Lohris, the members of which are the descendants of emigrants from Bhotan and Nepal.

Putuli, a synonym for Gandhabanik.

Puyi-rási, a section of Málos in Eastern Bengal.

Pyakarel or Pokharyál, a *thar* of the Gargya *gotra* of Nepáli Brahmans.

Pyo-chhembo, a *rui* or sept of Dejong Lohris, the members of which are the descendants of emigrants from Bhotan and Nepal.

R

Rábad, a section of Goálás in the North-Western Provinces and Behar.

Rabchháli, a *thar* or sept of Khambus in Darjiling.

Rabi-Dás, a synonym for Chamár.

Rachhuáni, a sept of Rájputs in Behar.

Rádháli, a worshipper of Rádhá, the favourite mistress of Krishna; a title of Vaishnavas.

Radhar, a sept of Kharwars in Chota Nagpur.

Rafugar, a professional shawl-mender; generally a Mahomedan.

Rághab, a section of the Mahmudábáz sub-caste of Nápits in Eastern Bengal.

Rághab Ghosháli, a *mel* or hypergamous sub-group of Rárhi Brahmans in Bengal.

Rághopurdih, a *mul* or section of the Naomuliá or Majraut sub-caste of Goálás in Behar.

Raghu, a family of the Kulin group of Jugis in Bengal.

Raghubansi, a sub-tribe and a sept of Rájputs in Behar; a bastard caste in Chota Nagpur, like Rautia, who act as servants and are said to have originated since the time of Maharaja Raghunath Shahi.

Raghunáthiá, a sub-caste of Utkal Brahmans in Orissa.

Raghunáthpurdiár, a *mul* or section of the Naomuliá or Majraut sub-caste of Goálás in Behar.

Ráhá, a title of Dakshin-Rárhi and Bangaja Káyasths.

Rahapál, a section of Kámis; a *thar* or sept of Mangars in Darjiling.

Rahdauriár, a *pur* or section of Sákadwipi Brahmans in Behar.

Rahpáchá, a *thar* or sept of Sunuwárs in Darjiling.

Rahtaur, a sept of the Surajbansi division of Rájputs in Behar.

Ráhu, a title of Dosadhs in Behar who worship the demon Ráhu.

Ráhul, a *thar* or sept of the Das-Gurung sub-tribe of Gurungs in Darjiling. The name is said to have arisen in consequence of Rahul, the ancestor of the *thar*, showing courage worthy of the demon Ráhu in certain tribal feuds.

Ráhut, a title of Dakshin-Rárhi and Bangaja Káyasths.

Rái, a *gáin* of the Bharadwája *gotra* of Bárendra Brahmans in Bengal; a title of Brahmans; a section of the Sribástab sub-caste of Káyasths in Behar; an honorary title of Káyasths and Subarnabaniks in Bengal; a title of Rájputs, Bábhans, Dhánuks, and Goálás in Behar; of Jugis, Baitis, and Sunris in Bengal; a section of Khambus; a hypergamous division of the Maghaya sub-caste of Barhis; a title of Chásádhobás, Kapális, Korás; a title and a sept of Thárus; an honorific title common among many other castes.

Raibhuiya Ghatwal, a well-to-do class of Bhuiyas, Rai being their title; some also call themselves Singh.

Raikwár, a sept of Rájputs in Behar.

Raini, a *kul* or section of Bábhans in Behar.

Ráipur, a section of Pátnis in Bengal.

Ráj, a title of Mayarás in Bengal.

Ráj, Rájmistri, Rájmajur, a mason or bricklayer, an occupation mostly followed by Kaibarttas, Chásádhobas, Bágdis, Chandáls, and Mahomedans.

Raja, a bird, a totemistic sept of Mundas in Chota Nagpur.

Rája, a family title of Kashta Baidyas and of Dakshin-Rárhi and Bangaja Káyasths.

Rájá, a section of the Magahiyá sub-caste of Doms in Behar.

Rajabin, a *thar* or sept of Khambus in Darjiling.

Rájáiswar, a section of the Kamár sub-caste of Dosádhs in Behar.

Rajak, a synonym for Dhobá in Bengal.

Rajandipur, a section of the Ariár sub-caste of Bais Baniyás in Behar.

Rájápáker, a *mul* or section of the Sátmuliá or Kishnaut sub-caste of Goálás and of the Kanaujiá sub-caste of Sonars in Behar.

Rájápákur, a section of Majraut Goálás in Behar.

Rajápati-Sobhni, a *mul* or section of the Naomuliá or Majraut sub-caste of Goálás in Behar.

Rajata-kausik, a section of the Uttar-Bárendra Brahmans in Bengal.

Rajbandh, a section of Ghásis in Chota Nagpur.

Rájbangsi, a Dravidian caste of Northern Bengal, originally Kochh, but now claiming to be an outlying branch of Kshatriyas.

Rájbansi, a synonym for Kochh, Rajwár, and for Tiyar; a sub-caste of Tiors in Behar who are said to wear the *janeo* or sacred thread; a sub-caste of Mauliks; a title of Bágdis in Western Bengal.

Rajbansi or *Rájá-Mál*, a sub-caste of Máls in Western Bengal.

Rájbansiá, a sept of Páns in Chota Nagpur.

Rájbhar, an up-country caste engaged in Bengal as gardeners and cowherds. They claim to be a distinct caste from the Bhars, with whom they do not eat or intermarry. In the North-Western Provinces they are engaged purely in agricultural pursuits, and rank socially with the Kurmis and Koiris.

Rajbhat, a sub-caste of Bháts, who are the hereditary bards and genealogists of the higher classes, and are said to wear the sacred thread.

Rájdom, a sub-caste of Doms who affect Brahmanical customs.

Rajgiri, Rájgrihi, a section of the Sátmuliá Maghaya sub-caste of Kándus and of the Kanaujiá sub-caste of Sonars in Behar

Raj Gond, a sub-tribe of Gonds in Chota Nagpur who affect Hindu customs.

Rájhans wild goose, a totemistic sept of Goálás in Chota Nagpur.

Rájhasia, swan, a totemistic sept of Páns in Chota Nagpur.

Rájib, a section of the Mahmudábáz sub-caste of Nápits in Eastern Bengal.

Ráj-Kástha, see **Kástha**.

Rájkuar, a sept of Rájputs in Behar.

Rájkumát, a sept of Rájputs in Behar.

Rájkurin, a section of Maghayá Dhobis in Behar.

Rájmahaliá, a sub-caste of Kumhárs in Dacca.

Rájmor, a section of Kurmis in Chota Nagpur and Orissa.

Rájpur, a *samáj* or local group of the Dákshinátya Baidik Brahmans in the 24-Parganás.

Rajput, a section of Ghásis; a sept of Mundas in Chota Nagpur.

Rájput, *Kshatriya*, *Chhatri*, *Chhettri*, the fighting and landholding caste of Northern India, who claim to be the modern representatives of the Kshatriyas of classical tradition, and who are in many cases entitled to appeal to their markedly Aryan cast of feature in support of their claim. Besides these Aryan Rájputs, the large group designated indifferently by the name Rájput or Chhatri includes many families of doubtful or non-Aryan descent, whose pretensions to membership of the twice-born warrior caste rest solely upon the circumstances that they have, or are supposed to have, some sort of proprietary dominion over land. It would be out of place to attempt to give here an exhaustive account of the Rájput community as it exists in Rájputana and North-Western India. The peculiar characteristics of the pure-blooded Rájput have been described by several competent observers. Among the most conspicuous are a pride of blood, which delights in endless genealogies and ranks every one according to descent; a strong passion for field sports, combined with an equally pronounced distaste for peaceful and prosaic means of earning a livelihood; and an exaggerated idea of the saving virtues of ceremonial purity and precision in the matter of food and drink.

Origin.

The same characteristics are doubtless to some extent traceable among the Rájputs of the Lower Provinces; but the pressure of different conditions of life has tended to obliterate many distinctions, and the eastern Rájput is far less peculiar than the Western. It is commonly said that the Rájput can only be studied in his original surroundings, and that an account of the tribe as it exists in Bengal must necessarily be valueless and misleading. There is much truth in this view: at the same time it may be observed that outlying branches of a tribe which have wandered far away from the original habitat often preserve survivals of usages which have died out among the original stock or have been overlaid and obscured so as to be no longer traceable. Again, if there is reason to believe, as several good observers think there is, that the Rájput tribe itself has been recruited now and again by irregular methods from men of alien lineage, may there not be a better chance of observing the working of this process in distant districts than in Rájputáná itself, where all departures from the strict theory of descent are speedily condoned and hidden by the operation of fiction?

In Chota Nagpur, for example, the methods by which many of the chief landholding families have transformed themselves into Rájputs may be traced beyond question at the present day. The Maharajas of Chutia Nagpur Proper, that is of the elevated table land forming the southern portion of the Lohardagá district, call themselves Nágbansi, and claim descent from a mysterious child found in the jungle, concerning whose origin a singular story is told. The myth of the birth of the founder of the Chutia Nagpur house from a Brahman mother and a snake father, with the picturesque incidents which Colonel Dalton relates, seems to be nothing more than an ingenious invention contrived to mask the fact that a family of Munda chieftains had assumed the rank of Rájput. To this day ladies of Nágbansi families will not employ a Munda to carry their palkis, because they say he is their elder brother-in-law (*bhaisur*), and they veil their faces before him as they would before an elder brother-in-law. The Pachete family call themselves Gobansi Rájputs and tell a strange story, analogous to the Nágbansi myth, of the birth of their progenitor from a cow in the jungle near Pachete. The zamindars of Barabhum, Patkum, Nawagarh and Katiar in Manbhum all claim to be Rájputs, and boldly affiliate themselves to the Raksel and Chandel clans. Some minor landholders of the Bhumij tribe who hold ghatwali tenures in Barabhum have followed the example of the zamindar of that estate, and call themselves Rájputs, though in some cases it can be shown by documentary evidence that their ancestors in the last generation called themselves Bhumij.

Traditions.

The traditions of the tribe go back to the dateless antiquity in which so many royal pedigrees seek refuge. Accordnig to the usually accepted version there are two branches of Rájputs—the Surajbansi or Solar Race and the Chandrabansi or Lunar Race. To these must be added the four Agnikulas or Fire Tribes. Surajbansi Rájputs claim descent from Ikshwáku, son of the Manu Vaivaswat, who was the son of Vivaswat, the Sun. Ikshwáku, it is said, was born from the nostril of the Manu as he happened to sneeze. The elder branch of the Solar race sprang from Ikshwáku's eldest son Vikukshi, and reigned in Ayodhyá at the beginning of the second or Tretá Yuga. Another son named Nimi founded the dynasty of Mithilá. The Lunar race affect to be descended from the moon, to whom they trace through Ayus, Pururavas and Budha or Mercury, the son of Soma by Rohini or by Tárá, wife of Brihaspati. The Agnikulas or Fire Tribes are supposed to have been brought into existence by a special act of creation of comparatively recent mythological date. After the Kshatriya had been slain by Parasu Ráma, gods and men, and more particularly the Brahman, began to feel the consequences of the loss of their natural protectors. The earth was overrun by giants and demons (*Daityas* and *Asuras*), the sacred books were held in contempt, and there was none to whom the devout could call for help in their troubles. Viswámitra, once a Kshatriya, who had raised himself to be a Brahman by the might of penance determined to revive the race that had been exterminated, and moved the gods to assemble for this purpose on Mount Abu in Rájputáná. Four images of *Dhuba* grass were thrown into the fire fountain, and called into life by appropriate incantations. From these sprung the four fire-tribes, Pramar, Sulanki, Parihár and Chauhán.

Turning from mythology to fact, the first point to be noticed about the Rájput tribe is that, in theory at any rate, it has no endogamous subdivisions. All Rájputs are supposed to be of one blood, and no distinctions are formally recognized among them as forming a conclusive bar to intermarriage. The groupings **Surajbansi**, **Sombansi** and **Agnikula** refer only to traditions of origin, and there is nothing to prevent a man belonging to one of these divisions from marrying a woman who belongs to another subdivision. It is no doubt the case that some exogamous divisions are of higher rank than others, and that to give a daughter in marriage into one of these groups degrades her family in respect of future marriages for a period of seven years. But with a few doubtful exceptions in outlying districts the principle of hypergamy has not been pushed to the point of forming strictly endogamous groups.

Internal structure.

The original septs of the Rájput tribe appear to be for the most part of the territorial type, that is to say, their names seem to denote the tract of country in which the sept or its founder had their earliest habitat. **Sesodia** and **Bhadauria** may be taken as examples of this type. Other names again, such as **Jadubansi**, clearly refer to descent from particular families or stocks. In addition to their original septs, long lists of which are given in Appendix I, the Rájputs of Behar also recognize the Brahmanical *gotras*, and the tendency is for the latter series to supplant and take the place of the latter. Usually where the original sept names are still held to govern intermarriage, the rule is that a man may not marry a woman who belongs to the same sept as his father or his mother, and the prohibition is often extended to the septs, of the paternal and maternal grandmothers. Notwithstanding this rule a case has been brought to my notice in which the son of a Salanki Rájput of Behar married a woman of the Chandel sept, although his father had married into the same sept. At the time of the betrothal a question was raised as to the correctness of the procedure, and the Brahmans held that, as the son's betrothal, though of the same *tribal sept* as his mother, belonged to a different Brahmanical *gotra*, the rule of exogamy would not be infringed by the marriage. The standard formula for reckoning prohibited degrees is also recognized by the Behar Rájputs, who in theory considered it binding down to seven generations on the father's, and five on the mother's side. A man may marry two sisters, but he must take them in the order of age, and he cannot marry the elder sister if he is already married to the younger.

Isogamy and hypergamy.

In theory, as has been already stated, the whole body of Rájputs constitutes a single tribe divided into a very large number of septs or clans of descent, each of which is supposed to be descended from a common ancestor. Marriage within the sept is of course interdicted to its member, and in theory a Rájput belonging to any given sept has the whole community to choose from in seeking a bride for his son or a bridegroom for his daughter. In fact, however, the field of selection is greatly restricted by the operation of the laws of isogamy and hypergamy, the nature of which has been explained in the Introductory Essay. In a society so organized as to give the fullest play to the idea of purity of descent and the tradition of ceremonial orthodoxy, it must needs be that offences should come, and should be deemed to affect not only the offender himself and his family in the narrower sense, but the entire sept to which he belongs, which is conceived as an enlarged family. Thus in course of time is developed an infinite series of social distinctions giving rise to complicated and burdensome obligations in respect of marriage. In the case of the Rájputs these distinctions have not led to the formation of endogamous groups, as commonly happens among other castes, nor have they hardened into fixed hypergamous groupings, such as are exemplified by the Kulinism of Bengal. But running through the entire series of septs we find the usages of isogamy and hypergamy which have exercised and continue to exercise a profound influence on Rájput society. Isogamy or the law of equal marriage is defined by Mr. Ibbetson* as the rule which arranges the septs of a given locality in a scale of social standing, and forbids a father to give his daughter to a man of any sept which stands lower than his own. Hypergamy or the law of superior marriage is the rule which compels him to wed his daughter with a member of a sept which shall be actually superior in rank to his own. In both cases a man usually does not scruple to take his wife, or at any rate his second wife, from a sept of inferior standing. It will be readily seen how the working of these rules must have given rise to all sorts of reciprocal obligations as between septs, and must have restricted the number of available husbands in any particular locality. The men of a higher sept can take their wives from a lower sept, while a corresponding privilege is denied to the women of the higher sept. Hence results a surplus of women in the higher septs and competition for husbands sets in, leading to the payment of a high price for bridegrooms, and enormously increases the expense of getting a daughter married. Under these circumstances poor families are under a strong temptation to get rid of their female infants by poison or intentional neglect in order to be saved the expense of finding them suitable husbands or the disgrace of being compelled to marry them to men of lower degree.

Infanticide.

There is no reason to believe that infanticide has ever been practised by the Rajputs of Bengal on the scale on which it has been known to occur in North-Western India. The sentiment which would tend to the commission of the crime is probably not so strongly developed among the Eastern Rájputs, who are, as has been indicated above, probably of much more mixed descent than the Rájputs of Rájputáná.

* Report on the Census of the Panjab, p. 356.

Marriage.

The demand being for husbands, not for wives, it follows that the negotiations leading to marriage are opened by the father or guardian of the girl, who sends his family priest and family barber to the boy's house to make inquiries and to answer any questions that may be asked. Sometimes a professional match-maker, *aguá* or *ghatak*, is employed. In any case these preliminary negotiations are known as *aguái* or *bartuhari*. If these results are satisfactory, and the girl's family find that their offers are likely to be accepted, the same emissaries pay a second visit to the boy's house, accompanied by the girl's father, and bringing with them her horoscope, which is compared by the Brahmans of the two families with the horoscope of the boy in order to ascertain whether the match is likely to be auspicious. When this point has been satisfactorily settled, the question of the bridegroom-price (*tilak* and *dahej*) to be paid by the girl's family is discussed, and a certain proportion of it, usually half, is paid on the spot by way of clinching the bargain This is called *bar chhenka* or *phaldán*, and by receiving it the boy's people are deemed to bind themselves to marry him to no other woman. Sometimes the father of the boy also pays a small sum (*sagun*) as earnest money to the family of the girl. This practice, however, is said to be unusual, and is only resorted to when it is thought that the girl's family may be disposed to evade fulfilment of their obligations. The first instalment of the *tilak* or bridegroom-price is paid by one of the girl's relations to the boy himself in the presence of the family Brahman. At the same time a cocoanut is presented to him and a mark (*tilak*) is made with curds on his forehead. Both the gift and the mark are supposed to bring good luck. The balance of the bridegroom-price is paid in two equal instalments later on—one before and one after the marriage. On the occasion of paying the first instalment of *tilak*, presents are made to the Bráhmans and barbers who have taken part in the proceedings, and a date is fixed for the celebration of the marriage, an interval of fifteen days being usually allowed.

A few days before the wedding *dhanbatti* takes place, a barber is sent from the girl's house to the boy's with a present of unhusked rice. The boy's guardian takes this, mixes with it some rice of his own, and has the mixture parched. Two days before the wedding the women of the family scatter this parched rice about in the courtyard, singing songs which are supposed to bring good luck. On the next day, that is the day before the wedding, the rite of *ghidhári* is performed in the houses of the bride and bridegroom separately. The parents and nearest relations of the latter put on yellow clothes, and in the presence of the family priests worship Ganesa, the deity, who presides over success in life. The bridegroom is then smeared with oil, turmeric and *ghi*, offerings are made to the family gods, and the hair of the bridegroom's mother or his nearest female relative is anointed with oil. The same ceremony is gone through in the house of the bride, the only difference being that her family clothe themselves in red for the occasion. On the day of the marriage, but before the wedding procession is arranged, the ceremony of *belonki mangna* is often, though not necessarily, performed. The parents of the betrothed couple distribute cakes to the neighbours, demanding in return small presents of money (*belonki*).

The marriage procession is formed at the house of the bridegroom, and makes a somewhat noisy progress to the house of the bride. There the entire party is entertained. The bride and bridegroom are seated under a *marwa* or wedding canopy, and after the recital of appropriate *mantras* or texts, the family priest of the bride's household fills the bridegroom's right hand with *sindur*, and makes a mark with it on the bride's forehead, the women of the family meanwhile singing songs to celebrate the event. Among the Rájputs of Tirhut this is deemed the binding portion of the ritual, and the practice of walking round the sacred fire, usually considered essential in the marriage of the higher castes, is said to be unknown. The married couple then leave the *marwa* and go to the *kohbar* or house, where the family deity has been placed for the occasion. They worship and make offerings to him, and this concludes the marriage. The bridegroom then returns to the *janwásá* or lodgings reserved for his party, while the bride remains in her own house. Early next morning they are brought out and each is made to chew betel with which has been mixed a tiny drop of blood drawn from the other's little finger. This usage in which we may trace an interesting survival of primitive ideas is called *sineh jorua*, the joining of love. When it is over the bride is taken to her husband's house where she remains. On the fourth day after her arrival she and her husband stand together on a yoke such as is used for oxen, and a washerwoman pours water over them. This symbolical washing is supposed to be the first occasion on which the couple see each other by daylight after marriage. Among the Rájputs of North-Western India, and in some parts of Behar, the bride and bridegroom do not live together until after a second ceremony (called *gauná*, or with reference to the bride's 'going' to her husband's house) has been performed, which may take place one, three, five or even seven years after the marriage, and is fixed with reference to the physical development of the bride. In Tirhut, however, the custom of premature consummation, mentioned by Buchanan as prevalent among the Rájputs of Behar, seems to have been introduced, and it is said to be unusual for a bride to be kept at home until she attains puberty. Another custom connected with marriage, which students of comparative ethnography will also recognize as a survival of more primitive ideas, may be referred to here. In Rájput families of Tirhut it is considered contrary to etiquette for a young married couple to see each other by day so long as the husband's parents are alive, and in particular they must avoid being seen together by the husband's parents, and must not speak to one another in their presence. It is of course extremely difficult to ascertain how far a rule of this sort is actually observed, but I am assured that young married couples are very careful to avoid infringing it, although as they grow older their solicitude on this point is apt to wear off.

The remarriage of widows is strictly forbidden among the Rájputs of Behar. Divorce is also prohibited, and when a woman is taken in adultery, she is summarily expelled from the caste, and either becomes a prostitute or joins herself to some religious sect of more or less dubious morality. In certain cases, however, where a married couple find themselves unable to live in harmony together, a separation is arrived at by mutual consent, each agreeing to look upon the other as a parent. In such cases the wife returns to her father's house, and the husband marries again. This is not, however, looked upon as a divorce.

Religion.

Rájputs are orthodox Hindus, and worship the Hindu divinities favoured by the sect to which they happen to belong. By the Surajbansi division, special honour is done to the sun, whom they regard as their eponymous ancestor. Among minor gods Bandi and Narsingh appear to be most in favour. Ancestors are worshipped with offerings of milk, flowers and rice. Mondays and Wednesdays are believed to be the most propitious days for this worship. On the 15th day of Asin married women offer cakes and oil to the souls of their mother-in-law, grandmother-in-law and great grandmother-in-law. This custom, known as the Jitia puja, has obviously been copied from the *sraddh* celebrated in honour of the three immediate descendants. The popular explanation of it is that it is intended to express the gratitude that every married women ought to feel for her good fortune in getting a husband. Mr. Grierson, in *Behar Peasant Life,** speaks of the jitiya puja as "a fast and worship performed by women on the 8th of the dark half of Kártik (late in October) for the benefit of their children. Further inquiry on the subject would perhaps bring out points of interest and might clear up the discrepancy of date

Disposal of the dead.

For religious and ceremonial purposes Rájputs employ Brahmans, who are received on equal terms by other members of the sacred order. The dead are burned and the ashes thrown into the Ganges or ones of its tributaries. *Sraddh* is performed on the thirteenth day after death, and on the fourteenth a feast is given to the Brahmans of the neighbourhood. It is followed by the *barki sraddh* on the first anniversary of the death, when the members of the dead man's family shave their heads and faces, and present a *pinda* to the deceased, while the Brahmans recite mantras. Then the priests and the members of the family partake of a feast. It is said to be a tradition that the expenditure on this ceremony must not exceed half of that incurred on the original *sraddh*. After the *barkhi* the *tarpan* or *nit-tarpan*, a daily offering of water is presented regularly by all the sons of the deceased, and particularly by the eldest. This practice, however, is observed only by highly-educated Rájputs, who know their religious obligations in this matter. On the first fifteen days of Asin the *pitri paksh* or ancestors' fortnight is observed with offerings of water to all deceased ancestors. If a man dies sonless, leaving a wife and daughter, the *sraddh* and the *barki* are performed by one of them, the other ceremonies being

---

* Page 402.

omitted. Failing these the nearest agnate *gotia* will take upon himself these pious duties. In the event of a man dying away from his people and being burned or buried without the proper rites, his body is burned in effigy by his relatives, and the other ceremonies are performed in the usual fashion. When a man has died a sudden or violent death, it is thought right for his son to make a pilgrimage to Gya and perform the *sraddh* ceremony there in order to secure the repose of his soul.

Occupation and social status.

The high-flown titles—Bhupál, Bhupati, Bhusur, Báhuja—in use among Rájputs, and the name Chhatri itself indicate the exalted pretensions of the tribe and their traditions concerning their original occupation. Many Rájputs still cling to the belief that Government and the trade of arms are their proper business in life; and these notions lead them to regard education, and more especially the higher education, in much the same light as a medieval warrior looked upon the clerkly studies of his time. For this reason the Rájputs as a body have rather dropped behind in the modern struggle for existence, where book-learning counts for more than strength of arm, and the more intelligent members of the tribe are quite conscious that their position is by no means what it was in the classical ages of Hindu tradition. Their relations to the land still help them to maintain a show of respectability and importance. Many of them are zamindars, and those who hold cultivating tenures claim in virtue of their caste a remission of rent of their homestead lands. The *jeth-raiyat* or headman of a Behar village is frequently a Rájput. He collects the rents and receives in return a yearly allowance, known as *pagri*, from the zamindar. Rájputs are never artisans, and it is unusual to find them engaging in any kind of trade. In theory their social status is second only to that of the Brahman, but in Bengal Proper, where great Rájput houses do not exist, popular usage would, I think, place them below the Baidya and the Káyasth. Even in Behar the Bábhans claim precedence over them on the ground that they will not touch the handle (*parihath* or *lagna*) of the plough, and that they use the full *upanayan* ritual when investing their children with the *janeo* or sacred thread, whereas the Rájputs plough and milk cows with their own hands, and shuffle on the *janeo* in a rough-and-ready fashion when a boy gets married.

In respect of diet the Rájputs conform generally to the practice of high-caste Hindus. The flesh of the goat, the deer and the hare, the pigeon, quail and ortolan may alone be eaten, and these animals, if not killed in hunting, must be slaughtered in a particular way (*jhataka*) by cutting the head off at a single stroke. Fish is lawful food. Wine is supposed to be forbidden. As regards the taking of food from members of other castes, the following rules are in force:—

A Rájput cannot take *kachchi* food, *i.e.*, rice or *dál* or anything that is cooked with water from anyone but a Brahman. *Pakki* food, such as parched grain, sweetmeats and the like, he may take from a man of any caste higher than his own or from a Dhánuk, Kurmi, Kahár, Lohar, Barhi, Kumhár, Goálá, Mallah, Hajjám, Máli, Sonár, Láheri, or Gareri, provided that no salt or turmeric has been used in the making. These condiments he will add himself. Water is governed by the rules applicable to *pakki* food. Rájputs may not use the hookahs of any other caste, but may smoke tobacco prepared by men of any caste except the Dosadh, Dom, Chamár, Musahar and Dhobi.

The following statement shows the number and distribution of Rájputs in 1872 and 1881:—

District.	1872.	1881.	District.	1872.	1881.
Bardwan	12,359	7,218	Noakhali	350	158
Bankura	9,180	13,987	Tipperah	2,161	1,162
Birbhum	7,028	8,344	Chittagong Hill Tracts ...	47	7
Midnapur	17,003	19,573	Patna	60,079	64,332
Hughli	6,983	5,539	Gya	102,918	114,402
Howrah		1,039	Shahabad	183,896	207,195
24-Parganás	8,683	12,604	Mozufferpur	237,236	167,594
Nadiya	5,017	6,047	Darbhanga		90,083
Jessore	1,114	903	Saran	213,348	243,972
Khulna	......	551	Champarán	69,614	80,764
Murshedabad	13,141	8,955	Monghyr	47,006	56,067
Dinajpur	1,813	2,887	Bhágalpur	52,579	60,191
Rajshahye	1,541	1,233	Purniah	23,663	48,465
Rangpur	2,404	2,338	Maldah	3,207	5,104
Bogra	3,426	872	Santál Parganás	33,337	28,124
Pabna	664	455	Cuttack	10,728	10,782
Darjiling	8,972	6,352	Puri	2,946	3,898
Jalpigori	523	1,269	Balasore	2,053	2,770
Kuch Behar...	......	3,107	Tributary States	6,510	3,551
Dacca	1,665	5,862	Hazaribagh	31,387	37,404
Faridpur	901	533	Lohardaga	37,762	47,471
Bakarganj	952	468	Singbhum	1,718	1,949
Maimansinh	2,470	2,167	Manbhum	16,588	16,942
Chittagong	359	1,040	Tributary States	2,389	5,258

Rajwár, a Dravidian cultivating caste of Behar, Western Bengal, and Chota Nagpur, who are probably a branch of one of the aboriginal races.

Origin.

This opinion was held by Buchanan, who went so far as to identify them with the Rachewárs or Rajawárs whom he came across in Mysore. Colonel Dalton reckoned them among the mongrel tribes. "Traditionally," he says, "they appear to connect themselves with the Bhuiyás; but this is only in Behar. The Rajwárs in Serguja and the adjoining States are peaceably-disposed cultivators, who declare themselves to be fallen Kshatriyas: they do not, however, conform to Hindu customs, and they are skilled in a dance called Chailo, which I believe to be of Dravidian origin. The Rajwárs of Bengal admit that they are derived from the miscegenation of Kurmis and Kols. They are looked upon as very impure by Hindus, who will not take water from their hands." The Rajwárs of Behar told Buchanan "that their common ancestor was a certain Rishi, who had two sons From the eldest are descended the Rajwárs, who became soldiers and obtained their noble title; from the younger are descended the Musahars, who have obtained their name from eating rats, which the Rajwárs reject." The suggestion of affinity with the Musahars seems to support Colonel Dalton's statement that the Rajwars connect themselves with the Bhuiyás, for Musahars and Bhuiyás are certainly closely related, if not one and the same. On the other hand, it should be observed that the Rajwárs of Gyá will not eat with Bhuiyás. The Rajwárs of Manbhum have a tradition that they came from Nagpur. They say that the king of that country had two daughters, the elder of whom was lawfully married to the elder of two brothers, while the younger daughter ran away with the younger brother. On the death of the king the brothers fought among themselves for the kingdom, but after a time it was settled that the one who came first to the capital on a certain morning should be king On his way to the city the younger brother saw a golden crab and dismounted to get it, tying his horse to a tree. As he was reaching for the crab, a kite screamed over his head. He mistook the kite's scream for the neighing of his horse, assumed that it had broken loose and went off to look for it. This took him so long that he never got to Nagpur at all, but gave up his claims to the crown and went home. The Rajwár caste are his descendants. The legend may well have been suggested by the name Rajwár or the title Rájbansi. The internal structure of the caste is shown in Appendix I. Some of the sections are totemistic —a fact which may be taken as certainly indicating Dravidian descent. The sub-castes are the following—Angrok or Angwár, Chapwár, Sikhariá, Sukulkárá, Bar-Gohri, Majhal-Turiyá, and Berra-Rajwár. The last three are found only in Lohardagá. The third occurs among several castes of Western Bengal, and refers to the tract of country between the Dámodar and Barákar rivers, east of the Parasnáth range of hills. The Doms of Behar have a section called Angwár. All the sections are exogamous, but in Behar the Marrik, Majhiyá, and Matwárá profess not to intermarry with members of the Bhogtá group. For the rest they follow the standard formula for calculating prohibited degrees.

Internal structure.

Marriage.

Rajwárs marry their daughters either as infants or as adults. In the latter case sexual intercourse before marriage is condoned, as with the Mundas and Oraons, provided that the lover marries the girl. An intrigue with a man of another caste would of course be punished by summary excommunication. The marriage closely resembles that in use among the Kurmis, *sindurdán* being the binding portion. Polygamy is permitted. A man may have as many wives as he can afford to maintain. A widow may marry a second time by the *sangá* form. She is not bound to marry her late husband's younger brother. Some Rajwárs of Gya and Shahabad assured me that only childless widows might marry again, and that the privilege was under no circumstances extended to a widow with children. This looks like a first step towards the introduction of further restrictions, but I doubt whether my informants were correct in their statement; or, if they were, whether the modified usage extended beyond a small number of families. Divorce is allowed for adultery or incompatibility of temper, and divorced wives may marry again.

Religion.

The members of the caste profess to be Hindus of the Vaishnava sect, and employ degraded Brahmans (Jyosi or Maithil) for religious and ceremonial observances. In Behar they also worship Goraiyá, Dihwár, Jagdambá, and the other standard minor gods. They burn their dead and perform a rather meagre *sráddh* ceremony on the eleventh day. A piece of bone is saved from the fire in order that it may be thrown into the Ganges or the Dámodar. The reverence thus shown for the latter river deserves notice, as it is always associated with the funeral rites of the aboriginal races.

Social status.

The social rank of the Rajwárs is low, and Brahmans will not ordinarily take water from their hands. Those Brahmans, however, who serve them as priests, and the Vaishnava ascetics, who act as their spiritual guides, will eat sweetmeats and similar *pakki* food in their houses. In virtue of their abstinence from beef and pork they believe themselves to be raised above the Bauris and Doms; while the fact that they eat fowls and the leavings of the higher castes, and indulge freely in strong drink, cuts them off from the respectable classes from whose hands Brahmans will take water. The Kurmis are the lowest caste from whom they will take cooked food. Agriculture is their sole occupation. Some of them are occupancy raiyats, but a large proportion have not risen above the condition of landless day-labourers.

The following statement shows the number and distribution of Rajwárs in 1872 and 1881:—

District.	1872.	1881.	District.	1872.	1881.
Bardwan	......	230	Patna	3,344	3,960
Bankura	......	61	Gya	39,484	43,773
Birbhum	......	135	Shahabad	4,451	6,802
Midnapur	......	10,265	Mozufferpur	72	531
Hughli	......	2	Saran	117	304
Howrah	......	133	Champaran	37	32
24-Parganás	......	469	Monghyr	114	......
Nadiya	......	113	Bhagalpur	289	354
Murshedabad	......	163	Purniah	218	62
Rajshahye	......	211	Maldah	......	23
Bogra	......	41	Santál Parganás	5,080	6,172
Pabna	......	4	Hazaribagh	1,265	9,291
Darjiling	......	20	Lohardagá	3,559	5,657
Faridpur	......	51	Singbhum	33	101
Chittagong	......	13	Manbhum	10,091	15,541
			Tributary States	11,510	14,475

Rajwár, a sept of Rájputs in Behar.

Rakhál, a *thar* or sept of Mangars in Darjiling.

Rakhali, a section of Khámbus in Darjiling.

Rakhi, a sub-caste of Kalwárs in Behar.

Raksa, a section of the Kanaujiá sub-caste of Goálás in Behar.

Raksáin, a sept of the Suryabansi sub-tribe of Rájputs in Behar.

Raksel, a sept of Rájputs in Behar.

Rakshit, *Rakhit*, a title of Baidyas, of Dakshin-Rárhi and Bangaja Káyasths; Báruis, Támolis, and Telis, of Mayarás and Sutradhars in Bengal.

Raksise, a *mul* or section of the Chhamuliá Madhesiá sub-caste of Halwáis in Behar.

Rakwár, a section of Rájputs in Behar.

Rám, (i) a title applied to Kurmis in Behar until by age or personal influence they attain a leading position in the village, when they are called Marár or Máhton; (ii) a title of Dosádhs; (iii) a section of the Mahmudáiriz sub-caste of Nápits.

Rámáiyá, an endogamous branch of the Chauan sub-caste of Kurmis in Behar who are said to have been outcasted for eating by mistake for a goat the body of a dog which had been roasted in a fire which burned down a village The Rámáiyás deny the truth of this story, but, while claiming to belong to the Chauan sub-caste of Kurmis, can assign no reason for their exclusion from rights of food and intermarriage.

Rámánuja, a sect of Vaishnavas.

Rámávat, a sect of Vaishnavas.

Ramayá, a section of Bábhans in Behar.

Rámáyat, Rámáth, a celibate sect of Vaishnavas who worship Rama and Krishna, wear the *paita*, and are usually treated as Brahmans.

Rámer-Dhobá, a sub-caste of Dhobás in Eastern Bengal.

Rámgarhiá, a sept of Bairágis and Mundas in Chota Nagpur.

Rámi dhámi ke asámi, a section of the Banodhiá and Jaiswár Kalwárs in Behar.

Ramjani, a caste of dancers, singers, and prostitutes, synonymous with Gandharvin.

Rámkisán, a section of the Biyáhut and Kharidáhá Kalwárs in Behar.

Rámpái, a section of Bábhans in the north of Manbhum to whom the members of other sections will not give their daughters in marriage, though they allow the men to marry Rámpai women.

Rámpuri, a section of Báis Sonárs in Behar.

Rámpuriá, a section of the Banodhiá and Jaiswár Kalwárs in Behar.

Rámudán, a section of Kámis in Darjiling.

Ráná, a title of the Bhar and Mayará castes; a *pangat* or section of Dosadhs; a section of the Surajbansi division of Rájputs in Behar; a title of Dakshin-Rárhi and Bangaja Káyasths; a title of Aguris and Sutradhars; of Kumhárs in Behar; of Mangars in Darjiling; a section of the Magahiyá sub-caste of Doms in Behar.

Ráná Lamsani, a *thar* or sept of the Das-gurung sub-tribe of Gurungs in Darjiling.

Ranasinha or *Samarsinha*, lion of the fight, a title of Khandáits in Orissa.

Ránauchhá, a *thar* or sept of Khambus in Darjiling.

Ranauni, a sept of the Suryabansi sub-tribe of Rájputs in Behar.

Ráncho, a section of Bágdis in Western Bengal.

Ráne, a section of Kanaujiá Lohárs in Behar.

Ranga, a title of Dakshin-Rárhi and Bangaja Káyasths.

Rángá, a sept of Dhimáls in the Darjiling Terai.

Rangataba, a yellow bird, a totemistic sept of Juángs in Orissa.

Rángdhári, Rangdháriá, a maker of tin (*rángá*) or pewter ornaments, an occupation followed by Mahomedans; also a synonym for Sonár.

Rangomung, a sept of Lepohas in Darjiling.

Rangpiár, a section of the Biyáhut and Kharidáhá Kalwárs in Behar.

Rangrez, *Rangráj*, a dyer, an occupation usually followed by Mahomedans.

Rangroz, a functional group of Jugis.

Rani Poka, a red worm, a totemistic sept of Mundas in Chota Nagpur.

Ranka, a section of Oswáls in Behar.

Rankankar, a sept of Kaurs in Chota Nagpur.

Ránki or **Kalál**, a sub-caste (Mahomedan) of Kalwárs in Behar.

Rankwár, a sept of Rájputs in Behar.

Ransadiyá, a section of Bábhans in Behar.

Ranubád, a section of Kumhárs in Singbhum.

Ranyacelunya, a sept of Chakmás in the Hill Tracts of Chittagong.

Ranyin, a sept of Chakmás in the Hill Tracts of Chittagong.

Ráorh, a section of Maghayá Kumhárs in Behar.

Ráori, a title of Kándus in Behar.

Raot, a totemistic sept of Doms and Chamárs in Chota Nagpur.

Raotiá, crab, a totemistic sept of Páns in Chota Nagpur.

Rápungchhá, a *thar* or sept of Khambus in Darjiling.

Rárh-ásram, a sub-caste of Mayarás in Central Bengal.

Rárher Rárhi, a sub-caste of Sunris in Eastern Bengal.

Rárhi, a sub-caste of Brahmans in the Lower Provinces of Bengal who derive their name from the Rárh, or the high-lying alluvial tract on the west bank of the river Bhagirathi. They claim descent from five Kanaujiá Brahmans brought by Ádisur to perform certain ceremonies which the local Brahmans, who are now known as Saptasatis, were incompetent to undertake; a sub-caste of Kewats in Orissa; of Kumhárs, Tántis, Telis; of Baidyas, Baruis, Kayasths, Goálás, Kaibarttas, Jugis, Subarnabaniks, and Sunris in Bengal; of Kámárs in Murshedabad, and in Pabna also called Dás-Samáj; a group of Phulkátá Mális.

Rarhi-Mál, a sub-caste of Máls in the Santál Parganás.

Rárhiya-Samáj, a sub-caste of Dhobás in Hughli.

Ráriá, a section of Goálás in the North-Western Provinces and Behar.

Rasáili, a section of Kámis; a *thar* or sept of Mangars in Darjiling.

Rasákmáre, a *mul* or section of the Naomulia or Majraut subcaste of Goálás in Behar.

Rásamba, mushrooms that grow on ant-hills, a totemistic sept of Juángs in Orissa.

Rasáunmare, a *mul* or section of the Naomulia or Majraut subcaste of Goálás in Behar.

Rás-rishi, a section of Gandhabaniks in Bengal.

Rást, a title of Goálás in Behar.

Rástogi, a trading caste of Behar, usually engaged in selling cloth and money-lending, but sometimes also dealing in grain and native medicines. They practise two peculiar forms of petty money-lending by *bahi*, that is by entry in books of account without the security of a separate bond. These are known as *augáhi* or *ugáhi* and *rozáhi*. Mr. Hoey gives[1] the following account of them :—

"*Augáhi* is lending of money to be repaid with interest at 20 per cent. in monthly instalments. Thus, if a Rástogi lends on the 1st January ten rupees, he receives one rupee on the first of each month for twelve months, and thereby realises twelve rupees, of which two rupees are interest. A Rástogi's *augáhi bahi* is a curiosity. It is ruled like a chess-board, but has twelve columns. As each month's instalment is realised, it is entered in a square until the twelve squares are filled. He generally keeps also a separate *bahi*, in which the principal is noted when lent. It may, however, be noted in the margin of his check-pattern account. *Rozáhi* is money lent to be realised in daily instalments with interest at 25 per cent. Thus, if a rupee be lent, one-half anna (*táká roz*) will be realised daily. The account of this money is kept in a similar way, but the account-book will be ruled in lines of 40 squares. A Rástogi keeps his accounts by locality, that is, he has several *khets*, as he calls them; one, say, is Saadatganj, another Hasanganj, a third Deori Agha Mir, and so on. Debtors are called *asámis*, and the amount to be collected is called *lagán*. A separate set of account-books is kept for each *khet*, and a servant (generally a Brahman on Rs. 3 per mensem) is employed to collect each *khet*."

Mr. Sherring mentions three sub-castes—**Amethi**, **Indrapati**, and **Mauhariá**, which do not intermarry. Rástogis marry their daughters as infants, forbid widows to remarry, and do not recognize divorce. In matters of diet they affect to be extremely punctilious, and thus married women of the caste will not eat food that has been prepared, or even touched by their husbands.

The following statement shows the number and distribution of Rástogis in 1881. They were not returned separately in 1872 :—

DISTRICT.	1881.	DISTRICT.	1881.
Patna	238	Champarun	21
Gya	8	Monghyr	206
Shahabad	186	Purniah	17
Mozufferpur	10	Hazaribagh	164
Darbhanga	36	Lohardagá	44
Saran	1,470		

Rat, a section of Awadhiá Hajjáms in Behar.

Rathiá, a sub-tribe of Kaurs in Chota Nagpur.

Rathitara, a section of the Páschátya Baidik Brahmans in Bengal ; a Kshatrapeta *gotra* or section of Brahmans.

Ratnábali, *a gáin* of the Bharadwája *gotra* of Bárendra Brahmans in Bengal.

Ratwariá, a section of Lohárs in Behar.

Rauná, a synonym for Rawáni, *q.v.*

Ráuniá, a section of the Sátmuliá Maghayá sub-caste of Kándus in Behar.

[1] *Trade and Manufactures of Northern India*, p. 144.

Rauniár, *Raunia, Noniár*, a sub-caste of Baniyás[1] in Behar. Writing of the members of this group in the North-West Provinces, Mr. Nesfield says:—"Raunia, more fully written Ravaniyá, is from *ravan*, which means the crying or hawking of wares for sale." In another place he adds:—"The Rauniá (which means literally a crier) moves in a circle of some eight or ten villages surrounding his own; and if he cannot get cash for his grain, he barters it for spices, sugar, condensed treacle, etc. In these days he is seldom able to live by trade alone, and in the intervals of business he raises his own crops. But trade, and trade only, was his original function."

Internal structure.

The Rauniárs of Behar profess to have come from the North-West Provinces, and their allegation is likely enough to be correct. They are divided into exogamous sections (*muls* or *gotras*), but the only section-names I have been able to ascertain are Ekadasi and Ekassi, referring possibly to the number of families comprised, or supposed to be comprised, in each section. Their titles are Sáhu and Modi, which are common to them and to many other trading groups. In Champáran they have broken up into two endogamous groups—Chhatri and Samri, the former of whom claim to be Rájputs from the North-West Provinces who were degraded for intermarrying with women of the Baniyá caste.

Marriage.

Rauniárs profess to marry their daughters as infants, but I am informed that cases of girls being married after puberty are not uncommon where the parents are poor or for any special reason there has been difficulty in finding a husband. It is clear therefore that the caste does not take the extreme sacerdotal view of the necessity of infant-marriage which prevails among Hindus of the higher classes, especially in Bengal Proper. Their marriage ceremony is of the standard type, and a price (*tilak*) is paid to the parents of the bridegroom. Polygamy is allowed, but is rarely resorted to in practice, except when the first wife proves barren. Widows are allowed to remarry by the *sagai* form, of which *sindurdán* is the binding portion. The widow is under no obligation to marry her deceased husband's younger brother. Divorce is not generally recognized; but in Champáran it appears to be the practice to bring cases of unchastity before a pancháyat, which makes an order of divorce; and if the offence has been committed with a member of the caste, the woman is allowed to marry again by *sagai*.

Religion.

In their religious and ceremonial observances the Rauniárs are orthodox Hindus and employ Brahmans, whose social position is in no way affected by serving them. Rauniárs are not conspicuous for adhesion to any particular sect, but in some parts of the country they are said to regard

[1] I have treated the Rauniár as a sub-caste of Baniyá, instead of as a separate caste, in order to avoid doing violence to popular usage. Both Natives and Europeans speak of the Baniya caste, and ignore the fact that the expression denotes a group comprising several distinct castes, which cannot now be traced to any common stock. The subject is discussed at greater length in the article on Baniyá.

Mahádeva as their tutelary deity. Like the Agarwals, they pay special reverence to Lakhsmi, and celebrate the Diwáli festival with great pomp. They also worship Bandi, Goraiyá, Sokhá, and Máhábirji as household or village gods.

Occupation.

Trading in grain, cloth, etc., and lending money, are their special functions, but of late years some of them have taken to agriculture, and a few have risen, probably as a consequence of money-lending transactions, to be zemindars. In Champaran Rauniyárs are found as occupancy raiyats, but such cases are rare.

Rausan, a synonym for Teli.

Raut, a sub-tribe of Kharwárs in Southern Lohardagá.

Ráut, *Rahut*, a title of Amáts, Chamárs, Dhanuks, Dosádhs, Gonrhis, Goálás, Kadars, Kumhars, Nágars, Pargahs, Rájputs, and Sunris in Behar; in Bengal of the Bhát Brahmans. As a title of Mális in Behar, it seems to be in process of development into a sub-caste, for the Ráut Mális intermarry among themselves; a title of Beldars, Nuniás, Barais, Kahárs, Binds, and of Dhobis in Behar; a section and a title of Kurmis in Behar; a sept of Thárus; a title of Gareris; a title of Chásás and Khandáits in Chota Nagpur and Orissa; a section of Dharkár Doms in Behar; a title of Bhuiyás; a sept of Mundas in Chota Nagpur.

Rautar, a section of Sonárs in Behar.

Rautár, a sub-tribe of Thárus in Behar.

Rauti, a section of Mahesris in Behar.

Origin.

Rautiá, a landholding and cultivating caste of Chota Nagpur, probably Dravidian in its original affinities, but since refined in features and complexion by a large infusion of Aryan blood. The name Rautiá suggests some connexion with Rajpúts, and Mr. Beames has noticed that the cognate term Ráut is used in some districts to denote an inferior Rajpút, "the corruption of the name betokening the corruption of the caste."[1] Their traditions say that they formerly dwelled in Sinhal-dwip (Ceylon), whence they migrated to Barhar, in Mirzapur. In the time of the Emperor Jahángir some Rautias were serving as sentinels in the fort at Gwálior when Maharája Durjan Sáh of Chutiá Nagpur was imprisoned there for failure to pay his tribute to Dehli.[2] During his confinement the Rautiás treated the Raja kindly, and he repaid their good offices on his release by giving them lands in parganá Panári of Lohardagá. Further grants of villages, groups of villages, and entire parganás were afterwards made to them in *jágir*, and many of these are in existence at the present day. The titles of Baráik, Gaunjhu, and Kotwár were at the same time conferred upon them.

---

[1] *Supplemental Glossary*, vol. i, p. 24.

[2] See extracts from *Tuzuk-i-Jahángiri* and MS. history of Chutiá Nagpur in *J. A. S. B.* for 1871, and *Statistical Account of Bengal*, vol. xvi, p. 447 *et seq.*

The Rautiás are divided into two endogamous sub-castes—Bargohri and Chhot-gohri. The origin of this division is obscure. The Rautiás themselves tell an absurd story to account for it. They say that the Bar-gohris were the first to arrive in their present habitat. When the Chhot-gohris came they were asked with what cooking pots and on what fire-places they had cooked their food after the Bar-gohris had started. On their replying that they had used the pots and fire-places left behind by the Bar-gohris, but had cleaned them, the latter straightway took offence, and from that time forth have refused to eat cooked food (*kachi*) with the Chhot-gohri. Following the analogy of similar schisms in castes formerly united, it seems more likely either that the Chhot-gohri were the first settlers and were outcasted for some such breach of caste rules as people are apt to commit, or to be taxed with committing, when they settle in outlandish parts of the country, or that the Chhot-gohri are the offspring of alliances between the Bar-gohri and women of inferior caste or purity of lineage. At the present day the Chhot-gohri eat fowls and wild pig and drink spirits, all of which things are forbidden for members of the higher group.

Internal structure.

Within each sub-caste we find a group called Berrá Rautiá, who are admittedly descendants of Rautiás by concubines of other castes. Although not strictly endogamous, the Berrás observe certain special restrictions in the matter of marriage. Thus a Berrá whose mother was a Rájput will not marry a girl whose mother was a Ghási.

Both sub-castes have a long list of sections (*páris* or *got*), which will be found in the Appendix. The fact that the list contains totemistic, eponymous, and territorial names, tells on the whole in favour of the view that the Rautiás are people of mixed descent. The rule that the totem is taboo to its bearers seems only to apply to the animal-totems, which may be named, but not killed or eaten; for a Rautiá of the sword or axe groups is not forbidden to use those weapons, nor is a man of the Kási group forbidden to touch the grass from which his section is supposed to be descended.

The section name goes by the male side, and the prohibition attached to it affects only a man's own section and does not prevent him from marrying a woman belonging to the same section as his mother. This simple rule of exogamy is therefore supplemented by a table of prohibited degrees made up, like our own, by enumerating the individual relatives whom a man may not marry, and not, as is more usual, by prohibiting intermarriage with certain large classes of relations or with the descendants within certain degrees of particular relations.

Marriage.

Girls are married either as infants or adults, usually between the ages of eight and eighteen. Sexual license before marriage is not openly recognized, as it is among the aborigines of Chota Nagpur; but I am informed that grown-up girls enjoy considerable liberty in this respect, it being understood that in case of pregnancy a husband will be at once forthcoming. In theory polygamy is allowed without any restriction being laid on the number of wives or any antecedent condition being insisted on, such as that the first wife must be barren or be inflicted with an incurable disease in order to entitle her husband to take another wife. In actual life, however, it is unusual to find a man with more than three or four wives. One simple reason for this is that few men can afford to keep many wives or have house-room to accommodate them, as by universal custom each wife must have a separate room.

A widow is allowed to marry again by the *sagai* form, and it is considered right for her to marry her late husband's younger brother. Under no circumstances can she marry the elder brother. If she marries an outsider, her late husband's brother, father, or uncle have the right to the custody of all her children, both male and female. In any case she acquires no rights in her late husband's property, the whole of which passes to his eldest son, subject to certain obligations to provide, by way of maintenance, for younger brothers. If a widow marries her late husband's younger brother, her children by him are not deemed the children of her first husband, nor have they any rights in respect of his property.

The ritual used at the marriage of a widow is very simple. Five married women whose husbands are living take a *sári*, a pair of lac bracelets, and a little vermilion (*sindur*) to the bridegroom and get him to touch each article. They then return to the bride, attire her in the *sári* and bracelets, and daub the vermilion on her forehead. As in the case of a regular marriage, the proceedings conclude with a feast to the friends and relatives of the newly-married couple.

A woman may be divorced for adultery or for eating with a member of another caste. For lighter offences than these, separation is the only punishment awarded; and in that case the husband is bound to maintain his wife. A divorced woman may not marry again. If she lives with a man, she ranks as a concubine and her children are illegitimate.

The ceremony performed at the marriage of a virgin bride contains several features of a primitive and non-Aryan character. In the first instance, both parties go through the form of marriage to a mango tree (*ambá bihá*). The essential and binding portions of the ritual are the knotting together of the clothes of the bride and bridegroom and *sindurdán*, which is effected by smearing on the bride's forehead a drop of blood drawn from the little finger of the bridegroom, and *vice versá*. Sákadwipi Brahmans officiate, and offerings are made to Gauri and Ganesa.

Marriages are arranged by the parents or guardians of the parties, who have no freedom of choice in the matter. Professional marriage-brokers are unknown. The first offer is made by the father of the bridegroom, and a bride-price (*dáli taká*), varying according to the means of the bridegroom's parents, is paid to the parents of the bride, by whom it is retained. No portion of the bride-price becomes the special property of the bride.

The Mitákshará commentary, which forms the personal law of most Hindus in Lohardagá, does not apply to Rautiás, who are governed by special customs of their own. The eldest son by a regularly-married (*bihái*) wife inherits the whole of his father's property, subject to the obligation of creating maintenance grants in favour of his younger brothers. These grants are not equal in value, but are supposed to decrease in the order of age of the grantees, so that each younger brother gets a smaller grant than his immediate elder, and so on. Instances, however, have occurred among the Bar-gohri Rautiás in which, with the consent of the eldest son, an entire property has been equally divided. Sons by a *sagai* wife are included in this arrangement, but get smaller grants than sons by a *bihái* wife. The rule that sons by a *bihái* wife take precedence of sons by a *sagai* wife is subject to the important exception that an elder brother's widow, though married by the *sagai* form, ranks in all respects as a *bihái* wife, and her sons have the full rights of succession to their father. This principle was affirmed by the Civil Courts in a case which occurred a few years ago. One of the Rautiá Baráiks of Basia died leaving a widow and infant son; the widow married in the *sogai* form her late husband's younger brother, who was already married to a *bihái* wife. Both of the wives bore sons, the *sagai* wife a few months earlier than the *bihái* wife. Meanwhile the infant son of the original proprietor died: the whole property passed to his brother, and on his death was disputed between his sons. It was held that the son of the *sagai* wife, being the eldest, was entitled to succeed under the custom of the caste, and that the son of the *bihái* wife had only a right to maintenance. It will be seen from this instance that a brother excludes a widow from succession. The latter is in fact entitled only to maintenance, and may forfeit even that by misconduct or infringement of caste rules. Brothers and uncles, or their descendants, exclude daughters and their descendants. Succession indeed is strictly agnatic throughout; the eldest male of the eldest line taking the entire inheritance subject to the obligation to provide maintenance for relatives within certain degrees on a scale progressively diminishing in relation to the age and propinquity in relationship of the claimants. The distinction between ancestral and self-acquired property, which has acquired such prominence in the standard Hindu law, does not seem to be very clearly recognized in the customary law of the Rautiás. I gather, however, that such property is not subject to the rule of primogeniture, but is ordinarily divided equally among the male descendants.

Succession.

Step-sons are not entitled to maintenance from the estate of their step-father. Owing, however, to the fact that a widow may marry her late husband's younger brother and may *not* marry his eldest brother, it happens that a large proportion of the step-sons among the Rautiás are really the heirs to the estates of which their step-fathers happen for the time being to be in charge. A *ghár dijuá*, or son-in-law who lives with his wife in his father-in-law's household, retains his claims on his natural father's property, but acquires no right to a maintenance grant from his father-in-law's estate.

Adoption is unknown—a circumstance from which we may either infer that the Rautiás are free from the curse of childlessness, so common in the higher ranks of Hindus, or that one of the inducements to adopt sons has been removed by the rule regarding land referred to in the next paragraph.

In the event of a Rautiá dying without male heirs, his immovable property reverts to his superior landlord or the legal representative of the person by whom the land was originally granted. In such cases the landlord is expected to make some small provision for the maintenance of the females of the family. His movable property goes to the person who performs his funeral rites.

An elder brother can transfer to a younger brother all his rights in the family property, but the effect of such a transfer is limited to his own lifetime, and does not curtail the rights of his son, who will succeed, in preference to the uncle on attaining his majority.

Religion.

The religion of the Rautiás may best be described as a mixture of the primitive animism characteristic of the aboriginal races and the debased form of Hinduism which has been disseminated in Chota Nagpur by a class of Brahmans markedly inferior in point of learning and ceremonial purity to those who stand forth as the representatives of the caste in the great centres of Hindu civilization. Among the Bar-gohri Rautiás many have of late years become Kabirpanthis; the rest, with most of the Chhot-gohri and the Berrás of both sub-castes, are Rámáyat Vaishnavas. A few only have adopted the tenets of the Saiva sects. Rama, Ganesa, Mahadeva, and Gauri are the favourite deities, whose worship is conducted by Sakadwipi Brahmans more or less in the orthodox fashion. Behind the fairly definite personalities of these greater gods there loom in the background, through a fog of ignorance and superstition, the dim shapes of Bar-pahár (the Marang Buru or mountain of the Mundas); Bura-buri, the supposed ancestors of mankind; the seven sisters who scatter cholera, small-pox, and cattle-plague abroad; Goraiá, the village god—a sort of rural Terminus; and the myriad demons with which the imagination of the Kolhs peoples the trees, rocks, streams, and fields of its surroundings.

To Bar-pahár are offered he-buffaloes, rams, he-goats, fowls, milk, flowers, and sweetmeats; the animals in each case being given some rice to chew and decked with garlands of flowers before being sacrificed. When offered in pursuance of a special vow, the animal is called *charáol*, and is slain in the early morning in the *sarná* or sacred grove outside the village; rice, ghi, molasses, vermilion, flowers, and *bel* leaves being presented at the same time. No female may be present at the ceremony. The carcase of the victim is distributed among the worshippers, but no part of it may be taken into the village, and it is cooked and eaten on the spot, even the remnants being buried in the *sarná* at the end of the feast. The head is eaten by the man who made the vow and the members of his family, but no others share in it, owing to the belief that whoever partakes of the head would thereby render himself liable to perform a similar *puja*.

When a buffalo is sacrificed, the Rautiás do not eat the flesh themselves, but leave the carcase to the Mundas, Kharias, and other beef-eating folk who may happen to be present.

To the seven sisters (*devis*) and their brother Bhairo a rude shrine (*devigarhi*) is erected in the centre of every village, consisting of a raised plinth five cubits square covered by a tiled or thatched roof resting on six posts of *gulaichi* trees (*Plumeria*). In the middle of the plinth, on a line running north and south, stand seven little mounds of dried mud, representing the seven goddesses, while a smaller mound on one side stands for Bhairo. In front of the *Devigarhi*, at some ten or fifteen cubits distance, is a larger mound representing Goraiyá, the village god, to whom pigs are sacrificed by the village priest (*páhan*) and by men of the Dosádh caste. Regarding the names and functions of the seven sisters there seems to be much uncertainty. Some Rautias enumerate the following :—

Burhiá Mái or Sitalá.
Kankárin Mái.
Káli Mái.
Kuleswari Mái.
Bágheswari Mái.
Mareswari Mái.
Dulhári Mái.

Others substitute Jwálá-mukhi, Vindhyabásini, Málat Mái, and Joginiá Mái for the last four. Jwálá-mukhi is a place of pilgrimage in the Lower Himalayas north of the Panjáb, where inflammable gas issues from the ground and is believed to be the fire created by Parbati when she desired to become a *sati*. Vindhyabásini is a common title of Sitalá Devi, who presides over small-pox throughout Northern India. I cannot find out which sisters are supposed to be responsible for cholera and cattle-plague. Kuleshwari (*kul* = 'tiger' in Mundári) and Bágheswari apparently have to do with the tiger. He-goats, flowers, fruit, and *bel* leaves are offered to the seven sisters in front of the *devi-gurhi*. Women and children are present at the worship. A Sakadwipi Brahman presides, but does not slay the victims.

The following are the festivals observed by the Rautiás :—

Festivals.

(1) Nawa Khani—eating new rice with milk, molasses, and ghi. On the 12th of the light half of Bhádon (middle of September) and the 15th of the light half of Aghan (middle of November). These periods correspond respectively to the harvesting of the low land and high land rice crops.

(2) Jitia parab.—On the 8th of the dark half of Asin (end of September). The females of the village, after fasting a day, bring a twig from a *jitia pipal* tree (*Ficus religiosa*) and an ear of rice, and plant them in the courtyard of a house, usually that of the chief man of the village. Vermilion, *arua* or rice husked without boiling, flowers, and sweetmeats, are offered to the twig. Dancing, singing, and processions of various kinds follow, and in

the morning, after watching the twigs all night, the women offer *múnr* or rice gruel to their deceased ancestors.

(3) Dasahará—corresponding to the Devi-pujá and Vijayá dasmi of the Hindus.—On the 10th of the light half of Ásin (early in October).

(4) Debathan—a fast, followed by eating various kinds of boiled fruit and roots—observed only by bachelors and spinsters on the eleventh of the light half of Kartik (middle of November).

(5) Ganesh Chauth.—On the 4th of the dark half of Mágh (middle of January). An image of Ganesa is made out of cow-dung and is worshipped with *laddus* or cakes of *til*, legends being recited at the same time.

(6) Phagua—corresponding to the Holi of the Hindus.—On the 15th of the light half of Phágun (middle of March), when ancestors are propitiated.

(7) Karma.—On the 11th of the light half of Bhádon (beginning of September). This festival is similar to the Jitiá, except that a branch of a *karam* tree (*Nauclea cordifolia*) is planted in the courtyard and the fasting is not continuous as in the *Jitiya Parab*.

The foregoing festivals are observed by all Rautiás. The more Hinduised members of the caste add to them the Rath-jatrá, the Janmashtami, the Rámnabami, and the Ind Parab.

Disposal of the dead.

The dead are usually disposed of by burning, except in the case of Kabirpanthi Rautiás, who are buried standing upright and facing to the north. In the former case the corpse, covered with a new cloth, is taken to the place of cremation (*masán*) and there shaved, bathed, and clothed in a new waistcloth and sheet. If the body be that of a woman whose husband is alive, it is bathed, anointed with oil, and dressed in a new *sári*. In the case of a widow the oiling is omitted. The corpse is then placed on the funeral pile with the head to the north, and the chief mourner, lighting a torch made of five dry twigs of a *bel* tree tied to the end of a bit of wood and soaked in *ghi*, walks round the pile seven times, applies the torch to the mouth of the deceased, and then sets fire to the pile. Before doing so however, he takes a portion of the sheet in which the corpse is dressed and wraps up in it a knife or a piece of iron. This piece of cloth must be kept for ten days. After the body has been consumed, the ashes are collected in a new earthen vessel (*ghánti*). On returning home the mourners wash their feet with water previously placed for them outside the house. Inside the courtyard a shallow brass dish (*tháli*) is laid ready with leaves of the *tulsi* (*Ocymum sanctum*) and *kareli* (*Momordica charantia*), one pice, and a vessel of water. Some person, not a member of the family, pours a little water into the hand of each mourner, who drinks it off. For ten days after the cremation the ashes of the deceased (*santh*) are hung up in the vessel in which they were placed. During this time the chief mourner must make daily libations to the ashes, and must keep on his person the piece of sheet and the iron already referred to. He may not change his clothes, sleep on a bed, or eat salt, and he can only take one meal a day, which he must cook himself. At the end of this time the ashes are either buried at the *masna*, or, where the family are wealthy enough to undertake the journey, are kept for transport to Benares or Gya. On the tenth day he and the other relatives bathe, shave, anoint themselves with a mixture of oil and oil-cake, and put on clean clothes. The chief mourner also offers to the deceased ten cakes (*pinda*) made of rice, milk, linseed, barley, and honey. On the eleventh day the regular *sráddh* ceremony is performed with the assistance of a Kanaujiá, or, failing him, of a Sakadwipi Brahman who mutters unintelligble nonsense, supposed to be Vedic texts, and the Kantáha or Mahábráhman is fed and receives presents. On the twelfth day Sakadwipi Brahmans and friends of different castes are entertained, and one *pinda* is offered in order that the deceased may be united to the company of ancestors. On the thirteenth day relatives are fed and final purification is obtained. The anniversary of the death is celebrated only once (*barkhi sráddh*). While this is going on no marriage can take place in the family; and in order to avoid this inconvenience the *barkhi sráddh* is often performed some months before a year has elapsed from the time of death. Offerings to ancestors in general (*tarpan*) are made through the agency of Brahmans on the 15th of the dark half of Asin (end of September), and by the people themselves at the Nawá Khání, Jitiá, and Phaguá festivals. Childless relatives, lepers, persons who die a violent death, and women who die in child-birth, get only one *pinda*, and are not counted as ancestors. Lepers are usually buried.

Ceremonies.

The Rautiás do not perform any of the ceremonies usual among other castes during pregnancy. At child-birth assistance is rendered by the Kusrain or Dagrin, who cuts the umbilical cord. The ceremonies of *chhatthi*, *barhi*, and *ekaisi* are performed on the sixth, twelfth, and twenty-first days after birth. If the child is born under an unlucky star (*asubh lagan*), a fourth ceremony, called *Jataisi*, is added on the twenty-seventh day, at which Brahmans are fed, and Gauri, Ganesa, Mahadeo, and the *Kul devatas* or family gods worshipped. The father of the child does not lie up after its birth, or give up his ordinary occupations, but he is supposed to contract impurity (*chhutka*) by reason of the event, and must keep away from his neighbours until after the sixth day, when, if a poor man, he is purified by bathing and by giving a feast to his relatives and to Brahmans. The richer a man is, the longer is his term of impurity. Tolerably well-to-do Rautias remain impure till the twelfth day, while the wealthier of the castes cannot get purified till the twenty-first.

When a child is six months old, its first meal of rice is commemorated—the ceremony of *munghuti*, followed by *mundan* or tonsure. The effect of this latter rite is to remove from the mother the last traces of the pollution of child-birth, and to qualify to eat flesh and to worship the family gods. *Karnabedh*, the boring of a boy's ears by the village barber, is done between the ages of six and fourteen, and is deemed to admit a boy among the grown men of the caste. Kabirpanthi members of the Bargohri sub-caste assume the sacred thread (*janeo*) when initiated into the tenets of the sect. The thread so worn is a *Chhatri janeo*, which differs from a Brahman's in the form of the knot with which it is tied.

Superstitions. Spirits.

The Rautias, though less plagued by the terrors of the unseen world than are the Mundas and Oraons, have certain superstitions which are worth recording. Women who die in child-birth, persons killed by a tiger, and all *ojhas*. or exorcists, are liable after death to reappear as *bhuts*, or malevolent ghosts, and give trouble to the living. In such cases an exorcist (*ojhá* or *mati*) is called in to identify the spirit at work, and to appease it by gifts of money, goats, fowls, or pigs. Usually the spirit is got rid of in a few months, but some are specially persistent and require annual worship to induce them to remain quiet. Spirits of this type, who were great exorcists or otherwise men of note during their life-time, often extend their influence over several families, and eventually attain the rank of a tribal god.

Babu Rakhal Das Haldar, Manager of the Chutia Nagpur estate, gives the following instance of exorcism from his personal experience. In December 1884, when the Manager was in camp at the foot of the Báragáin hills in Lohardagá, a Kurmi woman of Kukui was killed by a tiger, and the tiger-demon in her form was supposed to be haunting the village. An *ojhá* who was sent for to lay the ghost, took a young man to represent the tiger-demon, and after certain incantations put him into a kind of mesmeric condition, in which he romped about on all fours, and generally demeaned himself like a tiger. A rope was then tied round his loins and he was dragged to a cross-road, where the volent fit passed off and he became insensible. In this condition he remained until the *ojha* recited certain *mantras* and threw rice on him, when he regained his senses, and the demon was pronounced to have quitted the village.

Occupation.

Rautias believe military service to have been their original occupation, but this is little more than a distant memory of times long past, and at the present day most members of the caste in Lohardagá are settled agriculturists. The chief men of the caste hold *taluks*, *jágirs*, *báraik* grants, and similar tenures paying quit-rents direct to the Maharája of Chutia Nagpur, while the rank and file are raiyats paying light rents and possessing occupancy rights. A few only are found in the comparatively reduced position of tenants of *raja's* lands at full rents. In many of the tenures and occupancy holdings *khuntkáti* rights, entitling the tenant to hold at a low quit-rent, are claimed; while others are *korkar*, paying only one-half of the standard rates of rent.

Social status.

Socially the caste ranks fairly high, and Brahmans will take water and sweetmeats from their hands. Bargohri Rautias will not eat cooked food, smoke, or drink with any but members of their own sub-caste; but they will take sweetmeats from Brahmans, Rajputs, and Srawaks. Chhot-gohris are equally particular about cooked food, but will take water and sweetmeats from, and will smoke with, Bhogtás, Ahirs, Jhorás, and Bhuyiás. They also drink spirits and fermented liquors, and eat wild pigs and fowls, all of which are forbidden for the Bar-gohri sub-caste.

Representative assembly.

The Chhot-gohri Rautias have a representative assembly (*mandli*) for groups of from five to fifteen villages, which decides questions of caste usage. Each village sends one member to the *mandli*, which is presided over by an official called *mahant*, whose office is hereditary. When the *mahant* is a minor, his duties are carried on by an adult member of his family or by any Rautiá unanimously chosen for this purpose by the *mandli*. The orders of the *mandli* are enforced by fines, by refusing to eat and drink with the offender, and by depriving him of the services of the barber and washerman of the caste. Certain acts entailing ceremonial impurity, such as accidentally killing a cow or having incestuous intercourse (*gotra-badh*) with a woman of the same *gotra*, admit of being atoned for by giving a feast to Brahmans and the caste brethren. But the wilful slaughter of a cow, the repetition of the offence of *gotra-badh*, and the cardinal sin of eating with a person of low caste, cannot be expiated, and in such extreme cases the offender is turned out of the caste. The Bar-gohri have no standing assembly, and pancháyats are summoned to deal with caste questions as occasion requires.

Sorcery.

The services of the *ojhá* are also called in to ascertain what spirit (*bhút*) or witch (*dáin* or *bisáhi*) has caused a particular illness, and to prescribe the cure. On such occasions he comes after sun-down and demands a winnowing fan, a small earthen lamp, rags for a wick, a handful of *arwa* rice, and some oil. Having twisted a wick into the rude semblance of a hooded snake, the *ojha* lights his lamp and proceeds, by shaking the rice in the winnowing fan, to divine the name of the *bhút* or *dáin* who is to blame. This point having been cleared up, he is presented with a fowl to be sacrified to his own *birwat* or *ishta deva*, and he then performs the ceremony of *kat bándh*, by which he binds the patient or his family to the spirit or witch. This is supposed to put matters in train towards recovery, and the *ojhá* departs, receiving from the patient's family a promise of presents of goats, etc., in the event of the treatment proving successful. Rautiás are in great terror of witches, and believe, like many people, that they can act upon their victims through objects belonging to or intimately associated with them, such as bits of cut hair or nails; but no special care is taken to preserve or destroy such articles.

Dreams are believed to be caused by recently deceased relatives of the dreamer, who appear to him in sleep and complain of hunger and want of clothes, etc. Such importunate spirits are easily appeased by sending for a Brahman and giving him the things which have been demanded in the dream.

Among other curious superstitions may be noticed the notion that a woman in the early stages of pregnancy should not cross running water. The evil eye is believed in, but its influence is attributed to inordinate appetite on the part of the person who has overlooked any one. Its effects may be averted by mixing red mustard seeds and salt, waving the mixture round the head and then throwing it into the fire. To ward off the evil eye from the crops, a blackened earthen pot with rude devices scrawled on it in white paint is stuck up in the fields.

Oaths and ordeals are sometimes resorted to for the settlement of personal disputes and the decision of questions affecting caste. Ganges water, rice that has been offered to Jagannath, a mixture of rice and cow-dung or copper and tulsi leaves, are held in the hand and a solemn statement is made touching the matter in dispute. It is believed that some sort of misfortune will befall the person who under these circumstances speaks falsely, but the consequences of lying do not seem to be clearly defined. In former days a more severe test was in vogue: a ring was thrown into a deep pan of boiling ghi, and the person whose conduct was in question was required to take it out with his fingers.

Boys whose elder brothers have died in infancy are given opprobrious names, such as Akhaj, Bechan, Bechu (he who is for sale), Khudi, Chuni, Gandaur, Kinu, Lohar, Chamár, Dom or Doman, Mochi, Ghási, Mahili (names of low castes). Girls are called by the feminine forms of these names—Akhji, Chámin, etc. Rautias do not follow the custom, common among the higher castes, of giving two names—one for ceremonial purposes and the other for common use.

Lucky days for ploughing are the 12th of the light half of Kátik and the 5th of the light half of Aghán for low rice lands (*don*), and the 1st of the dark half of Chait for high lands. The 3rd of the light half of Baisakh is good for sowing; but if there is early rain, a Brahman may be got to fix a lucky day before this date. For transplanting the rice seedlings a lucky day may be arranged by a Brahman at any time between the 2nd of the dark half of Asár and the 11th of the light half of Bhádo. It is specially unlucky to plough during the Mrigdáh or Nirbisrá period, called Ambubáchi in Bengal, when the sun is for three days in the Mrigasirá constellation; during the Karam festival (10th—12th of light half of Bhádo); and on the day of the Sarhúl. Rain during the Mrigdáh brings bad luck; but rainy weather, while the sun is in the Rohini or Swáti constellation, betokens good fortune. When rice is transplanted, the village *pahán* performs the *bangari puja* to the god of the village. When a well is sunk a Brahman is consulted as to the site and the proper time for commencing work, and a *pratishthá* or dedicatory sacrifice is performed before the water is used.

The following statement shows the number and distribution of Rautiás in 1872 and 1881:—

DISTRICT.	1872.	1881.	DISTRICT.	1872.	1881.
Santál Parganás	......	12	Singhbhum	......	1
Hazaribagh	4	... ...	Manbhum	......	64
Lohardaga	16,387	18,583	Tributary States	8,242	8,204

Rautiá, a sub-caste of Koiris and a title of Cheros in Chota Nagpur.

Raut Mehter, a sweeper sub-caste of Doms in Behar.

Rawáni, a sub-caste of Kándus in Behar.

Rawáni or *Ramáni, Raoni, Roháni*, a sub-caste of Kahárs in Behar.

Rawanpur, a section of Kahárs in Behar.

Raworh, a section of Maghaiyá Kumhárs in Behar.

Ráya, a title of Bráhmans, Káyasths, and several other castes in Bengal and Behar; of Khairás in Chota Nagpur.

Ráyi, a *gáin* of the Bharadwája *gotra* and a *mel* or hypergamous sub-group of Rárhi Brahmans in Bengal.

Regálaunchhá, a *thar* or sept of Khambus in Darjiling.

Regmi, a *thar* of the Kausika *gotra* of Nepáli Brahmans.

Rekhaur, a sept of Rájputs in Behar.

Reláti-Madak, a sub-caste of Madhunápits in Bengal.

Renta, a sept of Páns in Chota Nagpur.

Reson, a synonym for Teli.

Retha, fruit, a totemistic sept of Lohárs in Chota Nagpur.

Riáng, a sept of Tipperahs in the Hill Tracts of Chittagong.

Richil, a *dugu* or section of the Kochh-Mandai in Dacca. The name indicates the original habitat of the group, probably a hill or village in Assam, and now-a-days has no bearing upon marriage.

Rigretsa, a sept of Maghs in the Hill Tracts of Chittagong.

Rijál, a *thar* of the Dhánjaya *gotra* of Nepáli Brahmans; a section of Kámis; a *thar* or sept of Mangars in Darjiling.

Rikhab, a section of Brahmans.

Rikhi, a section of Rajwárs and Rautiás in Chota Nagpur.

Rikhiásan, a sub-caste of Bhuiyas in Hazaribagh; a sept of Kharwars in Chota Nagpur; a section of Kádars and Musahars in Behar; a totemistic sept of Chiks in Chota Nagpur who may not eat beef or pork.

Rikhiásan or **Pátrise**, a section of Mauliks in Western Bengal.

Rikmun, a section of Musahars in Behar.

Rimál, a *thar* or section of Nepáli Brahmans.

Rimching, a *thar* or sept of Khambus in Darjiling.

Rimrimiá, a section of Kurmis in Chota Nagpur and Orissa.

Rishi, a title of the patit or degraded priests, who minister to the spiritual wants of the lower castes; a section of the Bhar caste in Manbhum. The term appears to have been borrowed from the Brahmanical system in comparatively recent times, as the caste has also a set of the totemistic sections characteristic of the Kolarian race.

Rishi, *Rishiputra*, a synonym for, and a title of, Muchis in Bengal.

Risyál, a *thar* or section of Nepáli Brahmans.

Riti, a title of Bangaja Káyasths.

Rochingáchhá, a *thar* or sept of Khambus in Darjiling.

Rohilá, a *pathi* or hypergamous sub-group of Barendra Brahmans in Bengal.

Rohini, a title of Káhárs in Behar.

Rohita, a section of Brahmans and Káyasths in Bengal.

Roh-Lutur, ear-pierced, a sub-sept of the Hansda, Hemrom, Kisku, and Tudu septs of Santáls.

Roht, *pánjaun* tree, a sub-sept of the Márndi sept of Santáls.

Roi, a title of Bangaja Káyasths.

Rojá, a title of Kaibarttas in Bengal.

Rondiar, a section of Mahilis in Chota Nagpur.

Rong, a sub-tribe of Lepchas in Darjiling.

Rorah, a sept of Rájputs in Behar.

Rori, a fruit, a totemistic sept of Oraons in Chota Nagpur.

Rosráit, a section of the Dhaprá sub-caste of Doms in Behar.

Rote, a sept of the Asuras in Chota Nagpur.

Rudra, a title of Baidyas and of Dakshin-Rárhi and Bangaja Káyasths in Bengal.

Rudrabagchhi, a *gáin* of the Sándilya *gotra* of Bárendra Brahmans in Bengal.

Rudrabanik, a title of Baniyás in Bengal.

Rudrabans, a synonym for Kumhár.

Rudrapal, a synonym for Kumhár in Bengal.

Rugri, a kind of mushroom, a totemistic sept of Mundas in Chota Nagpur.

Ruhidás, a title laid claim to by all Chamárs, as denoting their descent from a Bhagat ancestor of that name; also a title of Dosadhs in Behar.

Rui, a title of Khandáits in Orissa.

Ruichhung, a sub-tribe of Dejong Lhori or Bhotia of the south.

Ruidás, a title of Muchis in Bengal.

Rujál, a section of Kámis in Darjiling.

Rujichá, a *thar* or sept of Sunuwárs in Darjiling.

Rukái, a *thar* or section of Nepáli Brahmans.

Rukhar, a group of the Aoghar sect of Saiva ascetics founded in Guzerat by a Dasnámi mendicant named Brahmagiri. See Aoghar.

Rukhi, squirrel, a sept of Mundas in Chota Nagpur.

Rukhiár, a section of the Amashta sub-caste of Káyasths in Behar.

Rumbá, a section of Murmis in Darjiling.

Runda, fox, leopard (wild cat?), a totemistic sept of Mundas, Oraons and Lohárs in Chota Nagpur.

Rupakheti, a *thar* or section of Nepáli Brahmans.

Rutá, a tree, a totemistic sept of Mundas in Chota Nagpur.

S

Sabáiáre, a sept of the Agáni sub-tribe of Meches in the Darjiling Terai.

Sabar, a synonym for Savar.

Sabarkárá, a sub-caste of Muchis in Bengal.

Sábarna, a *gotra* or section of Baidyas, Brahmans, Gandhabaniks, Káyasths, Tántis, and Subarnbaniks in Bengal; a Brahmanical section of Bábhans in Behar.

Sábarnia, a sept of the Chandrabansi division of Rájputs in Behar.

Sabarnika, a section of Utkal Brahmans.

Sabhaiyár, a *pur* or section of Sákadwipi Brahmans in Behar.

Sabhá-Sundar, a title of Dhobás in Bengal.

Sabkota, a *thar* or sept of Mangars in Darjiling.

Saboktsa, a sept of Maghs in the Hill Tracts of Chittagong.

Sabor, a sub-caste of Goálás in Chota Nagpur.

Sabri, a section of Kanaujiá Lohárs in Behar.

Sábu, a section of Mahesris in Behar.

Sadá, a section of Sunris in Behar.

Sádá, a sub-sept of all the septs of Santáls.

Sadábarti, a section of the Banodhiá and Jaiswár Kalwárs in Behar.

Sádá Goálá, a hypergamous group of Goálás in Eastern Bengal.

Sadásankar, a *thar* or sept of Mangars in Darjiling.

Sadgop, *Satgop*, *Chásá*, a cultivating caste of Bengal Proper, who are supposed to have separated themselves from the Goálás by abandoning pastoral pursuits and taking exclusively to agriculture.

Origin and internal structure.

They are divided into two sub-castes—the **Paschim Kuliyá**, who live to the west of the Bhágirathi, and the **Purbba Kuliyá**, whose settlements are on the east of that river. The separation between the two is said to have taken place in the time of Ballál Sen, when the ancestors of the Paschim Kuliya group refused to accept the institution of Kulinism, which was introduced among them at a later date and in a somewhat different form. The Purbba Kuliyás, a much smaller body, adopted the new rules and parted on that account from the main body of the caste. Originally both sub-castes were strictly endogamous, but of late years the rule has been relaxed and marriages have taken place between members of the two groups. The Purbba Kuliyás. however, recognize a further division of their own sub-caste into the two endogamous groups of Ghosh and Sarbesia. The hypergamous divisions of both sub-castes and the sections of the Paschim Kuliyá are shown in the Appendix. One of the hypergamous groups, the **Konr Gop**, seems to have developed in comparatively modern times among the Sadgops of Murshedabad, and deserves special notice for the light it throws upon the mode in which hypergamous groups are formed. The Konr Gop are in no sense of purer lineage than their brethren. They are merely Sadgops who have grown rich and have risen above the necessity of cultivating with their own hands. They affect some sort of ill-defined social pre-eminence, and while taking their wives from among ordinary Satgops will not give their daughters in marriage outside their own circle. The Purbba Kuliyá have no sections, and regulate their marriage by the standard rules defining prohibited degrees.

Marriage.

Infant-marriage is in full force among the Sadgops, and it would be deemed an indelible disgrace for a girl to be unprovided with a husband before she reaches the age of puberty. Men, on the other hand, marry comparatively later in life, and the operation of the law of hypergamy, popularly known as Kulinism, sometimes puts men of the lower groups to considerable difficulty in finding wives. The marriage ceremony is of the orthodox type, the binding portion being *sátpák*, the carrying of the bride seven times round the bridegroom. Although this is technically the essential rite, the marriage is held to be complete at an earlier stage, as soon as the *ásirbád*, or blessing on the married pair, has been pronounced. Polygamy is recognized so far that if a man's first wife is barren or proves faithless he may take a second; but such cases are said to be rare, and for all practical purposes the caste may be regarded as monogamous. Widows are not allowed to marry a second time. Divorce is not formally recognized; but if a woman commits adultery or otherwise disgraces herself, her husband may get rid of her by undergoing the ceremony of *práyaschitta* or expiation for impurity and by performing her *sráddh* as if she were actually dead. Women so divorced may not marry again.

Religion.

The religious and ceremonial observances of the caste exhibit no departure from the average Hinduism of the middle classes in Bengal. Almost all Sadgops are Vaishnavas, Hari and Satya Náráyan being their favourite deities. Lakshmi is also regarded with special reverence as watching over their welfare, while Sashti and Mangalchandi are worshipped by the women of the caste. The Brahmans who serve them as priests are received on equal terms by other members of the sacred order. The dead are burned, and the *sráddh* ceremony is performed according to the orthodox system.

Occupation and social status.

Agriculture is their characteristic pursuit, and they are commonly spoken of and addressed as Chásá. In Central Bengal large numbers of them are engaged in rearing silk-worms and selling raw silk. The bulk of the caste are occupancy or non-occupancy raiyats. Some hold tenures, and a few, particularly in Midnapur, have risen to be zamindars of fairly high position. Their social rank is sufficiently defined by stating that they belong to the Nabasákha group, and that Brahmans will take water and certain kinds of sweetmeats from their hands. Their rules as to diet are the same as are observed by all orthodox Hindus in Bengal Proper. One curious custom may be noticed here. Sadgops will not eat pumpkin (*láu*) and *dál* in the month of Ashár, and by way of accounting for this prohibition tell the absurd story that they are descended from one Kálu Ghosh, who, being appointed by one of the gods to look after his cattle, killed and ate the sacred animals. Oddly enough, instead of being punished for his sacrilege, the story goes on to say that his descendants, who thenceforth applied themselves to cultivation, were permitted to rank above the children of the other brother, Murári Ghosh, who faithfully discharged his trust. Valueless as the legend is, it deserves notice as a specimen of the folk-lore current among the people regarding the origin of particular castes.

The following statement shows the number and distribution of Sadgops in 1872 and 1881:—

District.	1872.	1881.	District.	1872.	1881.
Bardwan	185,804	112,128	Faridpur	693	820
Bankura	17,971	45,201	Bakarganj	186	240
Birbhum	100,446	82,764	Maimansinh	581	680
Midnapur	157,998	126,260	Tipperah	158	456
Hughli	} 63,774	{ 61,025	Chittagong	35	167
Howrah		12,593	Noakhali	25	......
24-Parganás	38,068	20,570	Patna	......	21
Nadiya	17,506	16,177	Monghyr	37	.....
Khulna	......	6,021	Bhagalpur	......	12
Jessore	7,529	9,316	Purniah	11,674	1,323
Murshedabad	29,321	38,008	Maldah	1,385	1,548
Dinajpur	2,316	3,823	Santál Parganas	1,109	2,581
Rajshahye	385	732	Cuttack	218	338
Rangpur	136	603	Puri	9	18
Bogra	568	942	Balasore	2,097	7,694
Pabna	449	884	Tributary States	51	125
Jalpigori	276	500	Lohardagá	69	9
Kuch Behar	......	133	Singbhum	1,413	1,239
Dacca	1,085	2,381	Manbhum	6,415	2,955

Sádhak, a *mul* or section of the Ghosin sub-caste of Goálás in Behar.

Sádhu, a title of the Desá sub-caste of Gandhabaniks and of Tántis in Bengal.

Sádhubagchhi, a *gáin* of the Sándilya *gotra* of Bárendra Brahmans in Bengal.

Sádhupaliyá, a sub-caste of Kochhs in Dinajpur.

Sádhya, a hypergamous group of the Bárendra Káyasths.

Sádhya-Maulik or **Bahátture**, a hypergamous group of the Dakshin-Rárhi Káyasths in Bengal.

Sádhya-Srotriya, a hypergamous group of Rárhi Bráhmans in Bengal.

Sad-Kámár, a sub-caste of Kámárs who are cultivators.

Sad-Lohár, a sub-caste of Lohárs or Hindu blacksmiths in Lohardagá.

Sad-Munda, a sub-tribe of Mundas affecting to follow the Hindu religion.

Sadom, horse, a totemistic sept of Mundas in Chota Nagpur.

Sadonga, a sept of Chakmás in the Hill Tracts of Chittagong.

Sadra, a section of Mahesris in Behar.

Sáfi, cleaner, a synonym for Dhobi in Behar, only used by persons who are not members of the caste.

Ság, vegetable, a totemistic sept of Chiks in Chota Nagpur.

Sagáhut, a sub-caste of Sunris in Behar who permit widows to marry again by the *sagái* form, often opposed to *Biáhut*, who do not tolerate such a practice. They are ordinarily grain-dealers and shopkeepers.

Ságáin, a *gáin* or sub-section of Saptasati Brahmans in Bengal.

Ságarbansi, a synonym for Ságarpeshá.

Ságarpeshá, in Orissa a designation of the illegitimate offspring of a Brahman woman by a Káyasth man.

Sagela Bagela, a *mul* or section of Kesarwáni Baniás in Behar.

Saghár, "vegetable-eater," a title of the Bahiot sub-caste of Amáts and of Dhanuks in Behar who are employed as personal servants to the higher castes.

Ságí, a section of Lohárs in Behar.

Sagin, the name of female attendants in shops for the sale of opium and its compounds, said to be kept for the purpose of attracting customers, and believed not to be above reproach in matters of morals.

Ságmá, a totemistic sept of the Bhumij tribe in Manbhum.

Saguniá, a sub-caste of the Kraunchdwipi Brahmans in Behar.

Sagun-ure, a title of the Kochh caste in Northern Bengal.

Sáh, a section of Saraogis in Behar.

Sáhá, *Sáhu*, a title of the Desá sub-caste of Gandhabaniks in Bengal; a title of Nápits, Sonárs, Telis, and Sunris. The latter invariably style themselves Sáhás or Sauloks. Tradition says that they were created from the sweat of the trunk (*sunda*) of the elephant-mouthed Ganesa to guard the celestial nectar for his mother Durgá; and hence they were called Sundis (corrupted into Sunris). Ballál assigned to them such a low rank on account of their tribal arrogance.

Sahadar, a section of the Biyáhut and Kharidáhá Kalwárs in Behar.

Sáhál, a section of the Biyáhut and Kharidáhá Kalwárs in Behar.

Sáhani, a title of Malláhs in Behar.

Sahar, a section of Bháts.

Sáhari, a *gáin* of the Bátsya *gotra* of Bárendra Brahmans in Bengal.

Sáharik, a *gáin* of the Bharadwája *gotra* of Rárhi Brahmans in Bengal.

Saharwár, a section of Kamárkalla Sonárs in Behar.

Sahasnangiá, a section of Bábhans in Behar.

Sahbar, a section of Goálás in Behar.

Sahdauliá, a *kul* or section of Bábhans in Behar.

Sáhjáwán, a section of Goálás in the North-Western Provinces and Behar.

Sahmbahang, a sept of the Tambrkhola sub-tribe of Limbus in Darjiling.

Sahni, a title of Gonrhis in Behar.

Sáho, a title of the Ariár and Khandiwár sub-castes of Bais Baniyás; of Halwáis, Kahárs, Kalwárs, Kandus, Sonárs, Sunris, and Telis in Behar.

Sahrwár, a *mul* or section of the Naomulia or Majraut sub-caste of Goálás in Behar.

Sahsradih, a *mul* or section of the Naomulia or Majraut sub-caste of Goálás in Behar.

Sáhu, a title of Khatris; of Baniyás, Kalwárs, and Kándus in Behar; a title of Kewats in Orissa; of Sonárs in Behar; a section of the Kulsunri sub-caste of Sunris in Behar; a title of Láheris in Chota Nagpur.

Sáhul, a section of Khariás in Chota Nagpur.

Sahuliar, a section of the Sribastab sub-caste of Káyasths in Behar.

Sahun, a *mul* or section of the Biahut sub-caste of Kalwárs in Behar.

Sahuri, a *mul* or section of the Chhamuliá Madhesiá sub-caste of Halwáis in Behar.

Sái, a title of Brahmans.

Saidábád, a section of Pátnis in Bengal.

Saigal, a section of the Panchjáti sub-caste of Khatris in Bengal.

Sailum, porcupine, a totemistic sept of Mundas in Chota Nagpur.

Sáin, a *gáin* or sub-section of Saptasati Brahmans in Bengal; a title of Dakshin-Rárhi and Bangaja Káyastha.

Sáini, a sub-caste of Sutradhars in Noakháli.

Sainthwár, a sub-caste of Kurmis in Behar.

Sair, a small agricultural caste of Western Bengal, believed to be closely related to Bágdis.

Sais, a *mul* or section of the Maghayá sub-caste of Koiris in Behar.

Saisarunduar, a sept of Mundas in Chota Nagpur.

Sai Sonarwar, a sept of Kharwars in Chota Nagpur.

Sáitghariá, a sub-caste of Sutradhars in Noakháli.

Saitiya, a section of the Oswál Baniyás.

Saiva, a worshipper of Siva.

Saival, a *thar* or section of Nepáli Brahmans.

Sakaddi, a section of Sonárs in Behar.

Sákadwipi or **Sakaldwipi**, a division of Brahmans in Behar.

Sákalya, a title of Dhobás in Bengal.

Sakar-Ghore, a *mul* of the Sándil section of Maithil Brahmans in Behar.

Sakarpuriet, a *mul* or section of the Naomuliá or Majraut sub-caste of Goálás in Behar.

Sakarwár, a *mul* or section of Bábhans; of the Bhojpuriá sub-caste of Halwáis; a sept of the Chandrabansi division of Rájputs in Behar.

Sákati, a *gáin* of the Bharadwája *gotra* of Bárendra Brahmans in Bengal.

Sakerbasá, a *mul* or section of the Kamárkalla sub-caste of Sonárs in Behar.

Sákhá, a title of Brahmans in Western Bengal.

Sakhali, a sub-tribe of Mangars in Darjiling.

Sakhwait, a *kul* or section of Bábhans in Behar.

Sakin, a section of the Purbiyá Madesia sub-caste of Halwáis in Behar.

Sakmait, a section of Bábhans in Behar.

Sákori, a *mul* or section of the Chhamuliá Madhesiá sub-caste of Halwáis in Behar.

Sakráit, a section of Bánsphor Doms in Western Behar.

Sakraiwár-Harari, a *mul* of the Kásyapa section of Maithil Brahmans in Behar.

Sakraiwár-Tatail, a *mul* of the Kásyap section of Maithil Brahmans in Behar.

Sakraiwár-Chhámu, a *mul* of the Kásyap section of Maithil Brahmans in Behar.

Sakraul, a *mul* or section of the Naomuliá or Goriá sub-caste of Goálás in Behar.

Sakri, a *mul* or section of the Kanaujiá sub-caste of Sonárs and of Ghásis in Behar.

Sakrol, a *mul* or section of the Chhamuliá Madhesiá sub-caste of Halwáis in Behar.

Saksena, a sub-caste of Káyasths in Behar.

Sákta, a worshipper of the female principle in nature, of the female forms of the Hindu deities, and especially of Devi, the sakti or female energy of Siva. Sáktas are divided into two classes: Dakshináchári, or Dakshinamárgis, "followers of the right-hand path," and Vámácháris or Vámamárgis, "followers of the left-hand path." The former base their religion on the Puránas and do not practise mystical or secret rites; the latter derive their ritual from the magical treatises known as Tantras, and are addicted to practices of a grossly licentious character. The Tantras are said to be founded on the Kaula Upanishad, and the left-handed Sáktas are therefore called Kaulikas.

Sakti, a title of Dakshin-Rárhi Káyasths in Bengal.

Saktri, a *gotra* or section of Brahmans and Baidyas in Bengal.

Sakuntalá, a sub-caste of Brahmans in Behar.

Sál, fish, a totemistic section of Khandáits; a sept of Mundas and Oraons; a title of Dakshin-Rárhi Káyasths.

Sál or **Saula**, a section of Korás, signifying a fish.

Sálákhá, a synonym for Sherpa Bhotia of Nepal.

Sálák-khá, a merchant carrying on trade, a sub-sept of the Nah-pá sept of Sherpa Bhotias.

Sálangiá, a section of Goálás in the North-Western Provinces and Behar.

Salankáyana, an exogamous section of Baidyas in Bengal.

Sálbanwár, *sál* jungle, a totemistic section of Kurmis in Chota Nagpur and Orissa.

Salhariá, a *kul* or section of Bábhans in Behar.

Salkar, a kind of potato, a totemistic sept of Mundas in Chota Nagpur.

Sálkhini, a *mul* or section of the Naomuliá or Majraut sub-caste of Goálás in Behar.

Sálmáchh, fish, a totemistic sept of Savars in Orissa; a section of Máls in Midnapur and Manbhum.

Sálodiá, a section of Goálás in the North-Western Provinces and Behar.

Sálrishi or *Sálmách* (the *sál* fish), a section of Bágdis in Bengal and of Chásás in Orissa; a totemistic sept of the Bhumij tribe in Manbhum, the members of which will not touch or eat the *sál* fish; a section of Lohárs in the Santál Parganás.

Sálu, a root in pond, a totemistic sept of Mundas in Chota Nagpur.

Sálubi, a synonym for Pátikár, *q.v.*

Sám, Syám, a title of Dakshin-Rárhi and Bangaja Káyasths.

Sámá, a section of Korás in Chota Nagpur.

Samaddar, a title of Chásádhobás in Bengal and a hypergamous group of Kaibarttas in Bakarganj.

Sámagáu, a singer of the Sáma Veda, a title of Brahmans.

Samaiár, a section of Káyasths in Behar.

Samal, a title of Khandaits in Orissa.

Sámal, a title of Chásás in Orissa.

Samal or **Samar**, deer, a totemistic sept of Mundas.

Sámanta, a chief, a group of the Srotriya sub-caste of Utkal Brahmans; a title of Aguris, Brahmans, Khandáits, Rájputs, Sadgops, Telis, and some other castes.

Sámantasár, a *samaj* or local group of the Saunaka *gotra* of Páschátya Baidik Brahmans in Bengal.

Sámánya-Maulik, a hypergamous group of the Uttar-Rárhi sub-caste of Káyasths.

Samári, a sub-caste of Malláhs in Behar.

Sámariá, a synonym for Málé.

Samastipur, a *mul* or section of the Naomuliá or Majraut sub-caste of Goálás in Behar.

Samat, pestle, a totemistic sept of Korwas in Chota Nagpur.

Samdiá, a section of Khariás in Chota Nagpur.

Samdoar, a sept of Mundas in Chota Nagpur.

Samduar, a sept of Agariás in Chota Nagpur.

Sámigrihi, a section of Utkal or Orissa Brahmans.

Sámil Thákur, a section of Kanaujiá Lohárs in Behar.

Samjhar, a sept of Chiks in Chota Nagpur.

Sámp, snake, a totemistic sept of Korwas; a section of Turis; a section of Goálás in the North-Western Provinces and Behar.

Sámperiyá, Sámp-wálá, a sub-caste of Bediyas who catch and charm snakes.

Samswár, a sub-caste of Kurmis in Behar.

Samudra, a *gáin* of the Sábarna *gotra* of Bárendra Brahmans in Bengal.

Samudwar, a sept of Kharwars in Chota Nagpur.

Samundar-Khorá, a section of Sonárs in Behar.

Samwah, a sept of Limbus in Darjiling.

San, heron, a totemistic sept of Lohárs in Chota Nagpur.

Sán, a title of Chásádhobás in Bengal.

Sáná, a title of Dakshin-Rárhi Káyasths in Bengal.

Sanádhya, a sub-caste of Gaura Brahmans.

Sánágánthá, a sub-caste of Máls in Bankura.

Sanahiá, a title of Hindu Joláhas in Behar.

Sánchi, a sub-caste of Doms in Bengal.

Sanda, a *pangat* or section of Dosádhs in Behar.

Sandaliá, a section of Bábhans in Behar.

Sándh, bullock, a totemistic sept of Lohárs; a section of Goráits; a totemistic sept of Chamárs and Doms in Chota Nagpur.

Sandhawár, a section of the Amashta sub-caste of Káyasths in Behar.

Sandhoá, a synonym for Niyáriya, *q.v.*

Sandi, plough, a totemistic sept of Mundas in Chota Nagpur.

Sandiguriá, black monkey, a totemistic sept of Mundas in Chota Nagpur.

Sandil, full moon, a totemistic sept of Mundas in Chota Nagpur.

Sándil, a *gotra* or section of Bábhans in Behar, borrowed from the Brahmanical system and superadded to the original exogamous groups (*kuls*) characteristic of the caste; a section of the Kumhár caste in Western Bengal, apparently borrowed from the Brahmanical system and added to the totemistic sections characteristic of the caste; a section of Utkal Brahmans; a section of Cháins.

Sándil or **Sanrishi**, a bull, a totemistic section of the Paripál sub-caste of Sunris in Manbhum, the members of which do not castrate their own cattle, but purchase bullocks and sell their own bulls.

Sandilai, a sept of Pators in Chota Nagpur.

Sándilya, a *gotra* or section of the Aguri, Baidya, Brahman. Kámár, and Subarnabanik castes in Bengal; a section of the Sárák caste in Manbhum; of Kumhárs, Tántis, Telis and Káyasths in Bengal; an eponymous sept of Rájputs and Savars; a section of Goálás, Kaibarttas, Madhunápits, Mális, Mayarás, Muchis, Nápits, and Sunris in Bengal; an eponymous section of Barhis, Baruis, Rautiás, Chásádhobás, Gandhabaniks; a sept of Bhumij; a section of Sánkháris, Bháts; of Suklis in Midnapur; of the Paschim Kuliyá Sadgops; of Sutradhars and Támbulis in Bengal.

Sandipurti, cock, a totemistic sept of Mundas in Chota Nagpur.

Sandi Sarin, fowl, a totemistic sept of Mundas in Chota Nagpur.

Sandwipá, a sub-caste of Kumhárs in Noakháli.

Sanga, a title of Bangaja Káyasths.

Sangá, or *Sangoar,* sweet potato, a totemistic sept of Mundas in Chota Nagpur.

Sángá, a section of the Mahili-Munda sub-caste of Mahilis in Chota Nagpur.

Sangalwár, a sept of Lohárs in Chota Nagpur.

Sángbá, a section of Murmis in Darjiling.

Sángbah, a sept of Limbus in Darjiling.

Sang-behbo, a *rui* or sept of Dejong Lhoris, the members of which are the descendants of emigrants from Bhotan and Nepal.

Sang Chiria, a kind of bird, a totemistic sept of Mundas in Chota Nagpur.

Sangda, a sub-sept of the Murmu sept of Santáls.

Sángdan, a section of Murmis in Darjiling.

Sangi, a synonym for Málé.

Sángir, a sept of the Suryabansi sub-tribe of Rájputs in Behar.

Sangiri Thákur, a section of Kanaujiá Lohárs in Behar.

Sangma, a buffalo, apparently a totemistic sept of the Chhothar sub-tribe of Limbus in Darjiling. The buffalo is taboo to this *thar:* the legend is the same as that of the Khema *thar.*

Sangmi, a sept of Lepchas in Darjiling.

Sángpáng, a *thar* or sept of Khambus in Darjiling.

Sangskár, a performer of ceremonies, a title of Brahmans.

Sangtarás, stone-cutters of various castes.

Sangtarásh, a sub-caste of Gonrhis in Behar. They say they are not Gonrhis, and distinguish themselves as Gonrh. They work in stone.

Sangwe, a title of Aráiya Telis in Behar.

Sanhá, a section of the Biyáhut and Kharidáhá Kalwárs in Behar.

Sanhakiá, a section of Bháts.

Sanicherá, a sub-caste of the Kraunchdwipi Brahmans in Behar.

Sanichrá, a mul or section of Kalwárs in Behar.

Sanjokmah, a sept of Limbus in Darjiling.

Sankar, a title of Sannyásis and Bairágis.

Sankarjáti, a generic term for the castes supposed to have been formed by marriages or illicit connexions between members of the four primary castes.

Sankarpur, a *mul* or section of the Naomuliá or Majraut sub-caste of Goálás in Behar.

Sankarshan, a section of the Páschátya Baidik Brahmans in Bengal.

Sankarwár, a sept of Rájputs in Behar.

Sankatwár, a title of Dhánuks in Behar.

Sánkh, conch shell, a sub-sept of the Saren sept of Santáls.

Sankha, a section of Karans in Orissa.

Sankha-Asram, a sub-caste of Gandhabaniks in Bengal.

Sankhabanik, a synonym for Sánkhári in Bengal.

Sankhakár, a synonym for Sánkhári in Bengal.

Sankhalai, a sub-caste of Kámárs in the Santál Parganás.

Sánkhári, *Sankhakár*. *Sankhabanik*, the shell-cutting caste of Bengal, some of whom have taken of late years to working in gold and silver. Tradition ascribes the origin of the caste, as of the goldsmiths, jewellers and Kánsáris, to one Dhanapati Saudagar of Karnáta, from whose third son, Srikánta, the Sánkhári believe themselves to be descended. They claim to be Vaisyas, and say that up to the time of Adisur they wore the Brahmanical thread, but were degraded by him at the same time as the Subarnabaniks, because the latter had cut to pieces a golden cow which the king had given to certain Brahmans at the celebration of a special sacrifice. Sánkháris have the Brahmanical *gotras* and observe the same table of prohibited degrees as the higher castes. In Dacca they are divided into two sub-castes—**Bara-Bhágiya** or **Bikrampur Sánkhári** and **Chhota-Bhágiya** or **Sunargáon Sánkhári**. The latter are a comparatively small group, who work at polishing shells, which they purchase ready cut—a departure from traditional usage, which may account for their separation from the main body of the caste. In other districts, owing possibly to the smallness of the caste, no similar divisions seem to have been formed.

Tradition of origin.

Internal structure.

The Sánkhári, says Dr. Wise, have the character of being very penurious and unusually industrious, young and old working to a late hour at night. Boys are taught the trade at a very early age, otherwise their limbs would not brook the awkward posture and confined space in which work is carried on. When sawing, the shell is held by the toes, the semi-circular saw, kept perpendicular, being moved sideways. The caste are notoriously filthy in their domestic arrangements. A narrow passage, hardly two feet wide, leads through the house to an open courtyard, where the sewage of the household collects and is never removed. Epidemic diseases are very prevalent among them, and owing doubtless to their unhealthy mode of life the men as a rule are pale and flabby and very subject to elephantiasis, hernia, and hydrocele.

Character and habits.

Dr. Wise describes the women as "remarkable for their beauty, confinement within dark rooms giving them a light wheaten complexion. They are, however, squat, becoming corpulent in adult life, and their features, though still handsome, inanimate. They are very shy, but the fact that in former days their good looks exposed them to the insults and outrages of licentious Muhammadan officials is a sufficient excuse for their timidity. Even now-a-days the recollection of past indignities rouses the Sánkhári to fury, and the greatest abuse that can be cast at him is to call him a son of Abdúl

Razzáq or of Rája Rám Dás. The former was a zamindár of Dacca; the latter the second son of Rája Ráj Ballabh, Diwán of Bengal. It is stated that they frequently broke into houses and carried off the Sánkhári girls, being shielded by their rank and influence from any punishment."

Marriage.

Sánkháris marry their daughters as infants by the ceremony in use among the highest castes. It is the fashion for the bridegroom to ride in the marriage procession, while the bride, dressed in red, is carried in a palanquin. Polygamy is permitted subject to the same restrictions as are in force among the Brahmans and Káyasths. Widows are not allowed to marry again, nor is divorce recognized.

Religion.

Nearly all Sánkháris belong to the Vaishnava sect, and comparatively few Sáktas are found among them. Their principal festival is held on the last day of Bhádra (August–September), when they give up work for five days and worship Agastya Rishi, who, according to them, rid the world of a formidable demon called Sankha Asura by cutting him up with the semi-circular saw used by shell-cutters. Others say that they revere Agastya, because he was the *guru* or spiritual guide of their ancestor Dhanápati Saudágar. Rice, sweetmeats, and fruit are offered to him, and are afterwards partaken of by the Brahmans, who serve the caste as priests. These Brahmans act also as priests for the Kayasths, and are received on equal terms by other members of the sacred order. They also observe the *Jhulanjátrá* and *Janmáshtami* festivals in honour of Krishna, kept by all Bengali Vaishnavas. Sánkhárís burn their dead, mourn for thirty days, and perform *sráddh* in the orthodox fashion.

Social status.

In point of social standing the Sánkhárís rank with the Navasákha, and Brahmans will take water and certain kinds of sweetmeats from their hands. Their own rules regarding diet are the same as those of the highest ranks of Hindus. Many of them indeed are vegetarians, and abstain even from fish. Taken as a whole, the caste have been singularly constant to their hereditary occupation—a fact which is due partly to the smallness of their number, and partly to the steady demand for the articles which they produce. In Bengal Proper every married woman of the respectable castes wears shell-bracelets, which are as much a badge of wedded life as the streak of red lead down the parting of the hair. Of late years, however, a certain proportion of the Sánkháris have become traders, writers, timber and cloth merchants, and claim on that account to be superior in social rank to those who manufacture shell bracelets.

Occupation.

Dr. Wise collected from various sources the following interesting particulars regarding the traditional occupation of the Sánkháris:—

The shells used for manufacturing bracelets are imported from the Gulf of Manaar. Natives distinguish many varieties, differing in colour and size, but the ordinary conch shell is the Mazza or Turbinella napa. The trade in these shells has flourished from the earliest historical times. The "chank" is mentioned by Abù Zaid in the tenth century of our era. Tavernier includes shell bracelets among the exports of Dacca in 1666, and adds that in Patna and Bengal there were over two thousand persons employed in manufacturing them.[1]

Towards the end of the seventeenth century the shell trade became a monopoly in the hands of the Dutch. A French missionary in 1700 writes[2] :—"It is scarcely credible how jealous the Dutch are of this commerce. It was death to a native to sell them to any one but to the factory servants at Ceylon. The shells were bought for a trifle, but when despatched in their own vessels to Bengal, the Dutch acquired great profit."

The chank fishery[3] became a royalty of the English Government, yielding an annual revenue of 4,000*l*., but it is now open to all the world. In former days six hundred divers were employed, and in a single season four and a half millions of shells were frequently taken, of the gross annual value of 8,000*l*. The shells are imported by English merchants into Calcutta, purchased by rich Sánkháris, and retailed to the cutters.

On the arrival of the shells the remains of the mollusc (*pitta*) are extracted and sold to native physicians as a medicine for spleen enlargement. The base (*gherá*), the lip, and point of the shell are then knocked off with a hammer, the chips being used as gravel for garden walks or sold to agents from Murshedabad, where beads are made of the larger pieces, and a paint, *Mattiya Sindúr*, of the smaller. From two to eight bracelets are made from one shell. The sawdust is used to prevent the pitting of small-pox, and as an ingredient of a valuable white paint.

In the ordinary shell the whorls turn from right to left, but when one is found with the whorls reversed, "Dakshiná-varta," its price is extravagant, as it is believed to ensure wealth and prosperity. One belonging to a Dacca zamindar is so highly prized that he refused an offer of 300 rupees.

The following statement shows the number and distribution of Sánkháris in 1872 and 1881 :—

DISTRICT.	1872.	1881.	DISTRICT.	1872.	1881.
Bardwan	1,145	1,001	Dacca	853	1,217
Bankura	479	687	Faridpur	......	335
Birbhum	574	159	Bakarganj	1,157	793
Midnapur	1,513	1,438	Maimansinh	192	400
Hughli	968	533	Tipperah	171	85
Howrah		323	Chittagong	89	[illegible]
24-Parganás	1,226	366	Noakhali	252	240
Nadiya	175	73	Maldah	84	71
Khulna	......	218	Hazaribagh	52	......
Jessore	1,450	555	Lohardagá	153	......
Murshedabad	423	371	Singbhum	410	......
Dinajpur	179	31	Manbhum	859	40
Rajshahye	88	87	Cuttack	1,135	[illegible]
Rangpur	35	3	Puri	270	289
Bogra	12	67	Balasore	406	313
Pabna	158	93	Tributary States	57	165
Kuch Behar	......	1			

[1] Tavernior, part ii, book ii, 183-84.

[2] *Lettres Edifantes*, ii, 278.

[3] Accounts of this shell or "sea-horn" fishery are given by Jan Nieuhof in A. and J. Churchill's *Voyages and Travels*, vol. ii, 298, and, of a later date, in *Lettres Edifantes* x. 121 (ed. 1781).

Sankhi, a sub-tribe of Rájputs in Chota Nagpur.

Sankhwár, a section of the Kurmi caste in Chota Nagpur the members of which may not wear *sankuá* or shell ornaments. Another peculiarity of the section is that its members wear a *pagri* in the marriage ceremony, and are prohibited from wearing the ornamental head-dress (*mukut*) made of *solá* pith, generally used on such occasions.

Sánki, a sub-caste of Muchis in Bengal.

Sánkoá, a totemistic section of the Rajwár caste in Manbhum.

Sánkriti, a section of Brahmans.

Sankura, king crow, a totemistic sept of Mundas in Chota Nagpur.

Sankwá, a section of Rajwárs in Western Bengal.

Sanmaulik, a hypergamous group of the Uttar-Rarhi Káyasths in Bengal.

Sánnyál, a *gáin* of the Bátsya *gotra* of Bárendra Brahmans in Bengal.

Sannyási Atit, a class of Atit in Behar who adopt a purely ascetic and celibate life, and transmit their property to their pupils (*chelás*) by a sort of spiritual succession.

Sannyási or Kánphát, a religious group of Jugis.

Sáno or Kabátkoniá, a subcaste of Sudhás in Orissa.

Sánpu, a totemistic section of the Korá caste in Manbhum, the members of which will not touch or kill a bull.

Sanpuri, a sept of Mundas in Chota Nagpur.

Sánrári (Jaideb), a section of Majhraut Goálás in Behar.

Sansáit, a section of the Dhaprá sub-caste of Doms in Behar.

Sansári, an epithet applied by Christian Kolhs in Chota Nagpur to their heathen neighbours.

Sanswár, a sub-caste of Kurmis in Behar.

Santál, *Sonthál*, *Saontár*, a large Dravidian tribe, classed on linguistic grounds as Kolarian, which is found in Western Bengal, Northern Orissa, Bhágalpur and the Santál Parganás. According to Mr. Skrefsrud the name Santál is a corruption of Sáontár, and was adopted by the tribe after their sojourn for several generations in the country about Sáont in Midnapur. Before they went to Sáont they are said to have been called Kharwár, the root of which, *khar*, is a variant of *hor*, 'man,' the name which all Santáls use among themselves. As regards the derivation of the name of the tribe from Saont, an obscure village, somewhat off the main line of their recent migrations, it may be observed that Colonel Dalton suggested a doubt whether the name of the place may not have been taken from the tribe, and this view seems to derive some support from his discovery of a small tribe of Saonts in Sarguja and Keunjhar. The point, however, is not one of great importance. At the present day when a Santál is asked what caste he belongs to, he will almost invariably reply 'Mánjhi' (literally 'village

Origin and traditions.

headman,' one of the commonest titles of the tribe), adding 'Santál Mánjhi' if further explanation is demanded of him.

In point of physical characteristics the Santáls may be regarded as typical examples of the pure Dravidian stock. Their complexion varies from very dark brown to a peculiar, almost charcoal-like, black; the proportions of the nose approach those of the Negro, the bridge being more depressed in relation to the orbits than is the case with Hindus; the mouth is large, the lips thick and projecting; the hair coarse, black, and occasionally curly; the zygomatic arches prominent, while the proportions of the skull, approaching the dolichocephalic type, conclusively refute the hypothesis of their Mongolian descent.

Santál tradition traces back the origin of the tribe to a wild goose (*hâsdak*) which laid two eggs. From these sprang Pilchu Haram and Pilchu Burhi, the parents of the race, who begat the first seven sub-tribes. Their earliest abode was Hihiri or Ahiri Pipiri, a name which Mr. Skrefsrud derives from *hir* origin, and which others identify with parganá Ahuri in Hazaribagh. Thence they went westward to Khoj-Kaman, where all of them were destroyed for their wickedness by a deluge of fire-rain, except a single pair who were saved in a cleft of the mountain Hara. From Hara they went to Sasangbera, a plain on the banks of a great river, and after that to Jarpi, where is the great mountain Marang Buro, through which they could find no pass. Here they offered sacrifices to the mountain god, and prayed him to let them through. After a while they found a pass leading into a country called Ahiri, where they dwelled for a time, passing on to Kendi, Chai, and finally Champa. In Champa they sojourned many generations, and the present institutions of the tribe were formed. At last the Hindus drove them out of Champa, and they established themselves in Saont, and ruled there for two hundred years. Again pressed by the Hindus, they wandered on under a Raja called Hambir Singh to the eastern part of the Manbhum district near Pachet. Here after a while their Rajas adopted the Hindu religion and set up as Rajputs, so that at the present day they intermarry with the family of the Raja of Sarguja. But the people would not change their religion, so they left their chief to rule over Hindus, and wandered on to the Santál Parganás, where they are settled now.

Neither as a record of actual wanderings nor as an example of the workings of the myth-making faculty does this story of the wandering of the Santáls appear to deserve serious consideration. A people whose only means of recording facts consists of tying knots in strings, and who have no bards to hand down a national epic by oral tradition, can hardly be expected to preserve the memory of their past long enough or accurately enough for their accounts of it to possess any historical value. An attempt has indeed been made by Mr. Skrefsrud to prove from these legends that the Santáls must have entered into India from the north-west, just as Colonel Dalton uses the same data in support of his opinion that the tribe came originally from Assam. The one hypothesis is as tenable or as untenable as the other, and all that can be said is that there is not a fraction of substantial evidence in support of either. If, however, the legends of the Santáls are regarded as an account of recent migrations, their general purport will be found to be fairly in accord with actual facts. Without pressing the conjecture mentioned above, that Ahiri Pipri may be no other than pargana Ahuri in the north-west of Hazaribagh district, it is clear that a large and important Santál colony was once settled in parganás Chai and Champá in the same district. A tradition is noticed by Colonel Dalton of an old fort in Chai occupied by one Jaura, a Santál Raja, who destroyed himself and his family on hearing of the approach of a Muhamadan army under Sayyid Ibráhim Ali *alias* Malik Bayá, a general of Muhammad Tughlak's, who died in 1353. This tradition, so far as it refers to the existence of a Santál fort in Chai Champá, is to some extent corroborated by the following passage from the legends of the Southern Santáls collected by the Revd. J. Phillips and published in Appendix G to *Annals of Rural Bengal*, ed. 1868:—"Dwelling there (in Chai Champá) they greatly multiplied. There were two gates, the Ahin gate and the Báhini gate, to the fort of Chai Champá." If, moreover, the date of the taking of this fort by Ibráhim Ali were assumed to be about 1340 A.D., the subsequent migrations of which the tribal legends speak would fill up the time intervening between the departure of the Santáls from Chai Champá and their settlement in the present Santál Parganás. Speaking generally, these recent migrations have been to the east, which is the direction they might *primâ facie* have been expected to follow. The earliest settlements which Santál tradition speaks of, those in Ahiri Pipri and Chai Champá, lie on the north-western frontier of the table land of Hazaribagh and in the direct line of advance of the numerous Hindu immigrants from Behar. That the influx of Hindus has in fact driven the Santáls eastward is beyond doubt, and the line which they are known to have followed in their retreat corresponds on the whole with that attributed to them in their tribal legends.

Internal structure.

The internal structure of the Santál tribe is singularly complete and elaborate. There are twelve exogamous septs, (1) Hásdak, (2) Murmu, (3) Kisku, (4) Hembrom, (5) Marndi, (6) Saren, (7) Tudu, (8) Baske, (9) Besra, (10) Páuria, (11) Chore, (12) Bedea. The first seven are believed to be descended from the seven sons of Pilchu Haram and Pilchu Burhi or Ayo. The five others were added afterwards. All are exogamous. In order that members of the various septs may recognize each other when they meet, each sept, except Páuria, Chore and Bedea, has certain pass-words peculiar to itself, which are supposed to be the names of the original homes of the septs in Champá or in one of the earlier settlements of the tribe. The pass-words are as follows:—(1) Hásdak—Tatijhári, Gangijauni, Kárá Guja, Sohodoro; (2) Murmu—Champágarh, Bagsumbha, Naran Manjhi; (3) Kisku—Kundagarh; (4) Hembrom—Kunda, Khairigarh, Jalaghatia; (5) Marndi—Badoligarh, Jelen Sinjo, Dhano Mánjhi; (6) Saren—Aubali, Barha, Pero Pargana; (7)

Tudu—Simgarh, Sukrihutup, Baru Mánjhi; (8) Baske—Ranga, Chunuk-jhandu; (9) Besra—Dhokrapalania, Gulu, Phagu Mánjhi. These pass-words or shibboleths seem to serve among the Santáls the purpose for which Australian and North American savages tattoo the totem on the body. They preserve the memory of the tie of blood which connects the members of the sept, and thus furnish an additional security against unconscious incest. They further go to show that the sept in its earliest form must have been a group of purely local character analogous to the communal septs which have been mentioned in the article on Kandh. If due allowance is made for the causes which must tend in course of time to scatter the members of any particular sept over a number of different villages, it will be seen to be a remarkable circumstance not that so few local septs are now to be found, but that any traces of such an organization have survived to so late a period.

Concerning the origin of the five additional septs the following stories are told. The eighth tribe, Baske, at first belonged to the seven, but by reason of their offering their breakfast (*baske*) to the gods while the Santáls were still in Champá, they were formed into a separate sept under the name of Baske. The Besras (No. 9) were separated on account of the immoral behaviour of their eponym, who was called Besra, the licentious one. The tenth sept, Páuria, are called after the pigeon, and the eleventh, Chore, after the lizard; and the story is that on the occasion of a famous tribal hunting party the members of these two septs failed to kill anything but pigeons and lizards, so they were called after the names of these animals. The twelfth sept, the Bedea, was left behind and lost when the Santáls went up out of Champá. They had no father, so the story goes—at least the mother of their first ancestor could not say who his father was, and for this reason they were deemed of lower rank than the other septs. This sept is believed to have arisen during the time of Mando Singh in Champá when the Santáls had begun to come in contact with the Hindus. Some Santáls say the father was a Rájput and the mother a girl of the Kisku sept. There would be nothing antecedently improbable in the conjecture that the well-known gypsy tribe of Bedea may owe its origin to the *liaison* of a Rájput with a Santál girl; but the mere resemblance of the names is a slender foundation for any such hypothesis. Santáls are very particular about the honour of their women, so far at least as outsiders are concerned, and it is quite in keeping with their ideas that a sept formed by a *liaison* with a Hindu should have been looked down upon, and eventually banished from the community. Any way it seems to be clear that the legend need not be taken to indicate the prevalence of the custom of female kinship in the tribe.

Marriage.

No Santál may marry within his sept (*páris*), nor within any of the sub-septs (*khunt*) (shown in Appendix I) into which the sept is divided. He may marry into any other sept, including the sept to which his mother belonged. A Santál proverb says:—No one heeds a cow track or regards his mother's sept.

Although no regard is paid in marriage to the mother's sept, the Santáls have precisely the same rule as the Kandhs concerning the sub-sept or *khunt*. A man may not marry into the sub-sept or *khunt* to which his mother belonged, though it is doubtful whether the Santáls observe this rule for as many generations in the descending line as is customary among the Kandhs. Many of the sub-septs have curious traditional usages, some of which may be mentioned here. At the time of the harvest festival in January the members of the Sidup-Saren sub-sept set up a sheaf of rice on end in the doorway of their cattle sheds. This sheaf they may not touch themselves, but some one belonging to another sub-sept must be got to take it away. Men of the Sádá-Saren sub-sept do not use vermilion in their marriage ritual; they may not wear clothes with a red border on such occasions, nor may they be present at any ceremony in which the priest offers his own blood to propitiate the gods. The Jugi-Saren, on the other hand, smear their foreheads with *sindur* at the harvest festival, and go round asking alms of rice. With the rice they get they make little cakes which they offer to the gods. The Mánjhi-Khil-Saren, so called because their ancestor was a mánjhi or village headman, are forbidden, like the Sádá-Saren, to attend when the priest offers up his own blood. The Náiki-Khil-Saren, who claim descent from a náiki or village priest may not enter a house the inmates of which are ceremonially unclean. They have a *jáhirthán* or sacred grove of their own, distinct from the common *jáhirthán* of the village, and they dispense with the services of the priest who serves the rest of the village. The Ok-Saren sacrifice a goat or a pig inside their houses, and during the ceremony they shut the doors tight and allow no smoke to escape. The word *ok* means to suffocate or stifle with smoke. The Mundu or Badar-Saren offer their sacrifices in the jungle, and allow only males to eat the flesh of the animals that have been slain. The Mál-Saren may not utter the word *mal* when engaged in a religious ceremony or when sitting on a pancháyat to determine any tribal questions. The Jihu-Saren may not kill or eat the *jihu* or babbler bird, nor may they wear a particular sort of necklace known as *jihu málá* from the resemblance which it bears to the babbler's eggs. The *jihu* is said to have guided the ancestor of the sept to water when he was dying of thirst in the forest. The Sankh-Saren may not wear shell necklaces or ornaments. The Barchir Saren plant a spear in the ground when they are engaged in religious or ceremonial observances. The Bitol-Saren are so called because their founder was excommunicated on account of incest.

Girls are married as adults mostly to men of their own choice. Sexual intercourse before marriage is tacitly recognized, it being understood that if the girl becomes pregnant the young man is bound to marry her. Should he attempt to evade this obligation, he would be severely beaten by the Jag-mánjhi, and in addition to this his father would be required to pay a heavy fine. It is curious to hear that in the Santál Parganás, shortly after the rebellion of 1855, it became the fashion among the more wealthy Santáls to imitate the usages of high-caste Hindus and marry their daughters between the ages of eight and twelve. This fashion has, however, since been abandoned, and it is now very unusual for a girl to be married before she attains puberty. Polygamy is not favoured by the custom of the tribe. A man may take a second wife if his first wife is barren, or if his elder brother dies he may marry the widow. But in either case the consent of his original wife must be obtained to the arrangement. Instances no doubt occur in which this rule is evaded, but they are looked upon with disfavour.

There seem to be indications that fraternal polyandry may at some time have existed among the Santáls. Even now, says Mr. Skrefsrud, a man's younger brother may share his wife with impunity; only they must not go about it very openly. Similarly a wife will admit her younger sister to intimate relations with her husband, and if pregnancy occurs scandal is avoided by his marrying the girl as a second wife. It will of course be noticed that this form of polyandry need not be regarded as a survival of female kinship.

The following forms of marriage are recognized by the Santáls and distinguished by separate names:—(1) Regular marriage (*bapla* or *kiring behu*, literally bride-purchase); (2) *Ghardi jáwáe*; (3) *Itut*; (4) *Nir-bolok*; (5) *Sanga*; (6) *Kiring jawae* or husband-purchase. The negotiations antecedent to a regular marriage are opened by the father of the young man, who usually employs a professional match-maker to look for a suitable girl. If the match-maker's proposals are accepted by the girl's parents, a day is fixed on which the girl, attended by two of her friends, goes to the house of the jag-mánjhi or superintendent of morals, in order to give the bridegroom's parents an opportunity of looking at her quietly. A similar visit of inspection is paid by the bride's parents to the bridegroom's house, and if everything is found satisfactory the betrothal is concluded and an instalment of the bride-price is paid. The ordinary price of a girl is Rs. 3, and the bridegroom must also present a cloth (*sári*) to the girl's mother and to both her grandmothers if alive. If more than this is paid, the bridegroom is entitled to receive a present of a cow from his father-in-law. In the case known as a *golát* marriage, when two families, each having a daughter and a son of marriageable age, arrange a double wedding, one daughter is set off against the other, and no bride-price is paid by either party. For a widow or a woman who has been divorced the bride-price is only half the standard amount, the idea being, as the Santáls pointedly put it, that such women are only borrowed goods, and must be given back to their first husbands in the next world. As the second husband has the use of his wife only in this world, it is clearly fair that he should get her for half-price. In an early stage of the marriage ceremony both bride and bridegroom separately go through the form of marriage to a *mahuá* tree (*Bassia latifolia*) In the case of the bride a double thread is passed three or five times from the little toe of her left foot to her left ear, and is then bound round her arm with some blades of rice and stems of *dhuba* grass. The conjecture suggests itself that this may be a survival of some form of communal marriage, but from the nature of the case no positive evidence is available to bear out this hypothesis, or to throw any light upon the symbolism of the usage. The essential and binding portion of the ritual is *sindurdán*, the smearing of vermilion on the bride's forehead and on the parting of her hair. This rite, however, is supposed to have been borrowed from the Hindus. The original Santál ceremony is believed to have been very simple. The couple went away together into the woods, and on their return were shut up by themselves in a room. When they came out they were considered to be man and wife. A practice closely resembling this was found by Colonel Dalton to be in vogue among the Birhors, and it is quite in keeping with what is known of the doings of primitive man in the matter of marriage. The memory of it, however, only survives among the Santáls in the form of a vague and shadowy tradition upon which no stress can be laid. *Sindurdán*, on the other hand, is nothing but a refined and specialised form of the really primitive usage of mixing the blood of a married couple and making them drink or smear themselves with the mixture, and although it is possible that the Santáls may have borrowed *sindurdán* from the Hindus, there are certainly good grounds for believing that the Hindus themselves must have derived it from the Dravidian races.

The second mode of marriage, *ghardi jáwáe*, is resorted to when a girl is ugly or deformed and there is no prospect of her being asked in marriage in the ordinary way. An instance has been reported to me in which a girl who had on one foot more than the proper number of toes was married in this fashion. The husband is expected to live in his father-in-law's house and to serve him for five years. At the end of that time he gets a pair of bullocks, some rice and some agricultural implements, and is allowed to go about his business.

The third form, *itut*, is adopted by pushing young men who are not quite sure whether the girl they fancy will accept them, and take this means of compelling her to marry them. The man smears his fingers with vermilion or, failing that, with common earth, and, watching his opportunity at market or on any similar occasion, marks the girl he is in love with on the forehead and claims her as his wife. Having done this, he runs away at full speed to avoid the thrashing he may expect at the hands of her relations if he is caught on the spot. In any case the girl's people will go to his village and will obtain from the headman permission to kill and eat three of the offender's or his father's goats, and a double bride-price must be paid for the girl. The marriage, however, is legal, and if the girl still declines to live with the man, she must be divorced in full form and cannot again be married as a spinster. It is said that an *itut* marriage is often resorted to out of spite in order to subject the girl to the humiliation of being divorced.

The fourth form, *nirbolok* (*nir*, to run, and *bolok*, to enter) may be described as the female variety of *itut*. A girl who cannot get the man she wants in the regular way takes a pot of *hándiá* or rice-beer, enters his house and insists upon staying there. Etiquette forbids that she should be expelled by main force, but the man's mother, who naturally desires to have a voice in the selection of her daughter-in-law, may use any means short of personal violence to get her out of the house. It is quite fair, for example, and is usually found effective, to throw red pepper on the fire, so as to smoke the aspiring maiden out; but if she endures this ordeal without leaving the house, she is held to have won her husband and the family is bound to recognize her.

The fifth form, *sanga*, is used for the marriage of widows and divorced women. The bride is brought to the bridegroom's house attended by a small party of her own friends, and the binding portion of the ritual consists in the bridegroom taking a *dimbu* flower, marking it with *sindur* with his left hand, and with the same hand sticking it in the bride's back hair.

The sixth form, *kiring jáwáe*, is resorted to in the comparatively rare case when a girl has had a *liaison* with, and become pregnant by, a man of her sept whom she cannot marry. In order that scandal may be avoided, some one is procured to accept the post of husband, and in consideration of his services he gets two bullocks, a cow and a quantity of paddy from the family of the man by whom the girl is pregnant. The headman then calls the villagers together, and in their presence declares the couple to be man and wife, and enjoins the girl to live with, and be faithful to, the husband that has been provided for her.

A widow may marry again. It is thought the right thing for her to marry her late husband's younger brother, if one survives him, and under no circumstances may she marry his elder brother. Divorce is allowed at the wish of either husband or wife. If neither party is in fault, the one who wants a divorce is expected to bear the expenses. The husband, for example, in such a case would not be entitled to claim a refund of the bride-price originally paid, and would also have to pay a fine and give the woman certain customary dues. If, on the other hand, it is the wife who demands a divorce without just cause, her father has to make good the bride-price in addition to a fine for her levity of behaviour. The divorce is effected in the presence of the assembled villagers by the husband tearing asunder three *sál* leaves in token of separation, and upsetting a brass pot full of water.

Inheritance.

In the matter of inheritance Santáls follow their own customs, and know nothing of the so-called codes which govern the devolution of property among Hindus. Sons inherit in equal shares; a daughter has no claim to a portion as of right, but usually gets a cow given to her when the property is divided. Failing sons, the father takes; failing him, the brothers; after them, the male agnates. Failing agnates, the daughter inherits with succession to her children. If a man dies leaving young sons, his widow manages the property till all the sons are old enough to divide and start separate households. She then takes up her abode with the youngest. Should the widow marry outside the family, the male agnates take the property in trust till the sons are of age, and she gets nothing. If a man has male relatives, he cannot give away his property even to a son-in-law. Wills are unknown.

Religion.

According to Mr. Skrefsrud traces may be discerned in the background of the Santál religion of a *fainéant* Supreme Deity called Thakur, whom the Santáls have long ceased to worship for the sufficient reason that he is too good to trouble himself about anybody and does neither good nor ill to mankind. Some identify him with the Sun, whom the Santáls regard as a good god and worship every fifth or tenth year with sacrifices of slain goats. But this point is uncertain, and I am myself inclined to doubt whether a god bearing the Hindu name Thakur, and exercising supreme powers which mark a comparatively late stage of theological development, can really have formed part of the original system of the Santáls. However this may be, the popular gods of the tribe at the present day are the following :—(1) Marang Buru, the great mountain or the very high one, who now stands at the head of the Santál Pantheon, and is credited with very far-reaching powers, in virtue of which he associates both with the gods and with the demons (2) Moreko, fire, now a single god, but formerly known to the Santáls under the form of five brothers. (3) Jáir Era, a sister of Moreko, the goddess of the sacred grove set apart in every village for the august presence of the gods. (4) Gosain Era, a younger sister of Moreko. (5) Parganá, chief of the bongas or gods, and more especially master of all the witches, by reason of which latter functions he is held in especial reverence. (6) Mánjhi, a sort of second in command to Parganá, a personage who is supposed to be particularly active in restraining the gods from doing harm to men. The two latter are clearly deities constructed on the model of the communal and village officials whose names they bear. The idea is that the gods, like men, need supervising officials of this sort to look after them and keep them in order. All the foregoing gods have their allotted place in the sacred grove (*Jáhirthán*), and are worshipped only in public. Marang Buru alone is also worshipped privately in the family.

Each family also has two special gods of its own—the Orak-bonga or household god, and the Abge-bonga or secret god. The names of the Orak-bongas are (1) Baspahar, (2) Deswáli, (3) Sás, (4) Goraya, (5) Barpahar, (6) Saronawdi, (7) Thuntatursa. The Abge-bongas are the following :—(1) Dharasore or Dharasanda, (2) Ketkomkudra, (3) Champa-denagarh, (4) Garhsinka, (5) Lilachandi, (6) Dhunghara, (7) Kudrachandi, (8) Bahara, (9) Duárseri, (10) Kudraj, (11) Gosáin Erá, (12) Achali, (13) Deswáli. No Santál would divulge the name of his Orak-bonga and Abge-bonga to any one but his eldest son; and men are particularly careful to keep this sacred knowledge from their wives for fear lest they should acquire undue influence with the bongas, become witches, and eat up the family with impunity when the protection of its gods has been withdrawn. The names given above were disclosed to Mr. Skrefsrud by Christian Santáls. When sacrifices are offered to the Orak-bongas the whole family partake of the offerings; but only men may touch the food that has been laid before the Abge-bongas. These sacrifices take place once a year. No regular time is fixed, and each man performs them when it suits his convenience.

Human sacrifice.

There still lingers among the Santáls a tradition of a 'mountain-god' (Buru-bonga) of unknown name, to whom human sacrifices used to be offered, and actual instances have been mentioned to me of people being kidnapped and sacrificed within quite recent times by influential headmen of communes or villages, who hoped in this way to gain great riches or to win some specially coveted private revenge. These are not the motives which prompted human sacrifice among the Kandhs of Orissa, a tribe whose internal structure curiously resembles that of the Santáls. The Kandh sacrifice was undertaken for the benefit of the entire tribe, not in the interest of individual ambition or malevolence. It is curious to hear that one of the men credited with this iniquity was himself murdered during the Santál rebellion of 1855, by being slowly hewn in pieces with axes, just as his own victims had been—a mode of execution which certainly recalls the well-known procedure of the Kandhs.

Festivals.

The chief festival of the Santáls is the Sohrai or harvest festival, celebrated in Posh (November–December), after the chief rice crop of the year has been got in. Public sacrifices of fowls are offered by the priest in the sacred grove; pigs, goats and fowls are sacrified by private families, and a general saturnalia of drunkenness and sexual license prevails. Chastity is in abeyance for the time, and all unmarried persons may indulge in promiscuous intercourse. This license, however, does not extend to adultery, nor does it sanction intercourse between persons of the same sept, though even this offence, if committed during the Sohrai, is punished less severely than at other times. Next in importance is the *Baha puja*, kept in Phalgun (February–March) when the *sál* tree comes into flower. Tribal and family sacrifices are held, many victims are slain and eaten by the worshippers, every one entertains their friends, dancing goes on day and night, and the best songs and flute-music are performed. A peculiar feature of this festival is a sort of water-bottle in which men and women throw water at each other until they are completely drenched.

Mention may also be made of Erok-sim, the sowing festival kept in Asar (May–June); Hariar-sim, the feast of the sprouting of the rice in Bhadra (September–October); Trigundli nauai, the offering of the first fruits of the millets *iri* (Panicum millaceum) and *gundli* (Panicum frumentaceum) also in Bhadra; Janthar puja in Aghran (October–November), the first fruits of the winter rice crop; Sankránt puja on the last day of Posh, when bread and chira and molasses are offered to dead ancestors; Mágh-sim in the month of Mágh, when the jungle grass is cut. This is the end of the Santál year. S ants are paid their wages and fresh engagements are entered On this occasion all the village officials, the Manjhi, , Jag Manjhi, Jag-parámánik, Gorait Náiki and Kudam-naiki go through the form of resigning their appoinements, and all the cultivators give notice of throwing up their lands. After ten days or so the manjhi or headman calls the village together and says he has changed his mind and will stay on as manjhi if the village will have him. His offer is accompanied with free drinks of rice-beer, and is carried by acclamation. One by one the other officials do the same; the ryots follow suit, and after a vast amount of beer has been consumed the affairs of the village go on as they did before. The Sima-bonga or boundary gods are propitiated twice a year with sacrifices of fowls offered at the boundary of the village where these gods are supposed to live. Jomsim puja is an offering of two goats, or a goat and a sheep, to the sun. Every Santál ought to perform this sacrifice at least once in his life. After a year's interval it is, or ought to be, followed by Kutam dangra, when a cow is offered to the household god, and an ox to Marang buru and to the spirits of dead ancestors. Mak-more puja, literally 'the out five,' is a sacrifice of three goats and many fowls offered to More-ko, the god of fire, supposed to have been originally five brothers, on occasions of public calamity, such as a failure of the crops, an outbreak of epidemic disease, and the like.

The following statement shows the number and distribution of Santáls in 1872 and 1881:—

DISTRICT.	1872.	1881.	DISTRICT.	1872.	1881.
Bardwan	4,467	5,806	Dacca	1	......
Bankura	36,378	20,034	Maimansinh	75	......
Birbhum	6,954	726	Chittagong	4	12
Midnapur	96,921	568	Patna	4	......
Hughli	} 46	{ 36	Tirhut	6	......
Howrah		67	Monghyr	13,957	......
24-Parganás	814	31	Bhágalpur	16,468	42
Nadiya	6	29	Maldah	215	833
Jessore	23	55	Sántál Parganás	4,55,513	9,148
Khulna	......	19	Cuttack	3	...
Murshedabad	3,002	1,663	Balasore	1,176	380
Dinajpur	1,039	6,813	Tributary States	76,548	922
Rajshahye	5	139	Hazaribagh	35,306	......
Rangpur	......	7	Lohardaga	1,204	7
Bogra	75	252	Singbhum	51,133	51,954
Pabna	......	130	Manbhum	132,445	86,403
Darjiling	......	19	Tributary States	9	17,216

The communal organization of the Santáls is singularly complete.

Communal organization.

The whole number of villages comprising a local settlement of the tribe is divided into certain large groups, each under the superintendence of a *parganait* or circle headman. This official is the head of the social system of the inhabitants of his circle; his permission has to be obtained for every marriage, and he, in consultation with a *pancháyat* of village headmen, expels or fines persons who infringe the tribal standard of propriety. He is remunerated by a commission on the fines levied, and by a tribute in kind of one leg of the goat or animal cooked at the dinner which the culprits are obliged to give. Each village has, or is supposed to have, the following establishment of officials holding rent-free land :—

1. *Manjhi.*—Headman, usually *iardar* where the village is held on lease under a zamindar, collects rents, and allots land among the ryots, being paid for this by the proceeds of the *mán* land which he holds free of rent. He receives Re. 1 as *marocha* at each wedding, giving in return a full *handi* of rice-beer.

2. *Paramanik.*—Assistant headman, also holding some *mân* land.

3. *Jag Manjhi*
4. *Jag Paramanik*
} Executive officers, respectively, of the *manjhi* and the *paramanik* who, as the Santáls describe it, "sit and give orders," which the *Jag Manjhi* and *Jag Paramanik* carry out.

5. *Naiki.*—Village priest of the aboriginal deities.

6. *Kudam Naiki.*—Assistant priest, whose peculiar function it is to propitiate the spirits (*bhúts*) of the hills and jungles by scratching his arms till they bleed, mixing the blood with rice, and placing it in spots frequented by the *bhúts*.

7. *Gorait.*—Village messenger, who holds *mân* land and acts as peon to the headman. The gorait is also to some extent a servant of the zamindar. His chief duty within the village is to bring to the *manjhi* and *Paramanik* any ryot they want.

The communal circles of the Santáls seem to correspond closely to the *mutas* of the Kandhs and the *parhas* of the Mundas and Oraons. It is a plausible conjecture that among all these tribes this organization was once connected with marriage, as it is among the Kandhs at the present day.

Santari, a section of the Magahiyá sub-caste of Doms in Behar.

Sántaru, a *samáj* or local group of the Sábarna *gotra* of Páschátya Baidik Brahmans in Bengal.

Sántrá, *Sánt*, a title of Kaibarttas, Telis, and Bágdis in Bengal.

Santu Kusáet, a section of the Ghosin sub-caste of Goálás in Behar.

Sanuani, a sept of Dhenuárs in Chota Nagpur who cannot wear gold.

Sanuár, a section of Goálás in Behar.

Sanukra, a section of Ghásis in Chota Nagpur.

Sanwani, a sept of Kaurs and Rautiás in Chota Nagpur.

Sanwar, a goldsmith; a section of the Kámi caste in Darjiling.

Sanwasi, a section of Ghásis in Chota Nagpur.

Sánwát, a title of Cheros in Palamau.

Saoasi, a synonym for Pán and Tánti.

Sáolá, a sept of the Bhumij tribe in Manbhum.

Saonra, a title of Goálás in Behar; a sub-caste of Goálás in Chota Nagpur.

Saonsiá, a sept of Páns in Chota Nagpur.

Saontár, a synonym for Santál.

Sapankotyá, a *thar* of the Kanniá *gotra* of Nepáli Brahmans.

Sapdohá, a section of Bábhans in Behar.

Saphárk, a *pur* or section of Sákadwipi Brahmans in Behar.

Sápkotá, a section of Kámis in Darjiling.

Saptagrámi, a sub-caste of Nápits and Telis in Bengal.

Saptagrámi or *Kusadái*, a sub-caste of Támbulis in Bengal.

Saptagrámi or **Nadiyá**, a sub-caste of Subarnabaniks in Bengal.

Saptasati or **Sátsati**, a sub-caste of Brahmans in Bengal who numbered seven hundred when Adisur brought the five Brahmans from Kanauj in order to perform certain *jajna*, owing to their want of ceremonial purity. They have since become mixed with the later emigrant Brahmans, and consequently very few families of them are now recognized by the name of Saptasati.

Sápui, a title of Pods in Bengal.

Sápurya or *Bediyá-Mál*, a sub-caste of Máls in Midnapur and Manbhum.

Sar, a synonym for Savars.

Sár, a sub-caste of Rájus in Midnapur.

Saráf, a title of the Ariár sub-caste of Bais Baniyás.

Sarai, a jungle fruit, a totemistic sept of Korwas and of Mundas in Chota Nagpur.

Saráihát, a section of the Sátmuliá Maghayá sub-caste of Kándus in Behar.

Saraiyár, a section of Káyasths in Behar.

Sárák, *Sráwak*, a small caste of Chota Nagpur, who seem to be a Hinduised remnant of the early Jain people, to whom local legends ascribe the ruined temples, the defaced images, and even the abandoned copper mines of that part of Bengal. The temples and images indeed are proved by their well-marked and characteristic symbolism to be the handiwork of Jain artists, while there is nothing *primâ facie* improbable in the supposition that the mines also may be due to the energy of this comparatively civilised race, whose well-wrought stone pillars and lintels far surpass anything that the present inhabitants of the province can execute. Neither history nor tradition throws any clear light upon the causes which compelled these peaceful settlers to desert the picturesque valleys, where we find vestiges of their faith; but if we may suppose the majority of them to have been gradually driven out by the incursion of the non-Aryan races, nothing would be more likely than that the remnant who remained behind, surrounded as they were by barbarians of alien blood and religion, should have hardened into a caste such as the Sáráks form at the present day.

Origin.

The Sáráks have no sub-castes. Their sections are of the eponymous type, and this fact, coupled with their comparatively refined cast of features and light complexion, seems to confirm their claims to be deemed of Aryan descent. The prohibited degrees are the same as in the case of high-caste Hindus. They marry their

Internal structure and marriage.

daughters as infants, forbid widows to remarry, and do not recognize divorce. Polygamy is permitted in so far that a man may take a second wife if he has no hope of obtaining male issue by his first wife. The marriage ceremony is of the standard type.

Religion.

The Sáráks of Manbhum, while retaining the tradition that their ancestors were Jains, appear themselves to have completely adopted Hinduism. They worship the ordinary Hindu gods with the assistance of Brahmans; nor have they retained, as might perhaps have been expected, any of the characteristic *tirthankaras* or glorified saints of the Jains under the disguise of minor or household gods. In Lohardagá, on the other hand, Párswanáth, the twenty-third *tirthankara*, who is believed to have attained *nirvána* on Párasnáth Hill in Hazaribagh, is still recognized by the Sáráks as their chief deity, though they also worship Shyám Chánd, Rádhá Mohán, and Jagannáth. Brahmans officiate as their priests, and in no way forfeit their social reputation by doing so. In all Jain temples, indeed, the ministrant priests are Brahmans.

Occupation and social status.

Sáráks are skilful agriculturists, and are credited with having introduced sugarcane cultivation on the plateau of Chota Nagpur. Most of them are occupancy raiyats, and in parganá Sonpur of Lohardagá a few villages are held by Sáráks in permanency and at a fixed rent by the tenure known locally as *britt-bhandár*. In point of social standing they rank high, and Brahmans will take water and *pakki* articles of food from their hands. Sáráks themselves retain all the prejudices of the Jains in regard to eating the flesh of any kind of animal. Life may on no account be taken. Their diet therefore consists entirely of vegetables; and it is said that if in preparing their food any mention of the word 'cutting' is made, the omen is deemed so disastrous that every thing must be thrown away. Subject to these conditions, Sáráks will eat the leavings of Brahmans, and will take water or sweetmeats from Rájputs, Baidyas, and Kayásths.

The following statement shows the number and distribution of Sáráks in 1872 and 1881:—

District.	1872.	1881.	District.	1872.	1881.
Bardwan	......	38	Monghyr	......	27
Bankura	......	601	Santál Parganás	......	448
Rangpur	......	3	Hazaribagh	......	103
Patna	......	342	Lohardagá	1,659	1,515
Gya	......	123	Manbhum	8,327	8,218
Shahabad	......	5	Tributary States	......	56
Mozufferpur	......	8			

Sárálíá, a sub-caste of Kumhárs and Bhuinmális found in Noakháli.

Sáramba, a tigress, a totemistic sept of Juángs in Orissa.

Sarangi, a section of Utkal or Orissa Brahmans.

Sarángi, a *thar* or sept of Mangars in Darjiling.

Sárangihár, a religious group of Jugis.

Saraogi, a mercantile caste of Northern India closely allied to the Agarwals and Oswals. Like these, Saraogis are mostly adherents of the Jain faith. They profess to have 84 exogamous groups deriving their names from villages in Khandela and Shekhawati. In marriage they exclude both *gots*, like the Maheari, and reckon them on both sides.

Sarari, a title of Byádhs who kill birds by *sar* or arrows.

Sáras, a water-fowl, a totemistic sept of Bhuiyás and Kharwars in Chota Nagpur.

Sáraswat, *Sársath*, *Sársati*, a territorial division of the Pancha Gaura Brahmans found in Behar, said to derive its name from having originally dwelled in the country watered by the river Saraswati in the Panjáb.

Saraswati, a sect of Dasnámi Sannyásis.

Sarauli, a *mul* or section of the Chhamuliá Madhesiá sub-caste of Halwáis in Behar.

Sarbbánandi, a *mel* or hypergamous sub-group of Rárhi Brahmans in Bengal.

Sarbesia, a group of the Purbba Kuliyá Sadgops.

Sardak-peapi, a sub-sept of the Phejom sept of Limbus in Darjiling.

Sardár, a headman, a chief. (i) In Bengal Proper an ironical title of Tántis, Bágdis, Háris, Doms, Káhárs, and other low castes; (ii) in Manbhum a title of the Bhumij tribe, many of whom are headmen of *ghatwali* villages; (iii) in the Santál Parganás a title of Mal Pahariás and Santáls.

Saren, a sept of Santáls.

Sares Parganá Dadádih, a *mul* or section of the Naomuliá or Majraut sub-caste of Goálás in Behar.

Sárgátiá, a section of the Biyáhut and Kharidáhá Kalwárs in Behar.

Sargrámi, a *gáin* of the Kásyapa *gotra* or Bárendra Brahmans in Bengal

Sarihin, a sept of the Patar-Mahili sub-caste of Máhilis in Chota Nagpur.

Sarin, a section of the Dharkár sub-caste of Doms in Behar.

Sariswe-Khángor, a *mul* of the Sándil section of Maithil Brahmans in Behar.

Sariswe-Sakuri, a *mul* of the Sándil section of Maithil Brahmans in Behar.

Sariyál, a *gáin* of the Bharadwája *gotra* of Bárendra Brahmans in Bengal.

Sarjál, a sept of Kaurs in Chota Nagpur.

Sarjupari, see **Sarwariá**.

Sarkár, a title of Brahmans; of Kurmis in Manbhum, used both by members of the caste and by outsiders; of Jugis, Kaibarttas, Kayasths, Nápits, Pods, Sadgops, and Tántis in Bengal.

Sarkatá, a *mul* or section of the Kanaujiá sub-caste of Sonárs in Behar.

Sarki, the cobbler caste of Nepal.

Sarmá, a synonym for Brahman; a title of Dakshin-Rárhi and Bangaja Káyasths.

Sarnabanik, a synonym for Subarnabanik.

Sarna-Kámár, a sub-caste of Kámárs in Midnapur.

Sarnakár, *Sekrá*, the working goldsmith and silversmith caste of Bengal, an artisan group, probably traceable to the Karmakar and wholly distinct from the Subarnabanik, who never work in metal themselves. Sarnakárs are divided into four sub-castes: **Brahman-desi, Dakhin-Rárhi, Khatangi** and **Uttar-Rárhi**. They have five exogamous groups, three Brahmanical and two Sabanta-Rishi and Sa-rishi, suggestive of less distinguished associations. Girls are usually married as infants, but this is said not to be obligatory—a view which is to some extent borne out by the fact that a bride-price is paid, and the bridegroom-price characteristic of the full development of infant-marriage has not yet been introduced. The marriage ceremony is of the orthodox type; its essential and binding portion being the gift of the bride to the bridegroom and his formal acceptance of the gift. Widows may not marry again, and divorce is permitted only on the ground of the wife's adultery.

The religion of the caste is that of the average middle class Hindu—Sákta or Vaishnava as the case may be. The divine artisan, Viswakarmá, is reverenced as the special patron of the caste. The women have a special ceremony called Kulai, which is performed during the rains without the assistance of any priest. Brahmans are employed for religious and ceremonial purposes, but these are not received on equal terms by those members of the sacred order who serve the higher castes. The dead are burned, and the *sráddh* ceremony performed one month after death. The caste believe the business of a goldsmith to be their original occupation, but some of them engage in agriculture. Their social status is low. None of the higher castes will take water from them, and they admit that they will take water and sweetmeats from any one except the very lowest castes, such as Hári, Muchi and Dom.

Sarnar, a curry vegetable, a totemistic sept of Mundas in Chota Nagpur.

Sarniá, a sept of the Suraj-bansi division of Rájputs in Behar.

Sarno, a sept of Oraons in Chota Nagpur.

Sarpa, snake, a totemistic section of Jagannáthi Kumhárs in Orissa.

Sáru, a *thar* or sept of Mangars in Darjiling.

Saruá, a group of the Pandá sub-caste of Utkal Brahmans.

Sarwál, a section of the Panchjáti sub-caste of Khatris in Bengal.

Sarwariá or **Saryupari**, a sub-caste of Kanaujiá Brahmans and Telis in Behar.

Sarwat, a section of Kanaujiá Lohárs in Behar.

Sarwe, a section of Bábhans in Behar.

Sásani or **Srotriya**, a sub-caste of Utkal Brahmans in Orissa.

Sásankhar, a section of Kámis in Darjiling.

Sásmal, a title of Suklis and Kaibarttas in Midnapur.

Satal, a *thar* or sept of the Bárah-Gurung sub-tribe of Gurungs in Darjiling.

Satánandkháni, a *mel* or hypergamous sub-group of Rárhi Brahmans in Bengal.

Satapasti, Satpati, a group of the Srotriya sub-caste of Utkal Brahmans.

Satarwár, a *mul* or section of the Kanaujiá sub-caste of Hajjáms in Behar.

Satchásá, a synonym for Sadgop in Bengal.

Sáteswari, a *gáin* of the Sábarna *gotra* of Rárhi Brahmans in Bengal.

Sátghariá, a sub-caste of Nápits in Bengal.

Satgop, a synonym for Sadgop in Bengal.

Sat Gosáin, a sub-sect of Vaishnavas recruited from the higher castes and distinguished for their proselytising zeal.

Sáthiet, a *mul* or section of the Naomuliá or Majraut sub-caste of Goálás in Behar.

Sátisá, a sub-caste of Dhobás in Central Bengal.

Sátlakshe-Sataur, a *mul* of the Kásyapa section of Maithil Brahmans in Behar

Sátlakshe-Sátlaksha, a *mul* of the Kásyap section of Maithil Brahmans in Behar.

Sátling, a sept of Limbus in Darjiling.

Satola, a *thar* or section of Nepáli Brahmans.

Sátcriá, a section of Goálás in the North-Western Provinces and Behar.

Satrá, a section of Sunris in Behar.

Sátsaikiyá, a sub-caste of Aguris in Western Bengal.

Satsudra, a group of castes from whose hands a Brahman can take water.

Sáttá, a section of Pátnis in Eastern Bengal.

Sattyal, a *thar* or section of Nepáli Brahmans.

Sátun, a title of Barhis in Behar.

Satya, truth, a section of Jugis.

Sáu, a section of Goálás in Behar.

Sau or Chalita-Sau, a sub-caste of Sunris in Western Bengal.

Sauar, a *mul* or section of the Maghayá sub-caste of Kándus in Behar.

Saubarniá, a section of Babháns in Behar.

Sauchánd, a sub-caste of Kurmis in Behar.

Saudá Báek, a *mul* or section of the Satmuliá or Kishnaut sub-caste of Goálás in Behar.

Saudarpurái Mahiá, a *mul* of the Sándil section of Maithil Brahmans in Behar.

Saudarpurái-Katká, a *mul* of the Sándil section of Maithil Brahmans in Behar.

Saudarpurái-Jagaur, a *mul* of the Sándil section of Maithil Brahmans in Behar.

Saudarpurái-Sarso, a *mul* of the Sándil section of Maithil Brahmans in Behar.

Saudarpurái-Suket, a *mul* of the Sándil section of Maithil Brahmans in Behar.

Saudarpurái-Hansauli, a *mul* of the Sándil section of Maithil Brahmans in Behar.

Saudarpurái-Khoir, a *mul* of the Sándil section of Maithil Brahmans in Behar.

Saudarpurái-Digaun, a *mul* of the Sándil section of Maithil Brahmans in Behar.

Saudarpurái-Kanhauli, a *mul* of the Sándil section of Maithil Brahmans in Behar.

Saudarpurái-Mánik, a *mul* of the Sándil section of Maithil Brahmans in Behar.

Saudarpurái-Rohár, a *mul* of the Sándil section of Maithil Brahmans in Behar.

Saudarpurái-Sundar, a *mul* of the Sándil section of Maithil Bráhmans in Behar.

Saudarpurái-Dhaul, a *mul* of the Sándil section of Maithil Brahmans in Behar.

Saudarpurái-Baghát, a *mul* of the Sándil section of Maithil Brahmans in Behar.

Saudarpurái-Gaul, a mul of the Sándil section of Maithil Brahmans in Behar.

Sauiá, a sept of Hos in Singbhum.

Saukálin, a section of Brahmans and of Káyasths in Bengal.

Saul, fish, a sept of Páns in Chota Nagpur.

Sáulok, a general term for members of the Sáhá or Sunri caste.

Saunaka, a Kshatra-peta *gotra* or section of Brahmans.

Saundika, a synonym for Sunri.

Saunt, a section of the Bánsphor sub-caste of Doms in Behar.

Sauntia-Kandh, a sub-tribe of Kandhs in Orissa.

Saupáyan, a section of Brahmans and of Káyasths in Bengal.

Saur, a synonym for Savar; a *mul* or section of the Kanaujiá sub-caste of Sonárs and of Goálás in Behar; a totemistic section of Khariás and Turis signifying a fish; a totemistic sept of Doms and Chamárs in Chota Nagpur.

Saurástriya, a sub-caste of Brahmans found in Behar.

Sauriyá, a sub-caste of Mauliks in Chota Nagpur.

Saursambár, a section of the Sátmuliá Maghayá sub-caste of Kándus in Behar.

Savar,[1] *Sabar*, *Saur*, *Sar*, *Sayar*, *Suir*, *Swiri*, a Dravidian cultivating and servile tribe of Orissa, Chota Nagpur, Western Bengal, Madras, and the Central Provinces. Colonel Dalton regards them as Dravidian,[2] while Friedrich Müller,[3] General Cunningham,[4] and Mr. R. Cust,[5]

Traditions of origin.

---

[1] "The origin of the name of *Savara*," says General Cunningham, "must be sought for outside the language of the Aryans. In Sanskrit *savara* simply means a 'corpse.' From Herodotus, however, we learn the Scythian word for an 'axe' was *sagaris*; and as *g* and *v* are interchangeable letters, *savar* is the same word as *sagar*. It seems therefore not unreasonable to infer that the tribes who were so called took their name from their habit of carrying axes. Now it is one of the striking peculiarities of the Savaras that they are rarely seen without an axe in their hands. This peculiarity has been frequently noticed by all who have seen them."—*Archæological Survey*. xvii, 113.

[2] *Ethnology of Bengal*, p. 149.

[3] *Allgem. Ethnog.*, 462.

[4] *Arkæolog. Survey*, vol. xvii, p. 132.

[5] *Modern Languages of the East Indies*, p. 85.

place them on linguistic grounds in the Kolarian group of tribes. The evidence from language, however, is meagre and inconclusive; while on the other hand it is tolerably certain that the Savars, scattered and partially Hinduised as they are, represent the main body of an ancient race, an isolated fragment of which survives in the Málé or Saur of the Rajmahal hills. The Savars are usually identified with the Suari and Sabarai mentioned by Pliny[1] and Ptolemy.[2] General Cunningham shows in the paper referred to above that the tribe is very widely diffused at the present day; and local tradition ascribes to the Savars the conquest of the Cheros, and their expulsion from the plateau of Shahabad, in about the year 421 of the Sáliváhana era, or A.D. 500. A number of ancient monuments in the Shahabad district are still put down to the Savars or Suirs, who are supposed to have been driven south by the inroad of Rájputs under the Bhojpur chief, which made an end of their rule.

Physical characteristics.

A good observer[3] describes the Savaras near Mahendragiri in Ganjam as small but wiry, often very dark in colour and sometimes quite black, which agrees with Stirling's account.[4] "Their hair is generally tied in a top-knot, and sometimes it is cut short over the forehead, two long locks being permitted to hang over the ears. A few individuals have frizzled shocks, with which no such arrangement is attempted. Most of the men have small, square beards. The nose is in general broad, with wide nostrils. Of those races in Bengal with whose appearance I am familiar, they reminded me most strongly of the Bhumij, who belong to the Munda family; but I could also perceive in them some points of resemblance to the Dravidian Paharias of the Rajmahal hills. They have not, however, the manly bearing and good physique of the latter . . . . Their manner of dancing resembles that of the Rajmahal Paharias, as I have on one occasion witnessed it, rather than that of either the Santáls or Kols."

Internal structure.

The exogamous septs current among the Savars of Bankura are shown in Appendix I. The totems **Sálmachh** and **Kásibak** occur also among the Bágdis and several other Dravidian races of Western Bengal. The eponyms **Gargarishi** and **Sándilya** appear to have been borrowed from the Brahmanical system. The Savars of Orissa are said to have no septs, and it is possible that the Bankura branch of the tribe may have picked up their totemistic septs locally. The case of the Telingas (see article on that caste) rather bears out this view. Mention has been made in the article on the Málé tribe of the remarkable fact that they have no exogamous divisions, and regulate marriage by the more modern system of counting prohibited degrees. It follows from this that the section-names of the Savars throw no light upon their connexion with the Málé. Mr. W. B. Oldham,

---

1 *Nat. Hist.*, vol. vi, 23. "Suari, quorum Mons Mallus."

2 Ptolemy VII, 1, 80. Lassen states that Karkaradama, the most western of the cities of the Sabarai, was probably somewhere in Singbhum.

3 V. Ball, *Jungle Life in India*, p. 267.

4 Stirling, *Orissa*, p. 42.

however, considers the two tribes to be one and the same, and this view may, I think, be accepted as correct.

The Savars of the Orissa Tributary States are divided into four sub-tribes—Bendkar, Parirá, Jharuá, and Palli—which are strictly endogamous. The origin of the names is obscure, but it seems possible that both Palli and Parirá may have some reference to the practice of using leaves as clothing. Varáha Mihira, quoted by General Cunningham, speaks of the Parna or leaf-clad Savaras[1]; and a Savara messenger mentioned in the Kathá Sarit Ságara is a described as carrying a bow in his hand "with his hair tied up in a knot behind with a creeper, black himself and wearing a loin cincture of vilwa leaves."

Marriage.

Girls may be married either as infants or after they have attained the age of puberty. Infant-marriage is deemed the more respectable usage, but no social stigma attaches to a family which is unable by reason of poverty or any other cause to comply with the demands of fashion on this point. Sexual license before marriage, though vehemently condemned, is said to be tolerated, and if an unmarried girl becomes pregnant her fault is condoned by marriage to the father of her child. The Savars of Bankura observe a Hinduised ceremony, the binding portions of which are *gotrántar*, or the transf r of the bride from her own sept to that of the bridegroom, and the smearing of vermilion on her forehead and the parting of her hair. In Orissa the ritual is more simple, and appears to have been less affected by the influence of Brahmanical usage. On the arrival of the bridegroom at the bride's house he is met by her female relatives, who greet him with cries of *lu lu*, and burn ghi, rice, areca nuts, turmeric, etc., in his honour. This is followed by a curious practice, called *seka*, believed to be peculiar to the Savars, in which the bridesmaids warm the tips of their fingers at a lamp and press them on both cheeks of the bridegroom. The couple then pass on towards the *bedi*, a raised platform of earth, in the courtyard of the house, stopping on the way to sprinkle each seven times with a mixture of mustard seed and salt. On reaching the *bedi* they make two and a half turns round a pot of water, in which are mango leaves, after which an elder of the tribe, nominated as priest for the occasion, makes them sit down side by side, and binds their hands together with *durba* grass and leaves of the *borkoli* plum tree. This is the closing and essential part of the ceremony. The bride-price varies with the means of the families. Among the Bendkar Savars, according to Colonel Dalton, it comprises two bullocks—one for the girl's father and another for her maternal uncle—and a cloth and one rupee presented to her mother.

Polygamy is permitted, and no theoretical limit is set to the number of wives a man may have. Few Savars, however, indulge in more than two, and usually a second wife is only taken in the event of the first being barren. In Orissa (but not in Bankura), a widow may marry again, and is ordinarily expected to marry her

[1] Professor Kern identifies the Parna Savaras with the Pallitæ of Ptolemy, but explains the name to mean "feeding upon leaves," which seems improbable.

first husband's younger brother or cousin. No compulsion, however, is exercised in the matter, and a widow may marry any one she pleases, provided that she returns to her father's house and remains unmarried for a year after her first husband's death. No regular ceremony is ordained for use on such occasions, and the union is celebrated by a feast given to the relations of both parties. Divorce is permitted for adultery or any other serious conjugal offence. The case is considered by the members of the husband's family, who, if they find it impossible or unadvisable to effect a reconciliation between the parties, formally escort the woman to the house of her father or guardian and leave her there. Divorced wives may marry again in the same manner as widows.

Religion.

The Savars of Bankura have become thoroughly Hinduised, and Brahmans serve them as priests in the worship of the standard gods. These Brahmans are received on equal terms by the *purohits* of Bagdis, Koras, Kewats, and other low castes. In Orissa the original faith of the tribe has been less modified by the influence of Hindu usage. The worship of the Brahmanical deities is indeed gaining ground among them, but the elder gods, Thánpati, who dwells in the *thán* or sacred grove of the village, and "Bansuri or Thákuráini, no doubt the same as the blood-thirsty she-devil revered by the Bhuiyás,"[1] still receive offerings of goats or fowls at the hands of the elders of the community, who have not yet been supplanted in their office by the professional Brahman.

Disposal of the dead.

The Orissa Savars recognize both burial and cremation as proper modes of disposing of the dead. The Bankura branch of the tribe only burn, and perform the ceremony of *sráddh* more or less in accordance with regular Hindu usage.

Occupation.

The Savars believe their original condition to have been that of a wandering tribe, roaming through the hills of Orissa and Chota Nagpur, living on the fruits of the forest and acknowledging the rule of no recognized chief. The memory of this primitive state is almost the only tradition which the tribe still preserve, and it can hardly be doubted that this primitive mode of life must have lasted, at any rate among some branches of the Savars, down to comparatively recent times.

The bulk of the tribe have taken to plough cultivation and massed themselves in regular villages; but the Bendkars of Keunjhar still adhere in the main to the nomadic habits which their traditions describe. An interesting account of this branch of the Savars was given in 1842 by Colonel Tickell, of the South-West Frontier Agency, who found them inhabiting a tangled tract of hill and forest bounded on the north and north-east by the cultivated land of the Ho communities or *pirs* of Kotgarh and Bar. They had lost their primitive dialect, and spoke either Ho or Uriyá. In physical appearance they resembled the Bhuiyás of that part of the country, and were fair,

---

[1] Dalton, *Ethnology*, p. 149. Thakuráini, it should be stated, is the name of a range of hills in the north of Keunjhar.

well-made, and intelligent. They worshipped Káli, with several minor tutelary deities. In matters of food they appear to have been rather exclusive. A Bendkar would take water from a Ho, but would not eat with him, nor would he touch any food that had been cooked by a Hindu. Their material condition was extremely poor. They possessed no cattle, and only a few fowls. The houses were mere hovels, not massed together in villages, but dotted about on the hillside in separate groups of two or three, like those of Birhors in Palámau. The crops usually cultivated were maize, high-land rice (*gora dhán*), and gram (*chaná*), which were grown in straggling fields formed by banking up the hillside water-courses. Edible jungle products were largely used for food, and frequently made up an entire day's subsistence. They paid no rent for their land, but were liable to be called upon for *begári* or gratuitous labour by the Rájá of Kalikáprasád in Keunjhar. Their funeral ceremony consisted in simply burning the dead body; they did not collect the ashes from the pyre, nor did they, like the Kols, destroy any of the deceased person's property with his corpse.

Dancing.

In writing of the same people Colonel Dalton[1] specially notices their style of dancing:—"The girls dance with their heads covered, bodies much inclined, and faces looking to the ground or to their feet, which have to perform a somewhat intricate step; the right hand holds down at arm's length the portion of the dress that is thrown over the head. The men, playing on tambourines or half drums, sing as they dance. The girls appear too intent on their steps to respond to them; but their peculiar attitude in the dance, the steps, and the melody, are the same for all Bhuiyás, and are unmistakeable characteristics of the race from the Ganges to the Mahánadi. The Kolarian dances are quite different." It seems to me that the argument from similarity of custom to tribal affinity has in this case been pressed too far. Subject races everywhere have not been slow to imitate the usages of the dominant people with whom they were brought into contact, and the Savars have been too long under the virtual control of the Bhuiyás for it to be at all surprising that they should have adopted the dances characteristic of the latter. The Kolarian races, on the other hand, have either maintained their isolation and independence or have been brought in contact only with Hindus, whose ideas on the subject of dancing would certainly not commend themselves to a sociable non-Aryan community.

Mode of agriculture.

Regarding the Bendkar methods of agriculture, Colonel Dalton[2] observes—"When first I saw the Bendkar hand-plough it was of wood,—only a branch cut with a large piece of the stem, from which it sprung attached, and that shaped so as to give it the appearance of a miniature Native plough; but they have improved on this, and now insert a piece of iron as a share, in further imitation of the Native plough. The implement answers well enough in preparing for seed the light

---

[1] *Ethnology of Bengal*, p. 150.
[2] *Ditto*, p. 153.

vegetable mould of the forest, to which they confine their cultivation; but in a stiff clay it would be inoperative. The hill Bendkars cultivate *kangni* (Panicum Italicum), *kheri, khodo* (Eleusine coracana) or *maruá, gangoi makai* (Zea mays) or maize, a species of coxcomb, the seeds of which they eat, a cereal called *siko*, and a large bean, which is intoxicating or acts as an emetic if eaten raw, but is pleasant and wholesome when well cooked; also *urid.* They have ordinarily no rice cultivation. They know well and use all the spontaneous edible productions of the forests, and showed me some wild yams, which they largely consume; they take an immensity of cooking." Here the suggestion seems to be that the Bendkar plough was consciously shaped in imitation of the implement commonly in use in India. It is, however, possible, and I think on the whole more probable, that it represents the earliest form of the Indian plough—a type which, though improved out of all recognition in the plains, may still be traced back to the clumsy wooden hoe which the Bendkar drags after him through the light ashes of his plot of *jhum* land.

Social status.

The social position of the Orissa Savars, like that of many non-Aryan tribes, does not admit of precise definition. Hindus alone are recognized members of the caste system, and the Savars have not yet come to be admitted as members of the Hindu community, though their promotion to that position cannot long be deferred. Their first step will doubtless be to provide themselves with Brahmans, as the Savars of Bankura have already done. The latter affect to maintain a high standard of ceremonial purity, and will not take cooked food from the hands of any one except a Brahman. Their pretensions, however, are not admitted by their neighbours, and at present their social rank is certainly not higher than that of Bágdis, Lohárs, Koras, and similar castes who hang on the outskirts of the Hindu social system.

The following table shows the number and distribution of the Savar tribe in 1872 and 1881:—

District.	1872.	1881.	District.	1872.	1881.
Midnapur	......	1,402	Tributary States, Orissa...	36,845	20,871
Cuttack	16,589	20,217	Singbhum	277	494
Puri	14,179	17,238	Manbhum	......	197
Balasore	446	692	Tributary States	106	190

Savar-Munda, a sub-tribe of Mundas in Chota Nagpur.

Sawani, a sept of Gonds in Chota Nagpur.

Sáwant, a section of the Magahiyá sub-caste of Doms in Behar.

Sawási, a synonym for Pán.

Sayar, a synonym for Savar.

Sebak, a title of the so-called pure Sudras who perform personal service for Brahmans.

Sebaka or Murhia, a group of the Pandá sub-caste of Utkal Brahmans.

Seduah, a sept of Limbus in Darjiling.

Sege, a sept of Chakmás in the Hill Tracts of Chittagong.

Segmang, a *thar* or sept of the Bárah-Gurung sub-tribe of Gurungs in Darjiling.

Segul, a sept of Rájputs in Behar.

Sejagá, a *gáin* of the Sándilya *gotra* of Rárhi Brahmans in Bengal.

Sekowa, a sept of Chakmás in the Hill Tracts of Chittagong.

Sekrá, a synonym for Sarnakár.

Sekri, a sweeper caste of Eastern Bengal, now converted to Islam and admitted to worship in the mosque and to the privilege of burial in the public graveyard. With their conversion the Sekris have abandoned their original occupation and now taken to cultivation and to the manufacture of lucifer matches, or rather spills of wood tipped with sulphur. All of them assume the title Shaikh, of which Sekri may perhaps be a derivative. Their personal names are generally taken from the day of the week, or from the month in which they were born. Thus Shaikh Ramazán and Shaikh Itwári are common appollations.

Sekwahdeng, a sept of Limbus in Darjiling.

Sem, a title of Kaibarttas in Bengal.

Semanohangiar, a sept of Lohars in Chota Nagpur.

Semárbár, a sub-caste of Beldárs in Behar.

Semári, a sub-caste of Kaibarttas and Gonrhis in Behar.

Semarkanda, root, a sept of Mundas in Chota Nagpur.

Semarwár, a sub-caste of Nuniás in Behar.

Semerya, a sub-caste of Barais in Behar.

Semraián, a section of Bábhans in Behar.

Sen, a family title of Siddha Baidyas, Báruis, and Mayarás; of Dakshin-Rárhi and Bangaja Káyasths and of Subarnabaniks; of Báitis, Sánkháris, and of Támbulis in Bengal.

Senápat, a section of Maghaiya Kumhárs in Behar.

Senápati, general, a group of the Srotriya sub-caste of Utkal Brahmans; a title of Khandáits in Orissa.

Senbhumiá, a sub-caste of Telis in Western Bengal.

Sendara-Nagasia, a sub-tribe of Nágesars who use *sindur* at marriage.

Senduriár, a *pur* or section of Sákadwipi Brahmans in Behar.

Sene, a sept of Limbus in Darjiling.

Senel, a *dugu* or section of the Kochh-Mandai in Dacca. The name indicates the original habitat of the group, probably a hill or village in Assam, and has no bearing upon marriage.

Sengár, a sept of the Chandrabansi division of Rájputs in Behar.

Sengra, horse, a totemistic sept of Mundas in Chota Nagpur.

Senihang, sons of the snow-chief, a sept of the Phedab sub-tribe of Limbus in Darjiling.

Senpuriá, a section of Banodhiá and Jaiswár Kalwárs in Behar.

Senthá, a sept of the Rautár sub-tribe of Thárus in Behar.

Seonáráyani, a religious sect found in Behar. See *Sivnáráini*.

Seorniá, a sept of Mundas in Chota Nagpur.

Sepári, a sub-caste of Goálás in Behar.

Serhar, a kind of bird, a totemistic sept of Mundas in Chota Nagpur.

Serling, the thief, a sept of the Yangorup sub-tribe of Limbus in Darjiling.

Serma, rent-collector, a sept of the Pánthar sub-tribe of Limbus in Darjiling.

Serwa, a section of Mangars in Darjiling.

Set, *Seth*, a chief merchant, from Sanskrit *sreshtha*, 'best' or 'chief,' (i) a title of Telis; (ii) a leading banker or trader among the Marwari Baniyás, usually Jains; (iii) a section of the Oswál Baniyás.

Set or Set-tálwár, a section of the Chárjáti sub-caste of Khatris in Bengal.

Setarapa, dog-eater, a totemistic sept of Mundas in Chota Nagpur.

Seth, a section of the Banodhiá and Jaiswár Kalwárs in Behar.

Setisurwál, a *thar* or sept of Mangars in Darjiling.

Setu, a *gáin* of the Sábarna *gotra* of Bárendra Brahmans in Bengal.

Setu-Suruál, a section of Kámis in Darjiling.

Seuli, people of different lower castes in Central Bengal who extract the juice of the date-palm and prepare molasses from it. See **Siuli**.

Sewar, moss, a totemistic sept of Mundas in Chota Nagpur.

Shahá, a sub-caste of Sunris in Eastern Bengal who have given up their original and taken to other professions, and thereby raised themselves above their caste brethren who sell wine, so that at present they consider the Sunris to be a caste different from, and considerably inferior to, them.

Sháha, a synonym for Sunri.

Sháhá, see **Sáhá**.

Sháhi Ugrakhatri, a sub-caste of Aguris in Western Bengal bearing the title Sháh.

Shaini, a *dugu* or section of the Kochh-Mándái in Dacca.

Shakya Láma, a *thar* or sept of Gurungs in Darjiling.

Shalankyana, a *gotra* or section of the Baidya caste in Bengal.

Shang-dah-bo, a *rui* or sept of the Tongdu sub-tribe of Dejong Lhoris, whose ancestor was born at his maternal uncle's when some tutelary deities were being propitiated.

Shári, a synonym for Bhát.

Shehedpuria, a section of Maghayá Dhobis in Behar.

Shelo, sub-tribe of the Bhumij tribe in Chota Nagpur who are iron-smelters.

Sheo, a *thar* or sept of Mangars in Darjiling.

Sheor, fish, a totemistic sept of Kharwars in Chota Nagpur.

Sherbá Khor, a section of Murmis in Darjiling.

Shergarhiá, a sub-caste of Lohárs in the Santál Parganás.

Shewa, a *thar* or sept of Dámis in Darjiling, whose chief profession is sewing.

Shikhu Karmakár, a sub-caste of Kámárs in Noakhali.

Sikkhdar, *Shikdar, Sikdar,* a title of Sudras in Eastern Bengal; an honorary title of Káyasths and Nápits in Bengal; an officer in charge of a *shikk* or fiscal division under the Mahomedan revenue system; a title of Brahmans, possibly of families descended from some one who held the office of shikdar; a title of Kapális and Sunris.

Shirasina, a sub-caste of Sunris in Maldah.

Shoályiá, a sept of Chakmás in the Hill Tracts of Chittagong.

Shushichá, a *thar* or sept of Sunuwárs in Darjiling.

Shyag-chom-bo, a *rui* or sept of Dejong Lhoris, the members of which are the descendants of emigrants from Bhotan and Nepal.

Shyag-ding-pá or **Shyag-tshang-pá,** a *rui* or sept of the Rui-chhung sub-tribe of Dejong Lhoris or Bhotias of the south.

Shyag-tsangpá, a *rui* or sept of Dejong Lhoris, the members of which form the lowest class of Bhotias.

Shyah-pá, a *rui* or sept of Dejong Lhoris whose ancestor had emigrated from North Bhotan.

Shyang-ba, a *rui* or sept of Sherpa Bhotias of Nepal.

Siár, jackal, a totemistic section of Kurmis in Chota Nagpur and Orissa; a sept of Asuras.

Siárahá, a section of the Banodhiá and Jaiswár Kalwárs in Behar.

Siárik, a *gáin* of the Sábarna *gotra* of Rárhi Brahmans in Bengal.

Siár Tuyio, jackal, a totemistic sept of Mundas in Chota Nagpur.

Sibala, a sub-sept of the Besrá sept of Santáls.

Sibingáre, a sept of the Agniá sub-tribe of Meches in the Darjiling Terai.

Sib-rási, a section of Málos in Eastern Bengal.

Siddh, a *thar* or sept of Gurungs in Darjiling.

Siddha, a hypergamous group of the Bárendra Káyasths in Bengal.

Siddhal, a *gáin* of the Sábarna *gotra* of Rárhi Brahmans in Bengal.

Siddha-Maulik, a hypergamous group of the Dakshin-Rárhi Káyasths in Bengal.

Siddha-Srotriya, a hypergamous group of Rárhi Brahmans in Bengal.

Siddhi-putra, a synonym for Bhuinmáli.

Sidhpur, a *mul* or section of the Chhamuliá Madhesiá sub-caste of Halwáis in Behar.

Sidhyál, a *thar* or section of Nepáli Brahmans.

Sidup or Siduk, a bundle of straw, a sub-sept of the Saren sept of Sántals.

Sigadiá, a section of Goálás in the North-Western Provinces and Behar.

Sihari, a *gáin* of the Sándilya *gotra* of Bárendra Brahmans in Bengal.

Sihásme-Khor, a *mul* of the Sándil section of Maithil Brahmans in Behar.

Sihásme-Sihásam, a *mul* of the Sándil section of Maithil Brahmans in Behar.

Sihogiá, a section of Bábhans and a sept of Rájputs in Behar.

Sihoriá, a section of Bábhans in Behar.

Sihujiá, a section of Bábhans in Behar.

Sijapati, a *thar* or sept of Mangars in Darjiling.

Sikalgar, a section of the Maghayá sub-caste of Barhis in Behar; a title of Lohárs or Kámárs.

Sikári, a section of Kumhárs in Singbhum.

Sikáuriár, a *pur* or section of Sákadwipi Brahmans in Behar.

Sikbandhera, a section of the Ariár sub-caste of Bais Baniyás in Behar.

Sikcharo, a bird, a totemistic sept of Mundas in Chota Nagpur.

Sikdár, a sept of Mál Pahariás; a hypergamous group of Kaibarttas in Bakarganj.

Sikhariá, a sub-caste of Bauris, Karangás, Korás, and Kurmis in Chota Nagpur, who derive their name from Sikharbhum, the tract of country north of the Dámudar river, corresponding roughly to the limits of the Pachet estate. In this connexion it deserves notice that Samet Sikhar is an old name for Párasnáth Hill, which is conspicuously visible from every part of Sikharbhum, and may almost be looked upon as forming the western boundary of the tract. See Statistical Account of Hazaribagh, p. 217. In the case of the Bauris, the Sikhariá sub-caste is also called Gobariá, which may perhaps have some reference to *gobar*, 'cow-dung,' as Bauri women earn money by making the cow-dung cakes used for fuel; a sub-caste of Rajwárs, and of Doms in South Manbhum.

Sikhariá or Sindurtopá, a sub-caste of Telis in Western Bengal.

Sikhariyá or *Meno*, a sub-tribe of Bhumijs in Chota Nagpur.

Sikhoriá, a sub-caste of Sunris in Behar who deal in liquor.

Sikhwád, a section of Goálás in the North-Western Provinces and Behar.

Sikiá, a *mul* or section of the Chhamuliá Madhesiá sub-caste of Halwáis in Behar.

Sikilgar, a cleaner of weapons.

Sikiyá, chain, a sub-sept of the Murmu sept of Santáls.

Sikrá, hawk, a totemistic sept of Mundas and Páns in Chota Nagpur.

Sikrar, a *pangat* or section of Bánsphor Doms in Behar.

Sil, a title of Subarnabaniks and Nápits; of Dakshin Rárhi and Bangaja Káyasths and of Tántis in Bengal; a section of Oswál Baniyás in Behar.

Silaichiá, a section of Sonárs in Behar.

Ṣilári (Sansk. *Silá*, a stone), a magician employed in Eastern Bengal to protect crops from hailstones. Formerly the Ṣilárí, like the Gárapagárí of the Central Provinces, was a paid village servant; and officiated as priest at an annual festival performed for the benefit of the crops. Now the festival has fallen into disuse, and a member of any caste may become a Ṣilárí, being remunerated in kind—it is unlucky to give him money—according to the success of his enchantments. Chaṇḍáls, Jogís, and Bairágis are the ordinary Ṣilárís, but a Muhamadan often acts as one, his co-religionists believing as implicitly in this occult science as their Hindu brethren.

"At the present day," says Dr. Wise, "this magical art is falling into disrepute, and it is no unusual thing for the peasantry to punish a Ṣilárí who fails to protect their fields. The Ṣilárís confess that their skill is inadequate to call down a storm on a neighbour's crop, as was formerly done; but they still profess ability to drive away a cloud threatening any tract of country.

"As hailstorms in Bengal occur usually in March and April, when the Boro-dhán, or spring rice, is in the ear, the services of the magician are called for in low lands, where this crop is cultivated. When a storm is impending the Ṣilárí, summoned by the peasantry, rushes, almost naked, from his hut, with a rattan wand in his right hand. Invoking Parameṣwara, the supreme god, he ascends a mound, where, spreading abroad his hands, and waving his rod to indicate the direction the storm-cloud is to take, he recites one or other of the following doggerel incantations in the vernacular:—

I.

O Narasiṇha! Narasiṇha! mighty Narasiṇha! whom the fourteen gods fear;
On hearing the name Narasiṇha the gods and spirits bend their heads;
My Guru's name is Híra. Wherever you go that quarter of the world is subdued,
Whether it consists of hills or mountains, trees or jungle.
Should this charm of mine fail, Mahádeva's hair will be uprooted and fall off.

II.

Diamonds cut stones.
Rivers retire before them.
A gold knife is keen as a diamond.
I have cut it this day into thirty-two.
Begone to the mountains of the north
Having paid you tribute to the south.
Having scattered you, I go home.
My name is Siva Ṣankara.

"The above metrical rhapsody was obtained from Rái Chánd Bairági, a celebrated Ṣilári, residing at Shámgáon, in Tipperah."

Silewár, a sept of Rájputs in Behar.

Silhatia or *Sirotia*, a sub-caste of Dosádhs in Behar.

Silhotia or *Jeswar Kurmi*, a sub-caste of Dhánuks in Behar who call themselves *Kulin*.

Silli, a sept of the Patar sub-caste of Mahilis called after the ancestral burying place of the group; a kind of fish, a totemistic sept of Korwas and Páns in Chota Nagpur.

Silongchhá, a *thar* or sept of Khambus in Darjiling.

Silotháer, a section of Majraut Goálás in Behar.

Simalwál, a section of Goálás in the North-Western Provinces and Behar.

Simar, a section of Kamár-kalla Sonárs in Behar.

Simarlásá, a tree, a totemistic section of Ghásis in Chota Nagpur.

Simarloká, a sub-caste of Ghásis in Chota Nagpur.

Simbi, a *gáin* of the Bharadwája *gotra* of Bárendra Brahmans in Bengal.

Simkhárá, a *thar* or section of Nepáli Brahmans.

Simlái, a *gáin* of the Kásyapa and Bátsya *gotras* of Rárhi Brahmans in Bengal.

Simli, a *gáin* of the Bátsya *gotra* of Bárendra Brahmans in Bengal.

Sinágar, a *mul* or section of the Chhamuliá Madhesiá sub-caste of Halwáis in Behar.

Sincheuli, a *thar* or sept of Mangars in Darjiling.

Sinchiori, a section of Kámis in Darjiling.

Sindhikuriá, a totemistic sept of Páns in Chota Nagpur who cannot touch the horns of a bull.

Sindhurishi, a section of Telis in Bengal.

Sindhwatiá, a section of Bhats.

Sindur, a totemistic sept of Mundas in Chota Nagpur who do not use vermilion in marriages.

Sinduriá, *Sindurhár*, a class of Bania who sell *sindur* or vermilion; also a class of Brahmans or Kayasths who formerly practised as inoculators, but are now employed as vaccinators; a sub-caste of Máls in the Santál Parganás.

Sinduriá, a red paint, a section of Binjhiás; a sept of Rájputs.

Sing, a title of Khambus and Mangars in Darjiling.

Singá-ore, a section of Kámis in Darjiling.

Singar, a section of Murmis in Darjiling; a sept of Kaurs in Chota Nagpur.

Singauri, a *thar* or sept of Mangars in Darjiling.

Singden, a section of Murmis in Darjiling.

Singdiár, a *gáin* of the Sábarna *gotra* of Bárendra Brahmans in Bengal.

Singdyang, a sept of Lepchas in Darjiling.

Singh, a title of Oswál Banyás, Bábhans, Goálás, Kshatriyas, Kurmis, and Rájputs in Behar; a title of Subarnabaniks in Manbhum. Intermarriage is prohibited within the title. A section and a title of Káyasths in Behar; a section of Rajwárs; a sept of Mundas and Páns in Chota Nagpur whose totem is horn; a title of Támbulis in Bengal.

Singhal, a *gotra* or section of the Agarwáls in Behar.

Singháras, a section of Madhesiá Halwáis in Behar.

Singhazári, a sub-caste of Sunris and Telis in Western Bengal.

Singhi, fish, a sept of Páns in Chota Nagpur; a section of Oswáls.

Singh-rási, a section of Málos in Eastern Bengal.

Singhror, a section of Goriá Goálás in Behar.

Singi, horn, a totemistic sept of Chiks in Chota Nagpur.

Singjangkuk, a sept of Limbus in Darjiling.

Singjuk, a sept of Limbus in Darjiling.

Singogpa, a sept of the Phedáb sub-tribe of Limbus in Darjiling.

Singpuriá, a sept of Birhors in Chota Nagpur.

Singyál, a *thar* or section of Nepáli Brahmans.

Sing-yangma, a sept of the Phágu sub-tribe of Yakhas in Darjiling.

Sinha, lion, a title of Khandáits in Orissa; of Káyasths and Subarnabaniks in Bengal; of Rájus in Midnapur.

Sinhi, a section of Kumhárs in Singbhum.

Sinhiniá, a sept of Rájputs in Behar.

Sinjali, a *thar* or sept of Mangars in Darjiling.

Sinjhikhariá, a sept of Páns in Chota Nagpur.

Sinjikuria, a sept of Chiks in Chota Nagpur.

Sinkoi, a sept of Hos in Singbhum.

Sipáhi, a title of Rájputs in Behar.

Sipahiyá, a section of Bánsphor Doms in Western Behar.

Sir, arrow, a totemistic sept of Goálás in Chota Nagpur.

Sirá, a section of Maghayá Kándus in Behar.

Sirasinthi, a *gáin* of the Bharadwája *gotra* of the Uttar-Bárendra Brahmans in Bengal.

Sirasthán, a sub-caste of Kumhárs in Pabna.

Siriár, a section of Bábhans in Behar.

Sirkar, a section of the Bánsphor sub-caste of Doms in Behar.

Sirkiá, 'the dweller in a *sirki* hut,' a designation of Nats, Bediyás, and other wandering castes of the gipsy type, derived from the materials of the temporary huts which they build.

Sirmaur, a sept of Rájputs in Behar.

Sirmauriár, a *pur* or section of Sákadwipi Brahmans in Behar.

Sirnáit, a sept of the Surajbansi division of Rájputs in Behar.

Sirnet, a sept of Rájputs in Behar.

Sirniá, a sept of the Surajbansi division of Rájputs in Behar.

Sirotá, a sub-caste of Dhanuks in Behar.

Sirpur, a section of the Tirhutiyá sub-caste of Doms in Behar.

Sirsait, a section of Bábhans in Behar.

Siruar, a sept of Birhors in Chota Nagpur.

Sirwár, a section of the Dhaprá and Pachainyá sub-castes of Doms in Behar.

Sisab, a section of Karan Káyasths in Behar.

Sisaundiá, a section of Sonárs in Behar.

Sisauriá, a *mul* or section of the Ayodhiábási sub-caste of Sonárs in Behar.

Sisingi, a river fish with two thorns on its head, a totemistic sept of Kumhars in Chota Nagpur.

Sisodhiá, a sept of Surajbansi Rájputs in Behar.

Sisodiá, a section of Goálás in the North-Western Provinces and Behar.

Sisoniá, a sept of Rájputs in Behar.

Sisotár, a *mul* or section of the Chhamuliá Madhesiá sub-caste of Halwáis in Behar.

Sisungi, fish, a sept of Mundas in Chota Nagpur.

Sisutbansi Loharia, a sub-caste of the Lohar caste (iron-smith); also called Lohondia.

Sit, a title of Telis in Bengal.

Sitali, a *gáin* of the Sábarna *gotra* of Bárendra Brahmans in Bengal.

Sitár-Dhobá, a sub-caste of Dhobás in Eastern Bengal.

Sithung, a *thar* or sept of Mangars in Darjiling.

Siuli or *Seuli*, a sub-caste of Háris in Bengal; a title of Chandáls, Doms, Haris and similar lower castes, as well as Mahomedans who extract juice from date-trees for the manufacture of *gur*, molasses, or toddy.

Siva, a section of the Mahmudábáz sub-caste of Nápits; of Jugis and Kapális; of Rautiás.

Siva-bansi, *Sivakul*, a synonym for, and a title of, Kochh or Rájbansi, probably a vague term for worshippers of Siva, in use among natives of Kuch Behar, many of whom claim to be Sivabansi, descended from Siva.

Sivnáráini, a worshipper of Siva and Naráyan, a class of religious sectarians who live a secular life.

Siwarwár, a sub-caste of Nuniás in Behar.

Siyár, a section of the Pargah caste in Behar.

Skandhasura, a synonym for Karadh.

Smár, Swar, a title of Dákshin-Rarhi and Bangaja Káyasths.

Smatti, a sept of Pators in Chota Nagpur.

Smritiratna, a literary title of Brahmans.

Soa, a kind of vegetable, a totemistic sept of Mundas in Chota Nagpur.

Soai, a bird, a totemistic sept of Mundas in Chota Nagpur.

Soási, a synonym for Pán.

Sobarnarekhá, a sept of Mundas in Chota Nagpur.

Soberi, a *thar* of the Kausika *gotra* of Nepáli Brahmans.

Sobhádih, a *mul* or section of the Naomuliá or Majraut sub-caste of Goálás in Behar.

Sobhni Tajpur, a *mul* or section of the Naomuliá or Majraut sub-caste of Goálás in Behar.

Sochari, a section of Báis Sonárs in Behar.

Sodemba, the spy, a sept of the Phedáb sub-tribe of Limbus in Darjiling.

Soeka, a bush, a totemistic sept of Mundas in Chota Nagpur.

Sogani, a section of Saraogis in Behar.

Sohagrámi, a *gáin* of the Kásyapa *gotra* of Bárendra Brahmans in Bengal.

Sohanpur, a section of the Biyáhut and Kharidáhá Kalwárs in Behar.

Sohek, a kind of fish, a totemistic sept of Mundas in Chota Nagpur.

Sohidamochi, a title of Chamárs or Muchis.

Soi, spring, a totemistic sept of Mundas in Chota Nagpur.

Sokhait, a sept of the Rautár sub-tribe of Thárus in Behar.

Sokhwá, a sub-caste of Barais in Behar.

Sokiriá, a sub-caste of Sunris in Behar.

Sokoe, a kind of fruit, a totemistic sept of Mundas.

Sokulkárá, a sub-caste of Rajwárs in Chota Nagpur.

Solai, fish, a totemistic sept of Mundas in Chota Nagpur.

Soma, a family title of Kashta Baidyas and Kayasths in Bengal.

Somáj, a hypergamous division of the Paschim Kuliyá Sadgops.

Somal, deer, a sub-sept of the Kisku sept of Santáls.

Sombansi, a sept of Rájputs in Behar.

Somnidih Sagun Máhta Purukh, a *mul* or section of the Naomuliá or Majraut sub-caste of Goálás in Behar.

Somrishi, a section of Mayarás in Bengal.

Somwár, a sept of the Surajbansi division of Rájputs in Behar.

Son, a title of Bangaja Káyasths; a sub-sept of the Besrá sept of Santáls.

Soná, gold, a totemistic section of Kurmis in Chota Nagpur and Orissa; a totemistic sept of Goálás in Chota Nagpur who cannot wear gold.

Sonáchain, a section of the Chain sub-caste of Nuniás in Behar.

Sonaibar, a section of Bábhans in Behar.

Sonákánt, a section of the Biyáhut and Kharidáhá Kalwárs in Behar.

Sonaman, a section of Kanaujiá Lohárs in Behar.

Sonamati, a sept of Páns in Chota Nagpur.

Sonámdih, a *mul* or section of the Naomuliá or Majraut sub-caste of Goálás in Behar.

Sonaome, a sept of Lohárs in Chota Nagpur.

Sonápur Sakarwár, a *mul* or section of the Sátmuliá or Kishnaut sub-caste of Goálás in Behar.

Sonar, goldsmith, a sept of Bairágis and Kharwars in Chota Nagpur who do not wear gold.

Sonár, *Káin, Kainyá, Zargar*, the goldsmith caste of Behar; also engaged to some extent in money-lending and general trade. Concerning the origin of the caste little is known, and it appears to be an occupational group consisting of the members of respectable middle-class castes who adopted the business of working in the precious metals. Sonárs are not rich in traditions, and the few they have are of the ordinary mythological type, and throw no light on the antecedents of the caste. A common story is that in the beginning of time, when the goddess Devi was busy with the construction of mankind, a giant called Sonwa-Dwaitya, whose body consisted entirely of gold, devoured her creations as fast as she made them. To baffle this monster the goddess created a goldsmith, furnished him with the tools of his art, and instructed him how to proceed. When the giant proposed to eat him, the goldsmith suggested to him that if his body were polished his appearance would be vastly improved, and asked to be allowed to undertake the job. With the characteristic stupidity of his tribe, the giant fell into the trap, and having had one finger polished was so pleased with the result that he agreed to be polished all over. For this purpose, like Œetes in the Greek legend of Medea, he had to be melted down, and the goldsmith, who was to get the body as his perquisite, giving the head only to Devi, took care not to put him together again. The goldsmith, however, over-reached himself. Not content with his legitimate earnings, he must needs steal a part of the head, and being detected in this by Devi, he and his descendants were condemned to be for ever poor.

Traditions of origin.

The internal structure of the caste is shown at length in Appendix I. Both sub-castes and sections belong to the local or territorial type, and their names do not help us to trace a connexion between the Sonárs and other similar groups. The system of exogamy followed is very complete. A man may not marry a woman belonging to the same section as (1) himself, (2) his mother, (3) his paternal grandmother, (4) his maternal grandmother, (5) his father's paternal grandmother, (6) his father's maternal grandmother. In applying this set of prohibitions to any particular case, the sections of both parties are taken into account; so that if the proposed bride's mother belonged to the same section as the proposed bridegroom's maternal grandmother, no marriage would be possible, although the parties themselves both belonged to different sections. The standard formula for

Internal structure.

calculating prohibited degrees is also taken into consideration down to the seventh generation in the descending line.

Marriage.

All Sonárs who can afford to do so marry their daughters as infants; and when a girl's marriage is delayed after the age of puberty, poverty is usually the sole cause. The marriage ceremony corresponds in all essential particulars to that observed by the higher castes in Behar. In rich families it is considered right for the bridegroom to go on horseback to fetch the bride. Polygamy is permitted, but is rarely resorted to except when the first wife is childless. In the Kanaujiá, Ajodhia-puri, Mair, and Kamarkalla sub-castes widow-marriage is prohibited. The other sub-castes allow a widow to marry again, and ordinarily deem it incumbent on her to marry her late husband's younger brother. Among the Sonárs of Chota Nagpur the custom of widow-marriage is recognized in the devolution of property, which proceeds *per stirpes*, the shares being so divided that the sons of a *sagai* wife get six-sixteenths and those of a *bihai* wife ten-sixteenths between them. In Behar the ordinary law of inheritance is followed by the caste, but a daughter's son is excluded from succession by the nearest male of the same *kul* or section. The sub-castes which permit widow-marriage also allow divorce, which is effected with the sanction of the pancháyat when a woman is suspected of unchastity.

Religion.

The religion of the Sonár caste differs little from that of other orthodox Hindus of about the same standing in society. Some Vaishnavas are found among them; but most Sonárs belong to the Sákta sect, and pay especial reverence to Devi. The popular minor gods of Behar are also worshipped. For the service of the *di majores* of the standard Hindu Pantheon, Maithil or Tirhutiá Brahmans serve them as priests, and are received on equal terms by other members of the sacred order. In the cult of the minor gods, on the other hand, traces of a more primitive state of things may perhaps be discerned. Thus the offerings made to Goraiá are the perquisite of the Dosádhs, which looks as if the priests of the deity were at one time chosen from that caste; while the *pakwáns* or cakes given to Bandi are eaten by the members of the family. Some Sonárs worship a Mahomedan *pir*, Sháh Sharf-ud-din; and all offer up silver images of Bandi at marriages.

Disposal of the dead.

The dead are burned, and the standard ceremony of *sráddh* is performed on the thirteenth day after death. Libations for the benefit of ancestors in general are also presented in the first fortnight of Asin every year.

Social status and occupation.

The social standing of the caste is respectable, and their practice in the matter of diet does not differ materially from that of other orthodox Hindus in Behar. Brahmans take water and sweetmeats from the caste; while Sonárs themselves are on similar terms with Kewats, Dhánuks, and Goálás. In former days, it is said, they wore the sacred thread and abstained from spirituous drinks; but these marks of distinction have now fallen into disuse. Their chief occupations are working in metal, mostly in gold and silver, money-changing (*saráfi*), and *khichri-faroshi* or dealing in food-grains. In parts of the country where rent is paid in kind on the *bhaoli* system, Kanaujiá Sonárs usually act as weighmen, and receive an allowance of a quarter or half a seer to every maund weighed. A few Sonárs are landholders or cultivators themselves, but as a rule the connexion of the caste with agriculture is only the indirect one of lending money to the raiyat.

It is fair to add that the Sonár does not bear a high reputation for honesty. As a goldsmith he is suspected of substituting base metal for the gold or silver supplied to him in order to be made up into ornaments; as a money-lender he is charged with numberless devices for extorting money from his clients. A fair idea of the opinion held of the caste by the agricultural classes may be derived from the following verses :—

Kainyá dub dubiyá
Suthan le gai Tágo bhái
Ek Suthan menminuá ke dehu
Sab Suthan mangá lehu.

"As he crossed the ford the Kainyá was drowned,
The Bábhan stole his gold mohars away:
Give one to the Judge, and if justice be found,
You will get all the others within the day."

The story is that once upon a time a Sonár and a Bábhan went forth from the same village to seek their fortunes. Both returned at the same time and met on the road—the Bábhan almost penniless and the Sonár with a bag full of gold mohars. As they were crossing a river, the Bábhan decided to drown the Sonár and steal his money. The latter gave himself up to his fate, only asking his murderer to repeat the foregoing verses as his last message to his kinsfolk. The stupid Bábhan did so, and thus himself furnished the clue which led to the detection of the crime. The story affords a curious illustration of the popular estimate of the comparative intellectual capacity of the castes concerned. A somewhat similar tale, in which a Káyasth plays the part here assigned to the Sonár, is quoted in the article on Ghási.

The following statement shows the number and distribution of Sonárs in 1872 and 1881. In certain cases the figures of Sekrás and Subarnabaniks seem to have been included in the Census Reports.

District.	1872.	1881.	District.	1872.	1881.
Birbhum	......	715	Monghyr	13,348	18,167
Nadiya	......	1	Bhágalpur	9,646	16,917
Dinajpur	......	186	Purniah	9,419	8,000
Rangpur	......	1	Maldah	......	14
Pabna	......	20	Santál Parganás	3,758	4,281
Darjiling	......	865	Cuttack	13,987	117
Kuch Behar	......	16	Puri	5,990	832
Chittagong Hill Tracts ...	......	7	Balasore	4,297	671
Patna	21,101	23,278	Tributary States	4,670	457
Gya	16,258	15,909	Hazaribagh	4,352	6,822
Shahabad	14,997	18,139	Lohardagá	3,302	4,495
Tirhut { Mosufferpur ...	} 34,720	{ 23,899	Singbhum	178	251
Tirhut { Darbhanga ...		16,988	Manbhum	1,812	2,553
Saran	20,157	21,472	Tributary States	1,290	1,304
Champaran	11,288	15,037			

Sonár, a synonyn for Sarnakár or goldsmiths.

Sonārbaniá, a synonym for Subarnabanik.

Sonárekhá, a sub-caste of Korás in Chota Nagpur.

Sonarwa, a bird, a totemistic sept of Mundas in Chota Nagpur.

Sonarwar, gold, a sept of Kharwars in Chota Nagpur.

Sonaul, a *mul* or section of Kasarwáni Baniyás in Behar.

Sonbesra, a bird, a totemistic sept of Lohárs in Chota Nagpur.

Sonbhadriá, a section of Bábhans in Behar, so named after the village Sonbhadra; or who live on the banks of the Son river.

Soncheri, a section of Kanaujiá Sonárs in Behar.

Sone, a totemistic sept of Mundas in Chota Nagpur who cannot wear gold.

Sonechaurupekedándi, a *mul* or section of Kasarwáni Baniyás in Behar.

Sonerupekhichri, a *mul* or section of Kasarwáni Baniyás in Behar.

Sonewár, a *kul* or section of Bábhans in Behar.

Songbangphe, the new settler, a sept of the Pánthar and Phedáb sub-tribes of Limbus in Darjiling.

Songden, a section of Murmis in Darjiling.

Songyokpa, a sept of the Phágu sub-tribe of Yakhas in Darjiling.

Sonhar, a *mul* or section of the Chhamuliá Madhesia subcaste of Halwáis and of Biyahut and Kharidáhá Kalwárs in Behar.

Soni, a section of the Bárajáti sub-caste of Khatris in Bengal; a section of Oswáls and Saraogis in Behar.

Soniyár, a *pur* or section of Sákadwipi Brahmans in Behar.

Sonkhare, a section of Káyasths in Behar.

Sonkharihan, a place of worship before cutting grain, a totemistic sept of Mundas in Chota Nagpur.

Sonkhariká, a sept of Páns in Chota Nagpur.

Sonkoka, a sept of Pans in Chota Nagpur.

Son Maghaia, a sept of Lohárs and Mundas in Chota Nagpur.

Sonmain, a section of Maghaiyá Kumhárs in Behar.

Sonmanik, a sept of Chiks in Chota Nagpur.

Sonoár, gold, a sept of Agariás in Chota Nagpur.

Sonoáti, a sub-caste of Ghásis in Chota Nagpur.

Sonpur, a section of the Tirhutiyá sub-caste of Doms in Behar.

Sonpuri, a sub-sect of Vaishnavas.

Sonpuriá, a section of Lohárs and Sonárs in Behar.

Sonpursa, a section of the Dhusiá sub-caste of Chamárs in Behar.

Sonpuryá, a section of the Pachainyá sub-caste of Doms in Behar.

Son Tirki, a sept of Lohárs and a section of Goráits in Chota Nagpur.

Sonwan, a section of Ghásis in Chota Nagpur.

Sonwani, a totemistic sept of Goálás, Nagesars, who cannot wear gold; a section of Cheros in Chota Nagpur.

Sonwár, a synonym for Sunuwár.

Sonwasi, a sept of Chiks in Chota Nagpur.

Sonyokpa, the guardian of the new fort, a sept of Chaibisa sub-tribe of Limbus in Darjiling.

So-onkobu, a resident of So-onko, a sept of the Phedáb sub-tribe of Limbus in Darjiling.

Sorahaiyá, a synonym for Surahiyá.

Soraiyá, a section of Kanaujiá Brahmans.

Soraniá, a section of Cheros in Palámau.

Sorawár, a section of Bábhans in Behar.

Soriyár, a *pur* or section of Sákadwipi Brahmans in Behar.

Soso bheloa, a fruit, a totemistic sept of Mundas in Chota Nagpur.

Sote, Srotriya, a hypergamous group of Maithil Brahmans in Behar.

Sothángeh, a *thar* or sept of Khambus in Darjiling.

Sothiwár, a section of Lohárs in Behar.

Sothung, name of a village, a sept of the Phedáb sub-tribe of Limbus in Darjiling.

Soti, a *thar* or section of Nepáli Brahmans.

Sotri, a title of Bábhans in Behar.

Sowáni, a section of Mahesris in Behar.

Sparshan, a title of Muchis in Bengal.

Spashta Dáyaka, a sect of Vaishnavas, said to have been founded by one Rup Rám Kabiráj, a disciple of Krishna Chandra Chakravarti of Saidábád.

Srávak, literally, a hearer; (i) a lay member of the Jain religion; (ii) a Hinduised branch of Jains in Manbhum who appear to have lost their religion and become an ordinary caste.

Srávaka, a synonym for Sárák.

Srávak, a synonym for Sárák.

Sreshta-Khandait, a sub-caste of Khandáits in the Orissa Tributary States.

Srestikaran, (i) a title of traders generally; (ii) a title of the Madhyasreni Brahmans of Midnapur.

Sri, a sub-caste of Sutradhars in Noakháli.

Sriangabhatti, a *mel* or hypergamous sub-group of Rárhi Brahmans in Bengal.

Sribakariá, a section of Gonds in Chota Nagpur.

Sribarddhani, a *mel* or hypergamous sub-group of Rárhi Brahmans in Bengal.

Sribastab or *Bástar*, a sub-caste of Hajjams and Káyasths in Behar.

Sribitiá, a section of Madhesiá Kándus in Behar.

Sri-Gaura, a sub-caste of Gaura Brahmans.

Srikrishna, a sub-caste of Sutradhars in Noakháli.

Srimal, a section of Oswáls in Behar.

Srimaurhá, a section of the Banodhiá and Jaiswár Kalwárs in Behar.

Sringa, a *gáin* of the Bharadwája *gotra* of Bárendra Brahmans in Bengal.

Sringi, a *gáin* of the Sábarna *gotra* of Bárendra Brahmans in Bengal.

Sripáli, a *thar* or sept of Mangars in Darjiling.

Srisampad, a title of Brahmans.

Srishti-Karan, Bhatuntara, a sub-caste of Karans in Orissa.

Srisrimal, a section of Oswáls in Behar.

Srotriya, a hypergamous division of the Rárhi and Bárendra Brahmans in Bengal.

Srotriya or **Sásani**, a sub-caste of Utkal Brahmans in Orissa.

Srotriya, Sote, a hypergamous class of Maithil Brahmans in Behar.

Srutabati, a *gáin* of the Bátsya *gotra* of Bárendra Brahmans in Bengal.

Ssahoden, born in famine time, a sept of the Tambrkhola sub-tribe of Limbus in Darjiling.

Sser-Gomba, a *rui* or sept of Sherpa Bhotias of Nepal.

Sser-Lungchan, a *rui* or sept of Sherpa Bhotias of Nepal.

Sserpa, a *rui* or sept of Sherpa Bhotias of Nepal.

Sser-Phen-Zangná, a *rui* or sept of Sherpa Bhotias of Nepal.

Suá, a section of Goálás in Behar.

Suar, hog, a totemistic sept of Oraons; a section of Kahárs.

Suarait, a section of Bháts.

Suargane, a section of Bábhans in Behar.

Subansi, a sept of Chandrabansi Rájputs in Behar.

Subarna, a *gáin* of the Sándilya *gotra* of Bárendra Brahmans in Bengal.

Subarnabanik, *Baniá, Banik, Sarnabanik, Sonárbaniá*, a mercantile caste of Bengal Proper, who claim to be the modern representatives of the ancient Vaisya. In spite of the wealth and influence of the Subarnabanik, their high-bred appearance, and the notorious beauty of the women of the caste, their claim to this distinguished ancestry has failed to obtain general recognition. They are excluded from the ranks of the Nabasákha, or nine clean Sudra castes, and none but Vaidik Brahmans will take water from their hands. To account for the comparatively low status assigned to them the Subarnabaniks narrate a variety of traditions, some of which, however unsupported by historical evidence, deserve to be briefly mentioned here as illustrations of the kind of stories which would tend to grow up wherever the business talents and practical ability of a particular community advance it in the eyes of the world conspicuously beyond its rank in the theoretical order of castes. The Subarnabaniks say that their ancestors came to Bengal from Oudh during the reign of Adisura, who was struck by their financial ability and conferred on them the title of Subarnabanik, or trader in gold, as a mark of his favour. They then wore the Brahmanical

Traditions of origin.

thread, studied the Vedas, and were generally recognized as Vaisyas of high rank. The stories of their degradation all centre round the name of Ballál Sen, king of Bengal in 1070 (A.D.) His intrigue with a beautiful Pátni girl is said to have been ridiculed on the stage by some young men of the caste, while the Subarnabaniks in a body refused to be present at the penance whereby the king affected to purify himself from the sin of intercourse with a maiden of low caste. Another cause of offence is said to have been the refusal of a leading Subarnabanik to lend Ballál large sums of money to carry on a war with Manipur. Authorities differ concerning the method by which the king obtained his revenge. Some say that in the course of the penance already referred to a number of small golden calves had been distributed to the attendant Brahmans. One of these Brahmans was suborned by Ballál Sen to fill the hollow inside of a calf with lac-dye, and to take the figure to a Subarnabanik for sale. In testing the gold the Subarnabanik let out the lac-dye, which was at once pronounced to be blood. Having thus fastened upon the caste the inexpiable guilt of killing a cow, Ballál Sen publicly declared them and their Brahmans to be degraded, deprived them of the right to wear the sacred thread, and threatened with similar degradation any one who should eat or associate with them. Up to this time Subarnagram, near Dacca, had been the head-quarters of the caste in Bengal. Many had settled at Puri, in Orissa, beyond the jurisdiction of Ballál Sen, while others went to Gour in attendance on Lakhsman Sen.

In default of independent testimony to the accuracy of this tradition I do not see how it can be regarded as a narrative of historical events. It is no doubt conceivable that a despotic monarch might order the social degradation of a particular class of his subjects provided that it were not too numerous or too influential; and it is generally believed that Ballál Sen did effect some changes of this kind in the relative status of certain families of Brahmans. Notwithstanding this, the story of the depression of an entire caste from a very high to a comparatively low rank in the social system makes a very large demand on our belief, and inclines one to suspect that it may have been evolved in recent times to account for the position actually occupied by the caste being lower than that to which their riches and ability would entitle them to lay claim. From this point of view, Dr. Wise's conjecture that the Subarnabaniks are Hindustani Baniyás who lost rank by residing in Bengal seems to deserve some consideration.

Internal structure.

According to Dr. Wise the Subarnabaniks of Eastern Bengal recognize four sub-castes—**Banga**, **Dakhin-Rárhí**, **Uttar-Rárhí**, and **Saptagrámi** or **Nadiyá**. The Banga "claim to be descendants of Sonars resident in Bengal during the reign of Ballál Sen, and are undoubtedly the oldest branch of the family. Two Srenis are met with, Kulina and Varendra, or Maulika, inferior, which never intermarry. Every Maulika, however, asserts that he is a Kulina, and village Sonárs, by assuming similar claims, cause endless squabbles and feuds.

Ward distinguishes between the Sauvarna-kár and the Sauvarnabanik; the former being goldsmiths, the latter money-changers. It is remarkable that members of the Banga engaging in the caste profession of goldsmiths are styled Sankara, or mixed, baniks, and excommunicated from the society of their brethren. In the city of Dacca about forty families reside, twenty-five of whom belong to the pure town stock and fifteen to the Grámí, or rural. These two branches are still further sundered by having two distinct dals, or unions.

The Bangas have three gotras—Kásyapa, Gautama, and Vyása. The "Padavi," or titles, are—

Sena.	Borál.	Pál.
Dhar.	Maulika.	Sinha.
Datta.	Laha.	Aḍḍi.
Dé.	Chanda.	

The marriage ceremonies are copied from those observed at the wedding of Ṣrí Rámachandra and Ṣíta, while in Western Bengal the marriage service is that of Mahádeva and Párvatí. At the former the bridal pair, seated on stools, are carried round the court; at the latter the bridegroom stands while the bride is borne round him. The bride wears a red dress, as well as a lofty diadem (*mukuta*) with a red turban, from which tinsel pendants hang. The bridal attire becomes the perquisite of the barber; the dress worn on the second day falls to the Ghaṭaka.

The "Pradhán," or president of the caste assembly, is always a Kulina. The Kulina sometimes marries a Maulika girl when her dowry is large, but this alliance does not exalt her family.

The Banga Sonárs are jewellers, but as a rule do not manufacture ornaments. They are often bankers, traders, and shop-keepers. The poorer class accept employment as writers, but would sooner starve than cultivate the soil. The large majority are Vaishnavas, but a few follow the Tantric ritual.

In the city of Dacca reside about seventy families of the Dakhin-Ráṛhí sub-caste, who originally sought shelter in Eastern Bengal, along with the Uttar-Ráṛhí and Nadiyá Sonárs, from the Marhatta invasion of 1741. Among them rage interminable disputes about precedence, and the confusion is increased by the Padavis being the same as those of the Banga.

The houses of Nílámbara Datta and Potiráj Dé are reckoned the first of Kulinas, and next, but at a great interval, are the children of two brothers, Chanda and Madhu, who are Síls, and reside at Balgonah, in Burdwan. Families with the titles of Borál, Laha, Chand, and Aḍḍi are deemed more aristocratic than the Maulika.

The gotras of this division are—

Madhu Kulyá.	Sánḍilya.
Káṣyapa.	Savarṇa.
Gautama.	Bharadwája.

As a general rule the Dakhin-Ráṛhí do not intermarry with the Uttar-Ráṛhí, but take *púri*, or cake, from them, and even cooked food, if on friendly terms. The daughter of a Kulina marrying a Maulika bridegroom sinks to his level, but the daughter of a Maulika marrying a Kulina is raised to his. Dakhin-Ráṛhí women dress like other Hindu females of Eastern Bengal; the Uttar-Ráṛhí as women of Bardwan and Hughli.

The Dakhin-Ráṛhí worship Lakshmí daily, when rice, sugar, and flowers are offered, and no woman will touch food until this duty is performed. The "goddess of wealth" is also worshipped with especial honour four times every year.

The members of this subdivision are usually employed as writers.

Many peculiarities of their earlier home in Western Bengal are retained by the Uttar-Ráṛhí subdivision. The women still speak the Burdwan "Bháshá," or dialect, and their dress is that of Central Bengal. The gotras are many, and the following are the most important:—

Madhu Kulyá.	Kaṣyapa.
Ṣáṇḍilya.	Bharadwája.
Paráṣara.	Brahma Ṛishi.
Nága-Ṛishi.	Gautama.
Aliman.	Savarṇa.

The titles are the same as those of other Sonárs, but they have no Maulika. Their president is styled "Múrdhanya," a Sanskrit word for highest.

The Uttar-Ráṛhí still prepares the marriage space, called Marocha, which has been given up by the Dakhin-Ráṛhí, and the bride wears the lofty diadem and appendages of the Banga.

In Dacca there are about seventy families, the men being employed as clerks, accountants, and bankers. Only four annual festivals in honour of Lakshmí are kept, that on the Díwálí being omitted. Manasá Deví is propitiated with great ceremony, and on the Bhagíratha Dashará a branch of "Síj" (*Euphorbia ligularia*), sacred to the "goddess of snakes," is planted in the courtyard, and on every Panchamí, or fifth lunar day of each fortnight up to the Dashará of the Durgá Pújah, the Sonárs make offerings to it. On the great day of the feast, the Vijaya Daṣamí, the plant is plucked up and thrown into the river.

The Saptagrámi or Nadiyá subdivision constitutes a small body, numbering some thirty-five households. Driven from their former homes by the Marhattas, they crossed the Ganges and settled in Dacca.

The principal gotras are—

Madhu Kuliyá.	Savarṇa.
Nága-Ṛishi.	Ṣúra-Ṣrí.
Ṣáṇḍilya.	

The patronymics are Síl, Borál, Pál, Sena, Maulika, Dé, Harí, Priya Dás, and Karaṇa Varí Dás.

Being a small community, the Nadiyá Sonárs intermarry with the Dakhin and Uttar-Ráṛhí, and easily obtain wives by giving a large dowry.

While the Ták-sál, or Mint, was open at Dacca, the Nadiyá Sonárs worked as *Son-dhoas*, gold-washers, or Niyáriyás, infusing and purifying metals, but since its closure they have worked as Sondhoas on their own account. The dust and refuse (*gád*) of goldsmiths' shops are bought for a sum varying from eight annas to five rupees a *ser*, according to the amount or nature of the business. The refuse being carefully washed, the metallic particles in the sediment are transferred to shallow earthen pans, and the larger separated by a skilled workman, or *Kárigar*. The smaller, mixed with cow-dung and a calx of lead, form a ball named *pindi* or *perá*. This ball being placed in a hole partially filled with charcoal, fire is applied, and as the lead melts it carries with it all gold and silver filings, forming a mass called *liná*. This *liná* is then dissolved in a crucible, and the gold and silver, being unmelted, are easily separated."

Dr. Wise's interesting information regarding the Subarnabaniks was collected by him nearly twenty years ago from members of the caste residing in the city of Dacca. Since that time a tendency towards the amalgamation of sub-castes seems to have set in. The Subarnabaniks of the present day do not seem to lay much stress on the distinction between the Uttar-Rárhí and Dakhin-Rárhí groups, and sometimes include both under the designation Rárhí. Members of the Rárhí sub-caste may, as is mentioned by Dr. Wise, marry into the Saptagrámi or Nadiyá sub-caste, subject only to the condition that the titles or family names of the parties shall not be the same.

Marriage.

Subarnabaniks marry their daughters as infants, and observe the standard marriage ceremony in vogue among the higher classes of Hindus. Betrothal, *nándi sráddha*—performed on the forenoon of the day of gift, and the formal gift of the bride on the same night, are the essential features of the ceremony.

The rules regarding the avoidance of marriage within the *gotra* or section, and the practice in the matter of prohibited degrees, are the same as are followed by the higher castes. Polygamy is permissible, but is rarely resorted to except in the event of failure of offspring by the first wife. Widow-marriage and divorce are under no circumstances allowed.

Religion.

The great majority of the caste belong to the Vaishnava sect of Hindus. Rádhá, Krishna, and Chaitanya, the modern incarnation of the latter, are their favourite objects of worship. Rádhá, the favourite mistress of Krishna, is in their view identical with Lakshmi, and a grain-measure (*kátá*, *kunki*, or *khunchi*) filled with paddy and shells, and daubed with vermilion, is worshipped daily as her emblem by the females of the family. In Central Bengal the goddess of learning, Bageswari, is also worshipped on the day following a marriage. For religious and ceremonial purposes the Subarnabaniks employ Brahmans of their own, who are not received on equal terms by other members of the sacred order. They claim nevertheless to be the descendants of certain Vaidik Brahmans of the highest learning and sanctity, who were opposed to the policy of Ballál Sen and elected to follow the fortunes of the Subarnabaniks even at the cost of sharing in their degradation.

Disposal of the dead.

The caste burn their dead and perform the ceremony of *sráddh* in the orthodox fashion on the thirty-first day The obsequies of persons who die a violent death are performed on the fourth day.

Social status and occupation.

The social status of the caste, according to the recognized scale of precedence, is comparatively low. They rank below the Navasakha, and the Brahmans who serve the higher castes will not take water from their hands. There seems nevertheless to be a tolerably widespread feeling that the standing allotted to them by tradition is ludicrously incompatible with their wealth and abilities, and with the aptitude which they have shown of late years for taking advantage of English education. Trade has always been their chief function, and it was as successful merchants that the families of Sil, Mallik, and Laha first won for themselves a place among the leading citizens of Calcutta. In the present generation Subarnabaniks have come to the front as officials, and have attained some literary distinction. They number among their community a District Judge, an Inspector of Schools, four Subordinate Judges, five Deputy Magistrates, and fifteen Munsifs. The Revd. Lal Behari Dey is well known in Bengal as the author of the clever *genre* novel *Govinda Sámanta,* while Babu Bholanath Chandra's *Travels of a Hindu* has certain quaint merits of its own which seem likely to keep its memory alive.

The following statement shows the number and distribution of Subarnabaniks in 1872 and 1881. In certain districts the figures of Sekrás and Sonárs seem to have been included in the Census Report of 1872 :—

DISTRICT.	1872.	1881.	DISTRICT.	1872.	1881.
Bardwan	12,313	4,754	Dacca	4,696	3,965
Bankura	5,259	6,683	Faridpur	2,280	2,643
Birbhum	5,262	3,467	Bakarganj	2,144	1,458
Midnapur	11,499	7,723	Maimansinh	3,106	3,522
Hughli	} 8,887	{ 5,511	Tipperah	1,841	2,046
Howrah		2,464	Chittagong	5,165	4,446
24-Parganás	27,615	2,370	Noakhali	1,190	1,570
Nadiya	6,928	3,766	Chittagong Hill Tracts ...	......	4
Khulna	......	2,799	Maldah	440	196
Jessore	6,929	3,073	Santál Parganás	......	1,541
Murshedabad	5,348	3,286	Hazaribagh	1,778	73
Dinajpur	888	27	Lohardagá	2,736	2
Rajshahye	869	815	Manbhum	6,486	7,725
Rangpur	414	299	Singbhum	233	......
Bogra	490	150	Cuttack	13,967	10,39
Pabna	947	93	Puri	5,990	4,197
Darjiling	40	......	Balasore	4,297	5,200
Jalpigori	81	579	Tributary States	4,670	719
Kuch Behar	......	128			5

Subarnabisayi, a sub-caste of Telis in Bengal.

Subarniá-panchbhá, a section of Bábhans in Chota Nagpur.

Suberi, a *thar* of the Bharadwája *gotra* of Nepáli Brahmans.

Subha or **Suffah** (chief), a title of Limbus in Darjiling.

Subharájkháni, a *mel* or hypergamous sub-group of Rárhi Brahmans in Bengal.

Suchait, a section of Oswál Baniyás.

Suchári, a *mul* or section of Sonárs in Behar.

Sudhá, a small caste of Orissa, who believe their original occupation to have been personal service, but are now for the most part engaged in cultivation. In the census of 1872 they appear to have been recorded under the name of Amáyat or Amát, which is one of their titles, and which, taken in connexion with their traditions of occupation, rather goes to suggest some affinity between them and the Amáts of Behar. Sudhás are divided into four sub-castes:—Bara-Sudhá, Sáno or Kabátkonia Sudhá, Pailá-Sudhá, and Butká-Sudhá. Concerning their exogamous groups my information is incomplete. The Bara-Sudhá profess to have gotras and to observe the rule that a man may not marry a woman of his own gotra. But I have not been able to ascertain the names of the *gotras*.

The most primitive of the three sub-castes regarding which tolerably full data are available appears to be the Butká-Sudhá. They are a nomadic race, who believe themselves to have immigrated into Orissa from Kerákhol in the Central Provinces. They wander about reclaiming waste lands and tapping date and palm-trees for their juice. Having found a suitable spot for their operations, they build small huts of mats, bamboos, and any light materials that are available and settle down for two or three years, deserting the place and seeking a fresh locality as soon as the soil shows signs of becoming exhausted. Marriage is adult, and courtship is a recognized preliminary; but after the parents have given their consent to an engagement it is not etiquette for the young people to meet until the marriage is celebrated. The marriage ceremony is simple. The parties sit side by side before a *bedi*, or elevated platform of earth, the bridegroom having the bride on his right. The headman (Beherá) of the caste ties their right hands together with a piece of string, which is afterwards untied or cut by the brother-in-law of the bridegroom, or the younger sister of the bride, who receives a piece of cloth from the bridegroom for doing him this service. Then some old women—not less than three or more than seven—sprinkle *atap* rice and turmeric powder over the couple and give them their blessing.

Widows may marry again. No regular ceremony is performed. The headman of the caste and the woman's relatives take her to her new husband's house and make her over to him. A feast is given to the caste if the bridegroom can afford it. Divorce is permitted with the sanction of the caste panchâyat, and divorced women are permitted to marry again in the same manner and by the same form as widows.

The regular Hindu deities seem to be unknown to the caste. They worship a goddess, called Pancha-Khanda (five swords), with offerings of he-goats, fowls and rice, which are partaken of by the worshippers. The full moon of the month of Aghran is the proper time for this sacrifice. The Beherá or headman of the caste officiates as priest at this and all other acts of public worship. The Butká-Sudhás have no Brahmans. The dead are burned and the ashes left on the spot. No sráddh ceremony is performed. The caste abstain from beef, but eat the wild buffalo, the wild boar, and domestic fowls.

The Bara and Sáno-Sudhá sub-castes have travelled further than the Butká on the road towards orthodox Hinduism. The first-mentioned group have entirely adopted infant marriage, while the Sáno, though still permitting adult marriage, regard infant marriage as the standard to which all respectable people should endeavour to conform. Widow remarriage, however, still holds its ground. A number of women headed by the barber's wife give the widow their blessing along with some *atap* rice and *duba* grass, and a priest mutters a few mantras. Divorced women may marry again.

For the service of the regular Hindu gods, the celebration of *sráddh*, and the like, Brahmans are employed, who are received on equal terms by other members of the sacred order. The goddess Khambeswar, a divinity of a more primitive type, having her chief seat in the wild country of Bod, is worshipped every year in the month of Bhadra with sacrifices of goats. The goddess is represented by a wooden peg (*khamba*) fixed in the ground, and the Brahmans take no part in her worship, which is conducted by a Dehuri or tribal priest supposed to be specially acquainted with the way of the local gods.

Bara-Sudhás believe military or personal service to have been their original occupation. Some of them hold service-tenures under the Chiefs of the Orissa Tributary Mahals, and the fact that they bear the title Páik seems to show that they must have formed part of the rude militia which once existed in that part of the country. The Sáno-Sudhá believe that their original profession was the cultivation and management of date and palm-trees, and regard the *katári* or pruning knife as their characteristic implement. The social status of both groups is considerably higher than that of the Butká Sudhá, who can hardly be reckoned as coming within the pale of Hinduism at all. The higher caste of Orissa Brahmans, Chhatris, Karans and Goalas take water and sweetmeats from the hands of the Bara and Sáno-Sudhás, but the Bhandáris or barbers alone will receive boiled rice from them.

Sudra, the lowest and servile caste in the fourfold grouping adopted by early Indian writers, and, in theory at least, more or less recognized by the Natives of India at the present day. The opinion has been expressed by Lassen[1] and concurred in by Zimmer[2] that the name Sudra is not of Sanskrit origin, but was probably the tribal designation of one of the chief aboriginal races of Hindustan who adopted the Aryan faith and were admitted as servile members of the Aryan polity. Tribes who followed the example of the Sudras were naturally enrolled in the same class, and thus came to be called by the same

Origin.

[1] *Ind. Alt.*, i, 947.
[2] *Alt. Ind. Leben*, 216.

name. Weber, on the other hand, thinks that the Sudra caste "was composed of various mixed elements, partly, perhaps, of an Aryan race which had settled earlier in India, partly of the aborigines themselves, and partly, again, of those among the immigrants, or their Western kinsmen, who refused adherence to the new Brahmanical order." It would be foreign to the purpose of this book to enter upon a lengthy examination of the position of the Sudra in relation to the other three castes of the Manavic system, or to discuss the vexed question how far the precepts of the Mánava-dharma-sástra were at any time in correspondence with the facts of actual life. The following extract from Mr. E. W. Hopkins' work on the subject sums up the main features of the social status of the Sudra as represented by Manu:—

"The Sudra, once-born, is to be regarded in two lights—the one as general representative of his caste, irrespective of his master, where he is the abject slave of the twice-born, whose touch is unholy, in whose presence the Brahman may not remain, contact with whom is as polluting as with the lowest wretches and outcasts; on the other hand, as the settled servant of one master in whose house he is perhaps born, where his position is by no means so ignoble, though the fact of his slavery and lowness cannot be done away with. The personal contact with the Brahman is here greatly eased of the strict abhorrence with which the *dwija* is bound in general to regard the Sudra caste. As a servant his position is not in many respects different from the, indeed, not comfortable, because dependent and servile, yet still endurable and not very severe, position of an American house-slave prior to 1860. It is true that the Sudra has no mercy to expect on insulting his betters, and torture and death may be the consequence; but so long as he retains a respectful demeanour towards the upper castes, he is tolerably secure from danger. His master may give him advice, and bestow on him such old furniture and goods as are no longer fitted for the Brahman himself. He has his family, and his wife is as carefully guarded from freedom with other castes as the wives of the upper orders. His daughter or wife, if wronged by the upper castes, have the right of law, and a heavy fine is visited upon the offender. His master has, indeed, the right of punishing him, but only, as in the case of son and wife, for his own good. The striking is, moreover, limited in kind, and the fact that he may not be smitten upon the back shows that even he had an honourable part of the body.[1] He may not study, nor hear the Vedas recited, but he may be present at the small family sacrifices and religious ceremonies, and is indeed even praised for so doing. His legal privileges are few, but his rights are granted him with the other castes. He has the right of demanding redress for an injury of personal character even from the Brahman himself. He is held separate from the very lowest, the mixed castes, and should hold himself from their occupations till driven thereto by want. He represents his master in occasional business matters. As a matter

[1] In the last two particulars he stood, indeed, upon a higher level than the Negro!—E. W. H.

of principle he can have himself no property, as all belongs to his master, but practically he is a householder and receives a support suited to his need, and has property returned him if it is stolen. He is enjoined not to acquire very much, but evidently often managed to do so; and if his property in the eye of the law is dependent on the whim of the Brahman, it is at least in respect to other castes not regarded as a fiction. The rights of the Sudra are generally on a graded scale in respect to the other castes, and here no distinction is made between family-slave and general Sudra.[1] Distinct mention of Sudra as teacher when others fail, and the possibility of his being a king, show that he sometimes gained a position superior to the one he generally occupies."[2]

The modern use of the term Sudra is not easy to define. "In the present time," says Mr. Beames,[3] "there are no Sudras and no Vaisyas; no Kshatriyas except the Rájput: only the Brahman is recognizable. The lower castes fused more readily than the higher, and the Sudras probably were soon absorbed in the mixed classes, and ceased to have any distinct existence as Sudras." A Native writer[4] dealing with the same subject takes much the same view as Mr. Beames, admitting that the Kshatriyas are represented by the Rájputs, while in Bengal, at any rate, the Vaisyas have fallen to the rank of Sudras. The Sudras, again, he divides into the four following classes:—

i. Satsudra, including the Káyasths and the Nabasákh.
ii. Jalácharaniya Sudra, being those castes not technically belonging to the Nabasákh group from whom Brahmans and members of the higher castes can take water.
iii. Jalabyahahárya Sudra, castes from whose hands a Brahman cannot take water.
iv. Asprishya Sudra, castes whose touch is so impure as to pollute even Ganges water.

Here it seems to me that in the attempt to reconcile the existing state of things with the traditional system, and at any cost to unearth the survivors of the fourth caste, the author quoted has given to the term Sudra a wider significance than is warranted by popular usage. It may of course be argued that the scheme propounded by Manu treats all men who are not twice-born as Sudras, and that the same principle, if applied at the present day, requires us to include every caste below the Rájput in that category.

---

[1] How far the legal arrangements of fines in personal injuries, etc., contained in Manu were regarded as matters of fact and had a practical working, and how far they were held as legal fiction resulting from a desire to adjust and systematise the relations of all four castes before the law with arithmetical exactness, cannot be my purpose to determine. That Yajnavalkya, however, as a rule follows the arrangement of Manu, and settles such cases also according to higher or lower rank, so well by stated amounts as by general determination, shows the relative worth of these laws was as valid with him as with Manu.

[2] *The Mutual Relations of the Four Castes according to the Mánavadharma Cástram.* Leipzig, 1881.

[3] *The Races of the North-Western Provinces*, vol. i, p. 167.

[4] *Sambandhanirnaya.* By Lál Mohan Vidyánidhi, p. 89 ff.

Still I do not believe that the castes classed as Asprishya would be spoken of by any Hindu as Sudras at all, though the members of any particular group might possibly in a vague kind of way claim that title for themselves. At the other end of the scale the classification is equally open to criticism. No place is assigned to the Baidyas, Khatris, and Bháts; while the Káyasths, though not technically twice-born, invariably claim to rank above the Nabasákh, and by virtue of their wealth and intelligence occupy a position which fully bears out their claim.

Failing, then, any classical and authoritative definition, we have only to consider what is ordinarily understood by the term. Both in Bengal and Behar I think it is commonly used to denote the entire group of castes from whose hands a Brahman can take water. Káyasths, Baidyas, Bháts, and Khatris are not generally spoken of or regarded as Sudras, though persons of a pedantic turn of mind, who are bent on finding survivals of the original fourfold division, would probably set down both Káyasths and Baidyas as technically Sudras. In Orissa the definition by water offered above seems to hold good in the main, but the Karan, or writer caste, does not hold so high a status as the Káyasths of Bengal, and ranks as a Sudra in popular estimation.

Internal structure.

Although in most parts of the country the term Sudra is not strictly speaking a caste-name at all, but rather a general designation of a certain number of castes, there appears to exist in the eastern districts of Bengal a numerous body of people who call themselves **Sudras**, and are also known by the names of **Ghulám** (slave), **Káyasth**, **Shikdár**, and **Bhandári**. They form a distinct caste, and as a rule marry only among themselves, though in Maimansinh and Sylhet they marry women of the Sunri caste, and even bestow their own daughters on Sunri bridegrooms. In the latter case the girl forfeits her caste, but her family are not held to be degraded. The origin of the Sudras is obscure, and some say that they are descended from individuals belonging to the Sat-Sudra group, who sold themselves or were sold as slaves to Káyasth masters, and thus, by discharging the same functions as were assigned to the ancient Sudras, came to be called by the same name. The following deed of sale, given to Dr. Wise by Babu Brijo Sundar Mittra, a member of one of the oldest and most respected Káyasth families of Dacca, is quoted in illustration of this view :—

"I, Rám Kisto Pál, son of Túla Rám Pál, and grandson of Rám Deva Pál, do hereby execute this deed of sale :—

"Owing to the debts incurred at my marriage, and which I am unable to pay, I, in my proper mind, and of my own free will, sell myself to you on my receiving a sum of Púrojonodohomasi[1] rupees twenty-five, and I and my descendants will serve you as slaves as long as we are given subsistence allowance and clothing. You, your sons,

[1] Mr. J. D. Ward, C.S., suggests the following reading and interpretation :—Púra (full), jana, or gana, dáhá (ten), másha. Each rupee was to value ten full máshas. A "másha" equalled 17⅓ grains, and a rupee ten máshas.

and grandsons shall make us work as slaves, and have power to sell or make a gift of us to others. On these conditions I execute this bond.

"Dated 19th Kártik, 1201 B.S. (November 1794)."

Dr. Wise adds that, although slavery is illegal, and has been so for many years, the buying and selling of domestic slaves still goes on, and it may be safely said that there is hardly a family of any distinction which has not several Bhándárís on its establishment. The life of the Nafr, or Shahna, as the slave is called in other parts of the country, is most congenial to the Bengali. With rare exceptions he is kindly treated, and in return he regards the welfare and happiness of each member of the family as inseparable from his own. Owing to the deaths of their masters many thousands are scattered throughout Bengal, who are found working at all trades, and in Chittagong, Noakháli, and Tipperah do not consider themselves degraded by holding a plough or wielding a mattock. In Bikrampúr they are often boatmen, while in Dacca Sudras are employed as confectioners, coolies, braziers, shop-keepers, and vendors of *pán* and Indian hemp. Even at the present day, however, any Sudra who is rich and provident can raise his family by judicious marriages with pure Káyasths as high as the Madhalya grade of that caste. Such families drop the title Sudra, and after a generation or two become absorbed in the ranks of recognized Káyasths. This circumstance is the more remarkable as the Sudras are certainly to some extent recruited from among castes inferior in social standing to the Káyasths. So far as I am aware, no parallel instance can be quoted within the range of the modern caste system. Thus, according to Dr. Wise, Brahmans, Baidyás, Sunris, and Baniyas possess slaves, but none of these castes have ever permitted their servants to rise in rank or assume an equality with their masters. It is suggested by the Káyasths that the Sudras of the present day are the descendants of the tribe resident in Bengal before the advent of the Kanauj families; but this conjecture is erroneous, for not only are individuals being added even now to the servile branch, but admissions such as that of Rám Kisto Pál, the subject of the deed of sale, who was a Telí by caste, can be proved by existing documents.

Marriage.

In the case of a girl the Sudras deem infant-marriage indispensable, and it would disgrace a family to have a daughter unmarried at the age of puberty. Their sections are the same as those of the Brahmans, and they observe the same set of prohibited degrees. They have, however, no hypergamous groups, such as Kulin or Maulik. A bride-price (*pan*) is paid to the parents of the bride, and girls seem as a rule to be rather in demand. This is probably due to the fact that the lower grades of pure Káyasths take wives from among the Sudras, but do not give their daughters to men of that class. For this reason there is a slight surplus of males in the Sudra group, and Sudra men often marry comparatively late in life, and always have to purchase their wives.

Social status.

For the rest, Sudras conform on the whole to the customs of the Káyasth caste. Widows are not allowed to marry again, and divorce is not recognized.

The status of the caste is respectable, and they rank immediately below the Nabasákh group. Brahmans take water from their hands, and will as a rule permit them to eat in the same room with themselves. Káyasths, except the very orthodox, will eat cooked food prepared by a Sudra. In matters of diet Sudras themselves follow the same rules as Hindus of the higher castes. In former years they used to eat the leavings of influential Brahmans, Baidyas, and Káyasths in whose houses they were employed as servants. This custom, however, is now dying out.

The following statement shows the number and distribution of Sudras in 1872 and 1881:—

DISTRICT.	1872.	1881.	DISTRICT.	1872.	1881.
Bankura	......	17	Dacca	......	17,392
Midnapur	23	12	Faridpur	86	15,109
Jessore	131	......	Bakarganj	8,969	9,573
Murshedabad	31	6	Maimansinh	8,617	13,842
Dinajpur	......	5	Tipperah	2,513	9,199
Rajshahye	......	16	Chittagong	30,738	28,112
Rangpur	36	......	Noakhali	4,292	2,212
Pabna	......	1	Chittagong Hill Tracts ...	......	13

Suga, parrot, a totemistic sept of Korwas and Mundas in Chota Nagpur.

Sugáin, a *gáin* or sub-section of Saptasati Brahmans in Bengal.

Sugardhar, a section of the Biyáhut and Kharidáhá Kalwárs in Behar.

Sugargane-Loám, a *mul* of the Parásara section of Maithil Brahmans in Behar.

Suia, a kind of little bird, a totemistic sept of Bediás, Kharwars and Lohárs in Chota Nagpur.

Suir, a synonym for Savar.

Sukalnaki, a sept of the Suryabansi sub-tribe of Rájputs in Behar.

Sukalvála, a group of the Ádi Gaura sub-caste of Gaura Brahmans.

Sukarbár, a sept of the Suryabansi sub-tribe of Rájputs in Behar.

Sukhar, a group of the Aoghar sect of Saiva ascetics founded in Guzerat by a Dasnámi mendicant named Brahmagiri. See **Aoghar**.

Sukhong, a sept of Limbus in Darjiling.

Sukhsárá, a *pur* or section of Sákadwipi Brahmans in Behar.

Sukli, a sub-caste of weavers in Western Bengal ranking below the Tantis. They use a wooden shuttle; the Tantis an iron one. Brahmans will eat sweetmeats, etc., in a Tanti's house, not in a Sukli's.

Sukli, a small cultivating caste peculiar to the district of Midnapur. Suklis claim to be the descendants of a Sulanki Rájput named Bir Singh, who came to Midnapur about six hundred years ago and built himself

Origin.

a fort at Birsinghpur in parganá Kedárkunda. The remains of the fort are still visible. It is flanked by two large mounds, called Mundamárui and Gardámárui, the former of which is said to cover the heads, and the latter the bodies, of seven hundred Bágdis who were slain by Bir Singh because they could not pronounce the word *hesh*, meaning a mat made of date-leaves. The legend goes on to say that after a time Bir Singh himself was defeated, and that his followers then discarded the sacred thread, changed the name Sulanki to Sukli, and settled down as cultivators. The internal structure of the caste throws no light on its origin. It is divided into three sub-castes—**Barabháiyá, Báhattarghari**, and **Dasásai**. The first, which is reckoned the highest in rank, is supposed to be descended from the twelve grandsons of Bir Singh. Their sections are of the ordinary Brahmanical type.

Internal structure.

Suklis marry their daughters as infants, forbid widows to marry again, and do not recognize divorce. For religious and ceremonial purposes they employ Brahmans, who however are not received on equal terms by other members of the sacred order. Most of them are Vaishnavas. They burn their dead and perform the ceremony of *sráddh* in the orthodox fashion on the thirty-first day after death.

Marriage.

Notwithstanding their conformity with all standard observances, the social position of Suklis is very low. They rank with Pods and Dhobás, and Brahmans will not take water from their hands. Agriculture is their sole occupation. A few hold tenures and small zamindáries, the bulk of the caste being occupancy raiyats.

Social status and occupation.

In the Census Report of 1872 the Suklis were included with the Tántis. The following statement, however, shows their number and distribution in 1881 :—

Bardwan ...	20	Hughli ...	46
Birbhum ...	2	Howrah ...	1,326
Midnapur ...	19,886	24-Parganás ...	339

Sukru, potato, a totemistic sept of Mundas in Chota Nagpur.

Suksárini, probably a class of religious mendicants.

Sukul, a title of Kanaujiá, Sáraswata and Gaura Brahmans in Behar.

Sukulbans, a sept of Rájputs in Behar.

Sukuliyá, a sub-caste of Chásás in Orissa.

Sukwabah, a sept of Limbus in Darjiling.

Sukwár, a sub-caste of Gulguliás in Gya and Hazaribagh.

Sulankhi, a sub-tribe of Rájputs.—Tod's *Rajasthan*, i, p. 74; *Sher.*, i, p. 122; a sept of the Chandrabansi division of Rájputs in Behar; a bird, a totemistic sept of Bediás and Mundas in Chota Nagpur.

Sultánpuriá, a section of Sonárs in Behar.

Sulunkhi-Mahili, a sub-caste of Mahilis in Manbhum who are generally labourers and servants.

Sumai, a kind of fish, a totemistic sept of Dhenuárs in Chota Nagpur.

Suman, a title of Bangaja Káyasths.

Sumat, a totemistic section of Turis, signifying a deer.

Sumedhiar, a tree, a totemistic sept of Kharwars in Chota Nagpur.

Sunaka, a *gotra* or section of Brahmans in Bengal.

Sunam, a *thar* or sept of Dámis in Darjiling whose chief profession is sewing.

Sunári, a *thar* or sept of Mangars in Darjiling.

Sunáriá, a section of Goálás in the North-Western Provinces and Behar.

Sundar, a section of the Kishnaut sub-caste of Goálás in Behar.

Sundas, a *thar* or sept of Dámis in Darjiling whose chief profession is sewing.

Sundi, a synonym for, and a sub-caste of, Sunris in Bengal; a section of Goálás in Behar. In Chota Nagpur, a totemistic sept of Bediás, signifying *mahuá* flower.

Sundi Baniyá, a sub-caste of Baniyás in Behar.

Sundi Deogam, a sept of Hos in Singbhum.

Sundip, a sub-caste of Dhobás in Noakháli.

Sundipá, a sub-caste of Jugis and Nápits in Noakhali.

Sundipe, a sub-caste of Kaibarttas in Noakhali.

Sundriába, red mushroom, a totemistic sept of Juángs in Orissa.

Sung, a sub-sept of the Besrá and Tudu septs of Santáls.

Sungaru, a *thar* or sept of Dámis in Darjiling, the members of which are drummers by profession.

Sunga Sarbbánandi, a *mel* or hypergamous sub-group of Rárhi Brahmans in Bengal.

Sungdele, a *thar* or sept of Khambus in Darjiling.

Sungutmung, a sept of Lepchas in Darjiling.

Sunkewar, a sept of Rájputs in Behar.

Sunri, *Saundika*, *Sundaka*, *Sháhá*, a large and widely-diffused caste, found in most districts of Bengal and Behar, whose original profession is believed to be the manufacture and sale of spirituous liquors. Many of its members have now taken to mercantile pursuits, call themselves by the title Sháhá, and disown all connexion with those who still follow the characteristic occupation of the caste. Their striving for social advancement has as yet not been entirely successful, and in spite of their wealth and enterprise ancient associations still hold them down. The bond of tradition is hard to break. According to Hindu ideas distillers and sellers of strong drink rank among the most degraded castes, and a curious story in the Vaivarta Purana keeps alive the memory of their degradation. It is said that when Sani, the Hindu Saturn, failed to adapt an elephant's head to the mutilated trunk of Ganesa, who had been accidentally beheaded by Siva, Viswa-Karmá, the celestial artificer, was sent for, and by careful dissection and manipulation he fitted the incongruous parts together and made a man called Kedára Sona from the slices cut off in fashioning his

Traditions of origin.

work. This Kedára Sena was ordered to fetch a drink of water for Bhagavati, weary and athirst. Finding on the river's bank a shell full of water he presented it to her, without noticing that a few grains of rice left in it by a parrot had fermented and formed an intoxicating liquid. Bhagavati, as soon as she had drunk, became aware of the fact, and in her anger condemned the offender to the vile and servile occupation of making spirituous liquors for mankind. Another story traces their origin to a certain Bháskar or Bháskar Muni, who was created by Krishna's brother, Balarám, to minister to his desire for strong drink. A different version of the same legend gives them for ancestor Niranjan, a boy found by Bháskar floating down a river in a pot full of country liquor, and brought up by him as a distiller. Others, again, following the traditional method of accounting for the formation of castes, believe that Sunris are descended from a Vaisya man and a Tiyar woman.

Internal structure.

Putting these fables aside, we may, I think, find in the internal structure of the Sunri caste, and most of all in the number and diversity of its endogamous and exogamous divisions, some ground for believing that it probably comprises several independent groups, which have arisen in different parts of the country to supply the wants of the community in the matter of strong drink. In Manbhum, for example, eight sub-castes are said to be known: **Ariyár, Biáhut, Maghaiyá, Lakargarhá, Holongwár, Paripál, Sikhariyá, Chaturthán.** The first three admit intermarriage and have practically become amalgamated into a single endogamous group. These Sunris have totemistic sections, permit the adult-marriage of girls and the remarriage of widows, allow divorce by the tearing of a *sál* leaf, and generally show the characteristics of non-Aryan races who are beginning to come under the influence of Hinduism. In Behar, as a reference to Appendix I will show, the sub-castes and sections are very numerous; but the latter are mostly titular, and I cannot find that any totemistic usages are connected with the two (*Háthi* and *Bichhu*) which appear to bear animal names. In Bhagalpur the **Kul-Sunri** sub-caste is further subdivided into groups called *chatáis* (mats, hence those who sit together on the same piece of matting), the members of which may not intermarry. So far as I am aware, the *chatáis* have no distinctive names.

In Central and Western Bengal four sub-castes are found—**Rárhí, Bárendra, Bangá,** and **Magi.** In Eastern Bengal, according to Dr. Wise, the caste is subdivided into two sections, or Ṣreṇi Rárhí and Bárendra. The former are distillers, called Súnṛí; the latter traders, who have assumed the title of Sáhá or merchant, which is said to be a corruption of Sádhu, 'perfect, honest.' Sáhás usually object to being called Súnṛís, and affect to belong to a distinct caste from the latter. By some authorities, however, they are held to be descended from a Ṣúdra father and a Súnṛí mother. My own enquiries go to show that the sub-castes are now more numerous than they were in Dr. Wise's time.

The Magi or Maghaiya sub-caste of Central and Western Bengal seems to derive its name from some real or supposed connexion with Behar, and may possibly be composed mainly of immigrants from that province. In various parts of Eastern Bengal a Magi

Ṣreṇí, distinct from the Ráṛhi or Bárendra, and accounted fallen and outcaste, is to be met with. It is stated that in old days the Mags made marauding expeditions into this part of Bengal and outraged some Súnṛí women, whose offspring, defiled by the doubt as to their paternity, became the nucleus of a new sub-caste. The Súnṛí barber and washerman work for them, but they always have purohits of their own.

Sáha or Sháhá is the common title of the caste, but on becoming rich a merchant often adopts Dás as a surname by way of concealing the fact that he is a Sunri. Dr. Wise also mentions a case in which a well-known Sáha trader of Dacca selected Rái Chaudharí as his family name. In the Maimansinh district a colony of Sáhas have taken the title of Pánjha, but can give no reason for doing so. They are chiefly talukdárs, writers, and shopkeepers, who eat and intermarry with Sáhas in other parts of Bengal.

Exogamy.

In Bengal Proper the sections are comparatively few, and the rule of exogamy seems to be gradually falling into disuse and giving way to the less archaic system of reckoning prohibited degrees from a common ancestor. The Sunris of Chota Nagpur observe the simple rule that a man may not marry a woman of his own section, and supplement this by a rather meagre table of prohibited degrees. In Behar marriage within the section denoted by the title is usually forbidden, but it sometimes happens that the group included under one title has split into two by reason of a quarrel or in consequence of the number of families in the group having increased so as to render the prohibition of marriage within the group unnecessary or inconvenient. In such cases one would *primâ facie* expect the newly-formed groups to adopt new titles or to qualify the original titles so as to indicate the change; but I am unable to quote instances where this has taken place. For reckoning prohibited degrees on the mother's side the standard formula in use is calculated to seven generations in the descending line. On the father's side the rule is said to be that a man may not marry any of his *Kes-Kátá* female relatives, that is to say, any of the women whose male relations would have to shave their heads if a death occurred in the family of the person whose marriage is in question.

Marriage.

The Sunris of Bengal marry their daughters as infants, and strictly prohibit widow-marriage and divorce. In Behar and Chota Nagpur adult-marriages occasionally take place when the parents of the girl are too poor to arrange for her marriage before the age of puberty. When both parties are children, the question of age is not minutely enquired into, and the essential point is that the bridegroom should be taller than the bride. This fact is ascertained by actual measurement—a method which commends itself to illiterate people, who keep no record of their children's ages. In the negotiations which precede the marriage, height of the parties is stated in *girahs*, and it is said to be the right thing for a girl to be married when she is from 12 to 14 *girahs* high and a boy when he is from 12 to 16 *girahs*. It is unusual for a girl to be unmarried at 16 *girahs* or a boy at 17.

When a girl is considered marriageable, one of her relatives or a professional marriage-broker is deputed to look out for a suitable bridegroom and to conduct the preliminary bargaining with his family. If the broker's overtures are favourably received, the bridegroom's father, accompanied by some of his relations, visits the bride's house and puts a garland of flowers (*hár*) on her neck. This ceremonial visit is returned by the bride's father, who also sends a present (*tilak*) of money, clothes, etc., to the bridegroom. According to the custom of the caste, the *tilak* must not exceed Rs. 101 or be less than Re. 1 or a pair of *dhotis*. When the *tilak* has been presented, a Brahman astrologer is called in to fix a lucky day for the wedding. This takes place in the bride's house. The ceremony is of the orthodox type, and *sindurdán*, or the smearing of vermilion on the bride's forehead and the parting of her hair, is believed to be its binding portion.

Polygamy is permitted, but it is unusual for a man to have more than two wives, and a second wife is usually only taken when the first wife is found to be barren. By all sub-castes except the Biyáhut, a widow is allowed to marry again by the *sagai* or *chumauná* ritual. As a rule this consists merely of *sindurdán*, but sometimes, when the parties are rich, the ceremony is amplified by introducing some of the forms used at the marriage of a virgin bride. In Chota Nagpur divorce is effected, with the sanction of the panchάyat, by tearing a *sál* leaf in two as a symbol of separation. Divorced wives may marry again within the caste. In Behar divorce is not recognized, and a woman taken in adultery is simply turned out of the caste, and probably ends by joining some of the less reputable religious sects or becoming a prostitute. The Bengal Sunris follow the same rule, but also hold that the husband is polluted by the sin of the wife. They therefore require him to perform an expiatory ceremony (*práyaschitta*), which consists, according to tradition, of giving from three to eleven (*káhans*) of cowries to a Brahman. At the present day, however, one four-anna bit is given for each *káhan*.

Religion.

According to Dr. Wise almost every member of the caste is a follower of Chaitanya, and the rich are celebrated for the ostentatious observance of the Sankirttana chants in honour of Krishna after the decease of any relative. The chief rites observed in Eastern Bengal are the worship of Ganesa on the 1st of Baisákh (April-May) and the 1st of Aghan (November–December); of Gandheswari on the 10th of Asín (September–October); of Durga at the time of the Durga Púja in October; and of Gangá whenever their boats are starting on a trading voyage. The majority being Vaishnavas, animals are rarely offered to any deity, but when this is done the victim is afterwards released. Sháhás are very fond of pigeons, and in the courtyard of almost every house a dovecot is fixed, as they believe that the air fanned by pigeons' wings wafts them luck. They are also devoted worshippers of Kártikeya, the Hindu god of war, constructing annually in November a life-size effigy of the god, and keeping it within the female enclosure for a year. Other Hindu castes throw the image into the river immediately after the Kártik Puja, but the Sháhás allege that their special veneration of the god is often rewarded, the barren rejoicing and the husband becoming the joyful father of children. It is easy to understand in what way this figure gives rise to scandalous stories among Bengalis, and how the Sáha becomes a butt for the wit and sarcasm of his neighbours.

The Behar Sunris follow the average Hinduism of that part of the country, and worship most of the regular gods as occasion offers. Their minor gods are very numerous—Dharam Raj, Bandi, Goraiya, Govindji, Hanumán, Kari Panjiár, Joti Panjiar, Apurba Panjiarin, Mirá, Saiyad, Jalpá, Sokhá, Hasankhán, and the Panch Pir. Rice cooked in milk and sugar (*khir*), cakes of ghí (*puri*), and various kinds of fruit, are offered to them and afterwards eaten by the worshippers. Kids are sacrificed to Bandi. On Sundays milk and flowers are offered to the sun. In Bengal, says Dr. Wise, the Brahman, peculiar to the caste, boasts that he never accepts alms from any one not a Súnrí, but it is quite certain that none of the clean castes would present him with charity. These Brahmans, who assume the bombastic titles of Vidyáságar, Vidyálankár, Chakravarttí, and Páṭhak, like the purohits of other low castes, read the funeral service at the burning ghât, and are looked down upon by other members of the sacred order. The Súnrís of Behar are served by a low class of Maithil Brahmans, who also minister to the religious necessities of the Teli caste. No other Brahmans will eat and drink with these men, who are known by the contemptuous epithet of Teliá Bábhan. In Chota Nagpur the Brahmans who serve the Súnrís call themselves Kanaujiás, but they have no right to the name, and no other Brahmans will have anything to do with them.

Disposal of the dead.

Súnris burn their dead and perform the regular *sráddh* ceremony in Bengal on the thirtieth, and in Behar on the thirteenth day after death. The usual periodical oblations for the benefit of departed ancestors are poured forth on the new moon of Kártik (October-November).

Social status in Bengal.

Dr. Wise gives the following account of the social status of Súnrís in Eastern Bengal:—

"The Súnrí is a very degraded individual, indulging freely in intoxicating liquors. A Brahman may not utter his name before noon. The majority of the workmen in the Government Abkári, or Excise Department, are Súnrís, and most of the gánja shops are owned by them. The Hindustani distiller (Kalár, Kalwár) has nothing in common with the Súnrí, as he only manufactures spirit, and will not vend it—an occupation carried on by Kurmis, or Baniyas.

"The Sáha, again, is perhaps the most enterprising and prosperous community in Bengal, comprising a large number of the cloth merchants, salt-traders, wood-dealers, and bankers. They are usually known as *Amda-wálá*, or traders who import goods wholesale and sell them to petty dealers by retail. Mahájan, Goladár, and Aṛhatdár, or broker, are also common designations. Notwithstanding their improved position of late years, they are still utterly abandoned in the eyes of the Hindus. Even the Bhúínmálí, who works for them, will not touch their food, and a Chaṇḍál loses caste if he lays his hand on the stool on which one of them is sitting. There is a saying among Bengalís that if a Ṣúdra be walking down a narrow lane with only Súnrí houses on each side, and an elephant approaches, he ought to allow the elephant to trample him under foot rather than take refuge in a house of the accursed. The Dhobá and Nápit are members of the Súnrí caste, the Ṣúdra washerman and barber declining to work for them. Although the Ṣúdra Nápit occasionally shaves the Sáhas, he will not attend at any of their religious ceremonies. When a member of the caste has to be employed. A Súnrí will not cultivate the soil, although he does so in Central Bengal, nor will he ply as a boatman unless the boat belongs to his caste and is entirely manned by Súnrís. He is also prohibited from becoming a fisherman and from selling fish in the market." Some of the lower classes of Súnris have taken to working as carpenters and thatchers of houses.

In Behar.

In Behar the Darchúa Sunris, who manufacture, and the Ganjwár, Dhakankorá, Sikhariá, and Chaurthán Sunris, who deal in country liquor, are considered lower in point of social standing than Kul-Sunri, Sagáhut, and Biahut sub-castes, the members of which are usually shop-keepers or dealers in grain. The entire caste, however, occupies a low position in the Hindu social system, and Telis are the highest caste which will take water from their hands. As a rule they affect to observe the restrictions in matters of diet which are characteristic of the Vaishnava sect, but the Kul-Sunris of Bhagalpur admit that they eat mutton, goat flesh, all kinds of fish, and even field-rats. Most of them indulge pretty freely in strong drink. Many Sunris have taken to cultivation, but comparatively few appear to have risen above the grade of tenure-holder or raiyat with occupancy rights.

The following statement shows the number and distribution of Sunris in 1872 and 1881. In the former year the figures of the districts in Behar and Chota Nagpur include those of Kalwárs and Kaláls.

District.	1872.	1881.	District.	1872.	1881.
Bardwan	22,259	19,088	Chittagong	1,742	2,152
Bankura	12,667	21,155	Noakhali	5,896	5,981
Birbhum	21,173	15,841	Patna	16,666	7,899
Midnapur	3,084	7,666	Gya	9,246	6,643
Hughli	6,509	3,560	Shahabad	20,595	4,409
Howrah		1,771	Tirbut { Mosufferpur ...	94,189	22,656
24-Parganás	13,272	5,270	Tirbut { Darbhanga ...		25,440
Nadiya	10,188	9,495	Saran	23,533	1,163
Khulna	......	9,998	Champaran	32,566	422
Murshedabad	16,311	13,039	Monghyr	26,703	8,962
Jessore	34,146	17,170	Bhagalpur	36,851	12,102
Dinajpur	6,686	4,498	Purniah	18,724	14,139
Rajshahye	8,228	6,871	Maldah	4,792	7,233
Rangpur	7,692	4,939	Santál Parganás	18,242	20,204
Bogra	6,683	5,775	Cuttack	3,246	4,261
Pabna	29,728	25,319	Puri	1,976	1,769
Darjiling	467	84	Balasore	1,757	1,388
Jalpigori	1,116	1,447	Tributary States	8,465	9,383
Kuch Behar	......	667	Hazaribagh	13,277	17,576
Dacca	62,511	58,299	Lohardagá	9,984	9,312
Faridpur	26,677	34,491	Singhbhum	3,274	2,611
Bakarganj	26,160	16,846	Manbhum	19,060	18,246
Maimansinh	35,982	41,306	Tributary States	1,858	2,834
Tipperah	35,323	32,749			

Sunri Dhánuk, a sub-caste of Dhánuks in Behar.

Sunriet, a *mul* or section of the Ghosin sub-caste of Goálás in Behar.

Sunriwár-Solhni, a *mul* of the Parásara section of Maithil Brahmans in Behar.

Sunuwár, *Sonwár*, a cultivating tribe of Nepal, forming with the Mangar Gurung and Khas the class known as Mukhya or chief. Although in theory the Sunuwárs are a strictly endogamous group, intermarriage with Mangars and Gurungs is tacitly recognized. The ceremony cannot be performed in public, but such unions are admitted to be valid, and the children are counted in all respects as Sunuwárs, except that during the first generation Sunuwárs of the whole blood may not take rice or *dál* from their hands. In the second generation this disability ceases to have effect. Sunuwárs say that they came originally from Simungarh near Bara Chhatri in Western Nepal, and that wandering east they came to Chuplu on the Likhukhola river and took possession of it. Makwani Raja was then ruler of Eastern Nepal. Likhukhola and Khuntikhola are now the main settlements of the tribe.

Origin.

The internal structure of the tribe is shown in Appendix I. There are no sub-tribes. All the names of the septs end in *cha*, which is conjectured by Babu Sarat Chandra Dás, C.I.E., to be a corruption of the Sanskrit *ja*, born of. Presumably, therefore, they have reference to descent, and further analysis may show that they preserve the names or nicknames of the first founders of the septs. For the following derivations and explanations I am indebted to Babu Sarat Chandra Dás:—Jespucha means 'born of the Jespu,' a tree, called Kairal by the Khas of Nepal Proper, the flowers of which are eaten by the hill people. Káticha-Káti is the name of a place. Jirel is supposed to be a mixed sept arising from a cross with some tribe not belonging to the Mukhya group. Although it is reckoned as a sept or *thar*, pure Sunuwárs do not intermarry with its members, nor will they eat *dál* or rice cooked by them. For all that the Jirel have not become endogamous, but marry with half-bred Sunuwárs and other tribes of the Mukhya and Kiránti groups. In Nepal tribal distinctions are not so sharply drawn as in India, and the offspring of mixed marriages find plenty of people in much the same position as themselves. The Wángdecha sept is considered in some sense inferior to the rest. Although they are admitted to marry with the other septs, *dál* and rice are not taken from their hands. Wandeh is said to be a Tibetan word, and it may be that this sept immigrated from Tibet after the others had become familiar with Hindu ideas. Kyahbohcha means 'born from a Kyahboh' (Tibetan *Kyahpo*), a rope ladder used by the hillmen for descending the face of a cliff to get wild honey, of which they are very fond. The fact that the two septs, Leokicha and Jespucha, are both called Preticha or earth-born, and may not intermarry, does not suggest any inference as to the affinities of the tribe.

Internal structure.

In most cases girls are married after they are grown up to men of their own choice, and sexual intercourse before marriage is tacitly recognized on the

Marriage.

understanding that in the event of the girl becoming pregnant she will be married without delay. Infant-marriage, however, is sometimes resorted to by well-to-do families which have been infected by Hindu ideas. Polygamy is allowed, but is not largely resorted to. If a man's first wife has no children, he is held to be justified in taking a second, and the matter is often arranged by his marrying his first wife's younger sister—an arrangement which is naturally more conducive to domestic peace than the selection of an outsider. The marriage ceremony consists for the most part of ritual borrowed from the Hindus, and *sindurdán*, or the smearing of vermilion on the bride's forehead and the parting of her hair, is the essential and binding portion. In addition to the standard forms, we find the peculiar usage that the bride's parents wash her feet when they give her to the bridegroom and splash the water over their own heads. By doing this they believe that they wash from her, and as it were take back, the quality of membership of her original sept, and transfer her to the sept of the bridegroom. On the next morning the bride washes the bridegroom's feet, and drinks the water, saying at the time that she does this as a sign that she has entered his sept and is truly his wife. After this has been done, she is considered competent to cook rice and *dál* for her husband and the members of his sept. The Nepalese regard it as characteristic of the Mukhya group that they treat the son-in-law as a very important personage and in a way worship him ; while the Kirántis look upon him rather in the light of a servant. By Kiránti custom, if a young man runs away with a girl and is unable to pay the fine which is appointed for such cases, his children by her are regarded and may be claimed as slaves by her parents. It is curious to find that the girl's *maternal* uncle is deemed the proper person to demand payment of the fine. The explanation of the difference of the Mukhya and Kiránti points of view is probably to be found in the fact that the former have been more affected than the latter by Hindu ideas, which tend always to exaggerate the value of men and to depreciate women.

A widow may not marry again by the standard ritual ordained for the marriage of a spinster, but she may live with a man without going through any ceremony at all, and in such cases public opinion recognizes her as his wife. Her children are deemed legitimate, and their status is in no way inferior to that of children born from a woman married by the full ceremony. If the deceased husband leaves a younger brother, married or unmarried, he is held to have a prior claim on the person of the widow, and she may not take up with another man until he has decided not to exercise his rights. Divorce is permitted on the ground of the adultery or misconduct of the wife. Divorced women may marry again in the same manner as widows, and their children by second husbands are deemed legitimate. Usually the first husband keeps his own children, but if the divorced wife is allowed to take them with her, as sometimes happens, they are treated as the children of her second husband.

Religion.

In point of religion the Sunuwárs may be described as undeveloped Hindus, still retaining many traces of an earlier animistic faith. They offer rice, flowers, sandal wood and vermilion to Siva, and sacrifice goats to

Káli, when sickness or domestic trouble afflicts them. Bhim Sen, the second of the Pándava brethren, is worshipped with sacrifices of he-goats, buffaloes, ducks, fowls and pigeons; but buffaloes are offered only on rare occasions, and the minor victims are usually thought sufficient. Tuesdays and Saturdays are the auspicious days. Offerings of rice, flowers and *sital-patti* leaves are also made to the rivers and mountain torrents and to the main peaks of the Himalayas visible from Nepal. Upádhya Brahmans serve them as priests and are received on equal terms by other members of the sacred order in Nepal. Among the minor religious observances of the tribe may be mentioned their solemn worship of the cow under the name of Lakshmi on the new moon of the month of Kartik, and their practice of marrying banyan and the pipul when found growing side by side.

Disposal of the dead.

Most Sunuwárs bury their dead and observe the same funeral ceremonies as the Mangars; but some well-to-do people have of late years taken to the Hindu practice of cremation, and perform a regular *sráddh* on the tenth or twelfth day after death.

Occupation.

The tribe believe hunting to have been their original occupation, and many of them are still strongly addicted to the chase. The bulk of the tribe, however, live by agriculture and pastoral pursuits.

Supáhá, a section of Kanaujiá Lohárs in Behar.

Supahran, a *mul* or section of the Kanaujiá sub-caste of Sonárs in Behar.

Supá-Parghá, a sub-caste of Parghás in Behar.

Supárá, a sub-caste of Doms in Behar.

Supat, a section of the Chhajáti sub-caste of Khatris in Bengal.

Suphar, a section of Kaserás in Behar.

Supolia, a title of Doms who make *sup*, a bamboo work for separating the chaff from the grain.

Sur, a title of Dakshin-Rárhi and Bangaja Káyasths and of Sánkháris and Sadgops in Bengal.

Surabani, a section of Kumhárs in Singbhum.

Origin.

Surahiyá, *Suraiyá, Sorahaiyá, Kalwat-Malláh*, a boating, fishing, cultivating, and labouring caste of Behar. According to Dr. Wise their origin, like that of other boatmen, is traced to the fabulous hero Nikhád. There is a shadowy connexion between the Surahiyá and Cháin. The former use the water vessels and hookahs of the latter; but the Cháin, assuming a higher rank, will smoke, but will neither eat nor intermarry with Surahiyá. The Surahiyás have no traditions of their own, except the common one that their ancestors came 'from the west.'

Marriage.

Both infant and adult-marriage are in vogue, but the former is deemed more respectable. The marriage ceremony is the same as is used by most of the lower castes, *sindurdán* being the binding portion. Polygamy is allowed, but is not practised on a large scale. A widow may marry a second time. It is thought right for her to marry her late husband's younger brother if there is one, but she is not positively obliged to do so. Divorce is not recognized.

Religion.

In matters of religion the Surahiyás profess to be orthodox Hindus, and employ Maithil Brahmans for religious and ceremonial purposes. In practice, however, the greater gods of the Hindu Pantheon receive only occasional worship, and the working religion of the caste is concerned rather with the mysterious group known as the Pánch Piur, Koil Bába, the boatman's deity, and Amar Singh, a canonised Surahiyá, who seems to be their special patron. In his honour a part of the house is daubed with cow-dung on stated days in every month of the year except Paus (December-January) and Chait (March-April), and goats, rice, sweetmeats, ghi, etc., offered, and incense burned, the worshippers afterwards partaking of the offerings themselves.

Social status and occupation.

In point of social standing the Surahiyás rank immediately below the group of castes from whose hands Brahmans will take water. Thus Koiris, Barais, Gangotás, who belong to that group, will accept sweetmeats from Surahiyás, but will not eat boiled rice in their houses. The characteristic occupation of the caste is boating and fishing. Dr. Wise describes them as enterprising and hardy sailors often met with in Eastern Bengal during the cold season in large trading vessels laden with grain, pulse, or fuller's earth, which is sold to *mahájans* and a cargo of rice shipped for the return voyage. They are very muscular and large-boned, and their physique offers a striking contrast to that of the average Bengali boatman. Some Surahiyás have taken to cultivation, and hold land as occupancy and non-occupancy raiyats. Their number, however, is comparatively small, and there are at present no signs of their developing into a sub-caste: in fact, even cultivating Surahiyás are ready to engage themselves as boatmen.

The following statement shows the number and distribution of Surahiyás in 1881. The figures of 1872 were returned among those of 'others' of the Boating and Fishing castes.

DISTRICT.	1881.	DISTRICT.	1881.
Birbhum	166	Darbhanga	43
24-Parganás	24	Mozufferpur	44
Murshedabad	390	Champaran	3
Dinajpur	973	Monghyr	2,863
Rajshahye	163	Bhagalpur	2,199
Rangpur	3	Purniah	498
Maimansinh	4	Maldah	586
Patna	19	Santál Parganás	139
Shahabad	1,846	Singbhum	16

Surái. a *mel* or hypergamous sub-group of Rárhi Brahmans in Bengal.

Suraiyá, a synonym for Surahiyá.

Surajbansi, Surjabansi, a sub-caste of Tiyars; a synonym for Rajwár; a title of the Kochh tribe in Northern Bengal; a division of Rájputs; a sub-caste of Goálás in the North-Western Provinces and Behar. See Suryabansi.

Suraj-bansi. This title, properly denoting one of the two main stocks of Rájputs, has been assumed within comparatively recent times by a hybrid Mongoloid caste claiming to be the aborigines of Kamrup and now inhabiting the jungly tracts of Bhowál in Eastern Bengal. According to Dr. Wise, from whose notes this article is condensed, the Súraj-bansís were formerly regarded as akin to the Kochh-mandái, but the Brahmans, taking advantage of their credulity and ignorance, led them to believe that they were descendants of the Chhatrí who, by throwing away their sacred thread, escaped the axe of Parasuráma. Accordingly, in 1871, a body of representative Suraj-bansís went to the house of their zamíndár, Kálí Náráyana Rái, Rái Bahádur, a Ṣrotriyá Brahman, and requested him to reinvest them with the sacred cord. An offer of five hundred rupees was made, but declined. Disappointed at this unexpected rebuff, they retired to consult, and afterwards raised their offer to two thousand. This sum allayed the scruples of the Brahman, the sacred cord was with due solemnity presented, and ever since the Suraj-bansí have assumed the high rank of Chhatrí, to the great disgust of the Hindus of those parts.

The Kochh-mandái, who reside in the same jungle, assert that a few years ago the Suraj-bansí were known as Kochh-mandái, and even at present Bansí is their ordinary appellation. The Suraj-bansí are peculiar to Bhowál, and are not met with beyond the limits of the Dacca district. They are certainly allied to the Kochh-mandái, but have modified the Mongoloid type by marrying with low Bengali castes. Their original language, probably a dialect of Garo, has been forgotten, and Bengali is universally spoken. The Suraj-bansí is generally a darker and taller, but less muscular man, than the Kochh-mandái. Certain of them still retain the peculiar Mongoloid cast of features, with oblique eyelids and scanty growth of hair; but the majority have the common Bengali countenance, with bushy moustaches and voluminous cues, for they have adopted the Vaishnava fashion of wearing tho hair. They already call themselves worshippers of Vishnu, and have engaged the services of a Patit-Brahman as purohit. Twice a year, in Phalgun and Baisákh, they worship under a *sál* tree Kamakha Devi, the tutelary goddess of Kamrup. Durga, Manasa Devi, and Bura-Buri are invoked in seasons of sickness and domestic trouble, and especial honour is paid to the sun as the reputed ancestor and eponym of the caste. They have borrowed three *gotras*, Kasyapa, Aliman, and Madhu-Kuliyá, and marriages into the same *gotra* are strictly forbidden. Widow-marriage has been abandoned; divorce is prohibited, and the Hindu system of marrying girls before puberty adopted. Furthermore, having assumed the sacred thread of the Chhatrís, they imitate them in observing the *sráddha* on the nineteenth day after death.

By Hindus they are not admitted to belong to a clean caste, but the Súdra servants are beginning to work for them, and in a few years they will doubtless have secured an established position. The Kochh-mandái affirm that the Suraj-bansí secretly indulge in the forbidden luxury of pork, although to curious strangers the fact is stoutly denied. It is a familiar experience that this taste survives in many tribes long after they have adopted the external observances of Hinduism. Almost all Suraj-bansís are cultivators, growing rice, pulse, tobacco, mustard and cotton on clearings in the jungle. Fishing is deemed dishonourable. A few who have acquired a slight knowledge of Bengali are employed as traders or servants to landholders.

Surajdhaj, a sub-caste of Káyasths in Behar.

Suran, a section of Rautiás in Chota Nagpur.

Suraniá, a section of Khariás in Chota Nagpur.

Surat, a section of the Ghosin sub-caste of Goálás in Behar.

Suratwalá, 'a good looking man,' a synonym for Barnasankar. In Gyá an ironical designation of the illegitimate descendants of Gyawals by women of the Rájput, Bábhan, and Bhát castes, but not of lower castes.

Surává, a sub-caste of Malláhs in Behar.

Suren, a section of Turis in Chota Nagpur.

Sureswari, a *gotra* or section of Subarnabaniks in Bengal.

Suret, a *mul* or section of the Kanaujiá sub-caste of Sonárs in Behar.

Surgane, a *mul* of the Parásara section of Maithil Brahmans in Behar.

Surgriá, a section of Bábhans in Behar.

Surhi, a wild cow, a totemistic sept of Mundas in Chota Nagpur.

Suri, fly, a totemistic sept of Mundas in Chota Nagpur; a section of the Bahánnajáti sub-caste of Khatris in Bengal; a synonym for Sunri.

Surijhabu, a sept of Chiks in Chota Nagpur.

Suril, a totemistic sept of Mundas who do not propitiate the 'Churin Deota.'

Surin, a sept of Mundas in Chota Nagpur.

Surinwár, a section of Turis in Chota Nagpur.

Surjáhá, a section of the Biyáhut and Kharidáhá Kalwárs in Behar.

Surkhi, a sept of the Suryabansi sub-tribe of Rájputs in Behar.

Surnair, a sept of Rájputs in Behar.

Suruan, a sept of Páns in Chota Nagpur.

Surunia, neck ornament, a sept of Kharwars in Chota Nagpur.

Surwár, a sept of the Suryabansi Rájputs in Behar.

Suryabansi, *Surji*, 'descendant of the sun,' an honorific title assumed by many castes, particularly the Rájputs, and castes which, like the Dravidian Rájbansi Kochh of Northern Bengal, attempt to affiliate themselves to the Rájputs; a sub-tribe of Rájputs in Behar; a *thar* or sept of Mangars in Darjiling.

Suryabansi Láma, a *thar* or sept of Gurungs in Darjiling.

Surya-dwija, a sub-caste of Támbulis in Behar.

Susan, a sept of Mundas in Chota Nagpur.

Suswár, *Suswári*, a title given by the former Rajas of Rámgarh to some of their servants of the Hajjám or Kahár caste, whose duty was to superintend their master's stores of provision and edibles.

Suta, a sub-caste of Aguris in Western Bengal.

Suthrá Sahi, *Sutrasáhi*, certain sect of mendicants said to be worshippers of Nirgun—God, void of qualities. They attract notice when soliciting alms by beating two sticks together.

Sutihar, a low caste who spin cotton thread.

Sutihár, a synonym for Barhi in Behar.

Sutradhar, *Chhutár*, the carpenter caste of Bengal, named thread-holder, from the Sanskrit *sútra*, the thread, with which the course of the saw is marked. Sútradhars claim descent from Viswakarmá, or, according to others, from Karna, son of Kunti by the sun-god before her marriage to Pándu. Karna, as is stated in the Mahábhárata, was exposed by his mother on the banks of the Jumna, where he was found by Adhiratha, the charioteer of Dhritaráshtra. The Sútradhars seem to have adroitly taken advantage of the resemblance between the words *súta*, a charioteer, and *chhutár* or *sutár*, a carpenter, to equip themselves with a mythological pedigree of undoubted respectability. Their ingenuity, however, has availed them little. That shrewd observer Dr. Wise describes them as a very low caste, recruited from one of the aboriginal races of Eastern Bengal, and largely employed in boat-building. He also quotes the story that in the time of Ballál Sen the Sútradhars lodged a complaint against the Brahmans for not performing religious ceremonies for them until all other castes had been served, whereupon the king, to prevent all further controversy, enrolled them among the *nicha* or low castes, and gave them a special Brahman of their own. Another legend says that they were degraded for delay in supplying the wood required by the Brahmans for certain sacrifices.

Traditions of origin.

The internal structure is rather intricate, and they furnish a good instance of the tendency to multiply sub-castes, which has already been noticed as characteristic of the lower social groups in the Hindu system. No less than twenty-five sub-castes are shown in Appendix I, and though the materials at my disposal were fairly ample, I am by no means confident that the enumeration is exhaustive. Of these groups some are local, others occupational, while for many of the names no explanation at all is forthcoming. Thus the Western Bengal sub-castes are based on distinctions of locality, except the **Goálá-Bhuiyá**,

Internal structure.

a group of uncertain origin. In Dacca the Chhutár sub-caste make boats, household furniture, beams, wheels, and ploughs; the Chúrá-Kutí parch and husk rice, make wooden necklaces, and burn shells for lime; the Káthuriá make ploughs, tubs, platters, and wooden agricultural implements.

The Chhutárs claim, and are admitted to have, precedence of the other two divisions. They are all included in one *gotra*, the Alamyan, and invariably belong to the Vaishnava creed. The caste has a pancháyat, but no union (*dal*), and their headman, styled *Parámánik*, settles disputes between members. It is derogatory for a Chhutár to fell a tree, which is done by a class of Chandáls called *Karáti*, from the Sanskrit Kara-patra, a saw. Turning (*kund-kári*), however, is the legitimate occupation of a carpenter, and he is permitted to make moulds used by confectioners for preparing fancy sweetmeats, and by plasterers for ornamenting cornices and roofs. Chhutárs never cultivate the soil, but frequently carry on business as mahájans or wholesale traders. Muhamadan carpenters, unknown in Dacca, are common in Chittagong, where they are employed as shipwrights.

The members of the Churákuti sub-caste are gradually relinquishing their ancestral trade, and of late years have taken Muhamadan servants to husk rice, while they themselves act as grocers, selling pulse, grain, and oils, or as writers, servants, and shop-keepers. The only wooden article now made by them is the sandal wood necklace worn by all Hindus. The Purohit is distinct from the family priest of the other subdivisions. The headman is styled Pradhán, and the only gotra is Alamyan. The Chúrákuti are all Vaishnavas in creed, the guru being the Farídábád Gosáin. Their principal festivities are the Gandheswarí on the 10th Aswin (September), and New Year's day, on the 1st of Baisákh.

The Káthuriá subdivision, scattered throughout the Dacca district, is engaged in cultivating the soil, building boats, and manufacturing lime with the fresh water shells dredged from the extensive *jhils*, or marshes, in the interior of Bikrampur, being for this reason often confounded with the Báiti or Chunari caste, a perfectly distinct community. The Brahman of this sub-caste is an Achárji, who performs the same religious ceremonies as the priest of the other two. The headman is known as Sardár.

Similar distinctions appear under different names in the Santál Parganás, where the Ket Chhutár are ordinary carpenters working only in wood and making household furniture, palanquins, and the like; the Pátúrá are stone-cutters; the Nagare practise turning; and the Bhar-Chhutár parch and pound rice into *churá*.

Exogamy and hypergamy.

The sections have been borrowed from the Brahmanical system, and give no clue to the origin of the caste. They are not invariably exogamous, and the tendency seems to be for the Sútradhars of Eastern Bengal to regard the *gotra* as a sort of titular distinction and to regulate their marriages by the more modern system of counting prohibited degrees. This at least is the case with two out of the three sub-castes found in Dacca, while in Noakhâli the caste is stated to have no sections at all. In Western Bengal, on the other hand, the sections are still intact, and three of them—Alamrishi, Bánrishi, and Kásyapa—appear in that district to be clearly totemistic. The Alamrishi will not eat, and even pay some sort of reverence to the eel (*áind*), while members of the Bánrishi and Kásyapa sections observe a similar taboo in respect of the *bán* fish and the water-tortoise. This curious survival of primitive usage lends important confirmation to Dr. Wise's opinion that the caste is really of non-Aryan descent. No regular system of hypergamy has yet been developed among them, but the beginnings of one may perhaps be discerned in the fact that families bearing the title of Parámánik are held in special esteem, and are usually spoken of as Kulins. Such families have not as yet reached the point of refusing to give their daughters in marriage to persons who are not Kulins, but a higher bride-price is paid for Parámánik girls, and members of Parámánik families are treated with special consideration at wedding and funeral feasts. In Dacca the Sútradhars of Bikrampur affect a high degree of ceremonial purity, and demand a special bride-price on giving their daughters in marriage to Sútradhars coming from other places. In the Bishanpur estate in Bankura the superior families of Sútradhar pay a small fee to the Raja of Bishanpur for the privilege of calling themselves Kulins, and the Raja is supposed to have the power of punishing a breach of caste custom by depriving the offender of this coveted distinction. No instance has come to my notice of this power being exercised in recent times, and the fee still paid is doubtless a survival from days when the Bishanpur family possessed considerable authority in Western Bengal.

Marriage.

Sútradhars marry their daughters as infants by the standard Hindu ceremony, of which *sátpák*, or the carrying of the bride seven times round the bridegroom, is deemed to be the binding portion. A bride-price is paid, which varies with the rank of the families concerned. Polygamy is permitted, and there appear to be no theoretical objections to a man having as many wives as he can afford to maintain. Widows are not allowed to marry again, nor is divorce recognized. Sexual indiscretions are usually hushed up within the circle of the family in which they occur; but a woman whose infidelity gives rise to public scandal is summarily turned out of the caste, and ceases thenceforth to be a member of respectable society.

Religion.

The great majority of the caste belong to the Vaishnava sect, but worshippers of the Saktis are also found among them. Viswakarmá is regarded as their patron deity, and sacrifices are offered to him on the last day of Bhádra and in Mágh Panchami. Images of the god are sometimes made in the likeness of a white man with three eyes, wearing a crown, and bearing a club in his right hand; but usually he is represented by the tools which the worshipper uses in his trade. These are set up inside the house and decorated with flowers, and offerings are placed before them, while the god is besought to favour his votaries on their profession during the ensuing year. Sútradhars employ Brahmans for religious and ceremonial purposes, but these Brahmans belong to the *Barna* class, and are not received on equal terms by other members of the sacred order. The dead are burned, and the ordinary *sráddh* ceremony is performed on the thirty-first day after death.

Social status.

The social rank of the Sútradhar is low. Brahmans will not take water from their hands, and they may be said to occupy much the same position as the Jugi, Sunri, and Dhobá. In Western Bengal the village barber has no objection to shaving them, but he marks his sense of their inferior status by declining to cut their toe nails or touch their feet.

Occupation.

Carpentry is believed to be their original and characteristic profession, but besides the occupations already enumerated, Sutradhars are employed in cutting conch shells into bracelets, in making images of the gods, and in painting religious pictures. In Murshedabad, indeed, this last occupation seems likely to form the basis of a new sub-caste, for I am informed that painters (Chitrakár) do not intermarry with the members of the caste who work as carpenters and shell-cutters. In Noakháli some Sútradhars work as goldsmiths. Cultivating Sútradhars are usually occupancy or non-occupancy raiyats. None of them appear to have risen to be zamindars or tenure-holders: on the other hand, very few have sunk to the position of landless day-labourers.

The following statement shows the number and distribution of Sútradhars in 1872 and 1881:—

District.	1872.	1881.	District.	1872.	1881.
Bardwan	15,973	10,131	Jalpigori	73	831
Bankura	4,610	6,471	Kuch Behár	......	132
Birbhum	7,747	8,900	Dacca	15,907	15,295
Midnapur	10,585	14,784	Faridpur	5,086	5,200
Hughli	5,108	4,607	Bakarganj	2,081	1,151
Howrah		1,704	Maimansinh	21,479	27,468
24-Parganás	8,274	1,467	Tipperah	11,804	1,526
Nadiya	9,120	9,420	Chittagong	1,328	2,464
Khulna	......	1,632	Noakhali	2,768	3,554
Jessore	10,644	12,071	Maldah	2,180	2,757
Murshedabad	10,070	9,673	Singbhum	342	381
Dinajpur	678	1,019	Manbhum	2,027	1,927
Rajshahye	4,538	1,093	Tributary States	112	39
Rangpur	2,326	2,220	Cuttack	......	210
Bogra	1,569	1,567	Balasore	......	19
Pabna	10,282	12,714	Tributary States	......	1
Darjiling	159	106			

Sutrasáhi, a class of Baniyás in Behar. See *Suthrá Sahi*.

Suwahong, the mendicant, a sept of the Yangorup sub-tribe of Limbus in Darjiling.

Suyál, a *thar* or sept of Mangars in Darjiling.

Swáin, a title of Chásás in Orissa.

Swarna-kausik, a section of the Uttar-Bárendra Brahmans in Bengal.

Swártha, self-absorbed, a title of Brahmans and Vaishnavas.

Swarupsing, a group of the Fatehsing Telis in Murshedabad.

Swetbhadra, a *pur* or section of Sákadwipi Brahmans in Behar.

Swiri, a synonym for Savar.

T

Tabkáhila, a section of the Biyáhut and Kharidáhá Kalwárs in Behar.

Tabkar, a section of the Dhaprá sub-caste of Doms in Behar.

Tábria, a section of Mahesris in Behar.

Tag-tcg-pá, *tag* or *brag*, a rock—a dweller on cliffs, a sub-sept of the Nah-pá sept of Sherpa Bhotias.

Tahalkiá, a setion of Goálás in the North-Western Provinces and Behar.

Taiá, a sept of Rájputs in Behar.

Taijaung, a sept of Limbus in Darjiling.

Tailakár, a synonym for Teli.

Tailangi or **Andhra**, a territorial division of the Pancha Drávira Brahmans who live in the south of the Vindhya range, a country of the Telugu language.

Taili, a synonym for Teli.

Taingchait, a sept of Maghs in the Hill Tracts of Chittagong.

Taipál, a synonym for Teli.

Tairan, a *gotra* or section of Agarwáls.

Taitia, a sept of Nágeswars in Chota Nagpur.

Taitum, a sept of Mundas in Chota Nagpur.

Taiyá, a title of Hindu Joláhás in Behar.

Tajna, name of a river, a totemistic sept of Chiks in Chota Nagpur.

Takware-Ankusi, a *mul* of the Bátsya section of Maithil Brahmans in Behar

Takware-Nimá, a *mul* of the Bátsa section of Maithil Brahmans in Behar.

Talabáti, a *gáin* of the Kásyapa *gotra* of Rárhi Brahmans in Bengal.

Talahadába, palm-tree, a totemistic sept of Juángs in Orissa.

Táláiboná, a sub-caste of Doms in Bengal who make palm-leaf mats.

Talápátra, bottom of a pot, a title of Bárendra Brahmans in Bengal.

Tálkátá, a sub-caste of Háris in Bengal who extract the juice from *tál* trees.

Tálu, a *thar* or sept of Mangars in Darjiling.

Tamág, a *thar* or sept of Murmis in Darjiling. The term is sometimes used to denote the whole caste.

Tamagandiyá, a section of Turis in Behar.

Támár, a sept of Rájputs in Behar.

Tamáriya, *Murá*, or *Mánki-Murá*, a sub-tribe of Bhumijs originally settled in pargana Tamár of Lohardagá.

Támbá, copper, a sept of Kharwars and Mundas in Chota Nagpur.

Támberá, a sub-caste of Kaserás, braziers in Behar.

Támboli, a group of the Sri-Gaura sub-caste of Gaura Brahmans.

Támbrakhola, a sub-tribe of Limbus in Darjiling.

Támbuli, *Támuli*, *Támli*, a respectable trading caste of Bengal, Behar, and Orissa, whose original occupation is supposed to have been the selling of betel-leaf, Sanskrit *támbúla*. Tradition represents them as the descendants of a Vaisya father and a Brahman mother, but this legend clearly throws no light upon the true origin. It is possible that they may be an offshoot from one of the trading castes, whose usages have been transformed by contact with Brahmanical influences. The Támbulis of Behar have no sections, and regulate their marriages by the standard formula for reckoning prohibited degrees calculated to six generations in the descending line for *dhiania* relations and fourteen for *deádi*. In Bengal and Orissa the Brahmanical *gotras* are in use, Vyása being included among them. Instead, however, of following the ordinary law of exogamy, the Támbuli have a peculiar system of their own, which depends partly on the *gotra* and partly on the family name. Persons who belong to the same *gotra* are allowed to marry provided they do not bear the same family name, and persons of the same family name may marry if they belong to different *gotras*. Where, however, both family name and *gotra* are the same, the prohibition on intermarriage is absolute. Marriage between *sapindas* and *samánodakas* is also forbidden.

Origin.

The Támbulis of Bengal are divided into five sub-castes or *tháks* —Saptagrámi or Kusadáye, Ashtagrámi or Kataki, Chauddagrámi, Biyállisgrámi, and Bardhamáni. The first-named say that they came from Northern India, and that their chief settlement was at Saptagrám or Sátgáon, where they numbered about 1,400 families. An outrage committed on one of their maidens by the Mahomedan Governor of the place induced them to leave Sátgáon in a body and settle at Kusadábá, in the 24-Parganás, which they now regard as their head-quarters in Bengal. A similar origin is claimed for the Biyállisgrámi, the largest of the five sub-castes, who are supposed to have entered Bengal at a still earlier date. The Chauddagrámi, which is now reckoned the highest in rank, is said to owe its origin to one Sashthibar Singh, a member of the Biyállisgrámi group, who being turned out of his father's house for marrying the daughter of Srimanta Pál, a Támuli of the Bardhamáni sub-caste, took refuge with his father-in-law at Bainchi, in Hughli, and headed a faction of his own. Being a man of wealth and influence, he gained over to his side several leading families, and thus formed the nucleus of a new sub-caste, which comprised the Támulis of fourteen villages (*chauddagrám*). Some clue to the time when this took place is given by the inscription on a temple at Bainchi, which shows it to have been built by Gokul, the son of Sashthibar, in the Saka year 1504 = A.D. 1582. We may place the formation of the Chauddagrámi sub-caste some fifty years earlier. The Bardhamáni sub-caste are supposed to have had their earliest settlement in the Bardwan district, but they are now most numerous in Birbhum. The Ashtagrámi profess to have come from Upper India at the same time as the Saptagrámi, but residence in Orissa has cut them off from the rest of the caste, and their social rank is now comparatively low. The

Internal structure.

Behar sub-castes are shown in Appendix I, and demand no special notice here.

Marriage.

Támbulis marry their daughters as infants. The Asura form of marriage is in vogue, and the parents of the bridegroom pay a bride-price, which varies according to the status of the bride's family. *Kusandiká* forms part of the ritual, but the essential and binding portion is believed to be the formal gift of the bride and acceptance of her by the bridegroom. Yellow silk is the proper bridal dress, but should the family be poor a girl may be married in cotton dyed with turmeric. Polygamy is permitted, and in theory a man may have as many wives as he can afford to maintain. Such indulgence, however, is rare, and I understand that few Támbulis have more than one wife. A man may marry two sisters, but he must follow the order of age, and may not marry his wife's elder sister. Divorce is not recognized, and on the rare occasions when a public scandal occurs within the caste the offending wife is turned out to shift for herself. Widows are forbidden to marry again, and the custom of the caste compels them to lead a more strictly ascetic life than is usual among the other castes of the Navasákha. They are allowed only one meal a day, of which neither flesh nor fish may form part, and they must fast entirely twice a month. A Támuli widow indeed is subject to as severe ordinances of self-denial as a Brahman widow. These ascetic doctrines, however, hold good only in Bengal and Orissa. In Behar a widow may marry again, and is tied down by no special restrictions in her choice of a second husband, although it is deemed right and proper for her to marry her deceased husband's younger brother should such a relative exist. It deserves notice that among the Behar Támulis the ceremony used at the marriage of a widow, though called *sagai*, does not differ materially from that which is performed when a virgin is married. In most cases where widow-marriage is permitted, the ritual is extremely meagre, and usually consists of little more than the smearing of red lead on the bride's forehead. Divorce is effected with the sanction of the pancháyat, but divorced wives may not marry again.

Religion.

The religion of the Támbulis presents no features of special interest. Most members of the caste are Vaishnavas, and comparatively few worshippers of the Saktis are found among them. They employ Brahmans for religious and ceremonial purposes, who are received on equal terms by other members of the sacred order. Among the minor gods recognized by the caste in Bengal may be mentioned the sun and moon, to whom rice, plantains, etc., are offered occasionally; Chandi, Lakshmi, Sashthi, and Manasá. In Behar Bandi and Nar Singh are the favourite deities. The offerings presented to them are wheaten cakes, sweetmeats, curds, and plantains, which are afterwards eaten by the members of the household. On the Purnimá or full moon of Baisákh some Támbulis set up inside their houses a vessel of lime, some betel-leaves, and areca nut, with the scissors (*katári* and *jánti*) used for cutting the leaf and nut, and worship these as the emblems of their trade. The dead are burned, and the *ádya* or principal *sráddhá* performed on the thirty-first day after death. Those who are well off make a point of taking some of the ashes to the Ganges, but the poor merely throw them into the nearest stream or tank.

Occupation.

To prepare and sell betel-leaf, which they buy from the cultivators, is believed to be the original occupation of the caste, which they still adhere to in Behar and Upper India, often adding thereto the business of a *pansári* or druggist. In Bengal, however, the Támbulis have long since abandoned this special business, and taken to dealing in grain and petty shop-keeping. Some sell lime, others are employed as *gomáshtas* in large shops, a certain number hold land, and a few are Government servants, pleaders, *mukhtiárs*, doctors, clerks in merchants' offices, and schoolmasters. No Támbuli will hold the plough himself, and those members of the caste who have taken to agriculture are zamindárs, tenure-holders, and occupancy raiyats cultivating their lands by means of hired labour.

Social status.

The social rank of the caste is respectable. They are usually classed among the Nabasákha, and in most districts of Bengal Brahmans will take water from their hands. On this point, however, there seems to be some conflict both of ancient authority and of modern usage. The couplet of Parásara, which is usually cited as the *locus classicus* defining the Nabasákh or Nava-Sáyaka group, makes no mention of the Támbuli; and although it is alleged that the caste is included under the Teli, who also are descended from a Vaisya father and a Brahman mother, this seems rather a forced interpretation. On the other hand the Brahma Vaivarta Purána omits the Teli and gives the Támbuli a prominent place among the Sat-Sudras. So the Brahmans of Bengal, while usually according to the Támbuli a place among the Navasákha, do not invariably allow them the privileges attaching to this position; and a Támbuli gentleman,[1] to whom I am indebted for an excellent series of notes on the caste, informs me that neither Brahmans nor Rajputs will take water from their hands. Támbulis will partake of cooked food with none but members of their own sub-caste. Thus a Chauddagrámi will eat boiled rice only with a Chauddagrámi, and so on. Some, however, will eat the leavings of Brahmans. Their own rules regarding diet are the same as are followed by most orthodox Hindus. Among lawful animal food they admit goat's flesh, venison, and all kinds of fish ordinarily sold except the scaleless varieties known as *pángás*, *gorchá*, and *etá*. Some also drink wine, but those who abstain from both animal food and strong drink are deemed to follow a more excellent path. In Behar, where less attention seems to be paid to the dicta of writers of the Pauranic age, the Támbuli rank with the Koiri, and no question has arisen as to the propriety of Brahmans taking water from their hands.

The following statement shows the number and distribution of Támbulis in Bengal Proper in 1872 and 1881. The figures for

---

[1] Babu Shambu Chandra Dé, of Hughli, a member of the Chauddagrámi sub-caste.

Behar, Orissa, and Chota Nagpur are included in the table on Barais.

DISTRICT.	1872.	1881.	DISTRICT.	1872.	1881.
Bardwan	14,428	6,311	Rangpur	319	378
Bankura	12,084	16,097	Bogra	399	37
Birbhum	2,962	3,554	Pabna	390	139
Midnapur	9,369	11,582	Darjiling	181	7
Hughli	5,325	8,457	Jalpigori	1	242
Howrah		1,896	Dacca	200	323
24-Parganás	6,013	1,651	Faridpur	235	3
Nadiya	1,683	1,802	Bakarganj	68	611
Jessore	136	444	Maimansinh...	32	251
Khulna	......	261	Chittagong	1,116	136
Murshedabad...	1,172	732	Noakhali	29	1
Dinajpur	13	648	Tipperah	332	1
Rajshahye	410	201			

Támgáin, a section of the Biyáhut and Kharidáhá Kalwárs in Behar.

Tamgarihar, a sept of Mundas in Chota Nagpur.

Tamghuria, a sept of Mundas in Chota Nagpur.

Támi, a synonym for Dámi.

Támli, a synonym for Támbuli.

Támrá, a sub-caste of Kámárs in Midnapur.

Támuli, a synonym for Támbuli.

Tandan, a section of the Bárajáti sub-caste of Khatris in Bengal.

Tángbuáh, a *thar* or sept of Khambus in Darjiling.

Tángi, axe, a totemistic section of Rautiás in Chota Nagpur.

Tankol, a *mul* or section of the Naomuliá or Goriá sub-caste of Goálás in Behar.

Tannahpurái-Solhni, a *mul* of the Kásyap section of Maithil Brahmans in Behar.

Tannán, a sept of Rájputs in Behar.

Tánti, *Tantrabáya, Tantubáya, Tatwá, Tantwá*, the weaver caste of Bengal and Behar, probably a functional group developed under the pressure of the natural demand for woven cloth. A common tradition represents them as descended from Siva Dás or Ghám Dás, who was born from the sweat (*ghám*) that fell from Siva while he was dancing, and his wife Kushati, who was created by Siva from a blade of *kusa* grass. Siva Dás had four sons—Balarám, Uddhab, Purandar, and Madhukar, who were the ancestors of the four sub-castes bearing those names. Another story recounted in the Játi Kaumudi makes the caste the offspring of a Manibandha father and a Manikár mother; while a third supposes that the Tántis, in common with all the artisan castes, were begotten on a Sudra woman by the celestial artificer Viswakarmá.

Origin.

The internal divisions of the caste are shown in a tabular form in Appendix I, and need only a brief notice here. In Western Bengal the Áswini or Ásan-Tánti claim to be the original stock, from

Internal structure. — Bengal.

which the other sub-castes have diverged. The women of this group do not wear nose-rings, and this is regarded as a badge of social distinction. The Áswini sub-caste is very numerous, and has broken up into five subordinate endogamous groups, which appear to derive their names from particular localities. In the city of Dacca, says Dr. Wise, the Tántis have separated into two *sreni* or sub-castes, called **Bará-bhagiyá** or **Jhámpániya**, from the *jhámpán* or sedan chair in which the bridegroom sits when going to fetch the bride, and **Chhotá-bhagiyá**, consisting of Káyasths who on becoming weavers were expelled from their caste. The former are about ten times as numerous. They assume the title Basák, which was originally taken by rich persons who had given up weaving and become cloth merchants. A few titles inherited from their forefathers, who were employed as weavers in the East India Company's factory (*aurang*), are still preserved. Among these **Jáchandár**, appraiser; **Muhkim**, supervisor; **Dalál**, broker; and **Sardár**, head of a gang of workmen, are the most common. Family nicknames are believed to be commoner among the Tántis than in any other caste, and certain households are called **Mesha**, sheep, and **Chhagri**, goat. The popular explanation of the names is that the ancestors of the families accidentally killed these animals; but it seems at least equally likely that they are totems, which have survived as family titles. This view derives some support from the fact that among the Tántis of the Santál Parganás the titles **Lu**, **Chandra**, **Pál**, **Sil**, **Dás**, **Datta**, **Nandi**, **Bit**, and **De**, serve to denote exogamous groups. In Mag Bazár, a suburb of Dacca, there reside a peculiar subdivision of outcaste Tántis belonging to a Magi Sreni who, though excommunicated for the same reasons as the Magi Kumhars, conform to all the customs of the Súdra Tánti.

According to Dr. Wise, the Chhotá-bhagiyá, or Káyath-Tántis, formerly goldsmiths, took to weaving as a more profitable trade, and now eat with and visit the Basáks, although the latter do not reciprocate the politeness. The richer families, having always adopted the prerogatives of the Káyasths, have been recognized, and if wealthy receive wives from them. At present only from twenty to twenty-five houses in Dacca are occupied by them, and several households work as goldsmiths, bankers, and engravers (Naqqásh).

Dr. Wise mentions another class of Tántis, called **Bangá-Tántis**, settled in Eastern Bengal. These are quite distinct from the city weavers, and claim to be the descendants of the original Tántis of Bengal, who supplied the people with cotton fabrics for ages before the reign of Jáhángír. Although the superiority which they claim over the Basáks is not conceded, there can be little doubt that these Bangá Tántis were earlier settlers in Bengal than their rivals. The Bangá Tántis are chiefly settled at Dhámrái, an old town about twenty miles north of Dacca, where they occupy about two hundred and fifty houses. Their bridal dresses are white, and not of red or other coloured silk, as is the case with the Dacca weavers. They manufacture the native *sári* and *chadar*, as well as *doriyá* and *nau-batti* muslins, which are sent to Dacca to be embroidered. At Dhámrái the famous female spinners (*Kátani*), who used to wind the fine native thread, were still to be found in 1873; but in 1885, when Dr. Wise revisited Dacca, the art had died out. In illustration of the delicate touch of these spinners, the story is told that one of them wound eighty-eight yards of thread on a reel which only weighed one *ratí* or two grains. Now-a-days a *rati* of the finest thread equals seventy yards, which proves that either a coarser cotton is grown, or that the women have lost their delicate sensibility of touch.

Behar.

The Behar sub-castes of Tatwás, as the caste is generally called in that province, need little comment. We find among them the common territorial groups **Kanaujiá** and **Tirhutiá**. The names **Baiswárá** and **Uttarhá** seem also to have reference to locality. **Banaudhiá** occurs among some of the Baniyá castes; **Jaiswár** is a common sub-caste of the Kurmis, while the names **Chamár-Tántí** and **Kahár-Tántí** suggest, what is in itself by no means improbable, that some members of the Chamár and Kahár castes may have taken to the profession of weaving, and thus formed new endogamous groups loosely affiliated to the Tántis. In Orissa there appear to be three sub-castes. The **Mátibans-Tánti** weave coarse cloth from thread of English or native manufacture. Many of them have deserted their characteristic profession and become teachers in village schools, assuming therewith the titles **Abadhán** and **Khetiputra**. The **Gálá-Tánti** weave fine cloth, and the Hansi-Tántí make coloured cloth of various patterns.

Dr. Wise has the following remarks on the Behar Tántis settled in Dacca:—

"The Hindustání, or Mungírya, weavers are very common in Dacca, where they comprehend a large proportion of the 'Mothiás,' or coolies, street porters, pankha-pullers, gardeners, and packers of jute; while at home they are weavers and cultivators. Two divisions are met with—the Kanaujiyá and Tirhutiyá; the former, the more numerous, being of higher rank than the latter, who are despised and shut out from all social intercourse. The Tirhutíyá, degraded by carrying palanquins and by acting as musicians at their homes, collect in Dacca during the jute season, and are remarkable for their squalor and stupidity. They also work as syces, gardeners, boatmen, and musicians."

The exogamous sections of the Tántis are comparatively few in number, and throw no light upon the origin of the caste. In Bengal the Brahmanical *gotras* have been adopted; while in Behar only three sections are known, and those do not appear to be necessarily exogamous. In Western Bengal prohibited degrees are reckoned by the standard formula to three generations in the descending line except where *bhayádi*, or mutual recognition of family events, is kept up. In that case the prohibition extends to seven generations.

Marriage.

Except in Behar, where adult-marriage is still practised by the poorer members of the caste, Tántis marry their daughters before they have attained the age of puberty. The bride-price usually demanded for a girl does not exceed from Rs. 50 to Rs. 60, but it is deemed more respectable for a man to give his daughter free of price. The marriage ceremony is of the ordinary type. Polygamy is recognized to the extent that a man may take a second wife if the first proves barren. Tántis are usually too poor to regard plurality of wives as a luxury. Widow-marriage and divorce are forbidden in Bengal, while in Behar widows may certainly marry again without any restrictions being imposed on their choice, and the balance of authority seems on the whole to incline to the opinion that divorced wives may marry again by the *sagai* form, which is used at the second marriage of a widow. Others, again, say that divorce is not recognized: if a woman goes wrong with an outsider, she is turned out of the caste; but if she has an intrigue with a Tánti, her fault is condoned by the headmen and her husband is compelled to take her back. If the bridegroom—elect of a widow has not been married before, he must perform the ceremony of *matkorwa* in his own house, and must smear vermilion on a sword or a piece of iron before going to take his bride.

It should be mentioned here that instances are said to have occurred of women belonging to lower castes, such as Teli, Turha, and Gonrhi, being formally admitted into the Tánti caste. These women had become the mistresses of Tánti men, and the latter, having been excommunicated on account of this discreditable *liaison*, had afterwards prevailed on the *panchâyat* of the caste to admit them and their mistresses to social rights on the condition that a feast was given to the caste and substantial presents offered to the members of the panchâyat. Men of other castes can on no account be received in this fashion. In matters of inheritance, a daughter's son is excluded by the nearest male relative of the same *kul*.

The Tántis of Eastern Bengal are, says Dr. Wise—

Religion.

"With few exceptions, Vaishnavas, being probably the most obsequious disciples of the Khardah Gosáins. They have no *pancháit* and no headman, but the rich guide and instruct their poorer brethren, while the trade interests of the caste are secured by the supervision of powerful Dals, or guilds, presided over by a Dalpatí, or director.

"The Dacca Tántís have always been celebrated for the magnificent procession which parades the streets of the city on the Janmáshtamí, or birthday of their god Krishna, in Bhádra (August–September). As long as a Nawáb lived at Dacca, his troopers and band led the pageant, and at the present day, though divested of many of its attractions, it is still the most popular exhibition in Eastern Bengal. For many generations the Dacca weavers have resided in two quarters of the city, Tántí Bazár and Nawábpúr, and on the day following the birthday of Krishna a procession issues from each of these quarters and perambulates the streets. In 1853 the processions met, and a faction fight ensued. In 1855 the Government ordered that for the future they should never be permitted to come out on the same day, and each quarter, therefore, takes precedence on alternate years, the peace of the city having been so far assured. Krishna is worshipped by the Tántí Bazár section under the form of Muralí Mohan; by the Nawábpúr as the Sáligrám, or Lakshí Náráyana. At the present day the processions are preceded by a string of elephants, and a "Panja," or model of a hand, presented by a former Nawáb, is borne aloft, as at the Muharram pageant. The peculiar part of the cavalcade, however, are the "Misls," or raised platforms, carried on men's shoulders. On these are placed images of Hindu gods, figures, and often caricatures of local celebrities. On others are Nách girls and buffoons reciting comic songs and bandying chaff with the crowd. In fact, the anniversary and the show have come to be regarded as the occasion of a holiday, when thousands of villagers throng the city bent on pleasure and amusement, which are more considered than the deity in whose honour it is held.

"The Banga Tántís observe with especial pomp the Kámadeva Pújá, or worship of the Indian Cupid, which, though generally neglected in Bengal and entirely omitted by the Jhámpániya Tántís, is still kept up in Bhowál, Kámrúp, and the districts bordering on that country. It is undoubtedly a worship of earlier origin than that of Krishna. On the Madana Chaturdasí, or fourteenth day of the waxing moon of Chait (March–April), the festival is held, but it does not last for seven days as formerly. The purohit officiates, no victims being sacrificed. The Banga Tántís, moreover, celebrate the Janmáshtamí, but in a different way from the Basák. Two boys gorgeously dressed, representing Krishna and his foster-father, Nanda Gopa, are carried about in great state and with much discordant noise. The Visvakarma worship is observed on the usual day, and, as with the Basáks, the loom, shuttle, and other implements of weaving are adored."

In Western Bengal Vaishnavism is the characteristic belief of the caste. Lakshinarayan-Chakra and Rádhá Krishna Bigraha seem to be the commonest objects of worship. Reverence is also paid to Durgá and Siva, but no sacrifices involving the taking of animal life are offered to them. Viswakarmá is looked upon as the tutelary deity of the caste, and is worshipped twice a year with offerings of flowers, rice, molasses, etc., under the supervision of a *purohit*, who recites appropriate texts. Images are sometimes made, but more commonly the weaver's loom or some of the tools of the craft is regarded as the dwelling place or symbol of the god. In the Santál Parganás Rangadhári and Jaikhá are mentioned among the minor gods of the caste, but I have been unable to ascertain their precise functions.

Among the Tatwás of Behar Vaishnavism appears to have made but little way, and the majority of the caste are addicted to the grosser cult of the Saktis, or female forms of the great gods. Thus the Kanaujiá sub-caste worship Mahá-máya, or Durgá, and those settled in Bengal keep the ninth and tenth days of the Durgá Pújah as holidays consecrated to her. On a certain date in Kártik they proceed to an open plain and sacrifice a male goat to Káli, a *khasi*, or castrated goat, to Madhu Kunwár, who, they say, was a Tánti. On the sixth day after a birth the *chhathi* is held, and on the twelfth the mother goes to the well, smears red lead on the edge in the name of Kamalá (Lakshmí), then draws water and carries it within doors, when she is pronounced clean.

Káli, Durgá, and Mahádeva are worshipped by the Tírhutiá sub-caste, but the majority follow the teaching of one Buddh Rám, a Mochí of Tírhut, who founded a sect, differing in some slight respects from that of Nának Sháh. They observe few caste usages, but many superstitious rites, such as burning *ghi* in a lamp and adding resin, in execution of vows. Besides the regular minor gods of Behar—Bandi Goraiyá, Dharamraj, and the rest—Tatwás worship Saisyár and Káruchar, departed members of the caste, with sacrifices of sheep and goats on Wednesdays and Saturdays in the month of Sráwan. Brahmans do not preside at these animisitic rites, which are performed by the male members of the household, with the object of protecting themselves, their families, and cattle against the ill-will of powerful spirits.

Priests.

The Tántis of Bengal are served in religious and ceremonial matters by the Brahmans, who minister to the spiritual wants of the Nava-Sákha group. These Brahmans occupy at the present day a highly respectable position, and although some of the most select Brahmans affect to look down upon them as *Sudra-jájak*, high caste Kulins are willing to marry their daughters; and it may be affirmed on the whole that they are received on equal terms by other members of the sacred order.

In Behar a very different state of things prevails, which seems to indicate that the caste may have been developed locally at a comparatively later date, and may be composed to a great extent of non-Aryan elements. In many places Tatwas have no Brahmans at all, and their place is supplied either by members of the caste who have joined some religious order, or by the sister's son (*bhánjá*) of the person at whose instance, or for whose benefit, a particular religious office is performed. In either case, notwithstanding the ignorance of the person selected as priest, the title of Brahman is conferred upon him, and he is treated with extreme deference. These primitive methods of satisfying the religious needs of the caste seem, however, to be tending to die out, and Tatwas, like other low castes, are beginning to set up Brahmans of their own, usually low Kanaujiás or Maithils, who are not looked upon as a credit to the priestly order. Both in Bengal and Behar the caste burn their dead and perform a funeral ceremony modelled more or less on the observances of the higher castes. But by the Tatwas of Behar this ceremony is performed on the thirteenth day after death, while the Bengal Tántis, following orthodox Sudra usage, observe the thirty-first day.

Social status.

Although the caste holds a degraded position in Behar, and Brahmans will not take water from their hands, the Tántis have had sufficient influence in Bengal to raise themselves to the grade of clean Súdras, and take undisputed rank in the Nava-sákha group. The purity of a Tánti depends on the quality of the starch used in weaving. The Súdra weaver prepares starch from parchéd rice boiled in water, or *kái*, which is not, according to Hindu ideas, *ento* or, as it is called in Behar, *jhúthá*, leavings. Impure weavers, as the Jugís, make starch (*már*) by merely boiling rice—a process which is considered utterly abominable. The rules observed in matters of diet bear, as is usual, some relation to the social status of the caste. The Bengal Tántis abstain, or affect to abstain, from flesh and strong drink, and claim to be superior in these respects to other Nava-sákha castes. In Behar flesh and wine are deemed lawful for Tatwas, and whenever spirits are drunk a few drops are poured forth as an offering to Mahadeva. Tatwas, again, take both *kachhi* and *pakki* articles of food from the Gangota, the Barai, and generally the entire group of castes from whose hands a Brahman can take water.

Occupation.

Although Tántis admit weaving to be their immemorial profession, many of them have of late years been driven by the influx of cheap machine-made goods to betake themselves to agriculture. These cultivating Tántis are for the most part occupancy raiyats, or small tenure-holders, but in the Murshedabad district a member of the caste owns the zamindari right in a large property. It is difficult or impossible to say with any approach to accuracy what proportion of the caste have abandoned their original craft in favour of trade or agriculture. The Uttarkul Tántis of Western Bengal have on the whole adhered to weaving, and it is popularly believed that their comparative poverty is mainly due to their attachment to the traditional occupation of the caste. Among the Aswini and Máriáli about one-third are supposed to have given up weaving and settled down as regular cultivators. Some minor differences among weaving Tántis deserve a passing notice. The Uttarkul sub-caste weave only cotton cloth, and the Máriáli only silk, while the Aswini make either cotton or silk goods.

According to Dr. Wise, five different sorts of cloth were manufactured by the Dacca Tántis in their palmy days, but the art of making the finer qualities has been lost. The five varieties were—

1. *Malmal.* Muslins of the first quality included the *Abrawán*,[1] *Tanzib*, and *Malmal* made of Desí (country) cotton or Kapás; of the second quality were the *Shabnam*, *Khasah*, *Jhúna*, *Sarkár 'Ali*, *Ganga Jal*, and *Terindam*;[2] of the third were the coarser muslins, collectively called *Báftah*, comprising *Hammám*, *Dimti* (*? Dimyáti*), *San*, *Jangal Khasah*, and *Galá-band*.
2. *Doriyá*, striped and ribbed muslin, such as Ráj-kot, Dakhan, Pádsháhi-dár, Kunti-dár, Kághazí, and Kelápát.

[1] Abrawán, literally running water, was solely made for the Delhi zanánah, and the following stories regarding its gossamer-like texture are still told by the natives. A daughter of Aurangzíb, one day on entering the room, was rebuked for wearing immodest drapery, but justified her conduct on the plea that she was wearing seven suits (Jámá). Again, in the reign of 'Alí Vardí Khán (1742—56), a Dacca Tántí was flogged and banished from the city for not preventing his cow from eating up a web of Abrawán which had been laid out to bleach on the grass.

[2] Probably from Arabic *tarah*, 'mode,' and Persian *andám*, 'figure.'

3. *Char-Khanah*, checkered muslins, such as *Nandanshâhi*, *Anâr-dâna*, *Kabûtar-khopi*, *Sâ-Kuttâ*, *Bachhâ-dâr*, and *Kunti-dâr*.
4. *Jâmdâni*, by the early European traders called *Nain-sukah*,[1] or embroidered muslins. The different sorts are distinguished by the coloured flowers, sprigs, *búti*, or network pattern on them. The commonest are *Sháhbarga-búti*, *Chawal*, *Mel*, *Tirchhá*, and *Dublíjál*.
5. *Kushida*, or *Chikan*, muslins embroidered with Múgá, or Tasar silk ,generally dyed red, blue, or yellow. The commoner ones are *Katáw-Rúmi*, *Naubatti* or *Naubati*, *Yahúdi*, *Azizullah*, and *Samundar Lahar*.

The common Dhotí, Chadar, and Orhní, or wrapper with a coloured or embroidered end, were always regarded as distinct from the foregoing, being woven at their homes by weavers of various castes.

On glancing over the preceding list one is struck by the predominance of Arabic, Persian, and Hindi words, and the rarity of Sanskrit and Bengali. That weaving, like other Native arts, was known in Hindustán prior to the foundation of the Bengal kingdom is beyond a doubt,[2] and that the earlier settlers brought it with them into the Delta is likely; but it would seem that either the names given by the dominant Muhamadans displaced the native ones, or that the liberal Mussulmán rulers stimulated—it may be developed—the manufacture of the finer sorts of muslins. That the inhabitants of Bengal at an early period made cotton cloth of wondrous fineness is undoubted, for the two Muhamadan travellers of the ninth century mention that in an Indian country called Rahmi[3] were woven cotton garments "so fine that they may be drawn through a ring of middling size." Unfortunately we possess no further evidence until A.D. 1506, three hundred years after the Muhamadan conquest, when the Roman Vartomannus[4] visited the fabled city of Bengalla, where the finest cotton and silk in all the world were produced, and whence yearly sailed fifty ships laden with cotton and silk goods. The earliest traveller, however, who gives us the names of the fine cotton fabrics of Bengal is the Arab author of the "Muhít," written in 1554.[5] He mentions among the goods exported from Chittagong by his countrymen a fine cloth (*Chautár*), muslin sashes called *Malmal*, the finest being known as Malmalí Sháhí, terms which are Hindi and Persian. Furthermore, when Cæsar Frederick visited Chittagong (1563–81), "bombast cloth of every sort" was exported thence. After his day the authorities

---

[1] Nayana-sukha, pleasing to the eye.

[2] It is referred to in the *Rig* and *Atharva Vedas*. See *Zimmer Altind. Leben*, p. 254.—H. H. R.

[3] Rahmi, however, may not be Bengal, but as it was the country of elephants, of a shell currency, and of the "Karkandan," or unicorn (rhinoceros), the assumption is not altogether groundless.—Elliot's *History of India*, vol. i, 361.

[4] *Ludovici Vartomanni Navigatio*, p. 209.

[5] *Journal A. S. of Bengal*, vol. v, 467.

are numerous, and names identical with those in use in the present day are cited.

The conjecture that the Muhamadans merely developed an already flourishing trade is strengthened by the fact that the terms in use by the Dacca weavers for the warp, woof, shuttle, and loom generally are Sanskrit, while later improvements, such as the *sháua* or reed, the *charkhá* or spinning wheel, and the *daftí* or reed frame, are Persian.

The decline of the cotton trade of Eastern Bengal has been sketched by a former resident of Dacca, Mr. James Taylor,[1] while much curious information is contained in Mr. Bolts' *Considerations* and in the works of Edmund Burke. Under the Mughal Government, and even as late as the Nawábship of 'Alí Vardí Khán (1742–56), the weavers manufactured in perfect liberty, and the enterprising among them advanced money to promote the trade, but with Siráj-ud-daulah (1756-7) the decadence began, and during his eventful reign seven hundred families of weavers left their homes at Jangalbári, in Maimansinh, owing to oppression, and emigrated to other districts. Before 1765, when the English obtained the Díwání of Bengal, bullion was regularly imported from Europe to meet the requirements of the traders, but after that day advances were made from the provincial treasuries to buy the annual stock or "investment." This gave a new and unprecedented stimulus to weaving, and in 1787, the most prosperous year on record, the estimated prime cost of the cloths entered at the custom house of Dacca amounted to fifty lakhs of rupees, or 625,000*l*. This prosperity, however, was very deceptive, being founded on injustice and intolerable oppression. The first decline may be traced to the rapacity of the "banyans" and gomastas, who arbitrarily decided the quantity of goods each weaver was to deliver, the prices he was to receive, while his name being entered on a register, he was not permitted to work for any one but his own gomasta. When the annual supply was ready the gomasta held a bazár, at which the jáchandár, or appraiser, fixed the price of the goods, but the rascality, Mr. Bolts says,[2] was beyond imagination, and the prices were often fifteen per cent., often forty, below the market rate.

The deplorable condition of the weavers in 1773 is depicted in the following extract from a letter written by Mr. Rouse, the Chief of Dacca[3]:—"The weavers are in general a timid, helpless people, many of them poor to the utmost degree of wretchedness, incapable of keeping accounts, industrious as it were by instinct, unable to defend themselves if oppressed, and satisfied if with continual labour they derive from the fair dealing and humanity of their employer a moderate subsistence for their families."

The following incident that occurred in 1767 gives a vivid idea of the state of matters in Dacca at that period. Mr. Thomas Kelsall,

---

[1] *A Descriptive and Historical Account of the Cotton Manufacture of Dacca, in Bengal.* By A Former Resident of Dacca. London. 1851.

[2] *Considerations*, part i, 193.

[3] *Burke's Works*, Bohn's edition, iv, 73.

Chief of Dacca, being informed that a certain weaver, Krishna Pál Kumár, was suspected of selling muslins to the French factory, ordered him to be seized, but he found shelter with the French. His relatives, however, were imprisoned and beaten, and their houses pillaged.' Upon this the weaver gave himself up to the Díwán, Bhikam Lál Thákur, who ordered him to be flogged, after which he was confined in the factory for eleven days, during which time the peons fleeced him of forty-nine rupees and two pieces of cloth. By Mr. Kelsall's order his head was shaved, his face blackened "with lime and ink," and being mounted on an ox, he was paraded through Nawábpúr, where the brokers and Paikárs lived. After three more days the accused was forwarded to the Nawáb for trial, who, finding no fault, discharged him.

This hateful system was at last swept away, and the weavers for a short time enjoyed comparative freedom of trade and unusual prosperity; but in 1769 Arkwright obtained his patent, in 1779 Crompton invented the mule, and the cotton manufactures of Lancashire have gradually driven the finer and less durable fabrics of the Bengali weavers out of the market, and all but annihilated the trade."

The following statement shows the number and distribution of Tántis in 1872 and 1881 :—

District.	1872.	1881.	District.	1872.	1881.
Bardwan	46,647	20,913	Chittagong	3,799	4,894
Bankura	16,510	29,304	Noakhali	1,273	1,326
Birbhum	16,761	15,962	Patna	12,958	18,802
Midnapur	106,317	97,720	Gya	6,894	5,744
Hughli	39,079	29,647	Shahabad	8,156	10,338
Howrah		14,250	Tirbut { Mozaffarpur	82,496	56,656
24-Parganás	19,576	8,139	Tirbut { Darbhanga		20,913
Nadiya	9,416	6,806	Saran	4,806	10,826
Khulna	......	2,594	Champaran	11,406	21,186
Jessore	10,760	10,349	Monghyr	36,208	37,288
Murabedabad	17,409	19,814	Bhagalpur	63,037	59,584
Dinajpur	12,800	9,093	Purniah	35,307	29,273
Rajshahye	822	1,515	Maldah	16,360	6,503
Rangpur	3,235	4,553	Santál Parganás	4,656	10,949
Bogra	1,801	1,660	Cuttack	37,822	38,790
Pabna	4,069	4,110	Puri	14,154	14,215
Darjiling	644	428	Balasore	38,460	40,046
Jalpigori	4,034	5,453	Tributary States	13,706	19,947
Kuch Behar	......	1,457	Hazaribagh	541	854
Dacca	8,906	10,587	Lohardagá	5,837	11,340
Faridpur	3,410	3,304	Singbhum	20,758	21,260
Bakarganj	1,875	1,327	Manbhum	12,961	12,243
Maimansinh	7,392	8,430	Tributary States	......	5,121
Tipperah	1,792	1,540			

Tánti, a synonym for Jolhá and Pán.

Tánti-Mahili, a sub-caste of Máhilis in Manbhum who carry palanquins.

Tántiá, a section of Goálás in the North-Western Provinces and Behar.

Tantrabái, a synonym for Tánti.

Tantrabáya, a synonym for Tánti.

Tantubáya, a synonym for Tánti.

Tánuri, a *gáin* of the Bátsya *gotra* of Bárendra Brahmans in Bengal.

Tapaer, a section of Mahilis in Chota Nagpur.

Tapaspati, "Master of Penance," a title of religious mendicants.

Tarah, *Terri*, an up-country caste.

Tarat, a sub-section of the Bharadwája section of Utkal Brahmans.

Tári, a *mul* or section of the Chhamuliá Madhesiá sub-caste of Halwáis in Behar.

Táriál, a *gáin* of the Bátsya *gotra* of Bárendra Brahmans in Bengal.

Tariyá, a section of Saraogis in Behar.

Tarkanyark, a *pur* or section of Sákadwipi Brahmans in Behar.

Táróálá Bisi, a *gáin* of the Sándilya *gotra* of Bárendra Brahmans in Bengal.

Társi, a *mul* or section of Kasarwáni Baniyás in Behar.

Társuriya, a sub-caste of Pásis in Behar.

Tártar ke khirpuri, a section of the Biyáhut and Kharidáhá Kalwárs in Behar.

Tarwár, a sept of the Suryabansi sub-tribe of Rájputs in Behar; a totemistic sept of Mundas in Chota Nagpur who cannot touch a sword.

Tárzukmung, a sept of Lepchas in Darjiling.

Tatia, a kind of bird, a totemistic sept of Mundas in Chota Nagpur.

Tátoár, a *gáin* of the Sábarna *gotra* of Bárendra Brahmans in Bengal.

Tatwá, a synonym for Jolhá and Tánti.

Tatwa, a weaving caste in Behar, who apply caterpillars to trees for cocoons from which *tasar* silk is made. See *Tánti*.

Taulika, a synonym for Teli.

Taulo, earthen-pot, a title of Bárendra Brahmans in Bengal.

Taunr, a sept of Rájputs in Behar.

Taw, a sept of the Patar subtribe of Mahilis in Chota Nagpur.

Táyal, a *gotra* or section of Agarwáls.

Tej, a title of Dakshin-Rárhi and Bangaja Káyasths.

Tejaniá, a section of Sonárs in Behar.

Tek Bárá, a sub-caste of Gaura Brahmans.

Tekhá, a sept of the Chandrabansi division of Rájputs in Behar.

Tela, a section of Mahesris in Behar.

Telgá, a section of Khariás in Chota Nagpur.

Telhá, a sept of Binjhiás in Chota Nagpur who use oil at marriage.

Telhari, a group of Maghaiya Telis in Behar.

Teli, *Taili*, *Tailika*, *Tailakár*, *Tailpal*, *Kalu*, a large oil-pressing and trading caste of Bengal, Behar, and Orissa. Their original profession was probably oil-pressing, and the caste may be regarded as a functional group recruited from the respectable middle class of Hindu society. Oil is used by all Hindus for domestic and ceremonial purposes, and its manufacture could only be carried on by men whose social purity was beyond dispute.

Traditions of origin.

The Telis of Bengal have a variety of traditions, mostly of the mythological type, which are interesting for their attempt to account for the origin and comparative status of some of the main divisions of the caste. The creation of the first Teli is ascribed to the god Siva, who, being of a mind to rub himself after bathing with oil instead of with the wood ashes, which he generally used, made from the sweat of his arm a man named Rupnáráyan Teli or Manohar Pál, and inspired him with the idea of an oil-mill (*ghâni*). Some say that the original oil-mill was turned by two bullocks without blinkers, and that the Kalus were degraded for using one bullock only and blinding its eyes with blinkers. Another legend bearing on the same point is the following:—In the beginning of time the goddess Bhagavati made two men out of turmeric paste and ordered them to bring her oil. One came back very soon with a pot of oil; the other took much longer. When the goddess asked the reason of the delay, the latter explained that he had to soak up the oil with a bit of rag and squeeze it into a pot, while the former had stolen a march on him by using a mill with a hole at the bottom, through which the oil trickled out. On hearing this the goddess was much offended at the idea that she had used oil procured by a process resembling one of the baser functions of the human body, and condemned the more inventive of the two oilmen to pay the penalty of his ingenuity by being degraded to a lower caste. It would be quite in keeping with other cases of the growth of sub-castes that the Kalus should have been separated from the parent caste by reason of their having introduced an improvement in the primitive oil-mill; and the myth of Bhagavati's anger may well have arisen to account for their separation and for the lower social status assigned to them. There are, for example, two outcaste classes of oilmen in Eastern Bengal, who have been excommunicated because they manufacture oil in a novel manner: the first, or Gáchhuá Teli, express the oil by crushing the seed between wooden rollers; the second, or Bhúnjá Teli, parch the seed and then extract the oil. I do not know whether these groups have as yet started myths connecting their degradation with the displeasure of a god; but it is reasonable to expect that some such legend should in course of time be evolved.

Internal structure.

Concerning the origin of the sub-castes which bear the curious names of Ekádas and Dwádas Teli an interesting legend is current. The father of all the Telis, it is said, was Manohar Pál, a *beopári* or hawker who travelled about selling various wares. He had two wives. While he was away on a journey, a rumour reached his home that he was dead. Thereupon the elder wife broke her ornaments and performed the rites appointed for a widow, but the younger wife disbelieved the tale. In fact Manohar Pál was not dead, and returned home after a few days. From the two wives sprang the two sub-castes on. The Ekádas Teli are the the elder wife, and. Owádas Teli of the younger. In the elder wife breaking her ornaments on hearing of her husband's death, the Ekádas women do not wear nose-rings and do not tattoo their foreheads and arms. Each group claims precedence over the other. The Ekádas are of course the elder branch, and it is alleged that they represent the original stock of the Teli caste, which is stated in the list given in the Brahma-Vaivartta Purána to be derived from a Kumhár (potter) father and a mother of the builder caste, Kotak or Gharámi. It stands eleventh on the list, and this is the reason for the name Ekádas. The Dwádas Teli in their turn, while admitting the descent of the Ekádas from the elder wife of the founder of the caste, alleged that they have forfeited the precedence they might otherwise claim by submitting to be governed by Parámániks in all matters relating to caste, and by sending women of the bride's family to accompany her on her first visit after marriage to her husband's house. Another queer custom of the Ekádas group forbids them to wear moustaches, but English education is said to be breaking this down.

The Ghaná, Ghání, or Gáchhuá Telis work an oil-mill of primitive pattern. This machine has no hole for the removal of the oil, which has to be soaked up with a bit of rag tied on to a stick The Kalu, as has been explained above, use a mill with a hole to let out the oil. The status of the latter is very low, and their separation from the main body of the Telis is so complete that many regard them as a separate caste.

In Eastern Bengal, according to Dr. Wise, there are two great subdivisions of this caste: the Tail-pál, or Manohar Pál, and the Teli, the former being the richer and more numerous. The Tail-pál arefrequently distinguished by the epithet Do-paṭṭí, from having adopted the Sudra marriage custom of carrying the bride and bridegroom on stools. The Telí, again, are known as Ekgáchhí, from their planting a champa-tree, on which the bridegroom sits while the bride is carried round him several times, as is the custom with the Gandhabaniks.

Originally, it is said there were no divisions, and all oilmen belonged to one caste, but in course of time, as wealth accumulated in their hands, the richer families, ashamed of their ancestral occupation, have adopted a new name to conceal their parentage. Thus in the district of Central Bengal Telis who have grown rich call themselves Tilís, and affect to be of a higher lineage than the Telis, although they still retain the old family titles. Wealth and prosperity have made them give up the manufacture of oil, and led them to become Amdawáláh, or traders buying goods wholesale and selling them by retail. Some go the length of saying that Tili is a caste wholly distinct from Telí, but I doubt whether the process of separation has as yet gone so far as this.

In the northern parts of the Dacca district, beyond the limits of the country affected by the reforms of Ballál Sen, the oilman caste has hypergamous divisions, which are said to vary in almost every parganá. In Ráipúra, for example, there are four classes of this sort—

the Sa or seventeen families; the B enty-two; the Chaubís, or twenty-four; and the Chár, or —each taking rank in the order named. These differ from the standard Kulin grouping in that the competition is for wives, not husbands. Girls may marry in a class below their own, and large dowries are given by the three lower groups for wives belonging to the first class.

Marriage.

In Dacca city at the time of Dr. Wise's researches the Tail-páls and Telís used to intermarry, and were regarded as clean Súdras. The *gotras* common to both were Aliman, Ṣáṇḍilyá, and Kásyapa. In addition to the well-known Padavís, or family surnames, of Pál, Nandí, Dé, and Kúndu, Chaudharí, and Shikdar, honorary titles bestowed by the native government were common among them, while the headman was styled Mandal. In former days their unions (*dals*) were notorious for the faction fights which broke out whenever differences of opinion were expressed. No *dal* existed in Dr. Wise's time, but the Mandal used to summon a pancháyat when required.

The marriage arrangements of the Telis of Bengal are cast in the orthodox mould, and the attempt is to approach as closely as possible to the example furnished by the higher castes. The sections which regulate marriage are of the eponymous type; infant-marriage is fully established, and the marriage ceremony is in general conformity with the ritual prescribed in the Hindu scriptures. Widows may not marry again, and divorce is not recognized.

In other parts of the country the influence of orthodox tradition has been less powerful, and the aspirations of the caste are more modest. In Behar their sections belong to the titular or territorial types, while among the Telis of Chota Nagpur and Orissa totems are still held in reverence and regulate the intermarriage of members of the caste. Infant-marriage, though more usual than adult-marriage, is not reckoned absolutely essential; widow-marriage is permitted, the widow being usually expected to marry her deceased husband's younger brother. Divorce is recognized, and divorced women are permitted to marry again.

Religion.

In Bengal almost all Telis are Vaishnavas. Their principal festivals are those in honour of Lakshmi, Saraswati, and Gandheswari, the last being celebrated at the Dasahara in Áswin (September–October) and not on the full moon of Baisákh (April–May), as is the custom of the Gandhabanik caste. They employ as their priests Rárhi Brahmans, who are received on terms of equality by the Brahmans who minister to the spiritual wants of the higher castes. The Brahmans who serve the Kalus, on the other hand, are generally looked down upon, and occupy a position hardly higher than that of the degraded Brahmans who are the priests of the Kaibartta caste.

In Behar the worship of Vishṇu does not appear to be a special characteristic of the Telis, and the worship of the minor deities seems to hold a more prominent position than is the case in Bengal. Among these the Kanaujia Telis pay especial reverence to the Panch Pir and Goraya, while the Magahiyá sub-caste is more addicted to the cult of Kalihandi, Jalpait, and Dharam Ráj. To these rural divinities the former offer *khirpuri* sweetmeats and bread made of seven kinds of grain on Wednesdays during the light half of the month of Asin, while the latter observe a similar ritual on the same day during the light half of Sáwan and Mágh. If a vow is made or a special boon solicited from the god, a more sumptuous offering is needed, and in such cases the Maghayá Telis usually sacrifice a goat. On Tuesdays during the light half of Sáwan, the Kanaujiá Telis offer a sucking pig to Goraya. After the blood of the victim has been poured forth on the ground before the lump of dried mud which symbolises the presence of the god, the body is either buried under ground or given to a Dosádh, whose religious scruples do not deter him from a savoury meal. The practice may also be accounted for by the supposition, in itself by no means improbable, that the Dosádhs, like the Layas and Bhuiyas in Western Bengal, were generally recognized as the hereditary priests of the more primitive deities, and in that capacity were entitled to claim the offerings as their legitimate perquisite. An inferior class of Brahmans, spoken of contemptuously as "Tel-Bábhan," serve the Telí as priests.

In Eastern Bengal, according to Dr. Wise, the pure Telís only extract *til* oil from the sesamum seed, and caste is forfeited if any other oil be manufactured. The *ghání*, or oil-mill driven by bullocks, is never used, the oil being prepared in the following manner: The seeds are boiled and given to the Muhamadan Kútí to husk. After being sifted, the Telí puts them into large vats (*jálá*), boiling water being poured in, and the seeds allowed to soak for twelve hours. In the morning the liquid is beaten with bamboo paddles (*ghotná*) and left to settle, when the oil floating on the surface is skimmed off and stored, no attempts to purify it being made. The refuse (*khalí*) is given to cattle.

Social status.

The social standing of the Telís differs in different parts of the country and for different sub-castes. In Bengal, for example, the higher sub-castes of Telís, who have abandoned the oil trade and become bankers, money-lenders, cloth-dealers, and shop-keepers, take rank among the Nava-Sákha, or nine castes (now in fact fourteen) from whose hands a Brahman may take water, while the Kalus, or working oil men, are included in a lower group along with the Sutradhar, the Sundi, and the Kapáli. In Behar the entire caste seems to stand on this lower level, and no Brahman will take water from their hands.

Dr. Wise mentions that Krishna Kánta Nandí, better known as Kánta Babu, the banyan of Warren Hastings, was a Telí by caste, and did much to raise its position among the Hindus. On visiting Jagganáth he offered to provide an *atka* or assignment of land for the maintenance of the poor, but the *Pandá*, or presiding priest, refused to accept it from the hand of such an unworthy person. Against this decision Kánta Babu successfully appealed to the Pandits of Nadiyá and Hughli, who held that the Telí, by using the balance *Tula* in his trade, must necessarily belong to the Baniá, a clean Súdra caste. Kánta Babu died in 1780. He is said to have introduced the *nath*, or nose-ring, among the females of his caste, an ornament previously worn only by Brahmans and the higher Súdras. The present representative of his family, Mahárání Sarnamayí of Kásimbázár, is renowned for her munificent support of public and private charities, and her zealous efforts to further the intellectual advance of her countrymen and countrywomen.

The following statement shows the number and distribution of Telis in 1872 and 1881:—

District.	1672.	1881.	District.	1872.	1881.
Bardwan	123,275	51,199	Noakhali	2,954	4,489
Bankura	54,386	96.435	Tipperah	4,914	6,098
Birbhum	30,867	27,926	Chittagong Hill Tracts ...	......	8
Midnapur	75,840	77,339	Patna	47,509	53,880
Hughli	39,956	47,038	Gya	50,701	57,379
Howrah		15,492	Shahabad	41,440	47,836
24-Parganás	32,902	29,896	Mozaffarpur	136,208	82,856
Nadiya	30,119	32,335	Darbhanga		79,444
Jessore	21,443	14,280	Saran	55,138	63,087
Khulna	......	7,742	Champaran	42,916	52,842
Murshedabad	89,189	20,730	Monghyr	52,765	56,632
Dinajpur	6,955	6,044	Bhágalpur	64,103	66,946
Rajshahye	8,060	6,929	Purniah	38,701	38,136
Rangpur	3,262	3,379	Maldah	17,949	11,374
Bogra	1,946	2,740	Santál Parganás	27,954	36,915
Pabna	10,604	10,272	Cuttack	52,173	58,559
Darjiling	412	903	Puri	36,839	38,916
Jalpigori	2,728	2,471	Balasore	37,749	43,200
Kuch Behar	......	504	Tributary States	42,476	50,283
Dacca	13,711	16,201	Hazaribagh	29,876	42,319
Faridpur	7,818	14,490	Lohardagá	24.427	32,835
Bakarganj	12,184	7,280	Singbhum	3,904	4,110
Maimansinh	7,814	9,713	Manbhum	33,072	31,382
Chittagong	4,963	4,031	Tributary States	3,026	6,227

Telia, a tree, a totemistic sept of Mundas in Chota Nagpur.

Teliá-Nagasiá, a sub-tribe of Nageswars who use oil instead of *sindur* at marriage.

Teli Baniyá, a sub-caste of Baniyás in Behar.

Teligámia, a group of the Mihtar sub-caste of Telis in Behar.

Teliha, a section of Kamárkolla Sonárs in Behar.

Teling, the worker in cane, a sept of the Chhothar sub-tribe of Limbus in Darjiling.

Telinga, a small caste found in Bankura and believed to be the descendants of certain sepoys imported from Madras in the last century by one of the Rajas of Bishenpur. Curiously enough, they have adopted the totemistic sections used by the Bagdis and Bauris of Western Bengal.

Temdih, a *mul* or section of the Naomalia or Majraut sub-caste of Goálás in Behar.

Temrakoti, a *thar* or section of Nepáli Brahmans.

Tendun, a sept of Rájputs in Behar.

Tengrá, a section of Binjhiás in Chota Nagpur.

Tenshába, a bird, a totemistic sept of Juángs in Orissa.

Tentuliá, a section of Pátnis in Behar.

Tentuliá, *Tetuli*, a sub-caste of Bágdis in Bengal, named after the tamarind tree, and apparently totemistic.

Teor, a sub-caste of Bágdis in Bengal and of Kaibarttas who still serve as fishermen and boatmen.

Tera-Hazár or **Birbandhi**, a sub-caste of Cheros in Palámau.

Terahghariá, a sub-caste of Kurmis in Behar.

Tesá, a sept of Bhumijs in Chota Nagpur.

Tesong, a synonym for Limbu.

Teswár, a section of Doms in Behar.

Tetenga, bloodsucker, a totemistic sept of Parhaiyas.

Teteteyin or *Bagiár*, a section of Khariás in Chota Nagpur.

Tetiá, a sept of the Chandrabansi division of Rájputs in Behar.

Tetihá, a *kul* or section of Bábhans in Behar.

Tetong, a *thar* or sept of Murmis in Darjiling.

Teva Pánya, a *thar* or section of Nepáli Brahmans.

Tewan Raja, a kind of bird, a totemistic sept of Mundas in Chota Nagpur.

Tewári, **Tiwári**, a title of Kámárs in Bengal; of Brahmans and Bábhans in Behar; a section of Sribástab Káyasths and of Magahiyá Doms in Behar.

Tháda, a *thar* or sept of Mangars in Darjiling.

Thahráit, a section of the Kamár sub-caste of Dosádhs in Behar.

Thaini, a small labouring caste of Nepal.

Thákur, a synonym for Brahman; a section of the Sribástab sub-caste of Káyasths in Behar; a hypergamous division of the Maghayá sub-caste of Barhis; a title of Kanaujiá Lohárs, Bábhans, Brahmans, Rájputs, Kámárs, and of Hajjáms or barbers in Behar; a title of a respectable class of Tipperahs in Hill Tipperah.

Thákurmairar, a *pur* or section of Sákadwipi Brahmans in Behar.

Thákurta, an honorary title of Káyasths in Bengal.

Thambden, the stay-at-home, a sept of the Phedáb sub-tribe of Limbus in Darjiling.

Thampái-Mech, a sub-tribe of Meches in the Darjiling Terai.

Thamsong, a sub-sept of the Thekim sept of Limbus in Darjiling.

Thándár, a title of Haris and Chandáls in Bengal who serve as a village watch.

Thápa, a title of Mangars in Darjiling.

Thápángi, a section of Kámis in Darjiling.

Tharait, a section of Maghaya Kumhárs in Behar.

Tháriáme-Tháriám, a *mul* of the Kásyapa section of Maithil Brahmans in Behar.

Tharmáit, a *dih* or local section of the Maghayá sub-caste of Telis in Behar. The system of exogamy among this sub-caste of Telis seems, however, either to be dying out or to be of recent introduction, for some of the Maghayás say they have no *dihs*, but merely prohibit marriage within nine *pirhis* or degrees of relationship.

Thâru, a non-Aryan tribe of Behar and Upper India, whose scattered settlements are met with all along the Himalayan terai, from the Kosi river in Purniah to the Sárda between Kumáon and Nepal. In an exhaustive account of the tribe published in the *Calcutta Review*,[1] Mr. Nesfield has the following remarks on their name:—

"Absurd etymologies have been given for the name *Thâru*, some deriving it from *tahre*, "they halted" (after their alleged flight into the forest), others from *tar hua*, "wet," in allusion to the swampy nature of the tract they live in. One writer derives it from *áthwáru*, 'an eighth-day serf.'[2] But this implies what is not true. The Thârus are remarkable for their indolence, aversion to service, and incapacity for sustained field labour; and they have never been in the position of serfs to any landlords. Had this been the case, they would have sunk long ago into the ranks of Arakhs, Pâsis, Chamârs, Koris, and other Hindu castes of the lowest rank, who serve as field labourers or bond slaves to landlords in the open plain, and have lost the free life of the forest, which Thârus still enjoy. Another etymology suggested is from *thár*, which in the colloquial dialect of the lowest classes, but not in the language of books, signifies forest; and thus *thâru* would mean 'man of the forest,' a name which correctly describes the status of the tribe. On the whole, however, it is safer not to seek for any Hindi etymology, but to consider the name as sprung from the language of the tribe itself, which is now for the most part obsolete. An aboriginal name, underived from any Sanskrit or neo-Sanskrit source, is the fit appellative to an aboriginal, casteless, and un-Brahmanised tribe, whose customs have been only slightly modified by contact with those of the Aryan invader."

Traditions of origin.

The origin of the Thârus has formed the subject of much controversy. The Rautár sub-tribe claim to be the descendants of certain Rájputs of Chittor, who quarrelled with their chief after his defeat by the Mahomedans, divested themselves of the sacred thread, and took to agricultural

---

[1] *Description of the Manners, Industries, and Religion of the Thâru and Bogsha Tribes of Upper India.* By John C. Nesfield, M.A., Oxon. January 1885.

[2] The first etymology is alluded to in *Oudh Gazetteer*, 1877, vol. ii, p. 126; the second, in *North-West Census Report*, 1867, vol. i, p. 61; the third (the author of which is Raja Siva Prasad, C.I.I.), in *North-West Provinces Gazetteer*, 1881, vol. vi, p. 358.

pursuits. Mr. Nesfield, however, points out that—"Some Thárus know nothing about this tradition, and those who do are not able to tell you whether it was the sack by Alaudin (A.D. 1303), or that by Bahâdur Shah (A.D. 1533), or that by Akbar (A.D. 1567). The story is absurd on the face of it. Not the slightest allusion to Thârus in connection with any of these events is made by the Mahommedan historians. The fiction of having come from Rajputâna was invented by some of the clans merely to raise themselves in their own and their neighbours' estimation. There is scarcely any hunting tribe or caste in Upper India which has not set up a similar claim."

Putting aside the hypothesis of Rájput descent as wholly untenable, we may, I think, conclude from the physical appearance of the tribe that they are simply an aboriginal race, whose ancestors bore rule at one time in the valley of the Ganges, and were gradually driven up into the sub-Himalayan forests by the expansion of the Aryan community. Thus within the last two or three centuries they have been brought into contact with the Nepalese, and their physiognomy "has acquired in some instances a slightly Mongolian cast, which shows itself chiefly, but not to a striking degree, in slanting eyes and high cheek-bones. In other respects their physical characteristics are of the strictly Indian type. They have long, wavy hair; a dark, almost a black, complexion; and as much hair on the face and body as is usual with other natives of India.[1] In stature, build, and gait they are distinctly Indian, and not Mongolian; nor have they any traditions whatever which connect their origin with Nepal. A century's intercourse with the people of the hills is more than sufficient to account for the slight Mongolian cast which some members of the tribe have acquired." They belong, in fact, to the large group of aboriginal races who are classed as Dravidian or Kolarian, according to the character of the language which they speak. The Thárus having lost their language cannot be affiliated to one or other of these linguistic families; but Mr. Nesfield's description of their appearance, which agrees substantially with the accounts given by other observers, leaves little room for doubting their non-Aryan descent. The relations said to have sprung up in comparatively recent times between the Thárus and the Nepalese find a tolerably complete parallel in the intermixture which has taken place between the Dhimáls of the Darjiling Terai and some of the lower castes of Nepal.

Internal structure.

The internal structure of the tribe, so far as I have been able to work it out, is shown in Appendix I. My own researches, however, extend only to Behar, and the enumeration of sub-tribes and septs is probably not complete even for that province. The nomadic habits of the Thárus, and the great extent of forest-clad area over which their settlements are scattered, must in the long run tend to promote the formation of sub-castes, and at the same time to make it difficult for the most careful

[1] A Native correspondent, to whom I am indebted for some interesting notes on the Thárus of Champáran, remarks on the scantiness of their beards and moustaches, but this peculiarity may have been due to crossing with Nepalese or Mech.

inquirer to give an absolutely correct account of the internal divisions of the community, which in all likelihood are liable to continual variations.

In Gorakpur, according to Mr. Nesfield, the Thárus divide themselves into two classes,—the Purabi or eastern, and the Pachhami or western, the latter of whom call themselves Chattris, and refuse to eat with members of the eastern branch. The western Thárus again are broken up into an upper (*barka*) and lower (*Chhotka*) division. Further west, in the Gonda district of Oudh, we find the Dangaria sub-tribe, who eat pork, and the Kathāriá, who affect to abstain from it. In Behar the Rautár rank the highest, owing possibly to the belief, which their name may have helped to encourage, that they are somehow connected with the Rájputs. Rautárs will not eat food cooked by members of the other sub-castes. Chitwaniá or Chitauniá Thárus follow the profession of weavers, and say that their ancestors were Joláhás, who gave water to the Raja of Chittor when he was out shooting, and obtained from him the boon that good Hindus should ever afterwards take water from their hands. This sub-tribe is more common in Nepal than in British territory. Its members have certain peculiar usages, the reasons for which I cannot ascertain. They perform no *sráddh* after a death, nor do their women go through any purificatory ceremony after child-birth. The bridal procession (*barát*) is limited to four or five persons, who go on their way in silence and employ no musicians to proclaim their errand. Among their minor deities they worship the Raja of Chittor, to whom they owe their promotion from the comparatively low status of Joláhá.

The septs appear to be either titular or territorial, and throw no light upon the early affinities. The rule of exogamy followed is the simple one that a man may not marry a woman belonging to the same sept (*bán*) as himself. The standard formula for reckoning prohibited degrees is also observed to four generations in the descending line on either side.

Marriage.

Both infant and adult-marriage are in force, and sexual intercourse before marriage is said to be tolerated by the Chitwaniá Thárus. The traditional amount of the bride-price is supposed to be Rs. 9, but this is liable to vary according to the circumstances of the family. The marriage ceremony is modelled on the ritual in vogue among the lower Hindu castes. Slight traces of the form of capture may perhaps be discerned in it, but these are not very marked among the Thárus of Behar. Brahmans officiate as priests, and the brother-in-law (*ganjuá*) of the bride usually takes a prominent part in the proceedings. In the Mardaniá and Chitwaniá sub-tribes the bridegroom's party, instead of being entertained by the bride's people, are expected to feast the latter for three days before the bride is produced. No second ceremony (*gauná*) is performed when the bride goes finally to live with her husband. When she is married as an adult, she goes to her husband at once, and in all cases I understand it is deemed proper for her to spend one night at her husband's house immediately after marriage. On the occasion of this visit she and the relations who accompany her are entertained at a feast called *dulhi bhatáwan*, 'giving rice to the bride,' which celebrates her formal admission into the sept to which her husband belongs. If she is still an infant, she is taken back next day to her parent's house by her brother-in-law, and remains there until she has attained sexual maturity.

Polygamy is permitted, and there appears to be no definite rule limiting the number of wives a man may have. Widows may marry again, and are subject to no special restrictions in their selection of a second husband. Divorce is allowed, and appears to be extremely common. The bond of wedlock is held in light esteem among the Thárus, who countenance a degree of sexual laxity analogous to that which prevails among many of the Nepalese castes, and generally among the sub-Himalayan races. Divorced women may marry again by the same ceremony as widows, and both classes are distinguished by the designation *urari*, or 'selected,' from women who were married as virgins by the full ritual. The social status of an *urari* wife is respectable, though slightly inferior to that of a *byáhi* wife. Even this position, however, is not accorded to her unless she is married with the consent of the relatives of her second husband, which is signified by the ceremony of *bhatáná*, or formally admitting her to the *jus cibi* of the household. Unless this is done she is called a *suraitin*, or concubine, and her husband cannot take water or cooked food from her hands without endangering his own standing in the family. *Bhatáná* is also necessary when any one has been debarred from social intercourse for an offence against the customs of the tribe. There seems to be some difference of practice among the Tháru sub-tribes in respect of the admission of women from a different sub-tribe. Some groups receive women from any other group, others only from certain specified groups, while Rautárs decline to admit any outsiders to the privilege of *bhatáná*, although they allow a woman of another sub-tribe to be kept by a Rautár man as a *suraitin*. Such women, however, have no rights as members of the family, and their children belong to their mother's sub-tribe.

Religion.

The religion of the Thárus is a compound of the mingled animism and Nature-worship characteristic of the aboriginal races and of elements borrowed from popular Hinduism. A prominent place in their pantheon is taken by the hero Rikheswar, whom I suspect to be identical with the Rikhmun of the Musahar-Bhuiyas. According to the legend in vogue among the Thárus of Kheri, this deified founder was a son of the renowned aboriginal King Raja Ben, whose fame is still rife in many of the oldest cities of Upper India and Behar as one who held the rank and title of *Chakravarti*, or universal emperor, in the olden time. Rikheshwar or Raksha was banished, it is said, from his father's court, and ordered with his band of male followers to seek for a new home in the north, from which they were never to return. Setting out on their wanderings, they took as wives any women whom they could steal or capture on the road, and in this way the Tháru tribe was founded. It was not till they had reached the sub-Himalayan forest in which they still dwell that they decided to rest and settle. The soul of Raksha is still believed to hover among the people of his tribe. Just as in ancient days he led them safely through the wide wilderness into a new and distant settlement, so in the present day he is said to be the guardian and guide of men travelling on a distant journey. No Thâru ever sets out from his village for such a purpose without first propitiating him with gifts and promising him a sumptuous feast of flesh, milk, and wine on his return. His presence is represented by a mound of mud, with a stone fixed in the middle; and he delights in seeing the head of a live capon dashed against this stone, and to feel its blood trickling down the side. One peculiarity of this god is that he is deaf,—an emblem of his antiquity; and hence vows and prayers are addressed to him in a stentorian tone of voice. The title *gurua*, which is generally prefixed to his name, implies that during his residence on earth he was famous as a wizard or medicine-man, and acquired through this means the kingship or leadership of his tribe.

The animistic element in the Thâru faith being represented by Rikheswar, we may perhaps trace a mangled survival of Nature-worship in two other deities of some importance, to whom Thârus address their vows. One is Madadeo, the god of intoxicating liquor, especially of the rice-wine made by themselves; the other is Dharchandi, the patroness of cattle, though her name would imply that she was at first intended to impersonate the earth. Her shrine, like those of the other deities already named, is a mound of clay. The mound dedicated to Dharchandi is studded with short wooden crosses, on which rice, pulse, and other produce of the fields are offered, and always on plates of leaf. Her shrine is so placed that all the cattle of the village, together with the swine, sheep, and goats, pass it on going out to graze, and repass it on their return. When the cattle sicken or die, larger and more valuable offerings are made. Neither of these deities is known or worshipped by other natives of Upper India.

Fowls are offered to Dharchandi; he-goats to Mari, the patron goddess of Kanjars and, according to Mr. Nesfield, identical with Kâli. This, however, seems not to be the case in Behar. In Champâran Kua is worshipped as a village deity by casting sweetmeats down a well (*kuâ*) and smearing vermilion on its rim. All these primitive deities, however, are rapidly losing ground in the estimation of the people, and giving way to the more popular worship of Siva and his consort Kâli. It is likely enough that both of these are themselves merely elaborated forms of aboriginal objects of worship, which may well have been familiar to an earlier generation of Thârus. But Siva and Kali, as now revered by the tribe, have clearly been borrowed at quite a recent date from the Hindus, and cannot be regarded as indigenous deities.

The goddess who presides over life and death, and whom the Thârus believe to be the supreme power in the universe, is Kâlikâ,—one of the numerous forms of Devi, Durgâ, or Kâli, at whose name all India trembles, especially the low castes and the casteless tribes, amongst whom she originally sprung. Medicine-men look to Kâlikâ as the special patroness of their art. To the fair sex she is the goddess of parturition, and her aid is especially invoked by women who have had no children. All classes combine to give her a periodical ovation, accompanied with much dancing, banqueting, and drinking of wine at about the middle of October. Thárus also take part in the huge animal sacrifice performed at her celebrated altar in Devi Patan (Gonda district). Such is her thirst for blood, that at this time 20 buffaloes, 250 goats, and 250 pigs are slaughtered daily for ten days continuously. The sacrifice is vicarious, the blood of buffaloes, etc., being intended as a substitute for that of human victims. This loathsome festival is thronged with visitors from the plains of India and from the hills of Nepal, Sikkim, and Bhotan.

"Another deity revered by Thârus, and, like Kâlikâ, of indigenous or non-Aryan origin, is her consort Siva, known chiefly amongst Thârus by the name of Bhairava, the Terrible, or Thakur, the Lord, and amongst Hindus by that of Mahadev, the great god. He, like his spouse, is a god of destruction, and thirsts for blood; but he is chiefly worshipped by Thârus as the author of reproduction, of which a stone lingam, as amongst Hindus, is sometimes made the symbol. It is more usual, however, for a Thâru to erect a mud mound in front of his house and fix an upright pole in its centre to represent the presence of this phallic divinity."

Although modern Hinduism is fast displacing the earlier gods of the Tháru religion, it seems probable that the principles of their primitive belief will long survive in the strong fear of evil spirits which continually haunts the tribe. It is to the action of these spirits that fever, ague, cough, dysentery, fainting, headache, madness, bad dreams, and pain of all kinds are ascribed. In fact, the Thárus have no conception of natural disease, and no belief in natural death, except what is faintly conceived to be the result of natural decay. Their state, therefore, would be one of utter helplessness were it not for the reputed skill of medicine-men or sorcerers, who profess to have the power to control the spirits of the air or to interpret their grievances and wants. In the Tháru language these men are called *bararar;* but the titles of Guru, Guruâ, Bhagat, Nyotya, Ojhait, all of which are borrowed from Hindi, are now in common use, though even of these the last two are probably of aboriginal or non-Sanskrit origin. The power of the medicine-man is tremendous. He has a host of liege spirits at his command. Not only can he expel a fiend from the body of the sufferer, but he can produce suffering or death by driving a malignant spirit into the body of his foe. In order to exorcise an evil spirit, he holds in his left hand some ashes of cowdung, or grains of mustard seed, or wild nuts, and after breathing some mystical virtue into them by the utterance of a spell, he causes the patient to eat them, or has them attached to his arm. One of the spells uttered at such times is as follows. It is addressed to Kâlikâ, the Tháru goddess of death and patroness of the magical art:—

Gur hai gur sair Gur tantra mantra Gur: Lakhai niranjan; toka sohai phulka bhâr; Hamka sohai gun vidyâ kai bhâr: Yahân kai vidyâ nahin, Kamru Kâm kai vidyâ. Jaise vidyâ Kamru Kâm kai lâgai, waise vidyâ lâgai mor.

The language is that of bad and scarcely intelligible Hindi, and might be rendered thus:—

"The Guru (Kâlikâ) is great, she is everything, she is *tantra* "(magic by deeds), she is *mantra* (magic by words). She points out "the way to relief. Thou (oh Kâlikâ) deservest to be heaped with "flowers. I too deserve to be heaped with secret wisdom,—the wisdom "of Kamru Kâm, not the wisdom of this country. Whatever "effects the knowledge of Kamru Kâm produces, such effects let my "knowledge produce also."

Disposal of the dead.

"The burial rites of Thárus are of various kinds. Sepulture or earth-burial seems to have been the original custom; but the Hindu rite of cremation has now become common in many clans, except in the case of persons who have died of cholera or small-pox; and these are invariably buried in the earth. After cremation the ashes are scattered on the nearest river. Before, however, the corpse has been disposed of by either rite, it is usual to paint it with vermilion and expose it for one night on a mound outside the house. From this mound, as from a stronghold, the spirit of the dead is supposed to scare away wild animals from the corpse. Whether the body is buried or burnt, the ceremony is always performed on the southern side of the village—a notion probably borrowed from Hindus, who consider that the north is the region commonly frequented by divine spirits, and the south by human souls. The man who puts the first fire to the funeral pyre is considered to be unclean, from having brought himself within dangerous reach of the contagion of death. He is therefore kept at a distance for ten days after cremation, and compelled to live entirely alone.". . . . . "On the expiry of the tenth day (or the thirteenth, as some Thârus relate), the friends of the deceased meet at the house where he died, and after undergoing the ceremony of shaving they hold 'a feast of the dead.' The banquet prepared for this purpose consists of cooked flesh and wine, the scent and smoke of which are intended to refresh the departed soul: the solid parts—that is, the flesh and wine themselves—are consumed by the living."

"In certain rare cases the burial rite is performed in a manner distinct from either of those already described. A man noted above his fellows for wisdom in counsel, bravery in the chase, or knowledge of the magical and medicinal arts, is buried under the floor of the house in which he was living before his spirit departed. The house thenceforth becomes a temple, and ceases to be used as a dwelling place for man. The soul of the dead becomes its occupant, and it lives there to bless those whom it has left behind. At periods of three or six months after the death, the friends and neighbours of the deceased assemble around his grave or temple and make an effigy in clay, parts of which are painted in various colours, intended to reproduce the appearance of resuscitated life. His worshippers fall down weeping and wailing before the image, and place offerings of cooked flesh and wine at its feet. Presently, at a given signal, as soon as the soul of the dead is believed to have been propitiated by the scent of roast meat and the fumes of wine, they commence to dance and sing with every demonstration of joy; and the proceedings of the day are closed with consuming the solid parts of the offerings."

Social status.

The Thárus stand wholly outside of the Hindu caste organization, and their social status cannot be defined by any of the ordinary standards. No orthodox Hindu will eat with a Tháru or take water from his hands, and by the higher castes his mere touch would be deemed pollution. This comparatively degraded position is, however, due in great measure to the nomadic habits of the tribe, and to the fact that they come very little into contact with settled Hindu communities. Thárus follow the forest; their typical village is a line of huts in the middle of a clearing, and their favourite mode of husbandry was until lately the *jhum* method of burning the jungle and planting a crop in the ashes. The scanty crops obtained in this fashion are eked out by hunting and fishing, by gathering forest fruits and vegetables, and by grazing cows and buffaloes. Avoiding the larger villages of the plains, they live their own life on the outskirts of Hindu civilization, and no place has as yet been allotted in the Hindu social system. "Every little village," says Mr. Nesfield, "is a self-governing community. Disputes are decided by a council of elders; and this is sometimes presided over by a headman, who in the Thâru language was formerly called *barwaik*, but who is now dubbed even by themselves with the ordinary Hindi title of *chaudhari*. The office of headman is not hereditary. The man selected is one whose age, experience, and knowledge of the magical and medicinal arts entitle him to more respect than the rest; and he acquires the status of headman by tacit consent, and not by formal election. The decisions of the council or the headman are obeyed unreservedly, and there is no such thing known as a Thâru taking a fellow tribesman before a tribunal outside his own community. Litigation between Thárus and Hindus is equally unknown. Among themselves the Thárus are for the most part a peaceful and good-natured race, following without question, as if by a law of nature, the customs and maxims of their ancestors." Notwithstanding their comparative isolation, their customs show many signs of the influence of Hindu example. Their religious observances tend unmistakeably towards Sivaism; their marriage ceremony is framed on a Hindu model; they revere the cow, and scrupulously abstain from eating beef. Their ultimate reception into the standard social system seems therefore merely to be a question of time. In other respects their practice in matters of food falls short of the orthodox standard. They eat pigs and fowls, and make no distinction between the clean and unclean species of fish. Field-rats they will cook when pressed for food, and the porcupine (*sáhi*) is thought a delicacy, because his flesh resembles that of the pig. Mr. Nesfield mentions that when their stock of meat becomes larger than they can consume at once, they preserve it by cutting it into strips and drying it in the sun.

Occupation.

As agriculturists they are still for the most part in the migratory stage, cultivating the land on which they have put up their temporary houses till it has given proof of exhaustion, and then moving off to fresh grounds to make a new clearance. Formerly it was their custom not to crop the same land for more than two years together. But this is now no longer the case. The Government conservancy laws, which have come into force of late, have interfered very seriously with their freedom in the selection of new sites; and hence the present tendency of the tribe is either to move up into Nepal territory or to remain below for a longer period in the same place. The crop in which Thárus chiefly delight is rice—the grain best suited to the swampy nature of their fields and to the heavy rainfall of the months between June and October. The coarse red rice called *sáthi* is the quality preferred. In the rainless months they chiefly grow peas, a small black grain called *kodo*, and the pulse called *arhar*. Such crops require occasional irrigation; and this is effected, not by drawing water from wells or from tanks and marshes and conveying it into the fields through artificial channels, as is the custom of Hindu cultivators, but by the rough-and-ready process of damming up the nearest rivulet and thus inundating the crop.

The women do the largest share of the sowing, weeding, and harvesting, while the men engage in hunting, fishing, etc., which they consider the proper calling of their sex. Such has been the invariable instinct of savage tribes both in India and elsewhere. The men have an intense repugnance to regular manual labour, and nothing will induce them to hire themselves out as labourers to Hindu landlords. The only kind of service which a Thåru will undertake is that of elephant-driver to some neighbouring princelet or råja. Their skill as elephant-drivers is admitted everywhere; and latterly they have acquired the art of catching wild elephants from the forest and taming them for the prince who employs them.

The only kinds of art or manufacture which Thárus can be said to possess are the manipulation of leaves, reeds, and fibres, and a rude kind of carpentry. The latter is exemplified in making the wooden part of the plough, in shaping the handles of tools, dove-tailing the corners of wells, and in fixing up the sides and roofs and floors of their houses. The former is an accomplishment common to backward races in every part of the world, wherever the materials exist; and here in India it is practised by all the low castes of Hindus (Bhars, Påsis, Bhangis, Båris, Dharkars, etc.) whose stage of culture is scarcely, if at all, raised above that of the casteless tribes. The Thárus make strong and durable mats out of the fine *bankas* grass, which they gather in large quantities from the lower ranges of the hills in the first quarter of the year. Excellent twine and rope are made from the same material; and such twine is used for the manufacture of fishing nets, nooses, and snares, for drawing water from the well, for tethering cattle, and many other purposes. Not less skilled are they in making the funnel-shaped baskets in which fish are caught, or in thatching the roofs of their houses. They have even invented a kind of umbrella made of cane and mat work; so great is their aversion to the sun and to the open plains. For plates and drinking cups they skewer large leaves together to the shape required for either purpose; and for drawing and keeping water they use a hollowed gourd or tomri. Some who are better off than others use vessels made of clay or brass; but these can only be obtained from Kumhârs (potters) and Thateras (braziers), both of whom are Hindu castes; for there is no such thing as home-made pottery or brass work amongst the Tháru tribe.

The following statement shows the number and distribution of Thárus in 1872 and 1881:—

District.	1872.	1881.	District.	1872.	1881.
Darjiling	......	113	Champaran	21,450	18,395
Darbhanga	320	915	Bhágalpur	48	112
Saran	......	2	Purniah	45	1,510

Thâther or *Thathera*, a sub-caste of Kándus in Behar; a section of the Banodhiá and Jaiswár Halwáis in Behar.

Thatherá, *Thatheri*, a brazier; in Shahabad also called Kaserá, which properly means a brass founder. See **Kaserá**.

Thâthung, a *thar* or sept of Gurungs in Darjiling.

Thawai, a synonyn for *raj mistiri* or mason, in use in Saran and South Champaran.

Thazœpá, a *rui* or sept of the Ruichhung sub-tribe of Dejong Lhoris or Bhotias of the south.

Theguba, the son of the cliff, a sept of the Phedáb sub-tribe of Limbus in Darjiling.

Thehbeh, a sept of the Yangorup sub-tribe of Limbus. This is an eponymous *thar* named after Thehbeh, son of Srijanga, the powerful chief of the tribe, since deified, who fought against Prithi Nárayan, the founder of the present ruling dynasty of Nepal.

Thek, a synonym for Chakmá.

Thekim, he who works in wicker, including the sub-septs (*a*) Meongba, (*b*) Thamsong, (*c*) Chobegu, (*d*) Petehhimba, (*e*) Angbu, the forest-dweller, (*f*) Yakten, formerly doctors—a sept of the Pánthar sub-tribe of Limbus in Darjiling.

Thekra, a section of Binjhiás in Chota Nagpur.

Themjáni, a *thar* or sept of Gurungs in Darjiling.

Thengáit, a section of the Dhusiá sub-caste of Chamárs in Behar.

Thenglahbo, the native of Thenglah, a sept of the Ahtharai sub-tribe of Limbus in Darjiling.

Theni, a section of Utkal or Orissa Brahmans.

Thero, *Tharua*, a sub-tribe of Santáls in the south of Manbhum who employ Brahmans and have adopted portions of the Hindu ritual.

Theya, a sept of Chakmás in the Hill Tracts of Chittagong.

Thholáchá, a *thar* or sept of Sunuwárs in Darjiling.

Thing, a section of Murmis in Darjiling.

Thingal, a *gotra* or section of Agarwáls.

Thithio, a bird with long legs, a totemistic sept of Mundas in Chota Nagpur.

Thobukya, he who has skin disease, a sept of the Phedáb sub-tribe of Limbus in Darjiling.

Thogleng, the suicide, a sept of the Chhothar sub-tribe of Limbus in Darjiling.

Thogphelagu, he who wears the rhododendron flower, a sept of the Charkhola sub-tribe of Limbus in Darjiling.

Thokar, a section of Murmis in Darjiling.

Thokcháki, a *thar* or sept of Mangars in Darjiling.

Thollong, the ragged one, a sept of the Miákhola sub-tribe of Limbus in Darjiling.

Tholchá, a *thar* or sept of Sunuwárs in Darjiling.

Thomi, a synonym for Mangar.

Thongtha, *Thongcha*, or *Jumiá Magh*, a sub-tribe of Maghs in the Hill Tracts of Chittagong.

Thoreliá, a section of the Banodhiá and Jaiswár Kalwárs in Behar.

Thukrán, a section of Goálás in the North-Western Provinces and Behar.

Thulung, a *thar* or sept of Khambus in Darjiling.

Thumuchá, a *thar* or sept of Sunuwárs in Darjiling.

Thungong-hepta, a sept of the Phága sub-tribe of Yakhas in Darjiling.

Thupra, a sept of the Phágu sub-tribe of Yakhas in Darjiling.

Thupuku, a sept of the Yangorup sub-tribe of Limbus in Darjiling.

Thup-yumah, name of a place, a sept of the Tambrkhola sub-tribe of Limbus in Darjiling.

Tiar, a synonym for Tiyar; a sub-caste of Kewats in Orissa.

Tiár, a sept of Rájputs in Behar.

Tiar, *Teor*, a sub-caste of Malláhs in Behar.

Tiar or Dalai, a group of the Rájbansi sub-caste of Kochhs in Northern Bengal.

Tig, a monkey, which is the totem of a section of Oraon-Dhángars settled for several generations in North Bhagalpur.

Tihu, a sept of Hos in Singbhum.

Tiyra, a synonym for Mirshikár.

Tikaur, a sub-caste of Brahmans in Behar.

Tikká, a sub-sept of the Murmu sept of Santáls.

Tiklihár, *Trijattá*, or *Maghaiya Brahman*, a caste employed in making *tiklis*, the spangles, wafers, or glass patches worn upon the forehead by women. They permit widow-marriage and rank socially among the serving castes, such as Kahárs. In Patna the term *tiklihár* denotes merely the occupation described above, which is followed by Mahomedans.

Tilachhwar, a section of Bábhans in Behar.

Tiláiwár, a *mul* of the Sándil section of Maithil Brahmans in Behar.

Tilakchandi, a sept of Rájputs in Behar.

Tilak Dás, a sub-caste of Tiyars in Eastern Bengal; a sect of Vaishnavs who follow the tenets of Tilak-dás.

Tilatwár, a *mul* or section of the Naomulia or Majraut sub-caste of Goálás in Behar.

Tilautá, a sept of the Suryabansi sub-tribe of Rájputs in Behar.

Tilding, a sept of Limbus in Darjiling.

Tili, a worker in *til* (*sesamum orientale*), a synonym for Teli.

Tiliá, a section of the Baranwár sub-caste of Baniyás in Behar.

Timilsiná, a *thar* of the Mautkaha *gotra* of Nepáli Brahmans.

Tin, a sept of Hos in Singbhum.

Tinai Prabarái, a *thar* of the Basishtha *gotra* of Nepáli Brahmans.

Tindiha, a section of Bantariá Kándus in Behar.

Tingal, a *gotra* or section of Agarwáls.

Tingilmung, a sept of Lepchas in Darjiling.

Tinmuliá Madhesia, a sub-caste of Halwáis in Behar.

Tinriár, a section of the Amashta sub-caste of Káyasths in Behar.

Tior, a synonym for Tiyar.

Tipperah, *Triprá*, *Mrung*, a wandering tribe of Hill Tipperah and the Chittagong Hill Tracts, who live by the *jhúm* cultivation described in the article on the Magh tribe. Lewin identifies them with the Mrungs of Arrakan, who, according to Colonel Phayre, believe themselves to be the descendants of persons carried away from Tipperah by the Arrakan kings. The Maghs speak of the entire tribe by the name Mrung, and do not use the Bengali word Tipperah. Members of the Tipperah tribe have no general name for their race, and when speaking his own language a man describes himself by mentioning the sept to which he belongs. When speaking Bengali, however, he would say he was a Tipperah. It seems to follow from this that the term Tipperah is not a genuine tribal name, but a designation conferred by outsiders by reason of the tribe being specially numerous in Hill Tipperah. Whether this was their original habitat or not is uncertain, and some have supposed that they came from Manipur. To attempt to trace the earliest home of a wandering tribe who live by *jhúm* cultivation and have neither written records nor definite oral traditions must always be a somewhat hopeless task, and the most reasonable view of the matter seems to be that taken by Friedrich Müller and other German ethnologists, who class all the wild tribes of the Chittagong and Tipperah Hills under the head Lohitic, a word which denotes some sort of connexion with the Brahmaputra river, and describe them in general terms as standing in the same ethnic relation to the Burmese as the Himalayan

Origin.

races do to the Tibetans.[1] The classification into Toungtha and Khyoungtha, hill-people and river-people, adopted by Captain Lewin, however convenient for local use, fails, as Professor Virchow[2] has observed, to bring out the true racial affinities of the various tribes.

Internal structure.

The Tipperahs are described in a survey report by Mr. H. J. Reynolds as having strongly-marked Mongolian features, with flat faces and thick lips. They are of much the same stature as Bengalis, but their frames are far more muscular and strongly made. Many of them have fair complexions, scarcely darker than a swarthy European. The tribe is divided into a number of septs, which are shown in the Appendix. They appear to be exogamous, but on this point there is some difference of opinion. I have only been able to discover the meaning of one sept name, Kákulu, a kind of gourd, and with regard to this no one could tell me whether the members of the Kákulu sept were forbidden to eat this gourd or were subject to any kind of taboo in respect of it. The point seems to demand further inquiry in the Hill Tracts by some one thoroughly acquainted with the language of the tribe. The Riáng sept serve as palanquin-bearers, and are said to be looked down upon by the others; but it does not appear that they have on this account been excluded from the right of intermarriage with other septs. The Mahárájas of Hill Tipperah, who now put forward an untenable claim to be Rájputs, are believed to belong to the Áfang and Jumátya septs, the members of which frequently call themselves Rájbansi by way of recalling their relationship to the royal family. The Káli sept furnish the guards of the chief.

Intermarriage.

Tipperahs admit into their tribe Lushais, Maghs, and Hindus. The ceremony of admission consists simply of a feast given by the new member, at which a pig is served up and a huge quantity of drink consumed. The proselyte declares himself to have entered the tribe, and is treated thenceforth as if he had been a Tipperah by birth. The liquors drunk on these and similar occasions are *khung* (ferment from rice), *sipá* (fermented from *birni*), and arrack (distilled from rice).

Marriage.

Adult-marriage is the universal rule, and "great freedom of intercourse is allowed between the sexes, but a Tipperah girl is never known to go astray out of her own clan. An illegitimate birth, also, is hardly known among them, for the simple reason that should a girl become *enciente* her lover has to marry her. The girls are totally free from the prudery that distinguishes Mahomedan and Hindu women, and they have an open, frank manner, combined with a womanly modesty that is attractive. At a marriage there is no particular ceremony, but a great deal of drinking and dancing. A pig is killed as a sacrifice to the deities of the wood and stream, the crowning point of the affair being this: the girl's mother pours out a glass of

---

[1] F. Müller, *Allgemeine Ethnographie*, p. 405

[2] Riebeck's *Chittagong Hill-Tribes, Anthropological Remarks.*

liquor and gives it to her daughter, who goes and sits on her lover's knee, drinks half, and gives him the other half; they afterwards crook together their little fingers. If a match be made with the consent of the parents, the young man has to serve three years in his father-in-law's house before he obtains his wife or is formally married. During the period of probation his sweetheart is to all intents and purposes a wife to him. On the wedding night, however, the bridegroom has to sleep with his wife surreptitiously, entering the house by stealth and leaving it before dawn. He then absents himself for four days, during which time he makes a round of visits among all his friends. On the fourth day he is escorted back with great ceremony, and has to give another feast to his *cortége*. A Tipperah widow may remarry if it so seems good to her. Every lad before marriage has his sweetheart, and he cohabits with her whenever opportunity serves. This, however, is without the knowledge of the elders.

"Divorce," says Major Lewin, "can be obtained among the Tipperahs, as among all the hill tribes, on the adjudication of a jury of village elders. One such case I remember to have seen. The divorce was sued for by the wife on the grounds of habitual cruelty. The jury deliberated and found that the cruelty was proved, and that the divorce should be granted. Some check, however, they determined, must be put upon the woman, or otherwise every wife would complain if her husband raised his little finger at her. Accordingly they gave sentence that the divorce was granted, but that as the woman was wrong to insist upon abandoning her lawful husband, she should give up all her silver ornaments to him, pay a fine of thirty rupees, and provide a pig with trimmings, in the shape of ardent spirits, to be discussed by the jury."

Religion.

The religion of the Tipperahs is a debased form of Hinduism. They offer to Káli black goats, rice, plantains, sweetmeats, areca nut, curds, red lead, etc. The goddess has no image, but is represented for sacrificial purposes by a round lump of clay, the edges of which are drawn out into four points or legs, so that the whole, seen from above, bears a rough resemblance to sea-urchin with four arms. Satya-Náráyan is also worshipped, but in his case the offerings consist only of fruits or flowers. The tribe do not employ Brahmans, but have priests, or rather exorcists, of their own, called Auchái, whose office is hereditary.

Disposal of the dead.

"When a Tipperah dies, his body is immediately removed from within the house to the open air. A fowl is killed and placed with some rice at the dead man's feet. The body is burnt at the water side. At the spot where the body was first laid out, the deceased's relatives kill a cock every morning for seven days, and leave it there with some rice as an offering to the manes of the dead. A month after death a like offering is made at the place of cremation, and this is occasionally repeated for a year. The ashes are deposited on a hill in a small hut built for the purpose, in which are also placed the dead man's weapons,—a spear, *dáos* of two sorts (one his fighting *dáo*, the other his every-day bread-winner), arrow heads, his metal-stemmed pipe, earrings, and ornaments. The place is held sacred."

In connection with the beliefs of the Tipperahs regarding the spirits of the dead, Major Lewin speaks of a curious practice. He says:—"We were travelling once through the jungles, and the path led across a small streamlet. Here I observed a white thread stretched from one side to the other, bridging the stream. On inquiring the reason of this it appeared that a man had died away from his home in a distant village; his friends had gone thither and performed his obsequies, after which it was supposed that the dead man's spirit would accompany them back to his former abode. Without assistance, however, spirits are unable to cross running water; therefore the stream here had been bridged in the manner aforesaid."

Another use of the white thread mentioned by Lewin as practised by the Tipperahs and most of the hill races seems to be a survival of the primitive animistic belief which attributes all disease to the action of malevolent spirits, who nevertheless can be propitiated by the exorcist who knows the proper means of turning away their wrath. When an epidemic breaks out in a village, the Tipperahs and many other hill tribes call in an *Auchái* to appease the demon of sickness by a sacrifice. The entire village is encircled with a newly-spun white thread, and the blood of the animal sacrificed is freely sprinkled about. This is followed by careful sweeping and cleansing, and the houses and gates are decorated with green boughs. For three days afterwards the thread is maintained unbroken, and no one is allowed to enter or leave the village. The theory seems to be that if the demon who presides over the malady can be kept at bay for that time, he will go away disappointed, while a breach of the quarantine or *khang* would lead to a renewal of the outbreak.

Dress.

"The dress of the Tipperahs," says Lewin, "is of the simplest description. Among the men a thick turban is worn, and a narrow piece of home-spun cloth, with a fringed end hanging down in front and rear, passes once round the waist and between the legs. In the cold season they wear a rudely-sewn jacket. The males wear silver earrings, crescent-shaped, with little silver pendants on the outer edge. The dress of the women is equally unornate. The petticoat is short, reaching a little below the knee, and made of very coarse cotton stuff of their own manufacture. It is striped in colours of red and blue. If the woman be married, this petticoat will form her whole costume; but the unmarried girls cover the breast with a gaily-dyed cloth with fringed ends. The women never cover their heads; they wear earrings like the men; but in addition to this ornament they distend the lobe of the ear to the size of half a crown by the insertion of a concave-edged ring of silver, placed, not through, but in, the lobe. Both sexes have long, black, abundant hair, which is worn in a knot at the back of the head. The use of false hair is common among them, especially the women. The meshes of false hair are woven in among the back hair to make the knot look larger."

The following statement shows the number and distribution of the Tipperah tribe in 1872 and 1881 :—

District.	1872.	1881.	District.	1872.	1881.
Kuch Behar	......	1,128	Chittagong	45	225
Dacca	38	47	Noakhali	232	16
Faridpur	......	101	Tipperah	3,004	1,895
Bakarganj	217	45	Hill Tracts	11,800	15,654

Tipperah-Suryabansi, also called Rajbansi—a mixed class of Bengalis and Tipperahs.

Tipriati, a section of the Maghayá sub-caste of Barhis in Behar.

Tirango, a wild bird, a totemistic sept of Mundas in Chota Nagpur.

Tirhutiá, a sub-caste of barbers; of Hindu Joláhás (Tatwa or Tánti); and of Kumhárs in Behar, who say they can intermarry with the Maghayá and Desi sub-castes. The Maghayás, however, allege that all the sub-castes are strictly endogamous; a sub-caste of Thatherá or brass-chaser and of Láheris, Telis, and Támbulis in Behar.

Tirhutiá or *Chiraut*, a sub-caste of Dhánuks, Doms, and Hajjáms in Behar.

Tirhutiā or **Maithil,** a territorial division of Brahmans in Behar.

Tirkar, a maker of bows and arrows; a title of Doms; a title of Byádhs who originally killed birds and beasts and lived on meat obtained by chase, at present most of them have taken to agriculture.

Tirki, bull, a totemistic sept of Goálás, Asuras, Chamárs, Kharwars, Lohars, Mundas, Oráons, and Nágeswars in Chota Nagpur who cannot touch any cattle after eyes open; a section of Ghásis and Goráits; a totemistic section of Doms and Turis implying a mouse.

Tirkiar, tree-mice, a totemistic sept of Mundas in Chota Nagpur.

Tirkoár, a section of Khariás in Chota Nagpur.

Tirkuar, fruit, a totemistic sept of Oraons and Turis in Chota Nagpur.

Tiro, a small bird, a totemistic sept of Mundas in Chota Nagpur.

Tirsuliá, a sub-caste of Pásis in Behar.

Tirtha, a sect of Dasnámi Sannyásis.

Tirthjátri, a pilgrim.

Tirtia, a bird, a totemistic sept of Mundas and Oraons in Chota Nagpur.

Tiru, a kind of bird or fish, a totemistic sept of Mundas and Oraons in Chota Nagpur.

Tiruá, a section of Kámis in Darjiling.

Tiruar, arrow, a sept of Kharwars in Chota Nagpur; a section of Kurmis in Behar.

Tiruhar, a bird, a totemistic sept of Mundas in Chota Nagpur.

Tirusiá, a *mul* or section of Kasarwáni Baniyás in Behar.

Tisbaryá or *Teswár*, a section of the Pachainyá sub-caste of Doms in Behar.

Tisor, a section of the Sátmuliá Maghayá sub-caste of Kándus in Behar.

Tiswar, a *mul* or section of the Maghayá sub-caste of Koiris in Behar.

Titehiá, a section of Bábhans in Behar.

Tithi, a bird, a totemistic sept of Oraons in Chota Nagpur.

Titiá Bámbár, a *mul* or section of the Naomuliá or Majraut sub-caste of Goálás in Behar.

Titipi, a totemistic sept of Bediás in Chota Nagpur, signifying a night bird.

Tititihu, a section of Khariás in Chota Nagpur.

Tittal, a *gotra* or section of Agarwáls.

Titung, a section of Murmis in Darjiling.

Tiwári, see Tewári.

Tiyar, *Tiar*, *Tior*, *Rájbansi*, *Machhuá*, a Dravidian boating and fishing caste of Bengal and Behar, whom Mr. Beames seems disposed to identify with the Dhimar, a sub-caste of the Káhárs. It may be doubted, however, whether this opinion rests upon any surer basis than similarity of name and occupation; and the names appear to be distinct, Tiyar being a corruption of the Sanskrit *tivara*, 'a hunter,' while Dhimar is derived from Sanskrit *dhivara*, 'a fisherman.' The two groups, moreover, show marked differences of complexion and physical type. The Dhimar have a light-brown skin and fairly well-cut features, and are not noticeably below the average stature of Hindus of the middle class. The Tiyars, on the other hand, according to Dr. Wise, who had special opportunities of observing them, are short and muscular, with prominent cheek-bones, dark-brown—almost black—complexions, thick and generally projecting lips, and long coarse hair, worn in a cue, which has often a reddish tinge towards the tip—a peculiarity common to them and other low castes, which, although in the first instance produced by exposure, is now, if not hereditary, at least characteristic.

Origin.

Internal structure.

In Eastern Bengal, where no subdivisions exist, the Tiyars call themselves **Ráj-bansi**, or sometimes, as in Maimansinh, **Tilak Dás**, while those living on the Ganges lay claim to the title of **Suraj-bansi**. According to Buchanan, the Tiyars of Bhagalpur are divided into **Báman-jagya**, who are cultivators and clean Sudrás, and **Govaríya**, who fish, eat pork, drink spirits, and are outcastes. Wherever they are regarded as pure, a Dasnámi ascetic acts as guru and a Maithil Brahman as purohit; when impure, a Gosáin of Bengal is guru, and a Patit or degraded Brahman is purohit.

The sections of the Tiyars shown in the Appendix throw no light on the origin of the caste. It is indeed doubtful whether the section-names are in general use for the purpose of enforcing the practice of exogamy; and I believe that practice, at least in its primitive form, to have been abandoned in favour of the more modern system of simply specifying the relations whom a man or woman may not marry. For this purpose they make use of the standard formula *mamerá*, *chacherá*, etc., calculated to five generations in the descending line on the male side and three generations on the female.

Marriage.

Girls are usually married as infants, but cases sometimes occur in which, owing to the poverty of her parents, a girl's marriage is deferred until she has passed the age of puberty. Polygamy is permitted, and in theory at least there are no restrictions on the number of wives a man may have. In Behar a widow may marry a second time. She is not obliged to marry her late husband's younger brother, if such a relative exist, but it is considered a very proper thing for her to do so; and the fact that he has a right to the custody of the children by the first husband tends as a rule to induce the widow to agree to the arrangement. In Bengal widows never marry, but earn a livelihood by selling fish, by manufacturing string, and such like petty industries. Those who find such an existence too monotonous, and desire a change of life and scene, usually join one of the mendicant orders of the Vaishnava sect. In the matter of divorce the practice of the caste seems to vary. Bengal Tiyars do not recognize it at all, while in Behar it is permitted only with the sanction of the caste panchâyat, a well-organized body presided over by a headman (*manjhan*), whose jurisdiction is supposed to comprise the traditional number of twenty-two villages. Each *manjhan* has under him a *chharidár* or stick-bearer, whose business it is to procure the attendance of persons summoned to appear before the panchâyat, and generally to carry out the orders of the *manjhan*.

Among the Tiyars of Bengal three hypergamous groups are recognized, the highest being the Pradhán, or chief families; next the Parámániks; while the rest go to form the Gana, or lower orders. The last can only intermarry with the higher by paying a large sum of money, the father receiving in all cases money for his daughter, so that female children are more valued than among the true Hindus. Widows never marry, but either earn a livelihood by selling fish, by manufacturing string, or, if desirous of change of life and scene, by becoming Boistubis (Vaishnavis).

Religion.

Tiyars are almost to a man Vaishnava in creed, their religious ceremonies being always held beneath trees. The seorhá (*Trophis aspera*), a very common scrubby plant, is held in especial veneration by them, and its shade is usually selected as the scene of their worship; but should this tree be not at hand, the nim, bel, or gujáli (*Shorea robusta*) forms an efficient substitute. Hindustáni Tiyars sacrifice a goat to Káli on the Diwáli, but the animal, instead of being decapitated in the orthodox Hindu way, is stabbed with a sharp-pointed piece of wood —a practice universal among the aboriginal races of India, after which, as with the Dosádhs, the flesh is eaten by the worshippers. Bengali Tiyars, on the other hand, sacrifice a swine to Bura-Buri on the Paus (December–January) Sankránti, slaughtering it in the same way as their Hindustani brethren. They do not, however, eat the flesh. At the Gangá festival in Jeth (May) they offer a white kid, pigeon and milk to the spirit of the river, and adore with great solemnity Manasá Devi in the month of Srávan (July-August).

As was natural, the Tiyars have peopled the waters and streams with beneficent and wicked spirits, whose friendship is to be secured, and enmity averted, by various religious rites. Along the banks of the river Lakhya they worship Pir Badr, Khwajah Khizr, and, in fulfilment of vows, offer through any Musalmán a goat to Madár, whom they regard as a water god, but who may be identified with Sháh Madár Badi'uddin. In stormy weather and in bad fishing seasons they invoke Khala-Kumári, a naiad, to whom the first fruits are presented, in the same way as Hindus do to Lakshmi. In Behar Mangal Chandi, Jai Singh, and Lál are their chief minor gods.

In Purniah Tiyars worship a peculiar deity called Prem Rája or Pamiráj, who, they say, belonged to their tribe and was a celebrated brigand residing at Bahurágar, in Tirhut. Having been on many occasions favoured by the deity, he was translated (Aprakása), and disappeared along with his boat. In 1864 one Baijua Tiyar gave out that Pamiráj had appeared to him in a vision and ordained that the Tiyars should cease to be fishermen and devote themselves instead to certain religious rites, which would procure general prosperity. Great excitement ensued, and in February 1865 about four thousand Tiyars from Gházipúr, Benares, and the adjoining districts assembled at Gogra, in Purniah, and after offering holy water to a private idol belonging to Baijua, which he said came to him out of a bamboo post, 3,000 goats were sacrificed. Shortly afterwards another meeting of the tribe was held in the Benares district, at which a murder was committed. This movement was a repetition of a precisely similar one among the Dosádhs of Behar in 1863, and, like it, was short-lived and unsuccessful.

As is done by all Bengali fishermen, the Jal Pálani, on the "Tilwá" Sankránti in Mágh (January-February), when the sun enters Capricorn, is observed by the Tiyars. The close time lasts from two to fifteen days, but the demand for fish being steady, they catch on the eve of the festival an extra supply and keep them alive for purposes of sale, there being no offence in selling, although there is in catching, fish at that period, when prices being high profits are unusually good.

Social status and occupation.

In Behar and Bengal generally Tiyars are reckoned impure, and along the northern bank of the Ganges Tiyars employed in manufacturing mats of the *nal* reed, and known as Nal Tiyars, are considered so utterly vile that the fisher Tiyars repudiate any fellowship with them.

In Dacca the Tiyars occupy an uncertain position, in one part of the district being pure and Pancha-varta, having the five Sudra servants working for them, while in another, being unclean, these servants are members of their own caste. Tiyars in Eastern Bengal are usually fishermen, but where the fishery has become unproductive, or the river has silted up, they are found cultivating the soil, keeping shops, and acting as boatmen. They manufacture their own nets, but their long narrow boats, called "Jalká," are made by Chandáls.

The following statement shows the number and distribution of Tiyars in 1872 and 1881 :—

District.	1872.	1881.	District.	1872.	1881.
Bardwan	3,631	3,369	Tipperah	379	96
Bankura	62	846	Chittagong	1,128	......
Birbhum	307	1,775	Noakhali	190	......
Midnapur	16,304	14,099	Patna	1,185	1,036
Hughli	} 23,051	6,687	Gya	162	......
Howrah		15,623	Shahabad	243	16
24-Parganás	49,709	37,171	Tirhut { Mozaffarpur ...	} 878	130
Nadiya	12,483	2,362	Tirhut { Darbhanga ...		190
Khulna	.. ...	3,823	Saran	1,513	2,608
Jessore	4,565	239	Champaran	10	434
Murshedabad...	12,038	7,735	Monghyr	18,014	19,163
Dinajpur	17,364	2,224	Bhagalpur	6,678	4,296
Rajshahye	2,249	2,016	Purniah	18,208	16,040
Rangpur	141,213	92,790	Maldah	13,717	15,736
Bogra	5,530	298	Santál Parganás	2,837	2,281
Pabna	2,786	1,253	Cuttack	541	889
Darjiling	1	......	Puri	907	878
Jalpigori	......	35,896	Balasore	682	686
Kuch Behar	......	54,152	Tributary States	1,613	1,615
Dacca	7,968	6,654	Hazaribagh	77	96
Faridpur	866	1,374	Lohardaga	761	128
Bakarganj	696	68	Singbhum	......	123
Maimansinh	14,461	15,969	Manbhum	255	498
			Tributary States	......	158

Tiyar, a sub-caste of Malláhs in Behar.

Toeba, flower of *parás* tree, a totemistic sept of Mundas in Chota Nagpur.

Toewa, a kind of bird, a totemistic sept of Mundas in Chota Nagpur.

Toinya, a sept of Chakmás in the Hill Tracts of Chittagong.

Toipá, a *rui* or sept of Dejong Lhoris whose ancestor had emigrated from South Bhotan.

Toktiham, a sept of the Pánthar sub-tribe of Limbus in Darjiling.

Tolángi, a *thar* or sept of Gurungs in Darjiling.

Tolwar, a section of the Chhajáti sub-caste of Khatris in Bengal.

Tongar, a sept of Surajbansi Rájputs in Behar.

Tongbángboha, a sept of Limbus in Darjiling.

Tongdu-Ruishi, the most respectable sub-tribe of Dejong Lhoris or Bhotias of the south.

Tongsi, a bird, a totemistic sept of Mundas in Chota Nagpur.

Tono, a big tree-ant, a totemistic sept of Mundas in Chota Nagpur.

Topna, a tree, a totemistic sept of Mundas in Chota Nagpur.

Topo, a sept of Asuras; a section of Khariás in Chota N-gpur.

Topoar, a bird with a long tail, body mottled black and white, a totemistic sept of Mundas, Oraons, and Lohárs and a section of Goraits in Chota Nagpur.

Toppo, a totemistic section of Turis in Chota Nagpur denoting a bird.

Toril, a section of the Sátmuliá Maghayá sub-caste of Kándus in Behar.

Toringtapá, a *thar* or sept of Mangars in Darjiling.

Tormeg, a *thar* or sept of Murmis in Darjiling.

Totábari, a section of Páns in Chota Nagpur.

Totaka, a *gáin* of the Sándilya *gotra* of Bárendra Brahmans in Bengal.

Tow, a kind of bird, a totemistic sept of Mundas in Chota Nagpur.

Trayodás, a sub-caste of Bágdis found in the 24-Parganás, said to have come from Bankura.

Tribedi, a title of Kanaujiá Brahmans in Behar.

Trikoniá, a title of low castes of the North-Western Provinces and Panjáb.

Trilokpuria, a section of the Banodhiá and Jaiswár Kalwárs in Behar.

Tripáthi, a title of the Dákshinátya Baidik Brahmans in Bengal.

Tripáti, a section of Utkal or Orissa Brahmans.

Triprá, a synonym for Tipperah.

Tsak, a synonym for Chakmá.

Tsakma, a synonym for Chakmá.

Tsegkhim-pá, *tseg*, 'a wall,' and *khim*, 'a house'—a dweller in a stone or walled house, a sub-sept of the Nah-pa sept of Sherpa Bhotias.

Tshe-gyu-thah, the family which sprang from the Buddha of life, a *rui* or sept of the Tongdu sub-tribe of Dejong Lhoris or Bhotias of the south.

Tshendangkya, he who lives apart, a sept of the Ahtharai sub-tribe of Limbus in Darjiling.

Tsonbang, he who listens and profits, a sept of the Miákhola sub-tribe of Limbus in Darjiling.

Tsong, a synonym for Limbu.

Tsong-zubo, a *rui* or sept of Dejong Lhoris, the members of which are the decendants of emigrants from Bhotan and Nepal.

Tubká, a section of the Tirhutiyá sub-caste of Doms in Behar.

Tudi, Tudu, a sept of Hos and Santáls.

Tuduar, hen, a totemistic sept of Kharwars in Chota Nagpur.

Tukipitá dumuriá, *dumur* fig, a totemistic section of Kurmis in Chota Nagpur and Orissa.

Tulatiá, a sub-caste of Telis in Orissa.

Tulsi, a group of Maghaiya Telis in Behar.

Tulsiar, a kind of flower, a totemistic sept of Mundas in Chota Nagpur.

Tumaliá, a section of Kumhárs in Singbhum.

Tumárung, a totemistic sept of the Bhumij tribe in Manbhum.

Tumbangphe, the earth-born or *Bhuiphutá*, a sept of the Phedáb sub-tribe of Limbus in Darjiling. This *thar* claim to be *terræ filii*, and point out a huge rock which covers the spot where their founder sprang from the earth.

Tumbapo, the eldest, a sept of the Pánthar sub-tribe of Limbus in Darjiling.

Tumbli, a red flying ant, a totemistic sept of Mundas and Kumhárs in Chota Nagpur.

Tumbli, Berni, a section of Kumhars in Lohardagá.

Tumbrok, born of a step-mother, a sept of the Pánthar sub-tribe of Limbus in Darjiling.

Tumkohong, a sept of Limbus in Darjiling.

Tumling, a sept of the Yangorup sub-tribe of Limbus in Darjiling.

Tundak, a section of Goálás in the North-Western Provinces and Behar.

Tundal, a *gotra* or section of Agarwáls.

Tunduár, a tree, a totemistic sept of Kharwars and Mundas; a section of Kurmis and Mahilis in Chota Nagpur and Orissa.

Tungá, a sub-caste of Kàrangás and of Máls in Midnapur and Manbhum.

Tungbai, a sept of Tipperahs in the Hill Tracts of Chittagong.

Tungjainya, a sub-tribe of Chakmás in the Hill Tracts of Chittagong.

Tungohong, the discontented, a sept of the Chhothar sub-tribe of Limbus in Darjiling.

Tunru, a totemistic section of Máhilis in Manbhum, the members of which will not touch or cut the grass which the name denotes.

Tuntiá Kaibartta, a sub-caste of Kaibarttas in Bengal who cultivate mulberry and rear silk cocoons, and produce all sorts of vegetables which their women sell in the market.

Tura, a sept of Bairágis in Chota Nagpur.

Turáha, a low caste who blow horns and play on flutes.

Turáhá, *Turhá*, a sub-caste of Káhárs who carry palanquins, sell fish and fresh fruit and cultivate; a sub-caste of Nuniás.

Turania, a sept of Mundas in Chota Nagpur.

Turhá, players on the wind instrument called *turhi*.

Turi, a non-Aryan caste of cultivators, workers in bamboo, and basket-makers in Chota Nagpur. The physical type of the Turis, their language, and their religion, place it beyond doubt that they are a Hinduised offshoot of the Mundas. In Lohardagá, where the caste is most numerous, it is divided into four sub-castes—**Turi** or **Kisán-Turi**, **Or**, **Dom**, and **Domrá**—distinguished by the particular modes of basket and bamboo-work which they practise. Thus the Turi or Kisán-Turi, who are also cultivators and hold *bhuinhári* land, make the *sup*, a winnowing sieve made of *sirkí*, the upper joint of *Saccharum procerum*; the *tokri* or *tokiyá*, a large open basket of split bamboo twigs woven up with the fibre of the leaves of the *tál* palm; the *sair* and *nadná*, used for catching fish. The Ors are said to take their name from the *oriyá* basket used by the sower, and made of split bamboo sometimes helped out with *tál* fibre. They

Internal structure.

also make umbrellas, and the *chhotka dáli* or *dálá*, a flat basket with vertical sides used for handling grain in small quantities. Doms make the *harka* and scale-pans (*taráju*). Domrás make the *peti* and fans. Turis frequently reckon in as a fifth sub-caste the Birhors, who cut bamboos and make the *sikás* used for carrying loads slung on a shoulder-yoke (*bahangi*), and a kind of basket called *phunda*. Doms and Domrás speak Hindi; Turis, Ors, and Birhors use among themselves a dialect of Mundári. All these sub-castes profess to be strictly endogamous; but a Turi can marry the daughter of an Or provided that she is formally admitted into the Turi sub-caste. This is effected by her lover giving a feast to the leading men of the local caste community. Members of other castes who have taken to themselves Turi women and have been ejected from their own group may be admitted on similar terms.

Marriage.

The sections of the Turis shown in Appendix are for the most part totemistic, and correspond closely with those in force among the Mundás. The rule of exogamy extends only to a man's own section, and is supplemented by the standard table of prohibited degrees. Except in Hinduised and comparatively wealthy families, whose tendency is to affect infant-marriage, girls usually marry as adults. Free courtship is recognized, and sexual license before marriage tolerated. Both youths and maidens are said, however, to lead purer lives than the Oraons, owing, it is suggested, to the fact that they do not frequent the dancing ground (*ákhrá*), and are thus less exposed to the temptations of the flesh. Before a marriage can be celebrated the consent of the heads of the Mádalwár and Surinwár sections, who are known respectively as Rájá and Thákur, is obtained, and a bride-price of Rs. 2-8 is paid. The village *páhan* attends, and the head of the Charchágiyá section officiates as priest. *Sindurdán* is the binding portion of the ceremony. Polygamy is permitted, the only limit to the number of wives a man may have being his ability to maintain them. A widow may marry again by the *sagai* form, and it is usual for her to marry her husband's younger brother if there is one. *Sindur* is not used in the *sagai* ceremony as practised by the Turis. The essential points are the consent of the chief relatives and the presentation to the bride of a new cloth and a lac armlet. Divorce is allowed, and divorced women may marry again.

Religion.

The original religion of the Turis is beyond doubt closely akin to the form of animism current among the Mundás and described at length in the article on that tribe. In many villages, indeed, they hold the office of *páhan*. Baranda Bhut and Bura-Buri are held in special reverence. Of late years large numbers of Turis have embraced the tenets of the deistic sect, known to its members as Sri-Náráyani, from the name of God, and to outsiders as Siva-Náráyani, from the name of its founder, a Rájput of Gházipur, who lived early in the eighteenth century. Those, however, who call themselves Sri-Náráyan Panthis, have by no means broken with the animistic faith of their ancestors, and in cases of illness have recourse to the regular aboriginal methods on propitiating the spirit who is believed to be afflicting them.

Social status. Turis will eat cooked food with Mundás and Oraons, take sweetmeats from Ahirs and Telis, and water from the Or sub-caste. They will smoke only with members of their own sub-caste. For the rest they are as lax in matters of diet as the Mundás and Oraons. Sri-Náráyanis abstain from beef, from the flesh of animals which have died a natural death, and from spirituous liquors.

The following statement shows the number and distribution of Turis in 1872 and 1881:—

DISTRICT.	1872.	1881.	DISTRICT.	1872.	1881
Bardwan	47	44	Rangpur	......	91
Birbhum	65	3	Bogra	......	171
Midnapur	4	......	Pabna	407	125
Hughli	46	2	Faridpur	......	4
Howrah		51	Maimansinh	33	34
24-Parganás	92	1,854	Chittagong	......	4
Nadiya	336	447	Hazaribagh	11,136	17,520
Jessore	86	78	Lohardagá	4,778	6,530
Murshedabad	472	17	Singbhum	251	265
Dinajpur	66	492	Manbhum	......	75
Rajshahye	......	43	Tributary States	1,330	1,466

Turi or *Dakhiná*, a sub-caste of Doms in Behar.

Turiar, a sept of Agariás in Chota Nagpur.

Turk-Bhát, a sub-caste of Bháts.

Turkia, a sub-caste of Telis in Behar, who are Mahomedans.

Turkiá or **Shekh**, a sub-caste of Mahomedan Dhobis in Behar.

Turk-Kumhár, a class of Mahomedan Kumhárs in Behar.

Turk-Nauwá, a class of Mahomedan barbers in Behar.

Turk Pási, a sub-caste of Pásis in Behar who are Mahomedan by religion.

Turku, a sub-sept of the Saren sept of Santáls.

Turman, a section of the Chhajáti sub-caste of Khatris in Bengal.

Tursia, a sept of Mundas in Chota Nagpur.

Turu, squirrel, a totemistic sept of Mundas and Bediás in Chota Nagpur; a section of Mahilis.

Turuar, *pákur* fruit, a totemistic sept of Kharwars and Mundas in Chota Nagpur.

Turuwar, a section of Cheros in Palamau.

Tuti, a bird, a totemistic sept of Bhumijs, Mundas, and Kharwars in Chota Nagpur; a section of Khariás.

Tutiear, a section of Mahilis in Chota Nagpur.

U

Uber, a *mul* or section of the Maghayá sub-caste of Kándus in Behar.

Ubhar, a *mul* or section of the Chhamuliá Madhesiá sub-caste of Halwáis in Behar.

Uchchharakhi, a *gáin* of the Bharadwája *gotra* of Bárendra Brahmans in Bengal.

Uchring, an insect, a totemistic sept of Mundas in Chota Nagpur.

Udadhi, a section of Málos in Eastern Bengal.

Udaniyár, a *pur* or section of Sákadwipi Brahmans in Behar.

Udási, *Udásin*, a religious mendicant; a title of Brahmans and Sannyásis; an indifferent person; a stranger. In Census papers may either be a variant for Udásin, or may merely mean that the persons enumerated under this title described themselves as strangers (udásin), and the word was taken to be a caste designation.

Udbaru, a tree, a totemistic sept of Mundas in Chota Nagpur.

Uddhabi, a sub-caste of Tántis in Bengal.

Udhmatiá, a section of Kanaujiá Lohárs in Behar.

Udwar, water cat, a totemistic sept of Lohárs in Chota Nagpur.

Uengsa, a sept of Maghs in the Hill Tracts of Chittagong.

Ugahar, a *mul* or section of the Chhamuliá Madhesiá sub-caste of Halwáis in Behar.

Ugrakhatri, a synonym for Aguri.

Uh, a sub-sept of the Hemrom sept of Santáls

Ujáin, a sept of the Surajbansi division of Rájputs in Behar.

Ujalá, a *gáin* or sub-section of Saptasati Brahmans in Bengal.

Ujhá or *Ojhá*, a sub-caste of Bágdis in Western Bengal, probably descended from the priests of the tribal gods, who would naturally tend to form themselves into a sub-caste.

Ujhá, Ojhá, or **Jhá**, a title of Maithil Brahmans in Behar.

Ujini, a group of the Fatehsing Telis in Murshedabad.

Ujli, a synonym for Dhobi in Behar.

Ukhar, a group of the Aoghár sect of Saiva ascetics founded in Guzerat by a Dasnámi mendicant named Brahmagiri. For a fuller account of the sect, see **Aoghar**.

Ukniyál, a *thar* or section of Nepáli Brahmans.

Uksarri, a sept of Chakmás in the Hill Tracts of Chittagong.

Ulárk, a *pur* or section of Sákadwipi Brahmans in Behar.

Ulit, a sept of Rájputs in Behar.

Ulluk, a *gáin* or sub-section of Saptasati Brahmans in Bengal.

Ulwár, a *mul* or section of the Naomuliá or Majraut sub-caste of Goálás in Behar.

Umatwár, a section of Bábhans in Behar.

Umethwár, a *mul* or section of the Naomuliá or Majraut sub-caste of Goálás in Behar.

Unain, a *mul* or section of the Ayodhiá sub-caste of Hajjáms in Behar.

Undhil, a section of Goálás in Behar.

Undhuri, a *gáin* of the Sábarna *gotra* of Bárendra Brahmans in Bengal.

Upádhyáya, a sub-caste of Utkal Brahmans in Orissa; an endogamous division of Nepáli Brahmans; a title of Kanaujiá and Saraswat Brahmans and of Bábhans in Behar.

Upamanya, a section of Brahmans.

Uphaltopi, a *thar* or section of Nepáli Brahmans.

Uranga, ? *Uraun*, a synonym for Oraon.

Urdágainhi, a section of the Biyáhut and Kharidáhá Kalwárs in Behar.

Urdwar, a sept of Mundas in Chota Nagpur.

Uriar, a sept of Kharwars in Chota Nagpur

Uring, a wild bird, a totemistic sept of Mundas in Chota Nagpur.

Uriyá, a sub-caste of Pods.

Uriyá Dhobá, a sub-caste of Dhobás in Orissa.

Uriyá-Káet, a synonym for Karan.

Urmakhori, a sept of Páns in Chota Nagpur.

Urmakuli, a section of Páns in Chota Nagpur.

Urmi, a wave; a title of Jáliyas in Bengal.

Uruntá, a *thar* or sept of Gurungs in Darjiling who burn their dead on a hill top and then throw the ashes in the air.

Urwár, a *pur* or section of Sákadwipi Brahmans in Behar.

Usahiyárk, a *pur* or section of Sákadwipi Brahmans in Behar.

Usauth, a section of the Karan sub-caste of Káyasths in Behar.

Usrám, a *mul* or section of the Naomulia or Majraut sub-caste of Goálás in Behar.

Utamapur, a section of the Karan Káyasths in Behar.

Utardáhá, a *mul* or section of the Maghayá sub-caste of Kándus in Behar.

Utkal, a territorial division of the Pancha Gaura Brahmans, deriving its name from the Province of Utkala or Odra (Orissa).

Utkuli, a *thar* or section of Nepáli Brahmans.

Uttara-Sreni, a territorial group of Brahmans in Orissa.

Uttar-Bárendra, an endogamous division of the Bárendra Brahmans in Bengal.

Uttardáhá, a section of the Sátmuliá Maghayá sub-caste of Kándus in Behar.

Uttarhá, a sub-caste of Tántis in Behar.

Uttariyá, a sub-caste of Doms in South Behar who work in *sirki*, and regard this as an important distinction between themselves and the Maghayá Doms who work with bamboos.

Uttar-Kabát, north gate, a title of Khandáits in Orissa.

Uttarkul, a group of the Áswini Tántis in Bengal.

Uttar-Rárhi, a sub-caste of Káyasths in Bengal; of Kámárs in the 24-Parganás; of Chásá-dhobás and Nápits; a group of the Hole Kaibarttas and of Bará-bhágiyá Muchis in Bengal.

V

Vaidika, one of the five main sub-castes of Bengal Brahmans; a group of the Srotriya sub-caste of Utkal Brahmans in Orissa.

Vaishnaba, *Baishtab*, *Bairági*, a religious sect based upon the worship of Vishnu under the incarnations of Ráma and Krishna. Founded as a popular religion by Rámanuja in Madras, and developed in Northern India by Rámánand and Kabir, Vaishnavism owes its wide acceptance in Bengal to the teaching of Chaitanya, a Vaidik Brahman of Nadiya at the beginning of the 16th century. The contemplative devotion inculcated by this teacher as the ideal of the religious life was transformed by Vallabha-Swámi into emotional longings of a more sensuous type. The sects now included under the general name Vaishnava are the following:—

Rámánuja.

(1) **Rámánuja**, comprising three grades of disciples: the Brahmacharya, or novice; Upa Kurvvána, who lives as an udasi in the house of his guru; and the Naisthika, who practises a life-long asceticism. When undergoing the initiatory rite (tapta-mudrá), the disciple is marked with the *sankha* or conch-shell of Vishnu on the left shoulder and the *chakra* or wheel on the right, the stamp used being made of eight metals (ashta-dhátu), gold, silver, copper, brass, tin, lead, iron, and zinc. Rámánujas are most punctilious about the privacy of their meals, and should any one see or speak to them while they are eating, the food is either thrown away or buried. Silken or woollen garments, not cotton, must be worn at meals, and no one may taste food without permission of the guru. Rámánujas will only eat food cooked by a Brahman of their own sect, but they do not reject articles prepared with *ghi* by a Rámávat. They will not touch food cooked by a Kulin Brahman of Bengal, nor will they take water from the hands of a man of that caste.

Rámávat.

(2) **Rámávat**, a Hindustani sect, recruited mainly from among Kanaujiyá Brahmans, though persons of other castes are occasionally received on the understanding that it is open to any member of the sect to decline to eat with them. Vishnu or Ráma-Chandra is the patron god of the community, but in some cases his worship has been supplanted by that of Hari, who is identified with Krishna. Brindában is the head-quarters of those who revere the latter, and Ajodhyá of those who adhere to the worship of Ráma. Their sacred books are the Rámáyana, the Sri Bhágavat, and the Bhágavat-Gitá. Most of them, however, are very illiterate, and of those who can blunder through a Nagari book, few understand what they read. Pilgrimage is believed to be the chief duty of the sect. The Tápasi or penitential order of Rámávats, erroneously styled Jogis, a term properly reserved for Saiva ascetics, wander through India almost naked, smeared over with ashes and stupefied with ganja, living on alms, but lodging with no one and taking shelter under trees, in ruins, or among tombs

in preference to entering a human habitation. A rope round the waist and a scanty cloth round the loins form their sole attire. A few shave the head and beard, but most allow their hair to grow, and twist their matted locks round the head like a turban, or roll them into coils terminating in a large knot or chignon over the left ear. They wear necklaces of rudráksha wood (*Elæocarpus gianitrus*) containing seventeen, nineteen, twenty-one, fifty-four or a hundred and eight beads, and when indulging in long fits of abstraction, they support themselves with a bamboo crutch. At initiation a new convert is enrolled in a so-called 'gotra,' bearing the name Aichittra; but as all Rámávats belong to this, and in theory celibacy is strictly enjoined, the procedure is a mere form, and has no bearing on marriage or the relations of the sexes. Rámávat Sádhus are notorious for their dissolute and licentious character, and for their excessive indulgence in gánja, a drug which they smoke systematically in order to induce the dreamy sensual reverie regarded by them as the highest manifestation of religious sentiment. All forms of worship, except the unceasing repetition of the name Ráma or Hari, are deemed useless, but in every ákhárá or monastery of the sect an idol is tended at regular hours to the sound of *sankh* shells and gongs, while offerings of flowers and fruit are presented by the laity. A *tulsi* plant in the courtyard and a Sálagram in the shrine complete the religious furniture of the establishment.

Nimavat.

(3) **Nimavat**, recruited from among Hindustani Brahmans or members of those castes from whose hands a Brahman can take water. The mark of a Nimavat is a circular black patch on the forehead between two parallel yellow streaks. Mathurá and Jaipur are their most sacred places of pilgrimage, and the Bhágavat-Gitá is their chief religious book. The chief duty of the Biraktas or monastic members of the sect is to prepare and offer to the idols kept in the ákhárá *bhog* or food consisting of rice and pulse boiled together. Four times a day this compound is laid before the god, and is then eaten by the mahant and his disciples. The idols usually worshipped by Nimavats are Jagannáth, Madan-Gopál, Rádhá-Krishna, Balarám, and Subhadrá, the sister of Krishna.

Baishtam.

(4) **Vaishnava**, colloquially **Baishtam**, of Bengal, a class not very easy to define precisely, as the name Vaishnava includes (*a*) ordinary Hindus who, without deserting their original caste, worship Vishnu in preference to other gods, (*b*) ascetic members of the Vaishnava sect, commonly called Bairági, (*c*) Ját-Baishtam, Samyogi, or Bántási, an endogamous group formed by the conversion to Vaishnavism of members of many different castes. It will be convenient here to treat first of the last-mentioned group. The Baishtam caste includes members of several Vaishnava sects, and in theory intermarriage between these sects is prohibited. But if a man of one sect wishes to marry a woman of another sect, he has only to convert her by a simple ritual to his own sect, and the obstacles to their union are removed. Baishtams have no *gotras*, but they are divided into fifteen sections (*paribár*), supposed to be descended from the principal

disciples of Chaitanya, such as Adwaita-Paribár, Nityánanda-Paribár, Achárya-Paribár, Syám Chánd, Jagadish Pandit, Gadádhar Pandit, Bakkeswar Pandit, Adhirám Gopál, etc. Although these groups are supposed to stand to the Baishtams in the place of *gotras*, marriage between persons belonging to the same *paribár* is not forbidden, and the grouping has no more effect on marriage than the *quasi*-endogamous division into sects referred to above. Outsiders are freely admitted into the community, however low their caste may be, provided only that they are Hindus. Chaitanya is said to have extended this privilege even to Mahomedans, but since his time the tendency has been rather to contract the limits of the society, and no guru or mathdhári (superintendent of a monastery) would now venture on such an act. The ceremony of initiation is simple. The guru or mathdhári, known on this occasion by the title of Bhek-gosain, 'the ascetic of alms,' after worshipping Chaitanya, gives to the convert a string (*dori*), a piece of cloth (*kaupin*) just sufficient to cover his nakedness, and a *báhirbásh*, a larger cloth, to wear round his loins over the *kaupin*. At the same time he whispers in his ear the *mantra* or sacred word, usually a monosyllable, indicating a name or attribute of a god or goddess, which is to guide him through life and must never be divulged to any one. The novice then bows down, and a small necklace of wooden beads is hung round his neck, and a *karanga* or cocoanut shell given him for the purpose of collecting alms.

Marriage.

Baistams profess to marry their daughters as infants, and this may be taken to be the rule of the caste, although in many instances it is departed from, as might be expected in a community comprising so many heterogeneous elements. Sexual intercourse before marriage is not visited by any social penalties, nor are girls who have led an immoral life turned out of the caste. Only before they can be formally married, they must again pass through the ceremony of initiation described above. The standard Hindu ritual is not observed in marriage. A guru or gosain presents to Chaitanya flowers and sandal wood paste, and lays before him offerings of *málsábhog*, a compound of rice, fruits and other articles. Hymns (*sankirtan*) in honour of Krishna and Chaitanya are then sung to an accompaniment of the *mridanga*, an elongated drum, tapering towards the ends, and the *kartál* or brass cymbal. The guardian of the girl takes her right hand in his and gives it to the bridegroom, and the couple exchange small garlands of flowers and necklaces of beads. Sankirtan is sung once more, and the ceremony is over. Its essential and binding portion is the exchange of flowers or beads, technically known as *kanthi-badal*. Widows may marry again (*sangá*), and are in no way restricted in the selection of their second husband, except that they may not marry within the prohibited degrees originally forbidden to them The ritual is the same as that described above, except that no one gives away the bride. For a widow, as for a virgin, *kanthi-badal* is held to be the binding portion of the ceremony. Divorce is permitted at the option of either party, and divorced persons of either sex may marry again

Krishna is the tutelary deity of the caste, and most Baishtams worship him exclusively and disregard the other gods of the Hindu system. They also worship Chaitanya as the latest incarnation of Vishnu, Nityánanda as Balarám, and Adwaita as an incarnation of Siva. The following gurus rank as patron saints:—Swarup Goswámi, Sanátan, Bhatta Raghunáth, Srijiba, Gopal Bhatta, and Dás Raghunáth. To them are presented flowers of any colour but red, paste of sandal wood, *tulsi* leaves, *málsábhog*, parched rice, curds, sugar, cakes and sweetmeats of various kinds. Boiled rice and vegetable curry are sometimes offered. Báuls offer fish, and members of the Nerá-neri sect *masur dál* seasoned with onion. The twelfth day of every month and *janmashtami*, the birthday of Krishna, are the proper times for such offerings. The Kartá Bhajás, however, hold Friday to be especially sacred. After being laid before the god, the offerings are distributed among the worshippers present on the occasion. Although Baishtams do not consider it necessary to employ Brahmans for religious or ceremonial purposes, the gurus and goswámis who look after the religion of the caste are in fact usually members of the sacred order. But as their spiritual disciples come from low castes, and they themselves eat in their disciples' houses and take water from their hands, it follows that Baishtam Brahmans are not received on equal terms by the Brahmans who serve the higher castes, and the latter would as a rule decline to eat cooked food which had been touched by a Baishtam Brahman.

Religion.

Baishtams bury their dead in a sitting posture. Each of the several sects included in the caste is supposed to have a separate burial ground of its own; but it is not an uncommon practice to bury the dead within the precincts of the homestead. No regular *sráddh* is performed; Chaitanya is worshipped, and *málsábhog* is offered seven or eight days after death, and the relations of the deceased then indulge in a feast to show that the time of mourning is over.

Burial.

Baishtams eat cooked food only with people of their own caste; but they take water and sweetmeats from, and smoke out of the same hookah with, men of almost all castes except Muchis and sweepers. Their social standing is low, as the caste is recruited from among all classes of society, and large numbers of prostitutes and people who have got into trouble in consequence of sexual irregularities are found among their ranks. They have no characteristic occupation, and follow all professions deemed respectable by middle class Hindus.

Social status.

In the district of Midnapore the organization of the Baishtam caste seems to differ in some points from that described above. Two endogamous classes are recognized—(1) Játi-Baishnab, consisting of those whose conversion to Vaishnavism dates back beyond living memory, and (2) ordinary Baishnabs, called also Bhekdhári or 'wearers of the garb,' who are supposed to have adopted Vaishnavism at a recent date. The former are men of substance, who have conformed to ordinary Hinduism to such an extent that they are now Baishnabs in little more than name. In the matter of marriage they follow the usages of the Nabasákha; they burn their dead; mourn for thirty days; celebrate the *sráddh*, and employ high caste Brahmans to officiate for them for religious and ceremonial purposes. They do not intermarry or eat with the Baishnabs who have been recently converted. The latter are described to me by a correspondent as "the scum of the population. Those who are guilty of adultery or incest, and in consequence find it inconvenient to live as members of the castes to which they belong, embrace Vaishnavism, first, because they can by so doing place themselves beyond the pale of the influence of the headmen of their castes, and secondly, because their conversion removes all obstacles to the continuance of the illicit or incestuous connexions which they have formed."

Gosains.

With this attempt to define the extent to which Vaishnavism has developed into a caste, we may pass on to notice the more purely religious aspects of the Vaishnava community. Tradition has it that when Chaitanya died, his most zealous disciples formed a society consisting of six Gosains, eight Kabirajs, and sixty-four Mahants to organize the new teaching and to make proselytes throughout Bengal. In course of time there arose three great centres of the faith—Khardaha, between Calcutta and Barrackpur, the home of the Gosains or religious mendicants who traced their descent from Nityánanda, a devoted disciple of Chaitanya; Sántipur, on the river Bhágirathi in Nadiya, where Adwaitánanda or Adwaita, another zealous disciple, had settled; and Saidabad, in Murshedabad, the residence of Birbhadra, the son of Nityánanda. The Gosains or "Gentoo bishops," as they were called by Mr. Holwell, have now become the hereditary leaders of the sect. Most of them are prosperous traders and money-lenders, enriched by the gifts of the laity and by the inheritance of all property left by Bairágis. They marry the daughters of Srotriya and Bansaja Brahmans, and give their daughters to Kulins, who, however, deem it a dishonour to marry one of their girls to a Gosain. As a rule, they are tall and well-made men, of light complexion, fair specimens of the Aryan type as found in Bengal. The Adwaitánanda Gosains admit to the Vaishnava community only Brahmans, Baidyas, and members of those castes from whose hands a Brahman may take water. The Nityánanda, on the other hand, maintain that any such limitation is opposed to the teaching of Chaitanya, and open the door of fellowship to all sorts and conditions of men, be they Brahmans or Chandáls, high caste widows or common prostitutes. The Nityánanda are very popular among the lower castes, and hold a leading position among Vaishnavas. A *panjah* or silver hand is the badge of the family. The Gosains themselves worship Durgá, but their disciples do not follow them in this. They observe the birthday of Chaitanya on the 13th Phálgun, the Govardhan Pujá on the first day of the new moon in Kártik, and the Diwali on the night of the Káli Pujá. The Adwaitánanda Gosains are highly esteemed by the upper classes of Bengal, and it is very unusual for a Brahman or Baidya to enrol himself in the ranks of the other branch. They are said to be more sincere and more open to religious motives than the Nityánanda, and they avoid much scandal by refusing to initiate women.

For the purpose of making proselytes and governing the Vaishnava church, Bengal is divided into circles, each circle having its own Gosain with whose jurisdiction no other Gosain is supposed to interfere. Under the Gosain is the *adhikári* or superintendent, who acts as deputy, initiates disciples within a certain area, and collects fees. Under him again is the *faujdár*, called also *khuro* or uncle (the Gosain being the father), whose business it is to beat up proselytes, and whose activity is stimulated by a percentage of the fees. Lastly comes the *chharidár*, or usher of the rod, who is merely the messenger of the *faujdár*. Persons who join the Vaishnava communion pay a fee of twenty annas, sixteen of which go to the Gosain and four to the *faujdár*.

Mendicant Vaishnavas.

The mendicant members of the Vaishnava community, as distinguished from the Ját-Baishnabs or Grihi-Baishnabs on the one hand and the governing body of Gosains on the other, are, says Dr. Wise, "of evil repute, their ranks being recruited by those who have no relatives, by widows, by individuals too idle or depraved to lead a steady working life, and by prostitutes. Vaishnavi, or Baishtabi according to the vulgar pronunciation, has come to mean a courtesan. A few undoubtedly join from sincere and worthy motives, but their numbers are too small to produce any appreciable effect on the behaviour of their comrades. The habits of these beggars are very unsettled. They wander from village to village, and from one ákhára to another, fleecing the frugal and industrious peasantry on the plea of religion, and singing songs in praise of Hari beneath the village tree, or shrine. Mendicants of both sexes smoke Indian hemp (*ganjá*), and although living as brothers and sisters, are notorious for licentiousness. There is every reason for suspecting that infanticide is common, as children are never seen. In the course of their wanderings they entice away unmarried girls, widows, and even married women, on the pretext of visiting Sri Kshetra (Jagannáth), Brindaban, or Benares, for which reason they are shunned by all respectable natives, who gladly give charity to be rid of them.

The following account of an annual religious gathering in Bengal discloses the true character of these disreputable mendicants. Amid the ruins of ancient Gaur are large reservoirs of water, called Rupa and Sanátan, after the two distinguished Mahomedans converted by Chaitanya, on the banks of which the 'Rás Melá,' or 'Prem talá,' *i.e.*, real love, festival is held in the month of June. Crowds of Bairágis and Bairágins resort to this fair from all parts of Bengal, the latter being seated in long rows with their faces covered. Should a Bairági be in search of a companion, he pays the customary fee to the *faujdár* and a selection is made. He leads the female aside, raises her veil, and if satisfied takes her away, otherwise he refuses to allow another choice, unless the twenty-annas fee is again paid. It is a law with these licentious Bairágis that a man cannot put away the woman selected, even for adultery, until the next year's gathering comes round."

Báyán-Káupína.

(5) **Báyán-Káupína**, a sect of Vaishnavas, so called because, contrary to the usual custom, they wear the *kaupin* or loin cloth fastened on the left side

instead of on the right. The story goes that a guru while initiating a disciple tied the *kaupin* on the left side by mistake. He was about to change it when the novice insisted that Krishna himself must have pre-ordained the error, refused to have it corrected, and, going forth as he was, founded the Báyán-Káupíni sect. The members worship Rádhá-Krishna, but they are said to abstain from the immoral practices usually laid to the charge of those who worship this union of the male and female principles. Báyán-Káupínas abstain from flesh, fish and intoxicants, and only women of moral character are allowed to be initiated.

Kisori-Bhajana.

(6) **Kisori-Bhajana**, 'maiden-worshippers,' or Sáhuja, a sect of Vaishnavas concerning whose beliefs and ritual it is difficult to get any very precise information. The members seem to be aware that the equivocal name of their community lays them open to the suspicion of sexual immorality, and they are said to ward off curious inquiries by placing a book or an article of common use in a conspicuous part of the house and worshipping it as a symbol of their faith. The sect is supposed to be an offshoot of the Rádhá-Ballabhi, or, according to another account, of the Spashta-Dáyaka. The latter view is improbable. A Spashta-Dáyaka will not look upon a woman or take food from her; while the Kisori-Bhajana makes woman the chief object of worship. The sect is peculiar in having no Udási or mendicant class. The guru or pradhán initiates neophytes and conducts all religious services. The cult is said to be popular, especially with women and with the Sunri caste, and to have a large number of adherents. No distinctions of rank are recognized, and all converts, whether Brahmans or Chandáls, enter upon a footing of entire equality.

According to Dr. Wise, "at the initiation of a disciple a *mantra*, consisting of the word 'Hang-sha,' is whispered into his ear, and is believed to possess a certain mystical meaning, the first syllable typifying the air breathed, the latter the air expired. An indecent scene, in which a naked woman sits on the knee of the neophyte, is then rehearsed, as a crucial test of his having mortified the flesh and its lusts, and of his having become a worthy candidate for admission.

"The chief ceremony resembling the Rásmandalis of the Mahárájas of Bombay, which they have styled 'carnal love meetings,' is celebrated in a suitable room, where a long strip of white cloth is spread on the floor with plantain leaves laden with fish and rice, while flesh and spirits never appear.

"The feast being over, songs in honour of Rádhá-Krishna are chanted with the effect of often causing extravagant and violent excitement, terminating in hysterical weeping and convulsions. The pradhán then selects a woman, possibly the prettiest; the pair are dusted with sandal wood powder, crowned with flowers, and the company make adoration to them as the personations of Rádhá and her lover Krishna. Each man present then decorates himself with garlands, perfect silence being observed, and is presumed to fall into a dreamy sensuous condition, with mind abstracted and absorbed in the contemplation of the semblance of Rádhá at his side."

(7) **Jagat-Mohani**, an obscure sect founded about two centuries ago by one Jagat-Mohan of Mashulia in Silhet.

Jagat-Mohani.

The morals of its members are said to be exemplary. Women are not allowed to live in the monasteries, and the men are expelled on second conviction of immorality. As in most Vaishnava sects, there are two classes of votaries—the Grihi and Bairági, the former being house-holders, and the latter wandering about the country as beggars. The latter may not eat fish or flesh, and may not smoke ganja or tobacco or drink spirits. Corpses are usually thrown into a river, not burned, and burial is only resorted to at the express wish of a dying mahant. In such cases the patient is lowered into the grave before he actually dies, as it is considered lucky for him to die *in situ*.

(8) **Spashta Dáyaka**, said to have been founded by one Rup Rám Kabiráj, a disciple of Krishna Chandra Chakravartti of Saidabad.

Spashta Dáyaka.

Although Rádhá Krishna is the principal object of worship, the members of the sect affect a high standard of morality, and decline to take food that has been cooked by a woman. Women are admitted to the *mantra*, but not to the *bhek*. All castes including Chandáls are enrolled, but a preference is shown for the pure Sudras, from whose hands a Brahman may take water. The Spashta Dáyaka take alms from any Hindus, and even from Mahomedans, but reject the offerings of prostitutes and of Chamárs. They may not touch flesh or fish, or eat with any one not a member of their communion. They will not eat with Bairági Vaishnavas, but in this case the objections are said to be mutual. Their sectarian mark is a smear of ochre (*Gopi Chandan*) on the nose with two narrow lines drawn upwards to the roots of the hair. The sacred name of Hari is stamped on the temples, arms, chest, and shoulders. The dead are buried in a sitting posture, with a cloth (*námá-bali*) stamped with the name Hari wrapped round the head : the arms are folded across the chest, a necklace is hung round the neck, and a cocoanut shell (*karanka*), a wallet and a staff (*danda*) are placed by the side. If the dead man has had influence in the sect, and has left behind him many disciples, an ákhárá is built over his grave, religious rites are performed at his tomb, and his spirit is invoked for aid on occasions of trouble.

(9) **Kavi-Indra Paribár**, a small Vaishnava sect, claiming to be the Paribár or attendants of Vishnu Dás Kavi Indra, one of the original sixty-four mahants

Kavi-Indra Paribár.

who went out into the world to teach the doctrines of Chaitanya. The story is that this Vishnu Dás affected great humility and made a point of eating the leavings of Chaitanya's food. One day the teacher left nothing on his plate, and the disciple seeking to abase himself had to make the best of a grain of rice which Chaitanya had spat out. This he swallowed without noticing that it was tinged with blood. A rival observed this, and seeing his opportunity put to Chaitanya the question what should be done to a disciple who tasted the blood of his guru. Chaitanya unwarily answered that he should be excommunicated, and as the judgment could not be recalled, Vishnu Dás had to leave the original community and set up a dissenting society of his own. The doctrines of the Kavi Indra are much the same as those of the Vaishnavas. The office of mahant, however, is elective, not hereditary, and can only be held by a Sudra. There is no Bairági or Udási grade, and all the members are family men. All castes are admitted into the sect, and even Srotriya Brahmans are said to be occasionally enrolled as members.

Báola.

(10) **Báola** (*Sansk.* Váyula, crazed or inspired), a generic term including a number of disreputable mendicant orders which have separated from the main body of Vaishnavas, and are recruited mainly from among the lower castes. They call themselves Nitya, Chaitanya, and Hari Dás Báolas, after the great Vaishnava teachers. Differing from each other in minute points of ceremonial and social observance, the Báola sects agree in regarding pilgrimage to Vaishnava shrines as a sacred duty, and reverence the Gosains as their spiritual leaders. Flesh and strong drink are forbidden, but fish is deemed lawful food, and ganjá is freely indulged in. Báolas never shave or cut their hair, and filthiness of person ranks as a virtue among them. Ládu-Gopál, or the child Krishna, is the favourite object of worship; but in most ákháras the *charan* or wooden pattens of the founder are also worshipped. Báolas as a class are believed to be grossly immoral, and are held in very low estimation by respectable Hindus.

Darwesh-Faqir.

(11) **Darwesh-Faqir**, a recent and corrupt Vaishnava sect, founded in 1850 by Udaya Chánd Karmakár of Dacca. They worship Krishna, and distinguish their creed by the term Brahmadharma. When a novice is admitted, he receives a *kaupin* or loin cloth, a *khirka* or gown reaching to the ankles, and a cocoanut shell (*kishti*) in which he is to collect alms. Like the Aghoris and some of the Báola sects, he is required to taste various disgusting substances in order to show his superiority to ordinary prejudices. Darwesh-Faqirs never cut their hair or shave, and instead of washing with water, smear themselves and their clothes with mustard oil. Celibacy is professed, but not practised, and every ákhára or community of ascetics has several women attached to it, ostensibly to keep the place in order and cook the food. Nevertheless they affect great austerity and pretend to be the strictest of the Vaishnava sects. Animal life is never taken, and it is deemed sinful to break off the branches or even the leaves of a tree. Before the tombs of the founders, and on receiving a present, a very elaborate obeisance is made by kneeling, touching the ground with the forehead, and smearing the chest and face with dust.

Kartabhaja.

(12) **Kartabhaja**, an obscure sect believed to have been founded early in the eighteenth century by one Aul Chand, who was considered by his followers to be an incarnation of Chaitanya. Aul Chand observed no distinction of caste, and taught the worship of one god and certain moral precepts of a negative type. As Kartá or spiritual head of the caste, Aul Chand was succeeded by Ram Smaran Pal of Ghoshpára in Nadiyá, and the office is still held by members of the Pál family. Next in rank to the *Kartá* are the *Mahásays* or Deputies, of whom one acts as leader to every village congregration, his duty being to

collect the dues for the support of the Kartá, and to transmit or account for all amounts so received at stated dates. The religious ceremonies of the sect are kept secret and performed in private.

The following statement shows the number and distribution of Vaishnavas in 1872 and 1881:—

DISTRICT.	1872.	1881.	DISTRICT.	1872.	1881.
Bardwan	37,303	28,652	Noakhali	2,131	2,983
Bankura	10,250	20,325	Tipperah	5,347	6,104
Birbhum	23,243	21,411	Hill Tracts of Chittagong	......	5
Midnapur	96,178	81,888	Patna	2,062	717
Hughli	20,373	12,107	Gya	1,395	2,757
Howrah		15,284	Shahabad	1,070	1,842
24-Parganás	36,563	33,788	Mozaffarpur	6,720	4,744
Nadiya	10,889	21,330	Darbhanga		1,917
Jessore	13,039	14,861	Saran	3,777	2,320
Khulna	......	12,039	Champaran	2,606	2,346
Murshedabad	21,464	25,034	Monghyr	3,184	2,759
Dinajpur	16,710	10,349	Bhagalpur	13,196	2,703
Rajshahye	14,268	17,081	Purniah	1,809	3,412
Rangpur	24,541	26,974	Maldah	6,039	9,509
Bogra	8,013	11,111	Santál Parganás	6,400	6,346
Pabna	8,726	13,157	Cuttack	21,330	29,614
Darjiling	223	507	Puri	6,770	7,273
Jalpigori	1,877	3,420	Balasore	18,651	23,057
Kuch Behar	......	1,210	Tributary States	5,416	7,681
Dacca	11,896	17,239	Hazaribagh	789	441
Faridpur	6,204	7,658	Lohardaga	4,459	2,579
Bakarganj	5,799	6,149	Sinhbhum	2,733	2,868
Maimansinh	11,981	18,023	Manbhum	12,962	11,948
Chittagong	894	2,035	Tributary States	606	1,640

Vaisya, a caste of Eastern Bengal claiming to be the modern representatives of the Vaiṣyas of classical tradition. According to Dr. Wise, upon whose notes this article is based, they are most numerous in the Bhowal parganá of Dacca, and at Jahángirpur in Maimansinh. They can give no account of themselves, nor do they possess any traditions of their original home. They deny that Ballál Sen ruled over or reorganised them, and boast that no honorary titles inherited from ancestors serving the Muhamadan Government survive. For these reasons they regard themselves as exceptionally pure, having lived uncontaminated amid the changes of the country. The Vaíṣyas are generally short and squat, some having fine aquiline noses and prominent superciliary ridges, while others have broad cheek-bones, badly formed chins and lower jaws. Their physiognomy suggests cunning combined with intelligence, but many exhibit the inanimate vacant expression so common among Bengali low castes. The Vaíṣyas have relinquished many of the peculiar duties enjoined by Manu, though still wearing the sacred cord, composed of three strands knotted together, and another disconnected one of three threads, called Utarí. The ceremony of tonsure, Chúrá Karan, is observed before the thirteenth year, not postponed to the twenty-fourth, and on this occasion the youth is invested with the Brahmanical cord. Vaíṣyas profess to repeat the whole of the Gáyatrí, but the Brahmans assert that at the present day few know more than three-fourths of it, and not having full permission to bestow a blessing on the Ṣúdras, they twist the *Paitá* round the right thumb, and holding the right hand on a level with the navel confer the usual benediction. Vaíṣyas are permitted to read one of the four Vedas, and that always followed is the Yajur-veda. Each household celebrates by itself the Sáligrám, Chakra, and Vishnu Pújas, although Brahmans dispute their right to do so without requiring the services of the guru, or purohit, who are Ṣrotriyá Brahmans. In creed the caste is a Vaishnava one, yet a few Ṣákta worshippers are met with. The Vaíṣyas formerly committed the sin of marrying in their own *gotra*, or exogamous group, but of late years, in order to stay the scandal, new *gotras* have been formed.

They have no peculiar titles, but Gupta is often adde to their names, while individuals employed as assistants to merchants frequently assume the surname of Biswas, literally a holder of one-fourth share. Manu says that the first part of a Vaíṣya name should indicate wealth, the second prosperity; but the Bengali Vaíṣyas have ceased conforming to this rule, and the names ordinarily met with are Rám Kamár, Dev Náráyana, Ṣítala Chandra, or Rám Gopála, to which the surname Vaíṣya is always appended. Baidyás and Káyasths residing within the Ballálí country refuse to touch food prepared by the Vaíṣyas, but those living beyond those limits readily do so.

The Vaíṣya is generally a tolerable Bengali scholar, but few learn English, as it entails expense and delays the young from starting in life. In Maimansinh a few enter Government employ, but the majority are pleaders, mukhtárs, rent collectors and land surveyors. Formerly the cultivation of the soil was general, but now-a-days holding a plough is considered dishonourable, while managing a harrow is admissible. When a Vaíṣya meets a Brahman he does not, like other Hindus, make the salutation Praṇáma, as the Brahman bestows his benediction without it. Among Vaíṣyas the period of impurity after a death is fifteen days. All the Hindu festivals are observed by them, but the favourite one is that in honour of Lakhsmi, the goddess of wealth.

Vakat, a variant of Bhakat.

Vasta Gáin, a *thar* or section of Nepáli Brahmans.

Vátsa, see **Bátsya**.

Vedánta, he who knows the Vedas, a title of Brahmans.

Veni, a variant of Beni, a synonym for Baniyá.

Vidyádhara, a title of Kawális in Eastern Bengal.

Vishnu, see **Bishnu**.

Vishnumási, a section of Báruis in Bengal.

Vishnuswámi, a sect of Vaishnavs.

Viswál, a title of Chásás in Orissa.

Vumik, a variant for Bhaumik, a title of Kaibarttas.

Vyása, a section of Kaibarttas, Támbulis, Subarnabaniks, and Tántis in Bengal; of Gaura Brahmans in Behar.

Vyásokta, a title of those Rárhi Brahmans who perform religious offices for the Kaibarttas.

W

Wadsuesa, a sept of Maghs in the Hill Tracts of Chittagong.

Wahe, a section of the Panch-játi sub-caste of Khatris in Bengal.

Wáhsali, a *thar* or sept of Khambus in Darjiling.

Waientsa, a sept of Maghs in the Hill Tracts of Chittagong.

Wangdehchá, a *thar* or sept of Sunuwárs in Darjiling.

Warggu, a sept of Chakmás in the Hill Tracts of Chittagong.

Weh-ba, a *rui* or sept of Sherpa Bhotias of Nepal.

Winih, a section of Barhis in Behar.

Y

Yahián, a section of Naiyás.

Yakhá, a small agricultural caste of Nepal belonging to the Kiranti group.

Yak-kyukpa, a sept of the Phágu sub-tribe of Yakhás in Darjiling.

Yakpangden, the dweller on the pass, a sept of the Yangorup sub-tribe of Limbus in Darjiling.

Yakshoma, the guardian of the fort, a sept of the Ahtharai sub-tribe of Limbus in Darjiling.

Yaktachá, a *thar* or sept of Sunuwárs in Darjiling.

Yakten, formerly doctors, a sub-sept of the Thekim sept of Limbus in Darjiling.

Yakthumba, a synonym for Limbu.

Yamphu, a sub-tribe of Yakhás in Darjiling.

Yangdenba, he who paid his footing, a sept of the Pánthar sub-tribe of Limbus in Darjiling, said to be descended from a Mech, who got admission into the Limbu tribe by bribing the heads of the *thum-thum*.

Yángdi, a *thar* or sept of Mangars in Darjiling.

Yángmi, a *thar* or sept of Mangars in Darjiling.

Yangorup, a sub-tribe of Limbus in Darjiling.

Yangsoba or **Namlagpa**, the chief of the tribe, a sept of the Pánthar sub-tribe of Limbus in Darjiling.

Yeti, a *thar* or sept of Sunuwárs in Darjiling.

Yijám, the wanderer or eater, a sept of the Yangorup sub-tribe of Limbus in Darjiling.

Yithingu, the huntsman, a sept of the Yangorup sub-tribe of Limbus in Darjiling.

Yo-chang, a sub-sept of the Pon-po sept of Dejong Lhoris or Bhotias of the south.

Yoksuma, a sept of the Phágu sub-tribe of Yakhás in Darjiling.

Yong-tong-ba, a *rui* or sept of Dejong Lhoris, the members of which are the descendants of emigrants from Bhotan and Nepal.

Yongyah, a sept of Limbus in Darjiling.

Yongyahang, the son of a chief, a sept of the Yangorup and Charkhola sub-tribes of Limbus in Darjiling.

Yulsahb, a *rui* or sept of Dejong Lhoris, the members of which are the descendants of emigrants from Bhotan and Nepal.

Yul-then-bo, a *rui* or sept of the Tongdu sub-tribe of Dejong Lhoris whose ancestor was turned out of his fatherland.

Yungmá, the idler, a sept of the Yangorup sub-tribe of Limbus in Darjiling.

Yurumbang, they of the central village, a sept of the Phedáb sub-tribe of Limbus in Darjiling.

Z

Zamindár, a synonym for Bábhan.

Zamindár Brahman, a synonym for Bábhan.

Zargar, a synonym for Sonár.

Zargar, *Zardosi*, a maker of cloth of gold.

Zatti, a title of Kewats and Mallas in Behar.

APPENDIX I.

APPENDIX II.

APPENDIX III.

APPENDIX IV.

APPENDIX I.

LIST OF TRIBES AND CASTES WITH THEIR TITLES, SUB-CASTES AND SUB-TRIBES, SECTIONS AND SEPTS.

Agariá.

Titles :—Dhángar, Parja.

Sub-tribes.	Septs.
Pahária-Agaria.	Baheroar, a jungle fruit.
Brijia-Agaria.	Mahatoar, a title.
Assur-Agaria.	Samduar.
Lohar-Agaria.	Sonoar, gold.
	Turiar.

Agarwál, *Ágarwálá*.

Sub-castes.	Sections.	
Pachhainya.	Airan.	Mangal.
Purbiya.	Bátsil.	Mittal.
Dasá.	Bhaddal.	Singhal.
Bisa or Birádari Rájá.	Garg.	Tairan.
	Gáwál.	Táyal.
	Gobhil.	Thingal.
	Goil.	Tingal.
	Goin.	Tittal.
	Kásil.	Tundal.

Aguri, *Ugra Kshatri*.

Titles :—Kesh, Pai, Pál, Sámanta, Syám.

Sub-castes.	Sections.
Bághá.	Bharadwája.
Bardwániyá.	Gautam.
Chágnáya or Chánga.	Kásyápa.
Jáná.	Sándilya.
Kásipuriá.	
Sátsaikiyá.	
Suta.	

NOTE.—In order to facilitate reference to these lists, the names of endogamous groups are printed in red ink.

Amát.

Titles :—Ghibihár, Khawás, Saghár.

Sub-castes.

Gharbáit or Raut.
Bahiot.

Sections.

Larwár.
Narhan.
Parabwár.
Pataiwár.

Asura, *Agoria, Lohrá.*

Titles :—Májhi, Parjá.

Sub-tribes.

Agariá.
Birjiá.
Kolh-Asur.
Lohra-Asur.
Pahária-Asur.

Septs.

Aind, an eel.
Baroa, a wild cat.
Basriár, bamboo.
Beliár, *bel* fruit.
Kachua, a tortoise.
Kaitháwar, *kaithá* or *chichinga fruit.*
Kerketa, a bird.
Mukruár, spider.
Nág, a snake.
Rote, frog.
Siar, jackal.
Tirki, a bird.
Topo, a bird.

Bábhan.

Synonyms :— *Ajagyak Bráhman, Bhuinhár, Chaudhriji, Grihasti Bráhman, Maghayá Bráhman, Pachhimá Bráhman, Zamindár, Zamindár Bráhman.*

Titles :—Arápe, Bharsi-Misr, Chaube, Chaudriji, Dikshit, Dube, Mawár, Misr, Ojhá, Panchobe, Pánde, Páthak, Rái, Singh, Sotri, Thákur, Tiwári, Upadhiyá.

SECTIONS.

(*a*) *Territorial.*

Abkáhon.	Anarai.	Aswariá.
Aggechal.	Anwár.	Atrab.
Agnidhaut.	Araich.	Auigh baid.
Ailwár.	Arait.	Badoniá.
Ajaitiá.	Arewar.	Badramiá.
Ambariá.	Arnwait.	Bagauchiá.

(*a*) *Territorial*—concluded.

Bagri.
Balaiár.
Bandihá.
Banriá.
Barhambiá.
Barhampuriá.
Barnait.
Basmait.
Baswait.
Baurihá.
Begampuriá.
Belkuár.
Belonchá.
Bemwár.
Bhadsuhiá.
Bhaju Chakwar.
Bhalrait.
Bhalan.
Bheloriá.
Bhomápoli.
Bhunasware.
Bigahiá.
Bijalpuriá.
Bilkhari.
Chaksiár.
Chakwár.
Chandráwat.
Chasiwar.
Chauriár.
Chausá.
Chesiá.
Chiksoria.
Chilimár.
Chiwár.
Dabhinchhwár, Dabhauchwar.
Dalihare, Dullihará.
Darihare.
Dhakáit.
Dhanichhwár.
Dharan.
Dharwár.
Dhauráni.
Dighwait.
Dighwe.
Dipár.
Domkatár.
Donwár.
Dudhnait.
Dumráit.
Dundwar.
Gambhariá.
Gangtiait.
Garniá.
Gaur.
Ghatait.
Goait.
Harariá, foundling.
Hariambá.
Hartakia.
Hastgame.
Indrawar.
Jaitharia.
Jáji.
Jajim.
Jamraián.
Janwár.
Jesiwár.
Jethuliar.
Kadarai.
Kalemniá.
Kanchanbhár.
Karmuá.
Karnautiá.
Karnáyati.
Kestwár.
Katauniá.
Katewar.
Katiáin.
Kathautiá.
Kathwait.
Katthawa.
Kausonjhiá.
Kinwár.
Korache.
Koránch.
Kulhá.
Kumedwár.
Kunjalwár.
Ladilá.
Lamgoriá.
Larwariá.
Mahbariá.
Mahuari.
Mairiá.
Malikauliá.
Malitwár.
Manaria.
Manchia.
Mandra.
Mangrauni.
Maniksshariá.
Nanjorá.
Naradwár.
Niktawár.
Nonaitwár.
Okinwár.
Onwár.
Pachbhajuá.
Pachgotya.
Panchobe.
Parhape.
Parsaria.
Pilchwar.
Piliksawár.
Pilkhait.
Raini.
Ramayá.
Rampai.
Ransadiyá.
Sahasnanghiá.
Sahdaulia.
Sakarwár.
Sakhwait.
Sakmait.
Salhariyá.
Sandaliá.
Sapdohá.
Sarwe.
Saubarniá.
Semraián.
Sihogiá.
Sihoriá.
Sihujiá.
Siriár.
Sirsait.
Sonbhadriá, living on the banks of the Sone.
Sonewár.
Sorawár.
Suargane.
Surgriá.
Tetihá.
Tetihia.
Tilachhwar.
Umatwár.

(*b*) *Functional* or *Personal.*

Bhusbarát, husk-gatherer.
Chaubhaiá, born of four brothers.
Eksariá, born of one brother.
Jalewár, holder of fishing nets.
Kodáriá, worker with the spade.
Panchbhaiá, born of five brothers.

(*c*) *Brahmanical.*

Agnihotra.
Atharb.
Basisht.
Bharadwáj.
Garg.
Gautam.
Hárit.
Kásyapa.
Kaundin.
Kausik.
Parásar.
Sábarna.
Sándil.
Vátsa.

Bágdi, *Bágtit.*

Titles :—Bágh, Dhárá, Khán, Mánjhi, Masálchi, Mudi, Palankhái, Parámanik, Pherká, Puilá, Rái, Sántrá, Sardár.

Sub-castes.

1. Bájándáriá, found in Jessore.
2. Dandamánjhi.
3. Darátiá, found in Nuddea.
4. Duliá, a palanquin-bearing sub-caste.
5. Gulimánjhi.
6. Kasái kuliá, said to live along the banks of the Kasái river in Manbhum and Midnapur.
7. Kusmetia, Kusmátiá, or Kusputra, said to be named after the *kusa* grass, and apparently totemistic.
8. Let, found in Murshedabad.
9. Máchhuá, Mechhuá, or Mecho, a fishing sub-caste.
10. Malla metiá, Mátiá, or Mátiál, fishermen and earth-workers.
11. Nodá, found in the 24-Parganás, said to have come from Bankura.
12. Tentuliá, named after the tamarind tree, and apparently totemistic.
13. Trayodás, found in the 24-Parganás, said to have come from Bankura.
14. Ujha or Ojha, probably descended from the priests of the tribal gods, who would naturally tend to form themselves into a sub-caste. For a parallel case, see Mallik.

SECTIONS.

(a) *Totemistic*—	(b) *Eponymous*—
Ardi, fish.	Alamyán.
Bághrishi, the tiger.	Kásyapa.
Kachcháp, the tortoise.	
Kásbak, heron.	(c) *Uncertain*—
Pákbasanta, bird.	Bágri.
Pátrishi, the bean.	Dásya.
Ponkrishi, jungle cock.	Gadibhárat.
Sálrishi or Sálmachh, the *sál* fish.	Kál.
	Rácho.

Baidya, *Vaidya, Ambastha, Bhisak, Chikitsak.*

Sub-castes (Endogamous).

Rárhi.
Banga, *Bangaja.*
Barendra, *Varendra.*
Panchakoti.

Hypergamous groups.

Kulin.
Bangsaja.
Maulik.

Family titles (padabis).

Titles	Group
Dás, Gupta, Sen	Siddha.
Datta, Deb, Dhar, Kar	Sádhya.
Chandra, Kundu, Nág, Nandi, Raja, Rakshit, Soma	Kashta.

Sections (Exogamous).

Ádya.
Alamalaka.
Angira.
Atreya.
Baisvánara.
Basishtha.
Bátsya.
Bharadwája.
Dhanvantari.
Dhruba.
Gautama.
Ghritakausika.
Hingu.
Kásyapa.
Kausika.
Krishnátreya.
Madhukuliya.
Márkandeya.
Maudgalya.
Sábarna.
Saktri.
Salankayana.
Sándilya.
Vishnu.

Titles or popular designations of Baidyas practising medicine.

Used by themselves.
Baidya-nidhi.
Kabi-ballabh.
Kabi-bhushan.
Kabi-indra.
Kabiráj.
Kabiranjan.
Kabi-ratna.

Used by outsiders. Atai Baidya, doctor who defrauds the ignorant.
Chásá Baidya, plough doctor.
Deháti Baidya, village doctor.
Haturiá Baidya, a doctor who attends market, or, according to Wise, a quack, a meddlesome fellow.
Nári-tepá, pulse-feeler.

Bairági, *Jogi, Gosáin.*

Sub-tribes.	Septs in Chota Nagpur.
Nil.	Achut.
	Anaet.
	Anchit, tiger.
	Barandia.
	Bishnu.
	Dhobdhar, can't wash their clothes in child's birth ceremonies.
	Gobans, cow.
	Idri, a jungle fruit.
	Kansi, a kind of grass.
	Karanjea, an oil-seed.
	Nág, cobra.
	Ramgharia, a place.
	Sonar, can't wear gold.
	Tura.

Báiti, *Báoti, Chunári, Chuniyá, Barnak-Támuli.*

Titles:—Bhuiyá, Rái, Sen.

Sub-castes.	Sections.
1. Báiti of Dacca and Central Bengal.	Aliman.
2. Magi of Fáridpur.	Bághrishi.
	Kasyapa.
	Tilalochan.

Barhi, *Barhai.*

Titles:—Manjhan, Maraiya, Mistri, Rái, Sátun, Thákur.

Sub-castes.		Sections.
1. Kanaujiá.	(Work only in wood.)	(*a*) *Territorial*—
2. Kokás.		Bachberáit.
3. Maghayá.	(Work in wood and iron.)	Balbheráit.
		Bánsdih.

Sub-castes.	Sections.
	(a) *Territorial*—concluded.
4. Lohar. (Found in Bhágalpur. Work only in iron.)	Barhioth.
	Barnáit.
	Balhátt.
5. Kamár-Kallá.	Bharáii.
6. Mathuriá.	Charwa.
	Chaudhrána.
	Dasáonth.
	Dobháit.
	Gritári.
	Háthián.
	Kápri.
	Kharáit.
	Lakwár.
	Mukund.
	Parus.
	Pipriáti.
	Sikalgar.
	Winih.
	(b) *Eponymous*—
	Biskarma.
	Sándilya.
	Kásyapa.

Hypergamous divisions of the Maghayá sub-caste.

Thákur.
Rái.
Kuar.

IN BENGAL.

Bárui, *Barai, Baraji, Bárajibi, Latá-baidya.*

Titles:—Ain, Ash, Bawál, Bhadra, Bhaumik, Bhawal, Biswás, Chánd, Chaudhri, Dám, Dás, Deo, Datta, Dhar, Guha, Háldár, Hor, Kar, Khán, Khor, Kundu, Láhá, Majumdár, Mallik, Mandal, Mantrini, Mánná, Márik, Mitra, Náha, Nág, Nandan, Nandi, Pál, Rakhit, Rudra, Sarkár, Sen.

Sub-castes.	Sections.	
1. Rárhi.	Aliman.	Kanwamaharsi.
2. Bárendra.	Batsya.	Kásyapa.
3. Náthán.	Bharadwáj.	Madhukuliya.
4. Kotá.	Chandramaharsi.	Sándilya.
	Gautama.	Vishnumaharsi.
	Jaimini.	Vyása.

IN BEHAR.

Barai, *Mistri.*

Title :—Ráut.

Sub-castes.

1. Maghaya.
2. Jaiswár.
3. Chaurasiá.
4. Semerya.
5. Sokhwá.

Sections.

Kásyapa.
Nág.

Bauri, *Buno.*

Titles :—Digha, Mandal, Manjhi, Maulavi, Parámanik.

Sub-castes.

1. Dhuliá or Dhulo.
2. Jhátiá or Jhetiá.
3. Káthuriá.
4. Mallabhumiá.
5. Maluá or Máluá.
6. Mola.
7. Panchakoti.
8. Páturia.
9. Sikhariá or Gobariá.

Sections.

Aliman.
Kásyapa.
Madhukulya.
Májhi.

Bediá, *Bedeá, Bejeá.*

Title :—Mahto.

Sub-tribes.

Nil.

Septs.

Bar, the banyan tree.
Biha or Binjhá, a fish.
Chidra or Cherrá, squirrel.
Dhechua, a black bird.
Dian, a kind of fish.
Kachua or Kachchh, tortoise.
Khopchá, an owl.
Mahanadi, name of a river.
Mahua, *bassia latifolia.*
Mahukal, a bird with long tail.
Maina, a bird.
Nág, a cobra.
Parewá, a pigeon.
Pechâ, an owl.
Suiá, a bird.
Sulankhi, a bird.
Sundi, mahua flower.
Titipi, a night bird.
Turu, a bird.

Beldár.

Titles :—Gadahya, Marár, Ráut.

Sub-castes.	Section.
Bhojpuriá.	Kasyapa.
Chauhán.	
Kathautiá or Katháwá.	

Bhandári, *Nápit, Hajjám.*

Titles :—Bárik, Kshuri.

Sub-castes.	Section.
Bangáli.	
Dakhini.	
Desi.	
Khariá.	
Khurdá.	
Gola.	
Hatuá.	

Bhar.

Title :—Ráná.

Sub-castes.	Sections.
	(*a*) *Totemistic*—
1. Bangáli.	Bánsrishi, bamboo.
2. Maghayá.	Bel, *bel* fruit.
	Kachhap, tortoise.
	Mayur, peacock.
	(*b*) *Eponymous*—
	Agni.
	Brahmarishi.
	Rishi.

Bhát.

Titles :—Bhárata, Dasaundhi, Kabiji, Rái.

Sub-castes.	Sections.
Baram-Bhát.	Anal.
Ráj-Bhát.	Antahriá.
Turk-Bhát (Mahomedan).	Balbandhiá.
	Bharadwája.
	Gaighatiá.
	Kailiá.
	Kásyapa.
	Kunwar.
	Lakhsariá.
	Lohárkoriyá.
	Mahrajiá.
	Menwár.
	Sahar.
	Sándilya.
	Sanhakiá.
	Sindhwatiá.
	Suarait.

Atselá, Baruá, Bhatara, Chaurási, Chúngele, Dasaundhi, Gujriwálá, Jangira, Kailiá, Mahápátra, Nagauri, Sikatpúrea, are mentioned by Sir Henry Elliot as subdivisions of Bháts, but it is not stated whether these names denote sub-castes, sections, or merely titles.

Bhuimmáli, *Bhuimdar*, *Siddhi-putra*, *Hári*.

Sub-castes.		Sections.
1. Bara-bhógiyá.		Parásara.
2. Mitra Seni Behará.		Aliman.
3. Chhota-bhágiyá.		
4. Amarábádi	Found in Noakhali, and apparently peculiar to that district.	
5. Sáráliá		
6. Hátiá		
7. Bhuluá		

Bhuiyá, *Bhuinyá, Bhuiyán, Bhuinhár, Bhumiyá, Musahar, Náik Khandáyat, Khandáyat-Páik, Ghatwál, Ghatwár, Tikáyat, Rajwár, Rái-Bhuiyá, Ber-Bhuiyá, Sardár, Puran.*

Titles:—Bhogta, Chharidár, Kopát, Mahton, Mánjhi, Náik, Rái Singh, Thákur, Tikáyat.

Sub-tribes.

In Lohardagá—

Bichwár.
Deswáli.
Dundwár.
Junwár.
Khandait.
Maghaiyá.
Mahtwár.
Marheriá.
Rajwár.
Rikhiásan.
Tirwár.

In Keonjhar—

Mál or Desh-Bhuiyá.
Dandsena.
Khatti.
Rájkuli.

In Manbhum—

Dhorá.
Kátrás.
Musahar.

In Hazaribagh—

Ghátwár.
Tikáyat.

Septs.

Asura.
Bagáli.
Baliar.
Banini.
Banka.
Bankiar.
Banui.
Champiar.
Chirra or Rikhiasan, squirrel
Golari.
Jagdâ.
Jagorari.
Kach, tortoise.
Kaliar.
Kandni.
Kanrui.
Kenduari.
Keruri.
Kihar.
Kussum, a tree.
Kutar.
Lota.
Nág.
Naragi.
Narari.
Noah.
Pachoar.
Pansi.
Rái.
Ranangi.
Sani.
Satadi.
Sinhi.

Bhumij.

Titles :—**Mánki,**[1] **Matkum,**[2] **Mura,**[3] **Sardár.**[4]

Sub-tribes.	Septs.
Desi.	**Baddá Kurkutiá**, a kind of worm.
Tamáriá, Murá, or **Mánki-Mura.**	**Bárdá.**
Sikhariyá or **Meno.**[6]	**Bhuiyá**, fish.
Pátkumiá.[7]	**Chandil.**
Shelo, iron-smelters.	**Gulgu**, fish.
Barábhumiá, zamindar Bhumij.[8]	**Hánsdá**, wild goose.
	Hemrong, betel palm.
	Járu, a bird.
	Kásyab, tortoise.
	Leng, mushroom.
	Nág, snake.
	Obársári, a bird.
	Pilá.
	Ságmá.
	Sálrishi, *sal* fish.
	Sándilya, a bird.
	Sáolá.
	Tesá, bird.
	Tumárung, pumpkin.
	Tuti, a sort of vegetable.

[1] This title is common among the Mundas.
[2] Applied to the Bhumij of Dhalbhum.
[3] Mura is the common form of Munda in Manbhum.
[4] Possibly borrowed from the *ghatwali* system, the leading executive unit of which is the *sardár* or head of the subordinate *ghatwals* (*tabidars*) of a village.
[5] The two latter appellations clearly suggest Munda descent.
[6] This group is supposed to come from Manbhum.
[7] The Patkumiá and Tamáriá sub-tribes occasionally intermarry.
[8] Probably descended from members of the Barabhum zamindari family.

Bind.

Titles :—**Chaudhri, Mahto, Mukhiá, Ráut.**

Sub-castes.		Sections.
Khariát	In Behar.	(*a*) *Territorial*—
Awadhiyá	In Behar.	**Jarhuáit.**
Lodhiyá	In Behar.	**Jhauáit.**
Gondh	In Behar.	**Odaniá.**
Jutaut Bind	In Eastern Bengal.	
Nun Bind	In Eastern Bengal.	(*b*) *Eponymous*—
Bin	In Eastern Bengal.	**Kásyapa.**

Binjhiá, *Birjiá, Brijiá, Binjhwár.*

Titles :—**Baráik, Dandiá, Gaunjhu, Kárji, Mánjhi, Mirdáhá, Náik, Náth, Parja, Pradhán.**

Sub-tribes.	Septs.
Pahάriya-Binjhiá.	**Bair**, *zizyphus jujuba.*
Dand-Binjhiá.	**Bansetti**, don't touch bamboo at a wedding.
Agaria-Binjhiá.	**Bhair.**
	Cheruka, fish.
	Chidra, squirrel.
	Chingri, a river-fish.
	Chorka, a pond-fish.
	Chutia, rat.
	Dádul, bullfrog.
	Garai, a river-fish.
	Huru, paddy-bird.
	Kachua, tortoise.
	Kási, a kind of grass (*saccharum spontaneum*).
	Kuns, grass.
	Mangar, crocodile.
	Murgi, hen.
	Nág, serpent.
	Pusway, a river-fish.
	Sinduria, use *sindur*, a red paint, at marriage.
	Telha, use oil at marriage.
	Tengra, a river-fish.
	Thekra, a river-fish.

Birhor.

Title :—**Birhor.**

Sub-tribes.	Septs.
Nil.	**Hemrom**, a kind of fish.
	Jagsaria.
	Liluai.
	Mahli.
	Nág, cobra.
	Nagpuria.
	Singpuria.
	Sircar.

Bráhman, *Báman, Bipra, Dwija, Thákur, Sarmá, Deva-Sarmá, Bhudeva, Bhusur, Agraja, Maháráji, Bábáji, Gosáinji.*

Main divisions. *Territorial divisions.*

Pancha Gauriya—Sáraswat, Kányakubja, Gaura, Utkal, Maithil.

Pancha Drávira—Karnáti, Tailangi or Andhra, Gujráti or Gurjjara, Dráviri, Maháráshtriya.

Miscellaneous—Nepali, Vyásokta, Sákadwipi, Kraunch-dwipi (including Jausi, Jotkhi or Jyotshi, Dákantiá, Bhadariá or Bhareri, Jadwá, Saguniá, Sanicherá), Mágadha, Bandijan or Suta, Atharva, Máthur, Mahá Bráhman otherwise called Mahá-pátra or Kantáha, Lakhauria, Belontiá, Kathak, Kaláwat, Tikaur, Sakuntalá, Sawálákhi, Kashmiri, Kámrupi.

Tirtha Purohits, Debal or Pandá:—Gayáwál, Prayág-wál, Gangáputra, Dhámin, etc.

Sáraswat.

Sub-castes.		Sections.		
In the Panjáb.				
Four local divisions, divided into high, middle, and low endogamous groups.	1st division	High ...	50	The *gotras* are common to all Bráhmans.
		Low ...	172	
	2nd "	High ...	12	
		Low ...	23	
	3rd "	High ...	9	
		Low ...	48	
	4th "	High ...	11	
		Middle...	20	
		Low ...	124	
		Total ...	469	

In Behar they have the following titles, which are endogamous:—Misra, Sukul, Dube or Dobe, Tiwári, Páthak, Pande, Upádhyáya, Chaube or Chobe, Bájapeyi, Pandit.

Kánya Kubja, Kanaujiá.

Titles (*in Behar*):—Misr or Misra, Sukul, Tiwári, Dube or Dobe, Páthak, Pánre, Upádhyáya, Chaube or Chobe, Dichhit or Dikshit, Lakhnau or Bájapeyi, Sarwariyá or Saryupári.

Titles (*in Bengal*) :—Bhattáchárji, Ghatak, Chakrabartti, Bandya, Chatta, Mukhati, Rái, Munshi, Chaudhri, Sarkár, Majumdár, Háldár, Bidyáratna, Bidyábágis, Smritiratna.

Sub-castes.

In Bengal.

- Rárhi.
  - Piráli.
- Bárendra.
  - Uttar Bárendra.
  - Pánchuriá.
- Madhyasreni or Madyadoshi.
- Barna or Patita Bráhman.
- Agradáni.
- Achárji, Daibajna, Ganaka.
- Bhát or Bhatta.
- Maruiporá.
- Saptasati or Sátsati.
- Vaidik.
  - Páschátya.
  - Dákshinátya.

Sections or *gotras* common to all Bráhmans.

Abya.
Agastya.
Alamyán.
Anábrikáksha.
Angirasa.
Atreya.
Atri.
Baijáhmapadya.
Baiyághrapadya.
Basishtha.
Básuki.
Bátsya.
Bharadwája.
Bhárgava.
Bishnu.
Biswámitra.
Briddha.
Brihaspati.
Garga.
Gautama.
Ghritakausika.
Gotama.
Jábáli.
Jaimini.
Jájnabalkya.
Jámadagnya.
Kalvisha.
Kánchan.
Kanwa or Kánna.
Kásyapa.
Kátyáyan.
Kaundilya.
Kausika.
Kaustav.
Krishnátreya.
Kusal.
Maudgalya.
Maunas.
Parásara.
Paulastya.
Rikhab.
Rohita.
Sábarna.
Saktri.
Sándilya.
Sánkriti.
Saukálin.
Saupáyan.
Sunaka.
Upamanya.

Sections of Uttar Bárendras according to "Laghu Bhárat" and "Sambandhanirnaya."
- Swarna-Kausik.
- Rajata-Kausik.
- Ghrita-Kausik.
- Kaundilya-Kausik.
- Kausika.

Kshatrapeta or hybrid *gotras*.
- Saunaka.
- Kánwáyan.
- Rathitara.
- Agnibesma.

1. The Rárhi and Bárendra sub-castes have the following five *gotras* :—Kásyapa, Sándilya, Sábarna, Bátsya, and Bharadwája.

2. The Sátsatis have some of the *gotras* or exogamous sections in use among Baidik Brahmans.

3. There can be no intermarriage amongst persons of the following five *gotras* :—Jámadagnya, Bátsya, Sábarna, Maudgalya, Saupáyana, which are supposed to be of common ancestry and are therefore reckoned as one exogamous section.

4. The Madhyasreni or Madyadoshi Bráhmans of Western Bengal have the following *gotras* :—Sándilya, Bátsyaba, Kásyapa, Bharadwája, Sábarnya, Parásara, Gautma, Ghrita-Kausika.

5. The Bháts or Bhattas have the following *gotras* :—Kásyapa, Bharadwája, Sándilya, Ghrita-Kausika, Aurbba Rishi, Bátsya, Alimyán.

6. Each *gotra* has its *pravaras*, *i.e.*, a group of from three to five Rishis belonging to the same *gotra*. Intermarriage between persons having the same *pravaras* is in theory prohibited, but this rule is not now strictly observed.

Gáin or **Grámin** (56 or 59) of the Rárhi sub-caste under the five *gotras*:—

Sándilya Gotra (16).

Bandya.	Ghoshli.	Kadál.
Gargari.	Sejagá.	Kusári.
Kesarkuni.	Máschatak.	Kulisá or Kulkuli.
Kusumkali.	Barál.	Akás.
Párihál.	Basuári.	Dirgháti.
Kulabhi.		

Kásyapa Gotra (16).

Gur.	Palsái.	Pákrási.
Ambuli.	Har.	Simlái.
Bhuri.	Porári.	Pushali, Pushilál.
Talabáti.	Páladhi.	Bhatta.
Pitamundi.	Koári.	Mul.
Chatta.		

Bharadwája Gotra (4).

Mukhaiti.	Sáharik.
Dingsáin.	Ráyi.

Sábarna Gotra (12).

Gánguli.	Nandi.	Sáteswari.
Kundalál.	Báli.	Páriál.
Siddhal.	Siárik.	Ghanteswari.
Dáyi.	Pungsika.	Náyári.

Bátsya Gotra (8 or 11).

Mahintá.	Pippalái.	Kánjiári.
Ghoshál.	Putitunda.	Chautkhandi.
Simlái.	Purbba.	Dighál.
Bápuli.	Kánjilál.	

The Gáins whom Rájá Ballál Sen made—*Kulin*, *Gauna Kulin*, and *Srotriya* :—

Kulin (8).

Bandya.	Ghoshál.	Kánjilál.
Chatta.	Putitunda.	Kundalál.
Mukhaiti.	Gánguli.	

Gauna Kulin (14).

Ráyi.	Pippalái.	Párihál.
Gur.	Gargari.	Har.
Mahintá.	Ghanteswari.	Pitamundi.
Kulabhi.	Kesarkuni.	Dirgháti.
Chautkhandi.	Dingsái.	

The remaining 34 or 37 are **Srotriyas.**

Those Ghataks who reckon 56 Gains, include Porári among Gauna Kulins and exclude Dighal, Chautkhandi, and Purbba. Those who reckon 59, exclude Porári, Dighal, and Purbba from Gauna Kulin, and show 34 Srotriyas.

Hypergamous groups *bhába* and sub-groups *mel* of Rárhis formed by the famous social reformer Devibar Ghatak :—

Groups.	Mels or sub-groups, mostly endogamous.	
Kulin.	Phuliá.	Sribarddhani.
Bhanga Kulin.	Khardaha.	Satánandkháni.
Srotriya { Suddha.	Ballabhi.	Chhayi.
Srotriya { Sádhya.	Sarbbánandi.	Achambitá.
Srotriya { Kashta.	Panditratni.	Dasarath Ghataki.
Bansaja.	Bángál.	Subharájkháni.
	Surái.	Máládharkháni.
	Achárjya Sekhari.	Rághab Ghosháli.
	Gopálghataki.	Deháti.
	Chatta Rághabi.	Nariyá.
	Bijayapanditi.	Kákusthi.
	Mádhái.	Dharádhari.
	Bidyádhari.	Ráyi.
	Párihál.	Bhairab Ghataki.
	Sriangabhatti.	Parmánanda Misra.
	Pramodni.	Sunga Sarbbánandi.
	Báli.	Hari Majumdári.
	Chandrapati.	Chándái.

Gain or *Grámin* (100) of the Bárendra sub-caste under the five *gotras* :—

Kásyapa gotra (18).

Maitra.	Moáli.	Madhyagrámi.
Bháduri.	Kiral.	Mathgrámi.
Karanja.	Bijkunja.	Gangágrámi.
Bálayashthi.	Sargrámi.	Belgrámi.
Modhágrámi.	Sahagrámi.	Chamagrámi.
Balihári.	Katigrámi.	Asrukoti.

Sándilya gotra (14).

Rudrabágchhi.	Kámondra.	Subarna.
Láheri.	Sihari.	Totaka.
Sádhubágchhi.	Tároálá Bisi.	Pushána.
Champati.	Matasyási.	Beluri.
Nandanábási.	Champa.	

Bátsya gotra (24).

Sánnyál.	Simli.	Srutabati.
Bhimkáli.	Dhosáli.	Akshagrámi.
Bhattasáli.	Tánuri.	Sáhari.
Kámkáli.	Batsagrámi.	Káligrámi.
Kurmuri.	Deuli.	Kálihái.
Bháriál.	Nidráli.	Paundrakáli.
Laksha.	Kukkuti.	Kálindi.
Jámrukhi.	Borhgrámi.	Chaturábandi.

Bharadwája gotra (24).

Bhádar.	Bála.	Káchhati.
Láruli.	Sákati.	Nandigrámi.
Jhámál, Jhampati.	Simbi.	Gográmi.
Aturthi.	Bahál.	Nikhati.
Rái.	Sariyál.	Pippali.
Ratnábali.	Kshetragrámi.	Sringa.
Uchchharakhi.	Dadhiyál.	Khorjár.
Gochchhási.	Puti.	Goswálambi.

Sábarna gotra (20)

Singdiár.	Tátoár.	Khandabati.
Pákari.	Setu.	Nikari.
Dadhi.	Naigrámi.	Samudra.
Sringa.	Nedhuri.	Ketugrámi.
Medari.	Kapáli.	Jasográmi.
Undhuri.	Tuttari.	Sitali.
Dhundhuri.	Panchabati.	

Gáin of Uttar-Barendras according to "Gaure Brahman":—

Sándilya.	Kásyapa.	Bátsya.
Champati.	Bháduri.	Káláyi.
Bágchhi.	Karanjá.	Grihasodhani.
Lábar.	Simbi.	Madhugrámi.
Nandanábási.		
Sihari.		

Bharadwája.	Sábarna.
Rái.	Annásani.
Gopurbba.	
Sirasinthi.	
Jhámál.	

Kulins made by Ballál Sen:—

Láheri.	Maitra.	Kálihái.
Bágchhi.	Sannyál.	Bhádar.
Bháduri.	Misra.	

Srotriyas divided by Rájá Kansa Náráyan:—

(*a*) *Siddha Srotriya.*

Karanja.	Laruli.	Aturthi.
Nandanábási.	Champati.	Kálihái.
Bhattasáli.	Jhampati.	

(*b*) *Sádhya Srotriya.*

Uchchharakhi.	Sihari.	Bisi.
Jámrukhi.	Rái.	Karjjuri.
Ratnábali.	Goswálambi.	

(*c*) The rest are *Kashta Srotriyas.*

Hypergamous groups *bhába* and sub-groups *pathi* of Bárendras formed by the learned social reformer Udayanáchárya Bháduri:—

Groups.	Sub-groups.
Kulin.	Jonáli.
Srotriya { Siddha.	Nirábil.
Srotriya { Sádhya.	Bhushná.
Srotriya { Kashta.	Rohilá.
Kápa, Chhaghariá.	Kutabkháni.
	Aliákháni.
	Bhabánipuri.
	Beni.

Bárendra titles:—

Bágh, tiger.	Pánjá, heap of bricks.
Bherá, sheep.	Páthá, goat.
Dhol, drum.	Prachanda, furious.
Gappi, tell-tale.	Talápátra, bottom of a pot.
Gonj, peg.	Taulo, earthen pot.

Gáin of Saptasatis :—Ấrath, Báguri, Bálthubi, Bhágái, Dháin, Dhardhar, Háiui, Háturi, Jabagrámi, Jagái, Kálui, Kándare, Kántharâ, Kanyá, Kátádi, Kátáni, Káturi, Kusalá, Mulukjuri, Nálsi, Nánaksái, Pátári, Pharphar, Pithári, Ságáin, Sáin, Sugáin, Ujalá, Ulluk, etc.

Vaidik.

Sub-castes.		Sections (*gotras*).	Groups, *samáj*.
Páschátya Vaidik.	Jonári. Konári.	Sándilya	Ấkhará. Madhyabhág. Pánkunda.
		Basishtha	Joári. Gaurálí. Aládhi. Dadhichi.
		Sábarna	Sántaru. Brahmapur. Marichi Grám.
		Bharadwája	Chandradwip. Navadwip. Kotálipárá.
		Saunaka	Sámantasár.
		Local groups—	Purbbasthálí. Bishnupur. Bhátpárá. Purbba Banga.

Bráhmans of the following *gotras* came later on (1102 Sak or 1180 A.D.) and mixed up with the Páschátya Vaidiks :—Krishnátreya, Gautama, Rathitara, Kásyapa, Bátsya, Sunak; and still later on (1403 Sak or 1481 A.D.) came Bráhmans of the Ghrita-Kausika, Kausika, Ấtreya, Sankarshan, Parásara, Agnibesma, Maudgalya, Hárita, and Upamanyu *gotras*.

		Hypergamous groups.
Dákshinátya Vaidik.	Kásyapa.	Kulin.
	Gautama.	Bansaja.
	Bátsya.	Maulik.
	Kánwáyan.	
	Kausika.	Local groups or *samáj*.
	Ghrita-Kausika.	
	Játukarna.	Majilpur.
	Sábarna.	Rájpur.

The Dákshinátya Vaidiks have the following titles :—

Tripáthi, Misra, Páthak, Chakrabartti.

Gaura.

Sub-castes.		Titles.
Kevala Gaura.		Sukul.
Adi Gaura	Sukalvála. Joshi. Ojhá.	Pánde. Misra. Joshi.
Sanádhya	Chingala. Dáymia. Khandelvála.	Dube. Tiwári. Chaube.
Hariyána.		Vyása.
Sri-Gaura	Támboli. Adi Sri-Gaura.	
Gurjar Gaura.		
Tek Bárá.		
Chamár Gaura.		
Kritanay.		

Maithil or Tirhutiá.

Titles :—Majhrote, Misir or Misra including Chaudhari, Ráya, Parihasta, Khána and Kumára, Ojhá, Ujha or Jhá, Páthu, Pura including Bakriyár and Charviyár, Thákur, Pádri.

Hypergamous groups.	Sections. *Gotra.*	Sections. *Dih or Mul.*
Srotriya or Srotri. Jog. Panjibaddh. Nágar. Jaiwár.	Bátsa ...	1. Karmahe-Majhaurá. 2. Karmahe-Tarauni. 3. Karmahe-Naruái. 4. Karmahe-Behat. 5. Karmahe-Majhiám. 6. Karmahe-Alanpur. 7. Karmahe-Baghát. 8. Karmahe-Urará.
	Sándil	9. Karmahe-Ahpur.
	Bharadwája	10. Belaunche-Káko. 11. Belaunche-Ojhaul. 12. Belaunche-Sudai. 13. Belaunche-Ratpár. 14. Belaunche-Garh. 15. Belaunche-Dih.

Gotra.		*Dih* or *Mul.*
Bátsa	...	16. Hariáme-Rakhwári. 17. Hariáme-Sibá. 18. Hariáme-Balirájpur. 19. Hariáme-Katmá. 20. Hariáme-Ahil.
Bátsa	...	21. Paliwár-Mangrauni. 22. Paliwár-Mahesi. 23. Paliwár-Dibra. 24. Paliwár-Sakuri. 25. Paliwár-Haripur. 26. Paliwár-Samaul. 27. Paliwár-Kachhra. 28. Paliwár-Phuldáha. 29. Paliwár-Mahendra. 30. Paliwár-Jarhatyá.
Bátsa	...	31. Budhwáre-Mahesi. 32. Budhwáre-Sakuri. 33. Budhwáre-Dumrá. 34. Budhwáre-Balha.
Sándil	...	35. Saudarpurái-Mahiá. 36. Saudarpurái-Katka. 37. Saudarpurái-Jagaur. 38. Saudarpurái-Sarso. 39. Saudarpurai-Suket. 40. Saudarpurái-Hansauli. 41. Saudarpurái-Khoir. 42. Saudarpurái-Digaun. 43. Saudarpurái-Kanhauli. 44. Saudarpurái-Mánik. 45. Saudarpurái-Rohár. 46. Saudarpurái-Sundar. 47. Saudarpurái-Dhaul. 48. Saudarpurái-Baghát. 49. Saudarpurái-Gaul.
Kásyap	...	50. Darihare-Dih. 51. Darihare-Rájanpurá. 52. Darihare-Bargamiá. 53. Darihare-Ratauli. 54. Darihare-Sahasrám.
Bátsa	..	55. Anraiwár-Anrai. 56. Anraiwár-Usrauli. 57. Anraiwár-Jauá. 58. Anraiwár-Baingni.

Gotra.	Dih or Mul.
Kásyap ...	59. Baliáse-Narsam.
	60. Baliáse-Balha.
	61. Baliáse-Ási.
	62. Baliáse-Sakuri.
	63. Baliáse-Dharaurá.
	64. Baliáse-Suket.
	65. Baliáse-Baghánt.
Kásyap ...	66. Tannahpurái-Solhni.
Bátsa ...	67. Takwáre-Ankusi.
	68. Takwáre-Nima.
Kásyap ...	69. Khowáre-Nahás.
	70. Khowáre-Mahuá.
	71. Khowáre-Mahnaurá.
	72. Khowáre-Kokrahi.
	73. Khowáre-Khari.
	74. Khowáre-Murájpur.
Kásyap ...	75. Satlakhe-Sataur.
	76. Satlakhe-Satlakha.
Kátyáyan ...	77. Kunjilwár-Malangiá.
	78. Kunjilwár-Sater.
	79. Kunjilwár-Ullu.
	80. Kunjilwár-Bhakhren.
	81. Kunjilwár-Digaun.
	82. Kunjilwár-Bhakhrauli.
Sándil ...	83. Khanraure-Bhaur.
	84. Khanraure-Khutti.
	85. Khanraure-Gurdi.
	86. Khanraure-Ekmá.
Kásyap ...	87. Sakariwár-Harari.
	88. Sakariwár-Tatail.
	89. Sakariwár-Chhámu.
Sándil ...	90. Pagulwár-Barhiám.
	91. Pagulwár-Tarálohi.
	92. Pagulwár-Dhen.
Kásyap ...	93. Maráre-Sihol.
	94. Marare-Jagaul.
	95. Marare-Ukki.
	96. Marare-Barhampur.
	97. Marare-Adauri.
	98. Marare-Misrauli.
	99. Marare-Rajaurá.
	100. Marare-Jagatpur.
Sándil	101. Dighwe-Tipri.
	102. Dighwe-Nagar.
	103. Dighwe-Kankaurá.
	104. Dighwe-Sannahpur.
	105. Dighwe-Sakarpurá.

Gotra.	*Dih* or *Mul.*
Bátsa ...	106. Bahirarwár-Parhat.
	107. Bahirarwár-Punách.
	108. Bahirarwár-Párkhand.
	109. Bahirarwár-Kasiám.
Kásyap ...	110. Bisaiwár-Nanhpur.
	111. Bisaiwár-Bisphi.
Bharadwáj	112. Ekahre-Orá.
	113. Ekahre-Ruchaul.
	114. Ekahre-Kanhauli.
	115. Ekahre-Sagrám.
	116. Ekahre-Torne.
Sándil ...	117. Gangulwár-Sakuri.
	118. Gangulwár-Dumrá.
Kásyap ...	119. Kataiwár-Andhrá.
	120. Kataiwár-Phet.
	121. Kataiwár-Malangia.
	122. Kataiwár-Loám.
	123. Kataiwár-Maráchi.
Sándil ...	124. Sariswe-Khangor.
	125. Sariswe-Sakuri.
Bátsa ...	126. Ghusaute-Nagwár.
Bátsa ...	127. Babhanyáme-Katma.
	128. Babhanyáme-Karrain.
Kásyap ...	129. Kusmáre-Sabás.
	130. Kusmáre-Dhanauli.
Kásyap	131. Narwáre-Rámpur.
Gautama ...	132. Barhampurái-Barhampur.
Kásyap ..	133. Purue-Mahendra.
Sándil ...	134. Andarái-Nehra.
	135. Andarái-Laguniá.
	136. Andarái-Pirápur.
Sábarna ...	137. Panchaubhe-Khajuli.
	138. Panchaubhe-Jhauá.
	139. Panchaubhe-Birpur.
	140. Panchaubhe-Barhmaul.
	141. Panchaubhe-Bhithi.
	142. Panchaubhe-Dadri.
	143. Panchaubhe-Kariaun.
Bátsa ...	144. Jalaiwár-Jale.
	145. Jalaiwár-Maranchi.
	146. Jalaiwár-Ganraul.
	147. Jalaiwár-Máli.
Sándil ..	148. Jajwáre-Bharám.
	149. Jajwáre-Udanpur.
	150. Jajwáre-Jamuni.
	151. Jajwáre-Pachahi

Gotra.		*Dih* or *Mul.*
Kásyap	...	152. Pakaráe-Mahesi
Kásyap	...	153. Budhaure.
Kásyap	...	154. Bharhe.
Sándil	...	155. Gángaure.
Sándil	...	156. Bhatore.
Sándil	...	157. Sakarghore.
Parásar	...	158. Surganai.
Parásar		159. Sugarganai-Loám.
Kausika	...	160. Nekutwár-Barahi.
Sándil	...	161. Nonaitwár.
Sándil	...	162. Talaiwár.
Sándil	...	163. Sihásme-Khor. 164. Sihásme-Sihásam.
Bátsa	...	165. Kaiáre.
Kásyap	...	166. Ainwár.
Bharadwáj		167. Domtakarái.
Bharadwáj		168. Kanigáme Kanigám.
Kásyap	...	169. Bhandwâl.
Kásyap	...	170. Thariáme-Thariam.
Garg	...	171. Basahe.
Parásar	...	172. Sunriwár-Solhni.
Parásar	...	173. Naraune Teghrá. 174. Naraune Saktárápur.
Sándil	...	175. Chhatimane-Chhatman.
Sándil	...	176. Kodarie.
Krishnán	...	177. Bhusware.

Utkal.

Titles:—Nanda, Pate, Kara, A'chárya, Satpathi, Bedi, Senápati, Panigrahi, Nisank, Bainipati, Pandá, Padahári, Murhiá or Sebaka, Ghátiyá, Dája, Paya, Baghi, Muosi, Devatá, Dandapat, Mahanti, Dharsarmákar, Tripáti, Mahápátra, Misra, Rath, Dás, Sarangi, Sámágrahi, Hotá, Náth, Cheni, Pátra, Láik, Bahali, Pati, Pádhá Sálu, Páthak, Páni, Fakir, Feringi, Lau, Malo, Ghási, Ladu, Basu, Pakharpaila, Kantaru, Gorea, Tarat, Jayi, Karpur, Kandarpa, Parhatiá, Phunknali.

Sub-castes.	*Gotra* or sections.
Srotriya or Sásani—	
Sámanta.	Batsas. Kausika. A'treya. Kásyapa.
Bhatta Misra.	Kautsasa. Bharadwája. A'treya. Dattátreya. Krishnátreya.

Sub-castes.	*Gotra* or sections.
Vaidika.	Átreya.
	Kautsasa.
	Hárita.
	Kausika.
	Katyáyana.
	Maudgal.
	Sándil.
	Kaundinya.
	Gautam.
	Kásyapa.
	Bharadwája.
	Kapinjala.
	Sábarnika.
	Játukarna.
	Parásara.
Upádhyáya.	*Gotras* are all the same as in Sásani, except Batsas and Kausika.
Asrotriya—	
Sarua Pandá = Bardhusika or Paniár.	Bharadwája.
Murhiá Pandá or Debalaka.	*Gotras as of* Vaidiks.
Grám Jáchaka.	Ditto.
Mahasthán, Mastán, Saraibaliá or Háliá.	Balarám or Balabhadriá.
Jhárua.	
Dakshiná Uriyá or Dákhinátya.	
Jájpuriá or Uttar-Sreni.	
Raghunáthiá.	
Jaiá or Purbiyá.	

Besides those mentioned above, the following *gotras* or sections are found among Utkal Bráhmans :—

Ángirasa.
Autathya.
Baikháyana.
Basishtha.
Biswámitra.
Garga.
Jaimini.
Jámadagna.
Kaphalya.
Kámakáyan.
Kauchha.
Paithinasa.
Pautimanna.
Sánkriti.
Saunaka.
Taittiriya.
Uddalaka.
Upamanna.

Mr. John Beames gives the following scheme of the subdivisions of the Brahman caste in Northern Orissa,—first, according to the Veda, whose ritual they profess to observe, and secondly into *gotras* or families:—

I.—Dákhinátya Sreni or Southern Line.

1. *Rig-Veda.*

Gotra or Sections.	*Upádhi* or Titles.
Basishtha.	Sárangi.
"	Mahápátra.

2. *Sáma-Veda.*

Kásyapa.	Nanda.
Dharagautama.	Tripáthi.
Gautama.	Udgátá, *vulgo* Utá.
Parásara.	Dibedi, *vulgo* Dube.
Kaundinya.	Tripáthi, *vulgo* Tihári.

3. *Yajur-Veda.*

Bharadwája—	
a. Bharadwája.	Sárangi.
b. Sambhukar.	Misra.
c. Lándi.	Nanda.
Átreya—	
a. Dattátreya.	Ratha.
b. Krishnátreya.	"
Haritasa.	Mahápátra.
"	Dása.
Káuchhasa.	"
Ghritakauchhasa.	"
Mudgala.	Satpathi, *vulgo* Pathi, also Satpasti.
Batsasa.	Dása, Áchárya, Misra.
Kátyáyana.	Sárangi.
Kapinjala.	Dása.

II.—Uttara Sreni or Northern Line.

1. *Rig-Veda.*

Not represented.

2. *Yajur-Veda.*

Gotra or Sections.	*Upádhi* or Titles.
Kátyáyana.	Pandá.
Sándilya.	"
Krishnátreya.	" and Dása.
Bharadwája.	"
Barshagana.	Misra.
Kaphalya.	"
Gautama.	Kara.

3. *Atharva-Veda.*

Ángirasa.	Upadhyáya, *vulgo* Upadhya.

Of lower branches, and considered inferior to the above, are—

Sánkhyáyana.	Mahanti.
Nágasa.	Dasa, Mahanti.

Sákadwípí, *Bhojyak, Bhuist.*

Their *gotras* are the same as in the other sub-castes of Bráhmans.

Pur or sections.

Adriár.	Deorahiár.
Ahilásariár.	Dewárk.
Aiyár.	Dihwár.
Áwadhiár.	Dumariár.
Baghwár.	Gadahpurná.
Bariswár.	Gadrahá.
Barsái.	Gandark.
Barwár.	Gochhpuriá.
Batsauriark.	Gorhárk.
Batwákariyár.	Gunsaiyá.
Bhalauniár.	Hadauriár.
Bhedbakárár.	Hemriárk.
Bherápákri.	Jamuár.
Bholárk.	Jurhá.
Binsaiyá.	Juthibariár.
Budhwárk.	Karaiárk.
Chadchák.	Kausikárak.
Chandratiár.	Khajurák.
Chandrorh.	Khandarp.
Chhariyár.	Khantwár.
Chhathwark.	Khatsopárk.
Chhatrawár.	Konárk.
Chitauriár.	Korankárk.
Chonchwár.	Kukurbandhá.
Dadhpuriárk.	Kundárk.
Dakráhi.	Kurái.
Debkuliár.	Lokárk.
Dehlásariár.	Madhubaniá.
Deodhiár.	Madhurasiárk.

Pur or sections.

Mahdauriár.	Pundárk.
Maheswar.	Punrakhiá.
Mahrasiá.	Rahdauriár.
Makhaiwár.	Sabhaiyár.
Mákhpawár.	Saphárk.
Malauriár.	Senduriár.
Márkandárk.	Sikauriár.
Mauriyár.	Sirmauriár.
Nandark.	Soniyár.
Osiár.	Soriyár.
Pachhwár.	Sukhsárá.
Panchbatiar.	Swetbhadra.
Panchhai.	Tarkanyark.
Panchkanthi.	Thakurmairar.
Pandiár.	Udaniyár.
Pariár.	Ulárk.
Pathaiár.	Urwár.
Patiyár.	Usahiyárk.
Pawaiyár.	

Nepáli Brahmans.

Endogamous divisions.	*Gotra* or sections.	*Thar* or sub-sections.
Upádhyáya. Kamiya. Purabi.	Básishta ...	Bhatta Rái. Dawári. Chálisa, Chelisya. Bharári. Bisishta 'Sakti. Páráswar. Tinai Prabarái. Brahmimá Dhán.
	Dhánjaya ...	Rijál. Gura Gáin. Homya Gáin.
	Atrái ...	Parel, Poudyál. Arjel.
	Kausika ...	Regmi. Soberi.
	Kaundin ...	Acharjya. Párájuli. Neopáni, Nivipány
	Dhartá Kausik ...	Nepaliyá. Barál. Khodál or Khand

Endogamous divisions.	*Gotra* or sections.	*Thar* or sub-sections.
	Bharadwája	Suberi. Jámár Katyál. Bagalya.
	Bachh ...	Dohál. Langsál or Lamsál.
	Atri ...	Gautam. Khatiwára. Misra. Champágáin. Archnáni.
	Kásyap ...	Dhimire.
	Kasya ...	Adhikári.
	Agasti ...	Dhungiál.
	Mautkaha ...	Timilsiná. Kainrála.
	Upamanya ...	Dhákal.
	Kanniá ...	Sapankotyá.
	Gargya ...	Murtel. Pyakarel or Pokharyál.

In addition to the above, Hodgson's list contains the following *thars*:—

Khanál.
Nirola.
Maháráshtra.
Pakonyal.
Sattyal.
Rimál.
Devakotya.
Parbatya.
Kaikyal.
Rupakheti.
Desjá.
Rukái.
Saival.
Laiyál.
Dotiyál.
Danjál.
Singyál.
Bikrál.
Ukniyál.
Bhattvál.
Gajniyál.

Chavala Gáin
Vasta Gáin.
Banjára.
Dáji.
Soti.
Osti.
Utkuli.
Kandaria.
Ghartmel.
Ghartyál.
Temrakoti.
Uphaltopi.
Párijai Kavala.
Pandit.
Teva Pánya.
Kaphalya.
Gaithaula.
Gairaha Pipli.
Ghimirya.
Simkhárá.
Phuuvál.

Chámkasaini.
Purásaini.
Dhurári.
Bhurtyál.
Paneru.
Loityal.
Sidhyál.
Gotanya.
Ghorasaine.
Kisyál.
Dhongán.
Dulál.
Bajgáin.
Satola.
Ghurcholi.
Kelatoni.
Gilal.
Lahoni.
Muthbári.

Buná, *Banuá*, *Buno.*

Cháin, *Barcháin.*

Sub-castes.	Sections.
Nil.	Bharadwáji. Charanbansi. Kásyapa. Sándil.

Chakmá, *Tsakmá*, *Tsak*, *Thek* (Burm).

Sub-tribes.	Septs.
1. Chakmá. 2. Doingnak. 3. Tungjainya. Septs of the Chakmá sub-tribe.	Amu. Bámu, named after rivers. Barbora. Baruwa. Batalya, a chisel. Boga. Borsege. Bung. Bungza. Darjea. Dawin. Dhaona, he of the mended cloth. Dhurjya, the wearer of *bhimráj* feathers. Durjea. Ichapocha, the eater of rotten shrimps. Kalá, a plantain tree. Kengragati,[1] the giver of the big crab. Khambe. Khiongje. Kurá, named after rivers. Kurjya, the idle one. Kutua. Larma. Leba. Loskra. Molima, named after rivers.

The progenitor of this section is said to have presented to the head of the tribe a crab so large that a pig could cross the river Kanguli on its back.

Sub-tribes.	Septs.
Septs of the Chakmá sub-tribe—*concluded*.	**Molima-Sege.** **Phaksa.** **Phe-dang-sirri.** **Phedungsa.** **Phema.** **Pirabhanga,** the fat man who broke the stool. **Poa.** **Poma.** **Rangyacelunya,** the lover of shells or mother-of-pearl. **Ranyin.** **Sadonga.** **Sege.** **Sekowa.** **Shoályiá,** the jester. **Theya.** **Toinya.** **Uksarri.** **Warggu,** name of a river.
Septs of the Tungjainya sub-tribe.	**Aruyái,** the man as thin as a skeleton. **Bádál,** a chisel. **Bangál,** descended from a Bengali father. **Bhumar,** he of high back ribs. **Bolá,** he whose family was as numerous as the wasps. **Dunyá.** **Fariansa,** he who excelled in wickedness. **Gochalya,** the strong man. **Ichá,** he who was too fond of shrimps. **Kachui,** they who built their houses in a row. **Karuá.** **Lambacha.** **Lulang,**[1] the devil. **Millong.** **Monglá.** **Mo-u.** **Ongyo.** **Pumá.**

[1] A girl became pregnant, but would not name her lover. She was severely beaten, and was rescued by a devil, who was supposed to be the father of the child.

Chamár, *Chámár, Charmakár, Rabi-Dás.*

Titles:—**Beár, Bohit, Chunipárá, Kápri, Mahaldár, Mahara, Marar, Mehtariá, Náik, Panarha, Pradhán, Ráut.**

Sub-castes.		Sections.
Chamár-Tánti.	Of the Dhusiá sub-caste.	Hondagiá.
Dhárh.		Joriáhá.
Dhusiá.		Moghaliá.
Dohar.		Sonpursa.
Goria.		Thengáit.
Jaiswara.		
Janakpuri.		
Jaunpuri.		
Kháti-Mahará.		
Korár.		
Larkor.		
Magahia.		
Pachhián.		

Septs in Chota Nagpur.

Azghalla.
Dhusiá.
Harbans, cannot wear bones in any shape.
Kachuá, tortoise.
Karwa.
Kerketa, a bird.
Mahuá, *bassia latifolia.*
Mus, rat.
Nág, cobra.
Ráot.
Sándh, bull.
Saur, a fish.
Tirki.

Sub-castes enumerated by Mr. Sherring.

Jaiswara, servants.
Mangatiwa, professional beggars.
Dhusia or **Jhusia,** shoe-makers and harness-makers.
Katua, leather-cutters.
Kori, weavers, grooms, field-labourers.
Kuril, workers in leather.
Rangiya, leather-dyers.
Jatua, labourers.
Tantua, maker of leather strings.

Aharwar, Azimgarhia or **Birheria, Dakshinia, Dohar, Garaiya, Jaiswara, Jatlot, Jatua, Kaiyan, Kanaujia, Kuril, Kori** or **Korchamra,** are mentioned by Sir Henry Elliot and Mr. Beames.

Chandál, *Nama-Sudra, Nama, Changa, Chánrál, Kotál* or *Kotwál, Pratham-bákya, Swapacha, Nishád, Antebási.*

Titles:—**Bágh,** tiger, **Bhála, Biswás, Dás, Dáuk,** bird, **Dháli, Dule, Háit, Hajrá, Háldár, Háthi,** elephant, **Háuikar, Khán, Laskar, Mahará, Majumdár, Mandal, Mánjhi, Mirdada, Mistri, Namadháni, Padhwán** or **Pradhán, Pandit, Parámánik, Pátra, Phaliyá,** fish, **Rái, Sántrá, Sená, Seuli, Shumardar, Singh, Tengrá,** fish.

	Sub-castes.	Sections.
In Eastern Bengal.	Halwah. Ghási. Kandho or Behará. Karrál, Keral. Bári. Beruá. Pod. Baqqál. Sarálya. Amarábádi. Báchhár. Sandwipá.	Kásyapa.
In Central Bengal.	Dháni. Jáliá. Jiáni, Jiuni. Kárál. Nuniá. Siáli.	
In Western Bengal.	Chási. Helo. Jelo. Kesarkalo. Kotál. Májilá. Nalo. Nuniá. Pánphule. Saro. Siule.	Bharadwája. Lomasa. Sándilya.

Chása.

Titles:—Lenká, Puhár, Muduli, Swáin, Paridá, Padhán, Viswál, Náik, Raut, Jená, Sámal, Mahanti.

Sub-castes.	Sections.
Orhchásá or Mundi-chásá.	
Benátiyá.	Kásyapa.
Chukuliyá.	Sál-rishi.
Sukuliyá.	

Chásádhobá, *Chásádhopa*.

Titles:—Rái, Páik, Haladhar, Ballava, Sán, Sam..ddar, Biswás, Háldár, Házará, Mistri, Ráj-Mistri.

Hypergamous Groups.

Kulin. | Maulik.

Sub-castes.	Sections.
Uttar-Rárhi.	Alimán.
Dakhin-Rárhi.	Atulrishi.
Bárendra.	Bághrishi.
	Brihatbat.
	Dhabalrishi.
	Kásyapa.
	Sándilya.

Chero.

Titles:—Bábuán, Kanwár, Manjhi, Manár, Rautiá, Sánwát.

Sub-castes.	Sections.
Bára-Hazár.	(*a*) *Totemistic*—
Tera-Hazár or Birbandhi.	Besrá, hawk.
	Kachchhuá, tortoise.
	Kunwardár.
	Mahto.
	Mailwár.
	Sonwani.
	Soraniá.
	Turuwár.
	(*b*) *Brahmanical*—
	Kásyapa, etc.

Chik. *See* Pán.

Titles:—Baraik, Mahato.

Sub-tribes.	Septs.
	Aujana.
	Baghail, tiger.
	Bagti.
	Bajarpuriji.
	Bakura, paddy-bird.
	Balbandhiya, are bound to tie up their hair.
	Banichar.
	Bar, *Ficus Indica.*
	Bara.
	Barabhaia, ship.
	Bati.
	Bhengraj, kingcrow.
	Bhojraj, a kind of medicine.
	Bichwar, a centipede.
	Borá, a kind of snake.
	Chachet, a small bird.
	Chaenchair, a bird.
	Chand, moon.
	Chikanjari.
	Darká, born out of a crack in the earth.
	Dhan, paddy or rice soup.
	Dhandh, plum bushes.
	Dihbans.
	Dip, may not eat after lights have been lit.
	Dundoar, an owl.
	Gandha, flying bug.
	Gandhi.
	Ghatoar.
	Goherwar.
	Hanuman, monkey.
	Harin, deer.
	Induar, a kind of eel.
	Janamkiar.
	Kachua, tortoise.
	Kaita, curry vegetable.
	Kansi, field grass.
	Kara.
	Karhar, a fruit.
	Katri, subject to fits.
	Kechengia.
	Keora, a flower.
	Khamona, fork of a tree.
	Khukri.
	Korla, fig.

Sub-tribe.	Septs.
	Kotri, a small deer.
	Kowriar.
	Kulhai, a tiger.
	Kumharia, a tribe.
	Kusumni, a tree or its fruit.
	Loharbans, iron.
	Loyna.
	Maghi.
	Mahabaar, may not kill or chase the wild boar.
	Mahanadi, name of a river.
	Mahtoar, a title.
	Malta.
	Maria.
	Malua.
	Mawar, peacock.
	Munjaniar, a fruit from which oil is extracted.
	Mus, field-rat.
	Nág, cobra.
	Newra, mongoose.
	Nikharbans.
	Nimuani.
	Phul, flower.
	Phungune.
	Rikhiasan, may not eat beef or pork.
	Ság, vegetable.
	Samjhar.
	Saur, a fish.
	Singi, horn.
	Sinjikuria.
	Sonmanik.
	Sonwasi.
	Surijhabu.
	Tajna, name of a river.

Dámi, *Dam-yi, Támi, Kotwál, Nágarchi, Darji.*

Thars or Septs.

Bhusuwal.	Kala Kháti.	Panchkuti.
Burdewá.	Kurki Dholiar.	Shewa.
Damma Parriwár.	Kurno Beheri.	Sunam.
Darnal.	Mohara.	Sundas.
Dhuli.	Mutai.	Sungaru.

Dejong Lhori (Dejong Sikhim), *Lhopa Bhotia* or Tibetans of the south.

Sub-tribes.		*Rui, Thar* or septs.
Tongdu Rui shi. Bed (*d* silent) or Beh tshan-gye. Ruichhung.	Of the Tongdu Rui shi sub-tribe.	Guru Táshi, the blessed *rui*, of which Guru Pema was guide. Shang-dah-bo, ancestor born at his maternal uncle's when some tutelary deities were being propitiated. Tshe-gyu-thah, the family which sprang from the Buddha of life. Yui-then-bo, ancestor turned out of his fatherland.
Of the Bed tshan gye sub-tribe		Bangrongpá. Bhadpá. Dokhangpá. Ghingpá. Gnyambipá. Gyon-sah-pá, he of the new monastery. Khyung-toipá. Lagdingpá. Lin-dsen-bo. Nam-tsang-koba. Pon-po { Chhungpá. Lhasung, domestic priest of all the *ruis*. Nah-dik. Nambon. Yo-chang. } Pu-tsho-bo, a mixed progeny of Lepcha mother and Tibetan father.
Mixed septs of low origin[1] ...		Assampá. Chungyepá. Kah-tsho-bo. Mang-beh-pá. Namang-po.
Lowest septs of Bhotias[1] ...		Doh-rúhb-pa, one dwelling under the feet. Doh-zepá, living in rough and craggy rocks. Gangye-pa, dwelling behind a hill. Shyag-tsangpá.
Septs which emigrated from Tibet and North Bhotan[1] ...		Chhumbipá. Hah-po. Koyungpo. Shyah-pá. Toipá.

[1] These groups of septs form in each case endogamous aggregates, the members of which do not intermarry with the other sub-tribes.

Sub-tribes.	*Rui, Thar* or septs.
Septs which emigrated from Bhotan and Nepal[1] ...	Bendah. Bindumbo. Gah-oh, blacksmiths. Gurumbo, Gyu-rumbo. Ling-tamba. Ongdáhba. Parubo. Phensa-pá. Pu-tsibo. Pyo-chhembo. Sang-behbo. Shyag-chom-bo. Tsong-zubo. Yong-tong-ba. Yulsahb, of new country.
Of the Ruichhung sub-tribe ...	Dorompá. Khol. Lah-ogpá, dwelling below *la* or mountain-top or pass. Mang-tshang-wa. Nahmah-pá. Shyag-ding-pá or Shyag-tshang-pa. Thazoepá.

[1] These groups of septs form in each case endogamous aggregates, the members of which do not intermarry with the other sub-tribes.

Dhánuk.

Titles:—Mandar, Raut, Rai, Mahato, Kámati, Khawás, Ghibihár, Saghár, Bahíá, Bahiot, Sankatwár.

Sub-castes.	Sections.
Chhilatiá or Silhotia.	Kásyapa.
Magahyá.	Nág.
Banodhiá.	
Tirhutiá or Chiraut.	
Jaiswár.	
Kanaujia.	
Kahpariyá.	
Dudhwár or Dojwár.	
Sunri-Dhánuk.	
Kaṭhautiá.	
Khawásiá } In Purniah.	
Mandal } In Purniah.	
Gharbeta or Gharbait. } In Purniah.	

[1] Longbasta, Mathuriá, Katharia, Jaiswár, Magahyá, Dojwár, and Chhilatiya are given by Sir H. Elliot; Yasawar (Jaiswár), Magahi, Dojwar, Chhilatiyá are mentioned by Buchanan.

Dhenuar.

Sub-tribes.	Septs.
Nil.	Baiga, a tribe.
	Bard.
	Karwar, a tribe.
	Sanuani, can't wear gold.
	Sumal, a kind of fish.

Dhimál, *Dhemál, Maulik.*

Sub-tribes.[1]	Septs.
Agniá.	Chongá.
Láter.	Dauwá.
Dungiá.	Kauwá.
	Rángá.

[1] It is convenient to describe these groups as sub-tribes. They are not, however, strictly endogamous, as has been mentioned in the article on Dhimál.

IN BENGAL AND ORISSA.

Dhobá, *Dhopa, Dhupi, Dhávaka.*

Title:—Dás, Mistri, Rajak, Sabhá-Sundar, Sákalya.

Sub-castes.		Sections.
1. Rámer Dhobá	Eastern Bengal.	(*a*) *Totemistic*—
2. Sitár Dhobá		Nágasa (Orissa).
3. Sátisá	Central Bengal.	(*b*) *Eponymous*—
4. Athisá		Alamyán.
5. Hájará-Samáj		Kásyapa.
6. Niti Siná		Sándilya.
7. Bara-Samáj	Hughli.	
8. Chhota-Samáj		
9. Dhobá-Samáj		
10. Rárhiya-Samáj		
11. Bangali	Manbhum.	
12. Goriá		
13. Maghayá		
14. Khottá		
15. Bhuluá	Noakhali.	
16. Jugidiá		
17. Sundip		
18. Uriyá Dhobá ...	Orissa.	

IN BEHAR AND CHOTA NAGPUR, EXCEPT MANBHUM.

Dhobi, Ujli, Baithá, Sáfi.

Titles:—**Gozar, Mahto, Ráut.**

Sub-castes.	Section.
1. Kanaujiá.	Kásyapa.
2. Maghaya.	
3. Belwár.	
4. Awadhiyá.	
5. Bátham.	
6. Gorsár.	
7. Gadhayá, keep donkeys.	
8. Banglá, immigrants from Bengal.	
Turkia or Shekh, Mahomedan.	

Doai, *Doi, Chalànta, Baidya, Lakhiputra, Pátia Dás.*

Dom, *Domrá*, sometimes called *Chandál* by outsiders.

Titles:—**Malik, Marar, Mehalo, Mihtár, Marik, Mirdáhá, Raut.**

Sub-castes.

In Behar—

Bánsphor or Bánsbakurá, basket-makers: have nothing to do with funerals, and do not eat beef.

Chapariyá, make baskets and build the bamboo framework which supports the thatched roof of a house.

Dakhiná or Turi { Angwár. Deswár. }

Dháprá, sweepers.

Dharkár, workers in cane.

Gadahiá, breeders of donkeys.

Hári or Bangali, probably immigrants from Bengal.

Harkár, scavengers.

Larhorá or Purbál-Mihtár, scavengers and basket-makers.

Magahiyá, in North Behar cultivators and thieves; in Gya basket-makers.

Pachainyá.

Raut-Mihtar { Bhojpuriá, Ghar-Raut, Gházipuriá } sweepers.

Supárá.

Tirhutiyá.

Uttariyá, workers in *sirki* basket and mat-makers.

Sub-castes.

In Bengal—

Ankuriá or **Ankhuti**, basket-makers.
Bájuniá, musicians.
Bánukiá, breed silkworms and work in silk filatures in Murshedabad and Rajshahye.
Bisdeliá, make baskets and palm-leaf mats.
Dai-Dom, the men are day-labourers and the women serve as midwives.
Dhesiá Dhákál or **Tapaspuriá**, remove dead bodies, etc.
Dholá, supposed to come from Dhalbhum.
Ghaserá, cut grass for sale.
Kálindi, cultivators and basket-makers.
Kaurá, breed pigs and act as scavengers.
Magahiyá, musicians and basket-makers.
Mándároná.
Murdafarásh, remove dead bodies.
Sánchi.
Táláiboṇá, make palm-leaf mats.

In Behar—

	Sections.
Of the Bánsphor or Bánsbakurá sub-caste.	**Baithá.** **Chiranjiá.** **Dágri.** **Darbe.** **Gáin.** **Hát.** **Isar.** **Kotwal.** **Lakrihár.** **Mánjhi.** **Marar.** **Marik.** **Masrakhiyá.** **Nauriyá.** **Sakráit.** **Saunt.** **Sikrar.** **Sipahiyá.**
Of the Dakhiná or Turi sub-caste	**Angwár.** **Deswár.**
Of the Dhápra sub-caste ...	**Hári.** **Mukariá.** **Parwariá.** **Pusaitá.** **Rosráit.**
Of the Dharkár sub-caste ...	**Káibtár.** **Mánjhi.** **Mehtar.** **Ráut.** **Sarin.**

Sub-castes.	Sections.
In Behar—	
Of the Tirhutiyá sub-caste ...	Barbattá. Belsandi. Chanauli. Hánsá. Hár. Maggah. Mahwá. Murwá. Pusadih. Sirpur. Sonpur. Teswár. Tubká.
Of the Magahiyá sub-caste ...	Akhauri. Bèlsandi. Chaudhri. Chauhán. Hánsá. Jádu. Mánjhi. Mirdaha. Rájá. Ráná. Santari. Sáwant. Teswár. Tewari.
Of the Pachainyá sub-caste ...	Adhárpur. Barabatiá. Bargamáet. Belsandi. Bhojpuri. Bikrampur. Chahraitá. Chandaulyár. Dholi. Hánsá. Hansotá. Kanauli. Kolandh. Mohbaita. Murba. Pahasrait. Pohobait. Pusá. Pusetá. Sansáit. Sirwár. Sonpuryá Tabkar. Tibaryá or Teswar.

Sub-castes.	Septs.
In South Manbhum—	Azghala.
	Dhusia.
Aturá.	Harbans, bones can't wear in any shape.
Molá.	Kachua, tortoise.
Sikhariá.	Karwa.
	Kerketa, a bird.
	Mahua, a tree; wine is made from its flower.
	Mus, rat.
	Nâg, cobra.
	Raot.
	Sândh, bull.
	Saur, a fish.
	Tirki.

Dosádh, *Dusadh.*

Titles:—Chaukidár, Gorait, Hájará or Házará, Máhato, Mánjhi, Pásbán, Rái, Rám.

Sub-castes.	Sections.			
Magahiyá.	Of the Magahiyá sub-caste.	Agiyári.	Of the Pailwár sub-caste.	Bádsháhi.
Bhojpuriá.		Barbáik.		Bára Kharak.
Kanaujiá.		Bárik.		Panjiar.
Pailwár.		Beár.		
Kámar or Kánwar.		Bhadáiyá.		
Kurin, Kuri, or Kurmá.		Bhunsi Kurtho.	Of the Kámar sub-caste.	Aghráit.
Dhár or Dhárhi.		Darbe.		Amam.
Silhotia or Sirotiá.		Fotadár.		Amol.
Báhaiiá.		Hát.		Assiswar.
		Hazári.		Bhabániswar.
		Isar.		Busgarait.
		Khankarárá.		Kamláit.
		Kotwál.		Kariont.
		Kumarsan Bakri.		Lab Nagariá.
		Mahrána.		Madhupuriá.
		Mahton.		Mahabbat.
		Málti.		Mahesbaráit.
		Mandar.		Mainkisrár.
		Mánjhi.		Nabanápuriá.
		Marik.		Purukhinu Naráin.
		Mirdahá.		Rájáisur.
		Parbe.		Thahrait.
		Patwe.		
		Rái.		
		Rána.		
		Ráut.		
		Sanda.		

Gandhabanik, *Gandhabaniyá, Baniyá, Putuli.*

Titles:—Of the Desá sub-caste—Sáhá, Sádhu, Láhá, Khán; of the Áut sub-caste—Datta, Dé, Dhar, Dhár, Kar, Nág.

Sub-castes.	Sections.
Áut-Ásram.	Álamyán.
Chhatris-Ásram.	Bharadwája.
Desá-Ásram.	Kásyapa.
Sankha-Ásram.	Krishnátreya.
	Modgalya.
	Nrisingha.
	Ras-rishi.
	Sábarna.
	Sándilya.

Gangotá, *Gangaulá.*

Title:—Mandar.

Sub-castes.	Sections.
1. Jethkar.	Gangájhi.
2. Maghaya.	Jáhnavi..

Ganrár.

Sub-castes.	Section.
Nil.	Aliman.

Gareri, *Gadariya, Bhenrihar.*

Titles:—Kambliá, Kammali, Marar, Raut.

Sub-castes.	Sections.	
1. Dhengar.	Of the Dhengar sub-caste.	Chandel.
2. Farakhábádi.		Chaudhuriá.
3. Gangájali.		Kásyapa.
4. Nikhar.		Nánkar.

Chak, Chikwá (Mahomedan).

Ghási.

Sub-castes.	Sections.
Hári.	Ahir, a tribe.
Simarloka.	Air, a kind of fish.
Sonaáti.	Badhiria, bats.
	Bágh, tiger.
	Bhat, a tribe. Degraded.
	Bhuana, a tribe. Bhuiya.
	Bhuinkora, hog.
	Bhurungia, a kind of tree.
	Bunduar, a tribe.
	Chahubar.
	Chinear.
	Daspuria.
	Desoar, a tribe.
	Dhamna sap, a red snake, poisonless snake.
	Dowalbandhi.
	Golvar.
	Kachua, tortoise.
	Kalhia, Lohar.
	Kasiár, corruption of Kásyapa?
	Kewat.
	Loharbans, iron-worker.
	Malar, a tribe.
	Mohdiar, honey-bee.
	Mukhi, Mukhi is a person, one of five, who can reinstate outcastes by eating first with them. Mukhi can lose his own jat. Mukhi only wear pagri.
	Pandki, dove.
	Phansia.
	Rajbandh.
	Rajput, a tribe.
	Sakri.
	Sanukra, shell.
	Sanwasi, cobra.
	Simarlásá, gum.
	Simarloka, a tree.
	Sonwan, cannot wear gold.
	Tirki.
	Uraon, a tribe.

Goálá, *Goál, Goár, Gopa, Gopál, Pallab-Gopa. Áhir, Ábhir.*

Titles:—*In Bengal*—Bárik, Chomar, Dháli, Ghosh, Jana, Mandal, Parámánik.

In Behar—Bharari, Bhogta, Chaudhri, Ghoraila, Khirahá, Mahato, Mandar, Mánjhi, Marik, Panjiara, Rái, Rást, Saonra, Singh.

Sub-castes.		Sections.
In Bengal—		
Pallab or Ballabh.		Almasi or Alamyán.
Gaura or Go-baidya.		Bharadwája.
Gop or Ghosh Goálá.		Gautama.
Karanjá.		Kásyapa.
Kajol.		Madrisi or Madhukulya.
Bágre or Ujaini.		Sándilya.
Madhu Goálá.		
Rárhi.		
Gumia.		
Áhir or Mahishá Goálá.		
Magal or Mágadhi.		
Bárendra	Pallal. Láheri. Mula. Gáwá. Dágániá.	
Bhogá	Sádá Goálá Lál Goálá.	Hypergamous.
In Orissa—		
Dumala Jadupuria Goárá.		
Gaura or Gopopuria.		
Magadha Goárá.		
Mathurá or Mathurábási.		
In Behar—		
Goriá or Dahiára.		Bhadráj. Bhátásan. Chalasinghi. Chalasan. Dasil. Dhenu. Gaudhal. Jaliásinghi. Jethautiá. Kálásan. Láhágot. Mahraul. Nágásan. Nágráj. Pakra. Sakraul. Singhror. Tanokl.

Sub-castes.	Sections.
Majraut or Naomuliá.	Abhepur.
	Aganpuriá.
	Anrhráhi.
	Aunriá.
	Báergoá.
	Baini (Mhádes).
	Bájitpur.
	Bálágáchhpokrám.
	Bálgách.
	Barsám.
	Básáithi.
	Basárh.
	Bástiburhona.
	Baurám.
	Belwár.
	Bháonroá.
	Bheludih.
	Bhotieth.
	Chámuár.
	Chámuk-Sháhpur.
	Chánchar.
	Chándkatorá.
	Chaumukhdih.
	Chiksári.
	Dabhrait.
	Dahiet.
	Dháman.
	Dharampuria.
	Doálak.
	Dudhpuriet.
	Gángthaiá.
	Ghiuádhár.
	Gobargárhá.
	Golrám.
	Gotsobhni.
	Guábári.
	Habibpur-Phupidih.
	Hansi.
	Jagatpur.
	Jailok.
	Jháj.
	Kabái.
	Kailwár.
	Kámrám.
	Kánháiwár.
	Kátaiyá.
	Káthádularpur.
	Khájuri.
	Khánrsimáriá.
	Kherho.
	Khuthá-Bhagwánpur.

Sub-castes.	Sections.
	Kirtoliá.
	Kotsobhni.
	Labnagar-Kumet.
	Lágmetá.
	Lakshanpuriá.
	Láwápur.
	Lepuriet.
	Levátiá { Barar. Chhalor. Dámu.
	Lohár.
	Madhepuriet.
	Mahárano.
	Mahisirupján.
	Mailidhurlak.
	Mailwár.
	Mánickhak-dudhpuriá.
	Meghalbariárpur.
	Mehdipur.
	Mehmánpur.
	Mithoriá.
	Mogalkáchá.
	Nimáchandpurá.
	Pachhiparganá.
	Pátori.
	Pipret.
	Rághopurdih.
	Raghunathpurdiár.
	Rájápákur.
	Rájápatischhni.
	Rasákmárhe.
	Sahasradih.
	Sahrwár.
	Sakarpuriet.
	Sálkhini.
	Samastipur.
	Sankarpur.
	Sánrári (Jaideb).
	Saresparganá-Dádádih
	Sáthiet.
	Silotháer.
	Sobhádih.
	Sobhni-Tájpur.
	Somnidih.
	Sonám.
	Temdih.
	Tilatwár.
	Titiábámbár.
	Ulwár.
	Umethwár.
	Usrám.

Sub-castes.	Sections.
Kanaujiá.	Chaudhri.
	Gopa.
	Kaksa.
	Kásyapa.
	Khirahá.
	Mandar.
	Raksa.
	Raut.
Kishnaut or Sálmuliá.	Alakjaridárhuá.
	Banikarnauti.
	Bharduár.
	Chalasinghi.
	Dadhraut.
	Deseriet.
	Dhanu.
	Jeseriet.
	Kachásimar.
	Kátkiphulberiá.
	Kheláut.
	Laungijarhuá.
	Magháchewár.
	Májháliár.
	Málkarnauti.
	Málkiá.
	Nágrá.
	Páli.
	Rájápáker.
	Saudábáek.
	Sonápur-Sakarwár.
	Sundar.
	In general—
Bargowár.	Aindwár.
Dhanroár.	Baghwár.
Chauánlá.	Barhadaglá.
Chauthá.	Bella.
Goit.	Bhainsu.
Kantitáhá.	Bhant.
Puhoá.	Cher.
Sepárí.	Dhokasan.
Banpar.	Dumar.
Gujiár or Godágá.	Hát.
	Kachhuá.
	Kási.
	Khanduár.
	Kurji.
	Kutár.
	Lauriá.
	Lukhasan.

Sub-castes.	Sections.
	In general—
	Mahar.
	Mahtwár.
	Mongar.
	Muntri.
	Nág.
	Nagar.
	Pur.
	Sahbar.
	Sanuár.
	Sáu.
	Saur.
	Suá.
	Sundi.
	Tirki.
	Undhil.
Gáddi, Ghosi or Ghosin.	Argariá.
	Banrait.
	Barbariá.
	Bhádiswár.
	Bhindwár.
	Bhuskuliá.
	Biráji.
	Dárkhuriá.
	Dhurjhár.
	Goit.
	Káiwár.
	Kusieth.
	Lohutiá.
	Mádowán.
	Máhátmá.
	Marik.
	Mukhiá.
	Nágh.
	Parselá.
	Sádhak.
	Santu-Kusáet.
	Sunreit.
	Surat.
Ját.	Chitosiá.
	Gadhuál.

	Septs.
In Chota Nagpur—	
Bhogta.	Aind, a kind of eel.
Chauánlá.	Am, mango.
Goro.	Bacha, calf.
Kishnaut.	Bág, tiger.
Lari.	Bar, *Ficus Indicus.*

Sub-castes.	Septs.
In Chota Nagpur—concld.	
Majhwat.	Chownia, field-rat.
Sáonrá.	Demta, red tree-ant.
Sabor.	Diller.
	Gaegoal, *pakar* fruit forbidden.
	Garaur.
	Hasa, earth.
	Kachua, tortoise.
	Kaita, curry vegetable.
	Kamal, lotus.
	Kanojia, a tribe.
	Karam, a tree.
	Karsal.
	Karthia, a kind of grain or *dál*.
	Kasail, deer.
	Kasi, a grass.
	Maina, bird.
	Markam.
	Morpachi.
	Mus, rat.
	Nág, cobra.
	Phulwar.
	Rajhans, swan.
	Sir, arrow.
	Sona, can't wear gold.
	Sonwani.
	Tirki, can't touch any cattle after eyes open.

In the North-Western Provinces—

Sub-castes.	Sections.	
Desi.	Aphariá.	Bhánsriá.
Nandbansi.	Bachás.	Chabdiá.
Jadubansi.	Bachhwaliá.	Charkhiá.
Surajbansi.	Badgar.	Chikaná.
Goálbansi.	Badhwadiá.	Chitosiá.
Ahar.	Bághiá.	Chorá.
Kátha.	Bálwán.	Dágar.
	Bámboriá.	Dahmá.
	Bán.	Dámboriá.
	Báthotiá.	Deswál.
	Bháklun.	Dhaiá.
	Bhálkiá.	Dhorán.
	Bhámbasrá.	Dhundhiá.
	Bhángar.	Dhundhlá.

Sub-castes.	Sections.	
In the North-Western Provinces—concld.	Diá.	Kharsán.
	Dohán.	Khátádiá.
	Dudhliá.	Kheswá.
	Dumániá.	Khodiá.
	Dumdoliá.	Khosá.
	Dusád.	Kidat.
	Gadháriá.	Kosliá.
	Gadhojiá.	Lahaniá.
	Gahalá.	Lámbá.
	Garwál.	Lohchab.
	Ghumlá.	Luniwál.
	Gidad.	Máhakariá.
	Gigániá.	Mahalá.
	Gothwál.	Mahtá.
	Gumi.	Makadá.
	Guráh.	Mándhayá.
	Hádá.	Molán.
	Hadkwál.	Moldhiá.
	Hardá.	Motliá.
	Hudinwál.	Nadhiá.
	Jádu.	Nahadiá.
	Jadwál.	Nániá.
	Jánjdiá.	Nigániá.
	Jhádadiá.	Nikum.
	Jhagdoliá.	Nirbán.
	Kadayán.	Pacheriá.
	Kadián.	Padhániá.
	Kákas.	Parhar.
	Kakroliá.	Puháníá.
	Kaláliá.	Rábad.
	Kalganiá.	Rářiá.
	Kalinwál.	Sáhjáwán.
	Kaiot.	Sálangiá.
	Kalwadiá.	Sálodiá.
	Karirá.	Sámp.
	Káthá.	Sátoriá.
	Kátniá.	Sigadiá.
	Keswál.	Sikhwád.
	Khadoliá.	Simalwál.
	Khadotiá.	Sisodiá.
	Khadumiá.	Sunáriá.
	Khairwál.	Tahalḳiá.
	Khalhad.	Tántlá.
	Khámtá.	Thukrán.
	Kharniá.	Tundak.

Gond

Title :—Gaunjhu.

Sub-tribes.	Septs.
Gond.	Bágh, tiger.
Ráj-Gond.	Baghel, tiger.
Dhokar-Gond.[1]	Besrá, hawk.
Doroá-Gond or Náik.[2]	Bhainsá, buffalo.
Jhorá.	Bod, a big river-fish.
	Gaek, a kind of fish.
	Ganga, sea.
	Ghora, horse.
	Goh.
	Hansa, geese.
	Honti, a kind of fish.
	Jagaha, buffalo.
	Jagat.
	Jaipuria, name of a city.
	Kachhuá, tortoise.
	Káná Machhri, fish.
	Karma, a tree.
	Koput.
	Kusro.
	Loha, iron.
	Mahanadia, name of a river.
	Marai.
	Moti, a bead.
	Nág, snake.
	Naïtam, tortoise.
	Pachia.
	Phaguahi.
	Poia.
	Poiti.
	Porri, a kind of hawk.
	Sawani.
	Sribakaria.

[1] Also called Mángan-Gond from their begging habits.

[2] Colonel Dalton suggests that these may be the same as the Náik or Dhurwe Gonds of the Central Provinces.

Gonrhi, Malláh, Machhuá.

Titles:—Chaudhhri, Jethman, Mandar, Mukhiár, Nákhudá, Sahni.

Sub-castes.	Sections.
Banpar.	Bánt.
Cháb or Chábi.	Goráit.
Dhoár.	Jathot.
Khunaut or Khulaut.	Kásyapa.
Kolh.	Mandar.
Kurin.	Marar.
Parbatti-Kurin.	Mukhiyá.
Semári.	Pandit.
	Pánre.
	Parihár.
	Ráut.

Goráit, *Koráit, Baikar.*

Sub-caste.	Sections.
Nil.	Adra.
	Aindowár.
	Bagh, tiger.
	Baghuár.
	Bar, *Ficus Indicus.*
	Baroár.
	Induar, a kind of eel.
	Káchhuá.
	Kerketá.
	Khalkho, a fish.
	Kujri, a fruit, makes oil.
	Kujur.
	Nonoár.
	Pithoár.
	Sándh, bullock.
	Sontirki, gold.
	Tirki, cannot eat birds born blind, nor deep-setting eggs.
	Topoar, a kind of bird.

Gulgulia

Sub-castes.	Section.
Bantarl.	*Nil.*
Pachpaniá.	
Sukwár.	

Gurung, *Gurum, Gurungá, Gurungáh*

Sub-tribes.

Das-Gurung or Chár-Gotra.
Bárah-Gurung.

Thars or septs.

Bagálya.
Baráhi.
Bhumjan.
Bulung.
Byápri.
Chandu.
Chárki.
Dah Láma.
Dhakaren.
Dháren.
Ghárti.
Ghundáne.
Gohori.
Golángya.
Gonduk.
Gosti.
Gothi.
Guáburi.
Jimel.
Karámati.
Khangbha.
Khaptari.
Kháti.
Khulál.
Koki.
Láma.
Lámi Chhanya.
Leh Láma.
Lopáte.
Lotháng.
Madán.
Meghi.
Mengi.
Paindi.
Palámi.
Pengi.
Shakya Láma.
Siddh.
Suryabansi Láma.
Tháthung.
Themjáni.
Tolángi.
Uruntá.

Of the Das-Gurung sub-tribe:
Chheni-lama.
Ghaleh.
Ghoneh.
Kohli.
Korángi.
Lamsani Tongi.
Lhebo Lamsani.
Poinju-lama.
Pungi-lama.
Ráhul.
Ráná Lamsani.

Of the Bárah Gurung sub-tribe:
Buthuja.
Ghybrim.
Jhagreb.
Satal.
Segmang.

Hajjám, *Nái, Náu, Nauá.*

Titles :—Naheri, Ostá, Thákur.

Sub-castes.	Sections.
	Of Awadhiá Hajjáms—
Awadhiá.	Amraut.
Bangáli.	Barthoár.
Kanaujiá or Biáhut.	Beauran.
Magahiyá.	Beraut.
Sribástab or Bástar.	Bilsar.
Tirhutiá.	Chausar.
Musalmániá or Turk-Nauá.	Denrgamiá.
	Dharmáhu.
	Ekauniá.
	Gaya.
	Hargamiá.
	Jainagariá.
	Jaipur.
	Janágadhiá.
	Járdár.
	Jaru.
	Jaum.
	Jurvaunt.
	Kaisab.
	Kalaen.
	Kant.
	Kapur.
	Karaf.
	Karaunti.
	Katur.
	Khavur.
	Kopinyar.
	Koránch.
	Kujhariá.
	Kumair.
	Kundi.
	Kurnat.
	Mahrat.
	Manerar.
	Paithán.
	Parurá.
	Pauriár.
	Puráin.
	Rat.
	Samaiyar.
	Sansihar.
	Sisah.
	Telár.

Sub-castes.	Sections.
	Of Awadhiá Hajjáms—concld.
	Unri.
	Urkiser.
	Utrauniá.
	Of Kanaujiá Hajjáms—
	Baksar-Chausá.
	Kharpáik.
	Maura.
	Nipariá.
	Satarwár.

Halwái, *Mithiyá*.

Titles:—**Chaudhri, Dás, Modi, Sáhu.**

Sub-castes.		Sections.
Kanaujiá.	Sections of the Kanaujiá sub-caste.	Kachuá.
Magahiyá.		Kusmauliá.
Bantiriá or Balamtiriá.		Laskoriá.
Pachhainya[1] Madesiá.		Lukáthiá.
Purbiyá[2] Madesiá.		Santop Palwár.
Bhojpuriá.	Sections of the Bhojpuriá sub-caste.	Akhandhári.
Koránch.		Amghát.
Maltariá.		Básáriá.
		Básdebpur.
		Bharsahar.
		Bijaibanáras.
		Dhakais.
		Dharkiá.
		Gauli.
		Gauthάhá.
		Jábáliá.
		Kandwár.
		Káro.
		Kotsá.
		Naorakhiá.
		Nárauni.
		Pachάttar.
		Pachopát.
		Pátor.
		Sákarwár.
	Section of the Koránch sub-caste.	Pindwál.

[1] Also called Tinmuliá Madesiá.
[2] Also called Chhaumuliá Madesiá.

Sections of the Purbiyá Madesiá sub-caste.

Ájner.	Dariápár.	Kárkádo.	Naknesá.
Ákhanbári.	Dehádbanáras.	Kárni.	Ninghiám.
Ámi.	Deoghát.	Kásiáon.	Pachauta.
Ánar.	Dhákais.	Kátári.	Páchottar.
Ánokonwár.	Dhákait.	Káthej.	Paiharwáre.
Ánruá.	Dhanej.	Kesaur.	Phuli.
Ásármállá.	Dhemá.	Khontá.	Raksise.
Bádábasti.	Doem.	Kotsá or Korsá.	Sahuri.
Bijái.	Don.	Kurisár.	Sakarwár.
Baksár.	Gahunágáoná.	Kusarpákri.	Sakin.
Bakulári.	Gangápáli.	Lakhansariá.	Sakrol.
Bánebanáras.	Hátser.	Larauni.	Sarauli.
Baniápáthar.	Indri.	Lolutra.	Sidhpur.
Bansahar.	Jewel.	Máhepurá.	Sikiá.
Bátor.	Jirábasti.	Máil.	Sinhagarh.
Chánwár.	Kádá.	Manimanáras.	Sinharas.
Chausá.	Kalasdih.	Márar.	Sisotar.
Chilhár.	Kándár.	Maruá.	Sonhar.
Dádukli.	Kángkol.	Mohár.	Tári.
Dáhárak.	Kára.	Nágeswar.	Ubhar.
	Karar.	Nagneswar.	Ughar.

Sections of the Pachhainyá Madesiá sub-caste.

Ákhanbári.	Dighwárá.	Kachwár.	Kausár.
Básáriá.	Dumri.	Káhinwár.	Khirkatorá.
Bhárauli.	Gángauliá.	Kándeil.	Khoprihá.
Bijaibanáras.	Gauángahunár.	Kánpákar.	Maruáhá.
Chauberiá.	Gureni.	Kárádhánauta.	Nárauni.
Dhákáis.	Hánriáot.	Kárárihá.	Páchottar.
Dhánautá.	Jawáliá.	Káru.	Panthpákar.
Dhaneswar.			

Hári, *Mihtar, Harsantán*

Sub-castes.	Section.
Bará-Bhágiya or Káorá-páik.	*Nil.*
Madhya-bhágiyá or Madhaukul.	
Khore or Khoriyá.	
Siuli.	
Mihtar.	
Bangáli.	
Maghaya.	
Karaiyá.	
Purandwár.	

Ho, *Larka Kolh.*

Sub-tribes.	Septs.	
None.	Alru.	Jámulu.
	Angariá.	Janku Samrai.
	Babangá.	Kalundiá.
	Bandi.	Kisku.[1]
	Bansa.	Korá.
	Barpai.	Kuntiá.
	Biruá.	Lagori.
	Bodru.	Lamamaka.
	Buriali Kálundiá.	Marli.[1]
	Buri Sámat.	Munduia.
	Cháki Dukri.	Murmu.[1]
	Champiá Tubir.	Naguriá.
	Chatra Tuiu.	Parayá.
	Chorái.[1]	Pata Sayá.
	Echaghatu.	Pinguá.
	Emboro.	Podoro.
	Gagriá.	Purthi.
	Gatsorá.	Sauiá.
	Haiboru Lángi.	Sinkoi.
	Hánsda.[1]	Sundi Deogam.
	Hembaran.	Tihu.
	Hesá.	Tin.
	Hone-hogá.	Tudi.[1]

[1] These septs are common to the Hos and the Santáls.

Jáliyá, *Jeliá, Jele, Jálo, Jaluá, Málá, Málo, Dhibar, Machhuá, Mahifurosh.*

Titles:—Arash, Bág, Barddhan, Bárik, Berá, Bidyánto, Bisoi, Biswás, Borál, Chaudhri, Dás, Gal Guriá, Haldar, Kundu, Láhá, Mandal, Mánjhi, Mauna, Pakre, Pálde, Párai, Pátra, Pradhán, Rojá, Sántrá, Sarkár, Sasmal, Sem.

Sub-castes.	Sections.
In Noakhali—	
Chátgáon.	Áliman.
Bhuluá.	
Jhálo.	
Kaibartta.	

Jolha, *Joláhá, Juláhá, Momin, Tánti, Tatwá.*

Titles:—Lauki, Mahrano, Mahton, Mandar, Mandari, Manjhi, Marik, Mehter, Nuri, Pandit, Sanahiá, Taiyá.

Sub-castes.		Sections.
Tirhutiá.		Kachuá.
Kanaujia.		Parásar.
Chapota, Chanpadda.	Of the Chapota sub-caste.	Mánjhi.
Khatwe.		Marar.
		Parimanik.
		Purbe.

Juáng.

Sub-tribes.	Septs.
Nil.	Alemba, hailstones.
	Baitiriba, buffalo.
	Bálimba, mosquito.
	Bánaiba, bear.
	Bárátaba, boar.
	Dumriába, a kind of tree.
	Gághraba, paddy.
	Hatisalaba, elephant.
	Jarigámba, *jari* tree.
	Kálimba, tobacco flower.
	Kánchaba, dog.
	Kelobo, bee.
	Kerálaba, pumpkin.
	Kotábándab.
	Lihimba, dove.
	Mundiba, *mahua* tree.
	Munduáb, small mushroom.
	Odhalaba, fox.
	Rangataba, a kind of yellow-coloured bird.
	Rásamba, mushrooms that grow on ant-hills.
	Sáramba, tigress.
	Sundriába, red mushroom.
	Talahadába, palm tree.
	Tenshába, a bird.

Jugi, *Jungi, Jogi* or *Yogi, Náth.*

Titles:—Adhikári, Biswás, Dalál, Goswámi, Jáchandár, Mahanta, Majumdár, Náthji, Pandit, Rái, Sarkár.

Sub-castes.	Sections.
Rárhi.	Kásyapa.
Bárendra.	Siva.
Baidik.	Adi.
Bangaja.	Alarishi (Allamyán ?).
Khelenda.	Anádi.
Bhuluá.	Batuk.
Sundipá.	Birbhairab.
	Goraksha.
	Matsendra, king of fish.
	Min, fish.
	Satya, truth.

Functional groups.

Hálwa.
Kambule.
Manihári.
Rangroz.
Grihasth { Dhanái Mandal. Jnánbar. Bhagan Bhájan. Paban.
Ekádasi.
Másya.

Religious groups.

Bráhman.
Sannyási or Kánphát.
Dandi.
Dharmaghare.
Játh.
Kálipá.
Durihár.
Aghorpanthi.
Bhatrihari.
Sárangihár.

Hypergamous groups.

Kulin { Raghu. Mádhab. Nimái. Págmal.
Madhyala.
Bángál.

Kádar, *Bhuiyá.*

Sub-castes.	Sections.	
Kádar.	Báre.[1]	Mánjhi.
Naiyá.	Bárik.[2]	Maraiá.
	Darbe.[3]	Marik.[5]
	Hazári.	Mirdáha.[6]
	Kampti.[4]	Naiyá.[7]
	Kápari.	Raut.
	Mandar.	Rikhiásan.
	Mandri.	

[1] Will marry only with Mirdáha, Kampti, and Raut.
[2] Will not marry with Mandar, Mirdáha, Raut, and Báre.
[3] Will not marry with Marik and Báre.
[4] Will marry only with Bárik, Kápari, Marik, Darbe, Mánjhi, and Báre.
[5] Will only marry with Bárik, Kápari, Mánjhi, Mandar, and Naiyá.
[6] Will marry only with Darbe, Mánjhi, Kampti, and Báre.
[7] Will not marry with Marik, Hazári, Naiyá, Kampti, and Báre.

Kahár.

Titles :—Behará, Bhandári, Kamkar, Mahara, Mahato, Ráut, Sardár.

Sub-castes.	Sections.
Rawáni or Ramáni.	Alimán.
Dhuriá.	Bando, a small wild cat.
Dhimar.	Kanda, sweet potato.
Kharwárá.	Kansi, a kind of grass.
Turhá.	Kásyapa.
Jaswár.	Nág.
Garhuk or Garauwá.	Rawanpur.
Bisariá.	Suar, a pig.
Magahiyá.	

Kaibartta, *Kaibartta-Dás, Chási-Dás, Háliá-Dás, Parásar-Dás, Dhivara, Khyán.*

Titles :—*In Bengal*—Adaki, Arash, Bág, Bardhan, Bárik, Berá, Biswás, Borál, Chaudhri, Dás, Gharui, Giri, Haladhar, Háldár, Jáná, Kundu, Láhá, Máiti, Mallik, Mandal, Mánji, Mánná, Mete, Naskar, Pare, Patnáik, Pátra, Pradhán, Rojá, Sarkár, Sen, Sántrá, Sasmal.

In Orissa—Behará, Bhuiá, Dalái, Dás, Malhá, Mátiál, Náik, Sáhu.

Sub-castes.	Sections.
In Murshedabad—	
Pánchsata Baháttarghar.	Aládasi.
Chauddapárá Rárhibindus.	Almisi.
Rárhi.	Alamyán.
Bágri.	Kásyapa.
Bárendra.	Majlisi (Maudgalya)
Dakshini.	

Sub-castes.		Sections.	
In Midnapur—			
Hele-Kaibartta { Uttar-Rárhi.			
Dakshin-Rárhi.		Lál-Chátái.	Almál.
		Ekside.	Kástu-Rishi.
		Doside.	Kásyapa.
		Mákunda.	Madhukulya.
			Sándilya.
In Hughli—			Vyás.
Uttar-Rárhi.			
Dakhin-Rárhi or Marwar.			
Tutiya.			
Jeliya, Málá or Jaliyá.			
In Jessore—			
Málo or Málá.		Amrita-Rási.	
Rájbansi.		Kásyap-Rási.	
		Mesh-Rási.	
Mecho } Hypergamous.		Padma-Rási.	
Helo			
In 24-Parganás—			
Kaibartta.			
Dás.			
In Central Bengal—			
Chásá or Halwáha Kaibartta.			
Tutiyá Kaibartta.			
In Maldah—			
Hálik.			
Jálik.			
In Noakhali—			
Bhuluai.			
Sundipe.			
Karalái.			
Dántrái.		Kásyapa.	
Pátuá.			
Phirti.			
In Dacca—			
Dás, Jalwah Kaibartta.			
In Bakarganj—			
Háliá Dás, Parásar Dás,	Kálá Ráy	Hypergamous.	Alamyán.
or Chási Kaibartta.	Háliá Bálái		Bharadváj.
	Jádab Ráy		Ghrita-Kausik.
	Bhuban Kuri		Kásyap.
	Mánji		Parásar.
	Samaddár		
	Charmanái Ráy		
	Majumdár Bángál		

In Bakarganj—

Sub-castes.	Sections.
Kaibartta, Chandradwip.	Káwár, Mandal, Manjhi, Páthar, Sikdár — Hypergamous.
	Bángál.
Bára-Hazári.	

In Orissa—

Orh.	Dhamdi.
Rárhi.	Khauniá.
	Ghani.
	Gundi.
	Niáli.

In Behar—

Jethaut.
Garbetá.
Desi.
Semári.
Bangáli.

Kalwár.

Titles:—Abkár, Bhakat, Bhatthidár, Chaudhri, Goldár, Lála, Modi, Sáhu.

Sub-castes.	Sections of the Banodhia and Jaiswár sub-castes.	
Banodhiá.	Arddhálakhiá.	Kumhariá.
Biyáhut or Bhojpuri.	Bachhraián.	Lakhnauá.
Deswár.	Baniyá.	Mahátmá.
Jaiswár or Ajodhiá-bási.	Bardarhá.	Maurhiá.
	Barpaserá.	Modi.
Jasár.	Behnáhán.	Motrihá.
Khálsá.	Bhaiskayári.	Nagariá.
Kharidáhá.	Chailáha.	Nikthá.
Ránki or Kalal (Mahomedan).	Chamrauliá.	Rámi dhámi ke asámi.
	Chaubhaiá.	
	Chaurahá.	Rámpuriá.
	Dewán ke asámi.	Sadábarti.
	Gadahiá.	Senpuriá.
	Gaudanhá.	Seth.
	Ghorcharhá.	Siárahá.
	Harchanpuriá.	Srimaurhá.
	Hosainpuriá.	Tháther.
	Karaiáchor.	Thoreliá.
	Khalrihá.	Trilokpuriá.

Sections of the Biyáhut and Kharidáhá sub-castes.

Abkahilá.
Ami.
Bakat pánre ke pánre.
Baksariá.
Banárasiá.
Banráhá.
Báráha ke Máhto.
Barhariá ke pánre.
Baruár.
Básundár.
Bathuáke Máhto.
Bathuáke Ráut.
Battisi.
Beruke kisán.
Beruke Máhto.
Beruke pánre.
Bhádwariá.
Bhojpuriá.
Bhutáne.
Bihiá.
Chánre ke raut.
Chaugáin.
Chaugáinke pánre.
Chausá.
Datta ke ráut.
Daultá ke ráut.
Dhákáich.
Dhankháriá.
Dhobáhá.
Dhurfandá.
Ekauná.
Gádheyiá.
Gámel.
Gángdahiá.
Gareyiá.
Gharikárak.
Goá.
Gonr.
Hardwár.
Harnátar.
Hazári pánre.
Jagmanrá.
Jaintpur.
Jamuáon.
Kaithar.
Kálánuá.
Kamalsar.
Kámsar ke Máhto.
Kándh pákar.
Kaneil.
Kante ke rakmal.
Kante ke ras.
Karjáhá.
Kasarbáni.
Kasmal.
Kates.
Kateswar.
Kathariá.
Katherá.
Katsarwá.
Khan.
Khápráhá.
Kharknáke ke raut.
Khataiá.
Khereswarke pánre.
Krishán.
Laksham Seriá.
Lakshneswar.
Lamgariá.
Máhará.
Mahuári.
Májhaurá.
Mallik.
Maneriá.
Mángaf.
Masáre ke raut.
Mujniá.
Mulmaháli.
Nalakhiá.
Nunáon.
Nuneswar.
Nunhar.
Nunkhariá.
Osái.
Otoniá.
Pábai ke kisan.
Páchhnariá.
Pailáhá.
Pánihá chaur.
Pánkharayá.
Pánre ke Pánre.
Panthpákar.
Pariharbári.
Parlak Pánre.
Prási.
Rámkisán.
Rangpiár.
Sahadar.
Sáhál.
Sáhan.
Sanhá.
Sanichrá.
Sárgátiá.
Sohanpur.
Sonákánt.
Sonhar.
Sugardhar.
Surjáhá.
Tabkáhila.
Támgáin.
Tártar ke khir puri.
Urdágáinhi.

Kámár, *Kamár, Karmakár* (Bengal), *Lohár* (Behar), *Bhindhini* (Singbhum).

Titles:—In Bengal—Ari, Dás, De, Tewári: in Behar—Karuná, Mistri, Thákur.

Sub-castes.

In Bardwan—

Belási.
Máhmudpuriá.
Kámlá-Kámár.

Sections.

In Behar—

Bathuait.
Darsuriá.
Garbariá.

Sub-castes.	Sections.
In Midnapur—	*In Behar*—concld.
Lohár-Kámár } These two intermarry.	Godhanpurá.
Pitule-Kámár }	Harsariá.
Kánsari.	Hasanpuriá.
Sarna-Kámár.	Jakhalpuriá.
Ghatra-Kámár.	Jarangait.
Chánd-Kámár.	Jasiám.
Dhokrá.	Kalait.
Támrá.	Katosiá.
In 24-Parganás—	Marturiá.
Uttar-Rárhi.	Pokharmiá.
Dakhin-Rárhi.	Ratwariá.
Ánarpuri.	Ságí.
In Eastern Bengal—	Sonpuriá.
Bhusnápati.	Sothiwár.
Dhákái.	*In Bengal*—
Paschimá.	Alamyán.
In Murshedabad—	Bharadwáj.
Rárhi.	Kásyapa.
Bárendra.	Maudgalya.
Dhákáwál.	Sándilya.
Khottá.	*In Singbhum and the Santál Parganás*—
In Pubna—	Álam-rishi.
Rárhi or Dás-Samáj.	Bágh-rishi.
Bárendra or Panch-Samáj.	Bámuniá.
In Noakhali—	Kachhuá.
Játi-Karmakár.	Khujiriá.
Shikhu-Karmakár.	Manjari.
In Manbhum—	Nág.
Magahiyá.	Netriá.
Dhokrá.	Potá.
Lohsá.	Puraliá.
Básuná.	
In Santál Parganás—	
Ashtalai.	
Belálai.	
Churálai.	
Sankhalai.	

Kámi, *Kámiá.*

Sections.

Baráili.	Lohágun.
Darnál.	Lohár.
Devápáthi.	Lokándri.
Diáli.	Mangráti.
Dudhráj.	Parbaté.
Durál.	Pokhrel.
Gadáili.	Portel.
Gadál.	Rahapál.
Gahatráj.	Rámudán.
Gajmér.	Rasáili.
Ghám-ghotlé.	Rijál.
Gharti-ghauré.	Rujál.
Ghatáni.	Sápkotá.
Jár-Kámi.	Sásankhar.
Kairálá.	Setu-Suruál.
Kati-chioré.	Sin-chiori.
Kharkábáyu.	Singá-oré.
Kháti.	Thapángi.
Lámgádé.	Tiruá.

Kandh, *Kand, Kondh, Khond, Kui-loka, Kui-enju, Skandhasura.*

Titles :—Abbaye, Desauri, Jhankai or Jani, Máji, Málik, Muthá.

Sub-castes.	*Gochi* or septs.	*Klambu* or sub-septs.
Malua or Arria Kandh.		
Orh or Uriya Kandh.		
Beniah-Kandh.		
Betiah-Kandh.	1. Besringia	1. Besera. 2. Masara. 3. Boboto. 4. Binjarra. 5. Suna. 6. Motaro. 7. Mallika. 8. Murkuri. 9. Moku. 10. Dokeri.
Nikitia-Kandh.		
Sauntia-Kandh.		
	2. Bhetumendi.	
	3. Rasimendi.	
	4. Sagormendi.	
	5. Bankamendi.	
	6. Bidumendi.	
	7. Baloskuppa.	
	8. Grandimendi.	
	9. Gumalmendi.	
	10. Dutimendi.	
	11. Sandumendi.	

Sub-castes.	*Gorhi* or septs.	*Klambu* or sub-septs.
	12. Tuniamendi.	
	13. Bhetimendi.	
	14. Sidupari.	
	15. Delapari.	
	16. Kaliapari.	
	17. Rakodmoska.	
	18. Pundilkia.	
	19. Bogalkia.	
	20. Teridikia.	
	21. Koskirabi.	
	22. Domsing.	
	23. Kalabag.	
	24. Kutrengia ...	1. Kotringa. 2. Bisunga. 3. Damlunga. 4. Somanga. 5. Mongalka.
	25. Jehilingia.	
	26. Petingia.	
	27. Kerlingia.	
	28. Bakolmendi.	
	29. Dopsingia.	
	30. Sehelengia.	
	31. Dangnikia.	
	32. Adgirkia ...	1. Koskigan. 2. Panjurika. 3. Surumanega. 4. Pandega. 5. Sarenga. 6. Neringa. 7. Damanga.
	33. Lotpongia.	
	34. Danikia.	
	35. Robingia.	
	36. Mutungia.	
	37. Ganingia.	
	38. Behingia.	
	39. Dubosingia.	
	40. Dondikia.	
	41. Bhusangia.	
	42. Koinjabari.	
	43. Suramendi.	
	44. Bhursamendi.	
	45. Pobingia.	
	46. Gopingia.	
	47. Saitingia.	
	48. Pheringia.	
	49. Jorapongia.	
	50. Bobdengia.	

Kándu, *Kánu, Bharbhunjá, Bhunjá, Bhujári, Bhurji.*

Title :—Sáhu.

Sub-castes.	Sections of the Madhesiá sub-caste.	Sections of the Magahiya sub-caste.	
Madhesiá.	Baniápáthar.	Akán.	Khádhnu.
Magahiyá.	Bijaibanáras.	Akhgáon.	Kokras.
Bantariá or Bharbhunjá.	Dhanutá.	Ankuri.	Mahuli.
Kanaujiá.	Háthsukhá.	Aráp.	Máldhiá.
Gonr.	Kotá.	Bághákol.	Maner.
Koránch.	Pachtar.	Barhi.	Másaur.
Dhuriá.	Sribitiá.	Bere.	Mehaus.
Rawáni.		Bhárath.	Murti.
Bállamtiriá.		Bháter.	Nenijor.
Thather or Thatherá.		Bireri.	Neprá.
		Chhitni.	Páli.
		Datiyán.	Parsautiá.
		Gáger.	Pilich.
		Gánrol.	Rájgiri.
		Háthiákán.	Rauniá.
		Ichbariá.	Saráihát.
		Jiárwár.	Saursambár.
		Kánáp.	Sirá.
		Káneil.	Tisor.
		Kárián.	Toril.
		Kásiam.	Uttardáhá.
		Káteár.	

Sections of the Bantariá sub-caste. { Tindiha. Chaudihá.

Sections of the Koránch sub-caste. { Chási. Dehri. Háthiá Kándhá. Koriár. Muthá.

Kapáli.

Titles :—Bhuiya, Rai, Háldár, Málá, Mandal, Mánjhi, Mutabar (headman of *pancháyat*), Shikdár.

Sub-caste.	Sections.
Nil.	Kásyapa.
	Siva.

Karan, *Katki-Káel, Uriyá-Káet.*

Titles:—Dás, Mahanti, Mahápátra.

Sub-castes.	Sections.
Karan, Nauli-Karan.	Átreya.
Srishti-Karan, Bhatuntara.	Bharadwája.
	Kantsasa.
Hypergamous groups.	Kásyapa.
	Mudgul.
Khará.	Nágása.
Purá.	Parásara.
Chaián.	Sankha.
Kulina.	

Karangá, *Mistri.*

Titles:—Bishoi, Dalui, Kaur, Khán.

Sub-castes.	Sections.
Dhaluá.	Sálmách.
Máluá.	Kachchhap.
Sikhariá.	
Tungá.	

Kaserá, *Kanserá, Tamherá, Thatherá.*

Sub-caste.	Sections.
None.[1]	Banaudhiyá.
	Basaiyá.
	Chauarsá.
	Chaughará.
	Hariharno.
	Lakar-Mahauliyá
	Machhuá.
	Mahauliyá.
	Mauhariyá.
	Suariyá.
	Suppar.

[1] Mr. Sherring enumerates seven sub-castes—Purbiyá, Pachhawán, Gorakhpuri, Tank Táuchara, Bhariyá, Golar,—none of which appear to be known in Behar.

Kástha.

Sub-castes.	Sections.
Madhyasreni-Káyastha.	Same as of Kayastha.
Kastha.	

Kaur.

Sub-tribes.	Septs.
Chánti.	Bambai, a kind of eel.
Cherwa.	Banjar.
Dudh-Kaur.	Bhainsa, buffalo.
Paikará.	Chalenga, a kind of vegetable.
Rathiyá.	Kariar.
	Kolkatári.
	Motiomán.
	Pakar, a fruit.
	Pharsádhenti.
	Rankankar.
	Sanwáni.
	Sarjál.
	Singar.

Kawáli.

Titles:—Dháli, Háldár, Mála, Mánjhi, Vidyádhara.

Sub-caste.	Section.
Nil.	Aliman.

Káyasth, *Káet, Lálá.*

Titles:—Dás, Lál, Rái, Singh.

Sub-castes.		Sections.
Aithana.	In general ...	Kásyapa.
Amashta.		Dedhgawe.
Bálmik.		Kableár.
Bhatnágar.		Katariyár.
Gaur.		Katháutiár.
Karan.		Lakhauriár.
Kulsreshta.		Nandkiriár.
Máthur.		Narhatiár.
Nigam.		Nimandih.
Saksena.		Nuniyar.
Sribástab { Khare. Dusre.		Samalár.
Surajdhwaj.		Saraiyár.
		Sonkmare.

Sub-castes.	Sections.
Of the Amashta sub-caste.	Baidsáin.
	Bardiár.
	Bilwár.
	Birnáwar.
	Datkiliár.
	Dharkiliár.
	Gaprai.
	Gyásáin.
	Hargambai.
	Jaipuria.
	Jamuár.
	Kachgawai.
	Karpatne.
	Mahtha.
	Mandilwár.
	Pansain.
	Rukhiár.
	Sandhawár.
	Tinriár.
Of the Karan sub-caste.	Ajaidápál.
	Ambahlá.
	Atari.
	Badisámá.
	Bakhola.
	Baláin.
	Barhari.
	Battikbál.
	Benk.
	Garhbiwar.
	Ikahan.
	Kachhrá.
	Kánchanpur.
	Kothipál.
	Munga.
	Narangbali.
	Oari.
	Pakli.
	Sisab.
	Usauth.
	Utamapur.
Of the Sribástab sub-caste.	Kásyapa.
	Akhauri.
	Bakshi.
	Misir.
	Pánde.
	Rái.
	Sahuliar.
	Singh.
	Tewári.
	Thákur.

Káyastha, *Káet, Kait, Káyath.*

Sub-castes.	Sections.	
Uttar-Rárhi.	Agnibesya.	Kalvisa.
Dakshin-Rárhi.	Álambyán.	Kásyapa.
Bangaja.	Ári.	Kausika.
Bárendra.	Átreya.	Krishnátreya.
Madhya-sreni.	Baiyágrahapadya.	Kusik.
	Basishtha.	Maudgalya.
	Básuki.	Parásara.
	Bátsya.	Rohita.
	Bharadwája.	Sábarna.
	Biswámitra.	Sándilya.
	Gautama.	Saukálin.
	Ghritakausik.	Saupáyan.
	Jámadagnya.	

Titles arranged in Hypergamous Groups.

Dakshin Rárhi.

Kulin.—Basu, Ghosh, Mitra.

Siddha Maulik.—Dás, Datta, De, Guha, Kar, Pálit, Sen, Sinha.

Sádhya-Maulik or *Bahátture.*—Áditya, Áich, Ankur, Arnab, Ás, Baittash, Bal, Bán, Bandhur, Barddhan, Barmá, Bhadra, Bhanja, Bhui, Bhut, Bid, Bindu, Bishnu, Brahma, Chandra, Dáhá, Dáná, Dhanu, Dhar, Dharani, Gan, Ganda, Ghar, Guha, Gui, Guna, Gupta, Guta, Hem, Hes, Hor, Hui, Indra, Jas, Khil, Kirtti, Kshám, Kshem, Kshom, Kunda, Lodh, Mana, Nág, Nandi, Náth, Om, Pál, Pil, Ráhá, Ráhut, Rája, Rakshit, Ráná, Ranga, Rudra, Sáin, Sakti, Sál, Sám, Sáná, Sarmá, Sil, Som, Sur, Swar, Tej, Upamán.

Bangaja.

Kulin.—Basu, Ghosh, Guha, Mitra.

Madhyalya.—Datta, Nág, Nath.

Mahápátra.—Ádhya, Ankur, Bhadra, Bishnu, Chandra, Dás, Deb, Dhar, Kar, Kundu, Nandan, Nandi, Pál, Pálit, Ráhá, Rakshit, Sen, Sinha, Som.

Achal.—Abasakti, Aditya, Aich, Apa, Arnab, Baitosh, Bal, Bán, Bandhu, Barddhan, Barmá, Bed, Bhanja, Bhuin, Bhumik, Bhut, Bindu, Brahma, Chain, Chaki, Dáhá, Dám, Dáná, Dánri, Dhanu, Dharani, Dhol, Dhum, Dut, Gan, Gandak, Ghaniá, Ghár, Guna, Gupta, Háthi, Hem, Hes, Hom, Hor, Hui, Indra, Jas, Kachu, Karáiyá, Khil, Kirtti, Kshám, Kshem, Kshom, Lodh, Maguri, Mán, Mana, Nád, Náhá, Nalu, Pai, Pil, Pipi, Puin, Ráhut, Rája, Ráná, Ranga, Riti, Roi, Rudra, Sáin, Sanga, Sarmá, Sil, Smár, Son, Suman, Sur, Syám, Tej.

Uttar-Rárhi.

Kulin.—Ghosh, Sinha.

Sanmaulik.—Dás, Datta, Mitra.

Sámánya Maulik.—Dás,[1] Ghosh, Kar,[1] Sinha.

Bárendra.[2]

Siddha.—Cháki, Dás, Nandi.

Súdhya.—Datta, Deb, Nág, Sinha.

Hej.—Dám, Dhar, Gun, Kar.

Honorary titles:—Bakshi, Bhándári, Biswás, Chaudhri, Dastá-dár, Dháli, Kánungo, Mahallanavis, Majumdár, Mallik, Munsif, Mushrif, Mustaufi, Neogi, Pattadár, Rái, Sarkár, Shikdár, Thákurta.

---

[1] These two families are considered a quarter each, so the Uttar-Rárhis reckon 7½ out of 9 families.

[2] Originally the Bárendras had seven families, but now they count 7½ by adding the descendants of one Saramá, a Nápit, as a half family, besides many immigrant families from other parts of the country which go to swell the Hej group.

Kewat, *Kiot*, *Kaibartta*.

Titles:—*In Behar*—Bhandári, Cháudhri, Deradár, Jándár, Kámat, Kápar, Khawás, Mahto, Mandar, Marar.

Sub-castes.	Sections.
In Behar—	
Bahiáwak, Bahiot, or Ghibihár.	Bhadauriá.
Garbháit, Gorwáit, or Sághár.	Biswás.
Ajudhiábási.	Házará.
Játhot.	Itwár.
Machhuá.	Kápar.
Mahádanda.	Kásyapa.
	Maharná.
	Marar.
	Mukhiá.

Khambu, *Nau-lákh Khambu.*

Titles:—Dhan, Jimdár, Kiráti, Mandal, Mukhiá, Rái, Sing.

Thars or septs.

Bábhaunchhá.
Bángdel.
Barlós.
Bokhime.
Bonthárua.
Boyong.
Bumákámchhá.
Butepáchhá.
Chamlingeh.
Chaurási.
Chuiráchhá.
Dilpáli.
Dungmáli.
Haidibuthá.
Hatuwáli.
Homodimchhá.
Horongpáchhá.
Jubhingeh.
Kási.
Kháling.
Kheresanchhá.
Kuásanchhá.
Kulung.
Láphaunchhá.
Maiduchhá.
Maikam.
Male Kumchhá.
Mayáháng.
Mukáranchhá.
Mulukuas.
Námbochhá.
Námdung.
Nardauchhá.
Necháhli.
Nimámbaunchhá.
Ninauchhá.
Nomahang.
Paderáchhá.
Phlumáchhá.
Phulehli.
Phurkeli.
Plembochhá.
Rabchháli.
Rajabin.
Rákháli.
Ránauchhá.
Rápungchhá.
Regálaunchhá.
Rimching.
Rochingáchhá.
Sángpáng.
Silongchhá.
Sothángeh.
Sungdele.
Tángbuáh.
Thulung.
Wáhsali.

Khandáit, *Khandait-Páik, Khandáyat, Bhuiyá-Páik.*

Titles:

In Chota Nagpur:—Amáut, Arhá, Baráik, Behará, Gaunjhu, Kotwár, Mahápátra, Mánjhi, Mirdáhá, Náik, Ohdár, Pátra, Pradhán, Ráut.

In Orissa.

Bághá, tiger.
Báhubalendra, like the god Indra in strength of arm.
Dakhin-Kabát, south gate.
Daubárik, messenger or sentinel.
Garh-Náik or Sinha, leader or lion of the fort.
Háti, elephant.
Jená.
Maharath or Mahárathi, great charioteer.
Malla, wrestlers.
Mangaráj.
Náik, leader.
Paschim-Kabát, west gate.
Praharáj.
Ranasinha or Samarsinha, lion of the fight.
Raut, horseman.
Rui.
Sámanta, officer.
Senápati, general.
Sinha, lion.
Uttar-Kabát, north gate.

Sub-castes.	Sections.
	(*a*) *Totemistic*—
Bar-gohri. { Das-ghariá, in Saraṇda of Singbhum.	Kachhuá, tortoise.
Pachás-ghariá, in Chota Nagpur.	Kadam, *nauclea grandifolia*.
Pánchsau-ghariá, in Gángpur.	Mor, peacock.
Pandrasau-ghariá, in Gángpur, Bonai, Bámrá, and Sambalpur.	Nág, snake.
Chhot-gohrí, in Chota Nagpur.	Sál, fish.
	(*b*) *Eponymous*—
	Bharadwája.
	Kaundilya.
	Nágasá, etc.

Chásá or Orh-Khandait ... / Mahánáik or Sresta-Khandait	In Balasore and Cuttack.
Bhanja-Khandait ... / Harichandan Khandait ...	In Puri.
Khandait-Paik ... / Sresta-Khandait ...	In the Orissa Tributary States.

Khariá.

Titles :—Dhángar, Kisán, Kol, Parja.

Sub-castes.	Sections.
Berga-Khariá.	Bage, a bird.
Dhilki-Khariá.	Bar, *Ficus Indica*.
Dud-Khariá.	Bárlá.
Erenga-Khariá.	Baroá, an animal.
Munda-Khariá.	Bilung, Nun, or Noná Mailá, salt.
Oraon-Khariá.	Demtá, red ant.
	Dhán, paddy.
	Dhanuár, can't eat rice soup.
	Dhelki, a bird.
	Dungdung, Aind, or Indu, eel.
	Durang, a fish.
	Háthi, elephant.
	Kasi.
	Kerketá, a bird of that name.
	Kiro or Bágh, tiger.
	Kulu or Kachhuá, tortoise.
	Mailwar.
	Murgear.

Sub-castes.	Sections.
	Nág, cobra.
	Naik.
	Naniár.
	Pardhan.
	Pathal.
	Purti.
	Sáhul.
	Samdiá.
	Saur, fish.
	Suraniá, a rock.
	Telga.
	Teteteyin or Bagiár, a bird of that name.
	Tirkoár.
	Tititihu, a bird.
	Topo, a bird.
	Tuti, vegetable.

The above groups are found among the settled Khariás. I have been unable to ascertain whether the wild Khariás, commonly known as Ban-Mánush, 'men of the woods,' have any similar divisions.

Kharwár, *Kherwár.*

Titles:—Bhakat, Bhogta, Dás, Gaunju, Kapri, Mahto, Mandar, Manjhi, Ohdár, Panjiárá, Pradhán.

Sub-tribes.	Septs.
In Palamau—	Aind, a kind of eel.
Pátbandh.	Bág, tiger.
Daulbandh.	Bahera, a jungle fruit.
Khairi.	Baherwar, a tree.
	Bail, a fruit.
	Bair, plum.
	Bamnia, salt.
	Bandhia.
	Bania, a caste.
	Bar, *Ficus Indica.*
	Bhogta.
In Southern Lohardagá—	Binjoar.
Deswári-Kharwár.	Biserwar.
Bhogtá.	Bisra, a hawk.
Raut.	Chardiar, pineapple.
Manjhiá.	Chirra, squirrel.
	Chorant, a grass.
	Chundiar, a top-knot.
	Chuniar, lime.
	Demta, red tree-ant.
	Dhobi, can't touch washerman.

Sub-tribes. Septs.

Dolbandhi.
Dudul, a kind of bird.
Gai, cow.
Ghansi, a pond fish.
Hans, swan.
Hansarwar, duck.
Hasdajiá, a duck.
Hathi, elephant.
Hemremina.
Kachua, tortoise.
Kans, a grass.
Kanwad, a jungle fruit.
Karhar, a jungle fruit like 'bel.'
Kerketa, a bird.
Kesargia.
Khapu, a bird.
Khichengia, a fruit.
Kowriar.
Kuardar.
Kurdur.
Kussum, a fruit.
Maderwar.
Mahukal, a bird.
Mailwar.
Manjar.
Manjhi, a title.
Munga, coral.
Murgi, hen.
Murmurwar.
Mus, rat.
Nág, cobra.
Pátmurmurárá.
Radhar.
Rikhiasan.
Sai Sonarwar.
Samudwar.
Saras, a water-fowl.
Sheor, a fish.
Sonar, goldsmith.
Sonarwar, gold.
Suia, a kind of little bird.
Sumedhiar, a tree.
Surunia, neck ornament.
Tamba, copper.
Tirki, a bird.
Tiruar, Tirkuár, an arrow.
Tuduar, hen.
Tunduar.
Turuar, a fruit (*pakur*).
Tuti, a kind of bird.
Uriar.

Sub-tribes.		Septs.
	Septs of the Daulbandh sub tribe.	Behroár. Kaunsiár. Kauriár. Mánriár. Pát-murmu. Ráj-murmu. Sonoroár.

Khatik.

Sub-castes.	Section.
Khatik.	Kásyapa.
Dharamdási.	

Khatri, *Purbiyá Khatri.*

Titles :—Barman, Lál, Máhátá, Sáhu.

Sub-castes.		Sections.
Chárjáti.[1] Panchjáti. Chhajáti. Bárajáti. Bahánnajáti. Piruwal.	Of the Chárjáti sub-caste.	Kápur. Khánná. Meherá. Set or Set-tálwár.
	Of the Panchjáti sub-caste.	Beri. Birj. Saigal. Sarwál. Wahe.
	Of the Chhajáti sub-caste.	Bhale. Dhawan. Supat. Tolwar. Turman.
	Of the Bárajáti sub-caste.	Chaupre. Ghai. Kakkar. Meheden. Soni. Tandan.

---

[1] The Chárjáti sub-caste is again divided into Arhái-ghar and Chári-ghar, apparently hypergamous groups, the former of which is deemed superior to the latter. It seems probable that the first five sub-castes were originally hypergamous divisions, the order of precedence being that given above. Inter-marriage between members of different sub-castes is not unknown at the present day, but it is considered right for a man to marry in his own group, and the sub-castes are practically endogamous. The Piruwál sub-caste has always been endogamous for the reasons explained in the text.

Sub-castes.	Sections.
Of the Bahánnajáti sub-caste.	Behal. Chal-agge. Dhandhábe. Gayalpure. Handi. Keoli. Khosle. Kuchal. Marwáhe. Náiár. Nándi. Suri.

Brahmanical Gotras—

Angirasa.
Bátsya.
Bharadwája.
Hangsarishi.
Kásyapa.
Kausalya.
Lomasá.

Khatwe.

Title :—Mandar.

Sub-castes.	Section.
Bahio. Goro.	Kásyapa.

Khyán or Kolita.

Sub-castes.	Sections.
Nil.	Aladish. Alamyán. Agni batsya. Kánsári. Kasyapa. Kauchan rishi. Madhukulya. Mugrish.

Kochh, *Rájbansi, Sivabansi, Suryabansi, Mándái, Bhanga-Kshatı. Kshatri-Sankoch, Patita-Kshatri, Paliyá, Desi.*

Titles:—Bhaumik, Chaudhri, Dás, Mahat, Májhi, Tánti, Báns-árá, Sagun-ure.

Sub-castes.

In Northern Bengal—

Paliyá.
Sádhu.
Bábu, Byábahári.
Rájbansi.
Kántái.
Desi.
Tiar or Dalai.
Modásí.
Dobhásir.
Jáluá or Jháluá.
Bodo.

In Dacca—

Kochh-Mándál.

Sections.

Kásyapá.

Dugu or Sections.

Mekhun.	Darang-Chiachi.
Dásik.	Darang-Saudana.
Senel.	Darang-Dambuk.
Chisim.	Darang-Dakal.
Náphák.	Shaini.
Darang.	Doi.
Richil.	Durgu.
Parak.	Lori.

Koiri, *Muráo.*

Titles:—Mahto, Muráo (green-grocer), Marar, Dhelphor (clod-breaker).

Sub-castes.

Barki-Dángi.
Chhotki-Dángi.
Banáphar, Banapár.
Jaruhár.
Kanaujiá.
Magahiyá.
Tirhutiá.
Chirmait.
Kumárá.
Goita, Dhár } In Champaran.
Reutiá, Pauriá, Barákar, Palmohá } In Chota Nagpur.

Sections of the Banáphar sub-caste.

Bagwe.
Darbe.
Káno.
Kápri.
Mánjhi.
Marár.
Marik.
Panjiárá.

Sub-castes.	Sections of the Magahiyá sub-caste.
	Amrot.
	Gamaiyá Parganá Kharakpur.
	Kargaha.
	Maiketári beguná bágh.
	Mál.
	Sais.
In Chota Nagpur	Kásyap.
	Nág.
	Mujni.

Korá, *Kaorá*, *Khaira*, *Khayrá*, *Hári* (used inaccurately by outsiders only).

Titles :—Mudi, Rái.

Sub-castes.	Sections.
Dhalo.	Álu.
Molo.	Bárdá.
Sikhariá.	Butku, pig.
Bádámiá.	Hansdá, wild goose
Sonárekhá.	Kásyab, tortoise.
Jhetiá.	Kásibak, heron.
Guri-Báwá.	Sámá.
	Sál or Saulá, fish.
	Sánpu, bull.

Korwa.

Title :—Majhi.

Sub-tribes.	Septs.
Agaria-Korwa.	Ainduar, a kind of eel.
Dand-Korwa.	Amba, mango.
Dih-Korwa.	Asotoar.
Paharla-Korwa.	Bagher, tiger.
	Dhan, unhusked rice.
	Ginmuar.
	Ginuar, a kind of eel.
	Har, plough.
	Harrá, myrabolam.
	Hasda, wild goose.
	Huruj.
	Kerketta, a bird.
	Mujaniar.
	Muri, ancestors made a *chulá* of four skulls and cooked their dinner.
	Pakhua.
	Samat, pestle.
	Samp, snake.
	Sarai, a jungle fruit.
	Silli, a kind of fish.
	Suga, parrot.

Koshtá, *Máhárá.*

Title :—Dás.

Sections.

Baghál, tiger.
Bagutia.
Bhát, rice.
Bhatpáhári.
Chaudhri.
Chaur, yak's tail.
Gohi.
Khanda, sword.
Kurm, tortoise.
Mánik, gem.
Nág, snake.
Son.

Kotál, *Kotwál.*

Title :—Pradhán.

Sub-castes.	Sections.
Atpárá.	*Nil.*
Dhukursáni.	
Kutabpur.	
Manoharsáhi.	

Kumhár, *Kumár, Kumati, Kumbhakár, Kulál, Ghatakár, Ghatakárpur, Prajápati, Rudrabans, Rudrapál, Pandit.*

Titles :—Behárá, Biswás, Dás, Deuri, Kunkál, Máhato, Májhi, Marar, Marik, Mehrána, Pál, Ráná.

Sub-castes.	Sections.
In Jessore—	
Belgáchi.	Aladoshi.
Dáspárá.	Alamyán.
Nautana.	Hansa.
Bhushná.	Kanaka.
	Kásyapa.
	Rishi.
	Sándilya.
In Murshedabad and Hughli—	
Rárhi.	
Bárendra.	
Dáspári.	
Chaurási.	

Sub-castes.	Sections.
In Pabna—	
Sirasthán.	
Májhasthán.	
Chandan-sára.	
Chaurási.	
Daspárá { Prámánik. Pánpátra. Mujgarni. }	
In Dacca—	
Bara-bhágiyá } Lál.	
Chhota-bhágiyá } Sádá.	
Khatya.	
Rájmahália.	
Magi.	
In Noakhali—	
Bhuláiyá.	
Sarália.	
Chátgáinyá.	
Sandwipá.	
In Behar and Chota Nagpur—	
Maghaiyá.	
Kanaujiá.	
Tirhutiá.	
Desi, Deswár.	
Bardhiá.	
Biáhut.	
Ajodhyábási.	
Ardhauti.	
Godahiyá.	
Chápuá.	
Banaudhiá.	
Masawár.	
Bangáli or Rárhi.	
Turk-Kumhár.	

Of the Magahiyá sub-caste:

Asmait.
Baid.
Bárik.
Biswás.
Chaudhrián.
Gáim.
Jeruhet.
Kápar.
Kásyapa, Kaisab.
Kathalmalet.
Kheri.
Madhust.
Maháthá.
Mahátman.
Maheswar.
Mehtar.
Mukh.
Nág.
Pachmait.
Panjiár.
Parrarit.
Pharkiet.
Ráut.
Ráworh.
Senápat.
Sonmain.
Tharait.

Sub-castes.		Sections.
	Sections found in Singbhum.	Chána. Kharuá. Maher. Mandap. Natanya. Ranubád. Sikári. Sinhi. Surabanī. Tumaliá.
	In Manbhum	Báilhor. Kásyab. Min, fish. Nág, snake. Sándil.
	In Lohardagá	Bar, *Ficus Indica.* Garhatia. Hathi, elephant. Kansi, a grass. Parihar. Sisingi, a river-fish, has two thorns on its head. Tumbli, Berni.
	In the Santál Parganás.	Káchim, tortoise. Nág, serpent.
In Orissa—		
Jagannáthi or Urīya-Kumhár.		Bhad-bhadriá, sparrow. Goru, cow. Kaundinya, tiger. Kurma, tortoise. Mudir, frog. Neul, weasel. Sarpa, snake.
Khatya-Kumhár.		Kásyapa.

Kurmi, *Kunbi, Kurambi, Kurum, Kurumánik.*

Titles :—Chaudhri, Mahanta, Mahárái, Mahato, Mandal, Marár, Mukhya, Parámánik, Raut, Sarkár, Singh.

Sub-castes.	Sections.
(*a*) *In Behar—*	(*a*) *In Behar—*
Ayodhiyá or Awadhiyá.	Garain.
Chandel or Chandan.	Kásyapa.
Chanaur.	
Ghamela.	
Ghorcharhá.	

Sub-castes.

(a) *In Behar*—concld.

Jaiswár.
Kachaisá.
Katriár.
Kharchwár.
Rámaiyá.
Sainthwár.
Sanswár.
Sauchánd.
Terahghariá.

(b) *In Chota Nagpur*—

Adh-Kurmi or Madhyam-Kurmi.
Bagsariá or Bágsariá.
Khoriá.
Kurum.
Magahiá.
Nich-Kurmi.
Sikhariá or Chhota-Kurmi.

(c) *In Orissa*—

Bagsari.
Gádásari.
Gáysari.
Maisásari.

Sections.

(b) *In Chota Nagpur and Orissa*—

Andhachábár.
Andhachipá panariá.
Bághbanuár, tiger.
Bághwár, tiger.
Bagsariá, tiger.
Baherwár, a fruit.
Báns, bamboo.
Bánsriár, will not play the *bánsi* or bamboo flute.
Banuár, hunter.
Bendiár.
Bhokwár.
Bilár, cat.
Chhonch Mutruár, spider.[1]
Chilbindhá panariá.
Chilbinuár, kite.
Chiluár, kite.
Chorharuá.
Dugriár.
Dumuriá, *dumur*, fig.
Goriár.
Hánsdá.
Hásdagiá, wild goose.
Hastowár, tortoise.
Hemramiá, betel palm.
Henduár.
Homwár.
Jálbanuár, net.
Jhápábasriár.
Jhátideká.
Juruár.
Juthasankhwár.
Káchiári.
Káchimár.
Kaiobanuár.
Kairawár, illegitimate issues.
Kánbindhá, pierced ears.
Kárákátá Karwár, buffalo.
Katiár, will not wear silk cloth.
Kesariá, *Kesar*, grass.
Khechá Kesria.
Kundiár.

---

[1] In Midnapur Kurmis say that once upon a time water being needed to clear a place for some religious ceremony, a Kurmi there present made use of his urine for the purpose, and his descendants were therefore called Chhonch-mutruár.

Sub-castes.	Sections.
	Mangar, crocodile.
	Mantrawár.
	Mathrwár.
	Murmu, nilgao.
	Mus, rat.
	Nág, snake.
	Nágbasriár.
	Nángtoyár, give children their first rice naked.
	Nauákhuri.
	Punriár.
	Rájmor.
	Rimrimiá.
	Sálbanwár, *sál* jungle.
	Sankhawár, will not wear shell ornaments.
	Siár, jackal.
	Sona, gold.
	Tiruár.
	Tukipitá dumuriá, *dumur*, fig.
	Tunduár.

Laheri, *Laherá*.

Title :—Sahu.

Sub-castes.	Sections.
Dakhinhá.	Kási.
Tirhutiá.	Mahuriá.
Nuri.	

Lepcha, *Mon*.

Sub-tribes.[1]	Septs.
Rong.	Barphungpuso.
Khamba.	Adinpuso.[2]
	Singdyang.
	Tingilmung.
	Rangomung.
	Tárzukmung.
	Sungutmung.
	Námzingmung.
	Luksom.
	Sangmi.

[1] As stated in the text, these groups are not now endogamous.
[2] As stated in the text, Adinpuso is the only one of these groups which is now exogamous.

Limbu, *Das Limbu, Yakthumba, Tsong, Chang.*

Title :—Subha or Suffah (chief).

Sub-tribes (*thum* or *thum-thum*).

1. Pánthar ... ... 2. Chhothar ... ... 3. Ahtharal ... ... 4. Yangorup ... ... 5. Chaibisá	Classed as Kási-gotra, supposed to have immigrated into Nepal from Benares.
6. Miákhola or Terothar ... 7. Charkhola ... ... 8. Maikhola ... ... 9. Phedáb or Bhuiphuta ... 10. Tambrkhola ...	Classed as Lhásá-gotra, supposed to have come from Lhásá.

Septs (*thar*).

Of the Pánthar sub-tribe.

- Angdenba, lord of the forest.
- Chehmjom, a native of Chehm.
- Chikchábá.
- Chobegu.
- Hangsnemba.
- Ingmaba, he who kept fowls.
- Kerungma.
- Kokenamba, he who rises with the sun.
- Laoti, he who was obeyed.
- Luhá.
- Manglagpa,[1] the dancer.
- Mephagpa, the butcher, literally, pig-roaster.
- Phejom, the *kukri*-bearer, including (*a*) Nembong, (*b*) Sardak-peapi.
- Pheodan, the water-carrier.
- Phyagpa, the knife-grinder.
- Serma, rent-collector.
- Songbangphe, the new settler.
- Thekim, he who works in wicker, including the following sub-septs :—(*a*) Meongba, (*b*) Thamsong, (*c*) Chobegu, (*d*) Petehhimba, (*e*) Angbu, the forest-dweller, (*f*) Yakten, formerly doctors.
- Toktiham.
- Tumbapo, the eldest.
- Tumbrok, born of a step-mother.
- Yangdenba,[2] he who paid his footing.
- Yangsoba or Namlagpa, the chief of the tribe.

---

[1] The ancestor of this *thar* was ridden (possessed?) by a god, and danced.
[2] Descended from a Mech who got admission into the Limbu tribe by bribing the heads of the *thum-thum*.

Of the Chhothar sub-tribe.	Bargharri, the twelve brethren.
	Khema,[1] a pheasant. Apparently totemistic.
	Khojom, he who ate his earnings.
	Kurumbhong,[2] the divider of the village.
	Legma, the worker in mud.
	Maden, the son of his mother.
	Sangma,[3] a buffalo. Apparently totemistic.
	Teling, the worker in cane.
	Thogleng, the suicide.
	Tungohong, the discontented.
Of the Ahtharai sub-tribe.	Angbohang, king of the fir wood.
	Inglamphe, the liar.
	Kondongwa, the vagabond.
	Pomo, the large family.
	Thenglahbo, the native of Thenglah.
	Tshendangkya, he who lives apart.
	Yakshoma, the guardian of the fort.
Of the Yangorup sub-tribe.	Ingyaromba.
	Khebangba, the native of Khebang.
	Khingba, branch of the same sept may not intermarry.
	Lechenche, the dissolute one.
	Lekhogma, he with swollen testes.
	Lingden } Admitted from the Lepchas.
	Loksohm } Admitted from the Lepchas.
	Mahbho, branch of the same sept may not intermarry.
	Mangmu.
	Menyangbo, the unsuccessful one.
	Mongtupo.
	Phawahong, the name of a village.
	Pondha, the wanderer.
	Puktebu.
	Serling, the thief.
	Suwahong, the mendicant.
	Thehbeh.[4]
	Thupuku.
	Tumling.
	Yakpangden, the dweller on the pass.

[1] This *thar* will not eat a pheasant or fowl or any bird of that class. The story is that the founder went out to shoot pheasants in a fir copse, but found none, and vowed never to eat a pheasant again.

[2] The founder of this *thar* is said, for reasons not stated, to have divided his village into two parts by drawing a line down the middle.

[3] The buffalo is taboo to this *thar*: the legend is the same as that of the Khema *thar*.

[4] An eponymous *thar*, named after Thehbeh, son of Srijanga, the powerful chief of the Limbus, since deified, who fought against Prithi Náráyan, the founder of the present ruling dynasty of Nepal.

Of the Yangorup sub-tribe —*concluded.*	Yíjám, the wanderer, or eater. Yithingu, the huntsman. Yongyahang, the son of a chief. Yungmá, the idler.
Of the Chaibisa sub-tribe.	Lhoringten,[1] the chief of Morrung. Memophagpa. Papson, the adopted one. Pichagma,[2] the son of the monkey. Sonyokpa, the guardian of the new fort.
Of the Miákhola or Terothar sub-tribe.	Hangam, the king's officer. Líbang, the archer. Nahlibo,[3] he who chased his wife. Thoilong, the ragged one. Tsonbang, he who listens and profits.
Of the Charkhola sub-tribe.	Aktenhang, name of a domestic demi-god. Lingdam, admitted from the Lepchas. Mahbu,[4] the physician. Nembang, the swollen one. Photra. Thogphelagu, he who wears the rhododendron flower. Yongyahung, the aristocrat.
Of the Phedáb sub-tribe.	Chikkophung, he who planted the *brihati.*[5] Hupachongbang, he who was blessed and prospered. Isbo, name of a village. Khamapong, the dweller under the *bar* (*Ficus religiosa*) tree. Lokmahung. Lumphongma, those who shared the land. Maden. Musuhang, the lowland chief. Ninglehku, one who cuts poisonous plants. Obung-gyakpa, the dweller above the fountain. Phehim, the singer. Pho-omphu, the hangman. Phungthag, he who stole to order. Pongyangu, he who carries his goods on his back. Senihang, sons of the snow-chief.

---

1 This *thar* was formerly under the Morrung Raja.

2 This *thar* is said to have formerly worshipped the monkey.

3 The story is that the wife of the founder of the *thar* ran away from him, but he caught her and brought her back, and afterwards had a large family by her.

4 Literally a shaker; one who being ridden by ghosts or devils shakes himself free: hence a physician.

5 A thorny plant with a bitter berry used for medical purposes.

Of the Phedáb sub-tribe—*concld.*	**Singogpa.** **Sodemba**, the spy. **Songbangphe**, the dweller in the valley. **So-onkobu**, a resident of So-onko. **Sothung**, name of a village. **Thambden**, the stay-at-home. **Theguba**, the son of the cliff. **Thobukya**, he who has skin disease. **Tumbangphe**,[1] the earth-born or *Bhuiphuta*. **Yurumbang**, they of the central village.
Of the Tambrkhola sub-tribe.	**Legbahang.** **Lingkhim.** **On-chhombo**, the horse-seller. **Phenduá**,[2] the hammerer of iron. **Sahmbahang.** **Ssahoden**, born in famine time. **Thup-yumah**, name of a place.

Septs.

Angláh.	Nagen.
Anlábáng.	Nermáh.
Baidohang.	Nogo.
Bákhim.	Pálu.
Chempajong.	Párkhari.
Chungbáng.	Patálang.
Hemphá.	Pekhá.
Hukpáh.	Petungbah.
Ichommah.	Phalechhuah.
Ikteh.	Pheyak.
Ilámháng.	Ponthák.
Imsong.	Samwah.
Ithinku.	Sángbah.
Kámbáháng.	Sanjökmah.
Kámbáng.	Sátling.
Kephuk.	Seduah.
Khámthák.	Sekwahdeng.
Khobaipong.	Sene.
Khuadang.	Singjangkuk.
Kunbáhong.	Singjuk.
Laktomáháng.	Sukhong.
Lingdenbeh.	Sukwabah.
Linglámphen.	Taijaung.
Lugumah.	Tilding.
Mangoyak.	Tongbángboha.
Mangyong.	Tumkchong.
Muromah.	Yongyah.

---

[1] This *thar* claims to be *terræ filii*, and point out a huge rock which covers the spot where their founder sprang from the earth.

[2] This *thar* was formerly the blacksmiths of the tribe.

Lohár, *Kamár*.

Titles:—Mistri, Ráut, Thákur.

Sub-castes.

In Behar—

Kanaujiá.
Kokás.
Maghaya.
Kamár Kallá.
Mahur or Mahuliyá.
Mathuriyá.
Kamiá, immigrants from Nepal.

In Santál Parganás—

Birbhumiá.
Govindpuriá.
Shergarhiá.

In Lohardagá—

Manjhal-Turiyá.
Munda-Lohár.
Sad-Lohár.
Sisutbansi Loharia, Lohondia.

In Bankura—

Angariá.
Gobrá.
Jhetiá.
Pánsili.

Sections.

Of the Kanaujiá sub-caste.

Asesmeghrám.
Baswariá.
Begsariá.
Bermán.
Bhákur.
Biskarmá.
Bunichhor.
Chausáhá.
Damdariá.
Dhakaniá.
Gungambhir.
Kamtariá.
Kantithiá.
Kásyapa.
Kathár.
Kathautiá.
Kissauriá.
Kukurjhampar.
Kulthari Mallik
Pahlampuri.
Pánre.
Ráne.
Sabri.
Sámil Thákur.
Sangiri Thákur.
Sarwat.
Sonaman.
Supáhá.
Udhmatiá.
Sálrishi, *sál* fish.

Sub-castes.	Sections.
In Manbhum—	
Lohár-Mánjhi.	
Danda-Mánjhi.	
Bágdl-Lohár.	

Sub-tribes.	Totemistic septs in Chota Nagpur.
	Bagh, tiger.
	Bán, a kind of eel.
	Bando, wild cat, makes a loud noise at night.
	Báns, bamboo.
	Baroha.
	Beloar, fruit.
	Besra, a hawk.
	Bhengraj, kingcrow.
	Bhutkuar.
	Bodrâ.
	Bukru.
	Chouria.
	Churuar.
	Demta, red tree-ant.
	Dhan, rice soup forbidden.
	Dumria, fig.
	Gaintwar.
	Goloar, sweet potato.
	Gunj, a kind of fruit.
	Hardi, turmeric.
	Hastuar.
	Hatti, elephant.
	Hemrom.
	Induar, a kind of eel.
	Jalwar, net.
	Kachua, tortoise.
	Kaethoar, a curry vegetable.
	Kaisale.
	Kamal, lotus.
	Kanda, sweet potato.
	Kanojia, a tribe.
	Karhar, a jungle fruit.
	Karkosa, cow.
	Karkusa, a bird.
	Kaua, crow.
	Kerketta, a bird.

Sub-tribes.	Totemistic septs in Chota Nagpur.
	Kisnot, a tribe.
	Koeá, a wild beast.
	Kons, grass.
	Kusuar, a river-fish.
	Lalihar, a bird.
	Lumria, a fox.
	Maelwar.
	Maghaia, a place.
	Maghnia.
	Mahili Munda, a tribe.
	Mahili, a tribe.
	Mormu, deer.
	Mutriar.
	Nág, cobra.
	Pánru, a snake.
	Phutka, vegetable.
	Purti.
	Retha, fruit.
	Runda, a wild cat.
	San, heron.
	Sándh, bullock.
	Sangalwar.
	Saur, a fish.
	Semanohangiar.
	Sonaome.
	Sonbesra, a bird.
	Son Maghia.
	Son Tirki.
	Suia, a small bird.
	Tirki, can't touch any animals after their eyes open.
	Topoar, a bird.
	Udwar, a water-cat.

Madhunápit, *Madak.*

Sub-castes.	Sections.
Biswás-Madak.	Alamyán.
Játi-Madak.	Bharadwája.
Madhu-Madak.	Kásyapa.
Reláti-Madak.	Maudgalya.
	Parásara.
	Sándilya.

Magh, *Mag.*

Sub-tribes.	Septs.
Thongtha, Thongcha or Jumiá Magh.	Cherengtsa.
Marmá, Myammá or Roáng Magh.	Chingrisa.
Máramagri, Rájbansi, Baruá or Bhuiyá Magh.	Hroimajusa.
	Kaukdaintsa.
	Keophasa.
	Kogdengsa.
	Kolasa.
	Krong Khyungtsa.
	Kwinjusa.
	Kyaukmatsa.
	Kyaukpiatsa.
	Mahlaingtsa.
	Marotsa.
	Orá.
	Palainggritsa.
	Palaingtsa.
	Palása.
	Phrangroatsa
	Rigretsa.
	Saboktsa.
	Taingchait.
	Uengsa.
	Wadsuesa.
	Waientsa.

Maheśri.

Sub-caste.	Sections.	
Dasá.	Sabu.	Millak.
	Mundra.	Sadra.
	Rauti.	Gatáni.
	Sowáni.	Tela.
	Málpáni.	Loyá.
	Lakhotia.	Tábria.
	Palaur.	Murkia.
	Janwár.	Kalláni.
	Kábra.	
	Baoti.	

Mahili, *Mahuh.*

Titles:—Mánjhi, Mahoto

Sub-castes.	Sections.
Bansphor-Mahili.	Chardhagia.
Mahili-Mundá.	Chardhiár.
Pátar-Mahili.	Charhar, a tree.
Sulunkhi-Mahili.	Dhilki.
Tánti-Mahili.	Dumriár or Dungri, wild fig.

Sub-castes.	Sections.
	Goondli, a kind of grain, forbidden.
	Hánsdá or Hasdagiár, wild goose.
	Hemron.
	Induar, a kind of eel.
	Kantuár or Kánti, ear.[1]
	Karkusá.
	Khangar.
	Khariár.
	Kathargách, jack fruit tree.
	Kerketa, a kind of bird.
	Kundiar.
	Mahukal, a bird; its long tail.
	Mandriár.
	Marri.[2]
	Murmuár, nilgáo.
	Patariar.
	Pilua, a caterpillar.
	Rondiar.
	Sarihin.
	Silli.
	Tapaer, a bird.
	Taw.
	Tirki, bull.
	Tunduar.
	Turu, grass, cotton, fruit or seed.
	Tutiear.
Sections of the Mahili-Mundá sub-caste.	Bhuktuár. Láng Chenre. Sángá.

[1] Members of the Kantuár section may not eat the ear of any animal.
[2] Members of the Marri section do not allow their married daughters to enter their houses.

Mál.

Titles:—Háldár, Khámid, Machhuá, Mánjhi.

Sub-castes.		Sections.
Dhaliá Gobrá Kherá Rájbansi Sánágánthá	In Bankura.	Fenga, a bird. Garur, adjutant. Ghátu, a bird. Kachhap, tortoise. Nág, snake.
Dhunakátá Rájbansi Sápuryá or Bediya-Mál. Tungá	In Midnapur and Manbhum.	Pátrishi, bird. Penkál-máchh, fish. Sál-máchh, fish.

Sub-castes.		Sections.
Khuturiá Mallik Rájbansi	In Birbhum.	
Deswár Magahiyá Rajbansi or Rájá-Mál. Rarhi-Mál Sindurá	In the Santál Parganás.	

Málé. *Samariá-Málé, Sauriá, Savar Paháriá, Sámil Paháriá, Asal Paháriá, Sangi.*

Máli, *Málákár, Phulmáli.*

Title :—Ráut (in Behar).

Sub-castes.		Sections.
(a) *In Bengal*—		(a) *In Bengal*—
Phulkátá-Máli	1. Rárhi. 2. Bárendra. 3. Athghariá.	Alamyán. Kásyapa. Maudgalya.
Dokáne-Máli.		Sándilya.
(b) *In Behar*—		(b) *In Behar*—
None.		Bhandári. Mallik.

Málo, *Málo-Pátni.*

Titles :—Bepári, Jáliyá, Jálo, Jalwá, Mánjhi, Pátra.

Sub-caste.	Sections.
None.	Alimán. Bánarási. Bángas-rási. Bharan-rási. Khonrá-rási. Kártik-rási. Kulin-rási. Mesh-rási. Padma-rási. Puyi-rási. Singh-rási. Sib-rási. Udadhi.

Mál Pahária.

Titles :—Mánjhi, Náik, Sardár.

Sub-tribes.	Septs.[1]
Kumár or Komar-Bhág.	Ahriti, hunters.
Mál Pahária proper.	Dehriti, priests.
	Grihi, householders.
	Mánjhi, village headman.
	Pátra.
	Pujhor, priests.
	Sikdár.

[1] The names of the septs are said to denote the original occupations of their members at the time when exogamy was introduced. The Male tribe, of which, according to Buchanan, the Mál Pahárias are an offshoot, have no exogamous divisions.

Mangar, *Magar*, *Thomi*.

Titles :—Ráná, Sing, Thápa.

Sub-tribes.	*Thars* or septs.	
Atháráh Panth.	Achámi.[1]	Ghatani.
Buráthoki.	Agri.	Ghatráj.
Gharti.	Aleh, Alliá.[1]	Gonda.
Sakhali.	Arghaunle (?).	Granjá.
	Bareya.	Gurmáchhan.
	Bhujál.	Gyángmi.
	Braili.	Haio.
	Brangplagi.[1]	Jhángdi.
	Byángnási.	Jhári (?).
	Charmi, Chermi (?).	Kairálá.
	Chitauriá (?).	Kalalohár.
	Chumi.	Keli.
	Darnal.	Khápangi.
	Darrá Lámi.	Khaptari.
	Datt.	Khati.
	Devapáti.	Khulál.
	Dhamala.	Krubchhági.[1]
	Dhanuki.	Kyágchhági.[1]
	Dukhcháki.	Lahakpá.
	Gácha.	Lakándri.
	Gadaili.	Lamgadeh.
	Gadál.	Lámichanya.
	Gajamer.	Lamjál.
	Gandharma (?).	Lha-yo.[1]
	Geláng.	Lohágun.
	Gháli.	Lungyeli.[1]

[1] These seven *thars* besides one not known, are called the Bára Mangar, and hold the title of Thápa

Sub-tribes.	*Thars* or septs.	
	Magrathi.[1]	Sadásankar.
	Marsyángdi.	Sarángi.
	Máski.	Sáru.
	Meng.	Setisurwál.
	Namjáli.	Sheo.
	Pacháin (?).	Sijapati (?).
	Pánthi.	Sincneuli.
	Parbateh.	Singauri.
	Phyuyáli.	Sinjali.
	Pithákoteh.[1]	Sithung.
	Pongwar.[1]	Sripáli.
	Pulámi.[1]	Sunári.
	Pun.	Surya Vansi.
	Pung.	Suyál.
	Pusál.	Tálu.
	Rahapál.	Tháda.
	Rakhál.	Thokcháki.
	Rasaili.	Toringrapá.
	Rijal.	Yángdi.
	Sabkota.	Yángmi.

[1] These four *thars*, besides one not known, are called the Bára Mangar, and hold the title of Thápa.

Már, *Málwe Rájput*.

Sub-caste.	Sections.
Nil.	Aind, eel.
	Gandharb.
	Kási.
	Parás.

Maulik, *Láyá, Náyá*.

Title :—Bhumphor, peculiar to the Mál sub-caste.

Sub-castes.	Sections.
Chandana.	Belawahari, tree-rat.
Hariyán or Jehariyá.	Boro Sámp, rock-snake.
Mál or Már.	Dudhiá, snake.
Sauriyá.	Rikhiásan or Pátrisi, described as a small red bird with a long tail.
Rájbansi } Call themselves Hindus.	
Deobansi }	

Mayará, *Modak*, *Mairá*, *Kuri*.

Titles:—Ásh, Chandra, Datta, Barát, De, Dán, Gul, Indi, Láhá, Nág, Nandi, Rakhit, Ráj.

Sub-castes.	Sections
In Central Bengal—	
Rárh-ásram.	Álamyán.
Mayur-ásram.	Bharadwája.
Ajá-ásram.	Chandrarishi.
Dharm-ásram or Dharm-Sut.	Debrishi.
	Madhurishi.
In Dacca—	Kasyapa.
	Gautam.
Ekpátiá.	Majurrishi.
Dopátiá.	Ganesrishi.
	Nágrishi.
	Sándilya.
	Somrishi.

Mech, *Mechi*.

Sub-tribes.	Septs of the Agniá sub-tribe.
(*a*) *In Darjiling*—	
Agniá-Mech.	Bamodá.
Játi-Mech.	Bosmáthá.
	Chhongphtháng.
(*b*) *In Assam*—	Chongphrán.
	Isáre.
Agniá-Mech.	Kuktáiáre.
Assam-Mech.	Mochháre.
Kachrá-Mech.	Narjenáre.
Thampái-Mech.	Nobáiáre.
	Phádám.
	Sabáiáre.
	Sibingáre.

Muchi, *Rishi, Rishiputra, Nishi.*

Titles:—Darshan, Muchiram Dás, Patradás, Ruidás, Sparshan.

Sub-castes.	Sections.[1]
Bará-bhágiyá { Uttar-rárhi. Dakhin-rárhi. }	Kásyapa. Sándilya.
Chhota-bhágiyá.	
Chásá-Kurur or Chásá-Kolai.	
Betuá.	
Jugi-Muchi or Korá.	
Baitál.	
Kurur.	
Málabhumiá.	
Sabarkárá.	
Sánki.	

[1] These are not exogamous, and no sub-caste appears to have more than one section, Kásyapa or Sándilya, as the case may be.

Munda, *Mura, Horo-hon.*

Titles:—Bhuinhar, Dhangar, Kol, Konkpat, Mahato, Manki, Nagbansi.

Sub-tribes.	Septs.
Bhuinhár-Munda.	Aind, a kind of eel.
Karangá-Munda.	Amba, mango.
Khangar-Munda.	Ambras, a fruit.
Khariá-Munda.	Area, a kind of fish.
Kol-Munda.	Aru, yam.
Konkpát-Munda.	Arul.
Mahali-Munda.	Ashár, a month—June.
Mánki-Munda.	Asur Lohara.
Munda-Mánjhi.	Aura, fruit.
Nágbansi-Munda.	Baba, rice.
Oraon-Munda.	Bage, anything forbidden.
Sad-Munda.	Bagear, tiger.
Savar-Munda.	Baghela, quail.
	Baghtuar, a devotee.
	Bahera, a fruit.
	Bahomar.
	Balamdár, spearman.
	Balmus, a kind of insect which is found in the sand of rivers.

Sub-tribes. Septs.

Balum, salt.
Baman, may not touch or be touched by a member of the Brahman caste.
Banda, a kind of leaf.
Bando, small jackal.
Bar, *Ficus Indica.*
Barabhaiá, the twelve brothers' sept.
Barha, hog.
Bari, flower.
Barjo, name of an ancestor's village some miles south of Ranchi.
Barjoki, fig tree root.
Barla, a fruit.
Barukandal, the kussum tree.
Barunda, a big frog.
Barupendil, kussum tree.
Barwa, small cocoon.
Basaroar, a kind of small hawk.
Batkuar, a bird.
Beng, frog.
Besra, small hawk.
Bhaji Ság, vegetable.
Bhaonra, a large black bee or hornet.
Bhengra, a horse.
Bhingraj, kingcrow.
Bhinjo, a yellow bird.
Bhuina.
Bhutkuar.
Bihan, seed.
Binha.
Binjuar, a kind of eel.
Bisrot.
Bisru, a kind of bird.
Bocho, a bird.
Bodra, the ancestors of this sept did not wash their mouths after eating.
Bojra, a kind of grass.
Budh or **Budhwar**, Wednesday.
Buim, a worm.
Bukru, a kind of bird.
Chadil, place of worship of a headman.
Chadu, a kind of bird.
Chali, rice soup.
Champia, a bird.
Chata, umbrella.
Chauria, rats.
Chelekchela, a small bird.
Chilhia, kite.
Chirko, mushroom.

Sub-tribes. Septs.

Chitti, a kind of snake.
Chocha, a bird.
Chota, a kind of bird.
Chutia, a small rat.
Dáng, a big stick.
Dahanga, torch-bearer.
Dangarwar.
Dauru.
Demta, red tree-ant.
Dhan, paddy. To this sept rice and rice soup are forbidden; they eat only *gondli* or millet.
Dhechua, a kind of black bird.
Dhelakata, a kind of tree.
Dirwar, a wood fruit.
Dobongwar.
Dodrai, a kind of bird.
Dub Sag, vegetable.
Dumríar, figs.
Dundu, a kind of eel.
Dungdung, a river-fish.
Dura, a fruit.
Ergat, a kind of mouse which lives in plum bushes.
Gandura, a big bird.
Garabing, a big river-snake.
Gari, a monkey.
Garria, a kind of bird.
Ghager, field bird.
Ghi, clarified butter.
Ghunri, a kind of fruit.
Gidh, a vulture.
Gobolachan, may not eat beef.
Gondli, a kind of grain.
Goria, red earth.
Gua, areca nut.
Gundki, a kind of wood.
Gundri, a bird.
Gurni, a kind of vegetable.
Guru, may not eat beef.
Habin, a tree.
Hadung, big black tree-ant.
Hajeri, a kind of tree or bush.
Haluman, monkey.
Han, nest of ants.
Hanjait, a wild fruit.
Hanre, a bird.
Hansa, swan.
Hanthi, elephant.
Hardwar.

Sub-tribes. Septs.

Hargurra, bone.
Hari, ancestors did not wash their mouths after eating.
Harin, deer.
Hasada.
Hasará.
Hassa ara, a kind of vegetable.
Hausakar.
Heding, a bird.
Hembowar, ancestor.
Hemram, a kind of fish.
Hemromi, ashes.
Heride, a bird.
Herung, a kind of bird.
Hoduar, a bird.
Homjah.
Hong, a kind of bird with a long tail.
Horia, a wood bush.
Horo, a red ant on tree.
Hularbaha, a flower used to flavour curry.
Hundar, wolf.
Huni, mouse.
Hutar.
Imli, tamarind.
Indur katea, house-rat.
Ingaria, moonlight.
Jagdar.
Jago, tamarind.
Jamtuti, a kind of grain or vegetable.
Jangatras, the bone of a cow.
Jatrama.
Jatria.
Jhuri, dried bushes.
Jia, a river-fish.
Jirhul, a flower, used for curry.
Jitiapipar, a kind of fruit.
Jonk Haper, leech.
Kachhuá, tortoise.
Kakin, aunt.
Kamal, lotus.
Kanda, a kind of sweet potato.
Kandir, a bird.
Kandru, fish.
Kandurua, a fruit.
Karania, a kusum tree.
Karma, a tree.
Katea, a field-mouse.
Kaua, crow.
Kawnria, a water-snake.

Sub-tribes.	Septs.
	Kera, plantain.
	Kerketa, a bird.
	Khandania.
	Khondua.
	Khoyea, a wild dog with a long tail.
	Khukri, a kind of mushroom.
	Kiri, rice weevil.
	Kissi.
	Koá, cocoon.
	Kodoság, a kind of water vegetable.
	Kongaddi, crow.
	Kotah kaisi, a small vulture.
	Kujri, a fruit from which oil is made.
	Kukur, dog.
	Kukura.
	Kundula.
	Kurkuti, red ant.
	Kursi, fruit.
	Kusumbaha, kusum flower.
	Lang, a kind of bird.
	Lápung, a small bird.
	Larapa, monkey-eater.
	Larsunar.
	Lenda, earthworm.
	Lilla, a wild cow.
	Lipo, a tree.
	Litiya, a bird.
	Logna Kotra, small deer.
	Logo, a kind of animal.
	Lohrakhukhri, a kind of mushroom.
	Longa, a bird with a long tail.
	Lugniar, rabbit.
	Lugum, a tree.
	Lugun, a tree.
	Lugunki.
	Lupu, paddy husks.
	Luti, small black fly.
	Machli, fish.
	Madhuras, honey.
	Mahukal, a bird.
	Maina, a bird.
	Mar, new rice soup.
	Marmu.
	Matha Ság, a kind of vegetable.
	Mathia, brass bracelet.
	Maugh, fish.
	Mind.
	Minjur, peacock.
	Mowl.
	Muduk.

Sub-tribes.	Septs.
	Mundoraj, a tree. **Mundri**, quail. **Munga Ság**, a kind of vegetable. **Munri**, fried rice. **Murum**, stag. **Muri**, a wild fowl. **Musa** or **Musu**, mouse. **Mutri**. **Nadi Samp**, a river-snake. **Nág**, cobra. **Nagduar**, a water-insect. **Nagrua**, a kind of mud. **Nimak**, salt. **Nois**. **Oaria**, verandah. **Orea**, basket-maker. **Pakhora**. **Pamia**, a tree. **Pándar**, a tree. **Panduchone**. **Panduki**, dove. **Pankhi**, a bird. **Panr**, a tribe. **Pardhiel kokaw**. **Parsi**, a tree. **Parsu**, a bush. **Peo**, a bird. **Peroan**, pigeon. **Phurti**. **Phuti**, a rainbow. **Pikord**, a bird. **Porti**, crocodile. **Pussi**, cat. **Putam**, dove. **Raja**, a bird. **Ramgharia**. **Rani Poka**, a red worm. **Raut**, the Rautia caste. **Rugri**, a kind of mushroom. **Rukhi**, squirrel. **Runda**, leopard. **Rutá**, a tree. **Sadom**, horse. **Sailum**, porcupine. **Saisarunduar**. **Sal**, a big pond-fish. **Salkar**, a kind of potato. **Salu**, a root in pond. **Samal** or **Samar**, deer. **Samdoar**.

Sub-tribes.	Septs.
	Sandi, plough.
	Sandiguria, black monkey.
	Sandil, full moon.
	Sandipurti, cock.
	Sandi Sarin, fowl.
	Sanga, sweet potato.
	Sang Chiria, a kind of bird.
	Sangoar, sweet potato.
	Sankura, kingcrow.
	Sanpuri, a resident of Sanpur.
	Sarai, a tree.
	Sarnar, a curry vegetable.
	Semarkanda, root.
	Sengra, horse.
	Seornlá.
	Serhar, a kind of bird.
	Setampa, dog-eater.
	Sewar, moss.
	Siar Tuyio, jackal.
	Sikcharo, a bird.
	Sikra, hawk.
	Sindur, vermilion.
	Singh, horn.
	Sisungi, a kind of fish.
	Soa, a kind of vegetable.
	Soai, a bird.
	Sobarnarekha, name of a river three miles east from Ranchi.
	Soeka, a wood bush.
	Sohek, a kind of fish.
	Soi, spring.
	Sokoe, a kind of fruit.
	Solai, fish.
	Sonarwa, a bird.
	Sone, may not wear gold.
	Sonkharihan, a place where they worship before cutting grain.
	Son Maghia.
	Soso bheloa, a fruit.
	Suga, parrot.
	Sukru, potato.
	Sulankhi, a kind of bird.
	Surhi, a wood-cow.
	Suri, fly.
	Suril, do not propitiate the Churin Deota.
	Surin.
	Susan.
	Taitum.
	Támbá, copper.

Sub-tribes.	Septs.
	Tamgarihar.
	Tamghuria.
	Tarwar, may not touch a sword.
	Tatia, a kind of bird.
	Telia, a tree.
	Tewan raja, a kind of bird.
	Thithio, a bird with long legs.
	Tirango, a wood-bird.
	Tirki, a bird.
	Tirkiar, tree-mice.
	Tiro, a small bird.
	Tirtia, a bird.
	Tiru, a kind of bird.
	Tiruhar, a kind of bird.
	Toeba, flower of *parás* tree.
	Toewa, a kind of bird.
	Tongsi, a bird.
	Tono, a big tree-ant.
	Topna, tree.
	Topoar, a bird.
	Tow, a kind of bird.
	Tulsiar, a kind of flower.
	Tumbli, a red flying-ant.
	Tunduar, a tree.
	Turania.
	Tursia.
	Turu, squirrel.
	Turuar, a fruit—kussum.
	Tuti, a kind of vegetable.
	Uchring, an insect.
	Udbarn, a tree, the oil of which is not used by members of the sept.
	Urdwar.
	Uring, a wild bird.

Murmi, *Tamang, Isháng, Sain.*

Sub-caste.	Sections.	
Nil.	**Báibá.**	**Gábag.**
	Baju.	**Galan.**
	Bal.	**Gánthen.**
	Baltong.	**Ghale.**
	Bomjan.	**Ghising.**
	Bulun.	**Gole.**
	Chapen Khor.	**Gomdan.**
	Chumi.	**Gongbá.**
	Dumjan.	**Gothar.**

Sub-caste.	Sections.	
	Grandan.	Neki.
	Hopthen.	Nesur.
	Jimbá.	Pakhrin.
	Jongan.	Rumbá.
	Khâni Khor.	Sángbá.
	Kitung.	Sángdan.
	Khungbá.	Sherbá Khor.
	Kulden.	Singar.
	Lámá Khor.	Singden.
	Lo.	Songden.
	Lopchan.	Thing.
	Mármunba.	Thokar.
	Mekchan.	Titung.
	Moktán.	Tubah.
	Nárbá.	

Musáhar, *Mushar, Bhuiyá.*

Titles :— Mánjhi, Sádá.

Sub-castes.		Sections.
Bahtawár.	Of the Chanrwar sub-caste.	Ghurmutná.
Chanrwár.	Of the Chiksauriá sub-caste.	Giári. Kanghattá. Kosilwár. Mahatwár. Patwári. Phulwár. Sonwahi.
Chiksauriá.	Of the Magahiyá sub-caste.	Bálakmuni. Daitiniá. Gohlaut. Pail. Rikh-mun, Rishi-muni. Tisbariá.
Dhár.	Of the Tirhutia sub-caste.	Bánsghát Pahadi-nagar. Dhanháriá. Sarpurkhá—Chakbariá. Kasmetá. Mártariá.
Kanáujiá.		
Maghaiyá or Deswar.		
Nathuá.		
Pachhmá.		
Surajiá.		
Tirhutiá.		

Sub-castes.	Sections.
	Baiyár.
	Balgachhiá.
	Batwar or Batwári.
	Bhachhuár.
	Bhakhiásin.
	Bhuiyár.
	Churihár.
	Dhangpatiá.
	Diár.
	Dodhuár or Dodwár.
	Gáuriá.
	Genduá.
	Gibhári.
	Kásyap.
	Khatdhár.
	Mehári yá.
	Mandwár.
	Sandhoá.
	Sondhuár.
	Suruar.
	Tikait Bhogtá.
	Ulauriá.
	Upwariyá.

Nágar.

Titles :—Biswás, Chaudhri, Langi, Mahárána, Panjiár, Panch-námá-Mandar, Ráut.

Sub-castes.	Section.
Jethaut.	Kásyapa.
Pulauns.	
Nágbansi.	
Káthautiá.	
Bhátnágar.	

Nagesar, *Nágasiá, Kisán.*

Title :—Ban-Ganjhu.

Sub-tribes.	Septs.
Sendara-Nagasia, use sindur at marriage.	Amba, mango.
Telia-Nagasia, use oil instead of sindur at marriages.	Barla, *Ficus Indica.*
	Dhanki.
	Induar, a kind of eel.
	Mahto, a kind of eel.
	Manjhi, a title.
	Nág, cobra.
	Sonwani, can't wear gold.
	Taitia.
	Tirki, a bull.

Naiyá.

Title :—Pujáhá.

Sub-caste.	Sections.
Nil.	Bhulá.
	Chilkhor.
	Dhankoi.
	Kulkhwár.
	Yahián.

Nápit, *Nái Nauá.*

Titles :—Bárik, Bhandári, Baidya,[1] Chandra-baidya,[1] Dás, Khyaurakár, Khán, Nara-Sundar, Nandi, Parámánik, Síl, Biswás, Mazumdár, Mandal, Sháhá, Sarkár, Shikdár, Járdár.

Sub-castes.	Sections.
Anarpuriá.[2]	Alamyán.
Bámanbane.	Gargrishi.
Bárendra.	Kásyapa.
Uttar-rárhi.	Madhukuliya.
Dakshin-rárhi.	Maudgalya.
Paschim-rárhi.	Sándilya.
Mahmudábáz.[2]	Sections of the Mahmudábáz sub-caste: Bhagabán.
Saptagrám.	Daibaki.
Sátghariá.	Jádab-Mádhab.
Phul-Nápit.	Kánái-Madan.
In Noakhali—	Mahámandá.
Bhuluá-Nápit.	Rám.
Sundipá-Nápit.	Rághab.
In the 24-Parganás—	Rájib.
Háldar-Parámánik.	Siva.
Kola-Parámánik.	
Hansadáhá-Parámánik.	
Mujganji-Parámánik.	
Khottá.[3]	

[1] These titles are borne only by Napits who practise medicine.

[2] A few cases have occurred of marriages between members of these groups, but the breach of rule had in each instance to be expiated by giving a feast to the community.

[3] A designation of up-country barbers who have settled in Bengal. Such persons practically form a separate sub-caste, as Bengali barbers will not intermarry with them, and they are regarded as impure by the barbers of Upper India and Behar by reason of their having taken up their residence in Bengal.

Nuniá, *Lunuá, Noniyán, Núngoliá.*

Titles:—Beldár, Cháimarár, Chaudhri, Jamadár, Mahátmá, Mahton, Mandar, Marár, Mihtar, Ráut.

Sub-castes.

1. Awadhiá or Ayodhiábási.
2. Bhojpuriá.
3. Kharáont.
4. Maghayá.
5. Orh.
6. Pachainyá or Chauhán.
7. Semarwár.

Sections.

(*a*) *Totemistic*—

Andhigot.
Jamgot.
Nág.
Pechgot.
Phulgot.

(*b*) *Eponymous*—

Bachgot.
Bághgot.
Káchhgot.
Kásyapa.

Oraon, *Kurunkh.*

Titles:—Dhangar, Kol, Parjá.

Sub-tribes.

Berga-Oraon.
Dhanka-Oraon.
Kharia-Oraon.
Khendro-Oraon.
Munda-Oraon.

Septs.

Amri, rice soup.
Bagh, tiger.
Bandh.
Bando, a wild cat which barks at night.
Bakula, paddy-bird.
Bar, *Ficus Indica.*
Barwa, a wild dog.
Basa, a tree.
Bekh, salt.
Beanh, a large fish with thorns on its back.
Bhakla.
Chigah, a jackal.
Chirra, a squirrel.
Chouria Musa, field-rat.
Dhan, rice soup forbidden.
Dhechua, kingcrow.
Dirra, a kind of eel.
Dom Khakha, a raven.
Ekka, tortoise.
Ergo, a rat.
Gari, monkey.
Garwe, a stork.
Gede, a duck.
Gidhi, a vulture.
Gislihi, a bird.
Godo, crocodile

Sub-tribes.	Septs.
	Golaia.
	Gondrari, a tree.
	Induar, a kind of eel.
	Kachua, tortoise.
	Kaith, curry vegetable.
	Kanda, sweet potato.
	Kaua, crow.
	Kendi, a tree.
	Kenu, a fish.
	Keond, a fruit.
	Kerketa, a bird which makes a noise like "ket ket."
	Khalkhoa, cannot eat fish caught by baling water out of a tank or pool.
	Kheksa, curry vegetable.
	Khes, cannot eat plants that grow in ponds.
	Khetta, a cobra.
	Khoepa, a wild dog.
	Kinda, a date palm.
	Kispotta, pig's entrails.
	Kosuár, a kind of fish.
	Kujur, a fruit used to stain the horns of cattle at the Sohrai festival.
	Kundri, curry vegetable.
	Kusuwa, a fish.
	Lakra, a hyena.
	Lila, a kind of fish.
	Linda, an eel.
	Loha, iron.
	Mahato, a title.
	Minji, a kind of eel.
	Munjniar, a wild creeper.
	Murga, cock.
	Nagbans, cobra.
	Orgonra, a hawk.
	Pusra, fruit of kusum tree.
	Putri, a tree.
	Rori, a fruit or tree.
	Runda, a fox.
	Sâl, fish.
	Sarno.
	Suar, hog.
	Tig Hanuman, monkey.
	Tirki, young mice.
	Tirkuar, fruit.
	Tirtia.
	Tiru, a kind of fish.
	Toppoar, a bird with a long tail, and body mottled black and white.

Oswál, *Uswál.*

Titles:—Chánd, Dás, Dosi, Láb, Singh.

Sub-castes.	Sections.
Oswál proper.	Baid.
Dasá.	Baidmota.
	Chajia.
	Chaudalia.
	Chopra.
	Churáliye.
	Dháriwár.
	Gelra.
	Golchiá.
	Hinga.
	Jambar.
	Málkas.
	Methi.
	Nakat.
	Nolka.
	Ranka.
	Saitiya.
	Set or Seth.
	Sil.
	Singhi.
	Soni.
	Srimal.
	Srisrimal.
	Suchait.

Pán, *Pánwa, Pánr, Pab, Pánika, Chik, Chik-Baráik, Baráik, Mahato, Ganda, Sawási, Tánti.*

Sub-castes.	Sections.
In Manbhum—	Aind, a kind of eel.
Baráik.	Babunhathia.
	Bagh } a tiger.
	Baghel } a tiger.
In Lohardagá and Sarguja—	Bagti.
Chik or Chik-Baráik.	Bail.
Sawási or Tánti.	Bajar.
Ganda.	Balbandhi.
	Baleswar or Balasore.
	Bando, small wild cat.
In Orissa—	Banjor.
Orh-Pán or Uriya-Pán.	Bar, *Ficus Indica.*
Buna-Pán.	Barabihá.
Betra-Pán or Ráj-Pán.	Bardi.
Patradiá.	Bariaro.

Sections.

Bel, a fruit.
Beniaro, frog.
Benkurá.
Besrá, a small hawk.
Bhaisa, buffalo.
Bhanjor.
Bhata, brinjal.
Birár, a cat.
Bordi.
Buru.
Cherabesari.
Cherchete, a shrub jungle.
Chik, a tribe.
Chownr, yak's tail.
Dandpati.
Dásabigha.
Dasbihá.
Daskaria, wild fowl.
Demta, a red tree-ant.
Dhondh, a water-snake.
Dhunkro.
Dond-Chatra.
Gajbaniá.
Ghogor.
Ghorábach.
Goal, cow.
Hekoria, tomato.
Hunjar.
Hurjor.
Jia.
Kachua, tortoise.
Kansi, a grass.
Karunjua, a big black bird.
Kaua, crow.
Kesarari.
Kesrá, *rahar dál.*
Khechinjiá.
Khutibaran.
Kirki.
Kukuria.
Kulhai.
Kulhasia.
Kunjakuli.
Kunjasiri.
Kurai.
Kusum, a fruit.
Kutunjiá.
Loha, iron.
Lowa.
Machiwar.

Sections.

Mahánadia, name of a river.
Mahatoar, a title.
Mahua, *bassia latifolia.*
Malua.
Marai, wood-louse.
Mayur, peacock.
Mechari.
Mongri.
Mudu.
Mul.
Murchulia.
Mus, Musa, rat.
Nág, cobra.
Padowar.
Panchbiha, Panchbhia.
Panchhiah.
Purti.
Rájbansia.
Rajhasia, swan.
Raotia, crab.
Renta.
Saonsia.
Saruan.
Saul, a fish.
Sikra, hawk.
Silli, a place.
Sindhikuria, bull's horn.
Sing, horn.
Singhi, fish.
Sinjhikaria.
Sonamati.
Sonkharia.
Sonkoko.
Totabari.
Urmakhori.
Urmakuli.

Parghá, *Parighá.*

Sub-castes.	Sections.	
1. Supá-Parghá.	Kumár.	Pátar.
2. Paliyár-Parghá.	Mánjhi.	Rái.
	Marar.	Raut.
	Marik.	Siyar.
	Ojhá.	

Parhaiya.

Titles :—Kheroar, Gánju, Manjhi.

Sub-tribe.

Nil.

Septs.

Bâg, tiger.
Gachai.
Gidh, vulture.
Fanigâ, grasshopper.
Kauá, crow.
Mainá, a bird.
Nâg, cobra.
Ophia.
Tetenga, bloodsucker.

Pási.

Title :—Mahato.

Sub-castes.

1. Byádhá.
2. Gaiduhá.
3. Kámáni.
4. Tirsuliá.

Turk (Mahomedan).

Section.

Kásyapa.

Pátni, *Pátuni, Patauni, Dom-Pátni.*

Titles :—Gangáputra, Ghát-Mánjhi, Mánjhi, Pradhán.

Sub-castes.

1. Ját-Pátni.
2. Ghát-Pátni, Balami or Ghátwál.
3. Dom-Pátni, Machhwá or Nagárchi.
4. Bánsphor.
5. Dágará.

Sections.

(*a*) *Territorial*—

Bhadraghát.
Jhiniá.
Kálágáchi.
Káliwálá.
Naskarpurá.
Parámánik.
Práchir.
Ráipur.
Saidábád.
Sáttá.
Tentuliá.

(*b*) *Eponymous*—

Alyamán.

Pator.

Title :—Mahto.

Sub-tribe.

Nil.

Septs.

Bhengraj, kingcrow.
Charak, a festival.
Kachua, tortoise.
Katun.
Kerwári, a tribe.

Sub-tribe.	Septs.
	Maitbukru, place where he buries his bones, being his ancestral birthplace.
	Nág, cobra.
	Samatti.
	Sandilai.
	Sarihin.
	Silli, place where he buries his bones, being his ancestral birthplace.
	Taw.

Pod, *Padmaráj, Chási.*

Titles:—Baidya, Biswás, Háldár, Kayál, Laskar, Mandal, Mistri, Páik, Pátra, Pundari Kákhya, Sapui, Sarkár.

Sub-castes.	Sections.
Bágande.	Alamyán.
Banglá.	Dhánesri.
Chási-Pod.	Kásyapa.
Khottá or Mauná.	Maudgalya or Madhu Kulya.
Uriyá.	

Rájput, *Kshatriya, Chhatri* or *Chhetri, Báhuja, Bhupál, Bhupati, Bhusur.*

Titles:—Bábu, Baraik, Barman, Khán, Malik, Mandal, Rái, Ráut, Sámant, Singh, Sipáhi, Thákur.

Sub-tribes.	Septs.	
In Behar—		
Suryabansi, Surajbansi.	Amaithiá.	Chaubariá.
	Baghail or Baghel.	Chaubhán.
	Baráhi.	Dandwár.
	Baraiá.	Gaharwár.
	Bargáir.	Gautam.
	Besáin.[1]	Harihobans.
	Bhadariá.	Jasatbár.
	Bharsuriá.	Kachhwáh.
	Birwá.	Kákan.
	Chandail.	Kanwar.

[1] Besáin, Chaubhán, and Mahraur cannot intermarry, being supposed to be descended from the same ancestor.

Sub-tribes.	Septs.	
	Karnwár.	Ranauni.
	Kháti.	Sángir.
	Kinwár.	Sarniá.
	Kulchuliá.	Sirnait.
	Kulhariá.	Sirniá.
	Kurminiá.	Sisodhiá.
	Maulwar.	Somwár.
	Nikumbh.	Sukalnaki.
	Nimundih.	Sukarbár.
	Pamár.	Surkhi.
	Parihar.	Surwár.
	Raghubansi.	Tarwár.
	Ráhtaur.	Tilautá.
	Raksáin.	Tongar.
	Ráná.	Ujain.
Chandrabansi,		Bais.
Sombansi.		Banaudhiá.
		Barnár.
		Budhbansi.
		Damarwár.
		Dangar.
		Eh-Ár.
		Gahlaut.
		Kailwár.
		Kapur.
		Kausik.
		Kusbansi.
		Mahraur.[1]
		Narauni.
		Nauthni or Lautni.
		Nisán.
		Oh-Ár.
		Sabarniá.
		Sakarwár.
		Sengar.
		Subansi.
		Sulankhi.
		Tekha.
		Tetiá.
Agnikul.		
Bhojpuriá.		
Jadubansi.		
In Chota Nagpur—		
Malwe or Már-Rájput.		Chaudhriá.
		Mahto.
		Máli.

[1] Besáin, Chaubhán, and Mahraur cannot intermarry, being supposed to be descended from the same ancestor.

Sub-tribes. | Septs.

In Bardwan Division—

Bálgori.
Baradai.
Mulki.

The following septs are common to all the sub-tribes of Rájputs in Behar:—

Ahir-Páik.
Ataiá.
Athral.
Báchhil.
Banámpur.
Banáphar.
Bardhiá.
Bardiá.
Barhwatiá.
Barnlá.
Basbariá.
Bashariá.
Beruár.
Bhadaniá.
Bhalesultán.
Bhandári.
Bharchuihá.
Bhatgáiná.
Bhora.
Bhuthá.
Bichila.
Bijhuniá.
Binriá.
Bisokiá.
Bundelá.
Chakwán.
Chalhuk.
Dhán.
Dhaul.
Dhekhá.
Dhor.
Dikshit.
Donwár.
Dorowár.
Durgbansi.
Gáigwár.
Gáin.
Gajkesar.
Gandhauriá.
Ganhwariá.
Gargbansi.
Garhwár.
Gaudhaniá.
Gauláni.
Gaura.
Gehuaná.
Hárá.
Huddá.
Jádan.
Jádawár.
Jadubansi.
Kachnariá.
Kakir.
Kálhans.
Kámar.
Kanakwár.
Kandwár.
Karangarhyá.
Karcholiá.
Karjhuliá.
Karmwár.
Karsá.
Khánná.
Kharbahiá.
Khát.
Khechar.
Korwár.
Kuchhainá.
Kuká.
Kukurbans.
Kundail.
Kusbhabáni.
Lahtaur.
Láhuliá.
Lákat.
Lohtamiá.
Lukum.
Madhwál.
Mahuár.
Mándiár.
Maralbai.
Marhwár.
Mariár.
Maunachh.
Maunas.
Mehrá.
Mehri.
Mendru.
Nágbansi.
Nimri.
Pachhaniá.
Pachtariá.
Pailwár.
Pálki.
Phetiá.
Pundul.
Purubansi.
Rachhuáni.
Raikwár.
Rájkuar.
Rajwár.
Rekhaur.
Raksel.
Rankwár.
Rorah.
Sankarwár.
Segul.
Sihogiá.
Silewár.
Sinduriá.
Singhinlá.
Sirmaur.
Sirnet.
Sisoniá.
Sombansi.
Sukulbans.
Surnair.
Taiá.
Támár.
Tannán.
Taunr.
Tendun.
Tiár.
Tilakchandi.
Ulit.

The Rájputs also use the Brahmanical *gotras* or sections, of which the following are generally found in the caste:—

Baiághrapad.	Kásyapa.	Parásara.
Bátsya.	Kausika.	Prasidha.
Bharadwája.	Nág.	Sándilya.

Ráju.

Title :—Sinha.

Sub-castes.	Sections.
Dáiná or Chauán.	*Nil.*
Bainá.	
Sár.	
Bághái or Bághál.	

Rajwár, *Rájbansi.*

Title :—Máhato.

Sub-castes.	Sections.
Angrok or Angwár.	Bhogtá.
Chapwár.	Chápá.
Sikhariá.	Chirra, squirrel.
Sukulkárá.	Dorihár-jogi.
Bar-Gohri } In Lohardagá.	Karhar, a fruit.
Majhal-Turiyá } In Lohardagá.	Kásyapa.
Berrá-Rajwár } In Lohardagá.	Katwár.
	Kharakwár.
	Lathaur.
	Loharátengi.
	Majhiya.
	Marrik.
	Matwárá.
	Nág, cobra.
	Rikhi.
	Sankwá.
	Singh.

Rautia, *Raut.*

Titles:—Baráik, Gaunjhu, Kotwár.

Sub-caste.

1. Bar-Gohri.
2. Chhot-Gohri.

Sections (*paris* or *got*).

(*a*) *Totemistic*—

Aind, the eel.
Karsul.
Káshib, tortoise.
Kási, a kind of grass (*Saccharum spontaneum ?*).
Kátoár or Garur, vulture.
Kharak, sword.
Khariá, blade of grass.
Koyá, the wild dog.
Manjar, cat.
Nág, snake.
Rukhi, squirrel.
Sanwani.
Tángi, an axe.

(*b*) *Eponymous*—

Básudeo.
Chandramani.
Jogi.
Kumár.
Mánjhi.
Sándilya.
Siva.

(*c*) *Territorial*—

Baghel.
Kanthwár.
Kharakwár.

(*d*) *Uncertain*—

Chatgohri.
Kabar.
Kherkoar.
Kum.
Kundil.
Lachh.
Láthaur.
Suran.

Sadgop, *Salgop, Chásá.*

Titles:—Bákundi, Biswás, Dás, Ghosh, Konr, Neogy, Pál, Sarkár, Sur.

Sub-castes.	Sections.
	(Of Paschim Kuliyá.)
Paschim Kuliyá.	Alamyán.
Purbba Kuliyá { Ghosh.	Kásyapa.
Purbba Kuliyá { Sarbesia.	Maudgalya.
	Sándilya.

HYPERGAMOUS DIVISIONS.

(*a*) *Of the Paschim Kuliyá sub-caste.*

Kulin (Bhálki, Kánkshe, Praharáj, Siur).
Somaj.
Pratihár (Baugram and Gográm).
Maulik.

(*b*) *Of the Purbba Kuliyá sub-caste in Midnapur.*

Kulin (Biswás, Neogi, Sur).
Maulik.

(*c*) *Of the Purbba Kuliyá sub-caste in Murshedabad.*

Konr-Gop, who take their wives from other Sadgops, but give their daughters only in their own group.

Sánkhári, *Sankhakár, Sankhabanik.*

Titles:—Bandhu, Bhadra, Chandra, Das, Datta, Dhar, Kar, Kundu, Nág, Nandi, Sen, Sur.

Sub-castes.	Sections.
Bara-Bhágiya or Bikrampur Sánkharí.	Alyamán.
Chota-Bhágiya or Sunargaon Sánkharí.	Brahmarishi.
	Gautama.
	Gárgya.
	Kásyapa.
	Madnukulya.
	Mobrishya.
	Parásara.
	Sándilya.

Santál, *Sáontár*, *Kharwár* or *Safá-Hor*.

Titles:—Buná, Mandal, Mánjhi, Pradhán, Sardar.

Sub-tribes:—Deswáli Santál, Kharwár or Safá-Hor.

Septs.	Sub-septs.
Báski	Nij.
	Sádá.
Bediyá (sheep?)	*Nil.*
Besrá, hawk	Bundra.
	Kahu, crow.
	Kárá, buffalo.
	Nij.
	Sádá.
	Sibala.
	Son.
	Sung.
Chonre	*Nil.*
Hansda, Hasdak, wild goose.	Barwár.
	Chilbindhá, eagle-slayer.
	Jihu, a bird.
	Kerwar.
	Mánjhi-Khil.
	Niáki-Khil.
	Nij.
	Roh-Lutur, ear-pierced.
	Sádá.
Hemrom, Hembaram, betel palm.	Dántela, so called from their breeding pigs with very large tusks for sacrificial purposes.
	Guá, areca nut.
	Jahur.
	Kumár.
	Laher.
	Náiká-Khil.
	Nij.
	Roh-Lutur, ear-pierced.
	Uh.
Kisku	Abar.
	Ah.
	Kachuá, tortoise.
	Lát, bake meat in a leaf-platter.
	Nág, cobra.
	Nij.
	Roh-Lutur.
	Sádá.
	Somal, deer.

Septs.	Sub-septs.
Márndi, grass	Buru-birit, of the hills. Kekra, crab. Laher. Mánjhi-Khil. Niaki-Khil. Nij. Roht, *pánjaun* tree. Sádá.
Murmu, nilgái ...	Bitál. Boar, fish. Chopeár. Gánr, fort. Hándi, earthen vessel. Muro. Nij. Sádá. Sangda. Sikiyá, a chain. Tikká.
Pauriá or Pauliá ...	*Nil.*
Saren, the constellation Pleiades.	Barchi, spearmen. Hát. Jogi. Lát. Mál. Mundu or Badar, a dense jungle. Nij. Sánkh, conch shell. Sidup or Siduk, a bundle of straw. Turku.
Tudu	Agariá, charcoal-burners. Chigi, Chiki, impale. Dántela, breed pigs with very large tusks for sacrificial purposes. Lát, bake meat in a leaf platter. Manjhi-Khil. Naiki-Khil. Nij. Roh-Lutur, ear-pierced. Sádá. Sung.

Septs.	Sub-septs.
Adeb.	
Aind, a kind of eel.	
Bansdeo.	

Sárák, *Sráwak*, *Srávaka*.

Sub-caste.	Sections.
Nil.	Adyeb.
	Ananta.
	Machli, fish.
	Sándilya.

Saraogi.

Sub-caste.	Sections.
Nil.	Kastuwál.
	Sogani.
	Kodar.
	Pátni.
	Bhainsá.
	Chaunrá.
	Soni.
	Gadiyá.
	Dósi.
	Bakliwál.
	Koteri.
	Pátodi.
	Pándrá.
	Sáh.
	Kálá.
	Barjátya.
	Bilálá.
	Tariyá.
	Pápriwál.
	Chariwál.
	Jánjhri.
	Pahária.

Sarnakar, *Sekrá, Sarna-Kámár.*

Titles :—

Sub-castes.	Sections.
Bráhmandesi.	Bharadwája.
Dakhin-Rárhi.	Kásyap.
Khatangi.	Sabanta-Rishi.
Uttar-Rárhi.	Sándilya.
	Sarishi.

Sabar, *Sabar, Saur, Sar, Sayar, Suir, Swiri.*

Sub-tribes.	Septs.
Bendkar.	(*a*) *Totemistic*—
Jharuá.	Kásibak, heron.
Palli.	Sálmáchh, fish.
Parirá.	(*b*) *Eponymous*—
	Gargarishi.
	Sándilya.

Sherpa-Bhotia of Nepal, *Kham, Sálákhá, Nag-Chhang Shaksang.*

Rui, Thar or Septs.

Chah-ba.
Dong-ba.
Jing-ba.
Minag-pá.
Nah-pá ..
- Bhinásá, S. *Binása*, destroyed; occupier of a deserted village.
- Goleg-pá, *Go*, a head, and *leg*, good; the peaceful.
- Manding, *Man*, medicine; a practiser of medicine.
- Pang-Karmo, *Pang*, pasture, and *Karmo*, white; a dweller on pasture table lands.
- Sálák-khá, a merchant carrying on trade.
- Tag-tog-pá, *Tag* or *brag*, a rock; a dweller on cliffs.
- Tsegkhim-pá, *Tseg*, a wall, and *Khim*, a house; a dweller in stone or walled house.

Non-pá.
Shyang-ba.
Sser-Gomba.
Sser-Lungchan.
Sserpa.
Sser-Phen-zangná.
Weh-ba.

Sonár, *Káin, Rangdháriá, Zargar.*

Titles :—Chaudhri, Poddár, Sáhu.

Sub-castes.

Ajodhyábási.
Ajodhyápuri.
Bais.
Bhojpuriá.
Gaur.
Kamarkalla.
Kanaujiá.
Máir.
Oriá.

Sections.

Ainiá.
Aminápur.
Anril.
Aswariá.
Báguán.
Barmáit.
Barni.
Bathuet.
Belhá.
Bhaunrájpuri.
Bhekh.
Bibarhiá.
Bihári.
Bilar.
Bilauriá.
Borhá.
Chalhaká.
Chauswár.
Chithá.
Chonrhá.
Dánrsuriá.
Dhakaichhá.
Dhaundriá.
Dubaithiá.
Dumrahar.
Fatehpuri.
Ganesiá.
Ganet.
Garahiá.
Gehani.
Ghiohaddá.
Hamdábádi.
Hanumán.
Hardiwál.
Jakhalpuriá.
Jamálpuri.
Janakpuri.
Josiám.
Karbhaiá.
Kastuár.
Kási.
Kásyab.
Katalpuri.
Kokarsá.
Kothádomar.
Lohatiá.
Machhilhá.
Machi.
Makundpuri.
Marich-bhuswal.
Marj-bhuswal.
Mirchwan.
Musamiá.
Noinjorá.
Pachpákar.
Parián.
Prohá-Kerautá.
Rájgrihi.
Rámpuri.
Rautar.
Saharwár.
Sakaddi.
Samundar-Khorá.
Silaichiá.
Simar.
Sisaundiá.
Sochari.
Soncheri.
Sonpuriá.
Sultánpuriá.
Tejaniá.
Telihá.

Subarnabanik, *Baniá, Banika, Sarnabanik, Sonárbaniá.*

Titles :—Ádhya, Barál, Barddhan, Chandra, Dán, Dás, Datta, De, Dhar, Láhá, Mallik, Mandal, Nandi, Náth, Pál, Poddár, Rái, Sen, Sil, Sinha.

Sub-castes.

Bangaja.
Dakhin-Rárhi.
Uttar-Rárhi.
Saptagrámi or Nadiyá.

Sections.

Aliman.
Bharadwája.
Brahma-Rishi.
Gautama.

Sub-castes.	Sections.
	Kásyapa.
	Madhukulya.
Hypergamous groups—	Maudgalya.
	Nágrishi.
Kulin.	Parásara.
Maulik.	Sábarna.
	Sándilya.
	Sureswari.
	Vyása.

Sudhá.

Titles:—Amáyat, Beherá, Dehuri.

Sub-castes.	Sections.
Bara-Sudhá.	*Nil.*
Sáno or Kabátkoniá Sudhá.	
Pailá-Sudhá.	
Butká-Sudhá.	

Sudra, *Ghulám-Káyasth.*

Titles:—Bhandári, Shikdár.

Sub-caste.	Sections.
None.	Alimmán.
	Maudgalya.
	Vasishtha.

Sukli.

Sub-castes.	Sections.
Barabháiyá.	Alyamán.
Báhattarghari.	Kásyapa.
Dasasal.	Sándilya.

Sunri, *Hunri, Suri, Sundi, Saundika, Shaha, Chalita-Sau.*

Titles:—*In Bengal*—Bhakta, Bhuiyá, Chaudhri, Dás, Deori, Duryodhan, Kirttan, Majumdár, Mandal, Nirbhaya, Poddár, Pradhán, Rái.

In Behar—Bhandári, Chaudhri, Lál, Mandar, Mánjhi, Modi, Mohásib, Saho.

Sub-castes.	Sections.
In Bankura—	
Mandárane.	
Singhazári.	Kásyapa.
Jaibele.	
Dholo.	

Sub-castes.		Sections.
In Bardwan and Murshedabad—		
Sau or Chalita-Sau	Bárendra.	
	Rárhi.	Aládasi.
Sundi ...	Bich, distillers.	Bámrási.
	Palásram.	Gágarish.
Chaturásrám or Chaturthan, vegetable-sellers.		Sándilya.
Barnakule.		
In Maldah—		
Mani.		
Shirashina.		Alamyán.
Jogidasi.		
Duarbandha.		
In Eastern Bengal—		
Rárhi.		
Banga.		
Banger Rárhi.		
Rárher Rárhi.		Aliman.
Bárendra ...	Phul.	Gautama.
	Kul.	Kásyapa.
	Aichá.	Maudgalya.
	Panchsamáj.	
	Mahendra Khyáni.	
	Maughá.	
Majlishi.		
In Tipperah—		
Rarhi, Panchasiá.		
Barendra ...	Athárachurá.	
	Chhaphuliá.	
In Noakhali—		
Rárhi ...	Mul.	
	Phul.	
Bárendra ...	Mul.	
	Phul.	
In Santál Parganás—		
Bich.		Gágrish.
Bárendra.		Andrish.
Chaturthán.		Madrish.
Paripál.		Sándilya.
Kulsunri.		
In Monghyr—		
Sagáhut.		
Biyáhut.		
Gaunjhu.		

Sub-castes.	Sections.
In Bhagalpur—	
Kulsunri.	Bharwe.
Ganjwar.	Bichhu.
Dhukankorá.	Biár.
Barpárá.	Chaudhri.
Sagáhut.	Dobar.
Biyáhut.	Gáin.
Bitwár.	Gárá.
Maghaiyá.	Garain.
Banglá.	Háthi.
Darchuá.	Kapri.
Purbiya.	Kárak.
Sikhoria.	Kásyapa.
	Khán.
	Khárgá.
	Mahäset.
	Mahton.
	Mandar.
	Marar.
	Mehran.
	Náik.
	Panjiára.
	Pardhán.
	Parihár.
	Purbe.
	Ráut.
	Sadá.
	Satrá.
	Of the Kulsunri sub-caste: Kámti. Mandar. Mánjhi. Mehtar. Sahu.
In Tirhut—	
Maghaiyá.	
Sagahut.	
Biyáhut.	
Darchuá.	
Kalwár.	
Sokiriá.	
Chaurthán.	
In Patna—	
Biyáhut.	
Sagáhut.	
Khajkaliá.	
Bishtwár.	
Bhangerá.	
In Manbhum—	
Biyáhut.	
Lakargarhá.	
Ariyár.	
Maghaiyá.	
Sikhariyá.	
Chaturthán.	
Sagáhut.	
Paripál.	
Holongwár.	
	Of the Paripál sub-caste: Kásyapa. Andrishi, a rope of untanned hide, with which the yoke is fastened to the plough. Kách, crab. Madrishi, honey-bee. Bandrisi, fish. Nágrishi, snake. Sándil or Sánrishi, a bull. The members of the section do not castrate their own cattle, but purchase bullocks and sell their own bulls.

Sunu-wár, *Sonwár.*

Thars or septs.

Bráhmilchá.
Chhápátichá.
Durbichá.
Jeshkuchá.
Jespuchá.
Jijicha.
Jirel.
Kátichá.
Khyongpotichá.
Kintichá.
Kyahbohchá.
Liokichá.
Párgáchá.
Rahpáchá.
Rujichá.
Shushichá.
Thholáchá.
Tholochá.
Thumuchá.
Wangdehchá.
Yaktachá.
Yeti.

Surahiyá, *Suraiyá, Sorahaiyá, Kulwat-Mallah.*

Titles:—Jal Chhatri, Marar.

Section.

Kásyapa.

Sutradhar, *Chhutár.*

Titles:—Datta, De, Kar, Mistri, Kundu, Pál.

Sub-castes.		Sections.
Akrur-Paramánanda	In Murshedabad.	Alamrishi.
Chaturan-Khán ...		Alamyán.
Mán-Gauránga ...		Kásyapa.
Gopál-Kárikar ...		Sándilya.
		Bánrishi.
		Kanakrishi.
		Madhukulya.
Ket-Chhutár ...	In the Santál Parganás.	
Paturá-Chhutár ...		
Nagare-Chhutár ...		
Bhar-Chhutar ...		

Sub-castes.	Sections.
Chhutár	In Noakhali.[1]
Sáitghariá	
Challisghariá	
Sri	
Srikrishna	
Sáini	
Dáturiá	
Báni	
Duman	
Ari	In Western Bengal.
Mandaráná	
Bardwániyá[2]	
Kharipárá	
Goalabhuiyá[2]	
Chhutár	In Dacca.
Churá-Kuti	
Káturiá	

[1] The Chhutár appear to be carpenters properly so called, while the other eight groups are endogamous subdivisions of the Churá-Kuti sub-caste found in Dacca.

[2] Of late years these two groups have begun to intermarry.

Támbuli, *Támuli, Támli.*

Titles :— Chaudhri, Chail, Datta, De, Khur, Pál, Pánti, Rakshit, Sen, Singh (*in Bengal*).
Bhakat, Khili-wálá, Nágbansi, Paiti (*in Behar*).

Sub-castes.	Sections.
(*a*) *In Bengal*—	(*c*) *In Bengal*—
Saptagrámi or Kusadáye.	Kásyapa.
Biyállisgrámi.	Parásara.
Chauddagrámi.	Sándilya.
Bardhamáni.	Vyása.
Ashtagrámi or Kataki.	
(*b*) *In Behar*—	(*d*) *In Behar*—
Magahiyá.	None.
Tirhutiá.	
Bhojpuriá.	
Kanaujiá.	
Kurram.	
Karan.	
Surya-dvija.	

Tánti, *Tantrabáya, Tantubáya, Tutwá.*

Titles :—*In Bengal*—Barásh, Basák, Bhádya-bau, Bit, Chand, Chhagri (goat), Dalál (broker), Dás, Datta, De, Gui, Hansi, Jáchandár (appraiser), Kar, Lu, Mandal, Mesha (sheep), Muhkim (supervisor), Nandi, Pál, Prámánik, Sádhu, Sardár, Sarkár, Sil.

In Behar—Dás, Mahto, Manjhi, Marar, Marik.

Sub-castes.	Sections.
In Bengal—	
Aswini or Asan-Tanti. { Bardwáná.	Agastya Rishi.
Barna-kul.	Aladáshi.
Madhyakul.	Alamyán.
Mándaroná.	Attri-rishi.
Uttarkul.	Bararási.
Balarámi.	Bátsya.
Banga.	Bharadwáj.
Bará-bhágiyá or Jhámpániyá.	Biswámitra.
	Brahmárishi.
Bárendra.	Garga-rishi.
Chhota-bhágiyá or Káyath-Tánti.	Gautam.
	Janaráshi.
Káture.	Kásyapa.
Korá.	Kulyá Rishi.
Kshir.	Madhukulya.
Madhukari.	Parásara.
Magi.	Sándilya.
Mariáli.	Sábarna.
Nir.	Vyása.
Páttar.	
Purandari.	
Purbbakul.	
Rárhi.	
Uddhabi.	
In Behar—	
Baiswara.	
Banaudhia.	Chamártali.
Chamár.	Hinduá.
Jaiswár.	Kasyab.
Kahár.	
Kanaujiá.	
Tirhutiá.	
Uttarhá.	
In Orissa—	
Mátibans-Tánti.	
Gálá-Tánti.	
Hansi-Tánti.	

Teli, *Tili, Chakr, Garai, Kalu, Rausan, Tailakár, Taili, Tailika, Tail-Pál.*

Titles:—*In Bengal*—Chaudhri, De, Dhabal, Kundu, Koleman, Mandal, Masanta, Nandi, Pál, Parámánik, Parihara, Sádkhán, Sháhá, Sit.

In Behar—Behara, Chaudhri, Dafádár, Gorai, Kapri, Náik, Poddár, Sáhu, Sháhá, Tálukdár.

Sub-castes.		Sections.
		Aliman.
		Chandrarishi.
		Káchim.
		Kalmi.
		Kásyap.
		Madhukulya.
In Bengal—		
Anwarpuri.		Maudgalya.
Bárendra.	Bikrampur.	Nág.
	Chandradwip.	Niskalanka.
	Gangabisayi.	Niyárishi.
	Subarnabisayi.	Sándilya.
	Tulatia.	
	In Pabna—	
	Barapatti.	Sindhurishi.
	Chhotapatti.	
	Dáspárá.	
	Govindpuriá.	
Bhunjá Teli.		
Dwádas.	Bárahazári.	
	Bardwaná.	
	Chháguliá.	
	Mándaraná.	
	Maureswari.	
	Singhazári.	
Ekádas.	Chinpuriá.	
	Haludboná.	
Fatehsing.	Manoharsháhi.	
	Swarupsing.	
Gáchhuá or Kalu.	Ghaná Teli.	
	Desle.	
	Másle.	
	Pishle.	
Kutabpuri.		
Maghad Khandi.		
Rárhi.		
Saptagrámi.		
Senbhumiá.		
Sikhariá or Sindurtopá.		

Sub-castes.		*Bán* or sections.
In Oriss		
Abhi[illegible]n.		
Ekádas.		
Gáudá.		
Haldiá.		
Kalu.		
Tulatia.		
In Behar—		*In Shahabad*—
Aráiyá.		Demahá.
Barhári á.		Dhobahá.
Biáhut.		Jhagaráhá.
Desi.		Rath-charh-bagh-marwá.
Hermaniá.		
Janakpuri.		
Jaunpuri.		
Kanaujiá.		
Khuskhelia.		
Lathaur.		
Maghaiyá.	Sahu.	
	Naik.	Boria.
		Hárpati, 'plough-owner.'
		Khargpur.
		Musipur.
		Telhari.
		Tulsi.
	Kapri.	Bhusiwar.
		Kapri.
		Pata-Ratnauli.
	Gáim.	
	Garain.	
	Indrabárá.	
	Maháseth.	
	Mihtar.	Lálgámia.
		Mihtar.
		Pata-Ratnauli.
		Teligamia.
	Malik.	
	Mandar.	
	Mahto.	
	Panjiár.	
	Sangwe.	
	Tharmait.	
Masnath.		
Sarwariá.		
Tirhutiá.		
Turkiá.		

Sub-castes.	Sections.
In Chota Nagpur—	*In Lohardagá—*
Dakhini.	Kárak.
Haldia.	Kásyapa.
Hiapela.	Pándiáin.
Kanaujia.	*In Singbhum—*
Maghaya.	Nágasya.
Mathuria.	Pakhichátá.
	Barharoa, a fruit.
	Kachuá, tortoise.
	Kansi, a kind of grass.
	Nág, cobra.
	Pandki, dove.

Hypergamous groups in Bengal—

Parámánik.
Koleman or Kalu.

Thárū.

Titles:—Barwáik, Khán, Mahto, Rái.

Sub-tribes.		Septs.
In Behar—	Of Thárus in general.	Chaudhri.
Rautár.		Dahait.
Gaurihár.		Dás.
Marichwár.		Gauro.
Khawásiyá, including—		Guro.
Bábhan-Khawásiyá.		Káji.
Donrehá-Khawásiyá.		Khatait.
Dhotiyá-Khawásiyá.		Khojwár.
Khatkalá.		Mahaut.
Bantar, including—		Mahto.
Dhelphorwá-Bantar.		Patwári.
Kath Katwá-Bantar.		Rái.
Bot.		Raut.
Batewár.		
In Nepal—	Of the Rautár sub-tribe.	Bánth.
Chitwaniá or Chitaunlá.		Bhánr.
Belwadhiya.		Chautariá.
Kochila.		Chitaunihá.[1]
Iswájitauni.		Dahait.

[1] They are notorious for charms and spells.

Sub-tribes.		Septs.
In Nepal—concluded.		
Nauá.		
Purbiyá.		
	Of the Rautár sub-tribe—*concluded.*	Dangwaria.
		Danrehá or Gaunhá.
		Donwár.
		Gaharbári.
		Gaharwár.
		Gauro.
		Kachhriyá.[1]
		Káji.[2]
		Kanphatá.
		Kathariá.
		Khon.
		Kochilá.
		Konhar.
		Lampochhá.
		Mahto.[2]
		Majhiaur.
		Mardaniá, barber.
		Nawalpuriá.[1]
		Ojhaiyá.
		Patwári.[2]
		Rai.
		Senthá.
		Sokhait.

[1] They are notorious for charms and spells.
[2] These groups are said to have recently become endogamous.

Tipperah, *Triprá, Mrung.*

Sub-tribes.	Septs.
Nil.	Afang.
	Aialong.
	Fadung.
	Gaibing.
	Garjang.
	Harbang.
	Husoi.
	Jumátya.
	Kákulu.
	Káli.
	Keoya.
	Mising.
	Mongbai.
	Naithung.
	Nowattia.
	Osui.
	Puran.
	Riáng.
	Tungbai.

Tiyar, *Tiar, Tior, Rájbansi, Muchhuá.*

Titles :—Chaudhri, Chharidár, Malláh, Manjhan, Marar, Mukhíar.

Sub-castes.	Sections.
Rájbansi or Tilak Dás.	Itbál or Itbár.
Surajbansi.	Kásyapa.
Nal Tiyar.	Jai Singh.

Found by Buchanan in Bhagalpur—

Bámanjagya.
Govariyá.

Hypergamous Divisions—

Pradhán.
Parámánik.
Gana.

Turi, *Tori.*

Sub-castes.

Turi or Kisán-Turi.
Or.
Dom.
Domrá.

Sections.

(*a*) *Totemistic*—

Bar, *Ficus Indica.*
Charhad, tiger.
Hansdá, wild goose.
Hastaddá, eel.
Induar, a kind of eel.
Jariár, lizard.
Kachhuá, tortoise.
Kerketa, a kind of bird.
Samp, snake.
Saur, fish.
Sumat, deer.
Suren, a kind of fish.
Tirki, mouse.
Toppo, bird.

(*b*) *Uncertain*—

Bagehár.
Charchágiya.
Mádalwar.
Mal.
Panchbhaia.
Surinwár.
Tamagandiyá.
Tirkuar.

Vaisya.

Titles :—Arya, Bhumisprik, Bhumijivi, Dwija, Panik, Banik, Byanaharta, Uravya, Uruja.

Sub-caste.	Sections.
Nil.	Aliman.
	Kasyapa.
	Kátyáyana.
	Madhukuliya.
	Sándilya.

Yákha.

Sub-tribes.		Septs.
Phágu.	Of the Phágu sub-tribe.	Manem-ma.
Lhorong.		Mangthog.
Yamphu.		Okrabo.
		Sing-yangma.
		Songyokpa.
		Thungong-hehta.
		Thupra.
		Yak-kyukpa.
		Yoksuma.

APPENDIX II.

PROCEEDINGS OF CONFERENCE ON ETHNOGRAPHY OF NORTHERN INDIA, HELD AT LAHORE ON THE 18TH TO 22ND MARCH 1885.

Present :

MR. D. C. J. IBBETSON,
Director of Public Instruction, Panjáb.

" J. C. NESFIELD,
Inspector of Schools, Oudh.

" H. H. RISLEY,
On Special Duty, Bengal.

THE members of the Conference met at Mr. Ibbetson's office. Mr. Risley explained that he had come to Lahore, with the permission of the Government of Bengal, to consult Messrs. Ibbetson and Nesfield in consequence of certain demi-official suggestions received from Mr. FitzPatrick, Secretary to the Government of India in the Home Department. He stated that the Government of Bengal had decided to make an exhaustive enquiry into the castes and occupation of the people of these provinces, based upon the statistics recorded in the census of 1881, and had placed him on special duty for two years for that purpose. He laid before the meeting (*i*) a draft note setting forth the objects to be aimed at in the enquiry and the means to be adopted to obtain those objects, consistently with giving the minimum of trouble to the regular administrative staff; (*ii*) a set of ethnographic questions framed so as to facilitate the collection of fresh data in a systematic form through the agency of district officers, and of such private individuals as might be willing to give assistance in the matter. He asked the other members to assist him with such criticism as their experience of ethnographic enquiries might suggest. Messrs. Ibbetson and Nesfield, while ready and willing to assist to the best of their ability in discussing the papers in question, felt unable, without due leisure for consideration, to commit themselves to any final opinion as to the form that would be best suited for adoption in their respective provinces, should it eventually be decided to set such an enquiry on foot in those provinces.

In the absence of precise official instructions as to their functions, it appeared to the officers present that all they could usefully do was to indicate, with as much completeness as the circumstances under which they were called together admitted of, the direction in which ethnographic enquiries of the kind under description might best be pursued by any Local Government which might think it desirable to undertake them. With this view the members of the Conference prepared a note on certain difficult points of ethnographic terminology, a series of general questions calculated to elicit the salient characteristics of the several castes, and a set of special questions dealing with caste customs in greater detail, to be used by those whom inclination might lead to pursue the subject further. These papers form annexures A, B and C to these proceedings. It would remain for the Local Governments and Administrations concerned to determine in what manner the suggestions contained in them should be utilized.

At the present stage of the proceedings, and while the data have still to be collected, the members of the Conference did not feel prepared to consider the form in which the final results should be arranged and recorded.

DENZIL C. J. IBBETSON.
JOHN C. NESFIELD.
H. H. RISLEY.

A.

Suggestions regarding some doubtful points of Ethnographic nomenclature.

MUCH confusion is often caused by the indeterminate use of the various terms applied to the divisions upon which society in India is based. It seems that some attempt to define more precisely the nature of the groups to which these terms should respectively be applied might usefully be made, and the following is set forth as a suggestion.

The group organization commonly follows one of two main types—(1) the caste, (2) the tribe. The former may be defined as the largest group based upon community of occupation; the latter as the largest group based upon real or fictitious community of descent, or upon common occupation of territory.

Within the caste we find the *sub-caste*, and within the *sub-caste* the *section*. The *sub-caste* may be defined as the smallest *endogamous* group, and the *section* as the largest exogamous group, within the caste. No lower unit than the *section* need be regarded. The limits of the caste and *sub-caste* will occasionally be identical, there being no smaller endogamous groups included under a common caste name based on occupation.

Within the tribe we find many subdivisions. The smallest endogamous group within the tribe may be called the *sub-tribe*, which, as before, will occasionally coincide with the tribe. The largest exogamous group within the tribe may be called the *sept*, and no lower unit than this need be considered. Divisions intermediate between the sub-tribe and *sept* may, where they exist, be termed clans and sub-clans.

Some cases will occur in which the two types will run into each other, the caste based upon occupation being made up of tribes or tribal fragments based upon community of descent. In these cases the terminology of each type will be followed so far as the organization stands upon the same basis as the type, and no further.

It might be explained that the Brahmanical *gotras* have, in many cases, been adopted by or imposed upon castes and tribes in addition to their proper caste or tribal divisions. In such cases the *gotras* are not what is wanted: what is wanted is the organic divisions and subdivisions of the caste and tribe, not unusually called *got* by the people themselves, as distinguished from *gotra* in the strict Brahmanical sense. Occasionally these organic divisions and the *gotras* are identical; but where the latter are distinct from, and have been superimposed upon, the former, the *gotras* run through the divisions, the same division often, though not always, including several *gotras*, while, on the other hand, the same *gotra* is found in several divisions. The Brahmanical *gotras* are chiefly used by the officiating priest at marriage and the ceremony of *sankalp*, and are often unknown to the people themselves without reference to their priests.

DENZIL C. J. IBBETSON.
JOHN C. NESFIELD.
H. H. RISLEY.

B.

ETHNOGRAPHIC QUESTIONS.

General Series.

1. Write in English and vernacular the name of the caste with synonyms, if any, noting if any of these are used only by outsiders.

2. Write in English and vernacular the names of the exogamous subdivisions of the caste, if such subdivisions exist.

N.B.—By the term exogamous subdivision is meant a group from within which its male members cannot take their wives.

3. Show the endogamous divisions of the caste, if such divisions exist. If these divisions consist of groups of the subdivisions mentioned in question 2, show the grouping. If they are distinguished by separate names, write the names in English and vernacular.

N.B.—By the term endogamous division is meant a group from outside of which its male members cannot take their wives.

4. State the limits within or beyond which marriage prohibited, *e.g.*, that a man must marry within the caste, but must not marry into his own or certain other subdivisions, or within certain degrees of relationship, or may not marry two sisters.

5. Name any prohibitions on inter-marriage based upon (*a*) social status, (*b*) geographical or local position, (*c*) differences of religious belief or practice, (*d*) differences or changes of occupation.

6. State the popular tradition, if any exists, as to the origin of the caste, naming the common ancestor, if any, the part of the country from which the caste is supposed to have come, and the approximate time of its emigration, as marked by the reign of any particular king, or the occurrence of any historical event, together with the number of generations supposed to have intervened.

7. Is the habit of the caste settled or wandering? Have they any recognized head-quarters in the province? If wandering, over what tract of country do they wander? Are their migrations periodical or irregular, and what are the shape and material of their dwellings?

8. Do they admit outsiders into the caste? If so, from what classes, by what forms, and under what conditions?

9. Is marriage infant or adult? If the latter, is sexual license before marriage recognized or tolerated?

10. Is (*a*) polygamy, (*b*) polyandry, permitted; if so, under what conditions and within what limits? In the case of polyandry, must all the husbands be brothers?

11. What form of marriage ceremony is in ordinary use? Name the forms and state the essential and binding portion of the ceremony.

12. Is the remarriage of widows permitted? If so, is the widow obliged or expected to marry her husband's elder or younger brother? If she does not marry a brother, within what limits may she marry? What form of marriage ceremony is used, and what is the essential and binding portion of it?

13. Under what circumstances is divorce permitted, and by what form is it effected? May wives who have been divorced marry again?

14. Do the members of the caste follow the Hindu or Mahomedan law of inheritance, or a tribal custom of their own?

15. To what religion and to what sect within the religion do the caste belong? If Hindus, do they by preference worship any special one of the regular Hindu deities, and are there any reasons for this preference?

16. Name any minor gods or patron saints specially worshipped by the caste. State what offerings are made, on what days of the week, and what class of people receive them? Is the worship of any of these gods or saints confined to women and children?

17. Do the caste employ Brahmans for religious and ceremonial purposes? If so, are these Brahmans received on terms of equality by other Brahmans? If they do not employ Brahmans, what class of people serve them as priests?

18. Do the caste burn, bury, or expose their dead? If buried, in what position? Where are the bodies or ashes finally disposed of?

19. Are any ceremonies performed for the propitiation of (*a*) ancestors in general, (*b*) childless ancestors, (*c*) men who have died

a violent death; and if so, of what nature and at what seasons? Is the ceremony of *sráddh* performed or not?

20. Is the caste, or any of its subdivisions, named after any animal, plant, weapon or implement? Do they show their reverence for any such object either by special worship, or by abstaining from killing, eating, cutting, burning, using, or naming it?

21. What do the caste believe to have been their original occupation or group of occupations? To what extent have they or any sections of them departed from it? Describe their present occupation.

22. If they are agriculturists, state what position they usually occupy in the agricultural system, *i.e.*, are they—

(1) Zamindars;
(2) Tenure-holders, specifying the kind of tenures they hold;
(3) Occupancy or non-occupancy raiyats, stating whether they have or claim any privileges in respect of rent;
(4) Nomadic cultivators, specifying the mode of cultivation they follow;
(5) Landless day-labourers, stating the manner in which they are paid?

23. If their occupation is that of—

(*a*) *Artizans*, what is their industry, and in what special material do they work, or abstain from working;
(*b*) *Hunters*, do they catch game or vermin;
(*c*) *Fishermen*, do they catch fish only or also crocodiles and tortoises?
(*d*) *Sweepers*, do they remove night-soil or not?

24. Name any implement or mode of working which is characteristic of the caste, and also note whether there is any form or detail of their main occupation by abstaining from which they believe themselves to be raised above others of the same craft?

25. Do they habitually prostitute their (1) unmarried, (2) married women?

26. Which of the following articles of food do the caste eat or abstain from eating:—flesh, wine, monkeys, beef, pork, the flesh of cloven-footed or uncloven footed animals, fowls, scaly or scaleless fish, crocodiles, snakes, lizards, jackals, rats, other vermin, the leavings of other people? Is there any special article of food their abstaining from which tends in their opinion to raise them above some other caste which does not abstain from it?

27. Name the lowest well-known caste with which the caste will—

(*a*) Eat pakki.	(*c*) Drink.
(*b*) Eat kachhi.	(*d*) Smoke.

Name the highest well-known caste which will eat, etc. (as above), with the caste.

Sources of information.—Here should be noted the names, residence (village and thana), profession, caste, sub-caste, and section of the persons who answered the question. If any of them are *ghataks*, genealogists, heads of caste *panchayat*, or occupy any hereditary official position in relation to the caste, the fact should be stated. If the answers to the questions have been derived from any source other than personal enquiry addressed to members of the caste concerned, the source should be stated, and such references given as may enable the officer in charge of the enquiry to test the correctness of the answers.

DENZIL C. J. IBBETSON.
JOHN C. NESFIELD.
H. H. RISLEY.

C.

ETHNOGRAPHIC QUESTIONS.

Special Series.

INTRODUCTORY REMARKS.

The following questions have been drawn up in order to suggest lines of enquiry likely to prove interesting. They do not claim to be exhaustive, nor is it necessary that all of them should be answered. Some, for instance, will apply only to Mahomedans, others only to Hindus, and others again only to aboriginal[1] tribes. In making use of them various forms of bias on the part of the person questioned will have to be guarded against, such as—

(a) The wish to exalt his own caste or subdivision of his caste at the expense of other castes.

(b) The tendency to give ideal or book explanations of facts.

Care must also be taken not to tire the persons questioned by asking too many questions at a time and to check their statements occasionally by asking for actual instances of any specially remarkable custom. Questions should be put in as concrete a form as possible, in order to avoid the danger of people assenting out of laziness in order to save the labour of thinking.

It will be found in the case of many—perhaps of most—castes that there is a primary division into what may be called sub-castes, each of which is again divided into sections. Where several of these sub-castes are present side by side in the locality, their names will probably be given. But where all the local representatives of the caste belong to the same sub-caste, there is a danger of the sub-caste name being taken for granted and only the sections being named. Both groupings are required, the sub-castes being, if anything, the more important of the two.

I.—Constitution.

1. *Origin and internal organization.*—Write in English and vernacular the name of the caste, with synonyms, if any, giving its derivation if known.

2. If the caste has more names than one, explain their meaning and state which are used by the members of the caste, and which by other people.

3. Are any distinctions between the synonyms based upon the occupations of those to whom they are respectively applied, their place of origin, habitat, religion, or the like?

4. Is there any name used only by members of the caste?

5. State in detail any tradition that may exist as to the origin or foundation of the caste, the place from which they came, and their subsequent migrations.

6. Do they believe themselves indigenous in the district or to have come from elsewhere?

7. If from elsewhere, note any king's reign or historical occurrence contemporary with their migration, and how many generations are believed or ascertained from genealogical lists to have intervened.

8. Is there any place which they consider their head-quarters in Bengal?

9. Note particularly the name of the place from which they or their ancestors are believed to have come direct to their present locality.

10. Are any pilgrimages undertaken by the caste to places which purport to be their original habitat or serve to suggest its locality?

11. Is there any place in which the members of the caste are or should be buried?

12. Do they draw their priests, barbers, or genealogists from that place?

13. Do they trace their descent from a first ancestor or chief, and does he appear to have actually existed or to have been an eponymic personage invented to account for the existence of the tribe?

14. If any genealogical tree exists, trace the descent of the founders of the existing subdivisions from the common ancestor. Is there a shrine to him in the village or neighbourhood, and is it built on a brick or stone brought from elsewhere? If so, from where?

15. Do they consider any other castes to have branched off from them, or that they and others have come from the same national source?

16. Have they any tradition regarding changes of religion, introduction of new ceremonies, etc.?

17. Are there any local legends connecting them with any monuments, such as old tombs, mounds, forts, sites of villages, etc., in the district?

18. Is any light thrown upon the former movements of the tribe by the names of villages or by the existence of monumental stones? For instance, the Mundas of the Chota Nagpur plateau can be traced to places far distant from their present settlements by these

places bearing Mundari names and containing Mundari grave-stones, which are now worshipped by low-caste Hindus.

19. Write in English and vernacular the names of the exogamous subdivisions of the caste, if such subdivisions exist.

N.B.—By the term exogamous subdivision is meant a group from within which its male members cannot take their wives.

20. Write in English and vernacular the names of the endogamous divisions of the caste, if such divisions exist. If these divisions consist of groups of the subdivisions mentioned in question 19, show the grouping.

N.B.—By the term endogamous subdivision is meant a group from outside of which its male members cannot take their wives.

21. In the caste of both classes of divisions and sections explain the meaning of each name, and if the name denotes animals or edible substances, state whether the members of the subdivision bearing that name are prohibited from naming, eating, killing, cutting, burning or otherwise using the animal or substance denoted?

22. Cases may also occur in which the name of the subdivision is the name of an instrument which its members are prohibited from using; or conversely, where the caste is one of occupation, of a particular instrument or mode of working to which the members of the subdivision are hereditarily addicted.

23. Are particular subdivisions bound to observe or refrain from particular actions, such as the eating or burning of certain plants, the worshipping of certain trees, etc.?

24. Do the names of the subdivisions correspond with those of the subdivisions of any other caste, and if so, how is the correspondence explained?

25. Have, for instance, the members of the lower caste done service to the higher caste and adopted their subdivisions?

26. If so, is there any trace of their having had different subdivisions of their own, and are there any reasons for supposing that these were aboriginal and were abandoned in favour of a Brahmanical classification?

27. Have they any representative assembly or governing body?

28. What is it called?

29. How is it constituted?

30. What are its functions?

31. Who presides at its meetings?

32. How are its orders enforced?

33. Is there a permanent president?

34. If so, by what title is he called, and is the office hereditary?

35. If the hereditary president happens to be a minor, by whom are his duties carried on?

36. In the case of the trading and artisan castes the functions of the *panchayat* of the caste are of special interest and should be carefully ascertained, most of all where the occupation is followed by members of distinct castes united in a sort of trades guild, in which case the connexions and cases of conflict between the *panchayats* of the caste and guild should be investigated

37. *Rules of Intermarriage.*—State the limits within or beyond which marriage is prohibited, *e.g.*, that a man must marry within the caste, but must not marry into his own or certain other subdivisions or within certain degrees of relationship, or may not marry two sisters.

38. Give the formula (if any) defining the prohibited degrees of relationship.

39. Name any prohibitions on intermarriage based upon (*a*) social status, (*b*) geographical or local position, (c) differences of religious belief or practice, (*d*) differences or changes of occupation.

40. How far are differences of religion or sect a bar to marriage?

41. Can persons of different castes intermarry?

42. If so, of what castes, and by what form of marriage?

43. Note cases in which wives will be received from another subdivision or caste, but daughters will not be given in marriage to members of that subdivision.

44. Is the distinction referred to in the last question based mainly on social status or on what?

45. Is there any formal ceremony of admitting the bride into the husband's house, village or family by payment, after a mimic struggle, by eating together, or otherwise?

46. How many wives are allowed?

47. If more than one, is there any head wife, and what are her privileges?

48. Do the wives live together, or do they have separate dwellings?

49. Is concubinage permitted?

50. Is polyandry permitted?

51. If so, how are the husbands selected?

52. Must they all be brothers?

53. Are the women allowed much freedom before marriage?

54. Are they prostituted before marriage, or are some prostituted and others reserved for marriage?

55. In the case of a girl who has been prostituted, is any payment made to the parents or the community, or is any special feast given by the bridegroom?

56. At what age may marriage take place?

57. Is an infant marriage voidable, if not actually consummated?

58. Who arranges the marriage?

59. Are there professional marriage-brokers?

60. Whose consent is necessary to the validity of marriage (1) if both parties are minors, (2) if both are of full age?

61. Is there any freedom of choice on the part of the persons marrying?

62. Is any price paid (*a*) by the bridegroom's family for the bride, (*b*) by the bride's family for the bridegroom?

63. How is such price determined?

64. Does it or any part of it become the special property of either bride or bridegroom, and does it devolve by any particular rule of succession?

65. What physical defects will be sufficient ground for the annulment of a marriage which has actually taken place?

66. State whether idiocy or lunacy, impotence or mutilation are such sufficient grounds.

67. Is any distinction made if the party seeking annulment knew of the defect at the time of the marriage, or if the defect has arisen after the marriage was consummated?

68. Under what circumstances is divorce permitted?

69. What form of divorce is in use?

70. May wives who have been divorced marry again?

71. How are the offspring of (1) first marriages, (2) marriages of widows or divorced persons, (3) illicit connexions between parents of different tribes, castes, or religions now classed?

72. Do all inherit on the same terms, or are any excluded?

73. Do they follow the tribe and caste of the father or of the mother, or are they known by an entirely new name?

74. Is there any distinction between them and others born into the tribe or caste in a more usual or legitimate manner?

75. Are there any cases in which members of one subdivision cannot marry into another subdivision as being of common origin with themselves?

76. Do illicit connexions ever entail a change of caste on either of the parents?

77. Are there any caste or subdivisions of castes the origin of which is ascribed to connexions between members of two different castes?

78. Give particulars, and state the evidence on which the tradition is based.

79. Is it admitted by the members of the caste or subdivision in question?

80. May widows remarry?

81. If so, by what form of marriage ceremony?

82. Must the widow of an elder brother marry the younger brother, and may the widow of a younger brother marry an elder brother?

83. May the widow marry outside her husband's family?

84. If so, has her husband's brother a right to the custody of her children, and does the same rule apply to both male and female children?

85. If she marries an outsider, what rights in her husband's property accrue to—

(1) The widow,
(2) Her children by her first husband,
(3) Her husband's brother?

86. If she marries a brother, what rule of succession applies to her husband's property, *e.g.*, what right in it accrues to—

(1) The widow,
(2) The brother whom she marries,
(3) Her children by her first husband,
(4) Her children by her second husband?

87. Are children begotten of the widow by the brother of the deceased considered to be the children of her first or of her second husband?

N.B.—In illustration of the last eight questions, it may be noted that among the Jeswar Kurmis the widow of an elder brother usually marries a younger brother by the *sagai* form, but may marry an outsider. If she marries the younger brother, she gets half of her deceased husband's property. If she marries an outsider, she forfeits all claim not only to her husband's property, but to the custody of her children, except in the case of daughters, who stay with her till of a marriageable age, when she is bound to bring them back to be married from her husband's brother's house. The widow of a younger brother cannot marry an elder brother.

88. *Adoption.*—Is it necessary that the adopter should be destitute of a son, a son's son, and a son's grandson?

89. Must he obtain the consent of his heirs?

90. Is a daughter's son a bar to the right of adoption?

91. May a man adopt who has male issue, if such issue be disqualified by any legal impediment (such as loss of caste) from performing the exequial rites?

92. Can a man who had already adopted a son adopt another during the lifetime of the first?

93. Can the following persons adopt—

(1) A bachelor,
(2) A man blind, impotent, or lame,
(3) A widower,
(4) An ascetic who has renounced the world?

94. Can a woman adopt?

95. State whether it is necessary to the validity of an adoption by a widow that she should adopt with the permission, written or verbal, of her deceased husband, or with the consent of his kindred.

96. Can a widow adopt a son *as her own* without thereby making him a member of her late husband's family?

97. Can she adopt a son as her own in addition to a son adopted as the representative of her deceased husband?

98. In the event of the death of a son adopted by a widow with the sanction of her husband, may the widow adopt another person without permission of her husband to that effect?

99. May a man give in adoption—

(1) His only son,
(2) His eldest son,
(3) His brother?

100. Must the person adopted be less than any specific age?

101. If so, up to what age may a person be adopted?

102. In the case of the higher castes, can a person be adopted after tonsure or investiture with the sacred cord in his own family?

103. Can girls be adopted?

104. Is there any rule by which it is required that the person adopted should be related to the person adopting?

105. If so, what relatives may be adopted?

106. Is any preference required to be shown to particular relatives?

107. If so, enumerate them in order of preference.

108. Is it necessary that the adopted son and his adoptive father should be (1) of the same caste of tribe, (2) of the same *got*?

109. Is there any rule prohibiting the adoption of the son of a woman whom the adopter could not have married, such as his sister's son or his daughter's son?

110. Does an adopted son retain his right to inherit from his natural father?

111. Can he inherit from his natural father if the natural father die without other sons?

112. Describe the rights of an adopted son to inherit from his adoptive father.

113. What is the effect of the subsequent birth of natural legitimate sons to the adoptive father?

114. Will the adopted son take equal shares with them?

115. When a son-in-law leaving his own family takes up his residence permanently with his father-in-law as *ghar jamai*, what will be the effect on the rights of such son-in-law to inherit (1) from his father, (2) from his father-in-law.

116. *Succession.*—If a man die leaving a widow or widows, a son or sons, a daughter or daughters, brothers, and other relatives, upon whom will the inheritance devolve?

117. If there be more sons than one, will they take equal shares?

118. If the sons do not take equal shares, state upon what principle the shares are regulated.

(1) Is any regard had to uterine descent? Are the shares in the inheritance distributed according to the number of mothers?

(2) Is any regard had to the caste or tribe of the mothers, so that the sons by a wife of a high caste, or of the same caste, or tribe with the father take larger shares than the sons by the wife of a low caste, or of a different caste or tribe?

(3) Is any regard had to the age of the sons, so that (1) the eldest son, (2) the youngest son, would take a greater or less share than his brethren?

119. Can a father in his lifetime nominate a particular son as the fit person to take a larger share than his brethren after the father's decease?

120. When an estate has been held jointly by a father and his sons, and is distributed amongst them upon his decease, are acquisitions made by the sons exempt from distribution; or will all the sons share in all the joint estate, moveable or immoveable,

ancestral or acquired, whether or no any part of such estate have been acquired by any one or more of the sons, by gift or succession from a maternal grandfather or father-in-law, or other relative through a female?

121. Where there are male descendants who do not all stand in the same degree of kindred to the deceased, and the persons through whom the more remote are descended from him are dead, will the nearer descendants exclude the more remote, or are the more remote descendants entitled to succeed simultaneously with the nearer descendants?

122. If in the case stated in question 121 the more remote descendants succeed simultaneously with the nearer descendants, how is the estate to be divided?

Is it to be divided in equal shares amongst all the heirs; or is it to be divided into such a number of equal shares as may correspond with the number of the male lineal descendants of the deceased, who either stood in the nearest degree of kindred to him at his decease, or, having been of the like degree of kindred to him, died before him, leaving male lineal descendants who survived him?

123. Where there is no son, but where the male lineal descendants are all grandsons or all great-grandsons, will the estate be divided equally amongst all such grandsons or great-grandsons, as the case may be, or will the shares be allotted to the grandsons proportionately to the shares which the sons would have taken had they been living, or to the great-grandsons proportionately to the shares which the grandsons would have taken had they survived the deceased?

124. Do the principles stated in the replies to questions 121 and 122 apply to every case of the distribution of an inheritance; or is there any distinction when collaterals inherit; that is to say, does a son or grandson always take the share his father or grandfather would have taken, if such father or grandfather had survived the deceased, whether or no the share descend lineally or through a collateral relative?

125. Does the inheritance successively devolve upon all male lineal descendants, how low so ever; or is there any degree fixed in the descending line within which, if there be no male lineal descendants, the inheritance will devolve on other relatives. If so, state what that degree is?

126. If a man die leaving a widow or widows, and either a daughter or daughters, or brother or their descendants, or uncles or their descendants, or great-uncles or their descendants, but no male lineal descendants, within three generations, upon whom will the inheritance devolve?

127. If the estate devolve upon the widow, define her interest therein?

128. What rights has the widow to alienate by sale, gift, mortgage, or bequest?

(1) Are there any special circumstances or expenses under, or on account of, which alienation is permissible? If so, what are these?

(2) Is there any distinction in respect of moveable or immoveable, ancestral or acquired property, or in respect of alienation to the kindred of the deceased husband?

(3) Supposing alienation to be permissible, whose consent is necessary to make it valid?

129. As regards the right of a Mahomedan widow to alienate, is any distinction taken in respect of her legal share?

130. If there be several widows, do they take in equal shares?

131. Is any distinction made in respect of the rights of widows who are not of the same family with their deceased husband?

132. Is there any distinction in the rights of widows based upon the circumstance whether the husband was or was not associated with his brethren?

133. What is the effect of unchastity upon the right of a widow in respect of the estate of her deceased husband?

134. In the case of widows who are not Hindus, what is the effect of their remarriage?

135. Under what circumstances are daughters entitled to inherit? Are they excluded by the sons or by the widow, or by the near male kindred of the deceased? If they are excluded by the near male kindred, is there any fixed limit of relationship within which such near kindred must stand towards the deceased in order to exclude his daughters? If so, how is the limit ascertained? If it depends on descent from a common ancestor, state within how many generations relatively to the deceased such common ancestor must come.

136 Is there any distinction as to the rights of daughters to inherit (1) the immoveable or ancestral, (2) the moveable or acquired, property of their father?

137. (1) Under what circumstances are daughters entitled to be maintained out of the estate of their deceased father?

(2) What is the effect of (*a*) marriage, (*b*) residence in a strange village, upon the right of the daughter to inherit, or to be maintained?

(3) If a married daughter with her husband live with the father up to his decease, can the daughter inherit?

(4) Can daughters who are married and barren, or widowed, and without male issue, or mothers of daughters only, inherit the father's estate?

138. What is the nature of the interest taken by a daughter in the property she inherits? Define her rights of alienation, if any, by sale, gift, mortgage, or bequest.

139. After daughters, do daughters' sons succeed? If so, is the property equally divided amongst all the sons of several daughters, or are the shares proportioned to the number of daughters who leave sons?

140. When a man dies leaving no male lineal descendants, no widow, and no daughters or daughters' sons, upon whom will the inheritance successively devolve?

141. When the estate devolves upon the mother of the deceased, what is the nature of the interest she acquires?

142. Define her powers of alienation.

143. On the death of the mother, will the property devolve on the heirs of the son, or on her heirs?

144. When the property devolves on brethren, what, if any, regard is paid (1) to uterine descent, (2) to association? Do uterine associated brethren exclude all others? In what order succeed—

(*i*) Unassociated brethren of the whole blood?
(*ii*) Associated brethren of the half-blood?
(*iii*) Unassociated brethren of half-blood?

If a man die leaving a uterine brother separated and a half-brother associated, how will these two inherit?

145. When a man dies leaving associated brethren and unassociated brethren, and the property devolves on his brethren, have the associated brethren any preferential claim to acquired property, moveable or immoveable property, or to ancestral moveable property?

146. In default of brethren, does the property devolve upon their sons?

147. Does the property ever devolve upon sisters, or upon sisters' sons. If upon sisters' sons, how are their shares computed?

148. Where a wife dies holding property in her own right, is the husband entitled to succeed to such property, or any part of it?

149. Can the son by a former marriage of a woman who contracts a second marriage inherit from (1) his natural father, (2) his stepfather? If from his stepfather, is her share equal to, or less than that of, his stepfather's own sons?

150. Is any distinction taken as regards the stepson (*i*) if he be not born till after the second marriage of his mother, (*ii*) if the stepfather in his lifetime assign him a share by deed?

151. Are stepsons entitled to be maintained by their stepfather? If so, till what age?

152. Enumerate in the order of their succession the persons entitled to the estate of a man who dies intestate leaving no relations.

153. If a person voluntarily retires from the world and becomes a member of a religious order, what is the effect upon (*i*) his right to retain his property, (*ii*) his right to acquire property by inheritance? Upon whom will devolve property which he would have inherited if he had not retired from the world?

154. State any rules recognized by the caste governing the succession to—

(*a*) Zamindaries.
(*b*) Service tenures.
(*c*) Headships of villages.

155. In the case of tribes practising polyandry, state carefully the rules of inheritance, *e.g.*, does a man's property devolve upon his brother, his sister, or his sister's son?

156. *System of Relationships.*—Are any persons considered to be relations besides those who are descended from a common ancestor?

157. Are all or any of the kindred of the wife considered to be the relations of—

(1) the husband,
(2) the husband's relatives or children?

158. If so, state the persons who are relatives, with the names of the relationships.

159. How are generations reckoned?

160. Give a table of kindred with the local names of the generations up to the third degree in both the ascending and descending line.

161. By how many generations are the following persons said to be related to the person whose relatives are to be reckoned?

(1) Brother.
(2) Father.
(3) Uncle.
(4) Cousin-german, *i.e.*, uncle's son.
(5) Brother's grandson.
(6) Great-grandson.
(7) Great-grandfather.

162. Fill in the following tables with the local names of the relations.

A.—Relations, through the Father, whether of man or woman.

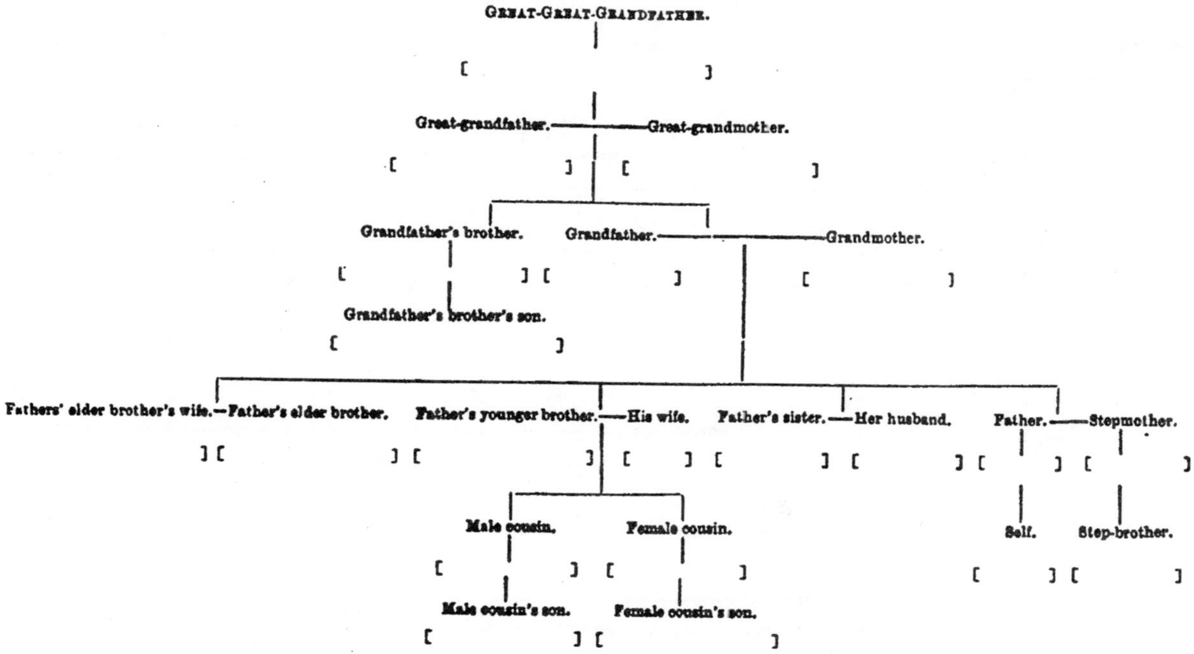

B.—Relations, through the Mother, whether of man or woman.

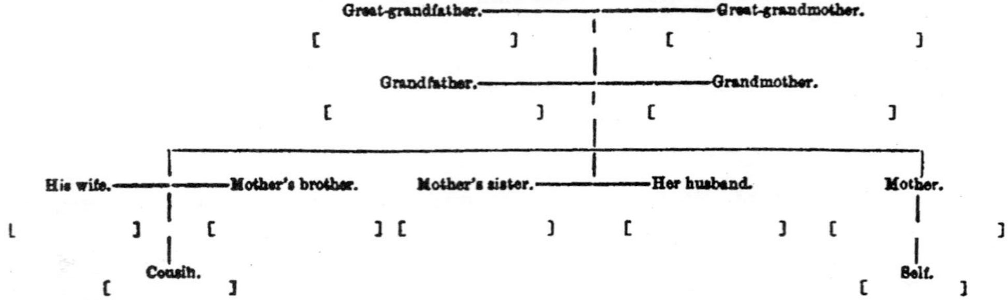

C.—Relations, through the Brother and Sister, whether of man or woman.

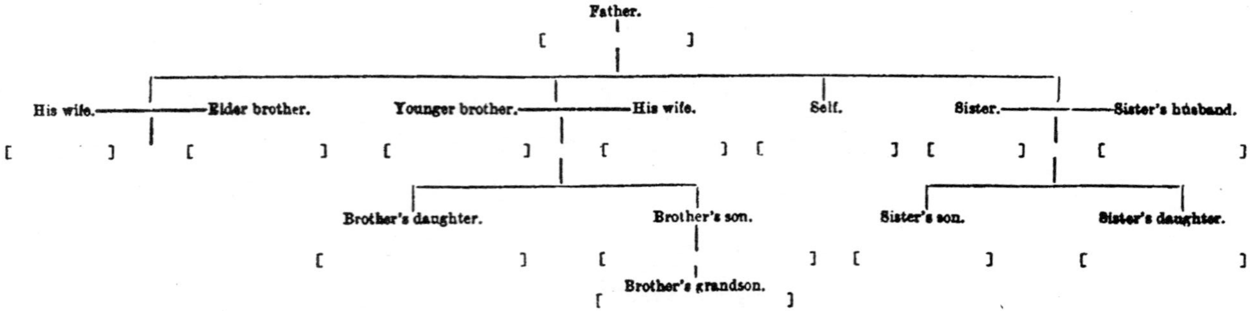

D (1).—*Relations, through the Wife, of a man.*

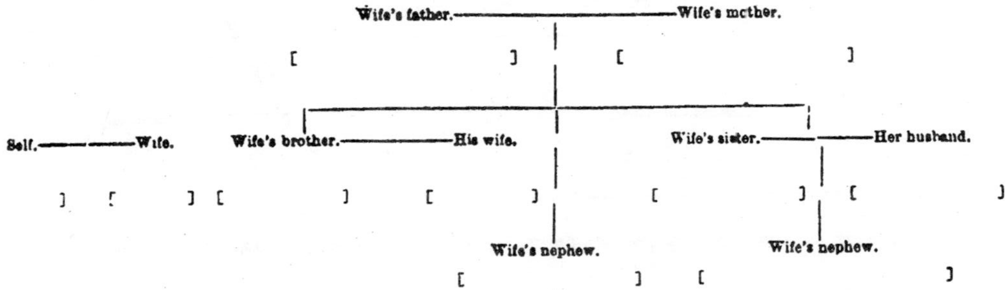

D (2).—*Relations, through the Husband, of a woman.*

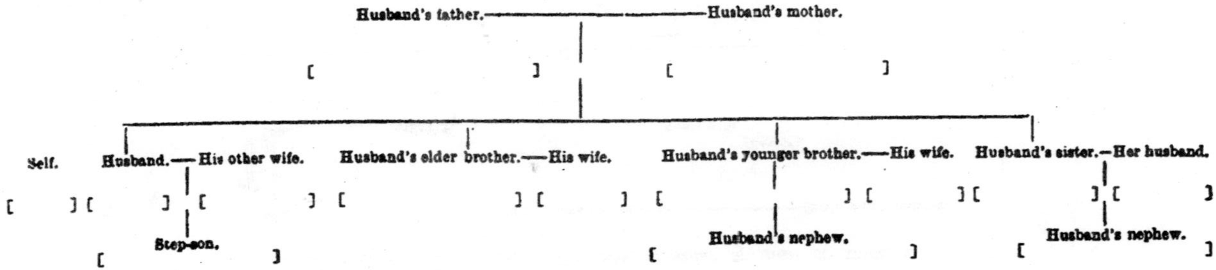

E (1).—*Relations, through the Son, whether of man or woman.*

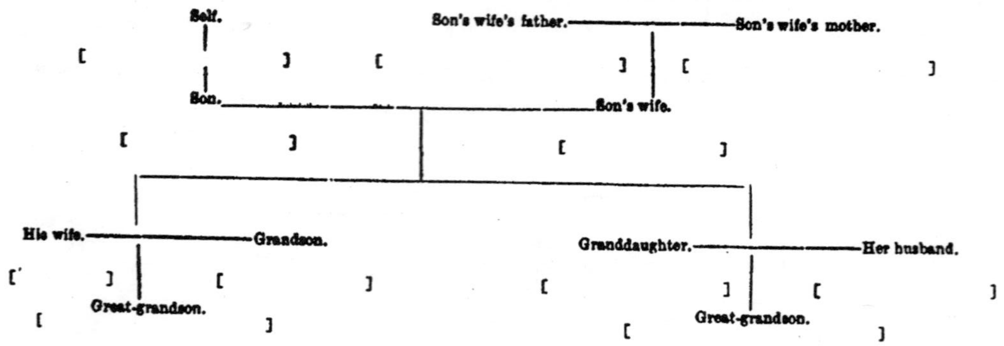

E (2).—*Relations, through the Daughter, whether of man or woman.*

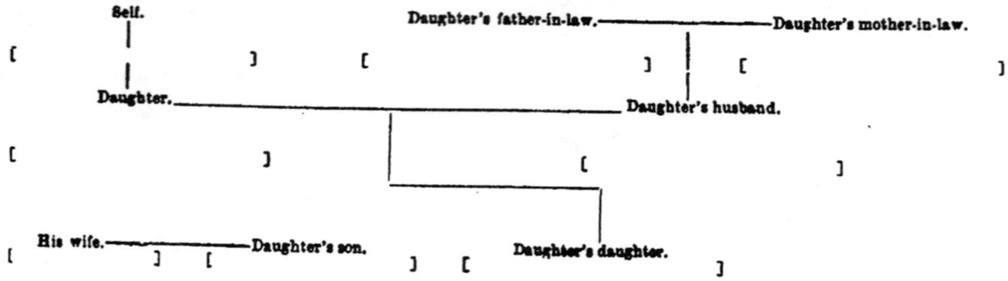

163. How is each group spoken of collectively by a man and by a woman?

164. Add any relationships not included in these groups for which there are special names.

165. Is a great-uncle distinguished from a grandfather's and a parent's cousin from a man's own cousin?

166. Into what classes are relations distributed?

167. Specify each class and the relations included in it.

168. Give the distinctions, if any—

(*i*) between sapindas, sakulyas, samanodakas, bandhus, and gotrajas.

(*ii*) between personal, paternal, and maternal kindred.

(*iii*) between legal sharers and residuaries, near and distant kindred, lineal and collateral relations.

169. State the various modes of addressing and speaking of particular relatives, *e.g.*, how do men and women address and speak of their husbands and wives respectively?

170. How does a man address and speak of his brother-in-law?

171. Are there any cases in which names originally denoting particular relationships are used in addressing or speaking of persons not related in the manner the name denotes? *e.g.*, a man sometimes speaks of another man as his *bhai*, when in fact he merely means that the other is a member of his own caste.

172. Are genealogies carefully kept?

173. Do they include the names of females?

174. Note any forms of adoptive relationships based upon friendship or on land (*e.g.*, *phulbahin* and *bhumbhai*), and state what consequences and obligations are annexed to them.

II.—Domestic Ceremonies.

175. *Birth and Pregnancy.*—Describe any ceremonies performed during pregnancy, and state what effect, if any, they are believed to have upon the mother or child.

176. What posture is adopted in accouchement?

177. Who attends on the mother (*a*) during her confinement, (*b*) after the confinement is over?

178. What ceremonies are performed on the birth of a child?

179. Are the ordinary occupations of the father given up or interrupted in any way in consequence of the birth of a child?

180. What reasons, if any, are assigned for such interruption?

181. Are there any special customs with reference to twins?

182. *Adoption.*—Describe the different ceremonies in use for adoption.

183. Does the validity of the adoption depend upon the performance of the customary ceremony?

184. Does the status of the person adopted depend upon the form of ceremony used?

185. If so, what is the effect of each of the different forms?

186. *Puberty or Adolescence.*—What ceremonies are performed when (*a*) a son, (*b*) a daughter, attains puberty?

187. In the case of a son, is there any ceremony purporting to admit him among the grown men of the caste?

188. *Betrothal.*—Describe the ceremony of betrothal.

189. What is considered the binding portion of the ceremony?

190. Is there any distinction between formalities after which the betrothal is reversible and formalities which are absolutely binding?

191. At what age does betrothal take place?

192. Whose consent is necessary?

193. If a betrothal be annulled, is there any custom as to the repayment of the expenses incurred?

194. *Marriage.*—Describe in detail the various kinds of marriage ceremonies in use, distinguishing between superior and inferior kinds?

195. What is considered to be the essential or binding part of each kind of ceremony?

196. In the marriage ceremony is there any pretence of capturing the bride, or does any part of the ceremony or of the previous or subsequent proceedings suggest that marriage by capture was formerly in vogue.

197. In the marriage ceremony is there any symbol of a previous marriage to any deity, *e.g.*, is the bride first married to a tree or to any natural object?

198. *Death and Burial.*—Do the caste burn, bury, or expose their dead?

199. If buried, in what position?

200. Where are the bodies or ashes finally disposed of?

201. Describe the ceremonies performed at the burning or burying of a corpse?

202. Are any ceremonies performed for the propitiation of (*a*) ancestors in general, (*b*) childless ancestors, (*c*) men who have died a violent death; and if so, of what nature and at what seasons?

203. Describe the ceremony of *sraddh*, and state whether the caste perform it or not?

204. Who officiates as priest at the funeral ceremonies and repeats formulæ of prayer (mantras, etc.)?

205. In the case of castes which do not employ Brahmans it should be enquired whether the sister's son or other relative on the female side officiates in the place of the Brahman.

206. *Purification.*—Are ceremonial purifications practised?

207. Are any persons at any time impure or unclean and requiring purification, as after child-birth, during menstruation, after funerals, etc.?

208. For how long does the ceremonial impurity last?

209. How are they purified?

III.—Religion.

210. *Worship, Priests, and Temples.*—To what religion, and to what sect within the religion, do the caste belong?

211. If Hindus, do they by preference worship any special one of the regular Hindu deities, and are there any reasons for this preference?

212. Have its members always professed that religion, or were they converted to it *en masse*, or gradually?

213. How did their conversion take place, and when—before their migration to their present abode or after?

214. Are members of the caste found in the neighbourhood professing the tenets of different religions or sects?

215. Do they affect a peculiar saint or shrine?

216. State the names, origin, and attributes of the minor village deities and local or patron saints whom they worship, describing, if possible, the shape and aspect of the shrine, the ceremonies observed in worship, the nature of the offerings made, the times, days, or seasons when they are made, the caste and subdivision of the officiating priests and of the persons who take the offerings.

217. Are any of these deities peculiar to women and children?

218. State any indications of ancestor worship, snake or tree worship, sun, moon, fire, or devil worship, which the religious practice of the caste suggests.

219. Is there any special shrine to which pilgrimages are made, and at what seasons?

220. Has any great religious teacher arisen in the caste? Give his name and state his peculiar tenets.

221. Is the caste, though nominally belonging to one of the main religions, excluded from any of the rites and ceremonies practised by other castes belonging to the same denomination, and is any specific reason assigned for this exclusion?

222. All cases of left-handed sect and worship of sexual principles, orgies, etc., should be noted.

223. Have they any ceremony of admission into the religious body corresponding to baptism or circumcision?

224. All cases of Hindus and Mahomedans, or their women and children, worshipping the same deities or saints, or frequenting the same shrines, should be carefully noted.

225. Do the caste employ Brahmans for religious and ceremonial purposes?

226. If so, to what caste or section of Brahmans do they belong, and are they received on terms of equality by other Brahmans?

227. If they do not employ Brahmans, what class of people serve them as priests?

228. Are there any family priests who perform ceremonial functions not connected with any particular deity?

229. Are particular persons or clans set apart as priests?

230. Is the same person often both priest and chief?

231. Do they practice austerities, observe chastity, etc.?

232. Is any special building set apart for worship?

233. Is it built in a particular position, as facing the east, etc.?

234. Has it any special shape, and is it called by a special name?

235. Are idols kept there?

236. What rites are performed?

237. Are all the rites public, or are any of the nature of mysteries or orgies?

238. *Sacrifice.*—Is sacrifice offered, to what deities, and of what animals?

239. May any one or only priests offer sacrifice?

240. Where is sacrifice offered?

241. After sacrifice, do the priests or worshippers consume or remove the objects offered?

242. Are substitutes used in sacrifice, such as part of an animal, an effigy or imitation?

243. Do worshippers sacrifice parts of themselves, such as hair, nails, drops of blood, etc.?

244. Is there any tradition of men, women, or children having been sacrified in former times to any deity?

245. If so, name the deity, and state all you can learn about the tradition.

246. Whence and in what manner was the victim obtained?

247. Enquire why the custom of human sacrifice was discontinued, how long ago, and what was substituted in its place?

248. *Festivals.*—Give a list of the festivals observed, stating the dates when each is celebrated.

249. What do they consist in—processions, games, dances, banquets, etc.?

250. Which are at regular periods and which occasional?

251. Are there annual religious festivals marking the months, seasons, equinoxes, solstices, seed-time, first fruits, harvest, etc.?

252. Is there an annual feast of the dead?

253. To what extent does the caste observe the great Hindu festivals?

254. Is there any great festival observed by the caste, but not observed by Hindus generally?

255. Are there festivals at which marriageable youths and girls mix, and matches are made?

256. Are any festivals specially connected with sexual relations?

257. Is drunkenness common on these occasions, and is the use of any particular intoxicating drink regarded as part of the festival.

258. *Fetichism.*—Do spirits or deities enter into or attach themselves to objects, such as sticks, bones, ornaments, etc.?

259. Are such objects kept sacred and believed to contain supernatural power?

260. Are blocks of wood, stones, etc., believed to be inhabited by deities, and worshipped accordingly?

261. *Worship of natural spirits, plants, and animals.*—Are there spirits especially attached to natural objects, such as rivers, springs, wells, rocks, trees, animals, etc.?

262. How are they worshipped?
263. Are fields believed to be haunted, and by whom?
264. Are groves and woods favourite places of worship or sacrifice?
265. If so, explain what gods are worshipped there, and note if the wood or grove is or is supposed to be part of a large forest which has been cleared, a portion being left as a refuge for the forest gods.
266. Are any beasts worshipped as gods? If so, describe the mode of worship.
267. *Ancestor worship.*—Are the souls of ancestors worshipped with prayers and sacrifices?
268. Describe briefly the ceremony in vogue?
269. Is the supposed primitive ancestor of the caste worshipped under the form of, or in connexion with, some sacred animal, plant or other object as a totem or clan deity?
270. Are animals sacrified at funerals; if so, with what object?
271. Are any funeral offerings given, so that the souls of the dead may become possessed of objects or their phantoms?
272. Are food, money, ornaments, etc., placed near the corpse, burnt or buried with it, or offered periodically at the place of burial?
273. Are the survivors in fear of the ghosts of the dead?
274. Do they attribute dreams to their influence, and do they take any means to get rid of them, or keep them off?
275. Do ghosts of the dead haunt houses or burial-places, and if so in what forms?
276. Does their doing so indicate that their bodies have not been properly buried?
277. How are ghosts propitiated?
278 Are there several kinds of them; if so, state the names, characteristics, and attributes of each?
279. Are any days sacred to ancestors, and what is done on these days?
280. Do the caste go to Gya or to any other well-known place of pilgrimage to perform the *sraddh* of their ancestors?
281. *Totems.*—Is the caste or any of its subdivisions named after any animal, plant, weapon, or implement?
282. Do they show their reverence for any such object either by special worship or by abstaining from killing, eating, cutting, burning, using or naming it?
283. Are there any cases of the object which the caste reverence being tattooed or painted on the body, possibly in a very conventionalised form, or of its representation being always carried about on the person?
284. If so, how do the members of the caste explain the practice?
285. Do the women of the caste pay special reverence to certain trees, by veiling their faces before them as if in presence of an elder relative, or worship them in the hope of getting children in the belief that the spirit of the ancestor inhabits them?
286. Are any trees or plants used or worshipped at weddings and similar ceremonies, and are children named after them?

IV.—Superstitions.

287. *Omens, etc.*—Do any superstitions prevail as to lucky and unlucky days, numbers, animals, places, houses, points of the compass, roads, physical functions, such as sneezing, spitting, etc., natural events, or calamities?

288. Are there any superstitions connected with stars, and may they be got over by burying a picture or rude representation of the star?

289. Is there any objection to crossing water under certain conditions? Is meeting a particular animal regarded as ominous, and does the character of the omen depend upon the direction in which the animal is seen? Are omens taken from accidents, such as stumbling, etc.?

290. Are there any peculiar customs as to wearing or abstaining from wearing particular kinds of dress, jewels, ornaments, etc.; as to using particular kinds of cooking vessels; or as to eating or growing particular plants or drugs?

291. In the case of plants, notice whether the name of the plant affected by the superstition corresponds with the name of a subdivision of the tribe?

292. Are there any superstitions as to the naming of children, *e.g.*, are two names given, one for every-day purposes and one for ceremonial use, or is a son whose elder brother has died given an approbrious name?

293. Do these practices apply to girls as well as to boys?

294. *Oaths and ordeals.*—Are any forms of oath in common use, and are they accompanied by any symbolic forms, such as swearing on a tiger's skin?

295. What consequences are supposed to be entailed by breaking an oath?

296. Are any ordeals in use, such as plunging into water, passing through fire, eating food under special conditions, etc.?

297. Are they used merely for the decision of personal disputes or for questions affecting the community, such as the boundaries of villages, etc.?

298. *Magic and witchcraft.*—Is the practice of magic arts confined to special sorcerers, witches, etc.?

299. Are these priests, etc., connected with religion, or is there jealousy or hostility between the priest and the sorcerer?

300. What are the functions of sorcerers and witches, and how are they generally regarded?

301. Are there any supposed arts by which it can be determined whether a particular individual is a witch or sorcerer or not?

302. Are spirits or demons called upon to give oracles, disclose secrets, do good or harm?

303. Is demoniacal possession believed in, and what remedies are resorted to in order to cure persons supposed to be possessed?

304. Is such possession regarded as a valuable quality; if so, how is it acquired; is it confined to particular castes or clans?

305. Are dreams regarded? Do they give information of the past and prophecy or omens for the future.

306. Are any special persons called upon to interpret them, and is there any recognised system of interpretation?

307. Are they ascribed to visits or communications from spirits, as, for instance, to persons recently deceased in the family of the person who has the dream?

308. Is there any mode of propitiating the spirits of persons recently dead so as to prevent them from causing dreams?

309. Is the effect of the evil eye believed in?

310. To what is it attributed?

311. How is it obviated?

312. Are sorcerers and witches supposed to act on their victims by objects belonging to them or intimately connected with them, such as cut hair or nails, or by making effigies or pictures of them and wounding the pictures in order that the victims may be affected?

313. Is special care therefore taken to destroy cuttings of hair or nails?

314. Is any kind of divination or astrology practised?

315. Who are its professors?

316. Describe the modes of divination and exorcism in use, and state what class of persons are resorted to as exorcisers.

317. Is disease attributed to the influence of spirits?

318. How is the particular spirit at work detected and how appeased?

Ceremonial Prohibition or Taboo.

319. Is any particular food, animal or vegetable forbidden, though obtainable and wholesome?

320. Do the whole caste abstain from it, or only certain families or individuals, or persons under some special circumstances?

321. Is the prohibition religious?

322. Is the animal or plant abstained from regarded as in any way divine, as a tribe fetish, the incarnation of a local deity, or personal guardian spirit or the soil of some ancestor?

323. Is it the animal or plant from which the caste or sub-division derives its name?

324. Give any explanation that may be current of the prohibition in question.

325. Do any members of the caste object to eating with, touching, speaking to, looking at, or calling by name other persons?

326. Do these prohibitions apply to persons of different rank, occupation, or caste?

327. Is any particular caste held in peculiar abhorrence, and if so, why? A good instance of what is meant is afforded by the fact that the Doms hold the Dhobis in special detestation. It is believed that other low castes have similar eccentric prejudices.

328. Are women and children specially prohibited from doing any particular religious acts, entering particular temples, performing particular acts of worship, etc.?

329. Do similar prohibitions apply between relations? And specially between relations by marriage, *e.g.*, does the husband's father avoid the wife's relations, *etc.*?

330. What appears to be the motive?

331. Is the person whose name may not be mentioned supposed to be holier than the other?

332. Is there an idea of magical harm, or is it merely a question of social separation?

333. Are the names of chiefs, dead persons, etc., avoided in conversation?

334. Are any special words or subjects considered improper?

335. Are there any cases in which gods, persons, or subjects whose mention by name is prohibited are spoken of under some honorific title?

336. *Agricultural Superstitions.*—Mention any remarkable superstitious beliefs connected with agriculture, such as the days on which ploughing, sowing, reaping, etc., must be begun, intermitted, or finished; the periods within which a shower of rain is specially lucky or unlucky; the customary number of times agricultural operations should be performed; the objects set up in the fields to avert injury to the crops, to frighten away demons, etc.?

337. Is any propitiatory or quasi-religious ceremony observed before the commencement or after the completion of any agricultural operations, such as the sinking of a well, sowing, reaping, or the like?

338. What times and seasons are lucky or unlucky for the commencement or completion of the various agricultural operations?

339. Are there any gods specially connected with particular crops?

340. If any of these are peculiar to the caste, the fact should be noted.

V.—Social Customs.

341. *Food and drink.*—Which of the following articles of food do the caste eat or abstain from eating:—flesh, wine, monkeys, beef, pork, the flesh of cloven-footed or uncloven-footed animals, fowls, scaly or scaleless fish, crocodiles, snakes, lizards, jackals, rats, other vermin, the leavings of other people?

342. Are there any seasons during which the use of special articles of food is forbidden?

343. Are such restrictions due to the desire to increase the stock of such article of food or to superstitious or sanitary causes?

344. Is the use of certain articles of food restricted to women or children, or to chiefs and persons of rank?

345. Are individuals or families prevented from eating certain animals and plants for superstitious reasons, such, for instance, as their being the totems of the individuals or family?

346. Does all the household eat together, or each person separately, or is there a distinction of ranks, sexes, or ages?

347. Do men and women eat together?

348. Are there any ceremonies used at the commencement of meals, such as offerings to the divinities, etc., or any religious rites connected with them?

349. Are there any marked peculiarities in the mode of eating and drinking of the caste, and how are these peculiarities explained?

350. State what spirituous liquors, drugs, and narcotics are in ordinary use.

351. Are any of them connected with particular religious ceremonies or festivals?

352. Are any of them supposed to have the effect of keeping off malaria?

353. How is the use of spirituous liquors and drugs regarded by the caste—for instance, is (a) drunkenness, (b) habitual indulgence in opium or ganja looked upon as disreputable?

354. *Customs of social intercourse.*—What customs prevails as to salutation?

355. Do they differ according to rank and relationship?

356. How do members of a family, friends and relations, and strangers greet one another?

357. What special processes of compliment and rules of precedence are in vogue?

358. How are guests, women, and aged or infirm persons treated?

359. What are the rules of hospitality as recognized between kinsfolk, neighbours, and strangers?

360. Are peculiar forms of language in use?

361. Are certain words or forms of address used or avoided in addressing certain people?

362. *Customs bearing on social status.*—Name the lowest well-known caste with which the caste will (a) eat paki, (b) eat kachhi, (c) drink, (d) smoke.

363. Name the highest well-known caste which will eat, etc., as in the last question with the caste.

364. Is there any special article of food their abstaining from which tends in their opinion to raise them above some other caste which does not abstain from it?

365. Mention any remarkable customs of the caste regarding dress, ornaments, implements of handicrafts, fishing or hunting, distinguishing marks, cutting of hair and beard, musical instruments, dances, etc., which affect their social status in relation to their neighbours.

VI.—Occupations.

366. What do the caste believe to have been their original occupation or group of occupations?

367. To what extent have they or any sections of them departed from it?

368. Describe their present occupation?

369. If their occupation is that of—

(a) *Artisans*—What is their industry and in what special material do they work, or abstain from working?

(b) *Hunters.*—Do they catch game or vermin?

(c) *Fishermen.*—Do they catch fish only or also crocodiles and tortoises?

(d) *Sweepers.*—Do they remove night-soil or not?

370. Name any implement or mode of working which is characteristic of the caste, and also note whether there is any form or detail of their main occupation by abstaining from which they believe themselves to be raised above others of the same craft?

371. Do they habitually prostitute their (1) unmarried, (2) married women?

372. Does a change of religion, such as conversion to Mahomedanism, or a joining a special sect of Hindus, usually involve a change or modification of occupation on the part of the convert?

373. In cases where an hereditary occupation is abandoned, do the persons changing their occupation change or modify their caste name, and are their ties with those members who adhere to their original occupation in any way broken or relaxed?

VII.—Relations to Land.

374. To what class of agriculturists do the caste or tribe usually belong, *e.g.*, are they—

(1) Zamindars;

(2) Tenure-holders, specifying the kind of tenures they hold;

(3) Occupancy or non-occupancy raiyats, stating whether they have or claim any privileges in respect of rent;

(4) Nomadic cultivators, specifying the mode of cultivation they follow;

(5) Landless day-labourers, stating the manner in which they are paid?

375. Have they any legend or tradition accounting for the position they occupy?

376. Have the caste any privileges in respect of land, *e.g.*, do they—

(a) hold at lower rates of rent than their neighbours;

(b) hold a certain proportion of their holdings rent-free;

(c) receive a certain proportion of the produce of each field or of particular crops in consideration of any kind of service?

377. Do they hold any peculiar kinds of tenures?

378. If so, have they any tradition accounting for the fact, such as that they are the descendants of the first clearers of the soil, of a former dominant race, or the like?

379. Do they claim special privileges in respect of land on the strength of traditional affinity to, or supposed contact with, the ancestors of the local zamindars?

380. Have they any hereditary right to perform certain services or receive certain fees?

381. Is it supposed that the ancestors of the local zamindars were members of the caste or tribe, and do they now admit this, or deny it?

382. Are there any traces among the caste or tribe of village communities, or of a communal organization embracing groups of villages?

383. Give all details that can be ascertained on this subject, or if the organization has already been described in print, quote the reference.

384. Does the system preserve its vitality, or is it dying out?

385. If the latter, state from what cause.

386. Are there any traces of the periodical redistribution of common arable land among the members of sections of the community?

387. If the communal organization has now fallen into disuse, can any trace of its previous existence be found in the character of distribution of the tenures now held by the caste or tribe?

388. Are there any restrictions upon the order in which certain fields are to be cultivated or certain crops sown?

389. Do communal rights of pasturage exist, or are they asserted over land which is private property?

390. Among hunting, fishing or wandering tribes does any apportionment of land or water exist between the divisions of the tribe, each division confining its operations to the tract allotted to it, and does the apportionment extend to the individual members of the division?

391. Does this custom obtain even where the land or water apportioned is not the property of the tribe?

Sources of information.—Here should be noted the names, residence (village and thana), profession, caste, sub-caste, and section of the persons who answered the questions. If any of them are *ghataks*, genealogists, heads of caste *panchayat*, or occupy any hereditary official position in relation to the caste, the fact should be stated. If the answers to the questions have been derived from any source other than personal enquiry addressed to members of the caste concerned, the source should be stated, and such references given as may enable the officer in charge of the enquiry to test the correctness of the answers.

DENZIL C. J. IBBETSON.
JOHN C. NESFIELD.
H. H. RISLEY.

APPENDIX III.

MR. DENZIL IBBETSON'S MEMORANDUM ON ETHNOLOGICAL INQUIRY IN THE PANJAB.

1882.

Memorandum for guidance in collecting Ethnological Notes.*

N.B.—Proper names and vernacular words should be very clearly and correctly written, and in vernacular as well as in English characters, if possible.

1. *Caste or Tribe—Clan—Locality—Tahsil—District.*—This information should always be given at the head of the note regarding the people from whose statements the note is compiled; and if they belong to a single village, it should be named in case of further inquiry being needed.

It is often difficult to decide what should be entered as the caste. Many clans, for instance, are called Jats in some districts and Rájpúts in others. A mere tradition of Rájpút origin, even though admitted by the Rájpúts of the neighbourhood, is not enough to warrant their being entered as Rájpúts, though the tradition and the fact of its admission should of course be stated; for a caste will often claim Rájpút origin, while readily admitting that they have lost the status which their ancestors enjoyed.

The real question is *whether they are, for practical purposes, looked upon and treated as Rájpúts at the present time by admitted Rájpúts of the neighbourhood.* The same test applies to claims to be classed as Patháns, Qoreshís, &c., &c. The claim, however, should always be noted, together with the considerations which may lead you to hold that it is inadmissible.

In any case the name by which the people are best known and most commonly spoken of among their neighbours, generally that of their clan, should always be prominently noted.

2. *Distribution.*—It is useful to state whether the particular caste or clan is numerous in the tahsil; where their local head-quarters are; and if few, where they are to be found in larger numbers. The provincial head-quarters, if any, should be named. The people will often tell you that they hold 27 villages in this and 84 in that tahsil, and so on, giving the old traditional number of villages rather than the number as they now stand. Such statements should be recorded.

3. *Subdivisions.*—The various grades of tribal subdivision to which the people belong should always be stated: for instance, they

---

* I need hardly say that I am indebted for many of the notes in this memorandum to the suggestions of friends who have been kind enough to help me in its compilation.

should be described as belonging to the A family of the B clan of the C tribe of the D race or caste. And especially it will be useful to give the traditional number of subdivisions of the tribe or clan under discussion, and to detail the names of as many of them as possible, as these names often appear in the census papers with nothing to indicate to what tribe they belong, and in such cases the barest list of names would be most valuable to me.

A tree showing the local subdivisions of a caste or tribe is always exceedingly useful, and should be accompanied by a detail of the vernacular terms used to denote the various degrees of subdivision; such as *zát, got, al, jad, pál, múhín, thok, movi, sútan, kuldevi, varri, bolak, tuman, páro, phalli, zai, khel, &c., &c.*

In the case of menial castes, it should be noted whether the name of their subdivision is the same as the clan name of the villagers whom they serve, or of the prevailing agricultural clan in the neighbourhood, or in the part of the country whence they came.

4. *Synonyms*—

(*a*) If the caste or clan is known by more thano ne name, all should be given; as *Jhínwar* and *Kahár*, *Juláha* and *Páoli*. So, too, if the name varies with the religion; as *Chúhrá* for Hindu, *Musalli* for Musalmán; and *Mazbi* for Sikh sweepers; *Mahra* for Hindu and Sikh, and *Jhínwar* for Musalmán *Kahárs*; *Rángar* for Musalmán Rájpúts, and so on. It should always be noted whether the synonyms are co-extensive or not; whether, for instance, the term Rángar is applied to all Musalmán Rájpúts, and to them only, or not.

(*b*) Too great caution cannot be exercised in accepting synonyms. To the educated and twice-born Native, every vagrant is a *Nat*, every outcast a *Chúhrá* or *Dúm*, and so on. The real test is whether, for instance, the same individual will call himself *Jhínwar* and *Kahár* indifferently; whether a Hindu *Chúhrá* would be called on conversion a *Musalli*; whether a *Juláha* from the east would, on settling in the west, be recognized as a *Páoli*; whether the people themselves accept and recognize the identity. Mere identity of *origin* is not sufficient. For instance, *Paráchas* are said to be converted *Banyas*; but no *Banya* could now become a *Parácha* by conversion; the caste is closed to outsiders, and has become separate and distinct.

(*c*) Names of occupations often give rise to most difficult questions of this sort. For instance, some say that *Jhínwar* and *Máchhi* are identical; and that all *Malláhs*, *Bhatyáras*, *Barbhúnjas*, and *Dáyás* are *Jhínwar* by caste, these words being the names of occupations only, and not of castes. Taking *Malláhs* only, the test questions would be something of this sort. Are there any *Malláhs* who never were *Jhínwars*; would a *Jhínwar*, on first taking to work as a boatman, call himself *Jhínwar*, or

Malláh, or both indifferently? What would his son call himself? What would he call himself if he reverted to working as a porter or village water-carrier or cook? Would he ordinarily marry a *Malláh* woman (1) while still working as a porter, (2) while working as a boatman, and *vice versâ*?

(*d*) Where the custom of the neighbourhood forbids marriage out of the caste, freedom of intermarriage is the best possible test of identity. But this is often not available. As to the general question, see section 21 below. Questions of this sort are the most difficult which have arisen in the classification of census figures, and a thorough examination of them is much needed.

5. *Origin or foundation of caste.*—The tradition as to the origin or foundation of the caste or clan, though often absurd, should always be given, together with any facts which may seem to bear upon its probable truth.

6. *Place of origin and course of migration.*—The ultimate place of origin, as stated by the people, should be recorded, together with such account as they may give of their subsequent stages. But especially the name of the village or neighbourhood from which their ancestors came direct to their present locality should always be stated, as this last can generally be relied upon, and enables us to trace them back, step by step, in their wanderings. It will often be found that they still make periodical pilgrimages to a place of origin, there to worship at a *satti*, or at the shrine (*jathera*) of their common ancestor.

The place of origin of their *Parohits* and *Náís* will often be a guide; and it is useful to know where their family genealogists (*Bhát*, *Jága*, *Cháran*, *Mírási*) live, and to what caste and religion they belong. These men should always be got hold of and examined if possible, as they are the repositories of all the traditions of the tribe.

The number of generations since immigration is often known, or can be got from the genealogical tree, and is useful as approximately fixing the date of arrival.

The people generally have a tradition as to who held the village or locality before their coming. These traditions often throw light on past movements of tribes, and should be examined into and recorded over as wide an area as possible.

7. *Religion*—

(*a*) Should be stated; and whether the same caste or clan is found of more than one religion in the neighbourhood. Original Musalmáns, who came into India as such, should be distinguished from those whose ancestors have been converted from Hindúism. The latter can often state who converted them, and when and where. [It is important to ascertain whether their conversion took place before or after their settlement in their present homes.]

(*b*) The sect, where it can be discovered, should also be stated. Whole villages of nominal Hindús or Musalmáns are sometimes adherents of a sect which practically eclipses the parent religion. It will often be found that the people affect a particular *gurú* or *pír* or *gurúdwára*, and will be of the sect to which he or it belongs (*see* further, section 20 *infra*); especially weavers, water-carriers, and other village menials are often devotees of some saint or shrine, local or distant; and in such cases the fact should be noted.

(*c*) It will generally be found that the peasantry worship minor village deities and local saints far more than the recognized gods of the Hindu Pantheon. Particulars regarding worship of this sort are especially valuable. The names, origin, and attributes of the deity, the shape and aspect of the shrine, the days of the week or year consecrated to him or her, the ceremonies observed in worship, the nature of the offerings made, and the class of people by whom they are taken, should be given.

(*d*) It should be especially noted whether any of these deities are peculiar to any particular sex, age, class, caste or clan, or their worship specially affected by them, or in any given locality.

(*e*) It is not impossible that the minor deities may be distributable into two classes, Aryan and Aboriginal, the former being worshipped by all, and the offerings made to them being pure and taken by Bráhmans, while the worship of the latter is often largely confined to women and children, and the offerings consist of fowls, pigs, *churmas*, and other impure things, and are taken by Jogis, Faqírs, Chúbras, and the like. The latter class are perhaps more often malevolent than the former.

(*f*) It should also be stated whether Sikhs or Hindús worship the same deities at the same shrines or not; and it will often be found that Musalmáns still worship these minor deities of the neighbourhood, *especially their women and children*.

(*g*) Customs forbidden, or not authorized by the nominal religion, are of special importance, as, for example, the worship of saints by Musalmáns, and of Musalmán saints by Hindús, the circumcision of females, and the like.

(*h*) It is particularly important to note the cases where a caste, though nominally Hindu, Sikh or Musalmán, is not recognized as such, and not admitted to a religious equality, or to a participation in public rites and ceremonies by others of the same denomination.

(*i*) Information regarding the religion and worship of the outcast and vagrant castes, such as sweepers and the various kinds of gipsies, is much needed.

Snake-worship and tree-worship will be found in full vitality in many parts of the province, and traces of fire-worship and devil-worship should be carefully looked for.

8. *Fairs, Fasts, and Festivals.*—These almost always have a semi-religious significance, and are of great sociological interest. The places at which they are held, and the fixed dates on which they fall, should be noted; and the name, history, and attributes of the saint or deity, if any, in whose honour they are instituted given; if none, the origin and significance attached to them by the people. It should be stated what sex and age, what castes or clans of people, and of what sect or religion, principally attend or observe them; what is the nature of the offerings made, and who takes these offerings. A rough estimate of the numbers usually attending a fair will be useful. Any tradition connected with the occasion should be narrated, and all rites and ceremonies observed should be minutely described.

9. *Omens and Superstitions.*—These are often peculiar to a clan or a locality, and are always interesting for comparison with those of other races. Divination; sooth-sayers (*bhagat syána, &c.*); witchcraft; the evil eye; the release of animals or scapegoats during epidemics; [the use and nature of charms, especially against small-pox and cattle-plague]; the sanctity of certain days, especially in connection with horned cattle; auspicious and inauspicious days, numbers, sights and events; and belief in and propitiations of ghosts (*bhút, paret, chhurel*) and fairies (*núri sháhpuri*) are some of the points on which information is needed; as also the worship of ancestors and the propitiation of those who die by violence (*upgat*) or childless (*gyál*), the custom of building little platforms with cup-marks (*bhorka*) for their worship, the custom of heaping up earth (*cf.* the cairns of Europe) in their honour, or in honour of some of the minor deities.

There is a large mass of superstitious custom connected with agriculture, such as the days on which ploughing, sowing, reaping, &c., must be begun, intermitted or finished; the rites observed or invocations employed at their commencement or completion; the ceremonies attending cotton-picking, cane-crushing, winnowing and division of grain, and commencement and completion of a well; the customary number of times which weeding should or should not be performed; the dimensions of wells and well-gear being measured in so many *and three quarter* hands, and the like.

The number 5 and its aliquot parts, as 1¼, 2½, will be found to run through many of the superstitious, and even of the religious, customs of the people.

10. *Use of Bráhmans.*—Musulmáns often still retain and fee the family Bráhmans, employing them especially at betrothals and weddings, in casting horoscopes and fixing lucky names and dates, and the like. This is valuable, as indicating Hindú origin. The *class* of Bráhman so employed should always be ascertained.

Some of the lower castes have a sort of outcast Bráhmans who minister to them only; and I understand that there are Musalmán Bráhmans (called Huseni) who perform hereditary offices for their converted clients. Any special order of priesthood of this sort should be described. Most of the frontier tribes include Levitical clans, who have the monopoly of priestly functions, and occupy a position somewhat similar to that of Bráhmans among Hindús.

More information is needed about the different classes of Bráhmans, as the *Achárj*, *Dákaut*, *Gújráti*, *&c.*, what position they hold in the sacerdotal ranks, what offerings they accept, what functions they perform, and what is the origin of the distinction into classes.

11. *Totemism.*—Signs of reverence for some animal or plant peculiar to the caste or clan will often be met with. Thus, some clans will not eat or burn certain plants; the women of others veil their faces before certain trees, as if in presence of an elder relative, or worship them in hope of getting children, in the belief that the spirit of the ancestor inhabits them; others use or worship certain plants at weddings and similar ceremonies; and some castes call all their sons after plants. A clandestine marriage round a fire made of certain wild plants, even though performed without the usual ceremonial, is sometimes considered to be of a peculiary binding nature. The clan name is sometimes derived from that of a plant or animal; and there is often a tradition connecting it with the clan and accounting for the reverence shown it. The people's explanation of the clan name, though often apparently absurd, should always be given.

12. *Social Customs.*—All social customs are exceedingly useful in tracing ethnic affinities, as they are marvellously persistent. The simplest method of recording them probably is to describe minutely any set of customs or ceremonies as practised by the principal tribe of the neighbourhood; and, taking that as a standard, to note the points in which the practice of other tribes departs from it—

(a) *Differential* customs, which are special to one tribe, and differ from the custom of other tribes in the neighbourhood, are most important of all.

(b) Birth customs; the giving two names, one for every-day wear, and one for ceremonial use; the meanings of names, often intended to deceive or frighten the small-pox goddess by depreciating or exalting the qualities of the child; name-jingles or rhymes within the family, perhaps marking the paternity in polyandrous families; the rites connected with the scalplock, puberty, and cuttings and offerings of hair in general, are all interesting and often important. The period of ceremonial impurity after birth and death (*sútak* and *pátak*) should always be given, as they vary with the caste.

(c) Marriage and betrothal customs are especially valuable. It will often be found that a Musalmán tribe will have identical marriage ceremonies with those of its Hindu neighbours, with the single exception of the substitution of the *nikáh* for the *pherá*, or even the addition of the former to the latter.

(d) Polyandry is practised, in a sort of half-recognized manner, far more generally throughout the Panjáb than is usually supposed. It may always be suspected where the custom is for the eldest only of a family of brothers to marry. Other curious forms of marriage will also be found in certain parts, such as the infant son marrying an adult woman who cohabits with the nominal father.

(e) It should always be stated whether the people burn or bury their dead; if the former, where the bones and ashes are finally bestowed; if the latter, whether they are buried lying or sitting, on the face or on the back, in a graveyard or at home; in both cases, in which direction graves or shrines face. In the case of menials, it should be noted whether they have a distinct custom proper to their caste, or whether they merely follow the custom of the village to which they are attached, which will vary with the religion of the villagers.

(f) All customs of committing corpses or ashes to local streams or tanks should be noted, and the origin and nature of the virtue these possess should be recorded. This practice is believed to be dying out in favour of the more orthodox localities.

13. *Karewá.*—It is of capital importance to know whether a tribe practises *karewá*, or the remarriage of the widow, as the existence of this custom helps to fix both origin and social status. The custom exists in two forms, which must be carefully distinguished :—

(1) The Levirate, in which the eldest surviving brother of the deceased takes the widow: this is either a remnant of past or a token of existing polyandry.

(2) Where the existing restrictions upon marriage out of the caste, &c., are relaxed in the case of widows, a marriage with almost *any* widow being permitted.

It should be noted which of these forms is practised; [and further, what rule of inheritance is observed, especially under the Levirate: whether, for instance, the son begotten of the widow by the younger brother of the deceased inherits as the son of the elder or of the younger brother.]

14. *Inheritance*—

(a) Minute details of the rules of inheritance do not generally bear upon our subject. But it is important to know whether the tribe follows the strict Islamic law of succession, or whether their rules, by denying rights of succession to females, tend to keep property in the clan.

(b) Primogeniture; equal division between sons; *Págband* and *Chúndaband*; succession of sons during the father's lifetime; distinctions between whole and half-brothers on the father's and mother's side respectively; succession of daughters; and inheritance by the son-in-law of a sonless father (*gharjawái*), are all points which may be usefully noticed, more especially when customs are found to differ on any of them.

(*c*) Any traces of inheritance through the female line, such as inheritance by brothers or sisters, or by sister's sons, should be carefully recorded.

(*d*) Traces of *vesh*, or the periodical redistribution by lot of common arable land among the households or adults of the community, are interesting.

15. *Relationship and its incidents.*—A table showing the terms used for the various kinds and degrees of relationship, and the people who are included under each, will often throw valuable light upon the ancient constitution of the family. It should be stated what relations may not be mentioned either by name, or by the term for the relationship; as for instance, that a woman may not name her husband, and that a man will not describe his brother-in-law (*sála*) as such.

The admission of strangers to inherit, the manner of and restrictions upon adoption, the relations arising from and destroyed by adoption, *gharjawái*, and foster kinship, and by the custom of making *bhúmbhai*, should all be noted.

Especially the relations which are created by marriage—(1) between the woman and the members of the family she marries into, (2) between the two families, are important. In the west of the Panjáb a woman changes her clan (*got*) by marriage; in the east she does not. It would be interesting to discover where the custom changes, and to note any facts bearing upon it; as, for instance, the custom of formal admission of the bride into her husband's clan. The functions which custom assigns to sisters' sons and husbands, brothers' wives, sister-in-laws' mothers and similar relations, in social ceremonials, such as marriage rites, are exceedingly interesting and instructive, and need further examination.

Further facts bearing upon the importance of eating together (*confarreatio*) in ceremonies where a new relationship is created, are needed. The custom often takes the form of a distribution of *gur* or sweetmeats.

16. *Intermarriage.*

(*a*) It is specially important to discover the limits within or beyond which marriage is forbidden; for instance, that a man must marry, in the first instance at any rate, within the caste; but must not marry into his own, his mother's or his paternal or maternal grandmother's clan, nor a girl, of whatever clan, who lives in a village marching with his own, and must not marry two sisters; or whether the prohibited degrees of Islám are the only limitations observed. It is important to know how far differences of religion or sect are a bar to marriage.

(*b*) It is also of great importance [as throwing light upon the possible mixed origin of some of our tribes and clans] to know how the offspring of—(1) first marriage, (2) *karewá* marriages, (3) illicit connexions between parents of different tribes, castes or religions are now classed; whether they follow the tribe and clan of the father or of the mother, or are known by an entirely new name; and what distinction, if any, is made between them and others who are born into the tribe and clan in a more usual or legitimate manner.

(c) Clans often cannot intermarry with certain other clans as being of common origin with themselves; for instance, the *Deswál*, *Mán*, and *Dalál* Jats, the *Mandhár*, *Kandhár* and *Bargújar* Rájputs, and so on. Ties of this sort should be carefully sought for and recorded.

(d) Castes and clans often refuse to, or are not allowed to, intermarry with certain others on the score of social status. In some cases wives will be received, but daughters will not be given in marriage. It is useful to give these particulars, as helping to fix the social standing.

17. *Social status.*—This is denoted in three ways:—

(a) by the customs regarding intermarriage just referred to;

(b) by the standing of the castes which will—(1) eat, (2) drink, (3) smoke with them, the Brahmanical distinction between *pakki roti*, or dry food cooked in ghi, and *kachhi roti* or food not so cooked, being noticed where it exists. Thus, in some parts of the province a *Gaur* Bráhman will eat *pakki roti* from the hands of a Hindu Jat, while he will not eat *kachhi roti* even from the hands of a *Sársút* Bráhman;

(c) by the general custom of the neighbourhood, which condemns certain castes to live in separate quarters, drink from separate wells, and so on.

18. *Occupation.*—The principal local occupations of the caste should be specified. It will often be found that change of religion affects the occupation. Thus a sweeper converted to Islám usually ceases to remove night-soil, while a Sikh Chamár will often leave leather work and take to weaving. It is often the case, moreover, that different clans pursue different branches of the occupation hereditary to the caste. Thus some Ghosi clans keep cattle and sell milk only; others buy milk and sell butter.

Instances of abandonment of hereditary occupation should be noticed, and whether in such cases the caste name is abandoned or altered, and the ties with the original caste broken or relaxed (*see* section 21 below).

19. *Minor peculiarities.*

(a) Customs prohibiting or enjoining the eating or growing of certain plants, as onions, turnips, indigo, &c., the eating of flesh, drinking of wine, smoking, and use of drugs, the use of vessels made of a particular metal or of earth, or ornamented with stripes or otherwise, often afford useful indications.

a Jat grandfather having now, by virtue of mere change of occupation, become Náís or Lohárs, and been admitted to caste privileges by the other Náís or Lohárs of the neighbourhood, are more common than is generally supposed. Nothing can be more important than a careful record of the actual facts in such cases; whether the people in question have risen or fallen in the social scale; how their position in respect of intermarriage with other sections of the community has been affected; whether they have adopted a new or are still known by the old name, and so on.

23. *Boundaries.*—It is important to define, as far as possible, the boundary which marks any change in religion, language, custom, or tribal distribution or nomenclature; such as the line at which Khatrís supersede Banyas or Aroras Khatrís, at which Bágri take the place of Dese Jats, Kutánas and Musallis of Chúhras, or Charhoas of Dhobis and Chhímpis, at which Juláha yields to Páoli, Ját to Jat, Hindi to Panjábí, Hinduism to Sikhism, at which the custom changes as to marriage within the caste but outside the clan, as to the hereditary nature of occupations, or as to the change of a bride's clan. The limits within which dialects are spoken also stand in great need of definition, though they are often by no means clearly marked. There is very generally an intermediate or neutral zone, within which the distinct dialects, tribes, or customs which prevail on either side of it are to be found in a state of intermixture or transition. Such zones should be defined as accurately aspossible.

24. *Tracts.*—It is useful to define the exact limits of the many local tracts into which the people themselves have divided the province; such as the Bágar, the Nardak, Hariána, Bhattíána, the Málwa, the Mánjha, the Pawád, the Bajwát, the Rohi, the Jangal-des, the Dogar-des, the Dáman, the Pachhád, and a hundred others. These divisions are permanent; and, unlike our artificially formed districts and subdivisions, represent natural features, either physical or ethnographical.

Information is also much needed regarding the limits of the old *parganahs*, *sarkárs*, *súbahs* and other ancient administrative divisions of the country; as in the absence of such information we cannot fully understand the statements of the old historians which refer to these divisions. The Sikhs often altered considerably the old units of Mughal administration; and it should always be stated to which of these two dynasties the facts given refer.

25. *Bibliography.*—Much information on the subject of the divisions of the people will be found in all the various Settlement Reports; while their religious and social customs are treated of in Mr. Lyall's Report on Kángra, paragraphs 66, 72 to 74, 112 to 119, 154, 160 to 169, in Mr. Barnes' Report on Kángra, paragraphs 253 to 294, in Captain Waterfield's Report on Gujrát, paragraphs 121 to 164, in Mr. Maconachie's Report on Delhi, paragraphs 143 to 150, in Mr. Channing's Report on Gurgaon, pages 34 to 37, and in my Report on Karnál (now passing through the Press), Chapters VI, VIII, IX, and part of VII. Elliot's Races of the North-West Provinces of India, edited by Beames (London, Trübner, 1869, two vols. 8vo., price 36*s.*), is a store-house of valuable information; as

are a little book on the Domestic Manners and Customs of the Hindús of Northern India by the Rev. Ishuree Dass (Benares, Lazarus, and London, Trübner, 1866), Wilson's Sketch of the Religious Sects of the Hindús (Calcutta, Bishop's College Press, 1846, cost about 5*s*.), and some of Colebrooke's Miscellaneous Essays (reprint of 1858, cost 6*s*.)

The constitution of the tribe and family can be studied in pages *i* to *c* of vol. II of Mr. Tupper's work on Panjab Customary Law; and in the earlier pages of Mr. Wilson's Code of Tribal Customs in the Gurgaon District (reprinted in the volume just mentioned).

The learner who is anxious to acquaint himself with some of the published results of sociological research cannot do better than begin with Sir John Lubbock's Origin of Civilisation (London, Longman, 1870, one vol., 8vo., price 16*s*.); while the following are a few less elementary works on the same and cognate subjects:—Tylor's Early History of Mankind (London, Murray, 1870, one vol., 8vo., price 12*s*.); Tyler's Primitive Culture (London, Murray, 1871, two vols., 8vo., price 24*s*.); MacLennan's Primitive Marriage (London, Quaritch, 1876, one vol., small 8vo., price 16*s*.); Morgan's Ancient Society (London, MacMillan, 1877, one vol., 8vo., price 16*s*.); Maine's Village Communities (London, Murray, 1872, one vol., 8vo., price 12*s*.); Maine's Early History of Institutions (London, Murray, 1875, one vol., 8vo., price 12*s*.)

26. *Finally*, I would remind you that *no notes can possibly be too fragmentary or too trivial to be worth sending me.* Incomplete as this memorandum is, a complete examination of even a single caste in a single district with regard to all the points noted would be a very serious undertaking. But it is only meant to suggest lines of inquiry, some of which will interest one person and some another. Even bare lists of clans and subdivisions, or a note that a certain single clan belongs to such a tribe, will be most useful. And *all* details regarding the customs of the people, however minute or apparently uninteresting, possess great ethnological value; and *especially points in which the customs of one people differ from those of another.* For instance, a statement which I have just seen that the temporary huts which the *Báwarias* build for themselves are circular in plan, at once suggests the inquiry where the pattern was brought from, and invites comparison with the bee-hive shaped tent of the nomad Mongols. It is always well to test and confirm any information which has been collected by inquiries from fresh individuals. But where this cannot be done, the information will still be of great value; for it can be tested by comparison or by subsequent inquiry, while, if not noted at once, it is lost. It is as well, however, in sending notes, to state how far the information has been tested and supported by repeated inquiry.

The primary distribution of the Panjab peoples among the aboriginal inhabitants, and the several great waves of immigration which have at different times swept into the country, can only be arrived at by a minute comparison of their various social and religious customs; and the immense question of the growth and nature of caste can only be elucidated by a study of the internal relations and economy of existing castes. The habits of the vagrant and outcast classes afford an almost untrodden field for the one inquiry; the exceedingly interesting and elaborate caste-organization of the menial castes, and of those numerous trade-guilds of which it is often so difficult to say whether they are castes or only occupations, affords equally unexplored material for the other. Work in either field, or indeed in any cognate direction, will help on the inquiry into the early history of social institutions which has lately assumed such great interest and importance. We in India have an inexhaustible store-house of facts at our very doors, and unequalled facilities for ascertaining and recording them. Every year sees some of the existing material disappear under the powerful solvent of contact with European thought and the appliances of civilization. We are probably too near our subject to generalise with success; but we, and we alone, can obtain the facts from which generalisations can be made.

APPENDIX IV.

LIST OF CORRESPONDENTS SELECTED TO TAKE PART IN THE ETHNOGRAPHIC SURVEY OF BENGAL.

Division.	District.	Names of correspondents.
BARDWAN ...	Midnapur ...	Baboo Bisseswar Banerji. ,, Kali Narayan Roy. The Deputy Inspector of Schools. K. C. Ghosh, Esq. Baboo Rajendra Lal Gupta. The Executive Engineer, Cossye Division.
	Bardwan ...	W. B. Oldham, Esq. Baboo Tara Prosad Chatterji. The Subdivisional Officer, Culna. Ditto ditto, Cutwa. Ditto ditto, Raniganj. Baboo Jaga Mohan Bhattacharji.
	Hughli ...	B. N. De, Esq. Baboo Kedar Nath Dutt. The Subdivisional Officer, Jehanabad. Baboo Aswini Kumar Bose.
	Howrah ...	Baboo Bankim Chandra Chatterji. ,, Prasanna Kumar Bose.
	Birbhum ...	Baboo Bhuban Mohan Raha. N. Warde-Jones, Esq.
	Bankura ...	Baboo Atul Chandra Chatterji. ,, Guru Das Barman. The Sub-Registrar of Khattra. Ditto of Kotalpur. Baboo Haris Chandra Rai.
PRESIDENCY ...	24-Parganás ...	Baboo Hem Chandra Kar. Kumar Gopendra Krishna Deb. Pandit Hara Prasad Sastri. Baboo Ranga Lal Mukharji.
	Calcutta ...	Dr. Rajendra Lal Mitra, C.I.E. Jagannath Khanna, Esq. Baboo Protab Chandra Ghosh. ,, Adya Nath Banerji. T. N. Mukharji, Esq. Baboo Protab Chandra Roy.

Division.	District.	Names of correspondents.
Presidency—*concluded.*	Nadiya ...	Baboo Tarini Kumar Ghosh.
		,, Ishan Chandra Ghosh.
	Jessore ...	Baboo Krishna Kali Mukharji.
		,, Kedar Nath Biswas.
		,, Bankim Chandra Chatterji.
		,, Chandi Das Ghose.
		,, Troylakya Nath Sen.
		,, Annada Prasad Sen.
		,, Kali Prasanna Sarkar.
	Khulna ...	Baboo Khagendra Nath Mitter.
		,, Bhubaneswar Sing.
		,, Narendra Nath Roy Chowdri.
	Murshedabad ...	Baboo Bansidhar Roy.
		,, Pran Kumar Das.
		,, Bipin Bihari Mukerji.
		,, Bijoy Krishna Bose.
		,, Srinath Gupta.
Rajshahye ...	Rajshahye ...	Baboo Mahendra Nath Bhattacharji.
	Dinajpur ...	Dr. U. C. Mukerji.
		Baboo Sarat Chandra Chatterji.
	Rangpur ...	Moulvi Abdul Khaleque.
		H. E. Ransom, Esq.
		J. T. Mackay, Esq.
		Baboo Sarada Prasad Chatterji.
		,, Kumud Bihari Samanta.
	Bogra ...	Baboo Bhubaneswar Gupta.
	Pabna ...	E. F. Growse, Esq.
		Baboo Barada Churn Mitter.
		,, Purna Chandra Gupta.
	Jalpigori ...	Baboo Priya Nath Mukerji.
		H. H. Heard, Esq.
		D. Sunder, Esq.
	Darjiling ...	Baboo Parbati Charan Roy.
		,, Sarat Chandra Das, C.I.E.
		Raja Tenduk Palgar.
		Baboo Mari Das Pradhan.
		,, Hathura Nath Chatterji.
		,, Gelong Nimsring.
	Kuch Behar ...	Baboo Calica Das Dutt.
Dacca ...	Dacca ...	Baboo Mati Lal Sarkar.
		,, Rajani Nath Ghosh.
		,, Syam Kishore Bose.
		,, Aswini Kumar Bose.
		,, Aditya Chandra Chakrabarti.
		,, Ram Chandra Dhar.

DIVISION.	District.	Names of correspondents.
DACCA—concld.	Dacca—concld.	Maulvi Mazharal Anwar. Baboo Nalini Nath Mitra. " Gopal Chandra Bose. E. B. Harris, Esq. Baboo Bagala Prasanna Mazumdar. " Raj Kumar Sen. " Dina Nath Dhar.
	Faridpur ...	Baboo Khetra Gopal Roy. " Girindra Nath Chatterji.
	Bakarganj ...	Maulvi Syed Obedulla. Baboo Jogadish Chandra Roy. " Umakishore Roy. " Sasi Sekhar Dutt. F. Wilcox, Esq. Baboo Pitambar Sing. " Aswini Kumar Dutt. " Parbatti Nath Ghose.
	Maimansinh ...	Maulvi Mohamed. Baboo Jogendra Nath Banerji. Mr. Ellison (missionary).
CHITTAGONG ...	Chittagong ...	Baboo Gaur Mohan Basak. " Radha Kishore Chakrabati.
	Noakhali ...	Baboo Jogendra Nath Chakrabati. " Satis Chandra Bose. The District Magistrate.
	Tipperah ...	Dr. J. ffrench-Mullen. Baboo Tarak Chandra Gupta.
	Hill Tipperah ...	Baboo Uma Kanta Dás.
	Chittagong Hill Tracts.	Baboo Braja Nath Shaha. " Hari Pada Ghosh.
BHAGALPUR ...	Bhagalpur ...	A. H. Giles, Esq. Baboo Ram Narain Banerji. " Mathura Nath Mukerji.
	Purniah ...	Baboo Karunamaya Banerji. Surji Kumar Agasti, Esq. Baboo Kastori Lal.
	Monghyr ...	Baboo Debi Prasad. The Subdivisional Officer, Begusarai. Ditto ditto, Jamui.
	Maldah ...	Baboo Shib Chandra Nag. Maulvi Zakir Hossein. H. R. Reily, Esq.

Division.	District.	Names of correspondents.
Bhagalpur—*concluded.*	Santál Parganás	Baboo C. N. Gupta. " N. C. Banerji. A. W. Stark, Esq. Syed Nejabat Hossein. Rev. L. O. Skrefsrud.
Patna	Patna ...	The District Superintendent of Police. Maulvi Majibar Rahman. Syed Zahiruddin. Baboo Bemala Charan Bhattacharji. " Sheo Nandan Lal Roy. C. N. Banerji, Esq. Maulvi Wahed Uddin.
	Gya ...	Dr. R. Macleod. Baboo Rajkishore Narain. " Radha Lal. " Sarada Prasad Ganguli.
	Shahabad ...	The District Superintendent of Police. " Subdivisional Officer, Buxar. J. R. Hand, Esq. The Subdivisional Officer, Bhabua.
	Darbhanga ...	The District Magistrate. " Subdivisional Officer, Tajpur. " ditto ditto, Madhubani. " Sub-Registrar, ditto. Maulvi Gowhar Ali. Baboo Dwarka Prasad. " Pramath Nath Chaterji. " Okhoy Kumar Chaterji.
	Mozufferpur ...	Baboo Ram Prakas Lal. H. W. C. Carnduff, Esq.
	Saran ...	The Deputy Inspector of Schools. A. Tytler, Esq. Baboo Raghunath Sahai. R. F. H. Pughe, Esq.
	Champaran ...	The Deputy Inspector of Schools. " Sub-Inspector of Schools. " Canungo at Sudder Station. W. R. Bright, Esq. The Sub-Deputy Collector, Bettiah. " Canungo at Bettiah.
Chota Nagpur	Hazaribagh ...	Baboo Girendra Nath Mitra. Rai Jadu Nath Mukerji.
	Lohardagá ...	Baboo Girindra Chandra Banerji. " Gagan Chandra Banerji. F. A. Slack, Esq. Baboo Rakhál Das Haldar. C. A. G. Lillingston, Esq. The Munsif of Palamow.

Division.	District.	Names of correspondents.
Chota Nagpur—*concld.*	Manbhum ...	Baboo Surya Kumar Guha. " Paresh Nath Ghosh. " Atal Bihari Moitra. Rev. A. Campbell. The Munsif of Bara Basar.
	Singbhum ...	The Deputy Commissioner, Singbhum.
	Tributary States	The Commissioner of Chota Nagpur.
Orissa ...	Cuttack ...	Baboo Ramakhoy Chatterji.
	Puri ...	The Senior Deputy Collector at head-quarters.
	Balasore ...	Baboo Rash Behari Naik. " Akhoy Kumar Chatterji. Hon'ble Kumar Baikant Nath De.
	Tributary States	The Tehsildar of Khandmals. " Manager of Nilgiri. " " of Dhenkanal. " " of Mohurbhanj. Rev. Father Schaff. Srinath Dutt, Esq.